The Role of the Supreme Court

The Role of the Supreme Court in American Government and Politics
1789-1835

CHARLES GROVE HAINES

"We are under a Constitution, but the Constitution is what the judges say it is."—CHARLES EVANS HUGHES

New York
RUSSELL & RUSSELL
1960

LAW AND PUBLIC POLICY

"The life of the law has not been logic: it has been experience. The felt necessities of the time, the prevalent moral and political theories, intuitions of public policy, avowed or unconscious, even the prejudices which judges share with their fellow-men, have had a good deal more to do than the syllogism in determining the rules by which men should be governed."

O. W. Holmes, Jr., *The Common Law* (Boston, 1881), p. 1.

⬦

"Our own Supreme Courts have long been drawing copiously and conscientiously from this unbounded field of public policy. The opinions are full of such discussions, and some of the greatest questions of the day have been settled with no more definite guidance and control."

John H. Wigmore, *Science of Legal Method,* Modern Legal Philosophy Series (Boston, 1917), IX: xl.

⬦

"The history of the Supreme Court would record fewer explosive periods if, from the beginning, there had been more continuous awareness of the role of the Court in the dynamic process of American society. Lawyers, with rare exceptions, have failed to lay bare that the law of the Supreme Court is enmeshed in the country's history; historians no less have seemed to miss the fact that the country's history is enmeshed in the law of the Supreme Court. ... This has had two unfortunate aspects. The public has been denied understanding of the intimate share of the Supreme Court in the affairs of States and Nation; the Supreme Court has been deprived of that healthy play of informed criticism from without which is indispensable for the vitality of every institution."

Felix Frankfurter, *Mr. Justice Holmes and the Supreme Court* (Cambridge, 1939), pp. 3, 4.

Preface

In a short introduction the general purpose and scope of this study will be briefly recorded. It is appropriate also to indicate the steps leading to the preparation of the volume and to note the aid I have received which made its completion possible. Beginning about two decades ago an analysis was made of the decisions of the Supreme Court in which there had been marked differences of opinion among the Justices and frequent dissents. It is well known that from dissents have come some of the most important constitutional trends and developments. This approach was followed by a consideration of the available biographical materials relating to the lives of the Supreme Court Justices. But so few biographies of Justices have been prepared that a consideration of the work of the Court through the membership of the Supreme Bench cannot be accomplished until many more thorough and reliable biographies have appeared. Finally there was begun an evaluation of the work of the Court in its relations to Congress, to the Presidents, to the states, and to the main currents and tendencies in American history. Much familiar ground relating to the activities of members of the Supreme Court had to be covered with some differences only in methods of approach and of interpretation. In parts of the treatise frequent and extensive use has been made of the leading works which have dealt with the Supreme Court as an agency in our constitutional development. Though credit is given throughout the study for those extracts and quotations used, I wish to recognize in this connection my great indebtedness to Charles Warren's *The Supreme Court in United States History,* and to Albert J. Beveridge's *The Life of John Marshall.*

Through grants from the funds of the University of California it was possible to secure the aid of research assistants. Vincent M. Barnett, Jr., rendered invaluable service in the preliminary analysis of the decisions of the Supreme Court having political significance. Charles Kummer prepared for my use a thorough and systematic treatment of the relations of Congress and the Supreme Court, particularly as portrayed in the Congressional debates. Foster and June Sherwood were of great assistance in the final preparation of the manuscript. A debt of gratitude is due also to the late Thomas W. Robinson, Librarian of the Los Angeles County Law Library, and to the present Librarian, Thomas S. Dabagh, for many favors and privileges granted to use the extensive collection of legal reports and treatises which this valuable library contains.

I am deeply indebted to Dean Emeritus Roscoe Pound of the Harvard Law School for his encouragement and assistance in the prosecution of the work. Though much preliminary work on the volume had been done, the completion of the manuscript was greatly facilitated by the award made through the aid of Dean Pound of a research grant from the Benjamin Fund of the Harvard Law School. This grant made it possible for me to spend the greater part of the academic year 1936–1937 working in the Harvard Law School, where the incomparable facilities of the Law Library and the Widener Library were available for the continuance of this study.

Los Angeles, March 15, 1943   CHARLES GROVE HAINES

Contents

Contents

Introduction

Introduction

THE SUPREME COURT of the United States has come to be regarded as the unique feature of the American governmental system. It is a feature which distinguishes the American government from practically all modern political systems. The Court's present position of independence and superiority in the interpretation of the laws and constitutional provisions was acquired gradually and through reverses which threatened the foundations of judicial power under the Constitution. Nearly a century elapsed before the attitude of adoration and almost worship of the Court, which is prevalent today, became general and customary among large groups of people.

The work of the Supreme Court has been treated in Charles Warren's extensive treatise[1] and in the lives of John Jay,[2] John Marshall,[3] Roger B. Taney,[4] Morison R. Waite,[5] Stephen J. Field,[6] and William Howard Taft.[7] And many works on constitutional law have presented historical and descriptive analyses of the Court's efforts to interpret and define the meaning of the terms and provisions of the Constitution. In most of these accounts the Court has been treated as a legal tribunal operating with only incidental relations to the main practices and tendencies of political life. The extent to which the members of the Supreme Judiciary and the tribunal itself have participated in and have influenced the political and partisan activities of the time has, in my opinion, received inadequate consideration.

Moreover, those who have attempted to evaluate the contribution of the Supreme Court to American legal and political thought have not infrequently viewed the development of American history from the standpoint of a bias favorable to one of the great political fac-

---

[1] *The Supreme Court in United States History,* 3 vols. (Boston, 1922).

[2] Frank Monaghan, *John Jay* (New York, 1935).

[3] Albert J. Beveridge, *The Life of John Marshall,* 4 vols. (Boston, 1919).

[4] Carl Brent Swisher, *Roger B. Taney* (New York, 1935).

[5] Bruce E. Trimble, *Chief Justice Waite: Defender of the Public Interest* (Princeton, 1938).

[6] Carl Brent Swisher, *Stephen J. Field: Craftsman of the Law* (Washington, 1930).

[7] Henry F. Pringle, *The Life and Times of William Howard Taft,* 2 vols. (New York 1939).

tions which has struggled for ascendancy and power. Thus, the story of the Court has usually been told in such a way as to defend and laud the federalist and nationalist policies and principles and correspondingly to depreciate and condemn the local, particularist, and democratic principles and traditions in the American way of life.

With the conviction that the role of the Supreme Court in American government and politics was deserving of more careful and systematic evaluation, an attempt has been made to consider the activities of the Justices, the decisions of the Court, and the relations of the tribunal to the other departments—in short, to present a survey of the political relations and implications of the work of the Court as it performed its significant functions as a balance wheel of the federal system inaugurated in 1789.

To understand the role of the Supreme Court in American government and politics, it is necessary to present the arguments and philosophy of the conservatives as well as those of the liberals and democrats. And there is at least a modicum of impartiality in the effort to present herein, fully and clearly, the arguments of both sides in the discussion of some of the underlying issues of American law and politics. But the fact that the work of the Supreme Court viewed from the conservative and nationalist viewpoints has been so frequently and so effectively treated by well-known historians, and that its work considered from the liberal and democratic approach has been so seldom and so inadequately handled has necessitated at times in the following pages more thorough and extended consideration of the critics rather than the defenders of the Court.

In view of the fact that the conservative and liberal or democratic approaches to political thinking have given color and direction to much historical writing, it becomes essential in considering the place and importance of the Supreme Court to recognize the different valuations which result when one or the other of the two fundamental approaches is given prominence.

No attempt has been made to present a nonpartisan account of the development of American constitutional law. Though historians are expected from an ideal standpoint to tell the story of events as they really occurred, this ideal is as far from attainment as it is to find a judge who is merely a mechanical mouthpiece to announce the law as applicable to a case. It is apparent today, if not always admitted, that personal peculiarities, predilections, and political leanings affect the writing of histories as they do the administration of justice. Personal views and political attitudes will be apparent to anyone who ventures to examine this study of the conflicts and controversies aroused by judicial decisions and of the place of the Supreme Court in the evolution of political and legal doctrines and practices. The belief, which was fostered and supported by the liberal and democratic groups at the time the American system of government was formed, that a free and acceptable government is one which derives its authority from the body of the people is approved with a frank recognition of its weaknesses and limitations. So also is the belief that the people are capable of self-government and that no other form of government is so well adapted to meet the needs of the American people.

Relatively few of the decisions of the Supreme Court have any political significance. The greater part of the cases which come to the Court involve questions relating to the interpretation of statutes which, however important to the litigants concerned, have only a slight effect on the economic and political life of the people. From the beginning the federal courts, except for the variety of cases which arose out of diversity of citizenship, were concerned primarily with questions of admiralty and maritime law, with the rights and privileges of the Indians, and with the interpretation of revenue laws. Eventually issues concerning bankruptcy, patents, copyrights, and some important matters of trade, navigation, and commerce came to be adjudicated. The annual record of cases appealed to the federal supreme tribunal is comprised, in large part, of the settlement of legal minutiae which in the long run are likely to have an important bearing on the growth of the law and on the determination of individual private rights. But it is not the day-by-day hearing of these controversies that has appealed to the interest and imagination of the people. The few cases which have not only determined individual rights but have also influenced governmental policies are the ones which have resulted in praise or condemnation of the work of the Court. It is to these cases that primary attention will be given in the ensuing pages.

To relate the story of the Supreme Court as it has participated in the political, economic, and industrial evolution of the people has required a reconsideration of many events and incidents of American history. Obviously in such a survey frequent use has been made of secondary sources. The larger part of the material included in the study, however, has been prepared in the process of a reëxamination and a reinterpretation of source materials, including the consideration of original documents, letters and diaries, Congressional debates, Executive papers and orders, and, finally, the decisions and opinions of the Justices of the Supreme Court. One who attempts to deal with such an extensive period of American history and to delve into the variety of sources relating to the Supreme Court keenly realizes the incompleteness and the inadequacies of any account of its work, and is fully aware of the limitations which condition an attempt to form judgments on the nature and significance of the work of the Court and its influence on the American ways of life and thought.

Part One

BACKGROUND FOR THE PREVALENCE OF
POLITICAL IDEAS AND PRINCIPLES IN THE
JUDICIAL INTERPRETATION OF THE
FEDERAL CONSTITUTION

CHAPTER I

Constitutional Law and Politics

AMERICAN constitutional law has frequently been treated in a detached and mechanical manner separated from the facts and historical conditions out of which it arose. The result of this treatment has been to surround the record of the development of this branch of the law with an atmosphere of certainty and logical exactness, thereby tending to conceal the underlying forces and motives which give color and life to the growth of the constitutional structure. If, as Justice Holmes observes, experience rather than logic is the life of the private law, is it not likely that political and social experience plays a prominent role in the molding of the main tenets and principles of public law? Though the method of the application of logic and of the criteria of legal rationalization to the evolution of constitutional ideas and doctrines has been fully explored by historians and legal scholars, the more elusive factors which are the mainspring of political and legal action with respect to the fundamental written law have received much less consideration. Sociological jurists and those who call themselves "realists" in jurisprudence have been inclined to attach less weight to the effect of logic and the syllogism than to personal, social, and political factors in the forming of judicial judgments. And the pragmatic or realist point of view has led to a reevaluation of some of the basic hypotheses of all legal thinking. One cannot proceed far in the analysis of constitutional law without the discovery that personal, social, and political factors have had a profound influence in its development. The imprint of politics may be found in almost all phases of constitutional law; and constitutional law has not infrequently, moreover, been the controlling and directing force in politics.

The consideration of the relation of constitutional law to politics requires, at the outset, an analysis of the issue which arose when written fundamental charters were formed, namely, whether the provisions of such documents may be regarded as law in the ordinary or conventional sense of that term, and also in what way the process of legal interpretation affects this branch of public law. Turning to the first of these issues: to what extent and under what conditions may the federal Constitution be regarded as "law"?

[9]

THE FEDERAL CONSTITUTION: "SUPREME LAW"
OR "POLITICAL DOCUMENT"

The American states began, in 1776, the practice of establishing governments on the basis of a written instrument or constitution. In 1789 was inaugurated the great experiment, as Washington and Hamilton called it, of conducting the central government for a union of these states in accordance with the provisions and requirements of a written fundamental law drafted at Philadelphia in 1787. A new form of polity was evolving in which men placed high value on the efficacy of written formulas to guide the conduct of public affairs and to preserve the liberties which were especially cherished. The adoption of written constitutions immediately raised some intricate and puzzling questions with respect to the significance or status of such instruments. What was the relation between the fundamental law and ordinary legislative enactments? And were the provisions of the written document to be considered as law in the usual sense and meaning of that term? Or were constitutions primarily political documents which must be interpreted and applied by political agencies, due consideration being given to the purposes and ideas contained in the instrument as well as the social, political, and economic conditions to which their provisions were to be applied?[1] Though, in the latter part of the eighteenth century, answers were not readily available to such fundamental questions, an attempt was made to give at least a tentative basis for the determination whether the federal Constitution was "law." The discussion of this issue first arose in connection with the proposal of Luther Martin in the federal Convention to include in the Constitution a supremacy clause.

The supremacy clause.—The federal Constitution, as framed and put into operation in 1789, declared that "this Constitution and the laws of the United States which shall be made in pursuance thereof . . . shall be the supreme law of the land, and the judges in every State shall be bound thereby, anything in the constitution or laws of any State to the contrary notwithstanding."[2] Luther Martin, one of the foremost advocates of the rights of the states in the Philadelphia Convention and opponent of the

---

[1] The terms "politics" and "political" throughout this treatise are considered in the broad sense to include political, social, economic, and personal factors so far as they bear on constitutional interpretation and in particular on the policy-determining activities of the Judges.

[2] Art. VI, sec. 2. "This declaration, therefore, taken on its face," says Andrew C. McLaughlin, "does not leave a shred of state sovereignty as a legal theory of the Union." *A Constitutional History of the United States* (New York, 1935), p. 184. As will appear later, the issue of state vs. federal sovereignty is not so readily disposed of, even as a "legal theory."

adoption of the Constitution, scarcely realized the import of these words when he proposed such a clause for insertion in the Constitution.[3] For not only has this clause been made the basis for the developing doctrine of federal supremacy in the establishment of interstate relations, but along with the provision declaring that judicial powers "shall extend to all cases in law and equity arising under this Constitution, the laws of the United States, and treaties made or which shall be made, under their authority,"[4] it has formed the groundwork for a type of constitutional legalism which scarcely has a parallel in the annals of modern government.

Though the significance of the "supremacy clause" and its relation both to state sovereignty and to the review of legislative acts by the courts will be considered in detail later, it is impossible to overestimate the importance of this clause in placing the imprint of a legalistic mode of thinking upon constitutional development in the United States. The Constitution was declared not only to be "supreme" but also to be "law." Though the language of the provision mentions state judges only, the principle was inscribed therein that "judges in the quiet of their own court rooms must maintain the authority of government and the binding effect of the Constitution."[5] There is, therefore, an implication if not an "inevitable basis" for the review and possible veto of acts of Congress by both the state and the federal courts.

With the gradual adoption of the principle of judicial review of legislative acts, the language of the federal Constitution as well as that of the state constitutions was considered to be "law." The judges interpreted and applied its terms as they did the language of statutes so that matters of great political import were passed upon apparently with the same ease, simplicity, and procedure as the interpretation of a contract or the defining of the rights of persons under a will.

The power of the courts, federal and state, which maintains the articles of the Constitution as the law of the land, and thereby keeps each authority within its proper sphere, A. V. Dicey observed, "is exerted with an ease and regularity which has astounded and perplexed continental

---

[3] Martin's original resolution was as follows: "That the legislative acts of the United States made by virtue and in pursuance of the articles of the Union, and all treaties made and ratified under the authority of the United States shall be the supreme law of the respective States, so far as those acts or treaties shall relate to the said States, or their citizens and inhabitants—and that the judiciaries of the several States shall be bound thereby in their decisions, anything in the respective laws of the individual States to the contrary notwithstanding." Agreed to unanimously on July 17 and amended on August 23 by adding "This Constitution" at the beginning. *The Records of the Federal Convention*, ed. by Max Farrand (New Haven, 1923), II: 28, 29, 381, 382.

[4] Art. III, sec. 2.   [5] McLaughlin, *op. cit.*, p. 184.

critics."[6] The explanation is, Dicey thought, that whereas the Judges control the action of the Constitution, they nevertheless perform purely judicial functions.[7] This duty which not only made the Judges the guardians but also the masters of the Constitution was responsible for the prevalence of the spirit of legality among the people; in fact, it stamped upon the American federal system the dominance of legalism.[8] The declaration that the Constitution was "law" and that the courts were to have cognizance of cases arising under the Constitution, combined with the prevailing concepts regarding the review of legislation by the courts, truly made of every legislature only a subordinate law-making body and placed definitive restrictions on all executive and administrative action.

The question may well be raised, then, whether the Constitution may be considered "law" in the ordinary use of that term. Constitutions framed and adopted in the United States from 1776 to 1800 had two primary objectives—first, to establish a form of government with the essential definition and distribution of powers and, second, to assure protection to certain individual rights. These charters, of which the federal Constitution became the prototype, may be essentially regarded as political documents.

The political nature of written constitutions.—In the first place, the provisions of written constitutions were based upon certain fundamental assumptions or theories which are essentially political in nature, such, for example, as the sovereignty of the people, governments based upon the consent of the governed, the right of revolution, and doctrines of inherent and inalienable rights. In the second place, throughout the instruments other political principles were imbedded in their provisions. Whatever its meaning, most of the American constitutions have inserted either expressly or by implication the Montesquieu principle of the separation of powers. This is in essence a political principle or theory of special import in American constitutional history. Moreover, the problem which the framers of the federal Constitution faced, that is, the distribution of powers between the states and the nation, is fundamentally political, though the courts may be called upon to aid in defining the distributing clauses.

To a certain extent the Supreme Court has recognized that parts of the Constitution are political in nature, and, hence, decisions of the other

---

[6] A. V. Dicey, *Introduction to the Study of the Law of the Constitution* (8th ed., London, 1927), p. 159.

[7] This contention is one which will not stand the test of strict analysis, as will appear in the following pages.

[8] Dicey, *op. cit.*, pp. 170–171.

departments of government arising thereunder are not deemed subject to judicial cognizance. Thus, the requirement that the states shall have a republican form of government has been left to the legislative and executive departments for determination.[9] Likewise, among other matters, the courts have declined to examine issues relating to the negotiation and termination of treaties, to the beginning and ending of war, or to the recognition of states or governments.[10] Many of the provisions relating to the organization and the operation of the Legislative and Executive departments of the federal government are considered as a matter of course outside the scope of the jurisdiction of the federal courts.[11] So significant and so extensive are these issues that this method of avoiding conflicts with the other departments has been suggested as the most reasonable and appropriate basis for the Court to decline to consider many of the controversial questions now arising under the due process of law clause.[12] At least the doctrine of the political nature of certain provisions of the Constitution is so well recognized that it would not be difficult or indefensible for the Court to extend its application. An examination of the provisions of the federal Constitution reveals that a large part of its provisions are governmental or political rather than legal in nature. The Judges are indeed the "cartographers who give temporary definiteness but not definitiveness to the undefined and ever-shifting boundaries between State and Nation, between freedom and authority."[13]

Phrases, such as habeas corpus, *ex post facto,* double jeopardy, infamous crime, unreasonable searches and seizures, and trial by jury, had fairly well-defined legal meaning when inserted in constitutions, but they comprise only a small part of the written instrument.[14] It scarcely seems necessary to note that the latter phrases come more readily within the scope of judicial interpretation and application than the former, though for the purposes of judicial review and the supremacy clause, they have been considered in the same category. Finally, constitutions contain phrases like "the law of the land" or "due process of law" serving as vague legal standards in the application of which wide differences of opinion arise. Provisions having essentially political meaning and implications

---

[9] Pacific States Tel. and Tel. Co. v. Oregon, 223 U. S. 118 (1912).

[10] Foster v. Neilson, 2 Pet. 253 (1829).

[11] See Oliver P. Field, "The Doctrine of Political Questions in the Federal Courts," 8 *Minn. Law Rev.* (May, 1924), 485.

[12] Maurice Finkelstein, "Judicial Self-Limitation," 37 *Harv. Law Rev.* (Jan., 1924), 338.

[13] Felix Frankfurter, ed., *Mr. Justice Holmes* (New York, 1931), p. 51.

[14] For classification of constitutional issues, see analysis by Felix Frankfurter, ed., *op. cit.,* pp. 48 ff.

and phrases of indefinite meaning require different treatment from the more exact legal terms which constitutions contain. But, as a rule, all the provisions of written constitutions are treated as law with the customary connotations attached to that phrase.

Any attempt to answer the inquiry whether or not the federal Constitution is "law" in the ordinary or conventional sense of the word must take into account also a difference in fundamental assumptions or postulates which is characteristic of the growth of written constitutions. With the assertion that the Constitution is law, it was soon assumed as a corollary to it that any action within its scope contrary to the Constitution was not law and that it was the duty of courts as custodians of the law, when such conflicts were discovered, to hold the challenged legislative or executive action void. Thus, the "supreme law" phrase appeared to make judicial review inevitable, and judicial review gave assurance that the Constitution would be declared and applied as law. With the Constitution being regarded as enforceable in the courts and to be treated as other laws are treated, it was assumed that no distinction should be made between provisions which were primarily political in character and those which had more exact legal import. With this attitude toward the Constitution—the written document being declared to be law—a chain of reasoning with seeming logical necessity and exactness was constructed. The assumption and the premises arising therefrom were presumed to be so clear and necessary to certain lawyers and jurists that the doctrine of review of acts of Congress was deemed to be expressly warranted by the language of the Constitution.

Since the framing of the federal Constitution many countries adopting written constitutions have accepted other assumptions which have given a different meaning to the provisions of these instruments. Vattel, who was one of the first writers to advocate a written constitution as a desirable medium for the embodiment of the fundamental laws of a society and who was frequently quoted in the formative period of American constitutional development, expressed the view which has become the dominant one in those countries in Europe where written constitutions still have validity and are enforced. "If," said Vattel, "there arise in the State disputes over the fundamental laws, over the public administration, or over the rights of the various powers which have a share in it, it belongs to the Nation alone to decide them, and settle them according to its political constitution."[15] In other words, disputes arising among the departments and over the distribution of powers were political in

[15] E. de Vattel, *The Law of Nations or The Principles of Natural Law*, trans. by Charles G. Fenwick from the edition of 1758 (Washington, 1916), p. 19.

nature and were to be settled by political methods similar to those by which the constitution was formed. Here, then, in germ at least, was a statement of what has come to be the prevailing doctrine of Continental Europe to the status and significance of written constitutions. The constitution is essentially *a political document*.

Where written constitutions are formulated and applied in Continental European countries, the constitution is regarded mainly as a document comprising groups of *political laws* which are in charge of the *political departments* to interpret in doubtful cases. Essentially, the guardianship of the constitution in these countries belongs to the legislative or lawmaking agencies of the government.

The theory of the separation of powers which is held by American judges to involve, of necessity, judicial review of legislative acts and the declaration of the supremacy of the constitution as law is, therefore, frequently considered to have exactly the opposite result. Following the principle that there are only two great functions of government, namely, to make and to execute the laws, and that, of necessity, these functions must be carried out with the closest unity and coöperation possible, the judiciary is regarded as subordinate to the other departments. Instead of establishing through judicial review, as American judges contend, a government of laws and not of men, European jurists and statesmen have claimed that under a constitutional regime it is precisely because the law is supreme that the legislature is placed above the other powers.

It follows, of necessity, then, that the provisions and limitations of the constitution are not *laws* in the ordinary meaning of the term and that they cannot form the basis of a case or contention before a court. A controversy regarding the meaning of a constitutional provision is not then *a justiciable controversy*. The basic assumptions, therefore, on which the American constitutional structure was founded—that constitutions are laws in the usual meaning of that term and that a case or controversy involving an alleged conflict between a constitutional provision and a statute or executive order is necessarily subject to judicial cognizance and review—have been regarded as legally unsound and politically impracticable.[16]

That the theory and practice with respect to written constitutions which were gradually adopted in Europe were familiar to American publicists is indicated on numerous occasions. Taking the opposite view from Chief Justice Marshall in *Marbury v. Madison*[17] and also that of

---

[16] See my article on "Some Phases of the Theory and Practice of Judicial Review of Legislation in Foreign Countries," 24 *Amer. Pol. Sci. Rev.* (Aug., 1930), 588 ff.

[17] 1 Cranch 137 (1803).

many other judges, Judge Bland of Baltimore maintained that the "right to enforce the observance of [constitutional] limitations rests with, and belongs exclusively to, the people, and cannot in any manner, be enforced by the judiciary. A constitutional limitation is then, the voice of the people addressed to the public agents respectively, in relation to their separate and distinct duties. . . . It is the business and duty of each department to attend to the constitution, only so far as regards its own proper checks and limitations, and not as relates to those of others."[18]

Failure to recognize these diametrically opposite assumptions and the implications involved in constitutional interpretation has had a marked influence on the development of American constitutional law. Starting with the assumption that the written constitution is comprised of laws and that when conflicts arise between these laws and the acts of other governmental agencies, the courts, whose duty it is to apply the law, must compare the two and must sustain the higher or supreme law in preference to that of any inferior agency, a train of reasoning was started which, by a peculiar type of legal logic, arrived at the essential features of the American doctrine of judicial supremacy. This assumption and its related postulates were used by Chief Justice Marshall in his opinion in *Marbury v. Madison* when he formulated what to him appeared to be a logical structure for the American doctrine of judicial review and which has become the standard for American legal thought relating to this matter.[19] Justice Gibson observed[20] that Marshall assumed the whole ground of the dispute and gave weak and inconclusive reasons for his judgment, but its mythical and fictional character has never been seriously questioned by the prevailing opinion among the bench and bar in the United States.

Judicial review and the legal nature of written documents.—With the acceptance of the reasoning and dicta of Chief Justice Marshall and others who agreed with him relating to the right of the courts to review legislative acts, the primary nature of a written constitution as a political document was not changed. Judges merely began to pass on questions political in nature and significance as if they were purely legal in char-

---

[18] *The Opinion of Judge Bland on the Right of the Judiciary to declare an act of Assembly Unconstitutional and also, on the Constitutionality of the Act investing County Courts with Equity Jurisdiction* (Baltimore, 1916), pp. 24, 25. For a brief analysis of Judge Bland's views regarding the nature of written constitutions, consult Charles Grove Haines, *The American Doctrine of Judicial Supremacy* (Berkeley, 1932), pp. 261 ff.

[19] For an analysis of Marshall's reasoning in this case, see below, pp. 249 ff.

[20] Eakin v. Raub, 12 S. and R. 330, 353. See also *The American Doctrine of Judicial Supremacy*, pp. 199 ff.

acter and as if legal methods and logic were the only factors employed in their interpretation. An analysis of the work of the Supreme Court indicates that to a considerable extent this effort to combine the political and legal phases of the Constitution under the same category by no means concealed the underlying political nature of many of the controversies with which the courts were concerned.[21] Furthermore, it is obvious that the acceptance of the usual European assumption that written constitutions are political laws and not within the jurisdiction of the courts would have changed the entire status of constitutions in the American political system.

How, then, did the foremost American legal theory develop that, at least for purposes of constitutional interpretation, the terms and phrases of a written constitution are to be considered "laws," that is, laws subject to judicial cognizance and application in the same manner as statutes or the phrases and principles of the common law to be applied by the courts? A satisfactory answer to this query may be found only in the history of the American doctrine of judicial review of legislation. This history, however, has been so carefully and systematically examined and discussed that it is unnecessary to give more than a short statement of the conflicting views which were expressed in the federal Convention and in the adoption of the Constitution.[22]

The notion that the provisions of written constitutions were laws, subject to interpretation as statutes were interpreted, was, no doubt, emerging as an incipient legal doctrine prior to the Convention's approval of Luther Martin's supremacy clause. Beginning with James Otis, the somewhat unreliable opinions and dogmas of Sir Edward Coke were quoted to the effect that the judges when they deem an act of Parliament as contrary to natural equity will declare it void.[23] A court in New Jersey had considered the Constitution as a superior law and refused to apply a statute regarded in conflict with it.[24] And James Iredell had presented to a North Carolina court the argument that the state constitution is

---

[21] The constitutionality of a statute, maintains Horace A. Davis, "is fundamentally a political and not a legal question" and, in his opinion, decisions of the courts which restricted legislation so far as they went beyond the specific language and express requirements of the Constitution were in effect constitutional amendments. *The Judicial Veto* (Boston, 1914), pp. 5 ff.

[22] See Charles A. Beard, *The Supreme Court and the Constitution* (New York, 1912), Edward S. Corwin, *The Doctrine of Judicial Review* (Princeton, 1914), and Haines, *The American Doctrine of Judicial Supremacy.*

[23] See Quincy *Reports*, pp. 521 ff.

[24] *Holmes v. Walton;* cf. *Amer. Hist. Rev.* (Apr., 1899), IV: 456, and *The American Doctrine of Judicial Supremacy,* chap v. For criticism of the view that *Holmes v. Walton* is a bona fide precedent for judicial review of legislative acts, see Louis B. Boudin, *Government by Judiciary* (New York, 1932), I: 534 ff.

to be considered law and any statutes deemed in conflict therewith must be considered by the judges as void. Following Iredell's argument the court held the act in question invalid.[25]

Gerry, King, Madison, Martin, Morris, and Wilson expressed opinions favorable to judicial review of legislative acts in the federal Convention.[26] In their official character, thought Martin, the judges will have a negative on the laws. So far as these men were responsible for the language of the Constitution, it is probable that the provisions on judicial powers were so worded as impliedly to sanction the exercise of power by federal courts, to a limited degree at least, and to declare laws of Congress invalid. It was perhaps deemed advisable by those favoring nationalism and the centralization of judicial power to allow the definite assertion of the right of judicial review to come through interpretation of the language of the Constitution rather than to arouse controversy and suspicion by incorporating a direct grant to the Judiciary.[27] In the state ratifying conventions John Marshall thought that when the Judges deemed an act as infringing the Constitution "they would not consider such a law as coming under their jurisdiction. They would declare it void."[28] Others who shared this view were Samuel Adams of Massachusetts, Grayson and Pendleton of Virginia, Martin and Hanson of Maryland, Wilson of Pennsylvania, Davie and Iredell of North Carolina, and Ellsworth of Connecticut.[29]

Mercer of Maryland, however, claimed "laws ought to be well and cautiously made, and then be uncontrollable." John Dickinson and Benjamin Franklin of Pennsylvania, Richard Spaight of North Carolina, and Gunning Bedford of Delaware expressed similar opinions. These men were among the group who agreed with Franklin that it would be improper to put it in the power of any man to negative a law passed by the legislature because it would give him control over the legislature.[30]

The issue whether the federal courts were to review and to declare invalid laws of Congress was not passed upon directly by the federal Convention. Among the resolutions presented in the Randolph plan was one providing for a council of revision modeled after the one in New York which authorized something in the nature of veto in a board

---

[25] Bayard v. Singleton, 1 Martin 44 (1787).

[26] See Farrand, *op. cit.*, I: 76, 97, 98, 109; II: 93, 299.

[27] *The American Doctrine of Judicial Supremacy*, p. 134.

[28] Elliot's *Debates* (2d ed.), III: 553.

[29] Farrand, *op. cit.*, pp. 548, 567; I: 189, 380; II: 131, 196; IX: 155, 156; and John Bach McMaster and Frederick D. Stone, eds., *Pennsylvania and the Federal Constitution, 1787–1788* (Lancaster, 1888), p. 354.

[30] Farrand, *op. cit.*, I: 109, and II: 298; Elliot's *Debates* (2d ed., 1888), V: 429.

comprised of executive and judicial officers. This plan twice met with disapproval.[31] Madison, who urged the adoption of the device of a council of revision, gave the reasons on which his view was based in his observations on the draft of a constitution for the state of Virginia. According to this draft, before measures under consideration were enacted into law they were to be separately submitted to the executive and judicial departments. If either department objected to the bill, a two-thirds vote would be necessary to pass the measure; if both departments objected, a three-fourths affirmative vote would be required. If either or both departments objected to a bill as violating the constitution, it was to be suspended until an election of members of the assembly had intervened and then reënacted by two-thirds or three-fourths votes of both houses, as the case may require. Neither the judges nor the executive were to have authority to declare a law thus enacted invalid.

Madison said the reasons for these proposals were as follows: "In the state constitutions and indeed in the federal one also, no provision is made for the case of a disagreement in expounding them; and as the courts are generally the last in making the decision, it results to them by refusing or not to execute a law, to stamp it with its final character. This makes the judiciary department paramount in fact to the legislature, which was never intended and can never be proper."[32]

It was the opinion of Charles A. Beard,[33] after an extensive analysis of data regarding judicial review of legislation, that the arguments and assumptions of the members of the Convention generally approved the view that the Judiciary would exercise considerable control over legislation. A similar analysis of the opinions expressed at this time has led to the conclusion that the issue of judicial review of acts of Congress was left undetermined by the Convention.[34]

The adoption of the supremacy clause, it is contended, not only settled the question of national sovereignty being paramount to State rights, but it also settled the Court's right of review of acts, both federal and state, to see if they conformed to the provisions of the Constitution. "If the Constitution is law," maintains Andrew C. McLaughlin, "nothing contrary to it can also be law," for judges are bound to recognize the Constitution and, in so doing, must treat it as law. Thus, he continues,

[31] Farrand, op. cit., II: 80, 298.
[32] Gaillard Hunt, ed., The Writings of James Madison (New York, 1900), V: 294, 295.
[33] Cf. The Supreme Court and the Constitution (New York, 1912), pp. 15 ff. For support of this opinion see Frank E. Melvin, "The Judicial Bulwark of the Constitution," 8 Amer. Pol. Sci. Rev. (May, 1914), 167 ff.
[34] Horace A. Davis, The Judicial Veto, chap. iii. Edward S. Corwin substantially agrees with this view; cf. 7 Amer. Pol. Sci. Rev. (May, 1913), 330.

"the Constitution is *plainly declared to be law, enforcible in courts,* to be handled as other law is handled, to be treated with the respect with which other laws are treated, to be enforced as other laws are enforced."[35] Though the state judges only are charged to be bound by the Constitutions as law, McLaughlin logically thinks that federal Judges must be likewise bound. In his opinion this logic was strengthened by something approaching an express grant when the federal courts were given jurisdiction over all cases arising under the Constitution and laws of the United States. The Martin resolution, it is argued, therefore not only made judicial review of acts of Congress inevitable, but, along with the clause granting jurisdiction to the federal courts, it gave express authority for its exercise. The only necessity, then, was to see that the Constitution was made law and had the qualities of fundamental law. It would then be the duty, not of the Supreme Court alone, but of all state and national courts, to recognize it as law and to apply it in controversies coming before them. This, then, was regarded as the great discovery made at the time of the formation and adoption of the Constitution.

Nor can Edward Channing see any other alternative than that which some members of the federal Convention saw; that is, the determination to establish a national tribunal with authority to decide the constitutionality of both state and national laws. The declaration that the Constitution and the laws and treaties made under it "shall be the supreme law of the land" could, as he sees it, "have only one meaning. Moreover, standing apart from the legislative branch and the executive, they set a Supreme Court with power to hear and determine all cases in law and equity arising under the Constitution. These phrases made the national Judiciary all powerful, and there can be little question that the members of the Convention so intended."[36] Claude H. Van Tyne, commenting on the supremacy clause, and declaring the Constitution and laws made in accordance therewith the law of the land and therefore enforcible in the courts together with the principle that the federal government might operate directly upon individuals, concluded that the issue of state

---

[35] *Constitutional History of the United States*, pp. 184, 185. At an earlier date McLaughlin wrote as follows: "Possibly the framers did not consciously intend by these words expressly to declare that the federal courts would have the right in all cases to declare a law of Congress void because exceeding constitutional limits. As to this it is hard to speak with absolute assurance. Certainly the Constitution was by this clause recognized and proclaimed as law, and we may at least assert that by force of logic, if not because of the full conscious purpose of the members of the Convention, this power was bestowed—the power to declare of no effect an act of Congress contrary to the law of the land." *The Confederation and the Constitution*, American Nation Series (New York, 1905), pp. 250, 251.

[36] *History of the United States* (New York, 1926), III: 497, 498.

sovereignty was settled by making the national government supreme and by leaving to the people nothing but the right of revolution.[37]

Extracts such as the above have been cited to show, in the opinion of historians, that there is good ground for the contention that the language of the Constitution expressly grants to the federal courts the authority to declare invalid acts of the state legislatures and of Congress deemed in conflict with the Constitution. Following this line of argument constitutional lawyers have recently asserted the view that since the Constitution authorized the state judges not only to consider the validity of acts of Congress but also the validity of the acts of their coordinate state legislatures, it can scarcely be presumed that it was not intended by this language to give the federal courts what was in effect granted by the twenty-fifth section of the Judiciary Act of 1789, that is, the authority to review such decisions. Any doubt which may arise regarding such presumption may, it is maintained, be resolved by reference to the grant of judicial power to all cases arising under the Constitution, laws, and treaties of the United States, and the express authorization of the Supreme Court to exercise appellate jurisdiction in such cases. When a state court passes on the validity of an act of Congress or interprets a provision of the Constitution, the Supreme Court must be conceded the power of review of such cases else the appellate power would not extend to all cases arising under the Constitution.[38] Thus, the supremacy and jurisdiction clauses of the Constitution are assumed to be equivalent to an express grant conferring upon national courts power to pass on the validity of acts of Congress.

Following the prevailing opinion among historians and jurists, William Draper Lewis says that one of the chief defects of the Constitution as drafted by the members of the federal Convention was its failure to designate the body having the power to decide—finally—disputed questions of constitutional interpretation. As a result of this defect there was, Lewis maintains, no authoritative interpretation of the effect of the provisions of the Constitution in limiting state action and no sanction was prescribed to compel state judges, executive officers, and legislatures to respect the supremacy of the Constitution, laws, and treaties of the United States.[39] An attempt was made, in part at least, to remedy this defect in the federal fundamental law by the passage of the twenty-fifth

---

[37] "Sovereignty in the American Revolution: An Historical Study," *Amer. Hist. Rev.* (Apr., 1907), XII: 529 ff.

[38] See book review by D. O. McGovney, 21 *Calif. Law Rev.* (Sept., 1933), 638 ff., and Hearings before the Judiciary Committee of the Senate on President Roosevelt's Proposal for Reform of the Federal Judiciary, Senate Bill 1392, Mar. 10 to 23, 1937.

[39] *Interpreting the Constitution* (Charlottesville, 1937), p. 11.

section of the Judiciary Act of 1789. For more than a quarter of a century the interpretation and application of this section was the cause of frequent political controversies between the federal government and the states.

Whatever may have been the intention of the framers of the Constitution, Congress, in the passage of the Judiciary Act of 1789 organizing the Supreme Court and the lower federal courts, took an important step toward the establishment of the legal significance and the supremacy of the Constitution as law. The twenty-fifth section of the act, which appears to have elicited little discussion in Congress, provided that cases may be reëxamined, reversed, or affirmed in the Supreme Court of the United States when an issue was raised in a state court regarding the validity of state action on the ground that the state act was repugnant to the Constitution, laws, or treaties of the United States, and when there was drawn into question the construction of any clause of the Constitution, treaty, or statute of the United States and the decision was against the title, right, privilege, or exemption claimed by either party.[40]

The purpose of this section was obviously to grant to the Supreme Court the right of review when a contention arose that a state court in its opinion and judgment failed to give the appropriate effect to the Constitution, laws, or treaties of the United States. From the language of this section "we are led to conclude," says Andrew C. McLaughlin,

that the federal Supreme Court could agree with the state tribunal as well as disagree; therefore the Judiciary Act, even though it makes no specific declaration of the power, assumes the right of a court, either state or national, to declare congressional acts void. As this fundamental statute was enacted by men, some of whom had been active in the federal Convention, we are entitled to gather from it evidence of the intention of the framers to recognize this important judicial power.[41]

McLaughlin thus expresses the view which many legal historians have been inclined to accept, namely, that the supremacy clause of the Con-

---

[40] *Statutes at Large*, I: 85–87. It was enacted "that a final judgment or decree in any suit, in the highest court of law or equity of a State in which a decision in the suit could be had, where is drawn in question the validity of a treaty or statute of, or an authority exercised under the United States, and the decision is against their validity; or where is drawn in question the validity of a statute of, or an authority exercised under any State, on the ground of their being repugnant to the Constitution, treaties or the laws of the United States, and the decision is in favor of their validity, or where is drawn in question the construction of any clause of the Constitution, of a treaty, or a statute of, or commission held under the United States, and the decision is against the title, privilege or exemption specially set up or claimed by either party, under such clause of the said Constitution, treaty, statute or commission, may be reëxamined and reversed or affirmed in the Supreme Court of the United States upon a writ of error." For an analysis of the debate in Congress on this act, see Charles Warren, "New Light on the History of the Federal Judiciary Act of 1789," 37 *Harv. Law Rev.* (Nov., 1923), 49.

[41] *Constitutional History of the United States*, pp. 236, 237.

stitution, the jurisdiction provision relating to the federal courts, and the twenty-fifth section of the Judiciary Act of 1789 are conclusive evidence that the makers of the Constitution expected the courts to pass on the validity of acts of Congress and of the state legislatures concerning whether or not they were in pursuance of the Constitution. But Mc-Laughlin, as well as other historians of the period, fails to point out that the crucial issue was not whether the federal courts could decide the validity of such acts, for it was taken for granted by most of the prominent men of the time that the courts should exercise such authority. The issue was whether a decision of the Supreme Court pertaining to the meaning of the Constitution was a final and conclusive decision on all points and, under all circumstances involved in the decision, bound the other coördinate departments of the government; and, if a question of ultimate political authority was concerned, bound the states. To concede the right of judicial review of legislation, whether it be looked upon as granted expressly or developed by implication from the language of the Constitution, is quite a different matter from the contention that a decision of a court—one of the coördinate branches of government—is such a final and authoritative exposition of the fundamental law that the other departments of the government were bound thereby. The view that the coördinate departments must accede to the interpretation of the Judiciary even with respect to the scope of their own powers was far from generally accepted at this time. Moreover, on the issue of the supremacy clause, the jurisdiction provision and the Judiciary Act of 1789 shed little light. This is the issue on which Hamilton and Marshall became the great proponents on the one side and Jefferson and Madison on the other. The arguments pro and con will be presented in later chapters.[42]

But the presumed inescapable logic leading to the American doctrine of judicial review will not bear critical scrutiny. The proposal to use force to bring into line a recalcitrant state, though included in both the Virginia and New Jersey plans for union, was soon abandoned, as was also the direct authority to veto or nullify state laws. Both of these means of coercion were obviated in part by the acceptance of the general principle that the federal government would operate directly on individuals rather than through the medium of the states. Speaking of the issue of federal supremacy, Oliver Ellsworth raised the query, shall it be a coercion of law, or a coercion of arms?—and indicated that he was "for coercion by law—that coercion which acts only upon delinquent individuals. This Constitution does not attempt to coerce sovereign

---

[42] For the consideration of the arguments on this issue, see especially chaps. x–xv.

bodies, States, in their political capacity. No coercion is applicable to such bodies, but that of an armed force."[43] Madison, also, in referring to the rejection of military power for the enforcement of state obligations, seemed pleased at the adoption of the alternative of "a government which, instead of operating on the States should operate without their intervention on the individuals composing them."[44]

The plan of coercion by legal methods over state acts in conflict with federal powers was undoubtedly the purpose of the supremacy clause. And it may be assumed from this clause, as was expressly provided by the twenty-fifth section of the Judiciary Act, that the federal courts might be called upon to review and revise the decisions of state courts so far as they undertook to interpret the grants of power to the federal government. That the general agreement concerning the principle of federal supremacy, with the Judges carrying the principle into effect, gave warrant to the federal courts to place an exclusive and final interpretation upon the Constitution, which was subject only to reversal by constitutional amendment, so far as the grant of powers to the coördinate departments was concerned, was a gratuitous assumption that had relatively meager evidence to support it and ran counter to the prevailing views and theories of the time.

It is necessary to recognize that the developing opinion regarding the authority of Judges to review legislative acts was designed, so far as the opinions of the conservatives were concerned, primarily as a check which the Judiciary might use to prevent legislative encroachments on judicial powers. It was part of the check and balance philosophy whereby the supremacy of the legislature was to be curtailed in a limited field. For the liberals such a check was especially desirable so that personal and individual rights should not be interfered with by overzealous officials. It formed part of the theory of confining government functions to the narrowest limits and was favored by Jefferson during the Revolutionary period. The idea that Judges might refuse to enforce arbitrary official acts was part also of the prevalent theory that it was the plain and unmistakable duty of all citizens, and to a special degree those charged with public responsibilities, to resist the enforcement of arbitrary and unwarranted acts. In this respect it was closely akin to the doctrine of revolution which held a foremost place in the political views of the time. In general, men thought of judicial review as a device to call attention to what appeared to be the unwarranted exercise of public powers in the hope that errors might be corrected. If the Judges found fault

---

[43] Elliot's *Debates*, II:196–197.
[44] *Letters* (1865 ed.), I: 344.

with an act of the legislature, it was done primarily to bring the matter to the attention of the legislature or to seek further instructions from the source of public authority—the people. Moreover, it was often necessary for the legislature to repeal the obnoxious act in order to release the people from the effect of its enforcement. The notion that judicial decisions bound the other departments and fixed irrevocably the meaning of the Constitution was seldom asserted before the debate on the Repeal Act of 1802 took place. Few men at this time considered judicial decisions in this field as having such a finality as was later claimed for them.[45]

The contention, then, that the terms and provisions of the federal Constitution are to be considered "law" according to the ordinary meaning and significance of that term can only be accepted with important qualifications and explanations. Parts of the Constitution may not be considered law in the usual sense of that term. Other parts have come to be regarded "law" only as the result of the general approval of certain postulates, when obviously the interpretation of the language of the Constitution in accordance with other postulates gives effect to its provisions as law only to a qualified and limited degree. The treatment of the entire Constitution as law to be interpreted by the courts and applied as such was not accorded general acceptance until the latter part of the nineteenth century.

With the developing doctrine of judicial review of legislation there was a growing tendency, particularly on the part of the conservative groups, to assert the doctrine that it was the duty of the courts to place final and authoritative interpretations upon the language of the written instruments. Judges called upon to make these interpretations followed the familiar methods and techniques of the common law. The process of legal interpretation, then, was the channel through which the provisions of the federal Constitution took their formal and definitive meaning. In more than three hundred volumes of the decisions of the Supreme Court of the United States, all but a few of the provisions have been explained and elaborated by the interpretative language of the decisions of the Court. The meaning of the Constitution has been so dependent upon such interpretation and elaboration by the Justices that the Supreme Court has frequently been called a continuous "constitutional convention."[46] The method and procedure of the Court in performing this func-

---

[45] See below, pp. 227 ff., and Don Ensminger Mowry, "Political and Party Aspect of the National Judiciary," *Amer. Hist. Mag.* (Jan., June, Sept., 1908), III: 83, 90.

[46] For an excellent summary of the changes made in the Constitution by the process of interpretation, see "The Constitution of the United States at the End of One Hundred Fifty Years," with an Introduction by Hugh Evander Willis (Bloomington, 1939).

tion have not been free from differences of opinion and sometimes acute controversy regarding the appropriate place and duty of the Judges in the interpretation and application of the fundamental law. To appreciate the role of the Supreme Court in the evolution of American government and politics it becomes necessary, therefore, to consider the process of legal interpretation.

THE PROCESS OF INTERPRETATION

Despite efforts to develop a science of interpretation of the law, the process is still an art and not a science, and, as Continental jurists contend, "it implies not knowledge but skill." Moreover, it is not always duly recognized that the so-called rules governing interpretation are not law and are seldom the result of the legislative will.

Interpretation is ordinarily understood to involve an attempt to find the meaning of a legal rule, especially a written rule, and an endeavor to discover the intention of its author. Interpretation in Rome had a different meaning. Roman jurisprudents, according to Puchta, were "intermediators, so to speak, between the letter of the statute and real life, and as such it was their business not to stick to the literal contents of the statute and the original intention of the legislator, but to adapt the letter to the needs of actual life and to make the application of the statute practicable."[47] But in the course of the development of the law interpretation has had other objectives.

The usual methods of interpretation as described by the commentators are the linguistic, the logical or systematic, and the historical.[48] The linguistic or grammatical method involves a search for the true import of the words in a statute as understood in customary usage. In general the application of the linguistic method led to the acceptance of a narrow and literal meaning of words according to their customary usage. But at times judges were inclined to extend the will of the legislature as much as possible and the theory was followed that a word is not, ordinarily, to be taken in a mere partial, narrow, or literal meaning. This resulted in the adoption of the principle of broad interpretation. The object of the

[47] Cf. Géza Kiss, "Equity and Law," *Science of Legal Method*, Modern Legal Philosophy Series (Boston, 1917), IV: 149 and Georg Friedrich Puchta, *Kursus der Institutionen* (4th ed., 1853), I: 316.

[48] Cf. Karl Georg Wurzel, *Science of Legal Method*, p. 359. From another approach three stages in the process of interpretation have been designated, as follows: first, the literal stage, when words are taken literally; second, the positive stage, when the will of the lawgiver is sought and carefully followed; and, third, the positive stage, when the text is not regarded as an all-sufficient guide and the opinions of judges are influenced by the exigencies of social life. Roscoe Pound, quoting Vandereycken, *Science of Legal Method*, p. 223.

logical or systematic method of interpretation is to arrive at the legislative intent or motive where the meaning may not be entirely clear from the words by comparing words or entire provisions of statutes with those of a similar character. This method often strives, where the purpose of the statute appears ambiguous, to discover in the language selected a single harmonious intent or purpose. By the historical method it is the aim of the interpreters to discover the sense or meaning which was intended to be attached to the words when they were originally discussed and approved in the legislature and inserted in the statute. Extensive use has been made of this method in the interpretation of constitutions and particularly in seeking the meaning of the provisions of the federal Constitution by referring to the debates in the Philadelphia Convention and in the state ratifying conventions.[49] In the process of constitutional interpretation the generally approved theory is that the primary object of the Justices is to discover the intent of the written document so that, with respect to collateral materials employed, they may be used merely to reveal or clarify the intent of the framers.[50] TenBroek gives ample evidence to demonstrate that this theory, which has frequently received judicial approval, does not stand in the way of the actual examination and use of extrinsic aids when the Justices regard such procedure advisable.

The conventional assumption that there is such a simple undifferentiated thing as the will of either a legislature or a constitutional convention is largely mythical.[51] Actually the provision to be interpreted was the result of the activities of a few individuals. Into the language which was put into the provision have gone the intent or will of these individuals, with the meaning they intended to convey, and the motive or motives for securing such legislative action.

Interpretation, which must be distinguished from mere application, whereby the judge determines whether the facts of a particular case fall within the rule, principle, or standard deemed pertinent, involves a mental process in which the words are mere symbols for intricate and complex modes of thought. The Judiciary must reconstruct these

---

[49] For a thorough study of the use of convention debates and related materials in constitutional construction see articles by Jacobus tenBroek on "Admissibility and Use by the United States Supreme Court of Extrinsic Aids in Constitutional Construction," 26 *Calif. Law Rev.* (Mar., May, Sept., 1938), 286, 437, 664; and 27 *Calif. Law Rev.* (Jan., May, 1939), 157, 399.

[50] Cf. Thomas M. Cooley, *Constitutional Limitations* (8th ed., 1927), I: 124, 125; and Joseph Story, *Commentaries on the Constitution of the United States*, I, sec. 405.

[51] "That the intention of the legislature is undiscoverable in any real sense is almost an immediate inference from a statement of the proposition," is the view of Max Radin, "Statutory Interpretation," 43 *Harv. Law Rev.* (Apr., 1930), 863, 870.

thought processes by the light of its own experiences. Language is not merely the instrument by which we think, but it directs our thinking into certain paths. Taking the words as symbols, the person whose duty it is to apply them must reëxpand or recreate the thought which was intended to be conveyed. In viewing the procedure of legislatures in the making of laws, and of courts in their interpretation, and taking into account the differences of personality and community interest, as well as the variations caused by the lapse of time and change of environment, we may well agree with John H. Wigmore that "words are far from fixed things; they are the most fluent and indefinite of things."[52] It was Justice Holmes who said that "a word is not a crystal, transparent and unchanged, it is the skin of a living thought and may vary greatly in color and content according to the circumstances and the time in which it is used."[53]

In private law the power of the judges over statutes is conceded to be very significant, both in common law and in civil law countries. Statutes, maintains John C. Gray, are merely points of departure for the judges to reproduce the thought of the law-giving body, and, instead of the process being merely mechanical, the meaning is derived, not by any exact and foreknowable methods of reasoning, but from the words according to the feeling of the judges. The freedom of judges in interpreting statutes is greater when legislation is rare and can only be secured with difficulty.[54]

The interpretation of constitutions is usually considered similar to the construction of statutes. Gray pointed out that in interpretation the real difficulty arises as a result of the members of legislatures or constitutional conventions failing to deal with a question or, having dealt with an issue, failing to indicate an intention. In cases of this kind the judges

---

[52] J. H. Wigmore, *Science of Legal Method*, Modern Legal Philosophy Series, IX: xxxv.

[53] Towne v. Eisner, 245 U. S. 425 (1917). According to Continental jurists words are like chameleons which take their color from their surroundings. Max Radin regards statutory interpretation as "not an exercise in logic or law but in creative imagination." 48 *Yale Law Jour.* (Apr., 1939), 1117.

[54] John C. Gray, *The Nature and Source of Law* (2d ed., 1921), pp. 170 ff.

"Whoever deals with juristic questions must always at the same time be a bit of a legislator." Ernst Zitelmann, quoted in *Science of Legal Method*, p. 208.

"The immensely greater portion of the facts and groups of facts with which lawyers have to deal were never anticipated by the intention of the legislator, nor were they part of the content of his mind, in such a way that they could be subsumed under his expressed concepts. The legislative will throws a bright light on just a few points in the vast field of life. . . . The illuminated places have but to serve the function of centers of attraction or convergence." Wurzel, "Methods of Juridical Thinking," *Science of Legal Method*, p. 356.

do not determine what is the will of the legislators or constitution makers but guess what they would have intended on a point not present to their minds, if the point had been presented.[55]

When law is crystallized into the unvarying text of a code or constitution, the flow of its expression is checked, though social progress continues its course. With a slow and cumbersome amending procedure the need of interpretation and elaboration is greater than in private law. Upon interpretation or periodic revision must depend the maintenance of harmony between the provisions of the written document and the practices of everyday life.[56] Owing to the extensive authority devolving upon the judges in their efforts to extract legal meanings from the inert language of statutes or constitutions, it has been deemed advisable to give credence to certain traditions or attitudes which would support and strengthen judicial powers.

One of the foremost problems of legal interpretation arises from the paradox that law shall at the same time have continuity with the past and be adapted to the present and the future. The history of the law, maintains Sir Maurice Sheldon Amos, "reveals a perpetual oscillation between the introvert ideal of stability and static perfection, with primary emphasis on the abstract rule, and the extrovert ideal, which commands that the law be remolded in conformity with the new interests and new moral standards of the outside world."[57] Mechanical jurists have tended to place uppermost the first of these ideals, and the school of free legal decision has been inclined to give emphasis to the second ideal. Each group of jurists has profoundly influenced American constitutional interpretation.

Mechanical jurisprudence.—A tradition that judges are somewhat in the order of supermen has been fostered by lawyers and judges and has gradually gained wide acceptance. It is customary for those who accept this tradition to insist not only that judges shall be free from executive and legislative control, but that they must also be nonpartisan and not be influenced by the political ideas and doctrines prevalent among the people. The domain of a court, said James M. Carter, is law, not politics; judges do not sit to decide political questions.[58]

Another phase of the tradition that judges are supermen is brought about by the contention that they must take a purely passive attitude

---

[55] Gray, *op. cit.*, pp. 172, 173.

[56] Cf. Layton B. Register, "Judicial Powers of Interpretation under Foreign Codes," 65 *Univ. of Penn. Law Rev.* (Nov., 1916), 39.

[57] "Roscoe Pound" in *Modern Theories of Law* (London, 1933), p. 102.

[58] "The Courts and Unconstitutional Law," Ill. Bar Assn. *Reports* (1912), p. 407; see also W. S. Carpenter, *Judicial Tenure in the United States* (New Haven, 1918), pp. 1–2.

toward the law.[59] Though the judges are the "mouthpieces" or the "living oracles" of the law, the prevalent theory or fiction is that they are not permitted to make law. In describing the function of the judge, Elihu Root observes "it is not his function or within his power to enlarge or improve or change the law."[60] Despite frank admissions or confessions by able members of the legal fraternity who have looked at the judicial process in a realistic way, the view is generally accepted that impersonal law is administered by judicial ministers who are impotent to change it.[61] The air of the courtroom and the legal forum is saturated with the dictum of Sir Edward Coke and approved by John Locke and his followers, namely, that only a law comprised of known, certain, definite, and established rules is tolerable in a civilized society. According to this view there is an ascertainable rule or formula prescribed in advance for every case that arises, and those rules or formulas are designed to provide for any condition or situation which may occur. Hence, one and only one

---

[59] Some typical expressions of the theory which Bentham called "decision without thought, or mechanical judicature," *The Works of Jeremy Bentham*, ed. by John Bowring (Edinburgh, 1843), VII: 246, are as follows:

"The judges of the nation are but the mouths that pronounce the words of law; inanimate beings who can moderate neither its force nor its vigor." Montesquieu, *L'Esprit des Lois*, Bk. 11, p. 106.

"The judiciary . . . can take no active resolution whatever. It may truly be said to have neither *force* nor *will* but merely judgment." Alexander Hamilton, *The Federalist*, No. 78 (Lodge ed.), 519.

The violation of a constitutional right ought to be as obvious to the comprehension of everyone "as an axiomatic truth; as that the parts are equal to the whole." Grimball v. Ross (Ga., 1808), T. U. P. Charlton 175, 178; see also Byrne v. Stewart (S. Ca., 1812), 3 De S. 466, 477.

The judicial department "has no will in any case. . . . Judicial power is never exercised for the purpose of giving effect to the will of the judge; always for the purpose of giving effect to the will of the legislature; or in other words, to the will of the law." Chief Justice Marshall in Osborn v. Bank of the United States, 9 Wheaton 738, 866 (1824).

"What is to become of constitutions of government if they are to rest, not on the plain import of their words, but upon conjectural enlargements and restrictions to suit the temporary passions and interests of the day. . . . They are not to be frittered away to please the demagogues of the day. They are not to be violated to gratify the ambition of political leaders; they are to speak the same voice now and forever." Justice Story in *Commentaries on the Constitution* (5th ed., 1891), II: 653.

Chief Justice Taney, in *Dred Scott v. Sanford*, said that whereas the Constitution remains unaltered, it must be construed now as it was understood at the time of its adoption; that it is not only the same in words but the same in meaning, "and as long as it continues to exist in its present form, it speaks not only in the same words, but with the same meaning and intent with which it spoke when it came from the hands of its framers, and was voted on and adopted by the people of the United States. Any other rule of construction would abrogate the judicial character of this Court, and make it the mere reflex of the popular opinion or passion of the day." 19 How. 393, 426 (1856).

"The judges make no laws, they establish no policy, they never enter into the domain

correct application of the law is possible—an application which should
be apparent to any reasonable-minded justice.

In the formative years of the common law it was recognized that the
personality of the judges could not be ignored in an attempt to understand the significance of the law. Though it was regarded expedient to
understand the decided cases, it was observed that "this cannot be done
without examining closely the personal characteristics of those who
decide them."[62] But the traditional attitude of the lawyer and judge
under the common law was to conceal or to ignore the personal elements
which entered into a judgment or decision. It was customary to portray
an ideal, passionless judge rendering justice in a wholly detached and
mechanical fashion.

The prevailing view regarding the settlement of a legal controversy
involved, therefore, the following steps: first, the finding of the facts
of the case; second, the classification of the facts according to certain

---

of public action. They do not govern. Their functions in relation to the state are limited to seeing that popular action does not trespass upon right and justice, as it exists
in written constitution and natural law." Justice Brewer in *The Movement of Coercion*
(1893), p. 12. See also Thomas M. Cooley, *Constitutional Limitations* (8th ed.), I: 124.

More recent expressions of this type are those of Justices Sutherland and Butler: "A
provision of the Constitution, it is hardly necessary to say, does not admit of two distinctly opposite interpretations. It does not mean one thing at one time and an entirely
different thing at another time. If the contract impairment clause, when framed and
adopted, meant that the terms of a contract for the payment of money could not be
altered *in invitum* by a state statute enacted for the relief of hardly pressed debtors
to the end and with the effect of postponing payment or enforcement during and
because of an economic or financial emergency, it is but to state the obvious to say
that it means the same now." Justice Sutherland, dissenting in Home Building and
Loan Association v. Blaisdell, 290 U. S. 398, 448, 449 (1934).

"There should be no misunderstanding as to the function of this Court in such a
case. It is sometimes said that the Court assumes a power to overrule or control the
action of the people's representatives. This is a misconception. The Constitution is
the supreme law of the land ordained and established by the people. All legislation
must conform to the principles it lays down. When an act of Congress is appropriately
challenged in the courts as not conforming to the constitutional mandate, the judicial
branch of the government has only one duty,—to lay the articles of the Constitution
which is invoked beside the statute which is challenged and to decide whether the
latter squares with the former. All the Court does, or can do, is to announce its considered judgment upon the question. The only power it has, if such it may be called,
is the power of judgment. This Court neither approves nor condemns any legislative
policy. Its delicate and difficult office is to ascertain and declare whether the legislation
is in accordance with, or in contravention of, the provisions of the Constitution; and,
having done that, its duty ends." Justice Butler, in United States v. Butler, 297 U. S.
1, 62, 63 (1936).

[60] "The Importance of an Independent Judiciary," 72 *The Independent* (1912), 45.

[61] Cf. Walter Nelles, "Towards Legal Understanding," 34 *Columbia Law Rev.* (May,
June, 1934), 862, 1041.

[62] Mr. Justice Darling in *Scintillae Juris and Meditations in the Tea Room* (6th ed.,
London, 1914), p. 9.

preëxisting legal categories; third, the selection of the rule, principle, or standard which was applicable to the relations involved; and, fourth, the decision or judgment which necessarily followed. According to this view a conclusion was reached by formal methods of legal thinking from which all individual prejudices and personal predilections were eliminated.[63] Thus, a method of interpretation was presumed to be involved which recognized nothing but formulated legal rules and the facts and circumstances of a specific case. Furthermore, it was assumed to be not only possible but also necessary to establish rules which, if properly understood and applied, would yield only one answer to legal controversies coming within their scope. In theory, then, the judge called upon to settle a legal issue must, after hearing the facts, select some rule or principle as his premise, apply this premise to the facts, and arrive at the decision dictated by a strictly logical process. Popular impressions strengthened by frequent confirmations of the bench and bar sanctioned the belief that judicial decisions were arrived at by logical deduction or subsumption from established legal rules. Though it made no difference how many other factors contributed to the result, juridical thinking, so it was asserted, must appear strictly logical in form. The judge was looked upon as a purely reasoning being—a sort of automaton pronouncing judgments.

In the prevalence of this point of view there was a tendency in legal thinking to ignore what are generally considered social ideas—ethical, political, and economic—as well as the forms in which these ideas manifest themselves. The legal rules to be applied need not therefore take into account the important influences and factors which operate in the ceaseless economic struggles of society. Nor are lawyers or litigants to give consideration to the bias or prejudices or the economic and political views of the judges. Law presumably becomes a scientific and detached phenomenon with personal views and feelings eliminated.

The mechanical or necessitous theory of legal interpretation and application has been lauded as a feature of the common law, for, in common law technique, the judgment, said Blackstone, "though pronounced or awarded by the judges is not their determination or sentence, but the determination or sentence of *the law*."[64] More than a century later Lord Esher insisted that there is in the English legal system "no such thing as judge-made law, for the judges do not make law,"[65] though he conceded that English judges frequently apply existing law to circum-

---

[63] Frederick Sherwood Dunn, *The Protection of Nationals* (Baltimore, 1932), p. 71, 72.
[64] 3 *Blackstone's Comm.*, 396.
[65] Willis and Co. v. Baddeley (1892), 2 Q. B. 324, 326.

stances to which it has not previously been authoritatively applied. Thus, it was observed that courts in the nineteenth century were unyielding in their faith that justice must be administered in accordance with fixed rules which could be applied by a mechanical process of logical reasoning to a given state of facts and made to produce an inevitable result.[66]

In the early decades of the interpretation of the provisions of written constitutions, it was not generally assumed that judges decided cases in such a mechanical or necessitous manner. Judges were selected as a rule from among those lawyers who were active in political life and were naturally partisan in their outlook and in their attitudes toward political problems. It was not deemed inappropriate for judges while serving on the bench to take an active part in politics and it was not uncommon for political views and principles to be stated in judicial decisions. The idea that judges stood aloof and were detached from partisan interests and activities, like many other ideas which have become prevalent in American political thought, came to be accepted gradually. And many jurists, lawyers, and judges did not find in the mechanical method of decision a satisfactory explanation of the mode of rendering legal opinions and judgments.

Two schools of jurists, the advocates of "free legal decision" in Europe and the realists in the United States, have especially emphasized the factual inaccuracies and the unreasonable implications of the traditional theory of legal interpretation.

Free legal decision.—During the latter part of the nineteenth century a group of European legal commentators became advocates of "free legal decision." This doctrine turned away from the method of strict interpretation of the code or statute or the binding effect of precedents and sought the real growth of the law through the creative activity of the judges. Claiming that all declarations or applications of the law involve of necessity a creative element, this school aimed to secure the guaranty of justice through the insight, feeling, and social perspective of members of the judiciary. François Geny, one of the foremost jurists of this period, thought of free judicial decision as a method by which the judges ought to decide cases primarily when there were gaps in the code or statutory law or when cases arose for which no express legal rule had been provided. Under such circumstances the judges were to be guided in rendering their judgments by their instinctive sense or feeling of justice as well as by their determination of what the social needs of

---

[66] Note on "Rule and Discretion in the Administration of Justice," 33 *Harv. Law Rev.* (May, 1920), 972.

the community required. Calling attention to the need of intuition or a feeling for justice in the exercise of the creative function of the judge, Geny favored "a process of reasoning which starts from an intuition supplemented by the feeling for what is just, and arrives at exact conclusions by a series of deductions under the constant guidance and control of practical common sense."[67]

Eugene Ehrlich, also a member of this school, looked upon every body of formulated rules as in its very nature incomplete and hence really antiquated the moment it was formulated. He could not see any hope for justice except through the personality of the judge.[68] "Sufficient stress has never been laid," Ehrlich asserted, "on the fact that the significance of law in the daily life of the people depends far more on the persons charged with its administration than on the principles according to which it is administered. The same rule is likely to have an essentially different meaning in different countries at different periods, for no other reason than that the persons sitting on the bench are differently trained, have a different temperament, hold a different official or social position."[69] Joseph Kohler also criticized the customary theory regarding interpretation because he deemed it the duty of the judge to seek the most reasonable meaning of the law and the one which will produce the most beneficial effect. Former types of interpretation, he maintained, failed to recognize that every work of the intellect is the product of social forces and that written texts contain ideas independent of the persons who drafted them.[70]

It is necessary to recognize that the theory and practice in civil law countries provides a system in which the code and statute furnish analogies and starting points for reasoning with judicial decisions, settling only particular points as applicable to concrete cases; whereas

[67] F. Geny, "Judicial Freedom of Decision," *Science of Legal Method*, pp. 17, 45. See also Geny, *Science et Technique en droit prive postif* (Paris, 1925), pt. iii.

[68] Ehrlich, *op. cit.*, pp. 61, 65, 72. "I do not doubt," said Ehrlich, "that the modern free-finding-of-law movement marks not only an advance in scientific insight, but also an actual shift in the relation of the state and society—a shift which has taken place long ago in other spheres." *Fundamental Principles of the Sociology of Law*, trans. by Walter L. Moll (Cambridge, 1936), p. 13. Cf. *ibid.*, pp. 130, 131, 172–174, 211–213.

[69] *Ibid.*, p. 48.

[70] Joseph Kohler, "Judicial Interpretation of Enacted Law," *Science of Legal Method*, pp. 187, 195. Kohler had little sympathy with the mechanical method of interpretation, for he said: "to think of a statute as a phenomenon the truth of which has to be sought, and to regard that truth as but a single deduction naturally flowing from the statute itself—all this is what constitutes scholasticism." *Ibid.*, pp. 193, 194.

In the Swiss Civil Code, Art. 1, the function of the judge is stated in different terms from those usually employed in describing the duties of a common law jurist. "The

in common law countries judicial decisions form the primary basis for reasoning, and it is the purpose of legislation to establish rules.[71] But despite these differences in the process of interpretation and application of the law, the European doctrine of free legal decision has many points in common with the interpretative procedure in Anglo-American jurisdictions. And there are some interesting points of comparison between the European advocates of free legal decision and the American school of realistic or experimental jurisprudence.

Realistic or experimental jurisprudence.—There have been persons in Anglo-American jurisdictions both in and outside of the legal profession who have regarded the accepted theory of legal interpretation and application in the nature of a fiction and hence not corresponding to the facts of everyday life. Some have agreed with Bishop Hoadly that "whoever hath an absolute authority to interpret any written or spoken laws, it is he who is truly the law-giver to all intent and purposes, and not the person who first wrote or spoke them"[72] and, therefore, they have turned to the personality of the judge as the pivotal factor in the administration of justice.

Foremost among those who recognized the significance of judge-made law in England is A. V. Dicey, who noted that "a large part and, as many would add, the best part of the law of England is judge-made law—that is to say consists of rules to be collected from the judgments of courts."[73] To John Chipman Gray, also, the judges are rather the creators than the discoverers of the law, and the law of a nation means primarily the opinions of a half-dozen old gentlemen.[74]

Justice Holmes was one of the first of American legal scholars and judges to point out the inadequacy of the traditional method of viewing

Civil Code applies to all cases for which it contains provisions, either according to its letter or its spirit. If the Code contains no provision applicable to the question at issue, the judge should decide according to customary law, and where that is also absent, according to recognized legal doctrine and science.

"In the absence of all these sources, he shall render judgment in accordance with such rules as he would enact if he were the legislator."

[71] See Introduction by Roscoe Pound, in Frederick J. de Sloovere, *Cases on the Interpretation of Statutes from Decisions of American and English Courts* (St. Paul, 1931), p. vi.

[72] Benjamin Hoadly, Bishop of Bangor, from sermon preached before the King, 1717.

[73] A. V. Dicey, *Lectures on the Relation between Law and Opinion in England During the Nineteenth Century* (London, 1930), pp. 361, 362.

[74] *The Nature and Source of Law* (2d ed.), p. 84. "Anglo-American history illustrates copiously how the judiciary have in fact occupied themselves at all times with declarations of law independent of the statute, i.e., with genuine legislation," J. H. Wigmore, Introduction to *Science of Legal Method*, p. xxx. At another time Dean Wigmore observed that "a judge may decide almost any question any way, and still be supported by an array of cases." See his *Treatise on Evidence* (2d ed., 1923), I: xv.

the law. In his work, *The Common Law,* published in 1881, he referred to "the felt necessities of the times, the prevalent political and moral theories, intuitions of public policy, avowed or unconscious, even the prejudices which judges share with their fellow-men" which, in his opinion, "have had a good deal more to do than the syllogism in determining the rules by which men should be governed."[75] Nearly twenty years later he criticized the teaching in the law schools by a method which he termed a combination of the inspirational and the logical and whereby postulates are taken for granted upon authority without inquiry into their worth, with logic then being used as the only tool to develop results. In his opinion "the life of the law has not been logic; it has been experience." He also objected to the tendency to deal with the law as if it were "a theological working out of dogma."

His realistic views were expressed in *The Common Law* in the often-quoted paragraph which will bear repetition in part here because of its direct bearing on the work of the Supreme Court in its influence on American political life. "The very considerations which judges most rarely mention, and always with an apology," said Holmes,

are the secret root from which the law draws all the juices of life. I mean, of course, considerations of what is expedient for the community concerned. Every important principle which is developed by litigation is in fact and at bottom the result of more or less definitely understood views of public policy; most generally, to be sure, under our practice and traditions, the unconscious result of instinctive perferences and inarticulate convictions, but none the less traceable to views of public policy in the last analysis.[76]

A group of American lawyers known as the realists or experimentalists, following in the footsteps of Holmes, have attacked the traditional mechanical type of interpretation of law from a different approach and with a different purpose than the European advocates of free legal decision. Looking upon the opinions delivered in the appellate courts as effusions of the judges explaining or excusing their decrees or judgments, which, incidentally, have little relation to the mental processes or motives in arriving at decisions, they contrast such "paper rules," as they call them, with the "real rules" or factors guiding judicial conduct.[77] The

---

[75] *The Common Law* (Boston, 1881), p. 1. See also *Justice Oliver Wendell Holmes: His Book Notices and Uncollected Letters and Papers,* ed. by Harry C. Shriver (New York, 1936), chap. 1.

[76] *The Common Law,* pp. 35, 36.

[77] "Do I suggest that . . . the 'accepted rules,' the rules the judges say that they apply, are without influence upon their actual behavior. I do not. I do not even say that, *sometimes,* these 'accepted rules' may not be a very accurate description of the judges' actual behavior. What I say is that such accuracy of description is rare. . . .

   " 'Real rules,' then, if I had my way with words, would by legal scientists be called

actual process of judicial decision, as they see it, instead of following the mechanical model, comes nearer to the procedure which Chancellor Kent described as applicable to his manner of deciding cases. After making myself master of the facts, Kent said, "I saw where justice lay, and the moral sense decided the case half of the time; and I then set down to search the authorities until I had exhausted my books; and I might once in a while be embarrassed by a technical rule, but I almost always found principles suited to my view of the case."[78]

The realists, then, place foremost in the process of interpretation the inescapable operation of the personal element in the administration of justice, despite the fact that by the tradition of the common law the injection of the personal element in court procedure is deemed to be an unmitigated evil. Why not recognize, contends Jerome Frank, that judges are fallible human beings and that prejudices and personal bias affect the reasoning of judges as they do the reasoning of other men? The factors which influence judges are, indeed, varied and complicated. Among these factors the most noteworthy, perhaps, are education, race, class bias, views of public policy, notions of the right and the just, as well as economic and social philosophies.[79] And, contrary to the usual assump-

---

the practices of the courts, and not 'rules' at all. . . . 'Paper rules' are what have been treated, as rules of law; the accepted doctrine of the time and place—what the books there say 'the law' is. The 'real rules' and rights—'what the courts will do in a given case, and nothing more pretentious'—are then predictions." Karl N. Llewellyn, "A Realistic Jurisprudence—The Next Step," 30 *Col. Law Rev.* (Apr., 1930), 431, 444, 448. Others who espoused the cause of legal realism were Walter W. Cook, "Scientific Method and the Law," 13 *Amer. Bar Assn. Jour.* (June, 1927), 303; Joseph C. Hutcheson, "The Judgment Intuitive: The Function of the Hunch in Judicial Decisions," 14 *Cornell Law Quar.* (Apr., 1929), 263; Max Radin, "Legal Realism," 31 *Col. Law Rev.* (May, 1931), 825; Dean Leon Green, "The Duty Problem in Negligence Cases," 28 *Col. Law Rev.* (Nov., 1928), 1014 and 29 *Col. Law Rev.* (Mar., 1929), 255; Karl N. Llewellyn, "Some Realism about Realism, Responding to Dean Pound," 44 *Harv. Law Rev.* (June, 1931), 1222; L. L. Fuller, "American Legal Realism," 82 *Univ. of Penn. Law Rev.* (Mar., 1934), 429, and Felix S. Cohen, "Transcendental Nonsense and the Functional Approach," 35 *Col. Law Rev.* (June, 1935), 809.

For criticisms of Legal Realism, see Dean Pound, "A Call for a Realist Jurisprudence," 44 *Harv. Law Rev.* (Mar., 1931), 697 and "Fifty Years of Jurisprudence," 51 *Harv. Law Rev.* (Mar., 1938), 785 ff.; H. Kantorowicz, "Some Rationalism about Realism," 43 *Yale Law Jour.* (June, 1934), 1240; and Walter B. Kennedy, "Functional Nonsense and the Transcendental Approach," 5 *Fordham Law Rev.* (May, 1936), 272.

[78] "Autobiographical Sketch of Chancellor Kent," 1 *Southern Law Rev.* (July, 1872), 389.

[79] *Law and the Modern Mind* (New York, 1930), pp. 105, 106, 145, 146. The practicing lawyer, says Dean Pound, "knows painfully how much depends on the particular judge on whose list his case chances to be; he understands well how much depends upon who argues a case before a given tribunal; he appreciates how much the result hangs upon the personnel of the appellate tribunal before which a decisive battle of law chances to be waged." *Interpretations of Legal History* (New York, 1923), p. 129.

tion, individual factors often are more important causes of decisions than political, economic, or moral biases. "The judge's knowledge of the rules," claims Frank, "combined with his reactions to the conflicting testimony, with his sense of fairness, with his background of economic and social views, and with that complicated compound loosely named his 'personality' to form an incalculable mixture out of which comes the court order we call his decision."[80]

Realists, functionalists, or experimentalists, as they are sometimes called, agree that it is a mistake to look upon law as primarily made up of rules. They view law in the process of its administration as the technique or method of the judges in rendering decisions. They urge that prime consideration be given, not to the written rationalizations of the judges, but to the actual facts of controversies to be determined and the judgments rendered in deciding these controversies. Referring to certain phases of the realistic movement, Dean Pound observes: "Where the last century stressed certainty and uniformity and ignored the falling short of these ideals, they stress the uncertainty and lack of uniformity, the influence of personal and subjective factors in particular cases, attributing to individual psychology the departures from an ideal of mechanical application of rules which are necessarily involved in the quite different process of choice of starting points for analogical reasoning and application of standards."[81] Though it has frequently been pointed out that the realists, like some of the sociological jurists, overemphasize the influence of personal factors in the administration of justice, on the other hand, it is admitted even by critics of the new school that its leaders have "brought home vigorously to the bench and bar in the United States the need of thinking about the judicial process."[82]

Thus, a group of American legal writers view the judicial process in the language of the French jurist, Raymond Saleilles, as a procedure in which not infrequently "one wills at the beginning the result; one finds the principle afterwards; such is the genesis of all juridical construction. Once accepted, the construction presents itself, doubtless, in the ensemble of legal doctrine under the opposite aspect. The factors are inverted. The principle appears as an initial cause, from which one has drawn the result which is found to be deduced from it."[83] As a matter

---

[80] Jerome Frank, "Are Judges Human?" 80 *Univ. of Penn. Law Rev.* (Nov., Dec., 1931), 17, 47. In the articles under this title and in his *Law and the Modern Mind,* Frank vigorously attacked the traditional doctrines concerning the function of judges in the process of the making and the interpretation of the law.

[81] "Fifty Years of Jurisprudence," 51 *Harv. Law Rev.* (Mar., 1938), 786.

[82] *Ibid.,* p. 796.

[83] *De la Personnalite Juridique* (2d ed., 1922), pp. 45, 46, and Benjamin N. Cardozo,

of fact, a not uncommon method of reasoning is for the conclusion or result to be anticipated or postulated and then data or principles to support this conclusion to be searched for.[84] According to this method constitutional interpretation follows the process which Pound finds applicable in the enforcement of the private law. The practice of our application of law is, he notes, to a large and apparently growing extent such as that of jurors or courts when they "take the rules of law as a general guide, determine what the equities of the cause demand, and contrive to find a verdict or render a judgment accordingly, wrenching the law no more than is necessary."[85] It is apparent, then, that for many cases at least, judges must choose the path of decision and such choices are often influenced by factors outside of the formal law.

Justice Cardozo, who takes judge-made law as one of the existing realities of life, observes that in the field of constitutional law the method of free decision has become the dominant one today. The great generalities of the Constitution have, he thinks, a content and significance which vary from age to age. And it is the method of free decision which sees through the transitory particulars and reaches what is permanent behind them. Interpretation, therefore, becomes more than the ascertainment of the meaning and intent of lawmakers. It supplements and fills the vacant spaces by the same processes and methods that have built up the customary law.[86] On another occasion Justice Cardozo tells of his efforts as a practitioner at the bar to find the pertinent authority and to fit it to the case at hand, and how this procedure failed not infrequently to bring the expected result, and how as a judge the problem stood before him in a new light. For, said he:

I found that the creative element was greater than I had fancied; the forks in the road more frequent; the signposts less complete. . . . Some cases, of course, there are where one route and only one is possible. They are the cases where the law is fixed and settled. They make up in bulk what they lack in interest. Other cases present a genuine opportunity for choice—not a choice between two decisions, one of which may be said to be almost certainly right and the other almost certainly wrong, but a choice so nicely balanced that when once it is announced, a new right and a new wrong will emerge in the announcement.[87]

The interpretation of the Constitution, like the process of the interpretation of statutes, is really a choice between a strict or a liberal and

---

The Nature of the Judicial Process (New Haven, 1922), p. 170. See also Max Radin, "Statutory Interpretation," 43 *Harv. Law Rev.* (Apr., 1930), 863, 864.

[84] Cf. Frank, *Law and the Modern Mind*, pp. 102 ff.

[85] Roscoe Pound, "Enforcement of Law," 20 *Green Bag* (Aug., 1908), 405, 406.

[86] Cardozo, *op. cit.*, p. 17.

[87] *The Growth of the Law* (New Haven, 1924), pp. 58, 59.

latitudinarian view of its phrases. Thus, two schools have waged a continual contest over the meaning and application of the Constitution. One group has maintained that the principles of the written law are so plain and unmistakable that the violation of a constitutional right ought to be as obvious to the comprehension of everyone "as an axiomatic truth; as that the parts are equal to the whole."[88] Justice Sutherland sponsored a similar view when he said the words of the Constitution "are pliable in the sense that in appropriate cases they have the capacity of bringing within their grasp every new condition which falls within their meaning. But their *meaning* is changeless; it is only their *application* which is extensible."[89]

Another group of jurists has recognized as a fundamental principle that judges, in interpreting and applying the terms of the written instrument, must of necessity participate in the process of legislation. Justice Holmes on many occasions presented the view that logic and general propositions do not suffice to decide concrete cases, but that the decisions are made by the judges and they must legislate. And Justice Brandeis, starting with the well-known dictum of Chief Justice Marshall that "it is a Constitution we are expounding," adopted the realistic approach when he said that the clauses of the Constitution must have a capacity of adaptation to changing conditions. This Court, said Justice Brandeis,

has repeatedly sustained the exercise of power by Congress, under various clauses of that instrument, over objects of which the Fathers could not have dreamed. We have likewise held that general limitations on the powers of government, like those embodied in the due process clauses of the Fifth and Fourteenth Amendments, do not forbid the United States or the States from meeting modern conditions by regulations which "a century ago, or even half a century ago, probably would have been rejected as arbitrary and oppressive." Clauses guaranteeing to the individual protection against specific abuses of power, must have a similar capacity of adaptation to a changing world. It was with reference to such a clause that this Court said in *Weems v. United States*,[90] "Legislation, both statutory and constitutional, is enacted, it is true, from an experience of evils, but its general language should not, therefore, be necessarily confined to the form that evil had theretofore taken. Time works changes, brings into existence new conditions and purposes. Therefore a principle to be vital must be capable of wider application than the mischief which gave it birth. This is peculiarly true of constitutions. They are not ephemeral enactments, designed to meet passing occasions. They are, to use the words of Chief Justice Marshall 'designed to approach immortality as nearly as human institutions can approach it.' The future is their care and provision for events of good and bad tendencies of which no prophecy can be made. In the application of a Constitution, therefore, our contemplation cannot be

---

[88] For citations supporting this view, see above, p. 30.

[89] Dissenting opinion in Home Building and Loan v. Blaisdell, 290 U. S. 398, 451 (1934).

[90] From opinion of Justice McKenna, 217 U. S. 349, 373 (1910).

only of what has been but of what may be. Under any other rule a constitution would indeed be as easy of application as it would be deficient in efficacy and power. Its general principles would have little value and be converted by precedent into impotent and lifeless formulas. Rights declared in words might be lost in reality."[91]

It is, indeed, where there are forks in the road that the predilection or training of the judge becomes a significant factor in the choice of paths. And there is a larger freedom of choice in the construction of constitutions than in ordinary statutes because constitutions are more likely to enunciate general principles and to contain phrases of political and economic rather than legal significance. Speaking of the contention of Chief Justice Marshall that the judge has no will in any case except "the will of the law," Justice Cardozo observed that "Marshall's own career is a conspicuous illustration of the fact that the ideal is beyond the reach of human faculties to attain. He gave to the Constitution of the United States the impress of his own mind; and the form of our constitutional law is what it is, because he molded it while it was still plastic and malleable in the fire of his own intense convictions."[92] Is it not pertinent, then, to direct attention to some phases of legal history where politics impinges upon law and where personal political convictions give direction to constitutional interpretation?

The Mingling of Politics and Constitutional Law

Not only did John Marshall mold constitutional law to accord with his own political convictions,[93] but also, contrary to the claims of the mechanical school, the Supreme Court has been an important political agency from the time of its establishment in 1789 to the present time.[94] Presidents Washington and Adams started the trend of constitutional interpretation along partisan lines by appointing all Federalist Justices under the first and second judiciary organization acts.[95] These Justices

---

[91] Dissenting opinion in Olmstead v. United States, 277 U. S. 472 (1927). See reference to the new method of interpretation the object of which is "to aid the evolution of institutions in the direction in which social phenomena are impelling them, solving the new cases that arise in harmony with that evolution." Alvarez, "Methods for Scientific Codification," *Science of Legal Method,* p. 449.

[92] Cardozo, *op. cit.,* pp. 169, 170.

[93] Recognizing "that the Constitution deals with great governmental powers to be exercised to great public ends, he went far towards erecting the structure within which the national spirit could freely move and flourish." Felix Frankfurter, ed., *Mr. Justice Holmes,* pp. 56, 57.

[94] In the ensuing pages evidence will be presented to substantiate these preliminary observations and comments relating to the mingling of politics and constitutional law.

[95] According to W. D. Coles, Washington "initiated the system of appointing political adherents, and political adherents only to places on the Supreme Bench. That system has seldom been departed from." "Politics and the Supreme Court of the United States," 27 *Amer. Law Rev.* (Mar.–Apr., 1893), 183.

with an unmistakable partisan bias lauded the policies of the Federalist party in their charges to grand juries, and, so far as was possible through their decisions, aided in sustaining these policies in the conduct of national affairs. The principles of the common law were interpreted as supplementary to the Constitution to serve as a basis for the courts to prevent the expression of opinions hostile to the Administration, and an effort was made to assert the doctrine of national sovereignty without a definite constitutional sanction. It required a constitutional amendment to put a temporary check upon nationalistic tendencies in constitutional interpretation. Commenting on the partisan activities of the Judges, Nathaniel Macon of North Carolina said in relation to the Memorial of Matthew Lyon on December 8, 1818: "the truth was, if the judge was a party man out of power, he would be a party man in. The office would not change human nature."[96] And referring to the attitude of the Judges in applying the Sedition Act, which he considered as unconstitutional, James Barbour of Virginia observed that "in times of violent party excitement, agitating the whole Nation, to expect that judges will be entirely exempt from its influence, argues a profound ignorance of mankind. Although clothed with the ermine, they are still men, and carry into the judgment seat the passions and motives common to their kind."[97] It was clearly recognized and understood that on issues involving the principles of constitutional construction the decisions of the courts would conform to that school of politics to which the Judge belonged and from which he was intentionally selected.[98]

The first Judiciary reorganization act was passed at the close of the Administration of John Adams to carry out partisan designs, particularly in the creation of new federal inferior courts and in the appointment of Federalist Justices to fill the newly created positions. It was strictly a partisan maneuver which brought John Marshall to the Judiciary in order to prevent a nomination to this high office by Thomas Jefferson. And the number of the Justices of the Supreme Court was reduced to retain the Federalist control over the Court. The Federalists used the courts to put into effect their political doctrines of judicial review of legislation, national supremacy over State rights, and the protection of property rights from disturbing legislative attacks. Chief Justice Marshall, as the head of the federal Judiciary, said Justice Story, was "a

---

[96] Thomas Hart Benton, *Abridgment of the Debates of Congress, from 1789 to 1856* (New York, 1857–1861), VI: 187.

[97] Daniel R. Goodloe, *Federalism Unmasked*, pp. 660, 661.

[98] George Mifflin Dallas, *Life and Writings of Alexander James Dallas* (Philadelphia, 1871), p. 78. See also Don Ensminger Mowry, "Political and Party Aspects of the National Judiciary, 1801–1835," *Amer. Hist. Mag.*, III: 331.

Federalist of the good old school," and in the maintenance of the principles of that school, "he was ready at all times to stand forth a determined advocate and supporter."[99] He used the Supreme Court openly and avowedly to announce Federalist doctrines. In a series of so-called "epoch-making decisions" Chief Justice Marshall gave a strongly nationalistic interpretation of the Constitution and helped to foster the bitterness which broke out in the relations between the nation and the states and led to the nullification of a federal law by South Carolina. In fact, the seeds from which the Civil War was germinated were, partly at least, sown and cultivated in the series of conflicts with the states in which Marshall extended federal powers by interpretations and by implications to cover the exercise of authority not granted by the Constitution.[100]

When the Supreme Court under the leadership of the foremost Federalist Justices, Marshall and Story, became out of harmony with the declared will and purposes of the nation as evidenced through the popularly controlled branches of the government, Presidents Jackson and Van Buren not only refused to support the Court in its pretensions of authority but also gradually brought the Court into accord with the people's will by seven new appointments to the Supreme Bench. Two of these appointments were rendered possible by the increase of the membership of the Court from seven to nine. From this time to the outbreak of the Civil War, the Democratic party controlled the Court, and its appointees were, with one exception, members of that party. During this period the decisions of the Court were in fairly close harmony with the general sentiment of the nation, so that, until an attempt was made to settle the slavery question by the Dred Scott decision, its work received public approval.

From 1860 to 1870 the Supreme Court was dominated by the coördinate branches of the government, and when the Justices undertook to assert their independence by declaring the Legal Tender Acts unconstitutional, the Republican party, through the President and Congress, moved to carry out the party's wishes.[101]

---

[99] Joseph Story, *Miscellaneous Writings,* ed. by W. W. Story (Boston, 1852), p. 683.

[100] For thirty-four years, it has been maintained, John Marshall labored unceasingly to counteract the political principles of Thomas Jefferson. See Martin Van Buren, *Inquiry into the Origin and Cause of Political Parties in the United States* (New York, 1867), p. 282.

[101] See Sidney Ratner, "Was the Supreme Court Packed by President Grant?" 50 *Pol. Sci. Quar.* (Sept., 1935), 343. Charles Fairman thinks that "the story that Grant packed the Court made a sinister mystery out of what can be very simply explained, and missed the real complexities which have now been recounted. The word 'pack' had an evil connotation but no precise meaning. The specific charge that Grant and Bradley made

Since 1870 the Court has been, until very recently, continuously under the control of the Republican party. Under this control the due process of law clauses of the Constitution were extended to the protection of corporations and the meaning of such phrases as due process of law and equal protection of the laws was broadened in such a way as to place the entire process of the regulation of public utilities under the domination of the courts. The authority of the states and the nation in the regulation of wages, hours of labor, as well as general social conditions affecting labor and industry were greatly restricted.[102] Since 1937 a change has taken place in the personnel of the Court together with a major shift in the mode of interpreting the Constitution, the effects of which cannot now be envisaged.

George P. Costigan, Jr., referring to the appointment of Howell E. Jackson, a Democrat, by Republican President Benjamin Harrison, expresses the opinion that this precedent will seldom be followed, owing to the fact that the political power of the Supreme Court is too great for Presidents to be willing to appoint Justices of opposite political faith. After assuring the reader that the ermine of the Court tempers partisanship, Costigan notes that though the judicial ermine ennobles the man it covers, the fact remains that the era of Marshall in the Supreme Court was of a different tenor from that of Taney and that of Taney of a different tenor from the period in which Chase, Waite, and Fuller have successively presided over the Court, the differences being explainable only by the political proclivities of the Justices. James Bryce is quoted, however, to the effect that the Judges may not be charged with the prostitution of their offices to party purposes but that "their actions flowed naturally from the habits of thought they had formed before accession to the Bench, and from the sympathy they could not but feel with the doctrines in whose behalf they had contended."[103]

From the time of its formation, the Constitution of the United States has been, to a considerable extent at least, a political document designed as the "vehicle of the life of a nation" and not a mere "lawyer's docu-

a bargain has been supported by absolutely nothing more than the loose invective of political opponents and a semblance of plausibility arising from an unusual concatenation of events." "Mr. Justice Bradley's Appointment to the Supreme Court and the Legal Tender Cases," 54 *Harv. Law Rev.* (May, 1941), 1142.

[102] See my articles, "Judicial Review of Legislation in the United States and the Doctrines of Vested Rights and of Implied Limitations on Legislature," 2 *Texas Law Rev.* (Apr., June, 1924), 257, 387, and 3 *Texas Law Rev.* (Dec., 1924), 1, and my treatise on *The Revival of Natural Law Concepts* (Cambridge, 1930).

[103] George P. Costigan, Jr., "The Supreme Court of the United States," 16 *Yale Law Jour.* (Feb., 1907), 265, 266, and Bryce's *American Commonwealth* (new ed., 1910), I: 274, 275.

ment."[104] As such a political document, it has been interpreted and applied in a political manner by all departments of the government, including the Judiciary. There is ample evidence to sustain the view that "Congresses and Senates, and Presidents have used the Supreme Bench as constituting a part of the political machinery of the great parties of the country."[105] Though there are marked evidences of partisanship in the process of constitutional construction, it is also apparent that certain fundamental assumptions or postulates give color and direction to the trend of interpretation; and these assumptions are the result of deep-seated personal convictions and attitudes which may have little relation to partisan views or political affiliations.

THE IMPORTANCE OF POSTULATES OR ASSUMPTIONS IN LEGAL ANALYSIS AND INTERPRETATION

It is generally recognized that the facts as well as the legal principles applicable to an issue or controversy which comes to a court for adjudication may be observed from various points of view, but the extent to which legal thinking is founded on postulates or assumptions is seldom fully appreciated.[106] Such basic generalizations or assumptions form the major premises of much judicial reasoning. It is assumed by Blackstone that the foremost purpose of the common law is to define and protect private property. All other ends of the law were to be subordinated to this primary object, and legal analysis was given the appropriate stamp to accord with this assumption. In both the common and statute law of England there was throughout the tacit and expressed assumption that in dealing with monopolies and contracts in restraint of trade it was desirable to preserve a competitive economic system. As constitutional law was molded in the atmosphere and in accordance with the underlying categories of the common law, both of these assumptions play an important role in the process of constitutional interpretation. One assumption becomes the standard and criterion for the development of doctrines of implied limitations against legislative action designed to restrict or interfere with acquired or vested rights. The other sanctions the philosophy and attitude which results in the formulation

---

[104] See Presidential Address of Woodrow Wilson, American Political Science Association, 5 *Amer. Pol. Sci. Rev.* (Feb., 1911), 10.

[105] John T. Morgan, "Partisanship in the Supreme Court," *North Amer. Rev.*, CXXXII: 181 (1881). "For politicians, if not for judges," says Abbot Emerson Smith, "Constitutional interpretation is little more than a rationalization of current prejudices." *James Madison, Builder* (New York, 1937), p. 129.

[106] "Every body of laws has undisclosed assumptions and emphasis not spelled out in words but familiar to those living under it." Felix Frankfurter and James M. Landis. *The Business of the Supreme Court* (New York, 1927), p. 16.

of a political and economic doctrine of *laissez faire* as embodied in the vague phrase due process of law.[107]

But the most significant assumption permeating all constitutional construction in the United States is involved in the belief or attitude which regards legislators as untrustworthy and as disposed to act inimical to the public welfare. Because of the ingrained fear of democratic or popular action as formulated and enacted by legislative chambers, it was taken for granted that constitutional limitations or inhibitions favorable to the protection of property and contracts could not be preserved unless courts acted as checks on these bodies to protect such rights. This was the undisclosed assumption in Chief Justice Marshall's reasoning in *Marbury v. Madison* to which Justice Gibson referred.[108] It is the only rational basis on which this opinion can be supported. This was the assumption on which Hamilton's reasoning was founded in his defense of judicial review of acts of Congress in the seventy-eighth number of *The Federalist*. Much of the argument in the cases leading to the establishment of the modern practice of judicial review of legislation is predicated on little else than this assumption.

Owing to this supposition constitutional interpretation in the United States is regarded as primarily a judicial function and for most purposes is not permitted either by legislatures or executives. A contrary assumption prevails in many countries. In England, Parliament may place an interpretation upon both the fundamental and ordinary law and thereby reverse judicial decisions.[109] The right of legislative interpretation of the fundamental written law was until recent years one of the recognized principles of French public law as well as the law of other countries which have followed the French model.[110]

The selection of the postulates in a legal issue is a matter of personal preference, inclination, and sagacity rather than of logic. As an exponent of legal realism, Walter Wheeler Cook maintains that when courts in applying the law read new meanings into old terms or rephrase the

---

[107] See Justice Holmes's contention that the Fourteenth Amendment did not enact Herbert Spencer's social statics, Lochner v. New York, 198 U. S. 45 (1905), and Justice Black's dissents in McCart v. Indianapolis Water Co., 302 U. S. 419 (1938), and in Connecticut General Life Ins. Co. v. Johnson, 303 U. S. 77 (1938).

[108] See *The American Doctrine of Judicial Supremacy*, pp. 282, 283.

[109] "The view that interpretation is exclusively a judicial function," declares Morris R. Cohen, "has no basis in the old common law or in the practice of any government." "The Process of Judicial Legislation," 48 *Amer. Law Rev.* (Mar.–Apr., 1914), 187.

[110] A recent instance of authoritative interpretation by the legislature in France is that act of April 13, 1908, reversing the judicial interpretation of the act regarding the separation of church and state of December 9, 1905. Cf. Gaston Jeze, *Jahrbuch für öffentliche Recht* (1910), pp. 495–497.

generalizations based on decided cases, their decisions are determined by the conscious or unconscious assumption of the desirability of certain consequences and by the assurance that the judgments rendered will promote those consequences. And these assumptions are considered as outside the domain of legal science.[111] With some of the basic factors and postulates which permeate legal thinking in mind, Justice Holmes, speaking of the law of a particular jurisdiction, said: "To one brought up within it, varying emphasis, tacit assumptions, unwritten practices, a thousand influences gained only from life, may give to the different parts wholly new values that logic and grammar never could have gotten from the books."[112]

In a preliminary study published in 1922 the mechanical method of judicial decision was compared with the method of free legal decision, particularly in reference to the procedure in the settlement of constitutional controversies.[113] Attention was then directed to the marked significance of extralegal influences in the development of constitutional law. Because an individual's views in political and legal matters are likely to be determined, in part at least, by his environment and training as well as by his associations and interests, it was pointed out that thorough and systematic studies of the lives of the Supreme Court Justices would shed light on the trend of decisions and on the judgments and opinions in many of the most important cases which came to the Court. But satisfactory biographies are available for only a few of the Justices and much original biographical work must be done before any attempt may be made to estimate the role of personal and individual views as factors affecting constitutional interpretation. Though the field of legal biography leaves much to be desired, a great deal of data is available bearing on the personal, political, and economic factors which have influenced the Justices in arriving at their judgments and conclusions on crucial issues, and it is with these data that we are chiefly concerned. William Draper Lewis observes that "the practice of the members of the Court generally, though not without exception, follows the principle that each judge has sworn to uphold the Constitution as he

[111] "The Legal Methods," in The Fifth Conference of Teachers of International Law (1933), p. 56. See also Cook, "Scientific Method and Law," 13 Amer. Bar. Assn. Jour. (June, 1927), 303, and H. Rottschaefer, "Legal Theory and the Practice of the Law," 10 Minn. Law Rev. (Apr., 1926), 382.

[112] Diaz v. Gonzales, 261 U. S. 102, 106 (1923). Cited with approval by Justice Brandeis, dissenting in Railroad Comm. of California v. Los Angeles Ry. Co., 280 U. S. 145, 164 (1929).

[113] Charles Grove Haines, "General Observations on the Effects of Personal, Political and Economic Influences in the Decisions of Judges," 17 Ill. Law Rev. (June, 1922), 96.

understands it, not as the prior decisions of the Court have interpreted it. . . . [This] means that by a change in the personnel of the Court, or, even without such a change in personnel, by a change in the opinion of one or more of the Judges, an earlier interpretation of the Constitution may be changed in a later case by the deliberate action of the Court itself."[114]

Not only have personal and political factors profoundly affected the decisions of the Supreme Court, but these decisions have also had far-reaching effects on the political and economic life of the people. It is appropriate, therefore, to give special consideration to the work of the Court where it impinges on the field of politics and becomes one of the foremost political agencies.

An attempt will be made in the following pages to deal with some of the fundamental problems of the statesmanship of the Bench and of the process of lawmaking by judicial decisions whereby the Judges have determined the pace of social change and have influenced the form of political and industrial organization.[115] For the eminent jurists who have sat upon the Supreme Court, Felix Frankfurter believes, constitutional interpretation has always been statecraft.[116] It is more accurate to say that to all of the Justices of the Supreme Court constitutional interpretation has to a large extent been statecraft, with differences only in degree among the Justices and in the objectives toward which the statecraft was directed.

Substantially it is assumed throughout this treatise that the observation of President Theodore Roosevelt was correct, namely, that "the chief lawmakers in our country may be, and often are, the Judges, because they are the final seat of authority. Every time they interpret contract, property, vested rights, due process of law, liberty, they necessarily enact into law parts of a system of social philosophy; and as such interpretation is fundamental, they give direction to all lawmaking. The decisions of the courts on economic and social questions depend upon their economic and social philosophy."[117] Confirming this view, Justice Harlan, speaking at a banquet in his honor, maintained that "the power of the Court, for good or evil can scarcely be exaggerated. If it cannot actually shape the destiny of our country, it can exert a commanding influence in that direction. It can by its judgments strengthen our institutions in the confidence and affections of the people, or, more

---

[114] *Interpreting the Constitution* (Charlottesville, 1937), p. 29.
[115] See Norman L. Meyers, "Walter Nelles," 46 *Yale Law Jour.* (June, 1937), 1280.
[116] *Mr. Justice Holmes, op. cit.*, p. 53.
[117] Message to Congress, December, 1908.

easily than any other department, it can undermine the foundations of our governmental system."[118]

The role of the Supreme Court in the development of the essential ideas and principles of American government and politics can be understood only in the light of and in relation to the acute and persistent political conflicts which have been waged from colonial times to the present day.

---

[118] 37 *Amer. Law Rev.* (Jan., Feb., 1903), 95. At the dinner honoring Justice Harlan after twenty-five years of service on the Supreme Court, President Theodore Roosevelt said: "During that time he has exercised an influence over the judicial statesmanship of the Court of a kind such as is possible only under our own form of government. For the Judges of the Supreme Court of the land must be not only great jurists but they must be great constructive statesmen, and the truth of what I say is illustrated by every study of American statesmanship, for in not one serious study of American political life will it be possible to omit the immense part played by the Supreme Court in the creation not merely the modification, of the great policies through and by means of which the country has moved on to her present position." *Ibid.*, p. 93.

CHAPTER II

Political Parties and Divisions during the War and the Critical Period and Their Influence on the Process of Constitution-Making

THE DETERMINATION of the Judges to regard written constitutions as "laws" and consequently to assume jurisdiction of issues which necessarily involved political factors and implications gave a political cast and significance to the federal Judiciary from the time of its establishment. Party divisions and affiliations during the Revolutionary War and the critical period of American history prepared the way for the political activities and functions of the Judges. It is necessary to review briefly some of the phases of the party history of these periods as a prelude to the early history of constitutional interpretation.

There have been essentially two schools of political thought in the United States, asserted Henry Cabot Lodge, and in his opinion "their struggle for supremacy has made the history of the country." One, the national school, believed in a liberal construction of the Constitution and in a strong and energetic federal government. The other, the school of State rights, believed in a strict construction of the Constitution and in restraining the federal government to the exercise of only such powers as were absolutely necessary. Alexander Hamilton founded one school and Thomas Jefferson the other. "The conflict between these opposing forces," observed Lodge, "began at the close of the Revolution, was ardent in the Convention which framed the Constitution, continued with ever-increasing intensity for seventy years, and then culminated in the Civil War. In that fierce battle the national principle, which had strengthened with every year from the time of the formation of the government, triumphed, and it is now supreme."[1]

These impressions of party divisions in the United States—with the central issue of political conflict one of constitutional interpretation—

[1] Henry Cabot Lodge, ed., *The Works of Alexander Hamilton* (Const. ed., New York, 1904), I: ix.

may well be cited as characteristic of a point of view which has permeated much of American political and legal history. Important as were the issues surrounding the distribution of powers between the nation and the states and the proper interpretation of that distribution, the primary party divisions and cleavages from colonial times to the present were along other lines.

EARLY PARTY DIVISIONS

Party divisions had their origins in colonial times when none of the colonies was democratic in political and social structure. Class distinctions brought from England were maintained and these distinctions implied political privileges. Three classes or factions were rather clearly differentiated in most of the colonies. The upper class consisted of merchants, the larger landowners, the clergy, the legal profession, and some of the most important public officials. This class, it is well known, "controlled the colonial assemblies, in certain colonies owned most of the land, sat on the county courts, directed the important economic activities, controlled credit by individual loans (for there were as yet no banks), and set the social and cultural standards."[2] Next in order was a middle class which comprised mostly the small farmers, the shopkeepers, and the better grade of workers. In most of the colonies this class was important and in some it dominated political affairs. Below this class were groups of freemen, sometimes called peasants, the lower ranks of laborers including the urban mechanics, and some who had come as indentured servants and had gradually found a place among the farmers or laborers. More than half of the men over twenty-one years of age were in the latter group. As a rule, the organization of the aristocratic group rested upon the feudal principle of personal relationships, and the usual designation of factions was the court party and the popular party.

Before the Revolution the colonial assemblies represented primarily the privileged or aristocratic groups and a large majority of people took no part in politics. As the colonies entered into the stage of rebellion against Great Britain, the assemblies were replaced by extralegal committees and congresses as the chief means for maintaining colonial rights. And it was this extralegal machinery that was "the open door through which the common freeholder and the unfranchised mechanic and artisan pushed their way into the political arena."[3] It was the entrance of this unfranchised class into politics that created the division between radicals and conservatives which continued during the Revolutionary

---

[2] Samuel Eliot Morison and Henry Steele Commager, *The Growth of the American Republic* (New York, 1937), I: 41, 42.

[3] Carl Lotus Becker, *The History of Political Parties in the Province of New York, 1760–1776* (Madison, 1909), p. 22.

War and the critical period. The Revolution gave an opportunity for participation in political affairs to many men who had previously been denied this privilege. Everywhere, as Morison and Commager maintain, "the Radicals were using the powerful lever of independence to oust the Conservatives and put themselves in control, and under cover of a popular war, push through their programs for radical reform."[4]

Among the main grounds for a division into parties were the differences in social and economic status (with the consequent participation or nonparticipation in the political activities of the colonies) and the fundamental differences in economic interests, point of view, and political outlook of those who lived along the seaboard and the lowlands and those who followed agriculture and the pursuits of frontier interests in the back country or among the uplands. Those who were active in politics in the seaboard or tidewater districts were inclined, as a rule, to be conservative, whereas those who lived in the interior or upcountry were usually self-reliant, independent, and democratic in political affairs.

The colonists who aided the Revolutionary movement, according to Allan Nevins, belonged to two main groups, as follows:

One was the alert, irrepressible proletarian element of the seaports from Boston to Charleston, who had been largely debarred from the ballot by a property qualification for voting. The other was the settlers of the back country, a great homogeneous population, rapidly increasing, but deprived of due political rights by unjust discrimination in the matter of representation. They had grievances also in the unfair administration of taxes and of justice. From the valley of the Susquehanna to that of the Savannah these inland settlers, in whose breasts a powerful individualism was nurtured by frontier conditions, were alike in two salient respects. Nearly all dissenters, having little formal education, and being of many European strains, they felt little attachment to England; while economic and other reasons made them eager for a due share in the government. They welcomed the opportunity the revolutionary movement gave them. In Pennsylvania they turned the scale for independence, and in South Carolina greatly assisted in doing so. But independence for them meant only the first milestone on a long road.[5]

The landowning and commercial aristocracy resented the entrance of the radicals into politics and condemned the extreme and sometimes violent methods which the new political groups employed. But despite the opposition of the older and more conservative leaders, the radicals formed organizations of their own, such as the "Sons of Liberty," and, as champions of the rights of the colonists, soon gained in strength and popular support. "The whole continent," George Bancroft said, "rang with the cheering name of the Sons of Liberty." But not all of the clubs

[4] *The Growth of the American Republic,* I: 79.
[5] *The American States During and After the Revolution, 1775–1789* (New York, 1924), pp. 114, 115.

which called themselves "Sons of Liberty" were founded to resist the Stamp Act—many of them "had been in existence for years and had been created with no thought of resisting the 'tyranny' of the mother country: their purpose was rather to combat the colonial aristocracy and give the unprivileged class a share in political power."[6]

Though the First Continental Congress was, in the beginning, controlled by the conservatives, the radicals were finally able to carry their program. They succeeded in having Congress approve a Non-Intercourse Association and adopt a plan whereby those who refused to follow the line of conduct proposed by Congress should be punished by social ostracism, commercial boycott, and confiscation of property.[7] As the colonies moved into the stage of open warfare with Great Britain, the radical party usurped the functions of government in some of the colonies and insisted on obedience to their authority. They were able to carry out their program because many of the conservatives joined the party rather than refuse to coöperate with the extralegal groups.[8] As the conservatives joined the movement, a new alignment of parties took shape between loyalists on the one hand and the Revolutionary party on the other. And the infiltration of conservatives tended toward the adoption of more moderate policies by the radical party which directed the military and civil affairs of the colonies engaged in the prosecution of war. It was not only in the conduct of the war that the radical and conservative parties contrived to gain political favor, but similar contests were waged between them over the formation of separate state governments.

State constitutions.—The division of people into radical and conservative groups was apparent in the adoption and early operation of the state constitutions. Debate over the adoption of the constitutions centered largely around the conflict between democratic and aristocratic notions. As a rule, the conservative party sought to secure a government of checks and balances with legislative powers limited, a reasonably strong executive who might direct the public administration, and an independent judiciary which might resist the tendency of the popular party to encroach on property rights. Governments were to be so devised that due respect was to be paid to wealth and the property-owning class

[6] John C. Miller, *Sam Adams: Pioneer in Propaganda* (Boston, 1936), p. 51. For an account of the organization and methods of the "Sons of Liberty," consult Miller, *op. cit.*, chap. iii.

[7] Becker, *op. cit.*, p. 154.

[8] In most of the states "the strength of the Revolutionary party lay most largely in the plain people, as distinguished from aristocracy," J. Franklin Jameson, *The American Revolution Considered as a Social Movement* (Princeton, 1926), p. 25.

would have a firm hold on the public purse. This group believed that "the inequalities of representation in some colonies, and the denial of the ballot to many freemen in others, were not abuses, but time-tested and valuable features of government."[9]

The radicals, opposing the attempts to establish a class control over public affairs, adopted the slogan "Let the people rule" and favored the concentration of power in a single-chamber legislative body, but where a bicameral system existed the radicals preferred that the greater authority be vested in the lower house which had championed the popular cause against the colonial governors. Governors were to be selected by the legislatures for short terms and judges were to be made subservient to the legislature, which, like the British Parliament, claimed final judicial powers.

Inadequate consideration has been given to the prevailing ideas concerning the supremacy of the legislatures and to the almost universal opinion that when written constitutions were adopted in the states the legislatures were the judges of their own constitutional powers. A theory of the separation of powers modeled after that of Montesquieu was inserted in certain state constitutions, but in practice legislative, executive, and judicial powers were frequently mingled—with the legislatures generally regarded as having supreme authority. Though, during the period from 1776 to 1787, many limits were placed upon the exercise of public powers, especially in the emerging bills of rights, few citizens at this time thought of the courts as guardians of these rights or that it was their duty to prevent violations of the constitutional guarantees. Legislatures elected annually or for a few years were conceded to have unlimited powers. In eight of the states the executive branch of the government was made subordinate to the legislature by making selection of the governor dependent upon the legislature. Judges were either selected by the legislature or in other ways were rendered subject to legislative dominance. The failure and excesses of supreme legislative bodies as well as the conservative distrust of popularly controlled assemblies combined to strengthen the movement to give the courts not only an independent position but also to encourage the judges to assert final and conclusive powers in the interpretation of constitutional provisions.[10] On the other hand, the claim that all of the state constitutions included a separation

---

[9] Nevins, *op. cit.*, pp. 139, 140.

[10] For further data relative to legislative supremacy in the states, see Charles Grove Haines, *The American Doctrine of Judicial Supremacy* (Berkeley, 1932), pp. 68 ff. In a constituted commonwealth, said John Locke, "there can be but one supreme power, which is the legislature, to which all the rest are and must be subordinate," *Second Treatise on Government*, chaps. xi, xiii.

of powers theory and that an attempt was made to carry the theory into effect is not supported by concrete evidence. The theory of the separation of powers was not included in some constitutions which made a tripartite division of government agencies. In other constitutions powers were so merged as to leave only a vestige of the separation principle. And in only a few states was the separation of powers theory so interpreted or applied as to have a substantial influence on the practices of the state governments. It was the failure to recognize and apply the separation of powers doctrine that led Madison in his defense of the Constitution to observe that the legislatures were not only increasing their powers but were inclined to dominate the other departments.

The radicals set about not only to democratize political institutions but also to destroy the social, economic, and religious privileges which had been inherited from Europe and which were fostered and strongly approved by the conservatives. Thus, the state-subsidized church, primogeniture and entail, methods of taxation which favored the rich, and unfair methods of apportionment favorable to the aristocracy of the seaboard and lowland districts were attacked.[11] The party divisions which prevailed throughout the colonies and the resulting conflict over governmental organization were exemplified especially in Massachusetts and Pennsylvania. In Massachusetts, where the radical party led by Samuel Adams and John Hancock dominated the political life of the colony during the Revolutionary period, the conservatives under the direction of the Essex Junto defeated a constitution prepared by John Hancock and adopted one largely drafted by John Adams. The Adams constitution embodying the conservative principle of checks and balances substituted for the prevailing legislative supremacy a bicameral legislature, an independent governor with most of the powers of the colonial governor, and an assured tenure for the judiciary.[12] The constitution of 1780 has been characterized as "a lawyer's and merchant's constitution, directed toward something like quarterdeck efficiency in government and the protection of property against democratic pirates." Property was given special protection in the suffrage, in the composition of the senate, and in the qualifications for officeholders. To Samuel Eliot Morison the real significance of the struggle over the adoption of the constitution of Massachusetts lies "in the conflict of opinion, and the victory of property over democracy that its adoption implied."[13] The con-

---

[11] Nevins, op. cit., pp. 165 ff.

[12] For John Adams' analysis of the check and balance doctrine, see The Works of John Adams, ed. by Charles Francis Adams (Boston, 1850), VI: 467.

[13] "The Struggle over the Adoption of the Constitution of Massachusetts, 1780," Mass. Hist. Soc. (May, 1917), pp. 353 ff.

servative elements gained control of the government of all the states except Pennsylvania, North Carolina, and Georgia.

The Pennsylvania constitution of 1776, drafted largely under the direction of the radicals, provided for a legislature of one house, a supreme executive council, and a judiciary dependent upon the legislature. Because of the liberal ideas contained in the document, it was immediately subjected to criticism and censure by the conservatives, who, as members of the commercial and planting aristocracy of the coast region, deemed the exercise of political power their special privilege. Opposing the constitution as too democratic, conservative leaders championed the principle of checks and balances to serve as a means to obstruct the progress of democracy or, as often expressed, of "protecting the few against the tyranny of the many."[14]

Party antagonisms in Pennsylvania from 1776 to 1790, it is claimed, were more consistently violent than in any other state.[15] The conservatives, mainly wealthy Quakers and Episcopalians, refused to coöperate in putting Pennsylvania's democratic constitution into effect. Though Georgia's constitution—with a single-chamber legislative body, a weak governor, and a dependent judiciary—worked fairly well, a similar document in Pennsylvania was under a constant fire of criticisms and condemnation by the anticonstitutionalists aligned chiefly with the Bank of Pennsylvania and the Bank of North America. When the federal Constitution was adopted in Pennsylvania by a *coup d'état,* which prevented the liberals and radicals from marshaling their forces and securing a free and open discussion of the merits and demerits of the document, the way was prepared for the adoption of a conservative type of state constitution.

The Pennsylvania constitution of 1790, drafted largely by James Wilson, contained all of the essential principles of the conservative party with its doctrine of separation of powers, the theory of checks and balances, and the principle of affording protection to property rights against democratic onslaughts. When historians maintain that the political leaders of the colonies, which had now become states, were not dissatisfied with the forms of government under which they had been living and desired so far as practicable to follow English customs and practices rather than to attempt political experiments, they have in mind primarily the theories and proposals of the conservatives. The types of

---

[14] W. Roy Smith, "Sectionalism in Pennsylvania During the Revolution," 24 *Pol. Sci. Quar.* (June, 1909), pp. 216 ff. and J. Paul Selsam, *The Pennsylvania Constitution of 1776* (Philadelphia, 1936).

[15] Consult Nevins, *op. cit.,* pp. 149 ff., for an account of the contest over the adoption of Pennsylvania's constitution.

government devised by the radicals represented, both in England and in America, marked departures from the prevailing political ideas and institutions.[16]

Conservatives were seeking, they contended, a "sufficient check to prevent the intemperate and unjust proceedings" of the legislatures. John Rutledge, a conservative, vetoing a new constitution for South Carolina, observed "the people also preferred a compounded or mixed government to a simple democracy, or one verging toward it," because, in his opinion, "however unexceptionable a democratic government may appear at first view, its effects have been found arbitrary, severe and destructive." A brief résumé of radical and conservative doctrines will aid in understanding the political cleavages during the Revolutionary and critical periods.

Radical and conservative doctrines.—With the exception of the loyalists, who participated only to a slight extent in the politics of the time, the people primarily aligned themselves during the Revolutionary War to one of two groups or factions. The radical group under the leadership of men such as Samuel Adams, Thomas Paine, Patrick Henry, Thomas Jefferson, Luther Martin, Richard Henry Lee, Elbridge Gerry,[17] and Benjamin Franklin advocated doctrines of the sovereignty of the people, government based upon the consent of the governed, the sanctity of individual rights as guaranteed by bills of rights, a theory of natural and inalienable rights which it was the prime duty of the government to protect, the contract theory of government, and the right of revolution. To this group government was to be reduced to a minimum, its chief function being to keep the peace and to protect communities from attacks by foreign foes.

Radical doctrines were put into concrete form in the Declaration of Independence, the Articles of Confederation, and the Ordinance for the government of the Northwest Territory. Summarized in a few sentences, some of the current doctrines of the radicals which Thomas Jefferson put into enduring phrases in the Declaration of Independence were:

We hold these truths to be self-evident, that all men are created equal, that they are endowed by their Creator with certain unalienable rights, that among these are life, liberty and the pursuit of happiness. That to secure these rights, governments

---

[16] See Homer C. Hockett, *Political and Social Growth of the United States* (New York, 1939), I: 242, 243.

[17] In the federal Convention, Elbridge Gerry first joined the advocates of a strong national government, then turned to the Anti-Federalist group, refused to sign the Constitution, and published a list of objections to it. Later he supported Hamilton's financial schemes and became a stockholder in the Bank of the United States. Patrick Henry also joined the conservative ranks in later years. See S. E. Morison, "Elbridge Gerry, Gentleman-Democrat," *The New England Quarterly* (1929), II: 6, 7.

are instituted among men, deriving their just powers from the consent of the governed. That whenever any form of government becomes destructive of these ends, it is the right of the people to alter or abolish it, and to institute new government, laying its foundations on such principles and organizing its powers in such form, as to them shall seem most likely to effect their safety and happiness.

In this Declaration a new political philosophy was formulated. The ideals or "glittering generalities," as they have frequently been called, were to serve as a basis for the future political and social programs of liberal groups in the United States. Visionary and chimerical as this political philosophy seemed to many of Jefferson's contemporaries and to those of suceeeding generations who have looked at politics and government from a conservative point of view, it is, nevertheless, a philosophy which has profoundly influenced American practices and modes of thinking.[18]

It was on the basis of such reasoning that Patrick Henry argued in the Parson's Cause that government was "a conditional compact, composed of mutual and dependent covenants, the King promising protection, the people promising obedience and support." A violation of this covenant by one of the contracting parties, Henry contended, discharged the other party from further obligations. An instance was then cited in which the King had violated his obligations under the mutual terms of the compact with the colonies, and hence it was maintained that the King had forfeited all rights to his subjects' obedience with respect to his invalid acts.[19]

The Articles of Confederation, like the state constitutions drafted by the radicals, provided for a diplomatic body or political debating society in which each state retained "its sovereignty, freedom and independence" and reserved the right to recall at any time its delegates sent to the Congress of the Confederation. Though the Articles were to be inviolably observed by every state and the union thus established was to be perpetual, it was provided that no alteration should be made in the Articles "unless such alteration be agreed to in a Congress of the United States and be afterwards confirmed by the legislatures of every state."[20] Designed to establish a weak type of government which was largely dependent upon the states for all important grants of power, the Confederate government was unable to formulate or to carry into effect

---

[18] For a consideration of the influence of the Declaration of Independence on American life and thought, see Carl Lotus Becker, *The Declaration of Independence: A Study in the History of Political Ideas* (New York, 1922), and T. V. Smith, *Notes on the American Doctrine of Equality* (Chicago, 1927).

[19] William Wirt Henry, *Patrick Henry* (New York, 1891), I: 38–42.

[20] Art. XIII.

national financial or commercial policies. It soon became a target for the attacks of the conservatives who began a campaign of criticism and vilification which resulted in the calling of the Philadelphia Convention and in the overthrow of the Confederation by a carefully planned and adroitly led revolution. Reference will be made later to the contributions of the Articles of Confederation in the establishment of constitutional government in the United States.

The ordinance which provided for the government of the Northwest Territory contained a number of features which were characteristic of the radical political philosophy. Provisions were made for a governor, legislative council, and house of representatives and for extending to the inhabitants of the territory "the fundamental principles of civil and religious liberty, which form the basis whereon these republics, their laws and constitutions, are erected; to fix and establish those principles as the basis of all laws, constitutions, and governments, which forever hereafter shall be formed in the said territory." Further provision was made for the establishment of states to be admitted on an equal footing with the original states.

Personal and individual rights were to be guaranteed to the inhabitants of the territory, such as the privilege of the writ of habeas corpus, the right of trial by jury, the "proportionate representation of the people in the legislature, and of judicial proceedings according to the course of common law." No man was to be deprived of his "liberty or property, but by the judgment of his peers, or the law of the land," and when property or services were demanded for public use "full compensation shall be made for the same," and no laws were to "interfere with or affect private contracts, or engagements, bona fide, and without fraud previously formed." Thus the ordinance contained in incipient form some of the provisions which were later embodied in the federal Constitution.

Indicating an interest in and solicitude for public education, Article III of the ordinance provided that "religion, morality and knowledge being necessary to good government and the happiness of mankind, schools and the means of education shall forever be encouraged." The utmost good faith was to be observed towards the Indians, and a significant clause prohibited slavery and involuntary servitude in the territory, except for the punishment of crimes. Thus, in the Declaration of Independence, in the Articles of Confederation, and in the Ordinance for the Northwest Territory some of the essential ideas of the radicals were put into concrete form.

The conservative party during the Revolutionary period was made up, first, of the loyalists who, though opposed to the activities of the radical party which carried the country into open revolt, still sympathized with the English cause but who remained sufficiently inactive not to be forced to emigrate. A second group of men, such as Alexander Hamilton, John Jay, George Washington, James Wilson, Gouverneur Morris, and Oliver Ellsworth, though aligned with the Revolutionary party during the war, later became affiliated with the conservatives. These groups favored the rule of the rich and wellborn or, as it was sometimes phrased, the "rich, the wise and the good." At the same time they disapproved of the principle of popular government or the rule of the majority of the people. The political philosophy of the conservatives was summed up by Alexander Hamilton in his argument for a life term of United States senators as follows:

All communities divide themselves into the few and the many. The first are the rich and well-born, the other the mass of the people. The voice of the people has been said to be the voice of God; and, however generally this maxim has been quoted and believed, it is not true in fact. The people are turbulent and changing; they seldom judge or determine right. Give, therefore, to the first class a distinct, permanent share in the government. They will check the unsteadiness of the second, and, as they cannot receive any advantage by a change, they therefore will ever maintain good government. Can a democratic assembly, who annually revolve in the mass of the people, be supposed steadily to pursue the public good? Nothing but a permanent body can check the imprudence of democracy. Their turbulent and uncontrollable disposition requires checks.[21]

Whereas the radicals or the incipient Democratic party founded their philosophy on the principle of popular sovereignty and placed uppermost the inalienable rights of the individual, the conservatives were primarily concerned with the protection of property and related interests and to this end desired a strong government to preserve these interests. They insisted that the minority should be protected from the dangers of popular rule and, with the admission of the democratic element into the body politic, wanted to be assured that their unstable and dangerous tendencies should be tempered by a system of checks and balances. It was generally assumed and occasionally expressed that there should be just enough concessions in favor of democracy to humor the people and keep them satisfied.

Fisher Ames, one of the ablest of the conservatives, contended that the chief duty of all governments is to protect the rights of property, for "the essence, and almost the quintessence, of a good government, is to protect property and its rights. When these are protected, there is scarcely any booty left for oppression to seize; the objects and motives to usur-

---

[21] Henry Cabot Lodge, ed., *The Works of Alexander Hamilton* (New York, 1904), I: 401.

pation and tyranny are removed. By securing property, life and liberty can scarcely fail of being secured."[22]

To the conservatives, the radicals and Democrats were "a set of men without reading, experience or principles to govern them." Maryland adopted an electoral plan for election to the upper house of the legislature to assure the representation of the "wealth, position and caution of the States." This plan was praised by Hamilton in *The Federalist*[23] because it placed a check upon "rash legislation demanded from vociferous, ill-educated voters." Everywhere the conservatives agreed with John Adams in supporting the dominance of "the rich, the well-born and the able."[24] Only men of education and fortune were considered to have the time for the study necessary to acquire an adequate knowledge of the interests of the state. It was held that this class only could understand the requirements and implications of a complex and carefully balanced form of government. The assertion of the conservatives, which has often misled the historians, that they were the "friends of order" and that those who disagreed with them were made up of "desperate, embarrassed, unprincipled, disorderly and disaffected men" was made in the early days of the development of American political ideas.[25] It was not difficult for the conservatives to believe that they were supporting "ideas of constitutional perfection" as against the "murky vapors of prejudice and malevolence." Hence, in the contest over the adoption of the federal Constitution in New York, it was made to appear as an issue between the "rough fringes of civilization" and the "wealth, education and conservatism of the American metropolis."

Party divisions in the state of New York followed the usual class basis. In one group were the great landowners who often lived in feudal splendor, the lawyers to whom in this state much deference was paid, and the merchants who were frequently enriched by illicit trade. In another group were the farmers and mechanics who were often made the dupes of the former class. The politics of the states at this time, E. Wilder Spaulding finds, is "the story of the struggle of a propertied, intelligent

---

[22] Seth Ames, ed., *Works of Fisher Ames* (Boston, 1854), II: 166.

[23] No. 63 (Lodge ed.), p. 398.

[24] John Adams, *Works*, IV: 290. "The rich, the well-born and the able, acquire an influence among the people that will soon be too much for simple honesty and plain sense, in a house of representatives." See also Dixon Ryan Fox, *The Decline of Aristocracy in the Politics of New York,* Columbia University Studies in History, Economics and Public Law (New York, 1919), chap. i on "The Few, the Rich and the Well Born."

[25] Edward Rutledge, writing to John Jay, referred in contemptuous language to the radicals, "I dread their low cunning, and those levelling principles which men without character and without fortune in general possess, which are so captivating to the lower class of mankind." Frank Monaghan, *John Jay* (New York, 1935), p. 83.

minority to maintain itself against a well-to-do, less sophisticated majority. The divisions between these two groups may be conceived as vertical, following geographical divisions; or as horizontal, following social and economic cleavages."[26] One group gradually became known as the Federalists and their opponents as the Anti-Federalists.

The merchants were almost invariably Federalist in their political beliefs and affiliations. Closely associated with them were the bankers and the lawyers, most of whom were staunch Federalists. It was truly observed that "trade and Federalism appeared hand in hand."[27] The commercial interests were the first to criticize the ineffectiveness of the Articles of Confederation. Chief among the complainants against the government as devised by the radicals were the great Federalist families which had become deeply involved in land speculation and were feeling the effects of the economic depression which was at its height about 1784.[28] "By 1783," notes Spaulding, "the Schuylers, the Hamiltons, the Jays, the Bensons, the Livingstons, and the Morrises were busy protesting to one another that the Confederation was hopelessly weak and that the state legislatures were disregarding all faith and credit."[29]

The politics of South Carolina followed similar lines. An aristocracy composed of the planters and the leading Charleston merchants controlled the state government.[30] The opposition came mainly from the clerks, artisans, and white laborers in Charleston and from the farmers in the uplands. Control by the planters was safeguarded by a constitutional gerrymander which gave their districts more than a proportionate representation in the legislature. The issue of the day, notes Phillips, "lay between classes of people differentiated by temperament, occupation and property-holding, rather than between sections antagonized by the pressure of conflicting geographical conditions and needs."[31]

The leaders of 1776 were mostly poor men, that is, small landowners or tenants and village shopkeepers. They revolted against the "small cliques and place hunters" who were in control of political affairs in most of the states. They protested against the established church, special privileges of all sorts, and commercial monopolies, whether in control of the British or Americans.[32] But these early proponents of democracy

---

[26] *New York in the Critical Period, 1783–1789* (New York, 1932), p. 84.

[27] Spaulding, *op. cit.*, p. 7.

[28] *Ibid.*, pp. 8 ff.

[29] *Ibid.*, p. 103.

[30] Ulrich B. Phillips, "The South Carolina Federalists," *Amer. Hist. Rev.* (Apr., 1909), XIV: 529–531.

[31] Phillips, *op. cit.*, p. 531.

[32] William E. Dodd, "The Struggle for Democracy in the United States," 28 *International Jour. of Ethics* (July, 1918), 465, 466.

made headway rather slowly against the vested interests of the day and the aristocratic groups in charge of colonial affairs. In Pennsylvania alone were they able to set up a real democracy. There an assembly based on popular suffrage controlled the government and the courts and carried out for a brief period the people's wishes. The rich and wellborn in the Philadelphia district were in revolt against this government until the conservative sentiment, which resulted in the adoption of the federal Constitution, afforded them a favorable opportunity to secure a "balanced" state charter designed to foster and preserve aristocratic interests. So, too, in other states, notes William E. Dodd,

the men who were in the majority and who fought England in part because of unequal and unfair representation of their interests and ideals in the British parliament were, by the nature of things compelled to submit at home to unequal and unfair representation. In order to free themselves from an intolerable state of things in the empire they were compelled to fasten upon themselves in almost every State constitutions which set up a privileged church in New England and a privileged slaveholding gentry in the South.[33]

By the end of the Revolution in 1783 there were large groups in each of the states who were opposed to majority rule in the state assemblies. A new party was in formation made up of the commercial men of the East, the officers of the army, the loyalists who were returning to their homes, the clergy of the established church of New England, and the planters of the South. These groups were led by George Washington, Alexander Hamilton, and the Pinckneys, and they soon were able to unite their following on a program to secure a strong government to counteract the rule which they characterized as that of the "ignorant, the poor and the vicious." As a result of effective organization and leadership, the Philadelphia Convention of 1787 was called, and a group of men who had little faith in the control of government by the people drafted a plan of government with intricate checks and balances so complex in its operation that few people could understand the plan or its implications. And the government which was organized under this written instrument had as its main feature that "at no time could the people intervene and change its policy, unless they could work up such a commotion that House, Senate, President and Court could all be changed at the same time—a feat which has never been performed."[34] Party divisions and the characteristic political methods of the time were much in evidence in the contests over the formation and adoption of the federal Constitution.

---

[33] William E. Dodd, *op. cit.,* p. 467.
[34] William E. Dodd, *op. cit.,* p. 471.

THE CONTEST OVER THE ADOPTION OF THE CONSTITUTION

Economic factors played a prominent role in the movement which resulted in the framing and adoption of the Constitution. The conflict between the rich and the poor, creditors and debtors, and between merchants and farmers centered largely on the questions of the issuance of paper money and on granting relief to debtors. Because the calling of the Convention came as a result of a political reaction and because the election of delegates was controlled by the conservatives, the small farmers, the debtors, and the advocates of paper money were absent from the Convention. Conservative sentiments were reflected in numerous provisions in the draft of the Constitution but especially in the clauses prohibiting the states from the emission of bills of credit and from passing laws impairing the obligation of contracts.

Referring to the Pennsylvania delegates selected to attend the Convention to revise the Constitution, the minority members of the state assembly observed that "a majority of our legislature appointed men to represent this State who were all citizens of Philadelphia, none of them calculated to represent the landed interests of Pennsylvania, and almost all of them of one political party, men who have been uniformly opposed to that [state] constitution for which you have on every occasion manifested your attachment."[35] Owing to the conservative control of the state, the South Carolina delegates to the federal Convention were from the Charleston district and all of them favored the new Constitution. Almost all of the delegates selected from the states that sent representatives to Philadelphia belonged to the conservative or aristocratic factions. Some of the leaders of the radical party declined appointments to serve as delegates to the Convention, whereas others who attended refused to participate actively in the discussions of the sessions, and a few of those of liberal or democratic views actively opposed the adoption and refused to sign the document approved by the Convention. The party divisions in the Convention were, therefore, mostly between the large and small states groups and between factions favoring or opposing particular provisions.

There was widespread alarm among the radicals and among those of liberal or democratic inclinations that the steps which were being taken toward the formation of a common or general government for the states would result in the permanent establishment of an aristocracy as the controlling element in the new society. Among other groups there was a

---

[35] John Bach McMaster and Frederick D. Stone, eds., *Pennsylvania and the Federal Constitution, 1787–1788* (Lancaster, 1888), p. 73.

strong sentiment for the formation of a monarchical type of government. The creation of a corrupt and oppressive aristocracy was more within the realm of probability and it was against the tendencies in this direction that the most active and virile opposition was directed by the liberal groups. Some of the fears were not without foundation, for it was frequently asserted that "men of education and property" were the only ones entitled to participate in the operation of government. It was property, rather than education, however, that was given primary consideration, for, as John Jay remarked, "those who own the country are the most fit persons to participate in the government of it."[36] Theodore Sedgwick, writing to Rufus King, expressed the opinion of those who controlled colonial affairs prior to the Revolution and who, having lost much of their political influence and prestige, were determined to regain what they deemed was rightfully their political heritage. "Every man of observation," said Sedgwick, "is convinced that the end of government security cannot be attained by the exercise of principles founded on democratic equality. A war is now actually levied on the virtue, property and distinctions in the community, and however there may be an appearance of a temporary cessation of hostilities, yet the flame will again and again break out."[37] And as the pages of American history are scanned, it is apparent that the "flame" has continued to break out.

Hamilton, in surveying the situation at the time the Convention draft was submitted to the states, predicted that the Constitution would have the good will of the commercial interests and of most men of property as well as the creditors who wish to see the debt of the union paid. In the opposition, holding offices under the state governments, he expected to see the debtors, those opposed to strong government, and those who were inclined to be alarmed at the development of institutions that might seem calculated to place the power of the community in few hands and raise a few individuals to stations of great preëminence. James Wilson, celebrating the ratification of the Constitution, exclaimed: "A people free and enlightened, establishing and ratifying a system of government which they have previously considered, examined, and approved. This is the spectacle which we are assembled to celebrate; and it is the most dignified one that has yet appeared on our globe."[38] But instead of the deliberate, careful, and enlightened consideration of the plan of the proposed government and the issues involved, we find in much of the deliberation what Elbridge Gerry called an inordinate

---

[36] See Monaghan, *John Jay*, p. 323 (Oct. 25, 1810).

[37] Charles R. King, ed., *The Life and Correspondence of Rufus King* (New York, 1894), I: 224.

[38] *Works* (Bird Wilson, ed., Philadelphia, 1804), III: 299.

zeal "to precipitate a blind adoption of the Constitution as proposed by the Philadelphia Convention."

It was in Pennsylvania that the strategy to secure an early adoption of the Constitution without full and free discussion was carried to the greatest extreme. On September 27 the Constitution was submitted to the states by the Congress of the Confederation without approval or disapproval. The Pennsylvania assembly which was then in session had resolved to adjourn *sine die* on Saturday, September 29, but the Federalists who had a majority in the body were determined that before adjournment a state convention should be called to consider the Constitution. Before the action of Congress was reported to the assembly and contrary to its own rules, the Federalists, through one of the members of the federal Convention, presented a resolution to call a convention in Philadelphia. This resolution was carried by a vote of 43 to 19. The assembly consisted of 69 members and 46 constituted a quorum. It was decided by the 19 members of the minority to refuse to attend a session called for Friday afternoon, thus leaving the day for the election of delegates and the choosing of the members unsettled. When the last session was held on Saturday morning and a quorum was not present, the sergeant at arms and the assistant clerk were ordered to summon the protestants to attend. Upon their insistent refusal the sergeant at arms secured the necessary aid from a mob of citizens and "broke into their lodgings, seized them, dragged them through the streets to the State House, and thrust them into the assembly room, with clothes torn and faces white with rage. The quorum was now complete."[39]

While the recalcitrant members were forcibly detained the election of delegates was called for November 6 and the meeting of the convention for November 21. The short time allotted for the consideration of the Constitution and the election of delegates rendered impossible anything approximating a thorough discussion of the advantages or disadvantages which might result from the adoption of the instrument. Evidently full and free consideration of the merits or demerits of the Constitution was not to be permitted. When the convention met in Philadelphia the Federalist majority followed similar tactics. Votes on separate articles of the Constitution were prohibited, no amendments could be proposed or adopted, and the reasons for dissent were not to be entered upon the minutes.[40] Only Federalist speeches were allowed to be printed and every

[39] McMaster and Stone, eds., *Pennsylvania and the Federal Constitution, 1787–1788*, p. 4.

[40] McMaster and Stone, *op. cit.*, p. 461. Of the abuse and ill-treatment of those who opposed the adoption of the Constitution, cf. Reasons of Dissent of the Minority, *ibid.*, pp. 456 ff.

effort was made to prevent the publication of the opinions of Anti-Federalists. Wilson must have had some other state than his own in mind when he portrayed in glowing terms the mode of the adoption of the Constitution. But the cause of the Constitution was improved by the fact that ratification was carried hastily, with little or no discussion, in Delaware, New Jersey, Connecticut, and Georgia. The small states looked forward to commercial and political advantages under the new system greater than they were likely to secure by any other plan for union.

It was not only in Pennsylvania that the course of affairs was not permitted to follow a natural channel. In Massachusetts, New York, and Virginia the majority of the delegates elected to the state conventions were Anti-Federalists. It was necessary, therefore, by argument and manipulation for the Federalists to win over a considerable number of votes in each state. Opposition to the Constitution in Massachusetts came mainly from those who distrusted the delegation of too much power to the people's agents, from the conflict of interests between the agricultural and commercial sections of the state, and from the pronounced antagonism between the aristocratic and democratic elements of society in this state.[41] The attempt to rush through an early adoption of the Constitution in Massachusetts as well as in other states was looked upon as an attempt of the "rich and wellborn" to obtain that domination of public affairs which they had not been able to accomplish in their respective states.[42] It was conceded that a majority of men of ability, of property, and of influence were in favor of the Constitution and that the opposition lacked effective leaders in some states.

By the year 1787, notes Samuel B. Harding, the antagonism of classes in Massachusetts had developed into an earnest, if not a bitter, contest between the forces of aristocracy and democracy for the control of the state government. Factors which fostered this antagonism were: the distrust by the liberals of the upper classes, which was partly a natural outgrowth of the democratic spirit that accompanied the Revolution, and the fact that so many of the professional men and men of property and education either remained loyalists or gave but lukewarm support to the measures of the patriot party; the natural antagonism of interest between the agricultural and the urban sections; and the economic and legal conditions of the time which brought into disrepute one of the most conspicuous elements of the aristocracy, namely, the legal class. Shays' Rebellion in 1786–1787 crystallized the existing class hostility

---

[41] Samuel B. Harding, *The Federal Constitution in Massachusetts* (New York, 1896), pp. 74 ff.

[42] McMaster and Stone, *op. cit.*, p. 627.

into definite political camps. Many who did not sympathize with the debt-repudiation views of the democratic party were nonetheless impelled toward democratic ideals because of the ultra-aristocratic views of the rich.[43] By the close of 1787, continues Harding,

we have in Massachusetts a democracy, incensed at what it considers the oppressions, actual and prospective, of the aristocracy, fairly united in its plans of political action, and abundantly confident of its power to decide all political matters whatsoever, unaided by the counsel or advice of the upper classes. The aristocratic element in the State had looked to the Convention at Philadelphia for such a federal Constitution as would enable it to maintain that ascendency in matters of government which had of old been the lot of men of wealth and education, but which of late had been seriously threatened by the encroachments of the jealous democracy. Though it did not get all that was desired at the hands of the Convention, the aristocracy found the new Constitution in the main acceptable. But just in proportion as it was welcomed by the upper classes, it promised to prove unacceptable to the populace. Under the influence of the existing antagonism of social elements, that which met with the favor of the aristocracy came shortly to be regarded with suspicion by the democracy; and, in the contest which ensued for ratification, the dread of irretrievably fastening upon themselves in some way the power of the aristocracy unquestionably formed the chief factor in determining the greater portion of the inhabitants of the State, especially those of the rural districts, in a fixed opposition to the adoption of the new system.[44]

Rufus King recognized that it was the fear of the aristocracy which threatened the adoption of the new system. He wrote to Madison: "An apprehension that the liberties of the people are in danger, and a distrust of men of property or education have a more powerful effect upon the minds of our opponents than any specific objections against the Constitution." And a week later he again wrote that the opposition arose chiefly "from an opinion that is immovable, that some injury is plotted against them—that the system is the production of the rich and ambitious, that they discover its operations and the consequence will be the establishment of two orders in the society, one comprehending the opulent and great, the other the poor and illiterate. The extraordinary union in favor of the Constitution in this State of the wealthy and sensible part of it is in confirmation of these opinions and every exertion hitherto made to eradicate it, has been in vain."[45]

With the assembling of the Massachusetts convention, it was evident that a majority of the delegates were opposed to the Constitution. According to the usual explanation, the Federalists won "a hard fought battle against ignorance and prejudice, honest doubt and opposition."[46]

[43] Samuel B. Harding, op. cit., pp. 8, 9.

[44] Harding, op. cit., pp. 13, 14.

[45] Life and Correspondence of Rufus King, I: 314, 317.

[46] Anson Ely Morse, The Federalist Party in Massachusetts to the Year 1800 (Princeton, 1909), p. 52.

But here as elswhere argument was aided by political manipulation. To secure the support of John Hancock and through him some of his friends and supporters, a bargain was made. The price paid was the promise of the support of Hancock by the Federalists for the next gubernatorial election with assurance of aid for his candidacy for the vice-presidency or the presidency. That such a bargain was made, says Harding, "there is not now the slightest reason to doubt."[47] On the results of the Federalist campaign in Massachusetts, Beveridge observes, "one hundred and sixty-eight held out against the Constitution to the very last, uninfluenced by the careful, able, and convincing arguments of its friends, unmoved by their persuasion, unbought by their promises and deals."[48] They regarded the plan of government proposed as "the production of the rich and ambitious" and as designed to establish two orders of society.

As a result of the arguments and political maneuvers, the motion to ratify the Constitution in Massachusetts was carried by the close vote of 187 to 168—a majority of 19 in favor of ratification. Because some of the delegates refused to obey their instructions and because it was largely the Anti-Federalist towns which were unrepresented, Harding does not regard this vote as truly representative of the sentiment in the state.[49]

Similar methods of argument together with political manipulation were used freely in New York and in Virginia. A majority of the people of Virginia were opposed to the new instrument of government. Estimates place the opposition as high as three-fourths.[50] The strength of the opposition no doubt accounts for the fact that the only real debate over the whole Constitution took place in this state. The Virginia constitutionalists, claims Beveridge, took no chances and neglected no precaution.[51] Though able arguments were presented on both sides, the shift of Governor Randolph to the side favoring the Constitution greatly weakened the opposition. His failure to present to the convention Governor Clinton's letter proposing that New York join Virginia in the call for a new federal Convention no doubt saved the Constitution from defeat. Randolph's change of view from determined opposition to defense of the Constitution without any proposals for amendment was ascribed to improper motives. His appointment to the position of Attorney General, thus giving Virginia the President and two members of the cabinet, gave color to the charge. Owing to "better tactics and

---

[47] Harding, *op. cit.*, p. 86. See also the rather unusual methods used to win the approval of Samuel Adams, *ibid.*, pp. 96 ff., and John C. Miller, *Sam Adams: Pioneer in Propaganda* (Boston, 1936), pp. 376 ff.

[48] Albert J. Beveridge, *The Life of John Marshall* (Boston, 1919), I: 344.

[49] *The Federal Constitution in Massachusetts*, p. 99.

[50] Beveridge, *op. cit.*, I: 321.

[51] Beveridge, *op. cit.*, I: 357.

stronger arguments," the constitutionalists won on three test votes by majorities ranging from 1 to 10. To accomplish this result 10 members voted in disobedience of the instructions of their constituents.

Most of the delegates to the convention in New Hampshire were instructed by their constituents to vote against the Constitution. Fearing a vote of rejection, those opposed to the Constitution were persuaded to agree to a plan of delay whereby "the illiberal and ignorant will be brought in to what is right and just." The delay had the desired effect, for, when the convention met a few months later, adoption was carried by a narrow margin.

In Dobbs County, North Carolina, the Federalists used illegal methods and force to elect their candidates to the ratifying convention. When the counting of the votes indicated that the Anti-Federalist candidates were winning, physical force was used to prevent further counting of votes. The sheriff, who had charge of the election, was knocked almost senseless, and the ballot box was forcibly taken from him and carried away. The boast was made by the Federalists that another and better election would be held. The Federalist governor was appealed to and he ordered another election in which the Anti-Federalists refused to participate. By the small number of 85 votes—about one-fifth of those who participated in the first election—five loyal Federalists were given certificates of election. Because of protests from both parties, no delegates from Dobbs County were permitted to sit in the convention.

When the convention met, the numerical advantage was on the side of the Anti-Federalists who had more than double the number favoring the Constitution. Contrary to the impressions usually given about the prevalence of wealth and ability on the side of the Federalists, it is claimed that there were many men of prominence and wealth among the Anti-Federalists. Moreover, "despite all of the efforts of the Federalists, there were only two delegates in the convention from the counties West of the mountains who voted for ratification of the Constitution."[52] The vote against the ratification of the Constitution without amendments was 184 to 93.

The Maryland convention, which was in control of the Federalists, afforded what Allan Nevins calls an illustration of a perfect "steam

[52] Louise Irby Trenholme, *The Ratification of the Federal Constitution in North Carolina* (New York, 1932), pp. 111, 115. In North Carolina the supporters of the Constitution were largely planters, merchants, and members of the learned professions. *Ibid.*, p. 138.

In South Carolina the Federalist leaders with but few exceptions were members of the old planter families of the lowlands, with the Democrats or Republicans being made up of the poor whites and the yeomanry of the piedmont districts. Phillips, *op. cit.*, pp. 529, 538.

roller."[53] Fearing obstructive tactics by the minority, the Federalists held a caucus prior to the meeting of the convention and agreed "that they and their constituents had enjoyed abundant leisure and opportunity for considering the proposed system of federal government, that it was not probable any new lights could be thrown on the subject, that (even if it were) the main question had already, in effect, been decided by the people in the respective counties, that, as each delegate was under a sacred obligation to vote conformably to the sentiments of his constituents, they ought to complete that single transaction for which they were convened, as speedily as was consistent with decorum." Hence the Federalist majority permitted discussion only on the Constitution as a whole, gave opportunity for the minority members to speak generally against the adoption of the document, and, without any attempt to answer the opponents, ratification was carried by a vote of 63 to 11.[54]

Rhode Island was the only state to hold a referendum on the Constitution. Of approximately 6000 men eligible to vote, 2708 voted against and 237 for the Constitution. It is claimed the Federalists did not go to the polls. Whether this surmise be true or not, Nevins remarks that "the commercial and professional groups owned most of the state's wealth, but their antagonists were far too numerous for them."[55]

Referring to New York's ratification of the Constitution by a vote of 30 to 27, Spaulding says: "The sectionalism of this vote is obvious, for no county north of Orange and Dutchess gave a single vote for the Constitution; and, with the one exception of Tredwell of Suffolk, no county south of those two gave a vote in opposition."[56] A line drawn parallel to the seacoast and fifty miles inland from it represented pretty accurately the Federalist area, in which resided most of the friends of the Constitution. West of this line were to be found the more democratic elements of the community. Few of the citizens of this region supported the Constitution.[57]

As a matter of fact, those who drafted the Constitution and secured its adoption did not regard the document as a perfect instrument. Many of them thought that as time and experience would point out its defects the states would be induced to call another convention to amend the document. It has been estimated that not more than 160,000 persons, or

---

[53] *The American States During and After the Revolution, 1775–1789,* p. 320.

[54] Bernard C. Steiner, "Maryland's Adoption of the Federal Constitution," *Amer. Hist. Rev.* (Oct., 1899, Jan., 1900), V: 22, 208, 211.

[55] Nevins, *op. cit.,* p. 237.

[56] Spaulding, *op. cit.,* pp. 267, 268.

[57] Channing, *op. cit.,* III: 522. In the contest over the Constitution, so balanced were the parties, claimed John Marshall, "that even after the subject had been discussed for a considerable time, the fate of the Constitution could scarcely be conjectured; and so

about five per cent of the adult male population, expressed an opinion on the new Constitution.[58] Thus the glowing tribute of James Wilson to a free and enlightened people, ratifying a system of government by their own deliberate choice after careful and systematic consideration, must be regarded as one of the fictions which was fostered by the conservatives to aid the cause of nationalism.

The class basis and the antidemocratic features of the Constitution have been fully considered and authenticated by modern writers in the fields of political science and history. About thirty years ago J. Allen Smith called attention to "the spirit of the Constitution, its inherent opposition to democracy, [and] the obstacles which it has placed in the way of majority rule." The so-called evils of democracy were, in his opinion, largely the result of the constitutional checks on popular rule which were inherited from the political system of the eighteenth century.[59]

Commenting on the general belief that the Constitution of the United States embodies a "democratic philosophy," Smith observed that this view is at variance with the facts, for "democracy—government by the people, or directly responsible to them was not the object which the framers of the American Constitution had in view, but the very thing which they wished to avoid." The efforts of the constitutional Convention were directed, he thought, to the task of devising a system of government which was just popular enough not to excite general opposition and which would give the people as little as possible of the substance of political power.[60] A few years later this interpretation of the ends to be attained by the adoption of the Constitution, which at first seemed rather shocking, was substantially confirmed in a study by Charles A. Beard of the economic interests of the members of the Philadelphia Convention. As a result of this study, Beard concluded:

The movement for the Constitution of the United States was originated and carried through principally by four groups of personalty interests which had been adversely

---

small, in many instances, was the majority in its favor, as to afford strong ground for the opinion, that, had the influence of character been removed, the intrinsic merits of the instrument would not have secured its adoption. Indeed it is scarcely to be doubted that in some of the adopting States, a majority of the people were in the opposition. In all of them, the numerous amendments which were proposed demonstrated the reluctance with which the new government was accepted; and that a dread of dismemberment, not an approbation of the particular system under consideration, had induced an acquiescence in it." *The Life of George Washington* (Philadelphia, 1804–1807), V: 132.

[58] Schuyler, *op. cit.,* p. 138.

[59] See preface to *The Spirit of American Government; A Study of the Constitution: Its Origin, Influence and Relation to Democracy* (New York, 1907).

[60] Smith, *op. cit.,* pp. 29, 30.

affected under the Articles of Confederation: money, public securities, manufactures, and trade and shipping. . . . The members of the Philadelphia Convention which drafted the Constitution were with few exceptions personally interested in, and derived economic advantages from, the establishment of the new system. The Constitution was essentially an economic document based upon the conception that the fundamental private rights of property are anterior to government and morally beyond the reach of popular majorities.[61]

Recent accounts of the political, economic, and social interests which dominated the process of constitution making, however, have merely confirmed and amplified the frank analysis by Charles Francis Adams of the reasons for the adoption of the Constitution. "In three southernmost States of New England only," said Adams,

was the whole community so inoculated with republican principles as to make the transition from the colonial to an independent state simple and easy. . . . The institutions of New York, Pennsylvania, and Virginia, had cherished a privileged class, which formed an obstacle to the reception of the new ideas, not to be removed without a serious rent in the social system. . . . It was the upheaving of the poorest classes to throw off all law of debtor and creditor, which brought about the successful effort to organize the federal government anew, as a bridle upon their license. They never favored it beforehand, nor cordially approved it afterwards, during their day and generation. The federal Convention was the work of the commercial people in the seaport towns, of the planters of the slave-holding States, of the officers of the revolutionary army, and the property holders everywhere. And these parties could never have been strong enough of themselves to procure the general adoption of the instrument which they matured, had it not been that the open insurrection in Massachusetts, and the assemblages threatening to shut up the courts of justice in other States, had thrown the intermediate body of quiet citizens of every shade of opinion, in panic, all on their side. It was under the effect of this panic, that the delegates had been elected, and that they had acted.[62]

The federal Constitution, Adams thought, was reduced in tone far below the level of opinion of one class, but it was still considered above that which prevailed in the country at large. Friends of the Constitution, in his opinion, "could never have succeeded in effecting the establishment of the Constitution, had they not received the active and steady cooperation of all that was left in America of the attachment to the mother country, as well as the moneyed interests, which ever points to strong government as surely as the needle to the pole."[63]

Richard Henry Lee, who opposed the adoption of the Constitution, gives some vivid impressions regarding the clash of interests and the main objectives of the conservatives in hastening the process of adoption. The country was, in his opinion, in a condition of peace; the exist-

---

[61] Charles A. Beard, *An Economic Interpretation of the Constitution of the United States* (New York, 1913), p. 324.
[62] *The Works of John Adams*, I: 441–443.
[63] *Ibid.*

ing governments were taking care of all exigencies except the regulating of trade, the securing of credit (in some instances), and the paying of interest on public debts. There was, as he saw it, no need for immediate action toward changing the form of government. But he saw that there were fraudulent debtors and embarrassed men on the one hand, and men unfriendly to republican equality on the other, who were producing an uneasiness among the people and preparing the way "not for cool and deliberate reforms in the governments, but for changes calculated to promote the interests of particular orders of men."[64] The abuse of power by the state legislatures, which had been charged as being due to the democratic ideas and principles prevailing, had furnished those with aristocratical inclinations with the means and weapons whereby they were rapidly attaining their primary objectives. There was an evident design, particularly on the part of a few men, to establish "one consolidated government." Lee doubted whether this object could be accomplished without convulsions and civil wars and, if attained, whether it would not seriously interfere with the liberties of the people.[65] Not being able to secure complete consolidation, the Convention proposed partial consolidation with a view to securing the gradual centralization of all important powers in one government.

Lee, referring to the disproportion in the democratic and aristocratic parts of the community as represented in the Philadelphia Convention, deplored the fact that some able men of democratic principles and outlook were unable to attend the Convention. If they had attended, it was clear to him that "the result of the Convention would not have had that strong tendency to aristocracy now discernible in every part of the plan." Together with most of the liberal and democratically minded men of the time, Lee saw grave dangers in the failure to include a bill of rights in the original draft of the Constitution. It is proper, he thought, that national laws should be supreme and superior to state or district laws, but "the national laws ought to yield to unalienable and fundamental rights—and national laws, made by a few men, should extend only to a few national objects."[66] The general presumption was that men who govern, will, in all doubtful cases, construe laws and constitutions most favorably for increasing their own powers. Lee wished to have the line clearly drawn between the powers which the people parted with and those that were reserved.

[64] "Letters of a Federal Farmer" in Paul Leicester Ford, *Pamphlets on the Constitution of the United States* (Brooklyn, 1888), pp. 279–281.

[65] *Ibid.*, pp. 282, 283.

[66] *Ibid.*, p. 312.

The most serious danger, Lee said, lurked in the provision for amending the fundamental law, and he expressed his apprehensions as follows:

While power is in the hands of the people, or democratic part of the community, more especially as at present, it is easy, according to the general course of human affairs, for the few influential men in the community, to obtain conventions, alterations in government, and to persuade the common people that they may change for the better, and to get from them a part of the power: But when power is once transferred from the many to the few, all changes become extremely difficult; the government, in this case, being beneficial to the few, they will be exceedingly artful and adroit in preventing any measures which may lead to a change; and nothing will produce it, but great exertions and severe struggles on the part of the common people. Every man of reflection must see, that the change now proposed, is a transfer of power from the many to the few, and the probability is, the artful and ever active aristocracy, will prevent all peaceful measures for changes, unless when they shall discover some favorable moment to increase their own influence.[67]

Describing the party line-up which was evident in the conflict over the adoption of the Constitution, Lee continued:

It is true there may be danger in delay; but there is danger in adopting the system in its present form; and I see the danger in either case will arise principally from the conduct and views of two very unprincipled parties in the United States—two fires, between which the honest and substantial people have long found themselves situated. One party is composed of little insurgents, men in debt, who want no law, and who want a share of the property of others; these are called levellers, Shaysites, etc. The other party is composed of a few, but more dangerous men, with their servile dependents; these avariciously grasp at all power and property; you may discover in all the actions of these men, an evident dislike to free and equal government, and they will go systematically to work to change, essentially, the forms of government in this country; these are called aristocrats. . . . Between these two parties is the weight of the community; the men of middling property, men not in debt on the one hand, and men, on the other, content with republican governments, and not aiming at immense fortunes, offices, and power. In 1786, the little insurgents, the levellers, came forth, invaded the rights of others and attempted to establish governments according to their wills. Their movements evidently gave encouragement to the other party, which, in 1787, has taken the political field, and with its fashionable dependents, and the tongue and the pen, is endeavoring to establish in a great haste, a politer kind of government. These two parties, which will probably be opposed or united as it may suit their interests and views, are really insignificant, compared with the solid, free, and independent part of the community. It is not my intention to suggest, that either of these parties, and the real friends of the proposed Constitution, are the same men. The fact is, these aristocrats support and hasten the adoption of the proposed Constitution, merely because they think it is a stepping stone to their favorite object. I think I am well founded in this idea; I think the general politics of these men support it, as well as the common observation among them. That the proffered plan is the best that can be got at present, it will do for a few years, and lead to something better. . . . Men who wish the people of this country to determine for themselves, and deliberately to fit the government to their situation, must feel some degree of indignation at those attempts to hurry the adoption of a system, and to shut the door against examination.

[67] Ford, *op. cit.*, pp. 317, 318.

The very attempts create suspicions, that those who make them have secret views, or see some defects in the system, which, in the hurry of affairs, they expect will escape the eye of a free people.

What can be the views of those gentlemen in Pennsylvania, who precipitated decisions on this subject? What can be the views of those gentlemen in Boston, who countenanced the printers in shutting up the press against a fair and free investigation of this important system in the usual way? The members of the Convention have done their duty—why should some of them fly to their States—almost forget a propriety of behavior, and precipitate measures for the adoption of a system of their own making? I confess candidly, when I consider these circumstances in connection with the unguarded parts of the system I have mentioned, I feel disposed to proceed with very great caution, and to pay more attention than usual to the conduct of particular characters.[68]

Instead of the customary fear of the rule of the people, Lee was chiefly concerned that "assuming and overbearing" men should be duly restrained. In this respect he agreed with Randolph who wanted a second convention called to propose amendments because he thought it better to amend the document while "we have the Constitution in our power and while the passions of designing men are not yet enlisted."

The federal Constitution was framed and adopted then, in large measure, as the result of the activities of factions comprising in the main the mercantile interests of the Atlantic seaboard, owners of bonds and public securities, property owners, and others who were vitally concerned in the preservation of property rights and the sanctity of contracts. The Constitution was opposed in large part in its formation and adoption by those who favored an indulgent attitude toward debtors, a liberal interpretation and relaxation of the terms of contracts, and a relaxed administration of justice, in the collection of taxes, and by those who espoused democratic principles and practices. It is apparent that the process of adoption of the instrument was accomplished by a sort of *coup d'état* whereby the conservatives took advantage of a fortunate set of circumstances and by a variety of political devices and maneuvers hastened decisions before the agrarian and debtor classes and those inclined to favor democratic ideas could satisfactorily organize their forces.[69]

---

[68] Ford, *op. cit.*, pp. 320–323.

[69] The Constitution, concludes Dr. Libby, "was carried in the original thirteen States by the influence of those classes along the great highways of commerce, the seacoast, the Connecticut river, the Shenandoah valley and the Ohio river; and in proportion as the material interests along these arteries of intercourse were advanced and strengthened, the Constitution was most readily received and most heartily supported. In other words, the areas of intercourse and wealth carried the Constitution. It was these sections that Hamilton rallied to support his far-seeing financial policy for continued national development. And it was in the interior and agricultural sections of the country that Jefferson found material for a party to oppose his great rival." Orin Grant Libby, *The Geographical Distribution of the Vote of the Thirteen States on the Federal Constitution, 1787–1788* (Madison, 1894), p. 49.

Historians have usually approved the second and largely peaceful revolution which, by means of the formation and adoption of the federal Constitution, transferred authority from the radical and democratic groups in control of public affairs from 1776 to 1789 to the conservative groups. Morison and Commager call this a "Thermidorean reaction" and describe it as follows:

There comes a time in every revolutionary movement when the people become tired of agitation and long for peace and security. They then eliminate the radicals, trouble-makers and war-mongers, and take measures to consolidate their government, hoping to secure what has already been gained through turmoil and suffering. . . . Naturally it was the men of property and education whose interests were primarily affected by the menace of disunion and who assumed leadership in the constitutional movement. But we are not to assume that it was for any exclusively selfish or class interest that they were acting. . . . Seldom has a class acted more wisely for the good of the whole, than the Federalists, the self-constituted party of property owners, publicists and professional men that framed the Federal Constitution, procured its ratification, and built a new federal state within its frame.[70]

The transformation took place, as Morison and Commager see it, quietly and peaceably and without "purges, exiles, executions or assassinations." But it is clear that the process was not wholly a peaceable one and that it was not without its persecutions and recriminations. It is obvious, moreover, that the customary laudatory accounts of the methods and procedure adopted by the leaders who directed and successfully carried out the second revolution is predicated upon the assumption that the end to be accomplished was a desirable one and that whatever means were necessary to attain this end were not only justifiable but also commendable.

THE RELATION OF THE JUDICIARY TO THE CONFLICT BETWEEN THE DEMOCRATIC AND ARISTOCRATIC GROUPS

So far as political and legal implications are concerned, the history of the United States records during the formative period the prevalence of two very divergent points of view or attitudes. One of these, taking its cue from an English and colonial background, aimed to preserve and foster the conservative and aristocratic ideals and conditions which were characteristic of the Anglo-American society of the eighteenth century. Government and social institutions were conceived as appropriate means for the furtherance of the interests of particular classes or groups. The ideal system of government was one of checks and balances in which ample provision was made for the protection of property and in accordance with which the popular democratic agencies were duly limited so

---

[70] *The Growth of the Republic*, I: 162, 163.

that the ownership and enjoyment of wealth might not be too seriously disturbed. Foremost among the doctrines of those imbued with the conservative faith was the notion there should be a single, strong, central government to provide a strategic political agency to control foreign relations, to preserve and protect the commercial and industrial interests of the people, and to keep in check the rising tide of populism which was beginning to loom up as a menace during the Revolutionary period. The doctrines of Federalism formulated during the Convention of 1787 and embodied in the federal Constitution and put into practice during the Administrations of Presidents Washington and Adams form the ideals and standards for the conservative tradition. Alexander Hamilton was the guiding spirit and the heroic character in the founding and establishment of this tradition. At the apex of the governmental system which Hamilton and his associates aimed to permanently entrench in the American way of life was an independent and for most important practical purposes a supreme Judiciary. It was the prime duty of this department to see that the weaknesses and follies of democratic rule would be held within reasonable bounds and the fundamental principles of the conservative faith would be fostered and maintained.

There was, in the year 1787 and afterwards, a working alliance of men of property and men of aristocratic views the purpose of which was the creation of a central government with coercive powers. In developing their political philosophy these groups made use of Harrington's notion of a delicately balanced system of checks whereby the aristocratic and democratic elements of society would offset one another, the result being a government of laws, not of men. Harrington's ideal government was one in control of the wisest and best citizens ruling under laws made in accordance with the limitations of a written constitution. To understand the aims and purposes of the written constitutions of the eighteenth century, it is necessary to consider a combination of Harrington's ideal government and Locke's notion that the great and chief purpose of government is the preservation of property. According to Locke the supreme power cannot take from any man his property without his own consent, for to invade property rights is to subvert the purpose of government.[71] From this set of ideas it was relatively easy for Hamilton and those who agreed with him to elaborate the philosophy that the primary concern of government was to assist industry and trade.[72]

To the proponents of the type of Federalism which was espoused by the conservative groups after the establishment of the national govern-

---

[71] See his *Second Treatise on Civil Government,* chaps. ix, xi.
[72] Vernon Louis Parrington, *Main Currents in American Thought* (New York, 1927), I: 292 ff.

ment in 1789, it was a plain and unmistakable duty to uphold the union as conceived and put in concrete form through the federal Constitution, to foster nationalism as against State rights and the undue influence of local politics, to defend the protection of the rights of property and contracts against democratic onslaughts, and to preserve the independence and supremacy of the Judiciary as the controlling check and balance department.

On the other hand, certain political leaders of ability and prominence in the formative years of American institutions had high respect for the judgment and sense of the common people and gave their sympathy and support to the development of democratic institutions in the United States. Unlike the Federalist aim, which was chiefly concerned with the establishment of checks on popular rule, this interpretation of American political and social life looked with favor upon the interests and agencies which aided in the process of securing democracy in all its phases—economic, political, social.[73] Though Jefferson became the leader and prototype for those who supported the democratic way of life, no one man so completely identified himself with the conservative and aristocratic point of view as did Hamilton. The currents which gave strength and direction to the democratic philosophy were in due course guided largely by Thomas Jefferson, Andrew Jackson, and Abraham Lincoln.[74] Under the leadership of Marshall the Supreme Court espoused the cause and aided in developing the program of Hamiltonian Federalism.[75]

---

[73] William E. Dodd, "The Struggle for Democracy in the United States," 28 *International Jour. of Ethics* (July, 1918), 465.

Democracy, said Dodd, "is equality, economic, political and even social in large measure. . . . [It is] a social organization in which all normal men and women have their proportionate voice in the determination of public policy, in which all have free opportunity to earn a livelihood, share according to capacity in the common prosperity, and bear their just portions of the burdens of war or other disaster. In such a society government flows from the decisions of the majority, whether those decisions are wise or not, and administration is not hindered or obstructed by executives or judiciaries." *Ibid.*

[74] Men, said Jefferson, "have differed in opinion, and been divided into parties by these opinions, from the first origin of societies, and in all governments where they have been permitted freely to think and to speak. The same political parties which now agitate the United States, have existed through all time. Whether the power of the people or that of the *aristoi* should prevail, were questions which kept the states of Greece and Rome in eternal convulsions, as they now schismatize every people whose minds and mouths are not shut up by the gag of a despot. And in fact, the terms of Whig and Tory belong to natural as well as to civil history. They denote the temper and constitution of mind of different individuals." *The Writings of Thomas Jefferson* (Mem. ed.), XIII: 279, 280.

[75] The doctrines of Hamilton and Jefferson, so far as they affected and conditioned constitutional interpretation, will be discussed in a subsequent chapter. See chap. xvii, below, for a consideration of Marshall's aid in advancing the cause of Hamiltonian Federalism.

But few writers who have discussed the undemocratic origins and purposes of the Constitution have indicated the extent to which the federal Judiciary was designed to accomplish one of the main objectives of the founders, namely, the placing of necessary restrictions upon the control of popular majorities to protect the interests of those possessing property and those engaged in the accumulation of wealth. J. Allen Smith, who portrayed more effectively than anyone else the undemocratic features of the American system of government, has an illuminating chapter on the federal Judiciary[76] in which he contends that the checks on popular rule which the founders wished to establish are, as we have them today, in large measure the work of the Supreme Court, for the Constitution "has been molded and developed by, and largely owes its spirit and character to the interpretation which that body has placed upon it." Though the methods by which the Judiciary has become a checking, guiding, and controlling department are merely suggested in cursory form in this work, the methods and devices by which such control in the interests of property and wealth has been accomplished are plainly indicated. For, says Smith, the Judiciary has not only claimed "the power to act as the final interpreter of the Constitution but also the right, independently of the Constitution, to interpret the political system under which we live, and make all legislative acts conform to its interpretation of that system."[77]

Confirming Smith's analysis, Nicholas Murray Butler recently maintained that the powers, position, and prestige of the Supreme Court must be upheld because it "is the only representative which the American people have to which they may turn for the protection of the underlying principles of their government."[78] The placing of the Supreme Court at the apex of the American system of government not only as the authoritative voice to expound the Constitution but also as the custodian and expositor of the underlying principles of government has come about both by design and by a fortuitous chain of circumstances. But whatever the process may have been, it has come to be true that "the fundamental division of powers in the Constitution of the United States is between voters on the one hand and property owners on the other. The forces of democracy on one side, divided between the executive and legislature are set over against the forces of property on the other, with the Judiciary as the arbiter between them."[79] In tracing the role of the

---

[76] *The Spirit of American Government*, chap. v.

[77] *Ibid.*, p. 106.

[78] New York *Times*, Apr. 19, 1937.

[79] Arthur Twining Hadley, "The Constitutional Position of Property in America," 64 *The Independent* (Apr. 16, 1908), 836.

Supreme Court in American government and politics, it will become apparent that, though a groundwork for such a development was laid in the express language of the Constitution, much the larger part of the functions the Court now performs in the political and quasi-political realm have been progressively constructed through the judicial process of interpretation. In this interpretation the Court, though assuming the role of a mechanical mouthpiece to express the language and meaning of the Constitution, has cast the weight of its prestige and influence on one side of the major and permanent party divisions in the United States. The story of the partisan and political activities of the Supreme Court will be revealed in its far-reaching decisions, the most important of which involved the relations between the nation and the states. Before undertaking an analysis of these decisions it is necessary to survey briefly the origin and early development of the central issue between the nation and the states—the location of sovereignty in the American federal system. This issue nearly brought about a drastic reduction in the powers of the Supreme Court to act as an umpire for the federal system and it was one of the main phases of the controversy which led to the Civil War and the consequent threats tending to destroy the union created by the Constitution.

APPENDIX

BECAUSE *Chief Justice Marshall had an opportunity to embody his political and economic views into federal judicial decisions, his comments on the party divisions at this time in his writings on the life of George Washington are of peculiar interest. When these observations on political parties were made, Marshall had definitely aligned himself with the party of which Hamilton was the acknowledged leader. Marshall wrote:*

At length, two great parties were formed in every State, which were distinctly marked, and which pursued distinct objects, with systematic arrangement.

The one struggled with unabated zeal for the exact observance of public and private engagements. By those belonging to it, the faith of a nation, or of a private man was deemed a sacred pledge, the violation of which was equally forbidden by the principles of moral justice, and of sound policy. The distresses of individuals were, they thought, to be alleviated only by industry and frugality, not by a relaxation of the laws, or by a sacrifice of the rights of others. According to the stern principles laid down for their government, the imprudent and idle could not be protected by the legislature from the consequences of their indiscretion; but should be restrained from involving themselves in difficulties, by the conviction that a rigid compliance with contracts would be enforced. They were consequently the uniform friends of a regular administration of justice, and of a vigorous course of taxation which would enable the state to comply with its engagements. By a natural association of ideas, they were also, with very few exceptions, in favor of enlarging the powers of the federal government, and of enabling it to protect the dignity and character of the nation abroad, and its interests at home. The other party marked out for itself a more indulgent course. Viewing with extreme tenderness the case of the debtor, their efforts were unceasingly directed to his relief. To exact a faithful compliance with contracts was, in their opinion, a measure too harsh to be insisted on, and was one which the people would not bear. They were uniformly in favour of relaxing the administration of justice, of affording facilities for the payment of debts, or of suspending their collection, and of remitting taxes. The same course of opinion led them to resist every attempt to transfer from their own hands into those of Congress, powers which by others were deemed essential to the preservation of the Union. In many of the States, the party last mentioned constituted a decided majority of the people; and in all of them, it was very powerful. The emission of paper money, the delay of legal proceedings, and the suspension of the collection of taxes, were the fruits of their rule wherever they were completely dominant. Even where they failed in carrying their measures, their strength was such as to encourage the hope of succeeding in a future attempt; and annual elections held forth to them the prospect of speedily repairing the loss of a favourite question. Throughout the Union, the contest between these parties was periodically revived; and the public mind was perpetually agitated with hopes and fears on subjects which essentially affected the fortunes of a considerable proportion of the society.

These contests were the more animated, because, in the state governments generally, no principle had been introduced which could resist the wild projects of the moment, give the people an opportunity to reflect, and allow the good sense of the Nation time for exertion. This uncertainty with respect to measures of great importance to every member of the community, this instability in principles which ought if possible to be rendered immutable, produced a long train of ills; and is seriously believed to have been among the operating causes of those pecuniary embarrassments, which at that time were so general as to influence the legislation of almost every state in the Union. Its direct consequence was the loss of confidence in the government, and in individuals.

. . . the continent was divided into two great political parties, the one of which contemplated America as a Nation, and laboured incessantly to invest the federal head with powers competent to the preservation of the Union. The other attached itself to the state authorities, viewed all the powers of Congress with jealousy; and assented reluctantly to measures which would enable the head to act, in any respect, independently of the members. Men of enlarged and liberal minds who, in the imbecility of a general government, by which alone the capacities of the Nation could be efficaciously exerted, could discern the imbecility of the Nation itself; who, viewing the situation of the world, could perceive the dangers to which these young republics were exposed, if not held together by a cement capable of preserving a beneficial connexion; who felt the full value of national honour, and the full obligation of national faith; and who were persuaded of the insecurity of both, if resting for their preservation on the concurrence of thirteen distinct sovereignties; arranged themselves generally in the first party. The officers of the army, whose local prejudices had been weakened by associating with each other, and whose experience had furnished lessons on the inefficacy of requisitions which were not soon to be forgotten, threw their weight almost universally into the same scale.[80]

Thomas Jefferson thought the party divisions thus described by Marshall might be briefly outlined as follows:

Within every society men form roughly into two groups for by their constitutions they "are naturally divided into two parties: 1. Those who fear and distrust the people, and wish to draw all powers from them into the hands of the higher classes; 2. Those who identify themselves with the people, have confidence in them, cherish and consider them as the most honest and safe, although not the most wise depository of the public interests."[81]

---

[80] John Marshall, *The Life of George Washington* (Philadelphia, 1804), V: 33–34, 85–87.
[81] Jefferson to Henry Lee, Aug. 10, 1824, *Writings* (Mem. ed.), XVI: 73, 74, 96.

CHAPTER III

The Issue of State versus National Sovereignty

THE CENTRAL ISSUE of American political and legal thought and the one around which the greatest constitutional controversies have been waged concerns the relations between the state and national governments and the distribution of powers between the two units of a federal system. A large part of the work of the Supreme Court has been devoted to the demarcation of the line between federal and state functions. Some of the most acute controversies concerning the functions of the Supreme Court in the American system have arisen in the performance of this duty. The first important case to come to the Supreme Court involving the interpretation of the federal Constitution, that of *Chisholm v. Georgia*,[1] centered around this issue. An estimate of the Court's work must give prominence, therefore, to the continuous conflicts arising over the distribution of powers in a federal state. But the issue is clouded by partisanship, propaganda, misrepresentation, and the bitterness engendered by civil strife, so that a fair and impartial discussion of different ideas relating to the subject is difficult to attain. No special claim of impartiality is made in this study. But an attempt will be made to present the two most prominent points of view or attitudes involved in the great national conflict, namely, whether sovereignty resided in the states or in the nation. Until after the Civil War the major questions of constitutional construction were concerned with this unsolved and perhaps unsolvable query.

For generations, observes Edward Channing, the people of each of the thirteen original colonies regarded themselves as forming distinct administrative entities. When the Revolution came and colonial ties with England were severed, the newly formed states assumed that being free from outside control they were sovereign in fact and in law. They acted as sovereign, free, and independent states and insisted on retaining all the rights of such states.[2] This belief in the right and duty of independent action is shown in the attitude of the states toward their first common agency, the Continental Congresses.

[1] 2 Dallas 419 (1793).   [2] *A History of the United States* (New York, 1926), III: 431.

EVIDENCE FAVORING STATE SOVEREIGNTY

The Continental Congresses and sovereign authority.—Contrary to the assertions frequently made, the First Continental Congress was mainly a "consultative and advisory body" and not "a government." Its chief objects were attained by a voluntary "association." Though Congress in certain respects had the appearance of a *de facto* government enforcing its own laws and undoubtedly exercising powers beyond the instructions to its members, there is little evidence that the members doubted their actual subordination to the colonial assemblies which had sent them to Philadelphia.

The claim that the First Continental Congress was organized "under the auspices and with the consent of the people, acting directly in their primary, sovereign capacity, and without the intervention of the functionaries, to whom the ordinary powers of government were delegated in the colonies"[3] is not substantiated by data concerning the selection of delegates or the instructions they received.[4] The delegates from two colonies, Rhode Island and Pennsylvania, were chosen by the legislatures, those of Massachusetts by the lower house, and in only six colonies were special conventions held. The instructions to the delegates of the First and Second Continental Congresses related rather to means of adjusting the unhappy differences with Great Britain, to a redress of grievances, and to a defense of colonial rights and liberties than to the setting up of an independent governmental authority. According to Van Tyne, these assemblies were not representative of all the people, but of the radical groups which were the first to think of independence and the formation of new states. If their instructions meant anything, these delegates were "unauthorized by the people to act as a national government."[5] Though these Congresses assumed some of the highest functions of sovereignty, such as the raising of an army and a navy, emitting bills of credit, and authorizing the capture and condemnation of prizes, all of these steps were taken with protestations of loyalty and expressions of attachment to the British King. Since loyalty to the King and a desire for an American national state were incompatible, Van Tyne thinks that "if Congress was doing seemingly sovereign acts, it was

---

[3] Joseph Story, *Commentaries on the Constitution* (5th ed.), I: 145.

[4] Claude H. Van Tyne, "Sovereignty in the American Revolution: An Historical Study," *Amer. Hist. Rev.* (Apr., 1907), XII: 529.

[5] Van Tyne, *op. cit.*, p. 532. The statement of Rutledge represented the prevailing view, "We have no legal authority; and obedience to our determinations will only follow the reasonableness, the apparent utility and the necessity of the measures we adopt. We have no coercive or legislative authority." John Adams, *Works,* II: 367.

merely in the capacity of a party committee leading a rebellious faction in the empire in an attempt to force the concession of its rights."[6] The powers and duties of the Second Continental Congress differed little in nature from those of the First Congress. In the main the delegates were expected to attend, meet and report, consult and advise, and determine means of obtaining redress from grievances.[7] Early use of the words "union" or "united colonies" was for the purpose of securing concessions which could be attained only by united efforts. Differences between the colonies and the English government, it was believed, should be temporarily adjusted until more satisfactory terms might be granted by the King and Council. And even the suggestion of establishing separate state governments was qualified as applicable "during the continuance of the present dispute between Great Britain and the colonies."[8]

From an examination of its journals and the language of its resolutions, it does not appear that Congress was intended to be nor considered itself an organ of government exercising national sovereignty. "The things that men said, the powers that they gave their state governments, the acts of those governments, and the conduct of the Congress itself, all show," says Van Tyne, "that in the minds of most men of the time, there were thirteen independent States which were temporarily acting together in the business of acquiring their individual independence."[9] There were a few men imbued with nationalistic or imperialistic notions and who occasionally spoke of the need of putting into objective form the idea of nationality. But how slight their influence was may be shown by the fact that the states had to be coaxed into a league of friendship.

"I am resolved," said Rutledge, "to vest the Congress with no more power than is absolutely necessary, and to use a familiar expression, to keep the staff in our own hands; for I am confident, if surrendered into the hands of others, a most pernicious use will be made of it."[10] Members of Congress appeared to have no doubts about their actual subordination to the colonial assemblies. When Congress suggested the establishment of courts by the states to consider prize cases, on the assumption that appeals might be made to Congress, the states replied by limiting appeals only to cases of capture by armed vessels fitted out under the direction

---

[6] Van Tyne, *op. cit.*, p. 534.

[7] See Instructions to Delegates, *Journals of the Continental Congress* (Ford ed.), II, *passim.*

[8] *Journals of the Continental Congress*, III: 319, 327. The formation of permanent governments was recommended on May 10, 1776, but some of the colonies acted slowly and reluctantly.

[9] Van Tyne, *The American Revolution*, American Nation Series (New York, 1905), p. 182.

[10] *Ibid.*, pp. 184, 185.

of the united colonies. Out of this limited Congressional authority, however, arose in 1780 the Court of Appeals—the predecessor of the Supreme Court of the United States. Congresses at first were convened merely to conciliate and secure redress of grievances, but as conditions drifted into war and independence was declared, they acted no longer as representatives of colonies but of independent states leagued together to overthrow the control of England and to secure the aid and recognition of other foreign states. To Congress, however, was yielded only a temporary and indefinite authority for war purposes, with the understanding that its future relations with the states would be determined by mutual agreement.

The juristic or political theory frequently advanced that there was at this time a general sentiment tending to create and demanding the establishment of a national government has little evidence to support it. Upon a relatively doubtful and insecure background, a philosophical theory was formulated by a few political leaders of the time who sustained the view that the mere act of breaking the bonds with Great Britain resulted in the formation of a nation with sovereignty vested in Congress. As a matter of fact, however, Congress was accorded powers only for effective common defense and was regarded primarily as a "superintending power." "So far as objective institutions were concerned, there were, at least until the Articles of Confederation were adopted," asserts Van Tyne, "thirteen independent and sovereign States which banded themselves together to fight a common enemy."[11]

The states showed their belief in their own authority and independence not only by refusing to accede to the proposals of Congress but also by asserting some of the essential powers of sovereign nations. They provided for their own armies and navies and asserted the right to make war and conclude treaties; they borrowed money abroad as if they were independent nations.[12] Nine states supported their own navies. State armies were used largely for state purposes. Much of the fighting early in the war in the South was carried on without the aid or advice of Congress.

Connecticut, adopting her old charter as a constitution, asserted "this republic is, and shall forever be and remain, a free, sovereign, and in-

---

[11] Van Tyne, *The American Revolution*, p. 177. According to Chief Justice Jay, however, "thirteen sovereignties were considered as emerged from the principles of the Revolution, combined with local convenience and considerations, the people nevertheless continued to consider themselves in a national point of view, as one people." Chisholm v. Georgia, 2 Dallas 419, 470 (1793).

[12] Allan Nevins, *The American States During and After the Revolution, 1775–1789* (New York, 1924), pp. 658–661.

dependent State." The New Hampshire constitution provided that "the people of this State have the sole and exclusive right of governing themselves as a free, sovereign and independent State." And the constitution of Massachusetts contained a similar provision. South Carolina in two constitutions authorized the government to make war and enter into treaties. Virginia ratified the treaty with France and sent her own agents to Europe for international negotiations and concluded a treaty with Spain relating to the western border. The Pennsylvania convention of 1776 resolved that reasons having been given by the Continental Congress for declaring "this, as well as the other United States of America, free and independent, ... we will ... maintain the freedom and independency of this and the other United States of America." From most of the indications of the time, the states deemed themselves sovereign and independent nations and their status was in all essential respects considered as unchanged by the adoption of the Declaration of Independence.

The Declaration of Independence and the transfer of sovereignty.— It has often been contended that the Declaration of Independence in effect consolidated the colonies into a unified state—in fact, made of them "a sovereign state and a member of the family of nations."[13] But the arguments and procedure at the time of the adoption of the Declaration do not sustain the nationalist theory. The claim was made in the debate on the resolution that "if the delegates of any particular colony had no power to declare such colony independent, certain they were the others could not declare it for them; the colonies being as yet perfectly independent of each other."[14] The vote on the Declaration was not taken until the delegates had received favorable instructions from their states, and New York did not deem herself bound until her own convention approved. Seven states by subsequent resolutions gave the Declaration the binding force of law within their respective jurisdictions.[15] And it was frequently asserted that the act severing the political connections with England erected the colonies into free and independent states. What was intended when the Declaration announced that "these United Colonies are ... Free and Independent States" may be inferred from the

---

[13] "The people of the country became henceforth the rightful sovereign of the country; they became united in a national corporate capacity, as one people." See George Tickner Curtis, *History of the Constitution of the United States* (New York, 1860), I: 52; cf. also Herman Edouard Von Holst, *The Constitutional and Political History of the United States,* trans. by John J. Lalor and Alfred B. Mason (Chicago, 1876), I: 8, 9.

[14] *Journals of the Continental Congress,* VI: 1088.

[15] Cf. Van Tyne, "Sovereignty in the American Revolution," *Amer. Hist. Rev.,* XII: 537, 538.

resolves of some of the state conventions or assemblies which voted on the Declaration. The Pennsylvania convention approved the action of Congress and declared "this, as well as the other United States of America, free and independent,"[16] and the Connecticut assembly adopted a similar proviso that "this Colony is and of right ought to be a free and independent State."[17] The belief in the political independence of the states was affirmed also in the debates on the adoption of the Articles of Confederation.[18]

From the time of its adoption there were, however, two points of view regarding the effect of the Declaration of Independence on the transfer of sovereignty. It was the opinion of one of the signers of the document— Chief Justice McKean of Pennsylvania—that there was a single body corporate. When it was argued in *Respublica v. Sweers*[19] that in 1779, prior to the acceptance of the Articles of Confederation, there was no body corporate known to law, McKean replied: "From the moment of their association, the United States necessarily became a body corporate; for, there was no superior from whom that charter could otherwise be derived." But the lack of agreement on this point is indicated by the view of Justice Chase, who, in speaking of the Declaration of Independence, said: "I consider this as a declaration, not that the United Colonies *jointly*, in a *collective* capacity, were independent States, etc., but that *each* of them was a sovereign and independent State, that is, that *each* of them had a right to govern itself by its own authority and its own laws, without any control from any other power upon earth."[20] Apparently it is not possible to determine from the nature and effect of the Declaration of Independence whether there was from that date one sovereign or thirteen sovereignties in the United States. But the uncertainty which arose from the indefinite language of the Declaration was removed by the express recognition of state sovereignty in the Articles of Confederation.

Sovereignty under the Articles of Confederation.—The issue between the advocates of state sovereignty and the proponents of an emerging

[16] Peter Force, *American Archives*, 5th series (Washington, 1837–1853), II: 10.

[17] *Records of the State of Connecticut*, I: 3. "We realize," says Nevins, "that when Americans thought of independence in 1775–76, they usually thought of it in terms of their own commonwealth, of Massachusetts, New Jersey, or Georgia, rather than in terms of the nation." *The American States During and After the Revolution, 1775–1789*, p. 115.

[18] *Journals of the Continental Congress*, VI: 1081.

[19] 1 Dallas 41, 44 (1779).

[20] Ware v. Hylton, 3 Dallas 199, 224 (1796). Separation from the mother country, Andrew C. McLaughlin maintains, meant that the colonies were no longer in the British Empire but were independent states. *A Constitutional History of the United States* (New York, 1935), p. 106.

nationalistic state is best portrayed in the adoption of the Articles of Confederation and in the operation, until 1789, of a central government under this instrument. Emerging through Franklin's draft of 1775, a select committee under the chairmanship of John Dickinson—considered by Congress to be a committee of the whole—adopted and submitted the Articles of Confederation to the states in November, 1777. The letter of submission of the Articles called attention to the efforts to combine "in one general system the various sentiments and interests of a continent divided into so many sovereign and independent communities, under the conviction of the absolute necessity of uniting all our councils and all our strength to maintain and defend our common liberties." After considerable delay owing to the controversy over the disposal of western lands which were claimed by certain states, the Confederation was adopted by Maryland in 1781. A "perpetual" union was formed with the proviso that "each State retains its sovereignty, freedom and independence, and every power, jurisdiction and right which is not by this federation expressly delegated to the United States in congress assembled."[21] The contention that the Articles of Confederation were deemed to be in the nature of a treaty between sovereign states is indicated from contemporary evidence aside from the Articles. The first draft of the Articles contained the clause that "the said Colonies unite themselves so as never to be divided by any act whatever," but this was struck out.

The Articles furnish an admirable measure of the sentiment for a nation and the contemporary desire to form a state. The idea of the

[21] On the article regarding the sovereignty of the states, Thomas Burke of North Carolina wrote: "It stood originally the third article: and expressed only a reservation of the power of regulating the internal police, and consequently resigned every other power. It appeared to me that this was not what the States expected, and, I thought, it left it in the power of the future Congress or General Council to explain away every right belonging to the States and to make their own power as unlimited as they please. I proposed, therefore, an amendment, which held up the principle, that all sovereign power was in the States separately, and that particular acts of it, which should be expressly enumerated, would be exercised in conjunction, and not otherwise; but that in all things else each State would exercise all the rights and power of sovereignty, uncontrolled. This was at first so little understood that it was some time before it was seconded, and South Carolina first took it up. The opposition was made by Mr. Wilson of Pennsylvania, and Mr. R. H. Lee of Virginia; in the end however the question was carried for my proposition, eleven ayes, one no, and one divided. The no was Virginia; the divided New Hampshire. . . . In a word, Sir, I am of opinion, the Congress should have power enough to call out and apply the common strength for the common defence: but not for the partial purposes of ambition. . . . The inequality of the States, and yet the necessity of maintaining their separate independence, will occasion dilemmas almost inextricable." Thomas Burke to the Governor of North Carolina, Apr. 29, 1777, in Edmund C. Burnett, *Letters of the Members of the Continental Congress* (Washington, 1923), II: 345–346.

state "in the consciousness of the people," which John W. Burgess asserts
to have been prevalent at this time, maintains Van Tyne, "is just what
I believe that the facts here submitted show not to have existed. Though
the whole logic of the situation seems to us now, and seemed to a few
leaders then, to point to the necessity of the formation of a national
state, yet the majority of men refused to see it, and hugged the delusive
phantom of independence and of sovereign statehood for each of the
thirteen colonies."[22]

Those who maintain the view that a national state existed from the
time of the First Continental Congress are obliged to demonstrate the
utter futility or unwarranted character of the Articles. The usual method
followed by exponents of the organic or nationalist theory of the interpretation of American politics is to claim that the states usurped the
legitimate and incipient national sovereignty which still existed even
though submerged during this period. Believing that the Declaration of
Independence made the united colonies a unit, and not separately free
and independent states, James Wilson maintained that it was not the
purpose of the Confederation to transfer any of the powers and rights
to which the united colonies were previously entitled to the particular
states.[23] Surveying the provision in the Articles relating to sovereignty
from the standpoint of the organic theory, Von Holst cannot see "how
this assumption was to be reconciled with the fact that the Congress had
been in existence for years, and had actually exercised sovereign power

[22] Van Tyne, *Amer. Hist. Rev.*, XII: 539. Cf. Washington's reference to "the bant-
ling—I had like to have said *Monster*—sovereignty," which had taken hold of the
states. Henry P. Johnston, ed., *The Correspondence and Public Papers of John Jay*
(New York, 1891), III: 239. According to Luther Martin, "the States, considered as
States, in their political capacity, are the members of a federal government; that the
States, in their political capacity, or as sovereignties, are entitled, and *only entitled*
originally to agree upon the form of, and submit themselves to, a federal government,
and afterwards, by mutual consent, to dissolve or alter it; that everything which relates
to the formation, the dissolution, or the alteration of a *federal* government over States
equally free, sovereign, and independent, is the *peculiar* province of the *States,* in their
sovereign or political capacity, in the same manner as what relates to forming alliances
or treaties of peace, amity, or commerce; and that the people at large, in their individual capacity, have no more right to interfere in the one case than in the other. That
according to these principles we originally acted, in forming our Confederation; it was
the States, as States, by their representatives in Congress, that formed the Articles of
Confederation; it was the States, as States, by their legislatures, ratified those articles;
and it was there established and provided, that the States, as States, that is, by their
legislatures, should agree to any alterations that should hereafter be proposed in the
federal government, before they should be binding; and any alterations agreed to
in any other manner, cannot release the States from the obligation they are under to
each other, by virtue of the original Articles of Confederation." Max Farrand, ed., *The
Records of the Federal Convention of 1787* (New Haven, 1923), III: 229–230.

[23] James Dewitt Andrews, ed., *The Works of James Wilson* (Chicago, 1896), I: 660.

from the first, while the individual States had assumed no sovereign attitude, theoretically or practically towards England or other foreign country."[24]

John W. Burgess, who also accepts the nationalist theory, says that when the revolutionary central government gave way to the government under the Articles of Confederation, "the American state ceased to exist in objective organization." It returned to its subjective condition merely as an idea in the consciousness of the people. From the standpoint of political science, what existed now as objective institutions was a central government and thirteen local governments.[25] Such nationalist interpretations represent, indeed, history made to order to suit partisan views. If the evidence does not fit the theory, it is convenient to overlook or declare the countervailing facts of no real value.

The general conclusion which may be formed from the best evidence of the time, including the records of the Continental Congresses, the opinions of public men of the period, and the general attitude and policies of the states, is that the states considered themselves sovereign, acted as though they were sovereign, and were considered by most of the men of the time to be independent states.[26] Public debates and expressions of opinion contain references to the belief that though the states were sovereign and independent units so far as internal affairs were concerned, the states could act only as a single or unitary sovereign so far as external or foreign affairs were concerned. Relative to the necessary unity of action in foreign affairs, Morison and Commager are of the opinion that despite the clauses indicating that a Confederation had been formed and the express retention of sovereignty and independence by the states, the powers conferred upon the central government, such as the authority to make war and peace, to send and receive ambassadors, to make treaties and alliances, to borrow money, to raise an army and equip a navy, as

---

[24] Von Holst, *op. cit.*, I: 23. "Congress exhorted the legislatures, by an act of public usurpation against the legal consequences of historical facts, to transform the Union into a league of States, and the legislatures recklessly responded to this demand. . . . Thus, in boldest opposition to facts, the Union appears, in the Articles of Confederation, as being first called into life by them [the states]." Von Holst, *The Constitutional Law of the United States* (Chicago, 1887), pp. 8, 9.

[25] John W. Burgess, *Political Science and Comparative Constitutional Law* (Boston, 1902), I: 101.

[26] "The unequivocal, voluntary, objective act of the people in adopting and maintaining the Articles affords conclusive evidence that the subjective sentiment of national unity ceased to exist, if, indeed, up to that time, it had ever existed . . . the testimony of history is overwhelmingly to the effect that, with practical unanimity, the people of those times held the contrary view and the reasonable interpretation of the facts supports them in their opinion." W. W. Willoughby, *The American Constitutional System* (New York, 1904), pp. 16, 17.

well as to decide disputes between the states, cast doubts on the reality of the separate sovereignty of the states.[27]

It is difficult to form an estimate of the Articles of Confederation and of the influence of this document in the development of a central or federal government for the states. Most of the interpretations or evaluations of the Articles were made by nationalists seeking to point out defects and aiming to secure either radical revisions or replacement of the form of government thereby established.[28] Summing up the prevailing impressions which the Federalists unfailingly presented regarding the weaknesses and inadequacies of the Articles, McLaughlin asserts "almost everything points in only one direction—toward the need of a competent central government and the necessity of finding a system of union which could maintain itself. . . . The whole story is one of gradually increasing ineptitude."[29] The chief causes of this weakness in the social and political philosophy of the radicals during the Revolutionary period and their desire to curb government functions, McLaughlin finds, were interstate jealousies, which placed uppermost local rights and privileges, and the economic and industrial depression which followed the Revolutionary War. The Confederation failed in its efforts to enforce the treaty of peace. It was unsuccessful in adjusting the commercial restrictions and irritations between the states, and, owing to the requirement of unanimity of action, requisitions upon the states for funds could not be collected. Moreover, efforts to adopt amendments to increase the powers of Congress failed of adoption. The chief interest in rehearsing such a distressing story, thinks McLaughlin, lies in the fact that it prompted "men of mind as well as men of property to strengthen the union and to create self-respecting government."[30]

The Articles of Confederation, now generally considered extremely crude and defective, were not so considered by the men who framed

---

[27] Samuel Eliot Morison and Henry Steele Commager, *The Growth of the American Republic* (New York, 1937), I: 142, 143.

[28] In the opinion of Charles A. and Mary R. Beard, "the chief sources of information bearing on the thesis are the assertions and lamentations of but one faction in the great dispute and they must, therefore, be approached with the same spirit of prudence as Whig editorials on Andrew Jackson or Republican essays on Woodrow Wilson." *The Rise of American Civilization* (New York, 1927), I: 302. For an interesting account of the conflict at this time between those who favored nationalism and the establishment of a strong central government and those who supported the independent rights and sovereignty of the states, see Merrill Jensen, *The Articles of Confederation: An Interpretation of the Social-Constitutional History of the American Revolution, 1774–1781* (Madison, 1940).

[29] McLaughlin, *A Constitutional History of the United States*, p. 137. "It is easy to pass these Articles by with an amused smile at their utter unfitness for the work at hand." McLaughlin, *The Confederation and the Constitution*, p. 49.

[30] McLaughlin, *A Constitutional History of the United States*, p. 141.

and adopted them. To Jefferson the Confederation was a "wonderfully perfect instrument considering the circumstances under which it was formed." He found only three serious defects which he thought should be remedied. These were: an ineffective plan for admitting states; an improper method of allotting a state's quota of money upon land instead of on a population basis; and defects of power over treaties, import duties, and commerce.[31] He thought the comparison of this form of government with the governments of Europe was like "a comparison of heaven and hell." Regardless of the customary views in condemnation of the Articles, historians are beginning to speak of them as "models of what articles of confederation ought to be, an advance on previous instruments of like kind in the world's history."

If one compares the Articles with the Constitution adopted at Philadelphia in 1787, he will find a similarity in the scheme of distribution of powers. A number of provisions in the Articles transferred to the Constitution are based on the supposition that the states stand in relation to one another as distinct sovereignties and hence are subject to the principles of international comity. The drafting of the Constitution was, indeed, greatly facilitated by the progress toward federation and union accomplished through the Articles. The defects of the Articles, particularly to those who favored a strong and efficient national government, became, however, distressingly apparent. Lack of power to levy and collect taxes and to regulate commerce between the states and an inadequate arrangement for the control of foreign affairs made men impatient to permit a fair trial of the system of government provided by the Articles. Despite these weaknesses in the governmental structure, the country was gradually recovering in order and prosperity from the rather distressing conditions of the economic and industrial depression which came soon after the signing of the Treaty of Paris.

Moreover, the objects of Shays' Rebellion, which greatly strengthened and consolidated conservative sentiment prior to the calling of the federal Convention, were not, in the light of subsequent developments during depression periods, so radical and preposterous as the commercial and planter classes made them appear. The leaders of the rebellion sought to scale down debts and generally to improve the status of debtors and laborers, to remove some of the privileges accorded to property, and to issue paper money. On the whole, it is apparent that it would have been possible to get along with a reasonable degree of satisfaction and success under the reputedly decrepit Articles. To the radicals, as Jefferson put it, the good of the Constitution of 1787 might have been couched

---

[31] *Works* (Ford ed.), V: 8.

in three or four new articles to be added "to the good, old venerable fabric, which should have been preserved even as a religious relic."

The extent to which the gloomy pictures of the social and political conditions of the so-called "critical period" are "but a phantom of the imagination produced by some undoubted evils which could have been remedied without a political revolution"[32] has not been adequately considered, though it must always be largely in the realm of conjecture. The chief discontented groups were the holders of government bonds, speculators in depreciated currency, and the soldiers of the revolutionary army. It is obvious that the financial, creditor, and commercial classes desired "a system of centralized political, judicial and economic control similar in character to that formerly exercised by Great Britain." They wished debts paid, a sound currency, commerce regulated, and western lands distributed.

In the welter of criticism, condemnation, and ridicule of the Articles by the conservatives, their advantages, their contribution to the formation of a permanent political union, and the important parts of the document which furnished a model for the federal Constitution have been largely ignored. The Articles were based upon a political philosophy to which many of the ablest men of the time adhered. To a not inconsiderable part of the people, the Confederation seemed to provide for an ideal confederation of states.[33] At most, only a few amendments were needed. There is good evidence to sustain the view of Jensen that "in spite of the paradoxes involved one may still maintain that the Revolution was essentially, though relatively, a democratic movement within the thirteen American colonies, and that its significance for the political and constitutional history of the United States lay in its tendency to elevate the political and economic status of the majority of the people. The Articles of Confederation were the constitutional expression of this movement and the embodiment in governmental form of the philosophy of the Declaration of Independence."[34] What would have happened if the design of the nationalists to replace the Articles legally or illegally had failed, can only be a matter of conjecture. It is fairly certain, however, that many of the dire predictions of disaster were much overdrawn.

[32] Charles A. Beard, *An Economic Interpretation of the Constitution of the United States* (New York, 1913), p. 48.

[33] Abbot Emerson Smith regards it not unreasonable to believe that more Americans approved the Articles of Confederation in 1785 than approved the Constitution in 1788. *James Madison: Builder*, p. 79. And, see comment of the French minister that but for the want of permanent revenue "the United States would be one of the best organized governments." George Bancroft, *History of the Formation of the Constitution of the United States of America* (New York, 1885), II: 411.

[34] Jensen, *op. cit.*, p. 15. See also *ibid.*, pp. 161–162, 239, 243–244.

And it is well known that following a disastrous economic depression prosperity returned under the Articles of Confederation in time to popularize and to gain ready acceptance for the new government established in 1789.

But John Jay, one of the members of the Congress of the Confederation from New York and a persistent and assertive nationalist, while serving as Secretary for Foreign Affairs, prepared a resolution relative to the case of *Rutgers v. Waddington*[35] which tended to sustain, in part at least, the nationalistic interpretation of the Articles. In expressing an opinion regarding a treaty entered into by Congress, Jay informed the states that he considered "the thirteen independent sovereign States as having, by express delegation of power, formed and vested in Congress a perfect though limited sovereignty for the general and national purposes specified in the Confederation. In this sovereignty they cannot severally participate (except by their delegates) or have concurrent jurisdiction. . . .When therefore a treaty is constitutionally made, ratified and published by Congress, it immediately becomes binding on the whole nation, and superadded to the laws of the land, without the intervention, consent or fiat of state legislatures." He therefore recommended that Congress formally deny the right of the state legislatures to enact laws construing a national treaty or impeding its operation in any manner. All state acts on the statute books contrary to the treaty of peace were to be repealed—the repeal to be in general terms. Local judiciaries were to decide all cases arising under the treaty according to the intent thereof "anything in the said acts . . . to the contrary notwithstanding."[36] Congress adopted Jay's resolution without a dissenting vote and transmitted it to the legislatures. The theory that the Articles of Confederation were for some purposes law and as such were enforcible in the courts would have given them a different status from the customary opinions and understandings. In this opinion there is in germ at least the idea that a written constitution is a supreme law and, as such, is to be interpreted and enforced by the Judiciary. Thus, in the concluding days of the Confederation, the revolutionary nature of the supremacy clause of the Constitution was foreshadowed, and an emerging nationalism was given official sanction. It should be noted, however, that the view that the

---

[35] See James Bradley Thayer, *Cases on Constitutional Law* (Cambridge, 1895), I: 63.
[36] *Journals of the American Congress* (Washington, 1823), IV: 730. See the report of the committee on the case of The Sloop *Active* claiming that Congress was invested with the supreme sovereign power of war and peace. *The Journals of the Continental Congress*, XIII: 134. At another time it was contended that the authority finally "to decide on all matters and questions touching the law of nations does reside and is vested in the sovereign supreme power of war and peace." *Ibid.*, p. 284.

Treaty of Paris was binding on the states was repudiated in New York and Virginia in such a manner as to leave little ground for the furtherance of Jay's nationalistic doctrines.[37]

EMERGING NATIONALISM

In any consideration of the question of the location of sovereignty during this period, or rather what men thought regarding such location, one is confronted with two conflicting or diametrically opposed theories, namely, the organic or nationalist theory and the State rights or particularist theory, the former being the one accepted by most legal and constitutional historians.[38] Proponents of the organic theory usually looked upon sovereignty as one and indivisible and assumed that the American colonies transformed into states were destined to form one nation or empire. To favor nationalism was an evidence of good judgment, sound principle, and statesmanlike vision. Contrary views were condemned by a variety of opprobrious epithets. The fundamental difference between the two points of view seems to rest largely on whether there was a sovereign nation because of social, economic, and political forces inevitably drawing the people together or whether the states were sovereign because the public acts of the period and the opinions of contemporaries seemed to indicate such a view.

The usual attitude of historians and commentators on the party divisions during this period may be illustrated in the following analysis:

Large state men and nationalists stood for *principle*.	Small state men stood for *power* and were "prating of sovereignty."
Strength of argument and national patriotism on one side.	Local pride and threats inspired by "sectional antagonisms and general discontent" on the other.

---

[37] Rhode Island also refused to comply with the request to repeal all laws repugnant to the treaty of peace with Great Britain, giving as the principal reason that it would be calling into question the propriety of their former measures. See letter of James Varnum to Washington, Farrand, *op. cit.*, III: 48.

[38] Concerning the beginnings of a nation and national consciousness, Albion W. Small noted many years ago that "the facts of American history were very early confounded with the definitions and doctrines of a dogmatic political philosophy. Before our Constitution was three score years old, it had been associated with a mass of theoretical and fanciful folk lore, whose authenticity was more vehemently asserted than were the facts themselves. A body of tradition grew up about the origins of our nationality, and it became the mold in which all conclusions from documentary sources must be cast. This apocryphal element obscured the genuine portions of our history, and became the criterion by which events were judged, instead of remaining an hypothesis which the examination of evidence should justify or destroy." *The Beginnings of American Nationality: The Constitutional Relations between the Continental Congress and the Colonies and States from 1774 to 1789* (Baltimore, 1890), p. 7.

Land and resources are chiefly in possession of the "well affected" and they as nationalists are entirely "devoted to the public good."	Opposition to Constitution attributed to "personal pique" and "mean-minded jealousy," or from surly localism—from those who could appreciate "liberty" but could not understand "government."
Nationalists had minds of "superior order," were "clear-headed," and were "seeing things face to face," or were not "narrow-minded men hemmed in by local patriotism or petty state jealousy."[39]	Democrats of the day made up of the "licentious," "destitute of education," and "void of principle." With these were associated the disaffected of every description.

It was the nationalists and the "well affected" who supported the organic theory or who insisted that a federation was in process of establishment.

The organic theory.—The idea of a single, sovereign, national state, mythical though it may have been, was, to use the historian's phrase, "emerging into consciousness." John Adams lauded the First Continental Congress as "that memorable league of the continent in 1774, which first expressed the sovereign will of a free nation in America."[40] Thus was begun the fiction of a nation in the making to which the historians have clung as the basis for the federalist and nationalist interpretation of the development of American constitutional law. A few examples of such interpretation may be pertinent.

Speaking of this Congress, Justice Story asserted that "the Congress thus assembled exercised *de facto* and *de jure* a sovereign authority; not as the delegated agents of the government *de facto* of the colonies, but in virtue of original powers derived from the people."[41] In the course of

---

[39] Andrew McLaughlin, *The Confederation and the Constitution,* pp. 300, 308, 313, and *The Constitutional History of the United States,* pp. 151, 175, and his article, "Social Compact and Constitutional Construction," *Amer. Hist. Rev.* (Apr., 1900), V: 467.

James Varnum, writing to Washington on June 18, 1787, from the standpoint of the conservative groups, deplored the attitude of Rhode Island in refusing to send delegates to the federal Convention. It was his observation that "the measures of our present legislature do not exhibit the real character of the State. They are equally reprobated, and abhorred by gentlemen of the learned professions, by the whole mercantile body, and by most of the respectable farmers and mechanics. The majority of the administration is composed of a licentious number of men, destitute of education, and many of them void of principle. From anarchy and confusion they derive their temporary consequence, and this they endeavor to prolong by debauching the minds of the common people, whose attention is directed to the abolition of debts both public and private. With these are associated the disaffected of every description, particularly those who were unfriendly during the war." Farrand, *op. cit.,* III: 47, 48.

[40] Thomas H. Benton, *Abridgment of the Debates of Congress* (New York, 1857), II: 404.

[41] *Commentaries* (5th ed.), I: 156.

time the nationalist fiction takes on impressive form. The transformation of the colonies into states was, asserted Von Holst,

not the result of the independent action of the individual colonies. It was accomplished through the "representatives of the United States"; that is, through the revolutionary congress, in the name of the whole people. Each individual colony became a State only in so far as it belonged to the United States and in so far as its population constituted a part of the people. . . . "One people" of the united colonies dissolved their political connection with the English nation, and proclaimed themselves resolved, henceforth, to constitute the one perfectly independent people of the United States. . . . Congress had, with the consent of the people, taken the initiative in the transformation of the thirteen colonies into one sovereign State.[42]

At a later date Burgess referred to the geographical and ethnical factors which were operating in the colonies and which were awakening in the people the consciousness of the fact that they had the natural conditions of a sovereignty—a state. "The impulse to objectify this consciousness in institutions," he maintained,

becomes irresistible. Its first enduring form was the Continental Congress. This was the first organization of the American state. From the moment of its existence there was something more upon this side of the Atlantic than thirteen local governments. There was a sovereignty, a state; not in idea simply or upon paper, but in fact and in organization. . . . The American state, organized in the Continental Congress proclaimed to the world its sovereign existence, and proceeded, through this same organization, to govern itself generally, for the time being, and authorized the people resident within the separate colonies to make temporary arrangements for their local government.[43]

Here then was the historical and juristic interpretation to sanction the view of Abraham Lincoln that,

The States have their *status* in the Union, and they have no other legal status. . . . The Union is older than any of the States, and in fact, it created them as States. Originally some independent colonies made the Union; and, in turn, the Union threw off their old dependence for them and made them States such as they are. Not one of them ever had a state constitution independent of the Union.[44]

A few men of the time thought of sovereignty in the organic sense as one and indivisible. Sovereignty is an integral thing, contended William Paterson of New Jersey, and hence we ought to be one nation.[45] Some agreed with Madison that the desired purposes of union could not be secured by a system founded on the principle of a confederation of sovereign states.[46]

---

[42] Von Holst, *The Constitutional and Political History of the United States,* I: 5, 6, 9.

[43] John W. Burgess, *op. cit.,* I: 100, 101.

[44] James D. Richardson, *A Compilation of the Messages and Papers of the Presidents,* Message, July 4, 1861 (Washington, 1911), V: 3228, 3229.

[45] Farrand, *op. cit.,* I: 27.

[46] *Ibid.,* p. 131.

Steps toward intercolonial coöperation and unity were, indeed, taken early in the colonial period. Despite the marked differences in industrial and social conditions and the primary interest in and concern for local affairs, various plans for union of the colonies were proposed prior to the convening of the Continental Congresses. The most important of these, the Albany Plan, which was largely the work of Benjamin Franklin, failed to secure the approval of either the colonies or the English Board of Trade. But conditions were tending in the direction of colonial unity. Similarity in language and in general political ideas and doctrines as well as similar habits of life and industry led in the direction of coöperative action. When political interests and economic needs called for unity the way was prepared for unity in thought and action.

The colonies or states—as they were beginning to be called—opposed in unison the new imperial policy of England. As associated units they enforced their rights by boycott; as united colonies they declared their independence and secured the status of a separate nation in the eyes of the European powers. So-called catch phrases as "our union is perfect" and "an indissoluble union" were not infrequently used but apparently with little idea of the underlying significance later attached to them.

Despite the prevalent opinions regarding state independence and sovereignty, there were liberals as well as conservatives who denied that the states ever possessed the essential rights of sovereignty.[47] They could not, argued King, make war, nor peace, nor alliances, nor treaties.[48] Gerry "urged that we never were independent States, were not such now, and never could be even on the principles of the Confederation."[49] Thus it has frequently been asserted that the United States never consisted of states wholly sovereign and capable of separate and independent action.[50] This view was recently expressed by Justice Sutherland in an opinion upholding the authority of the President to declare an embargo on the sale of arms and munitions to belligerents. Sutherland said:

powers of external sovereignty passed from the Crown not to the colonies severally, but to the colonies in their collective and corporate capacity as the United States of America. Even before the Declaration, the colonies were a unit in foreign affairs, acting through a common agency—namely the Continental Congress, composed of delegates from the thirteen colonies. That agency exercised the powers of war and peace, raised an army, created a navy, and finally adopted the Declaration of Independence. Rulers

[47] Cf. opinion of Madison reported in Yates' Minutes, Elliot's *Debates* (2d ed.), I: 461.
[48] Gaillard Hunt, ed., *The Writings of James Madison* (New York), III: 222.
[49] Farrand, *op. cit.*, I: 467.
[50] James Schouler, *Constitutional Studies, State and Federal* (New York, 1897), p. 82. But see evidence to the contrary above, pp. 88, 89.

come and go; governments end and forms of government change; but sovereignty survives. A political society cannot endure without a supreme will somewhere. Sovereignty is never held in suspense. When, therefore, the external sovereignty of Great Britain in respect of the colonies ceased, it immediately passed to the Union. . . .

The Union existed before the Constitution, which was ordained and established among other things to form "a more perfect Union." Prior to that event, it is clear that the Union, declared by the Articles of Confederation to be "perpetual," was the sole possessor of external sovereignty and in the Union it remained without change save in so far as the Constitution in express terms qualified its exercise.[51]

Justice Sutherland in this dictum was unaware of or chose to ignore the preponderant factual data for the opposite view of the location of sovereignty during the period of American history from 1776 to 1789.

A few of the prominent delegates to the federal Convention in Philadelphia argued in favor of the organic or nationalist theory. James Wilson and Alexander Hamilton could not accept the doctrine that when the colonies became independent of Great Britain they became independent also of one another. Both believed that the Articles of Confederation were drawn up by communities which were already institutionally bound together.[52] Rufus King, who opposed the idea of state sovereignty, argued that "a Union of the States is a union of the men composing them, from whence a *national* character results to the whole."[53] He joined with Hamilton and George Read of Delaware in not only favoring a consolidated or national government but also thought that it would be advisable to abolish or to greatly limit the powers of the states. When the friends of the states were outraged by such arguments, Hamilton hastened to assure them that he was not seeking the total extinguishment of the states, but that "a national government ought to be able to support itself without the aid or interference of the state governments, and that therefore it was necessary to have full sovereignty."[54] Wilson favored a national government with real sovereign powers but with the preservation of the state governments.[55] The assertion that Congress during the Revolution and under the Articles had

[51] United States v. Curtiss-Wright Corp., 299 U. S. 316 (1936).

[52] See *The Madison Papers*, ed. by Henry D. Gilpin (Washington, 1840), II: 907. Referring to the work of Congress both during the Revolution and under the Confederation, Hamilton wrote: "They have done many of the highest acts of sovereignty, which were always cheerfully submitted to: The Declaration of Independence, the declaration of war, the levying of an army, creating a navy, emitting money, making alliances with foreign powers, appointing a dictator, etc. All of these implications of a complete sovereignty were never disputed, and ought to have been a standard for the whole conduct of administration." *Works* (Const. ed., 1904), I: 214–215.

[53] Farrand, *op. cit.*, I: 323, 324.

[54] *Ibid.*, p. 328. For Read's comments, see *ibid.*, pp. 136, 141, 143, 202.

[55] *Ibid.*, p. 328. No state, Wilson contended, can remain sovereign when it becomes a member of a federal union. *The Madison Papers*, II: 835.

the attributes of a sovereign nation had, indeed, much less currency from 1776 to 1787 than might be inferred from the views of Hamilton, Madison, and Washington. Congress was, rather, as Randolph called it, "a mere diplomatic body."[56]

One of the chief contentions that a national government was being formed through the federal Constitution and that the states were being deprived of their sovereignty is based on the assertions of the liberal and democratic members of the Philadelphia Convention who declared that a "consolidated" government was being formed. Yates and Lansing, the delegates from New York who left the Convention in disgust, in recording their dissent to the measures adopted, set forth their opposition to a system which "had in object the consolidation of the United States into one government," and to the adoption of provisions which were designed "to deprive the state government of its most essential rights of sovereignty, and to place it in a dependent situation." They also commented upon "the insuperable difficulty of controlling or counteracting the views of a set of men (however unconstitutional and oppressive their acts might be) possessed of all the powers of government, and who, from their remoteness from their constituents, and necessary permanence of office, could not be supposed to be uniformly actuated by an attention to their welfare and happiness."[57]

Patrick Henry, too, thought it was clear that a consolidated government was being formed. So insistent was this charge that Madison deemed it well to assure the people that no such consequences as a complete consolidation would follow the adoption of the Constitution.[58] When the delegates were appointed, no legislature had any idea, said Gerry, that a scheme was to be adopted to destroy the state governments and offer a consolidated system. He had no sympathy with the efforts leading in the direction of the annihilation of the independence and sovereignty of the states.[59] "I meet with a national government, instead of a federal union of sovereign States," said Samuel Adams.[60] What right had they to say, "We, the people" instead of "We, the States," asked Patrick Henry, "if the States be not the agents of this compact, it must be one, great, consolidated, national government, of the people of all the States."[61] The fear that a single, national sovereign with authority to

---

[56] Madison, *Writings* (Hunt ed.), III: 181.

[57] Farrand, *op. cit.*, III: 244–246.

[58] Elliot's *Debates* (2d ed.), III: 34.

[59] *Ibid.*, V: 466.

[60] Letter to Richard Henry Lee, December 3, 1787, *Memoir of the Life of Richard Henry Lee* (Richard H. Lee, Philadelphia, 1825), II: 130.

[61] Elliot's *Debates* (2d ed.), III: 21, 22.

dominate the state governments was being established led many of the liberal and democratic citizens of the states to join with those who opposed the Constitution on other grounds.

To an ardent nationalist who deemed political unity for the United States of this day to be a necessity, it is relatively easy to read the events of the formative period of American institutions "from the viewpoint of the organic philosophy."[62] "There is absolutely no evidence," says McLaughlin, "to support the notion that they believed they were simply entering into a new order of things in which the States would have the right as before to refuse obedience and to disregard obligations, or from which they could at any time quietly retire when they believed the Union did not suit their purposes. Everything points to the fact that they intended to form a real government and a permanent union."[63]

In support of the organic or nationalistic theory, George Mason, in the Virginia ratifying convention, insisted that "this paper will be the great charter of America; it will be paramount to everything. After having once consented to it we cannot recede from it." And Richard Henry Lee, in his *Letters of a Federal Farmer* said: "It is to be observed that when the people shall adopt the proposed Constitution it will be their last and supreme act. It will be accepted not by the people of New Hampshire, Massachusetts, etc., but by the people of the United States; and wherever this Constitution, or any part of it, shall be incompatible with the ancient customs, rights, the laws or the constitutions heretofore established in the United States, it will entirely abolish them and do them away."[64] As is usual under such circumstances, the liberals were inclined to overstate what they regarded as the inevitable consequences of the adoption of the Constitution.

The organic point of view was emphasized particularly by those who favored the principle of the ratification of the Constitution by the people rather than by the states. Madison thought the difference between a system founded on the legislatures of the states only and one founded on the people was the real distinction between "a league or treaty and a constitution." Wilson's nationalist philosophy was based on the principle that "government ought to flow from the people at large." The plan of ratification of the Constitution by conventions rather than by the state legislatures was finally approved by a vote of 6 states to 5—the small state group, Delaware, Connecticut, Maryland, New Jersey, and New York voting against the proposal. In the minds of at least a few

---

[62] Cf. McLaughlin, "Social Compact and Constitutional Construction," *Amer. Hist. Rev.* (Apr., 1900), V: 488.
[63] *The Confederation and the Constitution,* p. 314.
[64] Willoughby, *op. cit.,* pp. 26, 27.

leaders the way was prepared for the development of a strong national government no longer dependent upon the states for its existence or its effective operation.

Though there were two fairly well understood points of view—one favoring the establishment of a single national sovereign with the states little more than subordinate administrative districts, and the other sustaining the theory of separate and independent states which were acting in unison merely to accomplish a few specific ends—as a matter of fact there was considerable vagueness and confusion in men's ideas relating to sovereignty. So far as certainty is concerned, the conflicting opinions and theories regarding sovereignty left much to be desired. Washington was led to complain that "the world must feel and see that the Union or the States are sovereign as best suits their purposes; in a word, that we are one nation today and thirteen tomorrow." And to complicate matters further, some men thought in terms of neither a single national sovereign nor of thirteen state sovereigns but rather of a mixed or divided sovereign.

The Notion of Divided Sovereignty and the Compact Theory

Early in the deliberations of the members of the federal Convention, it was decided that it was undesirable to give prominence to the word "national" and it was henceforth omitted from the formal resolutions.[65] Since the word "federal" was thought to tend toward state sovereignty and the word "national" toward national sovereignty, Madison contended that what was adopted was "neither a national nor a federal constitution; but a composition of both."[66] Even the nationalistically

[65] The first resolution of the Randolph plan for a new government submitted to the members of the Convention provided that "a national government ought to be established, consisting of a supreme legislative, judiciary, and executive." This resolution was amended and adopted on June 20, 1787, to read "that the government of the United States ought to consist of a supreme legislative, judiciary, and executive." As a result of this action, the word national was dropped from all the other resolutions of the Randolph plan. Elliot's *Debates*, I: 181–183; V: 214.

[66] Elliot's *Debates*, III: 94, 107. Expressing a noncommittal attitude relative to this matter, Madison wrote: "It has hitherto been understood that the supreme power, that is the sovereignty of the people of the States, was in its nature divisible, and was, in fact, divided . . . ; that as the States in their highest sovereign character were competent to surrender the whole sovereignty and form themselves into a consolidated State, so they might surrender a part and retain, as they had done, the other part. . . . Of late, another doctrine has occurred, which supposes that sovereignty is in its nature indivisible; that the societies denominated States, in forming the constitutional compact of the United States, acted as indivisible sovereignties, and, consequently, that the sovereignty of each remains as absolute and entire as it was then. . . . In settling the question between these rival claims of power, it is proper to keep in mind that all power in just and free governments is derived from compact." *Writings*, IV: 390, 391.

inclined members of the Convention, such as James Wilson, asserted that it was not the intention of the Convention to destroy the sovereignty of the states.[67] In this respect he agreed with Pierce Butler that something in the nature of a divided sovereignty was being established.

Because of the persistent advocacy of irreconcilable views regarding state sovereignty on the one hand, and consolidation or national sovereignty on the other, an effort was made to find a median position between the two extremes. Madison, who accepted a mild form of nationalism, tried to discover such middle ground when he wrote to Randolph on April 8, 1787, "An individual independence of the States is utterly irreconcilable with the idea of an aggregate sovereignty. I think, at the same time, that a consolidation of the States into one single republic is not less unattainable than it would be inexpedient. Let it be tried, then, whether any middle ground can be taken, which will at once support a due supremacy of the national authority, and leave in force the local authorities so far as they can be subordinately useful."[68]

When Dr. Johnson referred to sovereignty as being in the union, Colonel Mason replied, "The United States will have a qualified sovereignty only. The individual States will retain a part of the sovereignty."[69] In a proposal of a constitution for the thirteen states, Pelatiah Webster suggested a plan which, in his opinion, involved a division of sovereignty.[70] And Hamilton, apparently thinking in terms of a divided sovereignty, said he could not approve of an uncontrollable sovereignty in each state, since that would defeat the powers given to Congress and make the union feeble and precarious. In his opinion

[67] Farrand, *op. cit.*, III: 144. Wilson's exact words were: "When gentlemen assert that it was the intention of the federal Convention to destroy the sovereignty of the States, they must conceive themselves better qualified to judge of the intention of that body than its own members, of whom not one, I believe, entertained so improper an idea."

[68] Madison, *Writings* (Hunt ed.), II: 337–339. Madison, in a letter to Jefferson, commented on the nature of the work of the federal Convention as follows: "It was generally agreed that the objects of the Union could not be secured by any system founded on the principle of a confederation of sovereign States. A *voluntary* observance of the federal law by all the members could never be hoped for. A compulsive one could evidently never be reduced to practice, and if it could, involved equal calamities to the innocent and the guilty, the necessity of a military force, both obnoxious and dangerous, and, in general, a scene resembling much more a civil war than the administration of a regular government. Hence was embraced the alternative of a government which, instead of operating on the States, should operate without their intervention on the individuals composing them; and hence the change in the principle and proportion of representation." *Letters* (1865 ed.), I: 344. See also McLaughlin, *Confederation and Constitution*, chap. xv.

[69] Farrand, *op. cit.*, II: 347.

[70] McLaughlin, *A Constitutional History of the United States*, p. 143.

Congress should have complete sovereignty in all that relates to war, peace, trade, and finance.[71] John Jay also believed that the sovereignty of the nation is in the people of the nation and the residuary sovereignty of each state in the people of each state.[72] The notion that sovereignty was divisible and that it was in fact divided in the distribution of powers between the government of the United States and those of the states under the Constitution adopted in 1788 persisted in political and legal thinking. In fact, the notion of divided sovereignty was common during colonial times when the colonists were attempting to work out a formula whereby they could become free nations and at the same time remain in the British Empire. During the period of the Revolutionary War the theory was frequently advanced that legal sovereignty, if it existed at all, was divisible and that political sovereignty belonged to the people. There was no place in this reasoning for the concept of an absolute, unlimited, and indivisible power.[73] Not even a civil war fought largely on the issue of state versus national sovereignty could destroy the belief in the divisibility of sovereignty in a federal system such as that established by the Constitution. The dominant political philosophy of the time repudiated the doctrine that there could be any unlimited authority, and supreme legal powers were to be exercised within given fields— one field belonged to the national government, the other to the states.[74]

The compact theory, which was connected with the conflicting views regarding sovereignty and underlay the thinking of men in the federal Convention, later became a somewhat modernized version of the compact or contract theory of government. Certain ideas involved in the compact philosophy, namely, that the state is artificial and founded on agreement, that law is not the expression of a superior will but obtains its force by consent, and that sovereignty is divisible, profoundly affected constitutional interpretation at least until the period of the Civil War.

The compact theory gained its vogue because the political philosophy of the time was antiorganic or antimonistic. During the Revolution men spoke freely of a state of nature in which men had equal rights. When government was formed they gave up this equality and subjected themselves to a superior authority. But the superior authority or government must rule for the common good. Though the idea of compact as the basis for the formation of a state was broached on only a few occasions during

---

[71] *Works* (Const. ed.), I: 213 ff.

[72] Chisholm v. Georgia, 2 Dallas 471 (1793).

[73] Randolph Greenfield Adams, *Political Ideas of the American Revolution* (Durham, 1922), p. 173.

[74] McLaughlin, *op. cit.*, pp. 135, 136.

the formative days of the Constitution, two views appear at the out-set. Madison, though following in the main the nationalistic trend of thought, declared that in the formation of compacts there was a fallacy in the reasoning drawn from the theory of equality of sovereign states because of the failure to distinguish mere treaties from compacts by which authorities are created paramount to the parties and are author-ized to make laws for the government of them.[75] At this time Madison was apparently thinking of the form of a compact between each indi-vidual person and the whole body of the people collectively to form a government with authority to carry out the general will.

Luther Martin contended that in the recurrence to the people for the adoption of the Constitution and the establishment of a central govern-ment all of the people were "thrown into a state of nature," and there was involved a combination of each person with every other in the for-mation of a new body politic. But Martin saw the compact in a different light when he said: "It is, in its very introduction, declared to be a compact between the people of the United States, as individuals, and it is to be ratified by the people at large, in their capacity as individuals; all of which it was said would be quite right and proper, if there were no state governments, if all the people of this continent were in a state of nature and we were forming one national government for them as in-dividuals; and is nearly the same as was done in most of the States when they formed their governments over the people who compose them."[76]

Others thought in terms of a confederation or a league in which there was a mutual compact between each individual state and the states in their collective capacity. Certain proponents of the compact philosophy thought that when the states entered as parties into the compact for the formation of a general government they (the states) were the judges of whether the rights reserved by the states had been encroached upon.[77]

---

[75] *The Madison Papers,* II: 978.

[76] Farrand, *op. cit.,* III: 193. John Jay also approved the compact theory, observing that "every state constitution is a compact made by and between citizens of a State to govern themselves in a certain manner; and the Constitution of the United States is likewise a compact made by the people of the United States to govern themselves as to general subjects in a certain manner. By this great compact, however, many preroga-tives were transferred to the national government." Chisholm v. Georgia, 2 Dallas 471.

[77] Andrew C. McLaughlin, "Social Compact and Constitutional Construction," *Amer. Hist. Rev.* (Apr., 1900), V: 482 ff. Depreciating the significance of the compact theory in early American history, Edward S. Corwin maintains that "the idea of the Constitu-tion as a compact of the States was . . . first broached on the floor of the Pennsylvania ratifying convention, where it was repelled by Wilson most decisively. None the less, five years later the same idea is found to underlie Iredell's dissenting opinion in *Chisholm v. Georgia.* But the source of this dogma as a vital historical force, trans-forming the canons of constitutional construction, furnishing the fundamental premises

The Virginia ratifying convention gave its sanction to a form of the compact philosophy when it adopted the Constitution having the following proviso:

We the Delegates of the People of Virginia. . . . Do in the name and in behalf of the People of Virginia declare and make known that the powers granted under the Constitution being derived from the People of the United States may be resumed by them whensoever the same shall be perverted to their injury or oppression and that every power not granted thereby remains with them and at their will: that therefore no right of any denomination can be cancelled abridged restrained or modified by the Congress by the Senate or House of Representatives acting in any capacity by the President or any Department or Officer of the United States except in those instances in which power is given by the Constitution for those purposes: and that among other essential rights the liberty of Conscience and of the Press cannot be cancelled abridged restrained or modified by any authority of the United States.[78]

Similar resolutions were adopted by New York and Rhode Island.

But James Wilson took exception to the views expressed in this matter. When William Findley, leader of the Anti-Federalists in the Pennsylvania ratifying convention, spoke of the system of government framed by the Convention as forming a compact or contract of the greatest importance, Wilson replied, "I cannot answer for what every member thought; but I believe it cannot be said that they thought they were making a contract, because I cannot discover the least trace of a compact in that system."[79] On another occasion he spoke of "one great political compact" being in formation. It was not until the time of the controversy over the Kentucky and Virginia Resolutions that the compact theory of the formation of the Constitution became the center of argument in support of the doctrine of State rights.[80] Later this doctrine was ably defended by Spencer Roane and John Taylor of Caroline.[81]

The usual argument for State rights was based on the contention that the Constitution was the creation of the several states acting as separate and sovereign political entities. On this basis the confederate nature of the union and the legal right of secession were deemed to follow logically. All agreements between sovereign states are considered contractual in character. A constitution created by the union of wills of

---

of the doctrine of secession, is still other. It is the Virginia Resolutions of 1798, the work of James Madison who ten years earlier had been one of the foremost nationalists of the time." *National Supremacy: Treaty Power v. State Power* (New York, 1913), p. 102. It is apparent that the theory had a wider and more permeating influence.

[78] *Documentary History of the Constitution* (Washington, 1894), II: 145; cited by McLaughlin, *Constitutional History of the United States*, p. 218.

[79] Farrand, *op. cit.*, III: 166.

[80] For report to Virginia legislature by committee of which Madison was chairman, see below, pp. 167 ff.

[81] Cf. below, pp. 345, 362.

several states could not be other than of a nonlegal or conventional nature. The states united under it were bound only by practical or moral considerations. They were not subject to it as a legal superior.[82] Madison, who supported the nationalist theory at various times, appeared to sanction the state sovereignty assertions when he said: "Each State, in ratifying the Constitution, is considered as a sovereign body, independent of all others, and only to be bound by its own voluntary act. In this relation, then, the new Constitution will, if established, be a *federal*, and not a *national* constitution."[83]

It appears therefore that the view was generally accepted that the Constitution rested upon an agreement between the ratifying states, but this did not necessarily mean that they were establishing merely a common agent for a league or confederation of sovereign states but a national government exercising some of the powers of sovereignty. These two views, though they seem logically contradictory, were held by the people at the time.[84] The confusion of ideas which was apparent is seen in Madison's comment, when, after having asserted that the states as sovereign states would adopt the Constitution, he said that "this assent and ratification is to be given by the people, not as individuals composing one entire nation but as composing the distinct and independent States to which they respectively belong. It is to be the assent and ratification of the several States derived from the supreme authority in each State—the authority of the people themselves. The act, therefore, establishing the Constitution, will not be a *national* but a *federal* act."[85]

Expressing the views of Washington and the nationalist group in the Convention, Gouverneur Morris, in the letter submitting the completed Constitution to the Convention, observed that:

It is obviously impracticable . . . in the federal government of these States to secure all rights of independent sovereignty to each and yet provide for the interest and safety of all. Individuals entering into society must give up a share of liberty to preserve the rest. The magnitude of the sacrifice must depend as well on the situation

---

[82] Willoughby, *The American Constitutional System*, p. 12.

[83] Madison, in *The Federalist*, No. 39 (Lodge ed.), p. 249.

[84] Willoughby, *op. cit.*, p. 23. McLaughlin maintains that "if the states were not sovereign in the years *before* the adoption of the federal Constitution, no one could reasonably assert their possession of sovereignty *after* adoption; but if they were sovereign before such adoption, then one may find the starting point for an argument in behalf of state sovereignty afterwards." *The Constitutional History of the United States*, p. 131.

[85] *The Federalist*, No. 39 (Lodge ed.). In this number of *The Federalist*, Madison's discussion of the nature of the federal union to be established vividly portrays the complexity of the issues at stake in the attempt to merge sovereign states in order to form a national government. He also shows the prevailing vagueness and confusion of ideas relating to the location and division of sovereignty.

and circumstances as on the object to be obtained. It is at all times difficult to draw with precision the line between those rights which must be surrendered and those which may be reserved. And on the present occasion this difficulty was increased by a difference among the several States as to their situation, extent, habits and particular interests.

In all our deliberations on this subject we kept steadily in view, that which appears to us the greatest interest of every true American, the consolidation of our Union, in which is involved our prosperity, felicity, safety, perhaps our national existence.[86]

There was an evident disagreement about what was intended in the drafting of the Constitution between the particularistic notions of defenders of the rights of the states "as free sovereign and independent agencies" and the advocates of a permanent federal union with supreme and sovereign powers. The sentiment of the people and their fidelity and attachment to the states were such that it was generally agreed that an express declaration granting sovereign powers to the federal government would have rendered adoption of the Constitution impossible. It was necessary therefore to couch the principle of federal supremacy in language which left much to be desired from the standpoint of clarity and definite legal significance. The Constitution and the laws and treaties made in accordance therewith were to be the supreme law of the land. But was this "supreme law" in the normal legal sense of the term "law" and hence enforcible by the courts? It has been shown in a previous chapter[87] that to arrive at the conclusion that constitutional provisions were laws and could be judicially applied as such required the acceptance of assumptions which were contrary to the prevailing ideas and theories of both Europe and America. And even if the Constitution might in most respects be deemed law, would the fundamental questions of political power between the states and the federal government as well as the political relations between the departments of this government come within the category of law and hence be subject to judicial cognizance? Again postulates or assumptions were necessary to resolve the crucial issue.

The other provision of the Constitution on which federal supremacy was based, so far as this supremacy could be enforced by judicial action, was the clause that "the judicial power shall extend to all cases in law and equity arising under this Constitution, the laws of the United States, and treaties made or which shall be made, under their authority." But this language is extremely vague and indefinite. That this vagueness was intentional was the contention of Gouverneur Morris who, in referring to his part in the writing of the Constitution, said: "Having

---

[86] Farrand, *op. cit.*, II: 584, 666, 667.
[87] Chap. i.

rejected redundant and equivocal terms, I believed it to be as clear as our language would permit; excepting, nevertheless, a part of what relates to the judiciary."[88] The federal courts do not automaticaly acquire jurisdiction over cases in law and equity involving federal questions. The Supreme Court only is granted original jurisdiction and in relatively few cases may act on its own authority and initiative. All other jurisdiction is appellate and is dependent upon the establishment of courts by Congress and the grant of jurisdiction to hear and decide cases. In the establishment of inferior federal courts, in defining their jurisdiction, and in controlling the appellate jurisdiction of the Supreme Court, Congress was granted controlling authority by the express language of the Constitution. It is then largely for Congress to say when and to what extent the federal judicial power shall extend to cases in law and equity arising under the Constitution or other federal acts.

The Supreme Court was not placed by the Constitution above the other departments and above the Constitution. The departments were made coördinate and the people were to be the ultimate arbiters. Both Congress and the President were deemed to have the authority and duty to interpret the Constitution so far as their duties and powers were concerned. The federal courts were expected to check the exercise of unwarranted powers by the states and to aid in the preservation of personal and individual rights, but only a few extreme nationalists favored the idea of a final and authoritative interpretation of the Constitution by the courts. The judicial veto over acts of Congress was, therefore, not expressly provided for in the Constitution nor given specific sanction in federal legislation. But for obvious political reasons John Jay, Alexander Hamilton, and John Marshall set about to change the relations of the departments so as to assert a form of judicial supremacy.[89] Under the cloak of the Constitution as law the Justices have not only continued to assert their supremacy but also have extended their jurisdiction. In so doing organic or nationalistic doctrines were made an integral part of the federal Constitution. The steps by which the issue of nationalism versus State rights was decided in favor of the nation will require careful and systematic analysis.

[88] Jared Sparks, *The Life of Gouverneur Morris* (Boston, 1832), III: 323.

[89] "The Constitution ought to be the standard of construction for the laws, and whenever there is an evident opposition the laws ought to give place to the Constitution. But this doctrine is not deducible from any circumstance peculiar to the plan of the Convention, but from the general theory of a limited Constitution." Hamilton in *The Federalist*, No. 81 (Lodge ed.), p. 540.

Part Two

THE SUPREME COURT UNDER THE FEDERALIST REGIME

CHAPTER IV

The Federal Courts during the Administration of Washington

THE CONSTITUTION, as we have observed, was adopted as a result of a bitterly contested political campaign. Often it appears to to be taken for granted that the groups which fought so strenuously to secure or to oppose the adoption of the Constitution soon dissolved and that new party or sectional divisions arose. In the opinion of Edward Channing "there were no national political parties in the United States in 1789,—as we use the term today."[1] He thinks the definite party alignments which appear about 1796 were along new lines, though recognizing that there were rather well-defined political cleavages during the controversy over the formation and adoption of the Constitution and even after 1789 in support of and opposition to the policies adopted by Washington and Hamilton. But when Channing lists the issues on which the new parties divided, such as sectionalism due to divergent industrial conditions and, in particular, the differences between the capitalists and the agrarians and the divergent points of view between the conservatives and the radicals, the only new basis for party divisions appears to be the varying conceptions of the powers and functions of the new government.[2] After the completion of the ratification of the Constitution, maintains John Spencer Bassett,"Anti-Federalism died because its *raison d'etre* was gone."

O. G. Libby, in his survey of early political parties in the United States, confirms the views expressed by Channing and Bassett that there were no real party divisions during Washington's Administration. At this time, he maintains, "there was nothing which can be called a clear cut issue sufficient to produce national parties. Of factional division there was no lack, and sectional differences and personal animosities supplied abundant excuse for disagreement. But if one attempts to sift the evidence and examine the proof offered for the claims of party existence, he will in the end abandon the task as a profitless one."[3] Charles A.

[1] Edward Channing, *A History of the United States* (New York, 1927), IV: 50.
[2] See *ibid.*, chap. vi.
[3] "A Sketch of the Early Political Parties in the United States," and "Political Factions in Washington's Administration," *The Quarterly Journal of the University of North Dakota* (Apr., 1912), II, and (July, 1913), III: 295, 296.

Beard, analyzing the data from which Libby formed his judgments, comes to different conclusions. With reference to Libby's contentions, Beard observes that "contemporaries, no less capable than Jefferson, Hamilton, Washington, Madison, and Gerry, thought there were political parties. Men constantly spoke of the Federalist and Republican or Anti-Federalist parties. Organizations representing these two groups put up candidates in the important constituencies and soon began to wage hot electoral battles in behalf of their favorites. And after the elections the newspapers recorded so many votes for the Federalist and so many for the Republican candidates, and the mathematical politicians set to work to figure out the strength of the respective parties in Congress and in the state governments."[4] Commenting on the founding of the *National Gazette* by Philip Freneau in 1791, Bassett observes that the two parties, Federalists, on the one hand, and Democrats or Republicans on the other, were fairly launched, and that in 1792 the concealed dislike and distrust for one another led to an open break between the two party leaders, Hamilton and Jefferson.[5] As a matter of fact, party cleavages in Washington's Administration were strikingly similar to those that had prevailed during the Revolution and the critical period and they were apparent from the time of the establishment of the new government.

PARTY DIVISIONS DURING WASHINGTON'S ADMINISTRATION

Just as Alexander Hamilton sponsored the policies and became the leader of a newly inspired and directed conservative or Federalist party, so, men like William Maclay, Thomas Jefferson, and James Madison organized the former radical or democratic groups into a party taking the designation of Republicans. Hamilton, setting about to establish a strong national government, developed an effective and far-reaching alliance between the federal government and the industrial, commercial, and capitalist interests of the time. The means to accomplish this alliance were the establishment of a national bank, the funding by the national government of the confederate and state debts at their face value, and the adoption of a protective tariff with a comprehensive system of protection or bounties to aid industrial development in the United States. While this alliance was being developed, with the consequent enrichment of thousands of citizens who became enthusiastic supporters of the federal government, William Maclay, one of the senators from Pennsylvania, was keeping alive the sparks of liberalism and democracy until they could be rekindled by a greater political leader. From the

---

[4] *Economic Origins of Jeffersonian Democracy* (New York, 1915), pp. 12 ff., 32.
[5] *The Federalist System, 1789–1801* (New York, 1906), pp. 42, 46 ff.

somewhat acid and cryptic comments of his *Journal* it appears that Maclay tried to offset the tendency of the Federalists to emphasize form and ceremony by what he described as "republican plainness." He opposed any measure which would lead to the charge that those responsible for carrying on the affairs of the new government were attempting to assume powers not delegated. He vigorously opposed the funding scheme, the establishment of a national bank, and a revenue system designed to protect and foster infant industries. And he saw no reasonable grounds for setting up "a most expensive and enormous machine of a federal Judiciary."[6] The views of William Maclay, while he was a member of the Senate, were so cogently and convincingly presented that he may truly be regarded as the founder of the Democratic-Republican party— the party which aimed to secure the adoption of substantially similar policies to those sponsored by the former liberal and radical groups.

President Washington, whom Channing calls "a strong partisan,"[7] was fortunate in securing as his associates a majority of men who agreed with him in his political point of view and outlook. Most of those elected to the houses of Congress were friendly to the new Constitution and had aided in securing its adoption. The President selected for his cabinet Hamilton and Jefferson, two men of extremely divergent political opinions and affiliations, and for a few years attempted to follow a nonpartisan policy in the making of appointments. In the main, however, he selected those who were favorable to the Constitution and to the principles embodied in the document drafted in Philadelphia. As a general practice, the choice of Federalists, as those of Washington's party were coming to be called, was justified on the ground that to appoint men adverse to the measures which the general government was pursuing "would be a sort of political suicide."[8] The offices were filled with friends of the Constitution and friends of the Administration and this was especially true with respect to judicial appointments.[9] A similar policy was followed by the successor of Washington, John Adams. It was to be expected, therefore, that the federal courts established in 1789 would, to a certain extent at least, aid in carrying out Federalist policies.

To evaluate the work of the federal courts during the Administrations of Washington and Adams, it is necessary to indicate, at least in outline

---

[6] *The Journal of William Maclay* (New York, 1927), pp. 6 ff.

[7] "As a politician Washington was a strong partisan. He thought that only persons of 'sound politics' should be appointed to civil offices or be given commissions in the army." *History of the United States,* IV: 34.

[8] Worthington Chauncey Ford, ed., *The Writings of George Washington* (New York, 1889), XIII: 107.

[9] Channing, *op. cit.,* p. 53.

form, some of the important tenets and principles of the Federalist party as they had taken shape during the formation and adoption of the Constitution and as they were now to be applied in the administration of the new government. The first principle of the party was the one which favored a strong central government. Being unable to secure as complete and as extensive grants of power for the central government as was desired, the leaders of the party proposed to accomplish this purpose by the use of an implied-power doctrine and the expansion of federal authority by legislative, executive, and judicial interpretations of the Constitution. As a rule, Federalists insisted that the power and authority of the states should in most respects be curtailed. To take the necessary steps to counteract the growing tendency to extend the popular control over government was the second objective of the party program. For the accomplishment of this aim John Adams' device of checks and balances was deemed peculiarly appropriate. But a theory of the separation of powers and of the independence of departments was merely incidental to the main purpose to be attained. This purpose was the establishment of a judicial department which, through its interpretation of the laws and through its check on the other departments by keeping them within the limits of the Constitution, might place effective barriers in the way of the despotism of the rule of a majority. And the third main tenet of the Federalist policies was one which was beginning to emerge during the Administrations of Washington and Adams, namely, that it is the prime duty of the government to preserve property rights, and to this end the establishment of judicial supremacy in the interpretation of the Constitution and the laws was to be paramount. Alexander Hamilton, as the acknowledged leader of the Federalist party, supported these principles which were destined to lead the federal Judiciary into political channels.

The chief issue of the Federalist administrations on internal affairs was the espousal of nationalism or consolidation involving the development of a strong and energetic central government in opposition to State rights, the preservation of individual rights and privileges, and vigorous local and state governments. Hamilton and his party received the support of those who, "doubting the competency of the people to carry on the new government, sought to place it under the protection of an energetic and powerful chief,"[10] and of a second group to which John Marshall referred when he said regarding Hamilton's financial measures that "the public paper suddenly rose, and was for a short time above par. The

---

[10] Francis Wharton, *State Trials of the United States during the Administrations of Washington and Adams* (Philadelphia, 1849), p. 17.

immense wealth which individuals acquired by this unexpected appreciation, could not be viewed with indifference. Those who participated in its advantages regarded the author of a system to which they were greatly indebted with an enthusiasm of attachment to which scarcely any limits were assigned."[11]

Thus the Federalist party secured the support of the mercantile interests, public creditors, and large property owners—"a network of special interests,—almost all of them looking to government for encouragement of some sort."[12] It was the aim of these groups to have a strong government to protect property and contracts at home and to secure the confidence of foreign countries in order to have trade and commerce expand. For this reason the party favored an implied-power doctrine for the interpretation of federal authority so that the national jurisdiction could expand without the cumbersome process of amendment of the Constitution. It also aimed to secure, so far as property and contracts might be affected, implied prohibitions on legislative power which were deemed especially applicable to the states. The duty of seeing that federal powers might freely expand and that state powers might be properly delimited was to be placed to a large extent upon the Judges selected by appointment for life terms and armed with the weapon to declare legislative acts invalid. The leaders of the Federalist party proposed to lean heavily on the courts in the carrying out of some of the main features of their program. In a subsequent chapter the divergent principles and policies of the two great parties of the day, as exemplified in the writings of Hamilton and Jefferson, will be analyzed particularly with respect to their influence upon the interpretation and application of the Constitution.[13] For the present we are chiefly concerned with the organization and early development of the system of federal courts.

THE JUDICIARY ACT OF 1789

To the first Congress which met in 1789 had been elected a majority of members who favored the Constitution and who approved the features

---

[11] *The Life of George Washington* (2d ed., Philadelphia, 1840), II: 191. See also Bassett, *The Federalist System*, p. 31.

[12] Martin Van Buren, *Inquiry into the Origin and Cause of Political Parties in the United States* (New York, 1867), p. 226. According to Morison and Commager, "the old families, merchant-shipowners, public creditors, and financiers—in other words the Federalists who had procured the Constitution—must be welded into a loyal governing class, by a straightforward policy favoring their interests. That was the object of Hamilton's domestic and foreign policy. He proposed to use the federal government to enrich a class, in order that this class might strengthen the federal government." Samuel Eliot Morison and Henry Steele Commager, *The Growth of the American Republic* (New York, 1937), I: 219. See also Homer Carey Hockett, *The Constitutional History of the United States, 1776–1826* (New York, 1939), pp. 262, 263.

[13] See below, chap. vi.

therein designed to create a strong national government. Among the first acts to come before this Congress was the Judiciary Act of 1789, drafted by the Federalist Oliver Ellsworth, and supported by other prominent men of this party. With comparatively little opposition this act became law. Although the records of the debates on the measure are rather meager, it seems that the two features of the act which caused later criticisms and controversies were approved with little comment.[14] One of these was the provision which required the Supreme Court Justices to travel and to try cases on the circuits, many of which would later come before them again on appeal. The other was the twenty-fifth section of the act which regulated appeals to the Supreme Court. The effect of this section on the right of the Supreme Court to review and annul acts of Congress and the claim of finality for the decisions of Judges in the interpretation of the Constitution have been considered in a previous chapter.[15] It suffices to say that the grant of this authority to the federal courts is not so clear and specific as is frequently inferred from the language of the section.[16] Because only one section of an act of Congress was declared void under this section[17] before the *Dred Scott Case,* opposition to the grant of authority to the federal courts to review legislative acts came from the states whose acts were frequently annulled.

One of the main reasons for the establishment of inferior federal courts was the need of uniformity in the settlement of admiralty and maritime cases. James Wilson thought admiralty jurisdiction "ought to be given wholly to the national government, as it related to cases not within the jurisdiction of particular States, and to a scene in which controversies with foreigners would be most likely to happen."[18] Efforts were made at various times to confine the jurisdiction of the inferior federal courts to maritime cases.[19] The provisions in the Judiciary Act of 1789 for inferior federal courts with extensive jurisdiction over federal causes were enacted, in part at least, to insure the faithful collection of the national revenues.[20] Though from the beginning the jurisdiction of the inferior courts included admiralty and maritime causes, the trial of penalties and forfeitures under federal laws, and a limited authority over criminal causes, in the main, "to the Circuit Courts were allotted

---

[14] Charles Warren, "New Light on the History of the Federal Judiciary Act of 1789," 37 *Harv. Law Rev.* (Nov., 1923), 49.

[15] See above, chap. i.

[16] Cf. Morison and Commager, *The Growth of the American Republic,* I: 216.

[17] See *Marbury v. Madison,* below, pp. 245 ff.

[18] Farrand, *op. cit.,* I: 124.

[19] *The Journal of William Maclay,* pp. 83 ff.

[20] Max Farrand, ed., *The Records of the Federal Convention* (New Haven, 1923), I: 223, 224.

cases resting on diversity of citizenship, while the District Courts became the admiralty courts of the country."[21] It is apparent from the debate on the Judiciary Act that there were few who surmised how great the powers of the federal Judiciary would be or to what extent the Supreme Court would participate in the determination of the controversies over nationism and localism which were soon to absorb the interests and thought of the leaders of the political parties then in process of formation.

Soon after the passage of the Judiciary Act, Washington submitted to the Senate the names of John Jay, John Rutledge, James Wilson, William Cushing, Robert Hanson Harrison, and John Blair as nominations for the six Justices of the Supreme Court, and these nominations were promptly confirmed. Washington expressed a keen interest in securing "the first characters of the Union into the Judiciary"[22] and indicated a desire that the federal Judiciary should be not only "independent in its operations but as perfect as possible in its formation." He referred on one occasion to the Judiciary as "the chief pillar upon which our national government must rest."[23] That this exalted view of the place and function of the federal courts did not appeal to all of the appointees is indicated in the refusal of Robert Hanson Harrison to accept appointment on the ground that the Judiciary Act, particularly in relation to the circuits, was unsatisfactory and that his services would interfere with his private affairs. He preferred to continue as chancellor of the state of Maryland. James Iredell was nominated and confirmed for this place and the first panel of Justices was completed.

Commenting on the selection of a Chief Justice by President Washington, Charles Warren notes that the President "rightly felt that the man to head this first Court must be not only a good lawyer, but a great statesman, a great executive and a great leader as well."[24] Thus it was assumed from the beginning that the Supreme Court would not merely function as a court of justice, but it was also expected to take a prominent place in the politics and statesmanship of the country. John Jay, who was Washington's choice, and who had shown his abilities in the political and diplomatic fields rather than in the law, so conceived his duties as

---

[21] Felix Frankfurter and James M. Landis, *The Business of the Supreme Court* (New York, 1927), p. 12.

[22] Letter to Madison, *The Writings of George Washington*, ed. by Jared Sparks (Boston, 1855), X: 26; to Randolph he wrote, "I have considered the first arrangement of the judicial department as essential to the happiness of our country, and to the stability of its political system." *Ibid.*, p. 34.

[23] Hampton L. Carson, *The Supreme Court of the United States: Its History* (Philadelphia, 1902), p. 14.

[24] *The Supreme Court in United States History* (Boston, 1922), I: 33.

Chief Justice, and with the concurrence of his associates he asserted the role of an arbiter or umpire in determining the relations between the departments of the federal government and between the state and federal governments. He thus took an active part in some important political controversies.

THE FIRST TERMS OF THE COURT

In the February and August terms of 1790 and the February term of 1791 no cases were presented and decided by the Court.[25] Between the second and third terms of the Court the Virginia assembly passed Patrick Henry's resolutions condemning the federal act for the assumption of state debts as "repugnant to the Constitution of the United States, as it goes to the exercise of a power not granted to the general government." The Virginia assemblyman discerned a striking resemblance between Hamilton's funding system and that introduced into England at the time of the Revolution of 1689—a system which had resulted in an enormous national debt and in a greatly expanded executive power which was dangerous to English liberty. Since like causes produce like effects, the remonstrance pointed out that: "In an agricultural country like this, therefore to erect, and concentrate, and perpetuate a large monied interest, is a measure which your memorialists apprehend must in the course of human events produce one or the other of two evils, the prostration of agriculture at the feet of commerce, or a change in the present form of federal government, fatal to the existence of American liberty. . . . Your memorialists can find no clause in the Constitution authorizing Congress to assume the debts of the States."[26] Hamilton called upon the Judiciary to help counteract such political heresy.

"This is the first symptom," wrote Hamilton to Chief Justice Jay, "of a spirit which must either be killed or it will kill the Constitution of the United States. I send the resolutions to you that it may be considered what ought to be done. Ought not the collective weight of the different parts of the government to be employed in exploding the principles they contain?"[27] Despite Jay's strong Federalist sympathies and his attitude

---

[25] 2 Dallas 399–400. See Charles Warren, "The First Decade of the Supreme Court of the United States," 7 *Univ. of Chicago Law Rev.* (June, 1940), 631.

[26] Hening's *Laws of Virginia* (1619–1808), XIII: 234, and Morison and Commager, *op. cit.*, I: 223. Referring to the principle that powers not granted to the federal government are retained by the states, the Virginia assembly declared that "as guardians then of the rights and interests of their constituents, as sentinels placed by them over the ministers of the federal government, to shield it from their encroachments . . . they can never reconcile it to their consciences to acquiesce in a measure, which violates that hallowed maxim." *Ibid.*, pp. 237–239, and Herman V. Ames, *State Documents on Federal Relations* (Philadelphia, 1906), pp. 4–6.

[27] *Correspondence and Public Papers of John Jay* (New York, 1891), III: 405.

toward judicial functions as necessarily requiring him to support the
policies of the Administration, he refused to comply with Hamilton's
request. "Every indecent interference of state assemblies," he maintained, "will diminish their influence; the national government has only
to do what is right, and if possible, be silent."[28] It remained for another
Chief Justice with similar Federalist leanings to participate in the condemnation of what the party regarded as the "State rights heresy."

The first case to come before the Supreme Court, *West v. Barnes*,[29]
involving the paper money law of Rhode Island, was dismissed owing to
the irregular method of presentation of the petition. For the first two
and a half years after its establishment the Supreme Court's work was
confined to reading commissions, formulating rules, admitting lawyers
to practice before it, and hearing a few motions.[30] As an indication of the
prevailing attitude of indifference toward the Court, John Rutledge,
one of Washington's first appointees, did not attend a single session of
the Court. After trying a few cases on circuit, he resigned to accept the
position of chief justice of a state supreme court. Thomas Johnson of
Maryland was appointed in his place.

In the August term of 1792 the case of the *State of Georgia v. Brails-
ford* resulted in a close vote. This case involved an injunction to stay
money collected by a marshal on a judgment obtained by a British
creditor concerning a bond which had been sequestered under state law
until it should be determined to whom the money rightfully belonged.
Justices Iredell, Wilson, and Jay favored, whereas Justices Cushing and
Johnson opposed issuance of an injunction on the ground that there was
an adequate remedy at law.[31] When Attorney General Randolph moved
to dissolve the injunction, two Justices, Blair and Iredell, dissented from
the judgment of the Court, saying that there was no adequate remedy at
law. Iredell, however, took occasion to make the comment that "it is my
misfortune to dissent from the opinion entertained by the rest of the
Court upon the present occasion; but I am bound to decide, according
to the dictates of my own judgment."[32] The majority held that the state
should pursue its rights at common law. The same cause came up again
for determination at the beginning of the February term of 1794. The
Chief Justice disposed of the case by noting that the act of the state of

---

[28] *Ibid.*, p. 410.

[29] 2 Dallas 401 (1791).

[30] Frank Monaghan, *John Jay* (New York, 1935), p. 307.

[31] 2 Dallas 402, 415 (1792–1793); Wilson thought the state ought to have sued by writ
of error. It was in this case that Jay expressed the opinion that the jury was judge
of the law as well as the facts.

[32] 2 Dallas 415.

Georgia did not confiscate, but only sequestered, British debts, and the right to recover them revived when peace was restored. The treaty of peace was thus regarded as part of the supreme law of the land. "It is fortunate on the present, as it must be on every occasion," said the Chief Justice, "to find the opinion of the Court unanimous. We entertain no diversity of sentiment and we have experienced no difficulty in writing the charge, which it is my province to deliver."[33] This statement indicates the prevailing opinion that the judgments of the Court, in order to be effective and inspire respect, should be rendered by a unanimous court. But this result was not to be effectively accomplished until the appointment of John Marshall to the position of Chief Justice. Until this time opinions were usually rendered *seriatim* and disagreements were not infrequent. From these rather unpromising beginnings, the Supreme Court was soon called upon to take part in controversies semipolitical in character and to become involved in the carrying out of the partisan policies of the Federalist administrations.

During the first three years the Supreme Court had practically no cases to decide, though the Justices were called upon to settle a few important issues on the circuits. It was in the performance of their circuit duties and in particular in presenting charges to the grand juries that the Justices took sides on some of the political issues of the day, and it was here that the first friction arose between the federal Judiciary and the state agencies that were jealous of their rights and prerogatives. Much of the opposition to the Constitution on the part of the Anti-Federalists arose from the fear that federal tribunals would interfere with the state acts designed to meet the conditions of an economic depression, such as moratorium acts or paper money laws, and with legislation regarding the properties of loyalists or British subjects. The extreme sensitiveness of the states with respect to the probable intrusion of the federal inferior courts into their domain was shown by the rebuff administered to the federal Circuit Court in North Carolina.

On application to the Justice of the district for a writ of certiorari a case pending in a state court prior to the adoption of the Constitution was removed to the federal court. It was to this case that Nathanial Macon of North Carolina referred in a speech in the House of Representatives in 1802, when he said: "We have heard much about the judges, and the necessity of their independence.... Soon after the establishment of the federal courts, they issued a writ ... to the supreme court of North Carolina, directing a case then pending in the state court to be brought into the federal court. The state judges refused to

---

[33] 3 Dallas 4.

obey the summons and laid the whole proceedings before the legislature, who approved their conduct."[34]

The apprehension that the lower federal courts would soon interfere with the enforcement of state acts was not ill-founded, for, in May, 1791, the Justices on circuit held a law of the state of Connecticut void as an infringement of the clause of the treaty of peace relating to the obligations due to British subjects or to those who had joined the armies of Great Britain during the war.[35] And in June, 1792, a moratorium act of Rhode Island giving a creditor three years' time to settle his accounts with his creditors and providing for an exemption from arrest or attachment of property during this time was held void as impairing the obligation of contracts.[36] Acts of Pennsylvania[37] and of Vermont were also held invalid.

THE ENFORCEMENT OF A FEDERAL COMMON LAW

Speaking of the political trials which followed the adoption of the federal Constitution, Francis Wharton notes that "almost at the opening of the courts, we see the first Chief Justice of the United States, with the pen hardly dry with which the great contemporaneous commentary on the Constitution was partly, written, hurrying to Richmond to declare to the first federal grand jury that ever sat there, the doctrine, afterwards so precipitately abandoned, that, by the common law, the federal courts have power to punish offences against the federal sovereignty."[38]

Chief Justice Jay's charge to the grand jury in Richmond, May 22, 1793, to which Wharton referred, called attention to some of the controversial affairs of the day, as follows: "By their Constitution and laws, the people of the United States have expressed their will, and their will so expressed, must sway and rule supreme in our republic. . . . Every nation is, and ought to be, perfectly and absolutely sovereign within its own dominions."[39] Reading and commenting on Washington's Neutrality Proclamation, the Chief Justice instructed the jury to bring charges

---

[34] 7th Cong., 1st sess., p. 711. Cf. also Seth Ames, ed., *Works of Fisher Ames* (Boston, 1854), I: 91. Ames notes that the suit was against Robert Morris and that judgment was rendered against him for ten thousand pounds. Following the adoption of the Constitution by North Carolina, application was made to the federal Circuit Court for the district for a writ of certiorari to remove the case to the federal courts. It was this writ which the state judges refused to obey.

[35] Charles Warren, *The Supreme Court in United States History*, I: 65, 66. A similar decision was rendered by Justice Iredell in Savannah, Georgia, in 1792. *Ibid.*, p. 66.

[36] *Ibid.*, pp. 66, 67.

[37] Van Horne's Lessee v. Dorrance, 2 Dallas 304 (1795) and Warren, *op. cit.*, p. 69.

[38] Wharton, *State Trials*, p. 1.

[39] *Ibid.*, pp. 51, 56.

against those who violated the neutrality policy of the government. "What acts amount to committing, or aiding, or abetting hostilities," he declared, "must be determined by the laws and approved practice of nations, and by the treaties and other laws of the United States relative to such cases." Thus the law of nations was placed by the side of the treaties and laws of the United States as a basis for the bringing of charges and for the punishment of criminal acts.[40] The people were warned against becoming partisans for the interests or cause of any foreign nation. Adverting to the continuing discussion over the Constitution and the criticisms directed against it, the Chief Justice said:

The people of the United States, being by the grace and favour of heaven, free, sovereign and independent, had a right to choose the form of national government which they should judge most conducive to their happiness and safety. They have done so, and have ordained and established the one which is specified in their great and general compact or Constitution—a compact deliberately formed, maturely considered, and solemnly adopted and ratified by them. There is not a word in it but what is employed to express the will of the people; and what friend of his country, and the liberties of it, will say that the will of the people is not to be observed, respected and obeyed? To this general compact every citizen is a party, and consequently every citizen is bound by it. To oppose the operation of this Constitution and of the government established by it, would be to violate the sovereignty of the people, and would justly merit reprehension and punishment.[41]

The attitude and policy of the Federalists, later enacted into law to proscribe and punish those who expressed disagreement with or opposition to the federal officers exercising public authority, was suggested in this charge. And the doctrines announced by the Chief Justice were soon applied in the cases of Joseph Ravara and Gideon Henfield.

When, as a consequence of the French Revolution, all of western Europe became involved in war, Washington, in his Neutrality Proclamation and in his instructions to prosecuting officers, urged the officers to institute actions against all persons who within the cognizance of the courts of the United States violated the law of nations with respect to the powers at war.[42]

Acting on these instructions, the jury indicted Ravara in the District Court of Pennsylvania for sending threatening letters to the British Minister and others to extort money. Justices Wilson, Iredell, Peters, and Chief Justice Jay joined in holding that the Court had jurisdiction and

[40] Wharton, *State Trials*, p. 57.
[41] *Ibid.*, p. 58.
[42] Henry Flanders, *The Lives and Times of the Chief Justices of the Supreme Court of the United States* (New York, 1875), I: 390 ff.; also Wharton, *op. cit.*, p. 49; it is claimed that Jay was largely responsible for the drafting of the Neutrality Proclamation, George Pellew, *John Jay* (Boston, 1890), pp. 286 ff.

might punish for this offense under the common law of England. Ravara was tried before Chief Justice Jay and Justice Peters and was convicted but was later pardoned by the President.[43]

Under the advice and direction of the French minister, Gideon Henfield, a citizen of the United States, serving as an officer of a French privateer, brought to Philadelphia a British vessel taken as a prize. Henfield was apprehended and tried before the Circuit Court of Philadelphia, with Alexander Hamilton drafting the indictment and aiding in the trial.[44] In the argument of W. Rawle, district attorney, and of Edmund Randolph, Attorney General, it was contended that the law of nations is part of the law of the land. Hence, Henfield's acts being regarded as an offense against the law of nations, he was deemed punishable by indictment on information for his wrongful conduct.[45] The attorneys in defense contended that the indictment did not include an offense at common law, that the acts were committed before the President's Neutrality Proclamation was announced, and that since there was no statute giving jurisdiction in such a case, the court could not take cognizance of the offense.[46]

Justice Wilson, in the charge to the grand jury, supported the view of the Chief Justice and announced to the petit jury that it was the unanimous opinion of Justices Wilson, Iredell, and Peters that "the acts of hostility committed by Gideon Henfield are an offense against this country, and punishable by its laws."[47] Henfield's conduct was regarded as an offense against the law of nations or against the sovereignty of the United States under common law jurisdiction. The Justices apparently

---

[43] Wharton, *op. cit.*, pp. 90–92, and United States v. Ravara, 2 Dallas 297 (1793).

[44] Wharton comments on the *Henfield Case* as follows:

"We see Genet, to check whose depredations this prerogative was invoked, supplying an American skipper with the French flag; we see an English merchantman seized in the river Delaware by the vessel thus equipped; and we find a Connecticut day laborer magnified into a cause of war by the fact that, without casting off his American allegiance, he undertook to serve in the Gallicised privateer. The English minister demanded his arrest; the French minister insisted on his discharge; and all the Judges of the Supreme Court were summoned to give dignity and effect to his trial. By the court he was pronounced an offender against the Constitution and laws of the United States; by the jury he was decided to be an offender against neither; and, while Mr. Jefferson directed Mr. Morris to tender to the English ministry the charge of the court, as demonstrating that the federal government had power to punish offenders against the law of nations, Mr. Genet issued cards to a dinner in which many American dignitaries were invited to meet 'citizen Henfield,' and, where the position was boastingly taken, that by the verdict of a jury it was settled that the American people were hereafter to make war upon Great Britain, under the French flag." *Op. cit.*, pp. 1, 2, 49 ff.

[45] Wharton, *op. cit.*, p. 80.

[46] *Ibid.*, p. 83.

[47] *Ibid.*, p. 84.

placed the common law and the law of nations on the same plane. The jury, however, refused to convict the offender. Washington was so alarmed over the verdict of the jury in the case of Henfield that he submitted the query to his cabinet whether it might not be desirable to call a special session of Congress. The majority of the cabinet replied in the negative.[48]

The case aroused great excitement. The Democratic papers inquired what law had been broken and under what statute the indictment was supported. They inquired also whether the American people were ready to give a proclamation the force of a legislative act.[49] Thus an issue was raised on which the public men and federal Judges divided until the matter was set at rest by the rejection of the doctrine embodied in Washington's Proclamation and in Chief Justice Jay's charge to the grand jury. The view that the federal courts had common law jurisdiction in criminal cases was asserted in a number of cases,[50] but this phase of the court's work will be considered further in connection with the political activities of the Justices during the Administration of John Adams.[51]

THE REVIEW OF THE VALIDITY OF ACTS OF CONGRESS

It was assumed in the adoption of the Constitution, as has been previously indicated, that laws not in harmony with its provisions might be enacted by Congress and that such laws were to be considered as void. Whether these laws should be enforced by the courts until repealed by Congress was not expressly determined by the language of the Constitution. It was taken for granted by many who looked upon the Constitution as a fundamental law not to be violated that the Judges, in the first instance at least, might call attention to such a violation and possibly refuse to enforce the act. The first case to come before the federal courts involving the validity of an act of Congress was *Hayburn's Case*.[52] Congress passed an act to regulate claims to invalid pensions and authorized the Judges of the Circuit Courts to receive and determine upon the applications for pensions, subject to review by the Secretary of War and by Congress. In the New York circuit Justices Jay, Cushing, and Duane were of the opinion "that by the Constitution of the United States, the government thereof is divided into *three* distinct and independent branches, and that it is the duty of each to abstain from, and to oppose, encroachments on the other; that neither the *Legislative* nor the *Execu-*

---

[48] Sparks, *op. cit.*, X: 535.
[49] Marshall, *The Life of George Washington*, II: 273, 274.
[50] See U. S. v. Worrall, 2 Dallas 384 (1798).
[51] See chap. v.
[52] 2 Dallas 409 (1792).

tive branches, can constitutionally assign to the *Judicial* any duties but such as are properly judicial, and to be performed in a judicial manner."[53] In deference to the intention of the legislature, however, the Judges agreed to execute the act in the capacity of commissioners. The views of the Justices were sent to the President.

The Justices of the Pennsylvania circuit also wrote to the President referring to the theory of the separation of powers as implied in the language of the Constitution and stated that in their opinion the Circuit Court could not proceed under the act:

1st. Because the business directed by this act is not of a judicial nature. It forms no part of the power vested by the Constitution in the courts of the United States; the Circuit Court must consequently have proceeded without constitutional authority.

2nd. Because, if, upon that business, the Court had proceeded, its *judgments* (for its *opinions* are its judgments) might, under the same act, have been revised and controlled by the Legislature, and by an officer in the Executive department. Such revision and control we deemed radically inconsistent with the independence of that judicial power which is vested in the courts; and, consequently, with that important principle which is so strictly observed by the Constitution of the United States. . . . To be obliged to act contrary, either to the obvious directions of Congress, or to a constitutional principle in our judgment equally obvious, excited feelings in us, which we hope never to experience again.[54]

In the North Carolina circuit Justices Iredell and Sitgreaves addressed a similar communication to the President in which it was contended that the revision provided for in the act by the Secretary of War "subjects the decisions of the Court to a mode of revision which we consider to be unwarranted by the Constitution," and with regard to the provision permitting an ultimate appeal to Congress, the Justices said "we beg leave to add, with all due deference, that no decision of any court of the United States can, under any circumstances, in our opinion, agreeable to the Constitution, be liable to a revision, or even suspension by the Legislature itself, in whom no judicial power of any kind appears to be vested, but the important one relative to impeachments."[55] The Justices suggested that it might be possible to administer the act as commissioners but on this point they had grave doubts. As no application was made to the Justices in this circuit, there was no occasion for a decision on this issue.

The decision of the Judges in the Pennsylvania circuit led the Attorney General to appeal to the Supreme Court for a mandamus to compel the Judges to act on a petition by William Hayburn. The Court observed that they would hold the motion under advisement until the next term,

---

[53] 2 Dallas 410.
[54] *Ibid.*, pp. 411, 412.
[55] *Ibid.*, pp. 412, 413.

but, as the legislature at an intermediate session provided in another way for the relief of the pensioners, no decision was ever pronounced.[56] In the following year the Supreme Court decided that the Judges could not legally act in the capacity of commissioners under the act of 1792.[57]

Because this was the first case in which the Justices regarded an act of Congress invalid and refused to act officially under the act, there was considerable public discussion of the effect of such a decision. The House of Representatives appointed a committee to inquire and report upon the case. Those who looked upon the courts as the chief guardians of individual liberties usually applauded the action of the Justices. Among those opposed to the exercise of such authority by the Judges there was much talk of the desirability of impeaching the Judges for refusal to obey the law, and it was frequently insisted that in conflicts of this kind the issue should be submitted to the people.[58]

Following the customary attitude toward the Court[59] and the approval in particular of its exercise of semipolitical functions, Charles Warren notes that the refusal of the Justices to enforce an act of Congress "seems to have been heartily supported by the adherents of the political party which favored a strict construction of the Constitution and to have been opposed by the party which was devoted to nationalist theories." And he asserts that "whatever may have been the attitude of the Southern statesman at a later date, it is clear that at the outset they fully recognized and endorsed the exercise of judicial review."[60] Thus the conclusion is arrived at that statesmen of the North and the South were with few exceptions in favor of such review of acts of Congress as was favored by the Justices. To support this conclusion Warren quotes the opinions of members of Congress in 1789 on the proposal to make the Secretary of Foreign Affairs removable by the President. Though a number of Congressmen are quoted as regarding the courts as the "proper expositors" of the Constitution, the very significant opinion of Madison sustaining the authority of Congress to place its own authoritative and final interpretation on the Constitution is passed over without notice. Apparently the desired conclusion is more securely arrived at if the views of Madi-

---

[56] Hayburn's Case, 2 Dallas 409, 410. Cf. *U. S. Statutes at Large*, I: 324.

[57] United States v. Yale Todd, 13 Howard 52 (1851); note inserted by Chief Justice Taney.

[58] See extracts mostly favorable to the opinions of the Justices, Warren, *op. cit.*, pp. 72 ff.

[59] See my article, "Histories of the Supreme Court of the United States Written from the Federalist Point of View," *Southwestern Political and Social Science Quarterly* (June, 1923), IV: 1.

[60] *The Supreme Court in United States History*, I: 82, 83.

son, who was one of the most important members of the federal Convention, are ignored. These views will be presented later,[61] but attention may again be directed to the well-known fact that most of the prominent men of all parties favored some form of the review of legislative acts by the courts. It is the final and authoritative interpretation of the Constitution by the courts which becomes *ipso facto* binding on the coordinate departments of government as well as upon all persons that the Federalists proposed and defended. Such a principle of federal constitutional construction was not generally accepted until after the Civil War. The federal courts were authorized by the Judiciary Act of 1789 to review and declare state acts invalid so far as they were regarded in conflict with the federal Constitution, laws, or treaties, and there was an implication at least for the authority to pass in first instance in the settlement of private controversies on the validity of acts of Congress. The exercise of this authority, it was frequently insisted, did not result in a final and conclusive exposition of the Constitution binding the coördinate departments and private citizens as well.

Under the English practice at this time, it would have been entirely proper to call on the Judges for a service such as that required by the Invalid Pension Act, and under the colonial and state practice it was not uncommon for the legislature to place nonjudicial duties upon Judges. But a new theory of the separation of powers and judicial independence was emerging, and with this came a different concept of the relation of the Judges to the other departments of government.[62] This new concept was summed up in the doctrine that there was to be established in America "a government of laws and not of men."

In the declaration of rights formulated for the state of Massachusetts in 1780 is to be found this significant section:

In the government of this commonwealth, the legislative department shall never exercise the executive and judicial power, or either of them; the executive shall never exercise the legislative and judicial powers, or either of them; the judicial shall never exercise the legislative and executive powers, or either of them; to the end it may be a government of laws and not of men.[63]

The concluding phrase of this quotation was probably suggested by the famous passage of James Harrington in which he maintained that in a monarchy man is not governed by the law, but law by the man, whereas

---

[61] See below, pp. 215 ff.

[62] See especially Case of Judges, 2 Call. 139 (1789), and Kamper v. Hawkins, 1 Va. Cases 20 (1793).

[63] Francis Newton Thorpe, *The Federal and State Constitutions, Colonial Charters, and Other Organic Laws of the States, Territories, and Colonies* (Washington, 1909), III: 1893.

in a republic no man is governed by another man, but all in common are governed by the laws.[64]

Though the state constitutions of 1776 concentrated authority to a considerable extent in the legislature, a number of devices were inserted to prevent the influence of a personal element in government—to repress the inevitable tendency then thought to be evident for governments to become arbitrary and oppressive. Not only did some of these constitutions provide that the "legislative, executive and judiciary ought to be forever separate and distinct,"[65] but they also placed certain prohibitions and restrictions upon the exercise of governmental power. Such restrictions in the form of declarations of rights were to be jealously guarded and strictly preserved. Although in most of the states no provision was made for the enforcement of these restrictions, such as the Council of Censors of Pennsylvania and Vermont and the Council of Revision of New York, various remedies were proposed. Officers in the executive and legislative departments were to have short terms and were usually not to have the privilege of reëlection. The people were to have the right to petition the legislature, the right to call for a redress of grievances, and finally, when all other means of securing redress failed, there remained, so they held, the right "to reform the old or establish a new government." In the language of the Maryland constitution "the doctrine of non-resistance, against arbitrary power and oppression, is absurd, slavish, and destructive of the good and happiness of mankind."[66]

It remained for the Judges to give a new and largely unanticipated effect to these provisions by asserting their independence and by insisting upon their interpretation of constitutions as superior to that of other departments. A number of state courts had already taken steps in this direction. The extraordinary theory of judicial independence and semisuperiority which was emerging was not seriously opposed because of its limited scope and because in its earliest applications its chief object was to protect the Judiciary from the encroachments upon its domain by the other departments. The theory was championed primarily by Alexander Hamilton and John Jay and those who with them believed in strong government and preferred that government be removed so far as practicable from direct popular control.

As parties were taking shape in the formation of the Constitution and in the first years of Washington's Administration, the Justices, as

---

[64] James Harrington, *Oceana and other Works* (3d ed.), p. 386.

[65] Constitution of Maryland, Francis Newton Thorpe, *The Federal and State Constitutions* (Washington, 1909), III: 1687. Constitution of Georgia, *ibid.*, II: 778. Constitution of Virginia, *ibid.*, VII: 3813.

[66] *Ibid.*, III: 1687.

Federalists, were inclined to favor the views expressed by Hamilton regarding the right of courts to declare acts of Congress invalid. It was to be expected, therefore, that the Circuit Courts would favor an extreme view of the separation and independence of the judicial department, and that Congress would be rebuffed in its effort to carry out a laudable object at a small expense. It is interesting to observe that the very light duties of the Judges on circuit at this time would have rendered it possible to carry out the act of Congress without interference with regular judicial matters, and that it was not unusual to place similar functions upon Judges in foreign countries. But the Federalist views of the duties and responsibilities of the Justices were soon to involve the Supreme Court in a more fateful controversy—that of *Chisholm's Executor v. Georgia*.

STATE VERSUS NATIONAL SOVEREIGNTY

The issue whether a citizen or a corporation could bring suit against a state arose in one of the first cases presented to the Supreme Court[67] and in suits instituted against the states of New York[68] and Virginia.[69] A protest was submitted through a special committee of the Virginia legislature against the maintenance of a suit against the state. It was contended that the jurisdiction of the federal courts does not extend to such a case and the executive was requested "to pursue such measures as may seem most conducive to the interest, honor and dignity of the Commonwealth." But the first direct consideration of this question and the issuance of an order of the Court in connection therewith came when citizens of South Carolina on behalf of a British creditor filed a suit against the state of Georgia.[70]

This case raised before the Court the first issue of grave political significance. As a result of an action instituted in the August term, 1792, the state of Georgia was served with process by the Supreme Court. On refusal to appear[71] the Court at the next term made an order that judgment by default should be given against the state. The crucial question to be determined was whether the state of Georgia could be made a party in a case before the Supreme Court of the United States as a result of a

---

[67] Vanstophorst v. Maryland, 2 Dallas 401 (1791); Warren, *op. cit.*, p. 91.

[68] Oswald v. New York, 2 Dallas 401 (1792).

[69] Indiana Company v. Virginia, Warren, *op. cit.*, I: 92. Of the first nine causes seven were suits by individuals against states.

[70] Chisholm v. Georgia, 2 Dallas 419 (1793).

[71] For an extract from a resolution presented to the Georgia house of representatives declaring the action of the Supreme Court "unconstitutional and extra-judicial," see Herman V. Ames, *State Documents on Federal Relations*, p. 7.

suit instituted by a private citizen of another state. The Justices rendered their opinions *seriatim*, Justice Iredell alone supporting the view that a state was not liable to suit at the instance of a citizen of another state. According to Iredell, the issue of the case was determined by the Constitution and the laws of Congress. He found nothing in the Constitution or federal laws to support such authority in the federal courts[72] and said that "my present opinion is strongly against any construction of it [the Constitution] which will admit, under any circumstances a compulsive suit against a State for the recovery of money." He concluded his analysis of the question with this important observation:

I think every word in the Constitution may have its full effect without involving this consequence, and that nothing but express words, or an insurmountable implication (neither of which I consider, can be found in this case) would authorize the deduction of so high a power. This opinion I hold, however, with all the reserve proper for one, which according to my sentiments in this case, may be deemed in some measure extra-judicial. . . . Upon the question before us, I have no doubt. I have therefore nothing to do with policy. But I confess, if I was at liberty to speak on that subject, my opinion on the policy of the case would also differ from that of the Attorney General. It is, however, a delicate topic. I pray to God, that if the Attorney General's doctrine, as to the law, be established by the judgment of this Court, all the good he predicts from it may take place, and none of the evils which, I have the concern to say, it appears to me to be pregnant.[73]

Justices Blair, Wilson, Cushing, and Jay disagreed with this interpretation of the Constitution and laws. Blair thought, with respect to the attribute of sovereignty which exempts from suit, that "when a State, by adopting the Constitution, has agreed to be amenable to the judicial power of the United States, she has in that respect given up her right of sovereignty."[74] Owing to the serious consequences involved in a judgment by default against a state, he suggested further delay.

To Justice Wilson the real issue was: "Do the people of the United States form a nation?" He denied that the term "sovereign" might appropriately be applied to either the states or the federal government but that it could only be applied to the people.[75] After an analysis of the relations between the government established by the Constitution and the states, he concluded that *"as to the purposes of the Union, there-*

---

[72] Chisholm v. Georgia, 2 Dallas 432–435 (1793).

[73] 2 Dallas 449, 450. For commendation of Justice Iredell's views see Justice Bradley's opinion in Hans v. Louisiana, 134 U. S. 1, 12 (1890). William C. Coleman thinks that "since the suability of a State without its consent was a thing unknown to the law, its cognizance was not contemplated by those who wrote into the Constitution the clauses conferring jurisdiction upon the federal Judiciary." "The State as Defendant Under the Federal Constitution: The Virginia-West Virginia Debt Controversy," 31 *Harv. Law Rev.* (Dec., 1917), 216.

[74] 2 Dallas 452.   [75] 2 Dallas 454 ff.

fore, *Georgia is not a sovereign State,*" that the states could be bound so as to be liable for suit, and that the intent of the Constitution was to bind them.[76] He joined with Cushing in the contention that the language of the Constitution warranted a suit against a state by an individual citizen of another state. The basis for this contention was thought to inhere in the clause of the Constitution extending the judicial authority of the federal courts to controversies between states.

Chief Justice Jay likewise denied that sovereignty resided in either the federal or the state governments. Expanding the theory of Justice Wilson, he was of the opinion that the sovereignty of Great Britain had passed to the people of the United States and that the people as sovereigns had made the Constitution and had willed that the states should be bound.[77] "The sovereignty of the Nation," he continued, "is in the people of the Nation, and the residuary sovereignty of each State in the people of each State."[78] It was on the basis of this opinion that Jay's biographer characterizes his views as "even more advanced than the 'immortal nationalist opinions' of Marshall" and as designed to reduce the states to administrative units of the federal government.[79] Speaking for the Court, the Chief Justice ordered that the state shall either in due form appear or show cause to the contrary to this Court. In the absence of a constitutional provision relating to the matter, Jay and his colleagues, influenced by their nationalistic sentiments and contrary to opinions expressed by Hamilton, Madison, and Marshall,[80] rendered a decision which appeared to be "a frontal attack upon the sovereignty of the States. . . . Both the lawyers and the public were quite unprepared for any such decision."[81] Owing to the failure of state officials to execute the order, judgment was rendered for the plaintiff at the February term, 1794, and a writ of inquiry was awarded. The writ, however, was not executed.

---

[76] *Ibid.*, pp. 457 ff.

[77] *Ibid.*, pp. 470–471.

[78] *Ibid.*, p. 471.

[79] Monaghan, *John Jay*, p. 302.

[80] On the contention that individuals might bring suits against the states, Hamilton replied, "It is inherent in the nature of sovereignty not to be amenable to the suit of an individual without its consent. This is the general sense, and the practice of mankind; and the exemption, as one of the attributes of sovereignty, is now enjoyed by the government of every State in the Union." *The Federalist* (Ford ed.), p. 545.

"It is not in the power of individuals to call any State into Court." Madison, Elliot's *Debates* (2d ed.), III: 533.

"I hope that no gentlemen will think that a State may be called at the bar of the federal court. . . . It is not rational to suppose that the sovereign power should be dragged before a court." Marshall, *ibid.*, p. 555.

[81] Monaghan, *op. cit.*, p. 308.

The legislature of Massachusetts, called into special session by Governor John Hancock, urged upon Congress the adoption of amendments to the Constitution in order to change any provisions which might be "construed to justify a decision that a State is compellable to answer in any suit by an individual or individuals in any court of the United States." And the legislature of Virginia declared that the decision was "incompatible with and dangerous to the sovereignty and independence of the individual States, as the same tends to a general consolidation of these confederated Republics." Georgia took the most drastic action. The governor sent a message to the legislature condemning the proceedings of the Supreme Court and a bill was approved by the house of representatives declaratory of the retained sovereignty of the state. The house also approved another measure imposing the penalty of death upon anyone presuming to enforce the decree of the Supreme Court.[82] Because of the refusal of the senate to join in this action, the bill did not become a law. Two weeks after the decision was rendered, Congress submitted to the states an amendment providing that "the judicial power of the United States shall not be construed to extend to any suit in law or equity, commenced or prosecuted against one of the United States by citizens of another state, or by citizens or subjects of any foreign state." About four years later the amendment was ratified,[83] and the Court soon dropped all similar cases on its docket.[84] Since the Eleventh Amendment disposed of the controversy in a manner favorable to the state, there was no longer any fear that numerous suits against the states instituted by Tories and refugees might seriously interfere with the administration of justice. The chief significance of the *Chisholm Case* and the adoption of the Eleventh Amendment lies, in the opinion of Ulrich B. Phillips, "in the demonstration that the unanimous vote of the Georgia convention in 1788 was given in the understanding that the State remained in possession of all residuary rights and powers."[85]

Thus, the first significant case before the Supreme Court gave a fore-

---

[82] Cf. Ames, *State Documents on Federal Relations,* pp. 8–11.

[83] Eleventh Amendment.

[84] Hollingsworth v. Virginia, 3 Dallas 378 (1798).

[85] "Georgia and State Rights," in *Annual Report* of the American Historical Association, 1901, p. 28. The difficulties of the Court in connection with *Chisholm v. Georgia* led in another case where the state refused to appear to the postponement of a decision on the motion "in consequence of a doubt, whether the remedy to compel the appearance of a State, should be furnished by the court itself, or by the legislature." But an order was finally issued that "when process at common law or in equity shall issue against a State, the same shall be served upon the governor or chief magistrate, and the attorney general of such State." Huger v. South Carolina, 3 Dallas 339 (1796).

cast of the controversy which was waged with intermittent outbreaks until it was made the central political issue of four years of civil war. The main issue, so the Judges thought, was whether the government of the United States was a federation or a confederation. But this is scarcely the type of question a court would be expected to settle. It was the gravest type of political issue and one on which opinions were sharply divided during the Revolution, under the Confederation, and in the formation of the Constitution.[86] It is an issue on which historians still disagree concerning the effect upon it of the Articles of Confederation and the intention of the framers of the Constitution. There are those who regard the united colonies as in effect a federation from the time of the Declaration of Independence. Others find in the documents and political practices of the time ample evidence to support the contention that a confederation existed until the formation of the Constitution and that the fundamental characteristics of a confederation were not abandoned in the adoption of that instrument. The fact seems to be that it depended upon the individual, either nationalist or particularist, whether the emphasis was given to notions favorable to confederation or federation. To Hamilton, Madison, Bowdoin, and Wilson nationalist views were uppermost in the forming of the Constitution, whereas, according to many indications, the average citizen and political leader was still thinking in terms of a confederation and did not regard the adoption of the Constitution as bringing about a change in the location of sovereignty.

In view of the fact that this was the crucial political issue in men's minds during the making and adoption of the Constitution and that the controversy was beginning to rage anew in Congress, it might have been expected that the Supreme Court would pass the issue on to the political departments of the government. It was unusual, to say the least, that the Judges should attempt to settle through the judicial channel so fundamental a political question. But the members of the Supreme Court were Federalists, most of them were ardent nationalists, who believed that the existence and stability of the union depended upon a strong central government and that a liberal construction of the Constitution in the furtherance of that end should prevail. And to the Justices, only recently removed from the political forum, the opportunity appeared too pertinent to fail to give a judicial pronouncement favorable to nationalism as one of the prime Federalist principles. Most of the members of the Court adopted the latitudinarian view of the Constitution espoused by Hamilton and the leading Federalists and at-

[86] See chap. iii.

tempted to gather the nationalist intention from the general purport of the Constitution and from the implications of specific phrases.[87]

Justice Iredell, on the other hand, pleaded for a closer adherence by the Court to the Constitution and the laws. The opinion of Iredell was generally in accord with the views of Thomas Jefferson, as expressed in opposition to the establishment of a national bank, and met with warm commendation in the South.[88] Constitutional lawyers have generally regarded the Chisholm decision as unwarranted by the Constitution. In *Hans v. Louisiana*,[89] in which the principle of the majority view in the *Chisholm Case* was rejected, Justice Bradley commended the able opinion of Justice Iredell and remarked that "looking back from our present standpoint at the decision in *Chisholm v. Georgia,* we do not greatly wonder at the effect which it had upon the country."[90]

But loose constructionists who have followed in the footsteps of Hamilton and Marshall have supported the majority opinions. There is, says James O. Pierce, "no basis of comparison between the limited views of Iredell and the broad and masterly opinions of his colleagues Wilson and Jay."[91] Wilson, according to Hampton L. Carson, rose to heights of "judicial inspiration" in uncovering the basic principles of national sovereignty.[92] And to those holding similar views the case was decided on a "statesmanlike" basis. Whether the opinions of Justices were regarded as statesmanlike or narrow and reprehensible depends largely on the political bias of those who review them. Writers frequently laud Judges for statesmanship in decisions, that is, for exercising powers of

---

[87] Cf. Don Enswinger Mowry, "Political and Party Aspects of the National Judiciary, 1789–1801." *Amer. Historical Magazine* (Jan., 1908), p. 89; the Chisholm decision is "attributed entirely to the fact that the Constitution was regarded from a strongly federal point of view." W. D. Coles, "Politics and the Supreme Court of the United States," 27 *Amer. Law Rev.* (Mar.–Apr., 1893), 182, 188 ff.

[88] Griffith J. McRee, *Life and Correspondence of James Iredell* (New York, 1857), II: 379 ff. See opinions of Hamilton and Jefferson relative to the controversy over a national bank, below, pp. 203 ff.

The opinion of Iredell, says Hampton L. Carson, "enumerates either directly or by implication all the leading principles of what has since become known as states rights doctrine, and which as a mere legal argument was far superior in closeness of reasoning to Wilson's or Jay's. He confined himself strictly to the question before the Court." *The Supreme Court of the United States: Its History* (2d ed., Philadelphia, 1902), I: 174.

The adoption of the Eleventh Amendment demonstrated the correctness of Iredell's opinion with reference to the Constitution as then understood by the average voter and political leader.

[89] 134 U. S. 1 (1890).

[90] *Ibid.*, p. 12.

[91] James Oscar Pierce, "James Wilson as a Jurist," 38 *Amer. Law Rev.* (Jan.–Feb., 1904), 44, 57.

[92] "James Wilson and James Iredell: a Parallel and a Contrast," 7 *Amer. Bar Assn. Jour.* (Mar., 1921), 123, 129.

judicial legislation, and yet contend that Judges have no authority to participate in legislation. Evidently, if one agrees with the politics involved, it is a mark of statesmanship for a Judge to render an opinion on a political issue. Thus, the Supreme Court from the beginning was thrust in the midst of the political arena.

The question of state versus national sovereignty was passed upon adversely to the contentions of the states in *Penhallow v. Doane's Administrators*.[93] During the Revolution the *Susanna* had been captured by the brigantine *M'Clary*, a vessel owned by a citizen of New Hampshire. A New Hampshire court had ordered the vessel and cargo to be forfeited as lawful prize and the proceeds to be distributed according to law. The original owners appealed to the Continental Congress, under whose authority the *M'Clary* had been commissioned, and through their commissioners of appeals they took jurisdiction of the case. With the establishment of the Confederation it was decided to refer all cases regarding captures to the Court of Appeals of the new Congress. This court reversed the decision of the state court and ordered the property restored to the owners. Owing to the objections of the state this decree was not enforced. When the inferior federal courts were established under the Constitution the case was presented to the District and Circuit Courts for adjudication, and a decree was rendered ordering payment of damages and costs to the owners. From this decree the case was appealed to the Supreme Court, and eighteen years after the original cause had been decided in the state courts it was held that this decision was incorrect and must be reversed. Justice Paterson, in rendering the decision, adopted the organic or nationalistic interpretation of the events during the Revolutionary and critical periods.

With respect to the much controverted issue of the powers of Congress, Paterson said: "The powers of Congress were revolutionary in nature, arising out of events, adequate to every national emergency, and co-extensive with the object to be attained. Congress was the general, supreme, and controlling council of the Nation, the centre of union, the centre of force, and the sun of the political system." Referring to the acts of Congress in conducting the war, it was claimed that "these high acts of sovereignty were submitted to, acquiesced in, and approved by the people of America." And as in every government there must be one supreme will, Paterson asked where this supreme authority was during the war, and then said: "No one will hesitate to answer. It was lodged in, and exercised by Congress; it was there or no where; the States individually did not, and, with safety, could not exercise it. Disastrous would

---

[93] 3 Dallas 54 (1795).

have been the issue of the contest, if the States, separately had exercised the powers of war. For in such case, there would have been as many supreme wills as there were States, and as many wars as there were wills. Happily, however, for America, this was not the case; there was but one war, and one sovereign to conduct it. . . . As to war and peace, and their necessary incidents, Congress by the unanimous voice of the people, exercised exclusive jurisdiction, and stood, like Jove, amidst the deities of old, paramount and supreme."[94] The organic fiction of a single, supreme, and sovereign nation during the Revolution was taking definite shape and for the future was not likely to be disturbed by contrary facts or events.

Turning to somewhat firmer ground than the theory of national sovereignty, Justice Paterson noted that because the captain of the *M'Clary* obtained his commission from Congress, the legality of captures made under his direction must ultimately be determined by Congress. And since New Hampshire was a member of the Confederacy she was bound by the orders or decrees of its agencies. There was no other recourse for the state except to abide by the decisions of Congress or to withdraw from the Confederacy. It was pointed out also that New Hampshire had joined with the other states in condemning Pennsylvania for refusing to execute a decree of the Court of Appeals.[95]

Justice Iredell was not so sure that Congress represented the single, supreme, and sovereign will of the states, but, making a distinction between internal and external sovereignty, he thought Congress was the appropriate body to exercise external sovereignty, that is, to have control of affairs relating to war and peace. "I think all prize causes whatsoever," he said, "ought to belong to the national sovereignty. They are to be determined by the law of nations."[96] And, though Justice Iredell had not participated in the decision of the Supreme Court in the case of *Glass v. The Sloop Betsey*,[97] he indicated his approval of the decision so far as the vesting of the whole original jurisdiction in admiralty and maritime cases was concerned. The fact that no other court could exercise jurisdiction over prize cases left, he believed, no other alternative than to hold that the District Courts had such authority.

Despite the fact that the states had insisted on retaining their sovereignty and independence during the Revolution and had expressly reserved their rights as independent states under the Articles of Confederation, Justice Blair came to the conclusion that New Hampshire,

---

[94] 3 Dallas 80, 81.
[95] *Ibid.*, pp. 81, 82.
[96] *Ibid.*, p. 91.
[97] *Ibid.*, p. 6.

while a member of the Confederation, could not refuse to be bound by one of its committee's decisions; its only recourse was to withdraw from the Confederacy. Such reasoning can only be based on the assumption which the exponents of the organic theory have always made, namely, that the reservation of state independence in the Articles was a meaningless provision.

On the controversial issue of state versus national sovereignty, the Justices of the Supreme Court again chose the path of nationalism and decided that a federation was established when the Articles of Confederation was adopted. They proceeded to build up the case for nationalism by the process of interpretation which either ignored apparent facts or misconstrued them. The state legislature passed two remonstrances protesting vigorously against what it termed "a violation of state independence and an unwarrantable encroachment in the courts of the United States."[98] A notable beginning had been made in the assertion by judicial construction of national sovereignty in the federal government.

One of the most important controversies on which the Supreme Court was called upon to render a decision during Washington's Administration was that raised in *Ware v. Hylton*.[99] The case was ably argued and fully discussed by the Justices in their opinions. Differing from his argument in the state ratifying convention and his contentions in the case of *Marbury v. Madison*,[100] John Marshall, counsel for the state, asserted that "the legislative authority of any country, can only be restrained by its own municipal constitution: This is a principle that springs from the very nature of society; and the judicial authority can have no right to question the validity of a law, unless such jurisdiction is expressly given by the constitution."[101]

The nationalist philosophy which permeated some of the decisions of the Supreme Court was repudiated by Marshall, when he said: "It has been conceded, that independent nations have in general, the right of confiscation; and that Virginia at the time of passing her law, was an

---

[98] For copies of these remonstrances, see Ames, *op. cit.*, pp. 12 ff. In the first remonstrance the doctrine of state sovereignty and independence during the period of the Revolution was expressly avowed. The Congress of the Confederation was declared to be merely "an advisory body," the acceptance of its measures resting entirely with the several states.

[99] 3 Dallas 199 (1796). "The splendid eloquence of Patrick Henry, the great reasoning faculties of John Marshall at the bar, and the powerful dissenting opinion of Iredell were employed in vain to convince the Court that Congress had no power to make a treaty that could operate to annul a legislative act of any of the States, and thus destroy rights acquired under such act." Carson, *op. cit.*, I: 169, 170.

[100] 1 Cranch 137 (1803).

[101] 3 Dallas 211.

independent nation."[102] This view was approved by Justice Chase, who asserted that "all laws made by the legislatures of the several States, after the Declaration of Independence, were the laws of sovereign and independent governments."[103] After the states agreed to the Articles of Confederation, Chase thought the states retained all internal sovereignty and Congress "properly possessed the great rights of external sovereignty." Virginia therefore limited her sovereign authority by agreeing that the exclusive right to decide on peace and war belonged to Congress. To the contention that the provisions of the treaty of peace could not nullify state acts with respect to the confiscation of property, Justice Chase replied that, since the treaty-making power belonged to the Confederation and was granted to the federal government by the Constitution with the proviso that a treaty becomes the supreme law of the land, all acts of the state legislatures in conflict therewith must be deemed void.

The Justices differed concerning whether Virginia had the sovereign power during the Revolution to confiscate British property within its territory; but Justices Chase, Paterson, Wilson, and Cushing agreed that whatever power Virginia possessed, the acts of the state became subject to the treaty when it was ratified and the treaty must be enforced as the supreme law notwithstanding any state laws in conflict therewith. In fact, it was the judgment of the Court that all state acts in conflict with the treaty were to be considered null and void.

Justice Iredell, the only member of the Bench who though a Federalist had espoused some of the Democratic doctrines of the time, dissented, holding that "the acts of the legislature of the State, in regard to the subject in question, so far as they were conformable to the constitution of the State, and not in violation of any article of the Confederation (where that was concerned) were absolutely binding *de facto*" and that the subsequent adoption of the treaty of peace did not affect the rights involved.[104] He could see no other way to carry the fourth article of the treaty of peace into effect, so far as it enabled British creditors to bring suits and to recover the value of their debts, than for the states to repeal the laws constituting impediments to their recovery and to enact such laws as were necessary to give the recovery entire efficacy.[105] It was with this end in view, he thought, that the Congress of the Confederation recommended the repeal of all acts inconsistent with the due execution of the treaty.

---

[102] 3 Dallas 210.
[103] *Ibid.*, p. 225.
[104] *Ibid.*, pp. 256 ff.
[105] *Ibid.*, p. 271.

In answer to the contention of counsel, chiefly Marshall and Campbell, that a legislature could not destroy rights acquired by or vested in individuals, Chase replied "the legislatures of the States have often exercised the power of divesting rights vested, and in some instances of almost annihilating the obligation of contracts, as by tender laws." Although it was not necessary to render a judgment on this point, there is here a forecast of the great issue concerning the protection of vested rights which came before the Supreme Court when Marshall was Chief Justice.

Frequent references were made in this case as well as in a number of earlier opinions pertaining to the law of nations which some of the Justices contended was a part of law of the United States.[106] Said Justice Wilson, "when the United States declared their independence, they were bound to receive the law of nations in its modern state of purity and refinement."[107] If foreign relations were confided to the federal government and federal authorities were to be guided by the law of nations, a fruitful source was suggested for the expansion of federal functions. The gaps or silences of the Constitution on matters of vital public interest soon involved the Court in another controversy of political import.

ADVISORY OPINIONS

With England and France engaged in war and preying upon our commerce, President Washington had issued a Neutrality Proclamation. But the issuance of this proclamation did not deter the French Minister, Genet, who had the support and sympathy of many American citizens as well as numerous public officials, from fitting out vessels in our ports and setting up prize courts for the condemnation of captured ships. There was no provision in the Constitution for the determination of questions of this kind and no federal statutes had been enacted applicable to the circumstances. The issue came up for judicial determination when the sloop *Betsey*,[108] a Swedish vessel with a cargo owned jointly by Swedes and Americans, was captured by a French privateer and brought to the French consul at Baltimore for adjudication as a prize. A libel was filed by the owners in the District Court claiming restitution, but both the District and Circuit Courts upheld the captors' claim of no jurisdiction. District Judge Peters maintained that the Court could not take jurisdiction. He believed that courts were not the appropriate tribunals to vindicate the rights of nations and that remedies for na-

---

[106] Talbot v. Janson, 3 Dallas 133 (1795).
[107] Ware v. Hylton, 3 Dallas 281 (1796).
[108] Glass v. The Sloop *Betsey*, 3 Dallas 6 (1794).

tional insults and the invasion of territorial rights must be sought through other channels. President Washington refused to consider this decision as final and to avoid undue delay in settling the issues involved requested Jefferson to seek the advice of the Justices of the Supreme Court.

A series of questions relating to the rights of neutrals, the interpretation of treaties applicable thereto, and the pertinent principles of international law were submitted to the Justices for their legal advice and counsel. Doubtless being under the influence of the Chief Justice whose extreme notions of judicial independence and propriety were well known, the Justices declined to give their opinions on the legal questions involved. The departments being intended to be checks upon each other, noted Chief Justice Jay, "and our being Judges of a court in the last resort, are considerations which afford strong arguments against the propriety of our extra-judicially deciding the questions alluded to, especially as the power given by the Constitution to the President, of calling on the heads of departments for opinions, seems to have been purposely as well as expressly united to the executive department."[109] By thus declining to render an advisory opinion and by insisting that it could deal only with actual or concrete cases in which private or public interests were being litigated, it is often contended that the Supreme Court asserted its function as purely judicial in nature.

The practice of the King or the House of Lords, whether acting in their judicial or their legislative capacity, to request opinions from the Judges on questions of law[110] was familiar to the legal profession in this country. It was this practice which led the makers of the Massachusetts constitution of 1780 to include the provision that "each branch of the legislature, as well as the governor and council, shall have authority to require the opinions of the Justices of the Supreme Judicial Court upon important questions of law, and upon solemn occasions."[111] A similar provision was adopted by the states of New Hampshire, Maine, and Rhode Island and later by a number of southern and western states. In giving such opinions the Justices do not act as a court but as the constitutional advisers of the other departments of government.[112]

---

[109] Cf. Sparks, *op. cit.*, X: 359; John Marshall, *Life of George Washington* (1804–1807), V: 441.

[110] For instances of such requests, see James Bradley Thayer, *Legal Essays* (Boston, 1908), pp. 46 ff.

[111] Pt. II, chap. iii, sec. 2.

[112] For the history and operation of the practice of rendering advisory opinions, see Albert R. Ellingwood, *Departmental Coöperation in State Government* (New York, 1918).

Had it not been for the difficult and comprehensive nature of the questions propounded to the Justices and for the overzealous inclinations of the Chief Justice and his Associates to maintain the independence and aloofness of the Supreme Court from the other departments at the same time that the Justices were participating actively in the settlement of questions of a political nature, it is likely that the English and Massachusetts practice of giving advisory opinions might have been adopted by the federal Judiciary.

Where courts confine themselves to strict and narrow questions of the interpretation and application of the law, advisory opinions are infrequently sought and the practice of rendering such opinions appears to be on the decline. When a court such as the Supreme Court of the United States, which by the nature of its function as the expositor of the indefinite language of the written instrument, assumes to an increasing degree political or quasi-political functions in determining issues of public policy, there are urgent reasons for the giving of advisory opinions. The disastrous results and the great uncertainty involved in the recent declarations of the invalidity of acts of Congress have led to an effort to secure a reversal of the early precedent of the Supreme Court and an adaptation of federal legal procedure so that the members of the Supreme Court could give advisory opinions to Congress and to the President.

In the February term of 1794 the question of the jurisdiction of the federal courts to determine the legality of a capture and to order restitution of a prize, having been passed upon adversely by the inferior federal tribunals, was finally presented to the Supreme Court. It was contended on behalf of the captors that the jurisdiction of the District Court extended only to civil causes of admiralty and maritime jurisdiction and that this was not a civil case. But the Supreme Court, Chief Justice Jay rendering the opinion, decided that the District Courts had jurisdiction in such cases and that "no foreign power can of right institute, or erect, any court of judicature of any kind within the jurisdiction of the United States."[113] Hence the attempt of France to set up a prize court in the United States was held unwarranted. The President and his advisers had secured the desired result without Congressional or Executive action. By the device of judicial construction the rights of the United States as a sovereign nation were asserted.

When, on the instance of the French Republic, the Attorney General asked for a mandamus to be directed to Judge Lawrence of the District Court of New York for the issuance of a warrant thought to be denied through a misconstruction of a consular convention, the Supreme Court

[113] Glass v. The Sloop *Betsey*, 3 Dallas 6, 16.

administered a rebuke to the Executive department. "We are," says the Court, "clearly and unanimously of opinion, that a *mandamus* ought not to issue. It is evident, that the District Judge was acting in a judicial capacity . . . and, whatever might be the difference of sentiment entertained by this Court, we have no power to compel a Judge to decide according to the dictates of any judgment, but his own."[114]

A new theory of judicial independence was in process of formulation. It is the usual practice in other countries for the courts to serve the executive in the enforcement of the law. The courts, in fact, are frequently regarded as a part of the executive branch of the government and both executive and judicial officers are, to a considerable extent, under legislative direction and control. Such was the situation in England and in France when the peculiar American theory of judicial independence was being formulated.

When Chief Justice Jay returned from his mission to England, he was elected governor of the state of New York and, though he had retained his position on the Supreme Court during his absence, he now tendered his resignation. Washington desired to have Alexander Hamilton accept the position of Chief Justice as one "who was not to be scared by popular clamor or warped by feebleminded prejudices."[115] Hamilton, however, was not interested in a judicial appointment.

Hearing of the resignation of the Chief Justice, John Rutledge indicated in a letter to Washington that he would be willing to accept the position, if appointed. He was immediately nominated by the President, but owing to an address attacking Jay's Treaty the Senate refused to confirm the nomination. The Federalist opposition was based solely on partisan grounds, for, as Jefferson observed, "they cannot pretend any objection to him but his disapprobation of the treaty. It is, of course, a declaration that they will receive none but Tories hereafter in any department of the government."[116] After offering the position to Patrick Henry, who declined to serve, Washington nominated William Cushing, and his nomination was immediately confirmed. But Cushing also declined the position. The President then turned to Oliver Ellsworth, the author of the Judiciary Act of 1789, to whom the Federalists could find

[114] United States v. Judge Lawrence, 3 Dallas 42, 52 (1795).

[115] John C. Hamilton, *Life of Alexander Hamilton: A History of the Republic of the United States of America* (Boston, 1879), VI: 253.

[116] William Plumer in a letter to Jeremiah Smith expressed the Federalist point of view that "the conduct of the Senate will, I hope, teach demagogues that the road to preferment in this enlightened country is not to revile and calumniate government and excite mobs in opposition to their measures." See Warren, *op. cit.*, I: 137. William Plumer later joined the Democratic-Republican party and defended the principles of this party in the Dartmouth College controversy. See below, p. 381.

little objection. As a staunch partisan, it was thought he might save the country from approaching anarchy and confusion. In place of John Blair, who resigned in the summer of 1795, Washington nominated Samuel Chase of Maryland.

In view of the fact that the Justices had informed President Washington that they would not give an advisory opinion and that the Court would confine its action to the settlement of actual, bona fide controversies, the proceedings in the case of *Hylton v. United States*[117] are especially interesting. The question presented in the case was whether the federal tax on carriages was a direct tax and hence subject to the principle of apportionment among the states. Hylton, the defendant, asserted that his object was merely to determine a constitutional issue and was not to delay the payment of a public duty. The defendant owned one chariot on which the tax and penalty would have been only $16. In order to give the Circuit Court jurisdiction the sum of $2000 must be involved; hence a fictitious plea was entered that the defendant owned and kept 125 chariots, not to let out for hire, but exclusively for his own private use. It was agreed, however, in order that the fictitious plea would not work to the detriment of the defendant that "if the Court adjudged the defendant liable to pay the tax and the fine for not doing so and for not entering the carriages, then judgment shall be entered for the plaintiff for $2000 to be discharged by the payment of sixteen dollars, the amount of the duty and penalty." The effort to secure a decision on a constitutional question when there was no actual controversy involved was shown also by the report of the Secretary of the Treasury to the effect that an agreement was made with the defendant on the basis of which an appeal was taken to the Supreme Court. A condition of the agreement was that the United States should pay all the expenses incident to the appeal.[118] The subterfuge involved and the apparent lack of a real controversy did not deter three of the six Justices from rendering an opinion on the validity of the tax.

It was decided that a tax on carriages was not a direct tax such as was required by the Constitution. The extrajudicial part of the opinions expressed defined direct taxes under the Constitution as only two, a poll tax and a tax on land. The combined efforts of judges and economists have not yet made clear the distinction between direct and indirect taxes. It required an amendment to the Constitution to settle some of the difficulties involved in the definition of these terms as used in the Consti-

---

[117] 3 Dallas 171 (1796).

[118] *Amer. State Papers, Misc.* 1, 393. The attorneys, Campbell, Ingersoll, and Hamilton were paid by the federal government.

tution.[119] The issue stated in the case was whether an act of Congress is unconstitutional and void. And the Justices assumed that it was within their authority and jurisdiction to give a decision on this issue.

RIDING THE CIRCUITS

Not the least of the difficulties in the early years of the Supreme Court were inconveniences and hardships involved in trying cases on the circuits. The Act of 1789 provided for a District Court in each of the states and for three Circuit Courts. Two Supreme Court Justices and one of the District Judges of the circuit made up the membership of the Circuit Court. Sessions were to be held twice a year in the districts comprising the circuit. As early as December, 1790, Edmund Randolph, Attorney General, reported to the House of Representatives that the chief defect of the federal judicial system was involved in the circuit duties of the Justices. He regarded the duties of a Supreme Court Justice so difficult and comprehensive that it was impossible to perform such dual functions. Thomas Johnson objected to the disagreeable duties of touring the circuits, and Washington suggested that relief was anticipated from Congress.[120] Iredell thought that he was treated unfairly because of the refusal of Chief Justice Jay and the other Justices to ride the southern circuit which involved traveling over more than a thousand miles of country with roads scarcely worthy of the name and no other facilities for travelers.[121] Five of the Justices signed a statement in an appeal to the President for relief, saying:

That the task of holding twenty-seven Circuit Courts a year, in the different States, from New Hampshire to Georgia, besides two sessions of the Supreme Court at Philadelphia, in the two most severe seasons of the year, is a task which, considering the extent of the United States, and the small number of Judges, is too burdensome.

That to require of the Judges to pass the greater part of their days on the road, and at inns, and at a distance from their families, is a requisition which, in our opinion should not be made unless in cases of necessity.

That some of the present Judges do not enjoy health and strength of body sufficient to enable them to undergo the toilsome journies through different climates and seasons which they are called upon to undertake.[122]

The President sent the communication of the Justices to Congress with a letter giving the objections to circuit duties. An act giving partial relief

---

[119] See Pollock v. Farmers' Loan and Trust Co., 157 U. S. 429; 158 U. S. 601 (1894), and Sixteenth Amendment; also Hale v. Iowa State Board of Assessment and Review, 302 U. S. 95 (1937).

[120] Sparks., *op. cit.*, X: 182.

[121] See Griffith J. McRee, *Life and Correspondence of James Iredell*, II: 320, 321.

[122] *American State Papers*, I: 51, 52, 319.

only was passed. This provided that in touring circuits the Justices should be divided in pairs; each pair being confined permanently to one circuit. Only one Justice was required to attend each circuit except in special cases when the Supreme Court might assign two Justices to attend a circuit.[123] The relief afforded by this act was not deemed satisfactory. In response to a letter from President Washington, Chief Justice Jay called attention to deviations from the Constitution by the Judiciary Act, first, in that there was an incompatibility in the same Justices serving on the Supreme Court and on the Circuit Courts; second, that the assignment by act of Congress of the Justices of the Supreme Court to circuit duties was an exercise of power which constitutionally belonged to the President and Senate. Congress ignored the suggestions of the President and the Chief Justice and the matter was not again raised until the passage of the reorganization act in the closing weeks of Adams' Administration. The Act of February 13, 1801, eliminated circuit riding by the Justices. Other changes in the organization and jurisdiction of the federal courts which were passed at the same time will be considered later.[124] The repeal of this act before it took effect[125] restored the former system which the Supreme Court said in an opinion by Justice Paterson in 1803 had been confirmed by practice and acquiescence and that the contemporaneous interpretation of the Constitution was "too strong and obstinate to be shaken or controlled."[126]

President Adams, in his speech at the opening of the first session of the Sixth Congress in 1799, recommended a revision of the federal judicial system as "indispensably necessary."[127] Though a committee of the House of Representatives was appointed and a bill was reported, action upon it was finally postponed. The political implications of this bill were indicated by the comment of a member of the House in opposing the motion to postpone its further consideration that "the close of the present Executive's authority was at hand, and from his experience he was more capable to choose suitable persons to fill the office than another."[128]

The years when Chief Justice Jay presided over the Court were not eventful so far as the decisions on constitutional law are concerned. With the exception of the *Chisholm Case* in which the Court's decision was

---

[123] Act of March 2, 1793, 1 Stat. 333.

[124] 2 *U. S. Statutes at Large*, 89.

[125] *Ibid.*, p. 132.

[126] Stuart v. Laird, 1 Cranch 299.

[127] *Annals of Congress*, 6th Cong., pp. 188, 189.

[128] *Ibid.*, p. 648; cf. Max Farrand, "The Judiciary Act of 1801," *Amer. Hist. Rev.* (July, 1900), V: 683.

reversed by constitutional amendment, there were only a few cases of real significance in American legal history. The Chief Justice and his Associates, however, left a much greater impress on constitutional law than these few decisions would indicate and justified Madison's observation that the quiet subtlety of the Chief Justice is something to be watched and feared.[129] Though there was no definite decision on the right of the Court to review and hold void acts of Congress, the attitude which the Court would take when the issue arose in an actual case was manifested beyond reasonable doubt. The precedent was established that the Court would consider and render decisions in actual controversies only and hence would not render advisory opinions, though the unsubstantial nature of the controversy in the *Hylton Case* was slurred over. It was declared in a number of cases that the Court was not confined to the express language of the Constitution concerning its jurisdiction and the interpretation which would be placed upon the fundamental law. The federal courts were regarded as one of the chief agencies for the establishment of federal supremacy and for the checking of the pretensions and powers of the states. In fact, some of the most significant principles and theories developed through the process of constitutional construction had their origin during this period. The aristocratic notions of the Chief Justice, his exaggerated views regarding the aloofness and independence of judges, as well as his characteristic obstinacy, left a marked impression upon constitutional interpretation. The way was prepared for the peculiar American concepts of judicial supremacy and superiority. And above all, the Justices of the Supreme Court began the practice of settling questions of a political nature as envisaged under the general and often indefinite language of the written Constitution.

The lack of coördination between the Executive and the Legislature, which was characteristic of colonial times, was not engrafted upon the federal Constitution, but was soon injected into the American political mechanism by current ideas of political thought and practice. The Supreme Court played a significant role in making the departments separate and independent, thus evolving a check and balance philosophy of a different type from that envisaged by most of the members of the federal Convention. Two of the original and distinctive features of the American principles and practices of government are credited to the ability and ingenuity of the framers of the Constitution. These are the federal system of government and the delicately adjusted system of checks and balances. It does not detract, however, from the credit and honor due the statesmen of this time to recognize one of the primary

[129] Gaillard Hunt, ed., *The Writings of James Madison* (New York, 1900), VI: 110, 111.

facts of American legal history, namely, that the essential ideas and principles of federalism, as they are accepted and understood today, and the most significant phases of the modern concepts of the check and balance system were created through the process of constitutional interpretation. Chief Justice Jay took significant steps toward the adoption of some of the foremost doctrines of the Federalist party as an integral part of American constitutional law.

CHAPTER V

The Federal Courts during the Administration of John Adams

THE SUPREME COURT during the Administration of John Adams considered and decided only a few issues of political importance, but the work of the Justices in trying cases on circuit and in performing nonjudicial functions involved them in acrimonious political strife. It is sometimes asserted that the Court was subjected to relatively little criticism until, at the end of the Administration of President Adams, it was thrust into the political arena and became involved in the consideration and advocacy of some of the foremost doctrines of the Federalists. Federal common law jurisdiction, the interpretation of neutral rights, expatriation, and the notorious Alien and Sedition Laws—these and other matters of prime political import—came to the federal courts for determination.[1] Though the record of the federal courts for the first ten years scarcely warrants the contention that they were free from attack, it is true that beginning with 1799 they were subjected to persistent and sometimes severe partisan condemnation. Only three Justices, Paterson, Moore, and Washington, attended the August session in 1800. Chief Justice Ellsworth was in France on a special mission for the President. Cushing was ill, and Chase was speaking on behalf of Adams in the presidential campaign. Justice Chase's absence was the occasion, as Warren notes, of "a savage attack from the Anti-Federal newspapers."[2] But before turning to the major political issues of Adams' Administration, in which the Judiciary became involved, it is necessary to refer to some of the less controversial decisions.

On a question submitted by the Attorney General in the February term of 1797 whether, on the adoption of the Eleventh Amendment, all suits against any one of the United States by citizens of another state were to be dropped, the Court gave a unanimous opinion "that the amendment being constitutionally adopted, there could not be exercised any jurisdiction, in any case past or future, in which a State was sued by the citizens of another State, or by citizens or subjects of any foreign

---

[1] Cf. Charles Warren, *The Supreme Court in United States History* (Boston, 1922), I: 158, 159.
[2] *Ibid.,* p. 156, n. 1.

State.[3] The decision in *Chisholm v. Georgia*[4] having been reversed on a referendum to the various state legislatures there was nothing else for the Justices to do but to accept the result until a change in public sentiment might render it possible to mollify its rigor.

Ex Post Facto Laws and Retrospective Acts Affecting Private Rights

One of the few issues at this time touching the realm of political controversy arose in *Calder v. Bull*.[5] The legislature of Connecticut had passed a law setting aside a decree of a court of justice which had disapproved a will. As a result of the law a new trial was held by the same court and the will approved. Appeals to the superior and supreme courts of the state resulted in decrees affirming the decision of the trial court. In the meantime, more than eighteen months had elapsed and by the law of limitations the right of appeal to Caleb Bull and his wife had lapsed. It was contended for this reason that the Connecticut law was an *ex post facto* law and was prohibited by the federal Constitution. In deciding the case the Justices again followed the custom of delivering their opinions *seriatim*.

Justice Chase reiterated the view expressed in earlier cases that, as a self-evident proposition, the several state legislatures retained all the powers delegated to them by the state constitutions which were not expressly taken away by the Constitution of the United States. All the powers delegated by the people of the United States to the federal government were defined and no constructive powers could be exercised by it. After stating emphatically that all nondelegated powers remained with the states, Chase turned to the realm of political philosophy and defended the proposition that there were implied limitations upon the legislative power as a general principle of the social compact in the following dictum:

I cannot subscribe to the omnipotence of a state legislature, or that it is absolute and without control; although its authority should not be expressly restrained by the constitution, or fundamental law of the State. The people of the United States erected their constitutions, or forms of government, to establish justice, to promote the general welfare, to secure the blessings of liberty; and to protect their persons and property from violence. The purpose for which men enter into society will determine the nature and terms of the social compact; and as they are the foundation of the legislative power, they will decide what are the proper objects of it: The nature, and ends of legislative power will limit the exercise of it. This fundamental principle flows from the very nature of our free Republican governments, that no man should be compelled

---

[3] Hollingsworth v. Virginia, 3 Dallas 378 at 381 (1798).
[4] 2 Dallas 419 (1793).
[5] 3 Dallas 385 (1798).

to do what the laws do not require; nor to refrain from acts which the laws permit. There are acts which the federal or state legislature cannot do, without exceeding their authority. There are certain vital principles in our free Republican governments, which will determine and overrule an apparent and flagrant abuse of legislative power; as to authorize manifest injustice by positive law; or to take away that security for personal liberty, or private property, for the protection whereof the government was established. An act of the legislature (for I cannot call it a law) contrary to the great first principles of the social compact, cannot be considered a rightful exercise of legislative authority. The obligation of a law in governments established on express compact, and on Republican principles, must be determined by the nature of the power, on which it is founded. A few instances will suffice to explain what I mean. A law that punished a citizen for an innocent action, or, in other words, for an act, which, when done, was in violation of no existing law; a law that destroys, or impairs, the lawful private contracts of citizens; a law that makes a man a judge in his own cause; or a law that takes property from A and gives it to B: It is against all reason and justice, for a people to entrust a legislature with such powers; and, therefore, it cannot be presumed that they have done it. The genius, the nature, and the spirit, of our state governments, amount to a prohibition of such acts of legislation; and the general principles of law and reason forbid them. The legislature may enjoin, permit, forbid, and punish; they may declare new crimes; and establish rules of conduct for all its citizens in future cases; they may command what is right, and prohibit what is wrong; but they cannot change innocence into guilt; or punish innocence as a crime; or violate the right of an antecedent lawful private contract; or the right of private property. To maintain that our federal, or state, legislature possesses such powers, if they had not been expressly restrained; would, in my opinion, be a political heresy, altogether inadmissible in our free Republican governments.[6]

This dictum of Chase's was in accord with one of the primary objectives of the Federalists, that is, to limit legislative power with respect to contracts and property interests. Moreover, when constitutional provisions were not definite or specific enough to protect these interests from popular control, the theory of implied limitations was called into play in order to place limits on legislative powers not expressly inhibited by constitutions. Justice Chase's doctrine was frequently referred to and applied by the courts in developing by judicial construction a variety of implied restrictions on legislatures for the purpose of protecting vested or acquired rights.

But Justice Chase did not believe that the *ex post facto* clause of the federal Constitution was inserted to secure the citizen in his private rights of either property or contracts.[7] If the meaning of the words *ex post facto* were given the broad significance for which the plaintiffs contended, Chase observed, there would be no need of restrictions with respect to legislative acts affecting private rights, such as the prohibition on the states from passing laws impairing the obligation of contracts. In his judgment the term *ex post facto*, in accordance with long usage,

---

[6] 3 Dallas 387, 388.   [7] *Ibid.*, p. 390.

had acquired a technical meaning and was intended to be limited to acts regulating crimes and criminal procedure. Although Chase thought that the federal and state legislatures should not deprive citizens of rights vested in them by existing laws "unless for the benefit of the whole community; and on making full satisfaction," he believed that no vested right had been disturbed in this case. Justice Chase did not feel called upon to decide whether the act of the Connecticut legislature was void, but he indicated his attitude when he said: "If I ever exercise the jurisdiction I will not decide any law to be void, but in a very clear case."[8]

Justice Paterson, finding that it was the practice in Connecticut for the legislature to act as a final judicial body, agreed with the theories of Chase, and at the conclusion of his opinion remarked:

I had an ardent desire to have extended the provision in the Constitution to retrospective laws in general. There is neither policy nor safety in such laws; and, therefore, I have always had a strong aversion against them. . . . But on full consideration, I am convinced, that *ex post facto* laws must be limited in the manner already expressed; they must be taken in their technical, which is also their common and general, acceptation, and are not to be understood in their literal sense.[9]

Justice Iredell concurred in the result but not in the reasoning of these Justices. He expressed an opinion against the theory of implied limitations on the legislative power. Referring to the policy of the people of the United States when they framed their constitutions to define the objects of the legislative power and to restrain its exercise within fixed boundaries, he said:

If any act of Congress, or of the legislature of a State, violates those constitutional provisions, it is unquestionably void; though, I admit, that as the authority to declare it void is of a delicate and awful nature, the Court will never resort to that authority, but in a clear and urgent case. If, on the other hand, the legislature of the Union, or the legislature of any member of the Union, shall pass a law, within the general scope of their constitutional power, the Court cannot pronounce it to be void, merely because it is, in their judgment, contrary to the principles of natural justice. The ideas of natural justice are regulated by no fixed standards; the ablest and the purest men have differed upon the subject; and all that the Court could properly say, in such an event, would be, that the legislature, possessed of an equal right of opinion, had passed an act which, in the opinion of the Judges, was inconsistent with the abstract principles of natural justice.[10]

The judgment of the Court was against bringing the protection of vested interests under the *ex post facto* provision. Chase's dictum in the case of *Calder v. Bull,* which was gradually accepted as the correct legal meaning of the phrase *"ex post facto,"* is significant because it was necessary to find a basis for prohibiting legislative acts affecting civil rights retrospectively in the law of nature or of reason in the contract clause

---

[8] 3 Dallas 394, 395.   [9] *Ibid.,* p. 397.   [10] *Ibid.,* p. 399.

of the federal Constitution and, later, in the due process of law clause. And as opportunities arose, the Judges built up by the process of judicial construction a doctrine of implied prohibitions applicable to many types of retrospective legislative acts. It is doubtful whether Chase's definition of the term *"ex post facto"* is in accord with the intention of the framers of the Constitution. A careful examination of the debates in the federal Convention and in the state ratifying conventions reveals that many men at this time thought of the inhibition against the enactment of *ex post facto* laws as applicable to both civil and criminal acts. Chief Justice Marshall expressed doubt concerning the validity of Chase's interpretation.[11] Justice Johnson referred later to the "unhappy idea" that the phrase *"ex post facto* was confined to criminal cases exclusively; a decision which leaves a large class of arbitrary legislative acts without the prohibitions of the Constitution."[12] And this exposition of the term was approved by Justice Story.[13] But Chase's construction of the words used in the Constitution prevailed, and it remained for future Judges to find ways and means to prohibit legislative acts from having a retroactive effect upon acquired or vested rights.

In *Wilson v. Daniel*,[14] Chief Justice Ellsworth, speaking for the majority of the Court, adopted a latitudinarian view of the Judiciary Act of 1789 regarding appeals on a writ of error. As to the limit of two thousand dollars for issuance of such a writ the majority of the Justices thought the basis for determination was the amount involved in the original controversy. The minority, in the opinion of Iredell, believed the sum actually rendered in judgment should be the basis for the issuance of such a writ. When it was contended that an act of the legislature of Georgia passed in 1782 banishing the plaintiff from that state and confiscating his property was repugnant to the constitution of the state and relief was sought from the federal courts,[15] the Supreme Court refused to hold the act repugnant to the state constitution. Justice Chase in his remarks referred to the right of the Judiciary to declare a legislative act void. Though it is alleged

that all acts of the legislature, in direct opposition to the prohibitions of the Constitution, would be void; yet it still remains a question, where the power resides to declare

[11] Fletcher v. Peck, 10 Cranch 138 (1810).
[12] Satterlee v. Matthewson, 2 Peters 415, 416 (1829).
[13] *Commentaries on the Constitution* (5th ed.), II: 219; see also Oliver P. Field, "Ex Post Facto in the Constitution," 20 *Mich. Law Rev.* (Jan., 1922), 315, and my articles "Judicial Review of Legislation in the United States and the Doctrines of Vested Rights and of Implied Limitations on Legislatures," 2 *Texas Law Rev.* (Apr., June, 1924), 257, 387, and 3 *Texas Law Rev.* (Dec., 1924), 1.
[14] 3 Dallas 401 (1798).
[15] Cooper v. Telfair, 4 Dallas 14 (1800).

it void? It is, indeed, a general opinion, it is expressly admitted by all this bar, and some of the Judges have, individually, in the circuits, decided, that the Supreme Court can declare an act of Congress to be unconstitutional, and, therefore, invalid; but there is no adjudication of the Supreme Court itself upon the point. I concur, however, in the general sentiment, with reference to the period, when the existing Constitution came into operation.[16]

Justice Paterson thought the authority to declare a legislative act void could apply only "to a clear and unequivocal breach of the Constitution and not a doubtful and argumentative application"; whereas Cushing believed that courts possessed this power but did not regard this case as a proper instance of its exercise.[17]

The Circuit Court for the Pennsylvania district avoided some political complications by denying a motion for the holding of a special court for the trial of indictments against persons charged with high treason by levying war against the United States. As the trials arose out of the Whisky Insurrection in the western counties of Pennsylvania, the Court observed that "it is evident, that nothing but an armed force has recently been sufficient to quell the insurrection, and to arrest the insurgents; and, we hope, that it will never be expected from the exercise of a judicial discretion, that a court of justice shall be voluntarily placed in a situation, where the execution of its functions, and the maintenance of its authority, must depend on the same military auxiliary."[18] In the subsequent proceedings in this and other cases the Justices were not so adept in escaping political entanglements.

Bas v. Tingy[19] brought to the Court an issue arising out of the depredations upon American commerce by French privateers and the retaliatory acts of Congress. The questions raised were whether the act of March 3, 1799,[20] applied only in the event of a future general war and whether France was an enemy of the United States within the meaning of the law. The Court held that a state of hostility existed between the United States and France which was in the nature of limited warfare. France was, therefore, considered an enemy of the United States and the provisions of the act of Congress were applied. In view of the fact that the Anti-Federalists were generally favorable to France and its conduct toward the United States, the Court's decision was strongly condemned. Partisan resentment was such that impeachment of the Justices who rendered the decision was urged.[21] Similar objections were raised to the

---

[16] 4 Dallas 19.
[17] *Ibid.*, pp. 19, 20.
[18] United States v. The Insurgents, 3 Dallas 513, 514 (1799).
[19] 4 Dallas 37 (1800).
[20] 1 Stat. 742.
[21] See *Aurora*, Aug. 22, 23, 25, 1800.

view of Chief Justice Ellsworth in the Circuit Court that an American citizen had no right of expatriation because no such right was recognized under the common law of England.[22] The common law of this country, said the Chief Justice, remains the same as it was before the Revolution. It was in the sedition cases, however, that the administration of justice was characterized by extreme partisanship.

TRIAL OF CASES UNDER THE ALIEN AND SEDITION LAWS

Prosecutions for seditious libel against the government or its officers began before the passage of the Alien and Sedition Laws. These prosecutions were based on the doctrine announced by Judge Peters in 1798 that there was a common law of the United States which gave authority to the federal courts to punish crimes other than those defined by federal statutes and applied for the first time in the case of *United States v. Ravara.*[23]

In *United States v. Worrall,*[24] Justice Chase dissented on the ground that the federal government had no common law jurisdiction and that no indictment could be maintained in these courts for offenses merely at common law. But Judge Peters rendering the decision of the Court defended the common law jurisdiction of the federal courts as follows:

Whenever a government has been established, I have always supposed, that a power to preserve itself, was a necessary, and an inseparable, concomitant. But the existence of the federal government would be precarious, it could no longer be called an independent government, if, for the punishment of offences of this nature, tending to obstruct and pervert the administration of its affairs, an appeal must be made to the state tribunals, or the offenders must escape with absolute immunity.

The power to punish misdemeanors, is originally and strictly a common law power; of which, I think, the United States are constitutionally possessed. It might have been exercised by Congress in the form of a legislative act; but, it may, also, in my opinion be enforced in a course of judicial proceeding. Whenever an offence aims at the subversion of any federal institution, or at the corruption of its public officers, it is an offence against the well-being of the United States; from its very nature, it is cognizable under their authority; and, consequently, it is within the jurisdiction of this Court, by virtue of the 11th section of the Judicial Act.[25]

Alexander Hamilton[26] and Chief Justice Ellsworth supported Judge Peters' view. In his charge to the grand jury in Charleston, South Caro-

---

[22] *United States v. Williams,* Francis Wharton, *State Trials of the United States during the Administrations of Washington and Adams* (Philadelphia, 1849), p. 652, and *Connecticut Courant,* September 30, 1799.

[23] 2 Dallas 297 (1793). Cf. above, p. 126.

[24] *Ibid.,* p. 384 (1793).

[25] *Ibid.,* p. 395.

[26] Hamilton thought it would "be useful to declare that all such writings, etc. which at common law are libels, if levelled against any officer whatsoever of the United

lina, in 1799, Ellsworth advised the jury to bring indictments against those committing acts "manifestly subversive of the national government." Favoring the punishment of acts deemed criminal by the common law, whether or not they were defined as crimes by federal acts, he charged the jury to bring indictments against those committing acts regarded as "opposing the existence of the national government or the efficient exercise of its legitimate powers."[27] The efforts to secure the adoption of the doctrine of a federal common law supplementary to the Constitution and statutes indicates the extreme centralizing tendencies which were advocated by the Federalists in the early years of the American government.

It was the uncertainty and probable ineffectiveness of the prosecutions for seditious libel attempted under the common law that led to the enactment of the Alien and Sedition Acts. Though the most active steps to secure the enforcement of these laws were taken by Secretary of State Timothy Pickering, the Justices of the Supreme Court took no small part in the bringing of trials and in securing convictions. Grand juries were urged to bring indictments.[28] Justice Chase was particularly active in this respect. He was responsible for the bringing of an indictment against Thomas Callender and tried to secure similar action against the editors of Republican papers in Baltimore and Wilmington. Through the combined efforts of Administration leaders, federal district attorneys, and the Supreme Court Justices, proceedings were begun or attempted against "the editors of Republican newspapers, in each of the States, except New Hampshire and Rhode Island, where there were few Republicans, and in the States of the far South and West."[29] Because most of the indictments and prosecutions were directed against the proprietors, editors, or chief writers of the Republican papers, the laws were regarded primarily as a means of silencing the Republican press.

The treatment in *The Chronicle,* a Republican paper in Boston, of

States, shall be cognizable in the courts of the United States. To preserve confidence in the officers of the general government by preserving their reputations from malicious and unfounded slanders, is essential to enable them to fulfil the ends of their appointment. It is, therefore, both constitutional and politic to place their reputations under the guardianship of the courts of the United States. They ought not to be left to the cold and reluctant protection of the state courts, always temporizing and sometimes disaffected." Henry Cabot Lodge, ed., *The Works of Alexander Hamilton* (Const. ed., New York, 1904), X: 335, 336.

[27] See *Federal Gazette* and *Baltimore Daily Advertiser,* June 6, 1799.

[28] See Justice Iredell's charge to the grand jury at Philadelphia, April 11, 1799, Griffith J. McRee, *Life and Correspondence of James Iredell* (New York, 1857–1858), II: 551 ff.

[29] Frank Maloy Anderson, "The Enforcement of the Alien and Sedition Laws," Amer. Hist. Assn., *Annual Report,* 1912, p. 120.

the controversy over the Kentucky and Virginia Resolutions, according to Frank M. Anderson, "was a model for fairness and courtesy toward its opponents; measured even by the standards of today, there was little in its tone to which exception might fairly be taken." But such moderation did not prevent the persecution of its publishers. As the result of a charge to the grand jury by Chief Justice Dana of the state supreme court, indictments were brought against Thomas Adams, editor and publisher of *The Chronicle,* and Abijah Adams, a younger brother, employed in the office. Owing to a serious illness from which he soon died, Thomas Adams was not arrested; but his brother was apprehended and brought to trial.[30]

Charges of the unfairness of the federal Judges in the trials under the Sedition Law were frequently made. These charges related to the alleged packing of the juries, the unfair construction of the law by the courts, and the attitude of the Judges during the trials. One of the grounds for such charges was that the grand juries which brought the indictments were composed preponderantly, if not exclusively, of Federalists. Though information is lacking concerning the selection of the trial juries, there is evidence sufficient to show that something approaching the packing of the jury took place in the *Callender Case*[31] and that the juries were not impartial in other cases.[32] The constitutionality of the Sedition Law was assumed and no argument on or consideration of this issue was permitted. And the conduct of the Justices, though not devoid of bias, was generally not as objectionable as was the treatment accorded to political opponents by Justice Chase. The Federalists, observed Anderson, manifested, however, an imperious and intolerant attitude towards their Republican opponents, and the imprisonment of Abijah Adams indicates that they were ready "upon the slightest provocation to treat the opposition to the policy of the administration, whether federal or state, as a crime."[33] Some instances of the partisan practices of the Justices were such as to discredit the administration of justice in the federal courts.

Matthew Lyon of Vermont, Representative in Congress, was one of the first men against whom an indictment was brought under the Sedition Act. He had charged President Adams with a "continual grasp for power . . . an unbounded thirst for ridiculous pomp, foolish adulation

---

[30] Frank Maloy Anderson, "Contemporary Opinion of the Virginia and Kentucky Resolutions," *Amer. Hist. Rev.* (Oct., 1899), V: 61–63.

[31] Wharton, *State Trials,* p. 688.

[32] Anderson, Amer. Hist. Assn., *Annual Report,* 1912, p. 125, 126; and *Annals of Congress,* 8th Cong., 2d sess., pp. 195 ff.

[33] Anderson, *Amer. Hist. Rev.,* V: 229.

and selfish avarice." For this and other supposed indiscretions of speech, he was tried for bringing the President and government of the United States in contempt. Tried by a partisan jury and an unfriendly court he was sentenced to four months in jail and the payment of a fine of one thousand dollars. To complete his discomfiture and humiliation he was cruelly and brutally treated as a prisoner.[34]

While in charge of the second trial of Fries, Justice Chase allowed on the jury those men only who admitted they were unfriendly to the prisoner and who had expressed themselves as disapproving his conduct. When Chase informed the attorneys for the defense that he had made up his mind on the law of treason and distributed copies of his views, the attorneys, Dallas and Lewis, withdrew from the case.[35] As the trial proceeded without any attorney for the defense, Justice Chase informed Fries that he might ask the witnesses or the Court questions but warned him to "be careful to ask no question wherein you may possibly criminate yourself, for remember, whatever you say to your own crimination, is evidence with the jury; but if you say anything to your justification, it is not evidence."[36] The Philadelphia bar, after inquiring into Chase's behavior at this trial, resolved not to appear before him while on circuit.

Justice Chase had become odious even to his associates, for he was too ardent a partisan, trying cases like a political boss seeking revenge. As a Federalist, he was more outspoken both on and off the Bench than some of his associates. In the *Callender Case* the marshal was instructed not to put any Democrats on the jury. And every point on which the defense rested was promptly swept aside by the arbitrary decisions of Chase.[37] While holding court on circuit in Delaware, he assumed the role of prosecutor and tried to secure an indictment of the editor of the *Mirror of the Times and General Advertiser* published at Wilmington.[38]

Answering the contention that the courts should be guided and controlled by a legislative construction of the Constitution with respect to the meaning of treason, Judge Peters, in charging the jury in the first

---

[34] Wharton, *State Trials*, pp. 333 ff. See also trial of Thomas Cooper, *ibid.*, pp. 659 ff., at which an effort was made to compel President Adams to attend as a witness.

[35] Wharton, *op. cit.*, pp. 612 ff.

[36] Wharton, *op. cit.*, p. 629.

[37] Walter D. Coles, "Politics and the Supreme Court of the United States," 27 *Amer. Law Rev.* (Mar.–Apr., 1893), 182–191 ff.

[38] See *Annals of Congress*, 8th Cong., 2d sess., p. 87. Historians with nationalist leanings and an anti-Jeffersonian bias can find little in the conduct of Chase to condemn. To Channing, Chase "was abrupt and overbearing in his manner, but this was not a misdemeanor, much less a high misdemeanor or a high crime. He had tried to hasten matters that did not seem to him as important as they had to the defendants who were in court before him." *History of the United States*, IV: 288.

Fries Case,[39] stated the opposing view, which had now become one of the main tenets of the Federalist party. "The law, though established by legislative acts, or settled by judicial decisions," said he, "may be altered by Congress *by express words,* in laws consistent with the Constitution. But a mere legislative construction, drawn from any act by intendment, ought not to repeal positive laws or annul judicial decisions. The Judiciary have the duty assigned to them of interpreting, declaring and explaining—the legislature that of making, or altering, or repealing laws. But the decision of a question on the constitutionality of a law is vested in the judiciary department."[40] The doctrine that the courts were invested with authority to place final and conclusive interpretations on the meaning of the Constitution to which the other departments and political agencies were expected to submit was taking form.

In the *Callender Case* the attorneys defending Callender, Wirt and Nicholas, argued that since under the common law the jury had a right to decide the law and the fact, it was the duty of the jury, if they regarded the Sedition Law as contrary to the Constitution, to declare the law void and to refuse to convict a person under it. In supporting the doctrine of judicial review of acts of Congress, Judge Chase, who was presiding, held that the jury did not have such authority and that to concede such a right would be extremely dangerous.[41] "By the Constitution," continued Chase,

this right is expressly granted to the judicial power of the United States, and is recognized by Congress by a perpetual statute. . . .

Every man must admit that the power of deciding the constitutionality of any law of the United States, or of any particular State, is one of the greatest and most important powers the people could grant.

Such power is restrictive of the legislative power of the Union, and also of the several States; not absolute and unlimited, but confined to such cases only where the law in question shall clearly appear to have been prohibited by the federal Constitution, and not in any doubtful case. On referring to the ninth section of the first article of the Constitution, there may be seen many restrictions imposed on the powers of the national legislature, and also on the powers of the several state legislatures. Among the special exceptions to their authority, is the power to make *ex post facto* laws, to lay any capitation, or other direct tax, unless in proportion to the census; to lay any tax or duty on articles exported from any State, &c. &c.

It should be remembered that the judicial power of the United States is co-existent, co-extensive, and co-ordinate with, and altogether independent of, the federal Legislature, or the Executive. By the sixth article of the Constitution, among other things, it is declared that the Constitution shall be the supreme law of the land. By the third article, it is established "that the judicial power of the United States shall be vested

---

[39] Wharton, *State Trials,* p. 482.

[40] *Ibid.,* p. 584. For a similar opinion by Justice Iredell, see *ibid.,* p. 588.

[41] *Ibid.,* pp. 709 ff.

in one Supreme Court, and in such other inferior courts as Congress may from time to time ordain and establish; and that the judicial power shall extend to all cases in law and equity, arising under the Constitution and laws of the United States."

Among the cases which may arise under the Constitution, are all the restrictions on the authority of Congress, and of the state legislatures.

It is very clear, that the present case arises under the Constitution, and also under a law of the United States, and therefore it is the very case to which the Constitution declares the judicial powers of the United States shall extend.

It is incontrovertible that the Constitution is the supreme law, and therefore, it must be the rule by which the federal and state Judges are bound to regulate their decisions. By the sixth article of the Constitution, it is provided (among other things) that all members of Congress, and of the several state legislatures, and all judicial officers of the United States, and of the several States, shall be bound by an oath or affirmation to support the Constitution. By this provision, I understand that every person, so sworn or affirmed, promises that he will preserve the Constitution as established, and the distribution of powers thereby granted; and that he will not assent to any amendment or alteration thereof, but in the mode prescribed in the fifth article; and that he will not consent to any usurpation by any one branch of the Legislature upon the other, or upon the Executive, or by the Executive upon either branch, or by any department or officer of government, of the power granted to another; or that the power granted to either shall be exercised by others.

I also understand by this engagement, that the person taking it, promises also that he will oppose by his example, argument, advice, and persuasion, and by all other means in his power, force only excepted, any design, advice or attempt to impair or destroy the Constitution.

If this exposition of this solemn obligation is substantially correct, I cannot believe that any person having the same understanding of it, will maintain that a petit jury can rightfully exercise the power granted by the Constitution to the federal Judiciary.

From these considerations I draw this conclusion, that the judicial power of the United States is the only proper and competent authority to decide whether any statute made by Congress (or any of the state legislatures) is contrary to, or in violation of, the federal Constitution. . . .

I believe that it has been the general and prevailing opinion in all the Union, that the power now wished to be exercised by a jury, properly belongs to the federal courts.[42]

Justice Chase did not refer to any express language or requirement in the Constitution when he held that when the Justices have found a conflict between an act of Congress or of a state legislature and a provision of the Constitution and have indicated in their opinion that a legislative act is void, all other officers or agencies of the federal and state governments are required to accept the opinion and judgment of the federal Justices as conclusive and binding so far as all related official acts are concerned. From the standpoint of an effective national government the assumption of such authority was perhaps desirable. But it was an assumption of authority without any direct grant in the Constitution.

---

[42] Wharton, *State Trials*, pp. 715, 716.

When Matthew Lyon, defending himself on the charge of seditious libel, urged the jury to regard the Sedition Law as unconstitutional, Justice Paterson charged the jurors: "You have nothing whatever to do with the constitutionality or unconstitutionality of the Sedition law."[43] There appeared to be little doubt how the federal Justices would decide when a case arose involving the validity of an act of Congress.[44] The Alien and Sedition Laws, however, brought forth a direct and emphatic assertion of the independence and sovereignty of the states under the federal Constitution.

KENTUCKY AND VIRGINIA RESOLUTIONS AND THE DOCTRINE OF JUDICIAL REVIEW OF LEGISLATION

The opposition to the Alien and Sedition Laws brought to the forefront the issue whether, as claimed by the Federalists, it was the exclusive function of the Supreme Court of the United States to interpret the Constitution and whether its interpretation, when given, was binding on the coördinate departments of the federal government as well as upon the states. It was the adoption of the Kentucky and Virginia Resolutions which made the controversy on this matter one of national prominence. The Kentucky Resolutions, which were drafted by John Breckenridge and Thomas Jefferson,[45] stated the familiar compact philosophy as the

---

[43] *Ibid.*, p. 336.

[44] See also *ibid.*, p. 638. Historians are inclined to minimize the effect of the Alien and Sedition Acts. Channing asserts that "there were a few prosecutions under the Sedition Act, but not many. The trials aroused indignation, partly because the people were unfamiliar with the action of the federal Judiciary in criminal cases. . . . There was undoubtedly some harshness and some injustice to individuals as a result of the passage of the laws, but it was trifling in comparison with the harm done by Frenchmen in setting on foot expeditions against the Spanish dominions and in seeking to separate the American people from their chosen rulers." *History of the United States* (New York, 1926), IV: 222–224. James Truslow Adams believes that Channing's defense of the enforcement of the Alien and Sedition Laws was influenced by the war hysteria of 1917. See *The Living Jefferson* (New York, 1936), p. 288.

[45] Ethelbert Dudley Warfield in his work on *The Kentucky Resolutions of 1798* (New York, 1887) gives the following account of the authorship of these Resolutions:

"John Breckenridge was the responsible author of the Kentucky Resolutions of 1798. He formed the design of submitting such a series of resolutions to the Kentucky legislature, and sought and received assistance in the preparation of a suitable draught from various persons, but especially from Thomas Jefferson, who had independently conceived a similar design with regard to North Carolina, and probably also Virginia. At a conference at Monticello, Mr. Breckenridge, Mr. Jefferson, and Colonel Nicholas outlined the policy to be pursued, and Mr. Jefferson, at the request of his companions, embodied it in a draught, which passed into Mr. Breckenridge's hands. This draught he made the basis of the paper he offered in the legislature, but he subjected it to a searching revision, in the course of which it was altered and modified in important respects, and to a very marked extent. All this was done upon his sole responsibility,

basis for the formation of the federal union and the general doctrine of confining the federal government to delegated powers. Then it was asserted "that to this compact each State acceded as a State, and is an integral party, its co-States forming as to itself the other party; that the government created by this compact was not made the exclusive or final judge of the extent of the powers delegated to itself; since that would have made its discretion, and not the Constitution, the measure of its powers; but that as in all other cases of compact among parties having no common judge, each party has an equal right to judge for itself, as well of infractions as of the mode and measure of redress."

In a second set of Resolutions passed by the Kentucky legislature in 1799 it was declared: "That the several States who formed that instrument being sovereign and independent, have the unquestionable right to judge of its infractions; and that a nullification by those sovereignties of all unauthorized acts done under color of that instrument is the rightful remedy." This is one of the earliest uses of the idea of a nullification by the states of a federal act deemed to be unauthorized by the Constitution. In the Jefferson draft of the Resolutions a clause of similar purport was included: "Where powers are assumed which have not been dele-

---

and the document was offered as his, and, after a few verbal amendments, passed under his sponsorship." See p. 163.

For the views of Thomas Jefferson on his part in the preparation of the Resolutions, see his letter to J. Cabell Breckenridge, December 11, 1821. *Writings* (Ford ed.), VII: 290.

The following extract from Jefferson's draft for the Kentucky Resolutions relating to the question of finality in the interpretation of the powers of the nation and the states is of special interest:

"*Resolved*, That the several States composing the United States of America, are not united on the principle of unlimited submission to their general government; but that by a compact under the style and title of a Constitution for the United States, and of Amendments thereto, they constituted a general government for special purposes; delegated to that government certain definite powers, reserving, each State to itself, the residuary mass of right to their own self-government; and that whensoever the general government assumes undelegated powers, its acts are unauthoritative, void, and of no force: that to this compact each State acceded as a State, and is an integral party, its co-States forming as to itself, the other party. That the government created by this compact was not made the exclusive or final judge of the extent of the powers delegated to itself, since that would have made its discretion, and not the Constitution the measure of its powers; but that, as in all other cases of compact among powers having no common judge, each party has an equal right to judge for itself, as well of infractions as of the mode and measure of redress.

"*Resolved*, That the Constitution of the United States having delegated to Congress a power to punish treason, counterfeiting the securities and current coin of the United States, piracies, and felonies committed on the high seas, and offences against the law of nations, and no other crimes whatsoever; and it being true as a general principle, and one of the amendments to the Constitution having also declared, that 'the powers not delegated to the United States by the Constitution, nor prohibited by it to the States, are reserved to the States respectively, or to the people,' therefore . . . that the

gated a nullification of the act is the right remedy; that every State has a natural right in cases not within the compact (*casus non foederis*) to nullify of their own authority all assumptions of power by others within their limits."

Similar Resolutions adopted by Virginia which were drafted by James Madison also affirmed the belief in the compact theory and, regarding the aforesaid acts as unconstitutional, declared that "in case of a deliberate, palpable, and dangerous exercise of other powers, not granted by the said compact, the States who are parties thereto have the right, and are in duty bound, to interpose, for arresting the progress of the evil, and for maintaining, within their respective limits, the authorities, rights, and liberties, appertaining to them."[46]

Because of Jefferson's part in the drafting of the Kentucky Resolutions and his use of the word nullification, he has been criticized by historians partial to the doctrines of nationalism as being responsible for the preparation of the way for nullification and secession.[47] But proposals leading toward nullification and secession were too common and too extensive to be attributed to any man or group of men. Jefferson himself probably intended by such an extreme proposal to place a check

---

power to create, define, and punish such other crimes is reserved, and, of right, appertains solely and exclusively to the respective States, each within its own territory.

"*Resolved*, . . . that no power over the freedom of religion, freedom of speech, or freedom of the press being delegated to the United States by the Constitution, nor prohibited by it to the States, all lawful powers respecting the same did of right remain, and were reserved to the States or the people: that thus was manifested their determination to retain to themselves the right of judging how far the licentiousness of speech and of the press may be abridged without lessening their useful freedom, and how far those abuses which cannot be separated from their use should be tolerated, rather than the use destroyed. . . . That, therefore, the act of Congress . . . for the punishment of certain crimes against the United States, which does abridge the freedom of press, is not law, but is altogether void, and of no force. . . .

"*Resolved*, That the construction applied by the general government . . . to those parts of the Constitution of the United States which delegate to Congress a power 'to lay and collect taxes, duties, imposts, and excises, to pay the debts, and provide for the common defence and general welfare of the United States,' and 'to make all laws which shall be necessary and proper for carrying into execution the powers vested by the Constitution in the government of the United States, or in any department or officer thereof,' goes to the destruction of all limits prescribed to their power by the Constitution: that words meant by the instrument to be subsidiary only to the execution of limited powers, ought not to be so construed as themselves to give unlimited powers, nor a part to be so taken as to destroy the whole residue of that instrument. . . .

"*Resolved*, That, . . . where powers are assumed which have not been delegated, a nullification of the act is the rightful remedy." Draft of the Kentucky Resolutions. *Works* (Ford ed.), VIII: 458 ff.

[46] Elliot's *Debates* (2d ed., 1836), IV: 546, 547, and Madison, *Writings* (Hunt ed.), IV: 507.

[47] See Edward Channing, *History of the United States*, IV: 224 ff.

upon the tendency of the Federalists to claim almost unlimited powers for the federal government and to restrict in every way the authority of the states. Commenting to Madison on the tentative nature of these resolutions, Jefferson said: "I think we should distinctly affirm all the important principles they contain, so as to hold to that ground in the future, and leave the matter in such a train as that we may not be committed absolutely to push the matter to extremities, and yet may be free to push as far as events will render prudent."[48] So far as the doctrine of nullification was concerned, there was little difference between the Jefferson draft of the Kentucky Resolutions and the phrase, "interpose for arresting," selected by Madison, though it was not clearly indicated whether a state could act to arrest federal action on its own initiative or whether action by a majority of the states was necessary to take effective action. It was the latter interpretation to which Madison recurred when states threatening nullification based their right of action on the principles of the Resolutions of 1798 and 1799.[49]

The Kentucky and Virginia Resolutions were submitted to the other states for such action as seemed to them appropriate. In every state north of the Potomac the Federalists, being in a majority, secured expressions of disapproval for the proposals contained in the resolutions, and in most of the resolutions adopted the federal Judiciary was declared to be the proper authority to decide upon the constitutionality of the laws of Congress. The Republicans generally endorsed the protesting features of the resolutions and disapproved of the claim that the courts had exclusive jurisdiction to pass on the validity of acts of Congress, but many doubted the wisdom and expediency of giving the separate states the authority to declare a Congressional act void.[50]

---

[48] *Writings* (Ford ed.), VII: 301. The Kentucky Resolutions, as Homer Carey Hockett observes, "were more than a denunciation of the Alien and Sedition Acts for campaign purposes. Their permanent significance lies in the fact that they rest upon a theory of the Union which the Republicans, and Jefferson especially, were putting forward as the rival of the nationalistic theory which the Federalists and the federal judiciary were developing." *The Constitutional History of the United States: 1776–1826* (New York, 1939), pp. 289, 290.

[49] See chap. xv, appendix.

[50] Anderson, *Amer. Hist. Rev.*, V: 236, 237. The Federalist view of judicial powers of constitutional interpretation may be illustrated by extracts from some of the state resolutions:

"No state government by a legislative act is competent to declare an act of the federal government unconstitutional and void, it being an improper interference with that jurisdiction which is exclusively vested in the Courts of the United States."—Maryland.

This legislature "are persuaded that the decision of all cases in law and equity arising under the Constitution of the United States, and the construction of all laws made in pursuance thereof, are exclusively vested by the people in the Judicial Courts of the United States."—Massachusetts.   (Footnote continued on p. 169.)

Madison's report, prepared as chairman of a committee of the Virginia legislature to consider the replies from the other states, reaffirmed the doctrines of the original resolutions. Starting with the compact philosophy as a basis for the formation of government to which men recurred during the Revolution and the critical period, Madison defended the assertion of the third resolution that the powers of the federal government resulted from a compact to which the states, as states, were parties. The term state was defined as "the people composing those political societies, in their highest sovereign capacity." Thus, the people of each state instead of the people of the United States as a whole were regarded as the parties to the compact.[51]

Edward S. Corwin regards this defense of the compact philosophy as very significant from the standpoint of ideas of nullification. From the very moment that the notion was formulated, and not without vigorous protest from able spokesmen defending the older view in the Virginia legislature itself, Corwin says,

the doctrine that the Constitution was a compact of sovereign States moved forward to the high plane of the axiomatic in the popular consciousness. True the older view still, for more than a generation, found iteration and reiteration in the decisions of Marshall and Story, in the "Commentaries" of Story and Kent, and finally, and with prodigious force, in the orations of Webster. Nevertheless, the evidence is conclusive that, at least from the time of Jackson's election, the newer view had with the generality of Americans in all sections of the country become the dominant one. In the very act of assailing the doctrine of nullification in his famous Proclamation to the People of South Carolina, Jackson accepted the theory of the origin of the Union from which the right of nullification was deduced; and less than a decade later, the apostle of nullification brought the national Senate itself to declare by a vote of thirty-one to thirteen that the Constitution was a compact among state sovereignties.[52]

"The right to decide upon the constitutionality of laws passed by Congress belongs to the Judiciary, the assumption of that power by a state legislature is unwarrantable and dangerous."—New York.

The people of the United States "have committed to the Supreme Judiciary of the Nation the high authority, of ultimately and exclusively deciding on the Constitutionality of all legislative acts."—Pennsylvania.

The Constitution of the United States "vests in the federal Courts, exclusively, and in the Supreme Court of the United States, ultimately, the authority of deciding on the constitutionality of any act or law of the Congress of the United States."—Rhode Island.

See Frank Maloy Anderson, "Contemporary Opinion of the Virginia and Kentucky Resolutions," *Amer. Hist. Rev.* (Oct., 1899), V: 47–51, and Elliot's *Debates* (2d ed., 1888), IV: 532–539.

[51] Elliot's *Debates*, IV: 547.

[52] Edward Samuel Corwin, *National Supremacy; Treaty Power vs. State Power* (New York, 1913), pp. 102, 103; also Thomas Hart Benton, *Abridgment of the Debates of Congress, from 1789 to 1856* (New York, 1857–1861), XIII: 567 ff.

The compact theory of the formation of the federal union, it will be indicated later, had a very significant place in the early decades of American history.

The fourth resolution of the Virginia assembly was approved. It condemned the spirit manifested by the federal government to enlarge its powers by forced constructions of the constitutional charter and criticized the tendency to expound certain general phrases so as to destroy the plan of enumeration of powers in the federal government, because this method of interpretation led inevitably to the consolidation of the states by degrees into one sovereignty. In this connection Madison insisted that the authority granted to Congress to provide for the common defense and general welfare was not a separate and independent grant but was intended merely to extend and qualify the other powers conferred upon Congress. Emphatic exception was taken to the opinion of Hamilton in his report on manufactures that it was left "to the discretion of the national Legislature to pronounce upon the objects which concern the general welfare, and for which, under that description, an appropriation of money is requisite and proper. And there seems to be no room for doubt, that whatever concerns the general interests of learning, of agriculture, of manufactures, and of commerce, is within the sphere of national councils, as far as regards an application of money."[53] Nothing more would be necessary, asserted Madison, to consolidate the states into one sovereignty than to extend the authority of the United States to all cases of the "general welfare"—that is to say, to all cases whatever.[54]

In the course of this report Madison commented rather extensively on the question whether the Justices were authorized to place an authoritative interpretation upon the Constitution which would bind the other departments of government as well as individuals affected by the decision. He asserted:

It has been said that it belongs to the Judiciary of the United States, and not the state legislatures, to declare the meaning of the federal Constitution.

But a declaration that proceedings of the federal government are not warranted by the Constitution, is a novelty neither among the citizens nor among the legislatures of the States; nor are the citizens or the legislature of Virginia singular in the example of it.

Nor can the declarations of either, whether affirming or denying the constitutionality of measures of the federal government, or whether made before or after judicial decisions thereon, be deemed, in any point of view, an assumption of the office of the judge. The declarations in such cases are expressions of opinion, unaccompanied with any other effect than what they may produce on opinion, by exciting reflection. The expo-

[53] *The Works of Alexander Hamilton* (Lodge ed., 1885–1886), IV: 151, 152.
[54] Elliot's *Debates* (2d ed., 1888), IV: 550–553.

sitions of the Judiciary, on the other hand, are carried into immediate effect by force. The former may lead to a change in the legislative expression of the general will— possibly to a change in the opinion of the Judiciary; the latter enforces the general will, whilst that will and that opinion continue unchanged.[55]

But Madison did not regard such a finality of decision as either applicable or conclusive when political or nonjusticiable issues were involved. The report dealt with such a situation in these pertinent observations:

If the deliberate exercise of dangerous powers, palpably withheld by the Constitution, could not justify the parties to it in interposing even so far as to arrest the progress of the evil, and thereby to preserve the Constitution itself, as well as to provide for the safety of the parties to it, there would be an end to all relief from usurped power, and a direct subversion of the rights specified or recognized under all the state constitutions, as well as a plain denial of the fundamental principle on which our independence itself was declared.

But it is objected, that the judicial authority is to be regarded as the sole expositor of the Constitution in the last resort; and it may be asked for what reason the declaration by the general assembly, supposing it to be theoretically true, could be required at the present day, and in so solemn a manner.

On this objection it might be observed, first, that there may be instances of usurped power, which the forms of the Constitution would never draw within the control of the judicial department, secondly, that, if the decision of the Judiciary be raised above the authority of the sovereign parties to the Constitution, the decisions of the other departments, not carried by the forms of the Constitution before the Judiciary, must be equally authoritative and final with the decisions of that department. But the proper answer to the objection is, that the resolution of the general assembly relates to those great and extraordinary cases, in which all the forms of the Constitution may prove ineffectual against infractions dangerous to the essential rights of the parties to it. The resolution supposes that dangerous powers, not delegated, may not only be usurped and executed by the other departments, but that the judicial department, also, may exercise or sanction dangerous powers beyond the grant of the Constitution; and, consequently, that the ultimate right of the parties to the Constitution, to judge whether the compact has been dangerously violated, must extend to violations by one delegated authority as well as by another—by the Judiciary as well as by the Executive, or the Legislature.

However true, therefore, it may be, that the judicial department is, in all questions submitted to it by the forms of the Constitution, to decide in the last resort, this resort must necessarily be deemed the last in relation to the authorities of the other departments of the government; not in relation to the rights of the parties to the constitutional compact, from which the judicial, as well as the other departments, hold their delegated trusts. On any other hypothesis, the delegation of judicial power would annul the authority delegating it; and the concurrence of this department with the others in usurped powers, might subvert forever, and beyond the possible reach of any rightful remedy, the very Constitution which all were instituted to preserve.[56]

The states as states, Madison believed, reserved the right to place their own interpretation upon the Constitution on grave political issues involved in the distribution of powers. It was not clearly indicated

---

[55] Elliot's *Debates*, IV: 578.   [56] Elliot's *Debates*, IV: 549–550.

whether individual states possessed such authority or whether it was necessary for the states to act in unison in such an emergency.

In certain cases affecting the position and status of the states and the distribution of powers in the federal system, the report made the following proposal:

It appears to your committee to be a plain principle, founded in common sense, illustrated by common practice, and essential to the nature of compacts, that, where resort can be had to no tribunal superior to the authority of the parties, the parties themselves must be the rightful judges, in the last resort, whether the bargain made has been pursued or violated. The Constitution of the United States was formed by the sanction of the States, given by each in its sovereign capacity. It adds to the stability and dignity, as well as to the authority, of the Constitution, that it rests on this legitimate and solid foundation. The States, then, being the parties to the constitutional compact, and in their sovereign capacity, it follows of necessity that there can be no tribunal, above their authority, to decide, in the last resort, whether the compact made by them be violated; and consequently, that, as the parties to it, they must themselves decide, in the last resort, such questions as may be of sufficient magnitude to require their interposition.[57]

Thus, a view was expressed to which frequent references were made in later years, namely, that for the determination of conflicts of a political nature between the nation and the states no tribunal or umpire had been established by the Constitution. The constitutionality of the Alien and Sedition Laws was disposed of by the following dictum: "If no such power be expressly delegated, and if it be not both necessary and proper to carry into execution an express power; above all, if it be expressly forbidden by a declaratory amendment [First Amendment] to the Constitution—the answer must be, that the federal government is destitute of all such authority."[58] And the committee called attention to the declaration of Virginia made at the time of the ratification of the Constitution demonstrating that the powers of the federal government "being derived from the people of the United States, may be resumed by them whensoever the same may be perverted to their injury and oppression; and that every power not granted thereby remains with them, and at their will."[59]

After presenting an extensive argument in reply to the proceedings of the states in answer to the Virginia Resolutions of 1798, it was declared by the general assembly "to be their indispensable duty to adhere to the same, as founded in truth, as consonant to the Constitution, and as conducive to its preservation."[60] In this report Madison formulated and the legislature approved the political philosophy which was accepted and

[57] Elliot's *Debates*, IV: 548.
[58] *Ibid.*, IV: 573.
[59] *Ibid.*, p. 576.
[60] *Ibid.*, p. 580.

elaborated upon by Spencer Roane and John Taylor after Chief Justice Marshall had rendered some of his foremost nationalistic decisions.[61]

The debates on the Kentucky and Virginia Resolutions and the strong opposition to their adoption in some of the states show that the Democratic-Republican members of the legislatures did not accept the Federalist doctrine that the Supreme Court had authority to place a final interpretation on the Constitution which was binding on the states. Republicans usually agreed with John Taylor that "the Judges by the Constitution are not made its exclusive guardians." And the discussion of these resolutions brought out the fact that many Federalists as well as most of the Republicans accepted the compact theory as a basis for the formation of the federal union and were not averse to the doctrine of state sovereignty.[62] Frequently, however, they differed from the reasoning of the Kentucky and Virginia Resolutions with respect to the conclusion that each state may judge for itself regarding the violations of the Constitution. Votes on this as on other issues usually followed strict party lines. The dividing line between legislative and judicial functions was by no means clearly drawn either by the language of the Constitution or by the interpretations of this language by federal officials in the several departments.

There was in fact at this time a mingling of the judicial and political functions which would today be deemed quite inappropriate. Chief Justices Jay, Ellsworth, and Marshall saw no impropriety in combining their judicial offices with other executive appointments which necessarily made them partisans. While retaining the Chief Justiceship, Jay undertook the mission to England which kept him from the Bench from April 19, 1794, to June 29, 1795. On returning he resigned, not because he thought the Chief Justiceship was incompatible with other appointive offices, but because he was elected governor of New York. Ellsworth was sent as a Minister to France in February, 1799, but did not resign as Chief Justice until October, 1799, giving as the ground for his decision ill health. Marshall, while serving as Secretary of State, was nominated and confirmed Chief Justice. He presided during the February term of

---

[61] See below, pp. 343, 357, 438, 444. The passing of resolutions did not meet the situation according to John Taylor of Caroline who desired to have a law passed declaring the Alien and Sedition Acts unconstitutional. This step, he thought, would force the calling of a state convention. Jefferson disapproved of this plan and Taylor was unable to convince the legislature of the desirability of his proposal. See *Branch Historical Papers* (June, 1908), II: 226.

[62] Anderson, *Amer. Hist. Rev.*, V: 54, 242 ff. In their replies only one state, Vermont, undertook to deny the compact theory of the formation of the union. See John Spencer Bassett, *The Federalist System* (New York, 1906), p. 270.

the Court discharging the duties of the two offices until the inauguration of Jefferson, "on the same day issuing reports in the one capacity, and delivering judgments in the other."[63] But the Federalist members of the Judiciary took part in politics in other ways which were regarded as particularly offensive to the Republicans.

The Common Law in the Federal Courts

From a partisan standpoint, one of the most objectionable doctrines supported by the Justices at this time was the federal common law from which indictments might be brought in the federal courts under the common law jurisdiction as well as in accordance with federal statutes.

In the committee report to the Virginia legislature on the Alien and Sedition Laws, Madison considered the claim that in the prosecution of persons for sedition there was a "common or unwritten law" which might be applied by the federal courts. Reviewing legal conditions during the colonial period and under the Confederation it was declared that not a vestige of this extraordinary doctrine can be found. Nor do the provisions of the Constitution lend any support to such broad construction. The chief objection, he thought, to the concession of a common law jurisdiction in the federal government was that neither Congress nor the courts would be required to keep within the limits marked by the Constitution. Congress could legislate coextensive with the objects of the common law and the Judiciary would thereby acquire extensive legislative powers. After a thorough analysis of all the contentions to the contrary, it was concluded that "the common law never was, nor by any fair construction ever can be, deemed a law for the American people as one community."[64] Following a series of decisions and judicial pronouncements that there was a common law jurisdiction in the federal courts, the general assembly of Virginia sent a resolution to the members of Congress stating that "they would consider themselves unfaithful to the trust reposed in them, were they to remain silent, whilst a doctrine has been publicly advanced, novel in its principle and tremendous in its consequences: That the common law of England is in force under the government of the United States."[65]

But Jefferson expressed the most emphatic views against the assumption of powers involved in the construction of a federal common law by judicial interpretation. "I consider," he said, "all the encroachments made on that heretofore as nothing, as mere retail stuff compared with

---

[63] Wharton, *State Trials*, p. 46.
[64] Elliot's *Debates*, IV: 567.
[65] Tucker's *Blackstone*, I, appendix, p. 438.

the wholesale doctrine, that there is a common law in force in the United States of which and of all the cases within its provisions their courts have cognizance."[66] And at another time he wrote:

Of all the doctrines which have ever been broached by the federal government, the novel one, of the common law being in force and cognizable as an existing law in their courts, is to me the most formidable. All their other assumptions of un-given powers have been in the detail. The bank law, the treaty doctrine, the sedition act, alien act, the undertaking to change the state laws of evidence in the state courts by certain parts of the stamp act, &c., &c., have been solitary, unconsequential, timid things, in comparison with the audacious, barefaced and sweeping pretension to a system of law for the U.S., without the adoption of their Legislature, and so infinitively beyond their power to adopt. If this assumption be yielded to, the state courts may be shut up, as there will then be nothing to hinder citizens of the same State suing each other in the federal courts in every case, as on a bond for instance, because the common law obliges the payment of it, and the common law they say is their law.[67]

Justice Chase, differing from his associates, disapproved of the doctrine that an indictment could be maintained in the federal courts solely on common rules and principles.[68] It was this view which was later adopted by the Court.[69] But the most offensive evidences of partisanship were manifested in the charges of the Justices to the grand juries.

PARTISAN CHARGES TO GRAND JURIES

The ire of the Republicans was aroused more by the partisan charges to the grand juries than by any other activity of the Justices. Jefferson noted that the federal Judges have been inviting the grand juries "to become inquisitors on the freedom of speech, of writing and of principle of their fellow-citizens" and he urged the entering of protests against "this perversion of their institution from a legal to a political engine."[70]

A typical illustration of the political conduct of the federal Judges is afforded in the newspaper report of a charge to the grand jury by Justice Paterson at Portsmouth, New Hampshire, May 24, 1800. Judge Paterson, it is reported,

delivered a most elegant and appropriate charge. The *Law* was laid down in a masterly manner; *Politics* were set in their true light by holding up the Jacobins as the disorganizers of our happy country, and the only instruments of introducing discontent and dissatisfaction among the well meaning part of the community. *Religion* and *Morality* were pleasingly inculcated and enforced as being necessary to good government, good order, and good laws.[71]

---

[66] *Writings* (Ford ed., 1896), VII: 398.

[67] *Ibid.*, pp. 383, 384.

[68] United States v. Worrall, 2 Dallas 384, 394 (1798).

[69] See United States v. Hudson and Goodwin, 7 Cranch 32 (1812).

[70] *Writings* (Ford ed.), VII: 138.

[71] Wm. H. Hackett, "The Circuit Court for the New Hampshire District One Hundred Years Ago," 2 *Green Bag* (1890) 264.

Justice Iredell in his charge to the grand jury in the case of the North-ampton Insurgents referred to the peace and prosperity of the United States and the fortunate condition of the country and then observed: "But in the midst of this envied situation, we have heard the government as grossly abused as if it had been guilty of the vilest tyranny; as if common sense or common virtue had fled from our country; and those pure principles of republicanism, which have so strongly characterized its councils, could only be found in the happy soil of France."[72] And after having alluded to the Democrats who were criticizing the government, the Justice argued extensively in defense of the validity of the Alien and Sedition Laws. When the grand jury requested the privilege of publish-ing this charge to counteract the false philosophy and the dangerous and wicked principles spreading with rapidity, Iredell consented to its pub-lication in the hope that it might produce "a good effect." For, said he, "believing as I have long done, that the Constitution and laws of the United States afford the highest degree of rational liberty which the world ever saw, or of which perhaps mankind are capable, I have seen with astonishment and regret, attempts made in the pursuit of visionary chimeras, to subvert or undermine so glorious a fabric, equally con-structed for public and private security."[73]

In western Pennsylvania, Judge Addison of the state judiciary charged grand juries on such subjects as "Jealousy of Administration and Gov-ernment," "The Horrors of Revolution," etc., and pointed out the ter-rible things that were likely to happen if the people refused to uphold those in authority. Supreme Court Justices not only commended these political harangues but Justice Chase took the stump in the campaign against Jefferson and delivered to the grand jury at Baltimore a political invective against Jefferson and his party. Said Chase: "The late altera-tion of the federal Judiciary, by the abolition of the office of the sixteen Circuit Judges; and the recent change in our state constitution, by estab-lishing universal suffrage; and the further alteration that was then contemplated in our state judiciary, would, if adopted, take away all security for property and personal liberty." And it was predicted that our republican constitution will sink into "a mobocracy, the worst of all

---

[72] Wharton, *State Trials*, p. 466.

[73] Wharton, *State Trials*, pp. 481, 482. Regarding the practice of charging grand juries, it was claimed that "even if the judicial history of England, where the spirit of party has sometimes raged with the most dreadful consequences, you will find it difficult to trace any instance to countenance the political declamations, the party invectives, which have of late become a sort of a prelude to the commencement of every session of our courts of justice." George Mifflin Dallas, *Life and Writings of Alexander James Dallas* (Philadelphia, 1871), p. 82.

popular governments." The repeal of the Judiciary Act was condemned as shaking to its foundations the independence of the national Judiciary and it was contended that "nothing but a change in the representation of Congress, which the return of the people to correct sentiments alone can effect, will be sufficient to produce a repeal of this act, and thereby restore to its former vigor the part of the federal Constitution which has been thus impaired."[74] This political speech became the basis of one of the charges of impeachment brought against Justice Chase.[75]

Partisan influences prevailed also in the method of securing indictments and convictions. The United States marshals, who, like the Judges, were often Federalist politicians, when making up juries selected only persons of the same manner of thinking as that of themselves and the Judges. Hence, the juries often merely registered the opinion of the Judges and the district attorneys. "Certain state judges of the rabid Federalist type," says Albert J. Beveridge, "apostles of 'the wise, the rich, and the good' political religion, were as insulting in their bearing, as immoderate in their speech, and as intolerant in their conduct as some of the national Judges; and prosecutions in some state courts were as bad as the worst of those in the national tribunals."[76]

The conduct of the Judges during Adams' Administration was, indeed, "an amazing exhibition of headlong and reckless partisanship."[77] The Justices belonging to the aristocratic-conservative classes naturally lacked sympathy with the democratic-agrarian groups who formed the mainstay of the Democratic-Republican party. When they used their offices to expound the principles of their party they became the objects of invective and abuse. The Federalist Judges were indeed responsible for "dragging the Judiciary into the arena of politics" from which it has been removed in intermittent intervals only throughout the subsequent periods of American history. Congress also aided the design to use the courts as an agency to foster the policies of Federalism.

FEDERALIST JUDICIAL REORGANIZATION ACT

The crowning effort of the Federalists during Adams' Administration to use the Judiciary as a partisan agency was the reorganization act passed on February 13, 1801. Objections were raised from the beginning of the government regarding the organization of the federal courts as provided by the act of 1789. Attorney General Randolph, after consultation with

---

[74] Annals of Congress, 8th Cong., 2d sess., p. 148.

[75] See below, pp. 261 ff.

[76] The Life of John Marshall (Boston, 1919), III: 42–43.

[77] Henry Jones Ford, The Rise and Growth of American Politics (New York, 1900), p. 112.

the Justices, recommended changes which were approved by President Washington, but Congress failed to take any action. Judicial reorganization was again recommended by President Adams in 1799, and a measure which Hamilton is reputed to have drafted was considered in the Sixth Congress. One of the Federalist policies, that of ignoring the states in the establishment of new districts, was embodied in this bill. But the Republicans prevented action on this measure and the matter was deferred until the next session of Congress.

Jefferson, to whom Marshall felt "almost insuperable objections,"[78] was to be the third President of the United States. His foreign prejudices, thought Marshall, seemed to unfit him for the chief magistrate and "by weakening the office of President, he will increase his personal power. He will diminish his responsibility, sap the fundamental principles of government. . . . The morals of the author of the letter to Mazzei cannot be pure."[79] Chief Justice Ellsworth, writing from Paris, expressed the prevailing sentiment among the Federalists, that Jefferson was "a visionary man, an enthusiastic disciple of the French Revolution, and an enemy to whatever would encourage commercial enterprise or give energy to the government." If elected President, "there would be no national energy. Our character would sink, and our weakness would invite contempt and insult."[80] It is significant that the man who was to serve the country as its third Chief Justice looked upon the President, with whom, as the nation's head, he was to coöperate, with utter contempt. The Democrats, he said, "are divided into speculative theorists and absolute terrorists. With the latter I am disposed to class Mr. Jefferson."[81] Most of the leaders of the Federalist party agreed with Marshall's estimate of Jefferson, and many of them were so alarmed over the situation that, as we shall see later, they entered into a plot to secede from the union. Federalism and nationalism went hand in hand but nationalism did not at this time, even to the Federalists, envisage the doctrine that a state could not secede from the union.

With Jefferson's election to the presidency, new impetus was given to the proposals to reorganize the entire federal judicial system. Leading Federalists, such as Alexander Hamilton and Fisher Ames, recommended

---

[78] Beverage, *The Life of John Marshall*, II: 537.

[79] Letter of Jan. 1, 1801, in Hamilton, *Works*, ed. by J. C. Hamilton (New York, 1850), VI: 501, 502. For Jefferson's letter to Mazzei, see *Writings* (Ford ed.), VII: 75, 76.

[80] William Garrott Brown, *The Life of Oliver Ellsworth* (New York, 1805), p. 324. Brown comments on this judgment as follows: "This was a severe judgment, not a mere outbreak of partisan malice and fear, and it set forth correctly, though it may have exaggerated, the weakness of Jefferson's character." *Ibid.*, p. 325.

[81] Letter to Pinckney, March 4, 1801, Beveridge, *op. cit.*, III: 11.

the extension of the Judiciary department to disconcert, as they thought, the schemes of the enemies of the Constitution.[82] "The party of Washington, as a dominant and governing force in the development of the American nation," says Beveridge, "went down forever in a welter of passion, tawdry politics, and disgraceful intrigue." But all was not lost— the Judiciary remained. "No Republican was as yet a member of the national Judiciary."[83]

Before the first session of the Court to be held in the new Capitol in February, 1801, Chief Justice Ellsworth, still in France, resigned, giving as his reason ill health. President Adams, believing "the firmest security we can have against the effects of visionary schemes or fluctuating theories will be in a solid Judiciary," wrote to John Jay requesting him to again accept the position of Chief Justice. But Jay declined the nomination on the ground that the condition of his health did not permit the assumption of the strenuous duties of holding court on the circuits. In his letter of declination he took occasion to criticize the Judiciary Act of 1789 as accommodated to certain prejudices and sensibilities rather than to obvious principles of public policy. And since the expectations that the judicial department would be reorganized had not been realized, Jay said: "I left the Bench perfectly convinced that under a system so defective, it would not obtain the energy, weight, and dignity which are essential to its affording due support to the national government, nor acquire the public confidence and respect which, as the last resort of the justice of the Nation, it should possess."[84]

On the refusal of Jay to accept the position, Adams turned to his Secretary of State, John Marshall. The President observed that he was offering the place to "a gentleman in the full vigor of middle life, in the full habits of business, and whose reading of the science is fresh in his head"—a reading which Beveridge claims, however, was "extremely limited."[85] The Federalists were disappointed with the nomination and would have refused to confirm the appointment if they could have prevailed on the President to nominate their choice, Justice Paterson. Failing in this design, Marshall's nomination was confirmed without any enthusiasm on the part of the Federalists or special condemnation by the Republicans who deemed him "more distinguished as a rhetorician

---

[82] Hamilton, *Works* (Const. ed.), X: 329, and Samuel E. Morison, *The Life and Letters of Harrison Gray Otis, 1765–1848* (Boston, 1913), I: 202.

[83] *The Life of John Marshall*, II: 547.

[84] Henry P. Johnson, ed., *The Correspondence and Public Papers of John Jay* (New York, 1890–1893), IV: 285.

[85] John Adams, *Works*, ed. by Charles Francis Adams (Boston, 1856), IX: 93, 94, and *The Life of John Marshall*, II: 554.

and sophist than as a lawyer and statesman."[86] The President being un-willing to put another in Marshall's place as Secretary of State requested him to continue to discharge the duties of this office. Thus for one month Marshall served as a member of the President's cabinet while holding the office of Chief Justice. By refusing to accept the salary of the Secretary of State it was thought the constitutional objections to the holding of two offices would be obviated.

President Adams, in a message written by Secretary of State Marshall, urged the reorganization of the Judiciary as indispensably necessary.[87] The new act, as passed by Congress, contained features which carried out reforms recommended in the early years of Washington's Administra-tion and included provisions especially designed to continue and uphold the cause of Federalism. First, Supreme Court Justices were relieved of circuit duty, a part of their work to which persistent objections had been raised. Second, a new system of districts and circuits was provided. Prior to 1801 there were seventeen districts with one District Judge in each district. The act of 1801 established twenty-two districts in addition to one comprising the territories of Ohio and Indiana. Prior to 1801 there were three circuits—the Eastern, the Middle, and the Southern. Until 1793 courts were held in these circuits by two Supreme Court Justices and after this date by one Supreme Court Justice and a District Judge. The new act provided for six circuits with three judges in each of the first five and one judge for the Western circuit. A third feature of the act was the reduction of the number of Supreme Court Justices from six to five.[88] By a combination of circumstances, in part at least deliberately planned, the position of Chief Justice was now in the hands of one of the foremost Federalist politicians, and as another Justice might retire soon it was thought necessary to prevent an early appointment to the Court by the new President. This act has been appropriately described

[86] *Aurora,* June 12, 1800.

[87] This part of the message was as follows: "To give due effect to the civil administra-tion of government and to insure a just execution of the laws, a revision and amend-ment of the judiciary system is indispensably necessary. In this extensive country it cannot but happen that numerous questions respecting the interpretation of the laws and the rights and duties of officers and citizens must arise. On the one hand, the laws should be executed; on the other, individuals should be guarded from oppression. Neither of these objects is sufficiently assured under the present organization of the judicial department. I therefore earnestly recommend the subject to your serious con-sideration." James D. Richardson, *A Compilation of the Messages and Papers of the Presidents* (Washington, 1911), I: 279. It is well known that Marshall wrote this message. Beveridge referring to this fact says: "Marshall not only favored the President with his 'sentiments'—he wrote every word of the speech which Adams delivered to Congress and sent it to the distressed Chief Magistrate in such haste that he did not even make a copy." *The Life of John Marshall,* II: 530.

[88] Cf. Max Farrand, "The Judiciary Act of 1801," *Amer. Hist. Rev.* (July, 1900), V: 682.

as a "pure case of a political intrigue, of a defeated party striving to retain some semblance of power by interesting itself in the Judiciary."[89] The political motives which prompted the legislation were manifested during its enactment and in the hasty and unceremonious manner of filling the vacant positions with staunch partisans.

To see that the guns of the Republicans were securely spiked, so far as the administration of justice is concerned, President Adams hastened to send to the Senate a complete list of nominations to the new judge-ships created by the act and a list of 45 justices of peace for the District of Columbia, provided for in another act of Congress. All of the positions were filled by Federalists and places were found for three Senators and one Representative. There was, indeed, good grounds for the contention of Jefferson and the other Republicans that the Federalists "have retired into the Judiciary as a stronghold. There the remains of Federalism are to be preserved and fed from the treasury, and from that battery all the works of Republicanism are to be beaten down and erased. By a fraudu-lent use of the Constitution, which has made judges irremovable, they have multiplied useless judges merely to strengthen their phalanx."[90] As Secretary of State the Chief Justice saw no impropriety in assisting the President in securing good Federalists for the newly created judgeships which were established by the act reorganizing the Judiciary. In his position as Secretary of State he signed and sealed the commissions of these judges, including that of William Marbury as justice of the peace. It was the failure of Marshall and his secretary to deliver this commission which formed the occasion for the Chief Justice's first great constitu-tional decision.

As the Republicans took over the administration of the Executive and Legislative departments, the Federalists saw only the doom of the country through the reign of excessive democracy. And more than ever they turned to the Judiciary to save the nation for Federalism, as they thought there could be "neither justice nor stability in any system, if some parts of it were not independent of popular control."[91] Though Jefferson was

---

[89] W. A. Sutherland, "Politics and the Supreme Court," 48 *Amer. Law Rev.* (May–June, 1914), 394.

[90] *Writings* (Mem. ed.), X: 302. Henry Adams refers to the packing of the courts with "safe Federalists." *History of the United States of America during the First Administra-tion of Thomas Jefferson* (New York, 1921), I: 275. "I can say with truth," wrote Jefferson, "that one act of Mr. Adams' life, and one only, ever gave me a moment's personal displeasure. I did consider his last appointments to office as personally unkind. They were from my most ardent political enemies. . . . It seems but common justice to leave a successor free to act by instruments of his own choice." Letter to Mrs. John Adams, June 13, 1804. *Writings* (Mem. ed.), XI: 29.

[91] Beveridge, *op. cit.*, III: 12 ff.

beginning a revolution which was to change the government from one of aristocratic aloofness and arrogance in dealing with the people to one of frankness and democratic simplicity in which the interests of the people had a foremost place, the Federalists could see nothing but anarchy and a destruction of all that was good in American political life. To Jefferson these forebodings of ill were attributed to "the clergy, who have missed their union with the State, the Anglomen, who missed their union with England, and the political adventurers, who have lost the chance of swindling and plunder in the waste of public money, will never cease to bawl, on the breaking up of their sanctuary."[92]

After the inauguration of Jefferson the Federalist Judges and especially the new appointees of President Adams continued the policy of bringing prosecutions of libel against the editors of Republican papers. Since the Sedition Act had expired, such prosecutions could be brought only under the common law of libel. Though, owing to the opposition of the Republicans and the refusal of juries to indict, such proceedings proved to be ineffective, they indicated, nevertheless, the intention of the federal Judges, so far as was within their power, to continue to place restrictions on the freedom of speech and the press.[93] Since the design of the Federalists was to prevent, so far as possible, the carrying out of the public will as manifested in the election of the members of the Legislative and Executive departments, it was obvious to the Republicans that there was no way to deal with the situation except by a repeal of the new Judiciary Act. The steps leading to the repeal of this act and the arguments of the Federalists and Republicans regarding the place and significance of the federal courts under the Constitution, which will be presented in another chapter, give an illuminating analysis of some of the fundamental tenets of the two parties.

Only a few cases came before the Supreme Court during Adams' Administration and most of those related to minor points of procedure or to the jurisdiction of the federal courts. The total number of cases before the Court during the Administrations of Washington and Adams was small and required the time of the Judges for only a few weeks each year. About one-third of the total of sixty cases involved matters of admiralty and maritime affairs or questions growing out of war and foreign relations. These were regarded as coming naturally under the jurisdiction of the federal courts as the successor of the Court of Appeals under the Confederation. But even in this field Pennsylvania was soon to defy federal authority. Of the remaining forty cases a major part of them

---

[92] *Works* (Mem. ed.), X: 259.
[93] Cf. Warren, *op. cit.*, I: 195.

dealt with the explanation and interpretation of minor points of procedure growing out of the Judiciary Act or the rules of procedure announced by the Court. Only eight cases appear to be of more than passing importance.

During the Administrations of Washington and Adams it was the custom in the majority of cases for the Justices to render opinions *seriatim*. Such important issues as were raised in *Chisholm v. Georgia*,[94] *Hylton v. United States*,[95] and *Ware v. Hylton*[96] were determined by a common judgment arrived at through different methods of reasoning. No Justice had succeeded in becoming the oracle for the judgments and opinions of the Court.

The way of the Supreme Court to a position of respect and prominence was beset with difficulties and was marked by reverses which tended to shake the confidence of the people in the highest federal tribunal. Changing personnel, the mingling of the Justices in politics, and the long, wearisome, and sometimes dangerous trips on circuit during the first decades had not a little to do with the unpopularity of the Court. Chiefly because of the general feeling of uncertainty and distrust, Edmund Pendleton of Virginia, Robert Hanson Harrison of Maryland, and Charles Cotesworthy Pinckney and Edward Rutledge of South Carolina declined to accept commissions to positions on the Court. John Rutledge of South Carolina, Thomas Johnson of Maryland, John Blair of Virginia, and Alfred Moore of North Carolina resigned their positions and John Jay of New York and Oliver Ellsworth of Connecticut abandoned the office of Chief Justice. With a changing personnel, a reversal of one of the most important decisions by an amendment, with very few controversies of importance to pass on, it is not surprising to find that the Supreme Court did not make much of an appeal either to the interest or to the imagination of the people. The position and place of the Supreme Court in the American federal system continued to be uncertain and precarious during the Administration of Thomas Jefferson.

Speaking of the federal government, Hamilton wrote: "It must carry its agency to the persons of the citizens. It must stand in need of no intermediate legislations; but must itself be empowered to employ the arm of the ordinary magistrate to execute its own resolutions. The majesty of the national authority must be manifested through the medium of the courts of justice. The government of the Union, like that of each

---

[94] 2 Dallas 419 (1793).
[95] 3 Dallas 171 (1796).
[96] 3 Dallas 198 (1796).

State, must be able to address itself immediately to the hopes and fears of individuals; and to attract to its support those passions which have the strongest influence upon the human heart."[97] The Federalist party through its leaders aimed to carry out this policy, though in doing so they placed an interpretation upon the Constitution which differed no doubt in a marked degree from the views of many of those who participated in the drafting of the document and a large number of those who voted for its ratification. Definite indications of antinationalistic sentiment were shown in the adoption of the Ninth and Tenth Amendments confirming the principle of the enumeration of powers to the federal government and of the reservations of rights and powers to the states. And the announcement by the Supreme Court of the formation through the Constitution of an indissoluble union in which the sovereignty of the states had been merged and from which it might be inferred that the states could not withdraw from the union led to a speedy and emphatic reversal of the decision of the Court. Thus, three amendments were adopted with the primary purpose of checking the nationalistic tendencies of the Constitution and of its interpretation by the Federalists during Washington's Administration. When the federal government gave authority to the President to suppress the rebels of western Pennsylvania who refused to pay the excise tax on whisky—one of Hamilton's measures to bring the government to the people through the revenue agents—it was made clear that the resistance of individuals to the enforcement of federal laws would be suppressed, if need be, by force. This attempt to assert federal supremacy by an unwarranted display of military power aided in the crystallization of the sentiment for State rights. Indeed, the sentiment favorable to separation from the union or secession was so common at this time that Washington devoted a large part of his Farewell Address to a plea for unity in government and for support of the union. Channing believes that one of the main reasons why attempts to divide the union were unsuccessful was the adoption of the first eleven amendments. Though these amendments checked somewhat the marked trend toward nationalism, it soon became evident that they did not go far enough to adequately protect the rights of the states. The closing years of the Administration of John Adams called forth the first formal statement of the State rights philosophy.

Both Hamilton and Jefferson looked to the state legislatures as "not only vigilant but suspicious and jealous guardians of the rights of the citizens against encroachments from the federal government."[98] When

---

[97] *Works* (Const. ed.), X: 125, 126, and *The Federalist* (Ford ed.), p. 100.
[98] See *The Federalist* (Ford ed.), p. 166.

Jefferson became alarmed at the efforts to enlarge unduly the powers of the central government and to foster the interests of selfish minority groups, he developed the idea of vigilance into a theory of "sentinelship" whereby the states were regarded as the judges of the powers they had relinquished to the federal government. Moreover, Jefferson accepted and gave concrete application to the doctrine originally approved by Hamilton that in political matters and the settlement of ultimate questions on the division of powers between the states and the nation the Constitution had provided no judge to determine disputes that might arise. The Republicans in the election of 1800 denounced the Alien and Sedition Acts and in a general way approved the doctrines of the Virginia and Kentucky Resolutions. Jefferson's election was rightfully looked upon as an endorsement of the State rights interpretation of the "federal compact," as it was then commonly called, rather than the nationalistic interpretation as advocated by the Federalists. "The permanent significance of the [Kentucky and Virginia] Resolutions," maintains Professor Hockett, "is that they gave definite form for the first time to the Constitution as a compact made by mutual agreement of States as bodies politic. The Resolutions gave new life to the belief in state sovereignty, and from this time forward it showed great vitality."[99] Upon the election of Jefferson the extreme agitation for State rights declined until the embargo policy and the nationalist measures accompanying the War of 1812 brought the New England states to the verge of secession in defense of their sovereign rights and privileges. After this war and when the Supreme Court championed the cause of Hamiltonian nationalism, Spencer Roane, John Taylor of Caroline, and Thomas Jefferson led the Republicans in their efforts to protect and preserve what were regarded as the indefeasible rights and authority of the states. Whether or not the Federalists operated within the words and meaning of the Constitution as drafted and adopted in 1787–1788, they formed an enduring political structure which the Republicans and future political parties might transform in certain particulars but which continued to serve as the groundwork for a growing and increasingly assertive nationalism.[100]

[99] Homer Carey Hockett, *The Constitutional History of the United States, 1776–1826* (New York, 1939), pp. 295, 296.

[100] On the Federalist party Morison and Commager comment as follows: "The expanding forces of American life enveloped and overwhelmed them. Yet those forces had been so schooled and molded by twelve years of Federalist rule that, with John Marshall presiding at the supreme bench, even Jefferson and his 'wild men' (as the Federalists called them) were unable to do much more than throw the furniture about when the session opened." *The Growth of the American Republic* (New York, 1937), I: 277.

CHAPTER VI

Political Views and Theories of Constitutional Interpretation of Jefferson, Hamilton, and Madison

Partisan conflicts and political alignments prevailing during the Revolutionary War and the critical period continued with only minor modifications during the early administrations of the government under the federal Constitution. Despite a variation in grouping, in designations, and in the usual formulations of party policies, the fundamental and underlying division of parties in the United States has been manifested from colonial times to date in the clash of opinion and political conflicts between the conservatives, on the one hand, and the liberal, democratic, and sometimes radical groups, on the other.[1] Some years ago Charles A. Beard described the typical party machine in the United States as an effective office-filling and office-controlling device. And from the breakup of the early Federalist and Anti-Federalist parties, which, roughly at least, followed the normal trend of division between the conservatives and the liberals, the party names—Democrat, Republican, or Whig—frequently had little relation to the time-honored classification of political groups. But beneath the surface the contests of colonial and Revolutionary days continued to be waged between the conservative and the liberal and democratic groups. The characteristic devices of the conservative Federalist party checks and balances, separation of powers, and judicial supremacy gave the rising tide of democracy a fairly free rein to play the game of "hide and seek politics"—as Woodrow Wilson characterized it—in the choice and control of public officials; but judges, as the protectors of personal and property rights, were, in theory at least, to be kept as far as possible from the turmoil of parties. It was an independent Judiciary, armed with written constitutions, the principles and methods of the common law, and concepts of superiority of judicial interpretation applicable both to constitutions and laws, that was expected to preserve against democratic onslaughts the ramparts of conservatism.

---

[1] For evidence supporting this statement see Charles A. Beard, *Economic Origins of Jeffersonian Democracy* (New York, 1915).

By the end of the Administration of George Washington, as noted in the previous chapter, the lines were clearly drawn in the conflict between those who sought a strong, centralized government controlling the lives of the people for political and economic ends and those who aimed to have the government serve the interests of the people regardless of wealth, class, or position, and especially to limit governmental functions so that the individual would have as great a degree of personal liberty as possible.[2]

Political cleavages of the Revolutionary War and the critical period between the conservatives, on the one hand, and the liberals and radicals, on the other, were continued in the clash of opinions and the diversity of political practices between the Federalists under the leadership of Alexander Hamilton and the Democratic-Republicans directed by Thomas

[2] Though somewhat overdrawn, the analyses of party divisions under the Federalist regime by Madison and Jefferson are of interest in view of subsequent developments.

Madison described in 1792 the gradual rise of parties as follows:

"One of the divisions consists of those, who from particular interest, from natural temper, or from the habits of life, are more partial to the opulent than to the other classes of society; and having debauched themselves into a persuasion that mankind are incapable of governing themselves, it follows with them, of course, that government can be carried on only by the pageantry of military force. Men of these sentiments must naturally wish to point the measures of government less to interest of the many than of a few, and less to the reason of the many than of their weaknesses. . . .

"The other division consists of those who believing in the doctrine that mankind are capable of governing themselves, and hating hereditary power as an insult to the reason and an outrage to the rights of man, are naturally offended at every public measure that does not appeal to the understanding and to the general interest of the community, or that is not strictly conformable to the principles, and conducive to the preservation of republican government." Primarily the difference between parties, thought Madison, lay in their opposing views regarding the ability of men to govern themselves. Abbot Emerson Smith, *James Madison: Builder* (New York, 1937), pp. 187, 188; see also James Truslow Adams, *The Living Jefferson* (New York, 1936), pp. 18, 19.

Jefferson, writing to Mazzei, on April 24, 1796, characterized the situation concerning parties as follows:

"The aspect of our politics has wonderfully changed since you left us. In place of that noble love of liberty, and republican government which carried us triumphantly through the war, an Anglican monarchical, and aristocratical party has sprung up, whose avowed object is to draw over us the substance, as they have already done the forms, of the British government. The main body of our citizens, however, remain true to their republican principles; the whole landed interest is republican, and so is a great mass of talents. Against us are the Executive, the Judiciary, two out of three branches of the Legislature, all the officers of the government, all who want to be officers, all timid men who prefer the calm of despotism to the boisterous sea of liberty, British merchants and Americans trading on British capitals, speculators and holders in the banks and public funds, a contrivance invented for the purposes of corruption, and for assimilating us in all things to the rotten as well as the sound parts of the British model." *Writings* (Ford ed., New York, 1896), VII: 75, 76. It was this letter concerning which Marshall wrote to Hamilton that "the morals of the author of the letter to Mazzei cannot be pure." Hamilton, *Works,* ed. by J. C. Hamilton (New York, 1850), VI: 502.

Jefferson and James Madison. It is impossible to understand the underlying ideas and concepts of constitutional interpretation from 1800 to 1860 without a consideration of the divergent political views and theories of constitutional construction of these great political leaders. Some of the most significant of the political principles and practices which have prevailed in the United States were largely the product of the indefatigable work and the constructive contributions of two of this group—Hamilton and Jefferson. Since personal traits had a bearing on their political doctrines, a comparison of certain characteristics of the two men is appropriate.

DIFFERENCES IN PERSONAL CHARACTERISTICS AND ATTITUDES

Jefferson and Hamilton differed greatly in personal traits and attitudes. The former was frank, cordial, and sympathetic in his manner. He had confidence in his fellow men and was sanguine in his views of life. He despised pomp, ceremony, and court etiquette. As a man of culture he took delight in scientific and speculative studies. He was interested in plans for the uplift of mankind, and was essentially democratic in his point of view and his outlook on life.[3] Differing from the versatile Jefferson, Hamilton's mind was powerful only in the consideration of matters of government and finance. He had little confidence in the masses, and did not deem it desirable to seek equality among men, either social or political.[4] Hamilton regarded most men as unfit to govern themselves,

---

[3] "No other man in all our history," maintains James Truslow Adams, "has so contributed to the forming of the American spirit as Jefferson did by his life-long devotion to the principles of freedom, equality of opportunity, and of liberalism."*The Living Jefferson*, p. 127.

[4] Hamilton wrote to Washington that he had long since learned "to hold popular opinion of no value." *Works* (Const. ed.), VI: 457. We should, he thought, be "rescued from democracy." Cf. John C. Hamilton, *Life of Alexander Hamilton* (Boston, 1879), II: 487. "While property continues to be pretty equally divided, and a considerable share of information pervades the community, the tendency of the people's suffrages will be," Hamilton believes, "to elevate merit even from obscurity. As riches increase and accumulate in a few hands, as luxury prevails in society, virtue will be in a greater degree considered as only a graceful appendage of wealth, and the tendency of things will be to depart from the republican standard. This is the real disposition of human nature. . . .

"It is a harsh doctrine, that men grow wicked in proportion as they improve and enlighten their minds. Experience has by no means justified us in the supposition that there is more virtue in one class of men than in another. Look through the rich and the poor of the community; the learned and the ignorant. Where does virtue predominate? The difference indeed consists, not in the quantity, but kind of vices, which are incident to the various classes; and here the advantage of character belongs to the wealthy. Their vices are probably more favorable to the prosperity of the State than those of the indigent, and partake less of moral depravity." Speeches on the Compromises of the Constitution, June 21, 1788. *The Works of Alexander Hamilton* (Const. ed., New York, 1904), II: 26, 27.

and believed that the few ought to rule the many. "The people," he said, "are turbulent and changing; they seldom judge or determine right." As a consequence he urged that the "rich and well-born" should be given a permanent place in the government, for "nothing but a permanent body can check the imprudence of democracy. Their turbulent and un-controllable disposition requires checks." He had little tact, was not inclined to take people into his confidence, and often made enemies of those who should have been his friends.

Jefferson was in favor of giving the greatest possible scope to demo-cratic rule, believing that the common sense of the people would in the long run be the safest guide for public power. He had great confidence in his fellow men and favored a full and free expression of opinion on all matters.[5] Hamilton considered democratic government to be radi-cally defective.[6] To him most men were vicious and should be ruled with that theory in mind. He was in favor of repressing popular tendencies and keeping democracy restrained by the strong hand of authority. According to Jefferson "man was a rational animal, endowed by nature with rights, and with an innate sense of justice; and that he could be restrained from wrong and protected in right by moderate powers, con-fided to persons of his own choice, and held to their duties by depend-ence on his own will."[7] His fundamental postulate was a belief in the latent honesty and ability of the average man regardless of social posi-tion, education, wealth, or other opportunities.

Hamilton favored the development of a wealthy class and the encour-agement of the industrial and capitalist interests of the country. For, with his distrust of democracy, he believed that no government could endure which did not become identified with the interests of property. The opposition between Jefferson and Hamilton politically had its ori-gin in the belief of Jefferson that Hamilton was definitely planning and taking whatever steps to him seemed necessary to form a "permanent plutocracy based on money." And Jefferson noted that he had "never observed men's honesty to increase with their riches." Though it was impossible for Hamilton to secure the type of government he desired,

---

[5] "Every government degenerates when trusted to the rulers of the people alone. The people themselves therefore are its only safe depositories. And to render them safe, their minds must be improved to a certain degree." From Notes on Virginia, *Writings* (Ford ed.), IV: 64. At another time he observed that "The mass of the citizens is the safest depository of their own rights and especially, that the evils flowing from the duperies of the people, are less injurious than those from the egoism of their agents." *The Writings of Thomas Jefferson* (Mem. ed., Washington, 1905), XX: 23.

[6] "Republican government does not admit of a vigorous execution, it is therefore bad." John C. Hamilton, *op. cit.*, II: 488.

[7] *Writings* (Mem. ed), XV: 441.

it was generally conceded that the Constitution of 1787 was drawn in accordance with his wish with special provisions designed to favor the business and mercantile classes. In contrast to the plans and desires of Hamilton, Jefferson opposed monarchy, aristocracy, and special privileges. Disapproving of the use of corruption as a means of accomplishing political results, he hated chicanery and exploitation which were characteristic of the business practices of his day, and thought that every effort should be made to prevent the concentration in a few hands of the major part of the financial and economic resources of the country.

Whereas Jefferson was modest and had to be urged or prevailed upon to participate in public life, preferring his home and plantation where he could carry out his personal interests and desires, Hamilton had an overweening ambition. His aim was to be a prime minister, and, while a member of President Washington's cabinet, he was constantly interfering with the work of the men in the other departments. When he retired to private life he expected to be consulted on all important matters. According to James Truslow Adams, "Hamilton saw more clearly than Jefferson the springs which move men and the motives by which they are led and act. He took a much lower view of human nature than Jefferson, and in that he was right. On the other hand, Jefferson saw more clearly than Hamilton the ideals which the Americans cherished though they might not live up to them in practice."[8] The differences in political views and doctrines of the two men were as marked as the divergencies in personal characteristics.

COMPARISON OF POLITICAL VIEWS AND DOCTRINES OF HAMILTON AND JEFFERSON

Hamilton favored a government with an hereditary monarch and approved of the then constituted English system of government.[9] He presented a plan of government to the Constitutional Convention at Philadelphia, and in an elaborate argument defended the principles embodied in it. He did not expect his plan to be adopted, but offered it primarily, as he said, that those favoring Republican principles might be prevailed upon "to tone their government as high as possible." He proposed to have senators chosen by electors who were to be elected by the people, and the President was to be chosen by the electors to be chosen by other electors who were to be selected by landholders. This plan, though not seriously considered by the Convention, undoubtedly

---

[8] *The Living Jefferson*, p. 211.

[9] See Letters of Gouverneur Morris cited by Henry S. Randall, *The Life of Thomas Jefferson* (New York, 1858), I: 580 ff. "I believe the British government forms the best model the world ever produced." Hamilton, *Works* (Const. ed.), I: 400, 401.

helped to strengthen the views of the conservative party in the Convention. At the close of the Convention, Hamilton signed the Constitution for the state of New York with the reflection, however, that no man's ideas were more remote from the plan than were his; but, he inquired, "is it possible to deliberate between anarchy and convulsion on one side and the chance of good to be expected from this plan on the other?" After trying to increase the powers of the central government as provided by the Constitution in a period of despondency and despair, he referred to the document as "a frail and worthless fabric."[10] A constitution, Hamilton insisted, "cannot set bounds to a nation's wants; it ought not therefore to set bounds to its resources. Unexpected visitations, long and ruinous wars, may demand all the possible abilities of the country. Shall not our government have power to call these abilities into action? The contingencies of society are not reducible to calculations; they cannot be fixed or bounded, even in imagination. Will you limit the means of your defence when you cannot ascertain the force or extent of the invasion?"[11]

Jefferson, too, was not pleased with the draft of the Constitution as prepared by the Convention, and, although he expressed himself in favor of its adoption, he took an indifferent attitude, describing his position at one time as "nearly a neutral." Whereas Hamilton feared that the Constitution did not provide a sufficiently strong and secure government, Jefferson looked upon the plan as too strongly centralized and consolidated, unduly reducing the powers of the states. He was one of the first to see that the Constitution had been drawn to carry out the policies and to defend the interests of the business and commercial groups as against the agricultural interests. Hamilton became an ardent defender of the document, undoubtedly believing that it was possible to secure a government under it somewhat after the fashion of his own aristocratic notions. Jefferson favored conditional acceptance of the Constitution with active efforts to secure necessary amendments.[12] As a result of reflec-

---

[10] *Works* (Const. ed.), X: 425. See also Claude G. Bowers, *Jefferson and Hamilton* (New York, 1925), p. 29 ff. Hamilton's distrust of the people and contempt for democracy, notes Bowers, along with his "reliance on strong government supported by wealth, and, if need be sustained by standing armies, were carried by him into the Constitutional Convention and there proclaimed with all the tremendous force of his personality."

[11] Speech on June 27, 1788, Henry Cabot Lodge, ed., *The Works of Alexander Hamilton* (New York, 1885–1886), I: 471, 472.

[12] "At first I wished that when nine States should have accepted the Constitution, so as to ensure us what is good in it, the other four might hold off till the want of the bill of rights at least might be supplied. But I am convinced that the plan of Massachusetts is the best. That is, to accept, and to amend afterwards." Jefferson to William Carmichael, *Writings* (Ford ed.), V: 25.

tion and of the arguments of its proponents, Jefferson was gradually led to endorse the Constitution in 1789 as "unquestionably the wisest ever yet presented to men." He protested especially against the omission of a bill of rights. Some of his proposals were included in the first Ten Amendments adopted in 1791. Others, such as the prohibition of monopolies, limitations on a standing army, and restraints on the suspension of the writ of habeas corpus, were rejected. It was his conviction that the republican and democratic principles of the Constitution would come to prevail over the features which to him appeared monarchic in trend.[13] And though he was to a considerable degree a unionist, it was his view that neither the states nor individuals had surrendered all sovereign powers to the federal government.

To those who looked at the Constitution and the federal government organized under it, as did Jefferson, Hamilton was molding the Constitution by "administration" into a living form opposed to his deepest convictions. It was part of the policy of Hamilton to see that the Constitution should be "administered," that is, developed by interpretation rather than by amendment. Senator Lodge, a sympathetic biographer of Hamilton, wrote of his policy that it

was not merely to invigorate an existing political party or to evolve a new one, although such a result was incidental, important, and expected. Hamilton's scheme went farther, seeking to create a strong and, so far as was possible and judicious, a permanent class all over the country, without regard to existing political affiliations, but bound to the government as a government, by the strongest of all ties, immediate and personal pecuniary interest. . . . The full intent of the policy was to array property on the side of the government. That once done, the experiment, Hamilton felt, would succeed, and its powers, moreover, might then be much extended. He had been unable to introduce a class influence into the Constitution by limiting the suffrage for the President and Senate with a property qualification, but by his financial policy he could bind the existing class of wealthy men, comprising at that day the aristocracy bequeathed by provincial times to the new system, and thus, if at all, assure to the property of the country a powerful influence upon the government.[14]

Hamilton regarded the states as the bane of our political institutions. It was his purpose to reduce their power—to make them, if possible, merely administrative districts, in all important respects subservient to

---

[13] "It is my principle that the will of the majority should always prevail. If they approved the proposed Convention in all its parts, I shall concur in it cheerfully, in hopes that they will amend it whenever they shall find it works wrong." *Writings* (Ford ed.), IV: 479, 480.

"I see much precious improvement in it, but some seeds of danger which might have been kept out of sight of the framers by a consciousness of their own honesty and a presumption that all succeeding rulers would be as honest as themselves." *Writings* (Ford ed.), IV: 484.

[14] Henry Cabot Lodge, *Alexander Hamilton* (Boston, 1898), pp. 90, 91.

and dependent upon the nation. He believed in expanding the powers of the national government and hoped that eventually the federal government might "triumph altogether over the state governments and reduce them to an utter subordination, dividing the large States into smaller districts." Jefferson looked upon the states as the hope and promise of American life. Although a national government was necessary and indispensable, in his mind its functions were to be restricted so far as practicable to the narrowest limits. International affairs and interstate relations were regarded as federal matters, all else, especially those interests affecting the life, property, health, morals, and prosperity of the individual, were to be exclusively within the province of the states. Adopting to a certain extent the popular theory of divided sovereignty, Jefferson maintained that "the true theory of our Constitution is surely the wisest and best, that the States are independent as to everything within themselves and united as to everything respecting foreign nations."[15] The states, Hamilton hoped, would be compelled to relinquish powers until they would be stripped of all but administrative powers, whereas Jefferson wished to see them grow in power and prestige because to him they were the bulwarks of democracy against centralization and despotism.[16]

The greatest ability of Hamilton as a constructive statesman was shown in the development of the national finances. His fundamental measures, including the funding of the debt, federal and state, the establishment of a national bank and a mint, a system of taxation comprising customs duties and an excise tax, and a plan for the protection of American manufactures, were largely responsible for the success of the Administrations of Washington and Adams. These measures served to establish the credit of the United States with foreign countries and added materially to the prestige of the federal authorities at home. They established a foundation for the entire governmental system which has carried the nation through the stress and trials of a hundred and fifty years.

Hamilton favored the incorporation of a national bank, and in order

---

[15] *Writings* (Ford ed.), VII: 451. Foreseeing the encroachment of the state governments upon the powers of the national government, Hamilton referred to a disposition on his part toward "a liberal construction of the powers of the national government, and to erect every fence, to guard it from depredations, which is, in my opinion, consistent with constitutional propriety." *Works* (Lodge ed.), VIII: 263, 264.

[16] To Jefferson it was important to strengthen the state governments, and this could not be done by changes in the federal Constitution. He thought "it must be done by the States themselves, erecting such barriers at the constitutional line as cannot be surmounted either by themselves or by the general government." *Writings* (Mem. ed.), VIII: 276, 277.

to assure President Washington of the constitutionality of his proposal wrote an elaborate opinion on the interpretation of the Constitution, in which he argued for a loose construction of the Constitution and advocated the extension of federal authority under a doctrine of implied powers. He favored the funding of the state debts because in his opinion it would attach to the interest and support of the national government a large number of creditors in the states.[17] He recommended and secured the enactment of an excise tax because in his judgment the federal government could thus assert its authority directly in the states. Federal officials enforcing federal laws in the states were a prime necessity of the nationalism for which Hamilton stood.[18] A national debt, he claimed, if not excessive, would be "a national blessing," "a powerful cement of Union," "a necessity for keeping up taxation," and "a spur to industry."[19] The taxing power of the federal government was held to be plenary and complete without any direct limitations.

According to James Truslow Adams, "The most original feat of Hamilton was his realization of the fact that not only the national finances but the whole form and spirit of the government and fundamental law could be altered by a succession of fiscal measures."[20] Though he favored rapid industrialism, the encouragement of tariffs, and the granting of other privileges to the commercial classes, Hamilton himself did not foresee the huge concentration of wealth and the evils which his own economic system did so much to bring about. But his economic ideas—such as rapid industrialization, the fostering of immigration, the tariffs and other privileges given to certain groups, and above all the alliance between government and the privileged classes as a fundamental principle of political practice—were, in the opinion of Adams, "of profound importance in

[17] Regarding state debt assumption, Bowers notes that the largest unpaid debts were in the northern states. This fact led Patrick Henry to exclaim that "it seems to be a consistent part of a system I have ever dreaded and that the subserviency of Southern to Northern interests are written in Capitals on its very front." Claude G. Bowers, *Jefferson and Hamilton*, pp. 59, 60.

[18] Arguing on this point, Hamilton said: "The more the operations of the national authority are intermingled in the ordinary exercise of government, the more the citizens are accustomed to meet with it in the common occurrences of their political life, the more it is familiarized to their sight and to their feelings, the further it enters into those objects which touch the most sensible chords and put in motion the most active springs of the human heart, the greater will be the probability that it will conciliate the respect and attachment of the community." *The Federalist, Works* (Lodge ed), IX: 161.

[19] *Works* (Const. ed.), III: 40, 45.

[20] James Truslow Adams, *The Living Jefferson*, p. 229. According to Abbot Emerson Smith, Hamilton "created his aristocracy, his group of powerful persons who would find it to their *interest* to support and preserve the national government." *James Madison: Builder*, p. 160.

the insidious growth of that political immorality and lack of virtue in the individual citizens which have eaten into our national character like cancers. Much of the depravity and greed of our economic and political life is Hamilton's legacy to the Nation."[21] His work, indeed, laid the groundwork for government aid to business and the consequent business control of the government.

On taxation and finance, too, Jefferson was radically opposed to the doctrines of Hamilton. He objected to the funding of the state debts, finally lending his support to an arrangement with Hamilton which he later styled "a trick," and for which he frequently reproached himself. He shared the view commonly held at the time that funding the debt at face value was planned to bring extraordinary returns to speculators and to that group of capitalists which Hamilton was reputed to be serving. His opposition to the national bank was voiced in an opinion to Washington which presented his views on the meaning of the Constitution and the correct method of its interpretation. He regarded the excise tax as unnecessary and unduly calculated to arouse the people. He foresaw the opposition which resulted in the Whisky Insurrection on account of this obnoxious method of taxation. Hamilton's system of protection to American industries was held to require the exercise of authority beyond the jurisdiction of the federal government and was regarded as contrary to good policy. Finally Jefferson looked upon a national debt as a curse to a country and believed that a sound financial policy must aim to reduce the national indebtedness and keep expenditures within the limit of the revenues. The federal government, he thought, was limited in the field of taxation to the purposes stated in the Constitution. To him the financial measures of Hamilton appeared as "artful contrivances for keeping moneyed men and the administration in a close and profitable alliance," and for the establishment of a permanent plutocracy.[22]

The essential principle of Hamilton's reasoning with respect to the

---

[21] Adams, *op. cit.*, pp. 237, 238. Hamilton's plan for the administration of public affairs was characterized by Jefferson as a "government of wolves over sheep." The historian, Edward Channing, says that Hamilton was on intimate terms with the first well-defined group of speculators in American history and, in his opinion, "he was the organizer of exploitation, the originator of monopoly; but he did his work at the precise moment that exploitation needed to be organized and human ingenuity required exaltation by hope of monopoly." *History of the United States* (New York, 1926), IV: 66 and 96.

[22] Abbot Emerson Smith sums up the characteristic differences between the two men as follows: "Hamilton stood for the Industrial Revolution, for machines, cities, commerce, stock exchanges, England; Jefferson stood for agriculture, rural life, small holdings, hard money, France. Hamilton stood for capitalism, Jefferson for the rights of property. This was the real economic differences between parties." *James Madison: Builder*, p. 189.

formation of a stable government was predicated on a recognition of the class basis for the formation of a civil society and the necessity for the adoption of a check and balance theory. Assuming that the most important political conflicts would center around the interests of the few and the many and that it was necessary to check the imprudence or follies of the people,[23] Hamilton contended that:

It is of great importance in a republic not only to guard the society against the oppression of its rulers, but to guard one part of the society against the injustice of the other part. Different interests necessarily exist in different classes of citizens. If a majority be united by a common interest, the rights of the minority will be insecure. There are but two methods of providing against this evil: the one by creating a will in the community independent of the majority—that is, of the society itself; the other, by comprehending in the society so many separate descriptions of citizens as will render an unjust combination of a majority of the whole very improbable, if not impracticable.[24]

The principles which may be regarded as the foundation of the Jeffersonian philosophy were succinctly stated in his first inaugural address as follows:

It is proper you should understand what I deem the essential principles of our government and consequently those which ought to shape its administration. I will compress them within the narrowest compass they will bear, stating the general principle, but not all its limitations. Equal and exact justice to all men, of whatever station or persuasion, religious or political; peace, commerce, and honest friendship with all nations, entangling alliances with none; the support of the state governments in all their rights, as the most competent administrations of our domestic concerns and the surest bulwarks against anti-republican tendencies; the preservation of the general government in its whole constitutional vigor as the sheet anchor of our peace at home and safety abroad; a jealous care of the right of election by the people—and mild and safe corrective of abuses which are lopped by the sword of revolution where peaceable remedies are unprovided; absolute acquiescence in the decisions of the majority, the vital principle of republics from which is no appeal but to force, the vital principle and immediate parent of despotism; a well disciplined militia, our best reliance in peace and for the first moments of war, till regulars may relieve them; the supremacy of the civil over the military authority; economy in public expense, that labor may be lightly burdened; the honest payment of our debts, and sacred preservation of the public faith; encouragement of agriculture, and of commerce as its handmaid; the diffusion of information and arraignment of all abuses at the bar of the public reason;

[23] Speech in the Federal Convention, June 18, 1787. *Works* (Const. ed.), I: 401, 402; and above, p. 61.

"Take mankind in general, they are vicious, their passions may be operated upon. . . . Take mankind as they are, and what are they governed by? Their passions. . . . Our prevailing passions are ambition and interest, and it will ever be the duty of a wise government to avail itself of the passions, in order to make them subservient to the public good." From speech in Federal Convention, *Works* (Const. ed.), I: 408.

[24] *Works* (Lodge ed.), IX: 325.

freedom of religion; freedom of the press, and freedom of person, under the protection of habeas corpus, and trial by juries impartially selected.[25]

In this statement of his political principles and philosophy, Jefferson indicated the main lines along which his administration of national affairs was to be directed. It was on the whole a more moderate program than his political opponents expected and than many of his enthusiastic admirers deemed wise. Instead of a direct attack upon the major Hamiltonian measures which Jefferson disapproved and a program to crush the rising tide of aristocracy with its close affiliations with the national government, the principles of rationalism, common sense, and democracy which seemed so vital to Jefferson, were to replace the Federalist ideas and practices by a gradual process of infiltration. Moreover, prompted by a spirit of moderation and conciliation, Jefferson hoped that the bitterness and recriminations which had prevailed in the years preceding his election might be mollified and party lines less strictly drawn. For he wrote: "In every country where men are free to speak and think differences of opinion will arise . . . but these differences, when permitted, as in this happy country, to purify themselves by free discussion, are but as passing clouds overspreading our land temporarily, and leaving her horizon more bright and serene."[26] The Federalist leaders, he admitted, would continue to support wrong and in some instances vicious policies, but he thought their followers would gradually decrease in numbers and the party itself would disintegrate. Jefferson's prophecy of the decline and fall of the Federalist party was in the course of a few decades to be fulfilled. But, on the other hand, Jefferson did not realize how firm, solid, and enduring a structure the Federalists had built in the short term of their control of the national government.

---

[25] James D. Richardson, *A Compilation of the Messages and Papers of the Presidents* (Washington, 1911), I: 311, 312. The significance of Jefferson's contribution to American politics has been well stated by the historian, Andrew C. McLaughlin, as follows: "Whether we like the principles of Jeffersonian freedom or like them not, these are the principles which blossomed in America, and made America to be not Europe, but itself. To miss that fact is to miss, at the very least, half the story, to be blind to the spirit of freedom and hope, the creative spirit of developing liberalism and democracy." In review of Beveridge's *The Life of John Marshall*, 7 *Amer. Bar Assn. Jour.* (May, 1921), 231–233.

It is not the Constitution, thinks James Truslow Adams, "but the Declaration of Independence, Jefferson's first inaugural and Lincoln's Gettysburg address, which voice the inarticulate soul of the millions of Americans who in spite, often, of having their feet in the mire, have looked aloft and afar to dream the dream of America." *The Living Jefferson*, p. 305.

[26] *Writings* (Ford ed.), X: 236.

THE FEDERAL JUDICIARY AND DIVERGENT THEORIES
OF CONSTITUTIONAL INTERPRETATION

There was no issue on which the views of Hamilton and Jefferson were more diverse than on the organization and functions of the federal Judiciary. Hamilton not only advocated complete independence from other departments and a life term for the Judges, but he was also one of the first proponents of the doctrine that the courts should have authority to declare void acts of the legislature deemed in conflict with the Constitution. In fact, this doctrine was so cogently and forcefully stated in the seventy-eighth number of *The Federalist* that in the implied power doctrine John Marshall had only to adapt the language of Hamilton to the cases at hand to lay the foundation in constitutional law for the most distinctive features of constitutional interpretation. Hamilton, like many other prominent men of the time, looked to the courts as the champions of property rights and the bulwark of the aristocratic class which was, in his judgment, the only class qualified to take part in the government. A Constitution which effectively closed the avenues to change guarded by the federal Judiciary through the process of interpretation was one of the chief objectives in the program of Hamiltonian Federalism.

Favoring the convention plan of appointing Judges and providing for life tenure, Hamilton argued:

Whoever attentively considers the different departments of power must perceive that, in a government in which they are separated from each other, the Judiciary, from the nature of its functions, will always be the least dangerous to the political rights of the Constitution; because it will be least in a capacity to annoy or injure them. The Executive not only dispenses the honors, but holds the sword of the community. The Legislature not only commands the purse, but prescribes the rules by which the duties and rights of every citizen are to be regulated. The Judiciary, on the contrary, has no influence over either the sword or the purse; no direction either of the strength or of the wealth of the society; and can take no active resolution whatever. It may truly be said to have neither force nor will, but merely judgment; and must ultimately depend upon the aid of the executive arm even for the efficacy of its judgments.

This simple view of the matter suggests several important consequences. It proves incontestably that the Judiciary is beyond comparison the weakest of the three departments of power; that it can never attack with success either of the other two; and that all possible care is requisite to enable it to defend itself against their attacks. It equally proves that though individual oppression may now and then proceed from the courts of justice, the general liberty of the people can never be endangered from that quarter; I mean so long as the Judiciary remains truly distinct from both the Legislature and the Executive. For I agree that "there is no liberty, if the power of judging be not separated from the legislative and executive powers." And it proves, in the last place, that as liberty can have nothing to fear from the Judiciary alone, but would have everything to fear from its union with either of the other departments; that as all the effects of such a union must ensue from a dependence of the former on the latter, notwithstanding a nominal and apparent separation; that as, from the natural feebleness of the judiciary, it is in continual jeopardy of being overpowered, awed, or influenced by its coordinate branches; and that, as nothing can contribute so much to its firmness and independence as permanency in office, this quality may therefore be justly regarded as an indispensable ingredient in its constitution, and, in a great measure, as the citadel of the public justice and the public security.

The complete independence of the courts of justice is peculiarly essential in a limited Constitution. By a limited Constitution I understand one which contains certain specified exceptions to the legislative authority; such for instance, as that it shall pass no bills of attainder, no *ex post facto* laws, and the like. Limitations of this kind can be preserved in practice no other way than through the medium of courts of justice, whose duty it must be to declare all acts contrary to the manifest tenor of the Constitution void. Without this, all the reservations of particular rights or privileges would amount to nothing.

Some perplexity respecting the rights of the courts to pronounce legislative acts void, because contrary to the Constitution, has arisen from an imagination that the doctrine would imply a superiority of the Judiciary to the legislative power. It is urged that the authority which can declare the acts of another void must necessarily be superior to the one whose acts may be declared void. As this doctrine is of great importance in all the American constitutions, a brief discussion of the ground on which it rests cannot be unacceptable.

There is no position which depends on clearer principles than that every act of a delegated authority, contrary to the tenor of the commission under which it is exercised, is void. No legislative act, therefore, contrary to the Constitution, can be valid. To deny this would be to affirm that the deputy is greater than his principal; that the servant is above his master; that the representatives of the people are superior to the people themselves; that men acting by virtue of powers may do not only what their powers do not authorize, but what they forbid.

If it be said that the legislative body are themselves the constitutional judges of their own powers, and that the construction they put upon them is conclusive upon the other departments, it may be answered that this cannot be the natural presumption, where it is not to be collected from any particular provisions in the Constitution. It is not otherwise to be supposed that the Constitution could intend to enable the representatives of the people to substitute their will to that of their constituents. It is far from rational to suppose that the courts were designed to be an intermediate body between the people and the legislature, in order, among other things, to keep the latter within the limits assigned to their authority. The interpretation of the laws is the proper and peculiar province of the courts. A constitution is, in fact, and must be regarded by the Judges, as a fundamental law. It therefore belongs to them to ascertain its meaning, as well as the meaning of any particular act proceeding from the legislative body. If there should happen to be an irreconcilable variance between the two, that which has the superior obligation and validity ought, of course, to be preferred; or, in other words, the Constitution ought to be preferred to the statute; the intention of the people to the intention of their agents.

Nor does this conclusion by any means suppose a superiority of the judicial to the legislative power. It only supposes that the power of the people is superior to both; and that where the will of the Legislature, declared in its statutes, stands in opposition to that of the people, declared in the Constitution, the Judges ought to be governed by that latter rather than the former. They ought to regulate their decisions by the fundamental laws, rather than by those which are not fundamental . . . the prior act of a superior ought to be preferred to the subsequent act of an inferior and subordinate authority; and that accordingly, whenever a particular statute contravenes the Constitution, it will be the duty of the judicial tribunals to adhere to the latter and disregard the former.[27]

As Hamilton's argument forms the groundwork and standard for all future efforts to support the peculiar function to be allotted to the Judges in the American system of constitutional interpretation, it requires brief analysis and comment. The argument is founded on the assumption that the Judiciary is essentially a weak department and needs protection from the other more politically motivated departments and that the liberties of the individual may more safely be entrusted to Judges rather than to the officers of the other departments. Recognizing that the Constitution was a superior and fundamental law—a doctrine concerning which there was almost universal agreement—it was assumed that such law must be considered as law in the ordinary sense and that courts might take jurisdiction to determine whether conflicts had arisen between the statutory and constitutional provisions. From the standpoint of jurisdiction and interpretation constitutional law and statutory law were thus placed on the same plane. Hamilton formulated in its essential features the primary method and hypothesis of the mechanical school of interpretation. All that was necessary was to place the higher and lower law side by side and if there was a conflict the higher law prevailed, the lower law being *ex necessitate* invalid. Two other hypotheses formed essential links in the argument. First, that although the Court passed judgment on the validity of an act given the impress of authority of law by two coördinate departments, it did not thereby assert a superiority over these departments. The Court, it was assumed, was merely doing its plain and unmistakable duty as a coördinate branch of the government. Second, though a few life appointees on the bench were expected to exercise the prerogative of review, they were in effect carrying out the real will of the people in insisting that the Legislature keep within the limits assigned by the Constitution.[28]

---

[27] *The Federalist* (Ford ed.), pp. 520–523.

[28] Referring to Hamilton's arguments in *The Federalist* relating to the independence and superior powers of the Judiciary, J. Allen Smith observes "it is, to say the least, strange that the misstatement of historical facts, false analogies and juggling of popular catch-words which constitute the defence of the federal Judiciary should have been so often referred to as an example of faultless logic and a complete vindication of the system. Hamilton's interpretation of the Constitution as contained in these articles was merely for popular consumption, and not a frank and unequivocal expression of what he himself really believed." *The Spirit of American Government* (New York, 1912), pp. 78, 79.

Hamilton's argument was made in defense of the Constitution in which he indicated a number of times he had relatively little confidence. Believing as he did in government by the few, his model government would have followed the general lines of the English monarchy. Not being impressed with the demand for special rights and privileges on the part of the people, it was natural for him to turn to the Judges as the appropriate interpreters of constitutional provisions. Moreover, it soon appeared that he favored such a plan of judicial review because he believed the Judges would aid in the process of expansion of federal powers by construing its provisions on broad and loose lines. And, finally, Hamilton looked to the Judiciary for effective protection of property and vested rights. Judicial review of acts of Congress as well as of the state legislature was, then, to him, the foundation principle for the establishment of a series of significant checks upon popular government. The popular will might be made to prevail through constitutional amendments, but in the opinion of Hamilton and other conservatives the method adopted for this purpose prevented too free use of this extraordinary authority.[29]

To the claim that the Judges in interpreting the Constitution would warp the language to accomplish the objects which to them seemed desirable, Hamilton replied:

It can be of no weight to say that the courts, on the pretence of a repugnancy, may substitute their own pleasure to the constitutional intentions of the legislature. This might as well happen in the case of two contradictory statutes; or it might as well happen in every adjudication upon any single statute. The courts must declare the sense of the law; and if they should be disposed to exercise *will* instead of *judgment*, the consequence would equally be the substitution of their pleasure to that of the legislative body. The observation, if it prove anything, would prove that there ought to be no judges distinct from that body.

If, then, the courts of justice are to be considered as the bulwarks of a limited Constitution against legislative encroachments, this consideration will afford a strong argument for the permanent tenure of judicial offices, since nothing will contribute so much as this to that independent spirit in the Judges which must be essential to the faithful performance of so arduous a duty.[30]

[29] Though Hamilton stated the theories and postulates involved in the generally accepted practice of judicial review of legislative acts, he indicated doubts, so far as acts of Congress are concerned, about the nature and scope of such review. Answering the question, who was to judge of the necessity and propriety of the laws to be passed by Congress, Hamilton replied that the national government would be judge in the first instance and the people in the last, thereby neglecting to mention the Judiciary as an intermediary authority to interpret the Constitution. Discussing the supremacy clause with the phrase requiring acts to be in pursuance of the Constitution, Hamilton came near to the acceptance of a doctrine of nullification. It will not follow from this provision, he said, "that acts of the larger society which are *not pursuant* to its constitutional powers, but which are invasions of the residuary authorities of the smaller societies, will become the supreme law of the land." *The Federalist* (Lodge ed.), pp. 192, 193.

[30] *The Federalist* (Ford ed.), p. 523. Continuing the same line of argument, Hamilton

Hamilton not only supported the plan of life-appointed Judges who were to be the authoritative interpreters of the provisions of the Constitution and the correlative principle that the Judges were to aid in establishing limits on legislative powers for the protection of property, but he also expected the Judiciary to adopt methods of construction which would give the federal government a free rein for the expansion of national authority.

In the consideration of the powers of Congress during the Philadelphia Convention, Hamilton proposed that Congress should have the authority "to legislate in all cases for the general interest of the Union." Failing to secure approval for such broad powers, Hamilton believed that in essence the same authority might be interpreted as comprehended within the phrase included under the taxing powers of Congress "to provide for the common defense and the general welfare." In his report to Congress on manufactures in 1791, Hamilton, as has been noted, argued that Congress could appropriate money for any object which concerns the general welfare. Thwarted in his attempt to give unlimited legislative powers to Congress in the Convention, he sought to secure the same result by his construction of the words "general welfare."

But the first direct clash of opinion between Hamilton and Jefferson came when the Secretary of Treasury proposed the establishment of a national bank, as one of the features of his financial program. President Washington submitted the question of the constitutionality of such a measure to the members of his cabinet. In his reply Jefferson said:

I consider the foundation of the Constitution as laid on this ground: That "all powers not delegated to the United States, by the Constitution, nor prohibited by it to the States, are reserved to the States or to the people" [Tenth Amendment]. To take a single step beyond the boundaries thus specially drawn around the powers of Congress, is to take possession of a boundless field of power, no longer susceptible of any definition.

The incorporation of a bank, and the powers assumed by this bill, have not, in my opinion, been delegated to the United States by the Constitution.

I. They are not among the powers specially enumerated. . . .

II. Nor are they within either of the general phrases, which are the two following:

1. To lay taxes to provide for the general welfare of the United States, that is to say, "to lay taxes for *the purpose* of providing for the general welfare". . .

---

said: "It may in the last place be observed that the supposed danger of judiciary encroachments on the legislative authority, which has been upon many occasions reiterated, is in reality a phantom. Particular misconstructions and contraventions of the will of the legislature may now and then happen; but they can never be so extensive as to amount to an inconvenience, or in any sensible degree to affect the order of the political system. This may be inferred with certainty, from the general nature of the judicial power, from the objects to which it relates, from the manner in which it is exercised, from its comparative weakness, and from its total incapacity to support its usurpations by force." *Ibid.*, p. 542.

This grant of power, said Jefferson, does not give Congress power to do anything they may wish for the general welfare, but only to lay taxes for that purpose. If this is a general grant of power all of the specific enumerations of power become meaningless. And he continued:

> It would reduce the whole instrument to a single phrase, that of instituting a Congress with power to do whatever would be for the good of the United States. . . . Certainly no such universal power was meant to be given them. It was intended to lace them up straightly within the enumerated powers, and those without which, as means, these powers could not be carried into effect. It is known that the very power now proposed *as a means* was rejected as *an end* by the Convention which formed the Constitution. . . .
>
>   2. The second general phrase is, "to make all laws *necessary,* and proper for carrying into execution the enumerated powers." But they can all be carried into execution without a bank. A bank therefore is not *necessary,* and consequently not authorized by this phrase.
>
>   It has been urged that a bank will give great facility or convenience in the collection of taxes. Suppose this were true: yet the Constitution allows only the means which are *"necessary,"* not those which are merely *"convenient"* for effecting the enumerated powers. If such a latitude of construction be allowed to this phrase as to give any non-enumerated power, it will go to every one, for there is not one which ingenuity may not torture into a *convenience* in some instance *or other; to some one* of so long a list of enumerated powers. It would swallow up all the delegated powers, and reduce the whole to one power, as before observed. Therefore it was that the Constitution restrained them to the *necessary* means, that is to say, to those means without which the grant of power would be nugatory.[31]

Madison also agreed with Jefferson that the language of the Constitution did not warrant the establishment of a national bank, and, in a speech in the House of Representatives on April 6, 1796, remarked that according to his memory a motion had been made and negatived in the federal Convention for giving Congress a power to grant charters of incorporation.[32]

In replying to the arguments of Jefferson and Madison on the constitutionality of a proposal to establish a national bank, Hamilton claimed that this general principle is inherent in the very definition of government, namely, "that every power vested in a government is in its nature *sovereign,* and includes by *force* of the *term,* a right to employ all the *means* requisite and fairly applicable to the attainment of the ends of such power, and which are not precluded by restrictions and exceptions

---

[31] *Writings* (Ford ed.), V: 284–289.

[32] Max Farrand, ed., *The Records of the Federal Convention of 1787* (New Haven, 1923), III: 373. Madison's motion "to grant charters of incorporation where the interest of the United States might require and the legislative provisions of individual States may be incompetent," after being specified and limited to the case of canals was defeated by a vote of 3 states to 8. Farrand, *op. cit.,* II: 615, 616.

specified in the Constitution; or not immoral, or not contrary to the essential ends of political society."

Following this line of reasoning, Hamilton thought that in addition to the powers expressly granted to the federal government there were implied or resulting powers without which the government could not function effectively. Hence, when the Constitution referred to "laws necessary and proper for carrying into execution the foregoing powers," *necessary* meant not merely those things without which the government could not function but all means which are "needful, requisite, incidental, useful or conducive to" the carrying out of the express powers. The criterion of what is constitutional, then, is, maintained Hamilton, "the end to which the measure relates as a *means*. If the *end* be clearly comprehended within any of the specified powers, and if the measure have any obvious relation to that *end* and is not forbidden by any particular provision of the Constitution, it may safely be deemed to come within the compass of national authority."[33] It was this argument in particular to which Madison took exception.[34]

The opposition to the establishment of a national bank led Hamilton to defend the proposition that sovereignty, for certain purposes at least, was confided to the national government. Writing to Robert Morris, he contended that it was necessary for those who opposed the exercise of such a power

to show that a rule which, in the general system of things, is essential to the preservation of the social order, is inapplicable to the United States. . . .

If it would be necessary to bring proof to a proposition so clear, as that which affirms that the powers of the federal government, as to *its objects* were sovereign, there is a clause of its Constitution which would be decisive. It is that which declares that the Constitution, and the laws of the United States made in pursuance of it, and all treaties made, or which shall be made, under their authority, shall be the *supreme law of the land*. The power which can create the *supreme law of the land* in *any case*, is doubtless *sovereign* as to such case.

This general and indisputable principle puts at once an end to the *abstract* question, whether the United States have power to erect a corporation; that is to say, to give a *legal* or *artificial capacity* to one or more persons, distinct from the *natural*. But it is

---

[33] Writing to Robert Morris, Hamilton observed: "It is not denied that there are *implied*, as well as *express powers*, and that the *former* are as effectually delegated as the *latter*. And for the sake of accuracy it shall be mentioned that there is another class of powers, which may be properly denominated *resulting powers*. It will not be doubted that if the United States should make a conquest of any of the territories of its neighbors, they would possess sovereign jurisdiction over the conquered territory. This would be rather a result from the whole mass of the powers of the government, and from the nature of political society, than a consequence of either of the powers specially enumerated." *Works* (Lodge ed.), III: 184.

[34] See below, pp. 211, 376.

unquestionably incident to *sovereign power* to erect corporations, and consequently to *that* of the United States, in *relation* to the *objects* intrusted to the management of the government.[35]

Jefferson not only argued against the constitutionality of the proposal to establish a national bank but he also came to a different conclusion from that of Hamilton regarding the authority of the courts to declare legislative acts void. During the Revolutionary period, being concerned primarily with the preservation of personal and individual liberties, Jefferson was inclined to favor a judicial power which "ought to be distinct from both the legislative and executive, and independent upon both, that so it may be a check upon both, as both should be checks upon that."[36] Approving the desirability of a check on public powers, he included in his draft for a constitution for Virginia in 1783 a plan for a council of revision. And favoring a bill of rights for the federal Constitution, Jefferson wrote to Madison as follows:

In the arguments in favor of a declaration of rights, you omit one which has great weight with me, the legal check which it puts into the hands of the Judiciary. This is a body, which if rendered independent and kept strictly to their own department merits great confidence for their learning and integrity. In fact what degree of confidence would be too much for a body composed of such men as Wythe, Blair and Pendleton?[37]

In the same letter referring to the federal Constitution, he noted that "this instrument forms us into one state as to certain objects, and gives

---

[35] *Works* (Lodge ed.), III: 181, 182.

Concerning the debate on the constitutionality of Hamilton's proposal to establish a national bank, John Marshall remarked that the "wishes, affections, and general theories" of the disputants had a decisive influence with respect to their arguments. Thus, in Marshall's opinion, personal and political factors played a prominent part in the determination of a constitutional issue. It was without doubt the same factors which influenced Marshall when later as Chief Justice he was called upon to pass judgment on similar constitutional questions. See Charles A. Beard, *Economic Origins of Jeffersonian Democracy* (New York, 1915), p. 159.

[36] See letter to George Wythe, July, 1776, *Writings* (Ford ed.), II: 59. In his notes on Virginia, Jefferson commented as follows:

"All the powers of government, legislative, executive, and judiciary, result to the legislative body. The concentrating of these in the same hands is precisely the definition of despotic government. It will be no alleviation that these powers will be exercised by a plurality of hands, and not by a single one. One hundred seventy-three despots would surely be as oppressive as one. Let those who doubt it turn their eyes on the republic of Venice. As little will it avail us that they are chosen by ourselves. An elective despotism was not the government we fought for, but one which should not only be founded on free principles, but in which the powers of government should be so divided and balanced among several bodies of magistracy, as that no one could transcend their legal limits, without being effectually checked and restrained by the others." *Writings* (Ford ed.), III: 223.

[37] *Writings* (Mem. ed.), VI: 132, 133.

us a legislative and executive body for these objects. It should therefore guard us against their abuses of power within the field submitted to them. . . . The Executive in our government is not the sole, it is scarcely the principal object of my jealousy. The tyranny of the Legislatures is the most formidable dread at present, and will be for long years. That of the Executive will come in its turn, but it will be at a remote period."[38] Though Jefferson thought that the laws of the land administered by upright Judges would protect individuals from the exercise of powers unauthorized by the Constitution, he anticipated that public officers would seek to increase their powers; and, hence, he favored the principle that the powers of government should be divided and balanced among several "bodies of magistracy," so that no one of them could transcend their legal limits without being effectually checked by the others. It was, however, limitations on the powers of officials and not on the powers of the people that Jefferson wished to see established. The Federalists, on the other hand, were primarily concerned that checks be placed on popular authority and control.

When it was maintained, however, in the controversy over the Alien and Sedition Acts and over the Judiciary Repeal Act, that the judicial department was to have the authority to place a final and authoritative interpretation upon the Constitution to which all other departments must submit, Jefferson became an uncompromising critic of the Supreme Court. He insisted that not a word in the Constitution had given the power of final interpretation of that instrument to the Judges rather than to the Executive or Legislative branches.[39] In a paragraph omitted from the final draft of his message to Congress on December 8, 1801, Jefferson noted that:

Applications from different persons suffering prosecution under the act usually called the Sedition Act, claimed my early attention to that instrument. Our country has thought proper to distribute the powers of its government among three equal and independent authorities, constituting each a check on one or both of the others, in all attempts to impair its Constitution. To make each an effectual check, it must have

[38] *Writings* (Mem. ed.), II: 163.

[39] Edward S. Corwin, making the usual charge of inconsistency in Jefferson's earlier and later views on judicial review, says: "I cannot find that Jefferson ever actually denied the right of the Supreme Court to judge of the validity of acts of Congress." It was obviously not to judicial review of Congressional acts to which Jefferson objected, but to the somewhat arrogant claims of superiority of the decisions of the courts over the views of the other coördinate departments on matters of constitutional construction and on the settlement of political questions. See chap. i, above, p. 23, and Corwin, "The Supreme Court and Unconstitutional Acts of Congress," 4 *Mich. Law Rev.* (June, 1906), 629; also Charles Warren, *The Supreme Court in United States History* (Boston, 1922), I: 264 ff.

a right in cases which arise within the line of its proper functions, where, equally with the others, it acts in the last resort and without appeal, to decide on the validity of an act according to its own judgment, and uncontrolled by the opinions of any other department. We have accordingly, in more than one instance, seen the opinions of different departments in opposition to each other, and no ill ensue. The Constitution moreover, as a further security for itself, against violation even by a concurrence of all the departments, has provided for its own reintegration by a change of the persons exercising the functions of those departments. Succeeding functionaries have the same right to judge of the conformity or non-conformity of an act with the Constitution, as their predecessors who passed it. For if it be against that instrument it is a perpetual nullity. Uniform decisions indeed, sanctioned by successive functionaries, by the public voice, and by repeated elections would so strengthen a construction as to render highly responsible a departure from it. On my accession to the administration, reclamations against the Sedition Act were laid before me by individual citizens, claiming the protection of the Constitution against the Sedition Act. Called on by the position in which the Nation had placed me, to exercise in their behalf my free and independent judgment, I took the act into consideration, compared it with the Constitution, viewed it under every aspect of which I thought it susceptible, and gave to it all the attention which the magnitude of the case demanded. On mature deliberation, in the presence of the Nation, and under the tie of the solemn oath which binds me to them and to my duty, I do declare that I hold that act to be in palpable and unqualified contradiction to the Constitution. Considering it then as a nullity, I have relieved from oppression under it those of my fellow-citizens who were within the reach of the functions confided to me.[40] In recalling our footsteps within the limits of the Constitution, I have been actuated by a zealous devotion to that instrument. It is the ligament which binds us into one Nation. It is, to the national government, the law of its existence, with which it began, and with which it is to end. Infractions of it may sometimes be committed from inadvertence, sometimes from the panic, or passions of a moment. To correct these with good faith, as soon as discovered, will be an assurance to the States that, far from meaning to impair that sacred charter of its authorities, the general government views it as the principle of its own life.[41]

From this excerpt it appears that Jefferson ascribed to each department the power to judge for itself, "within the line of its proper functions," the constitutionality of the acts of the other departments. Again,

---

[40] At another time Jefferson wrote that "I discharged every person under punishment or prosecution under the Sedition Law, because I considered, and now consider, that law to be a nullity, as absolute and as palpable as if Congress had ordered us to fall down and worship a golden image." Letter of July 22, 1804, to Mrs. Adams, in *Memoir, Correspondence, and Miscellanies from the Papers of Thomas Jefferson*, ed. by Thomas Jefferson Randolph (2d ed., Boston, 1830), IV: 23.

[41] Jefferson MSS. Library of Congress; quoted in Albert J. Beveridge, *The Life of John Marshall* (Boston, 1919), III, Appendix A, pp. 605, 606. See also Gilbert Chinard, *Thomas Jefferson* (Boston, 1929), p. 383. This passage was first brought to public attention by Charles A. Beard in the *Economic Origins of Jeffersonian Democracy*, pp. 454, 455. This paragraph was included in the rough draft of Jefferson's first inaugural address but was finally omitted as indicated on the margin because "capable of being chicaned, and furnishing something to the opposition to make a handle of. It was thought better that the message should be clear of everything which the public might be made to misunderstand."

in another reference to the Sedition Act, Jefferson asserted the same doctrine. Writing to Mrs. John Adams in 1804, Jefferson said:

You seem to think it devolved on the Judges to decide on the validity of the Sedition Law. But nothing in the Constitution has given them a right to decide for the Executive, more than to the Executive to decide for them. Both magistracies are equally independent in the sphere of action assigned to them. The Judges, believing the law constitutional, had a right to pass a sentence of fine and imprisonment; because that power was placed in their hands by the Constitution. But the Executive, believing the law to be unconstitutional, was bound to remit the execution of it; because that power has been confided to him by the Constitution. That instrument meant that its coordinate branches should be checks on each other. But the opinion which gives to the Judges the right to decide what laws are constitutional, and what not, not only for themselves in their own sphere of action, but for the Legislature and Executive also, in their spheres, would make the Judiciary a despotic branch.[42]

The purchase of Louisiana and the subsequent government of the territory acquired put to the test some of Jefferson's ideas relating to constitutional interpretation. When the opportunity was presented to secure for a relatively small payment an extensive addition to the territory then under the jurisdiction of the United States, Jefferson authorized the representatives of the nation to conclude a treaty for the acquisition of Louisiana. This treaty, wrote Jefferson,

must of course be laid before both Houses, because both have important functions to exercise respecting it. They, I presume, will see their duty to their country in ratifying and paying for it, so as to secure a good which would otherwise probably be never again in their power. But I suppose they must then appeal to *the Nation* for an additional article to the Constitution, approving and confirming an act which the Nation had not previously authorized. The Constitution has made no provision for our holding foreign territory, still less for incorporating foreign nations into our Union. The Executive in seizing the fugitive occurrence which so much advances the good of their country, have done an act beyond the Constitution. The Legislature in casting behind them metaphysical subtleties, and risking themselves like faithful servants, must ratify and pay for it, and throw themselves on their country for doing for them unauthorized what we know they would have done for themselves had they been in a situation to do it. It is the case of a guardian, investing the money of his ward in purchasing an important adjacent territory; and saying to him when of age, I did this for your good; I pretend to no right to bind you: you may disavow me, and I must get out of the scrape as I can: I thought it my duty to risk myself for you. But we shall not be disavowed by the Nation, and their act of indemnity will confirm and not weaken the Constitution, by more strongly marking out its lines.[43]

In accordance with the views suggested in this letter, Jefferson had a draft prepared for a constitutional amendment; but the members of Congress, fearing that the delay in confirming the provisions of the treaty by the cumbersome method of amendment to the Constitution

[42] *Writings* (Ford ed.), VIII: 311.
[43] *Writings* (Ford ed.), VIII: 244.

might result in Napoleon's withdrawal of the proposal to sell the territory, preferred to give their approval to the treaty and to drop the plan to amend the Constitution. Some years later when Jefferson's conduct in this connection was criticized, he justified his action under what has come to be known as the emergency power doctrine. The question proposed, said he,

whether circumstances do not sometimes occur, which make it a duty in officers of high trust, to assume authorities beyond the law, is easy of solution in principle, but sometimes embarrassing in practice. A strict observance of the written laws is doubtless *one* of the high duties of a good citizen, but it is not *the highest*. The laws of necessity, of self-preservation, of saving our country when in danger, are of higher obligation. To lose our country by a scrupulous adherence to written law, would be to lose the law itself, with life, liberty, property and all those who are enjoying them with us; thus absurdly sacrificing the end to the means.

The line of discrimination between the instances when an officer should follow the strict letter of the law and those rare occasions when there is warrant to overleap the law, Jefferson admits, is difficult to draw; but he thinks "the good officer is bound to draw it at his own peril and throw himself on the justice of his country and the rectitude of his motives."[44]

Thus, it is claimed that Jefferson, like Hamilton, was willing to stretch the scope of constitutional grants to accomplish what he deemed worthy national objects. In evaluating this precedent, for which Jefferson has been condemned for violating his own canons of constitutional construction, it is well to note that although Jefferson presented in its most cogent form the doctrine of a strict or narrow interpretation of the grants of power to the federal government, there were other political doctrines more fundamental and pervasive which influenced his conduct as President. Laws and constitutions were mere instruments or means to carry out the wishes of the people. He preferred a strict construction of constitutional grants to the federal government because he believed the people of the states desired and expressly provided for the retention of the more important powers of government in their own hands. If by a clear expression of their will the people were willing to transfer particular powers to the federal government he would not object. His disposition to bow to the superior will of the people and to mold constitutions freely to accord with that will is shown in his comments on the process of constitutional amendment for the state of Virginia, as follows:

Some men look at constitutions with sanctimonious reverence, and deem them like the arc of the covenant, too sacred to be touched. They ascribe to the men of the preceding

[44] Letter to John B. Colvin, September 20, 1810, *Writings* (Ford ed., New York, 1898), IX: 279–282.

age a wisdom more than human, and suppose what they did to be beyond amendment. I knew that age well; I belonged to it, and labored with it. It deserved well of its country. It was very like the present, but without the experience of the present; and forty years of experience in government is worth a century of book-reading; and this they would say themselves, were they to rise from the dead. I am certainly not an advocate for frequent and untried changes in laws and constitutions. I think moderate imperfections had better be borne with; because, when once known, we accommodate ourselves to them, and find practical means of correcting their ill effects. But I know also, that laws and institutions must go hand in hand with the progress of the human mind. As that becomes more developed, more enlightened, as new discoveries are made, new truths disclosed, and manners and opinions change with the change of circumstances, institutions must advance also and keep pace with the times. We might as well require a man to wear still the coat which fitted him when a boy, as civilized society to remain ever under the regimen of their barbarous ancestors. . . . Let us, as our sister States have done, avail ourselves of our reason and experience, to correct the crude essays of our first and unexperienced, although wise, virtuous, and well meaning councils. And, lastly, let us provide in our constitution [that of Virginia] for its revision at stated periods. What these periods should be, nature herself indicates. . . . [Every generation of nineteen years.] If this avenue [of legal revision] be shut to the call of sufferance, it will make itself heard through that of force, and we shall go on, as other nations are doing, in the endless circle of oppression, rebellion, reformation; and oppression, rebellion, reformation, again; and so on forever.[45]

By this time, Jefferson had come to feel that the peculiar security of the American people was in the possession of a written constitution; but he did not wish to make the document "blank paper by construction." He preferred to go on perfecting the document by amendment and, if necessary, increasing the powers of the federal government so far as time and trial demonstrated its powers to be inadequate. Since each generation has a right to choose for itself the form of government it believes most promotive of its own happiness, a constitution should be changed every nineteen or twenty years "so that it may be handed on, with periodical repairs, from generation to generation, to the end of time, if anything human can so long endure."[46] Thus, the written Constitution was, according to the views of Jefferson, to change by the natural and normal processes of amendment and revision, rather than by the covert and indirect method proposed by Hamilton—the method of judicial construction.

Though the opinions of James Madison relating to constitutional construction accord in the main with those of Jefferson, there are differences in point of view which are of peculiar interest. In the federal Conven-

---

[45] Letter to Samuel Kercheval, July 12, 1816, *Writings* (Ford ed.), X: 42–44.

[46] *Writings* (Mem. ed.), X: 419 and XV: 42. At another time he wrote: "I set out on this ground, which I suppose to be self-evident, that the *earth belongs in usufruct to the living;* that the dead have neither powers nor rights over it." *Writings* (Mem. ed.), VII: 454.

tion, and until the early years of Washington's Administration, James Madison was in most respects a nationalist. He disapproved during the Convention debates some of the most important provisions which were incorporated in the draft of the Constitution, but he favored the adoption of the Constitution and argued ably in its defense. After the government was put into operation it was not long until he took issue with Washington and Hamilton because he believed they were aiming to secure by indirection powers for the federal government which the Convention had deliberately and expressly refused to grant. Speaking of the gradual evolution of Madison's thought in the direction of the formation of a strong central government, Abbot Emerson Smith observes that "the construction of this system meant . . . that building of a social order in which commerce and finance, merchants and bankers, might rise to a position of dominance. It meant the eventual destruction of the social and economic system out of which Madison had come and for which he stood." Not long after 1789 Madison realized that "he had helped to create something which held disastrous possibilities for him and his kind."[47]

Madison was the first to object to what he regarded as Hamilton's desire to "administer" the government in the form he desired it to take. Madison later observed that it was his wish "to make it conform to the Constitution as understood by the Convention that produced and recommended it, and particularly by the state conventions that *adopted* it."[48] During the debate over Hamilton's proposal to establish a national bank, Madison wrote that the arguments in favor of the bank increased his dislike for it because "they were founded on remote implications, which strike at the very essence of the government as composed of limited and enumerated powers."[49] Commenting on Hamilton's proposal in his report on manufactures that Congress can do whatever in its discretion can be done by money and will promote the general welfare, Madison wrote to Pendleton, "I consider it myself as subverting the fundamental and characteristic principle of the government; as contrary to the true and fair, as well as the received construction, and as bidding defiance to the sense in which the Constitution is known to have been proposed, advocated, and adopted, the government is no longer a limited one, possessing enumerated powers, but an indefinite one, subject to particular exceptions."[50] Madison's opposition to Hamilton's proposals grew more pronounced as he became convinced that there was a deliberate inten-

---

[47] Smith, *James Madison: Builder,* p. 94.
[48] Randall, *The Life of Thomas Jefferson,* III: 595.
[49] Smith, *op. cit.,* p. 176.
[50] Smith, *op. cit.,* p. 182.

tion on the part of the Federalists to create a "moneyed interest" which was expected to be the most powerful support of the government. Though Madison preceded Jefferson in his attacks on the Hamiltonian system, it was Jefferson who made the attack popular and became the leader of the opposition party. For this reason it is customary to contrast the Hamiltonian and Jeffersonian theories of constitutional construction and to treat the views of Madison as supporting and amplifying those of Jefferson.

MADISON'S VIEWS ON CONSTITUTIONAL INTERPRETATION

Agreeing with most other men of the time, Madison believed that governmental authority should be limited by a superior or fundamental law. He regarded the Constitution as the formulation of such a superior law, and he considered the courts as better qualified than other departments of the government to expound the ordinary meaning of the provisions of the Constitution. Thus, Madison noted in the course of the Convention debates that "a law violating a constitution established by the people themselves would be considered by the Judges as null and void."[51]

In his earlier views on judicial review of legislative acts, Madison appears to be chiefly concerned with two phases of the exercise of this authority, namely, the protection and preservation of individual rights and the necessary control over certain state acts. Speaking of the power of the courts with respect to the amendments designed to constitute a bill of rights, Madison observed that as "independent tribunals of justice the courts would consider themselves in a peculiar manner the guardians of those rights; they will be an impenetrable bulwark against every assumption of power in the Legislative or Executive; they will be naturally led to resist every encroachment upon rights expressly stipulated for in the Constitution by the declaration of rights."[52]

Recognizing that the states had other methods than a judicial recourse to assert their rights, Madison thought the jurisdiction claimed for the federal Judiciary is truly "the only defensive armor of the federal government, or, rather, for the Constitution and laws of the United States. Strip it of that armor, and the door is wide open for nullification, anarchy, and convulsion."[53] To him the natural and reasonable method for the settlement of controversies between the nation and the states for the controversies that might arise in the normal course of the administration

---

[51] Farrand, *op. cit.*, II: 93.
[52] *Annals of Congress*, I: 439.
[53] *Writings* (Cong. ed.), IV: 296, 297.

of public affairs was an appeal to the federal Judiciary.[54] For the settlement of major issues concerning the division of powers and for controversies tinged with questions of policy and expediency, he turned elsewhere for an official recourse.

Though Madison accepted the principle of judicial review of legislative and administrative acts, the limitations with which he surrounded the exercise of such authority are especially significant. In the federal Convention, Madison expressed doubt regarding the advisability of a grant of judicial power to apply generally to cases arising under the Constitution and thought that jurisdiction should be limited to "cases of a judiciary nature" or what we would consider today as justiciable questions. "The right of expounding the Constitution in cases not of this nature," he said, "ought not to be given to that department."[55] And he frequently referred to the principle that Congress is the judge of the expediency of the means or measures to carry out the powers granted to it by the Constitution. For, said he, "The Court certainly cannot be so; a question, the moment it assumes the character of mere expediency or policy, being evidently beyond the reach of judicial cognizance."[56] Indicating his disapproval of a general doctrine of judicial review, he commented on a proposal for a council of revision in Virginia similar to that of New York to the effect that

it should not be allowed to the Judges or the Executive to pronounce a law thus enacted unconstitutional and invalid. In the state constitutions, and, indeed, in the federal one also, no provision is made for the case of a disagreement in expounding them; and as the courts are generally the last in making the decision, it results to them, by refusing or not to execute a law, to stamp it with its final character. This makes the judiciary department paramount in fact to the legislature, which was never intended and can never be proper.[57]

The Supreme Court of the United States should not, he thought, have authority to decide controversies between the central government and the states so far as the delineation of the respective spheres of each is concerned. As a safeguard against transgressions of the rights of the states by the federal government and as a check upon the exercise of powers in excess of the constitutional grants, the protection to be afforded by the judicial department was considered ineffectual. In such cases and

---

[54] "It is true that, in controversies relating to the boundary between the two jurisdictions, the tribunal which is ultimately to decide, is to be established under the general government . . . some such tribunal is clearly essential to prevent an appeal to the sword and a dissolution of the compact." Madison, in *The Federalist* (Ford ed.), XXXIX: 251.

[55] Farrand, *op. cit.*, II: 430.

[56] *Writings* (Hunt ed.), VIII: 449.

[57] *Writings* (Cong. ed., 1865), I: 194.

no matter from what department the violation proceeded, the people in the states, as the parties to the constitutional compact, had the ultimate right to decide the nature of the violation and the remedy to be imposed. In the report on the Virginia Resolutions he stated his doctrine as follows:

The States, then, being the parties to the constitutional compact, and in their sovereign capacity, it follows of necessity that there can be no tribunal above their authority to decide, in the last resort, whether the compact made by them be violated; and consequently, as the parties to it, they must themselves decide, in the last resort, such questions as may be of sufficient magnitude to require their interposition.[58]

By this reasoning the people of the states, having been the original source of the division of sovereignty between the nation and the states, retain the right, in extreme cases, to settle issues pertaining to that division. Madison, however, denied the right of the individual state to nullify federal laws. Only the states collectively could construe the constitutional compact.[59]

Madison also denied that the courts had authority to decide issues with any degree of finality when major departments of the government were concerned. The three branches of the government were made coördinate by the Constitution and were equally bound to support the Constitution, and, in his opinion, "each must in the exercise of its functions be guided by the text of the Constitution according to its own interpretation of it; and consequently in the event of irreconcilable interpretations, the prevalence of one or the other department must depend on the nature of the case, as receiving its final decision from the one or the other, and passing from that decision into effect, without involving the functions of any other."[60]

In the first session of Congress, discussing the question whether the head of the Department of Foreign Affairs should be removable from office by the President, Madison stated his views regarding the authority of Congress to interpret the Constitution clearly and emphatically. "I feel the importance of the question," he said, "and know that our decision will involve the decision of all similar cases. The decision that is at this time made, will become the permanent exposition of the Constitution; and on a permanent exposition of the Constitution will depend the genius and character of the whole government."[61] He referred to the

[58] *Writings* (Hunt ed.), VI: 349.
[59] Edward M. Burns, "Madison's Theory of Judicial Review," 24 *Kentucky Law Jour.* (May, 1936), 420 ff.
[60] Burns, *op. cit.*, p. 421, quoting Manuscript, *Madison Papers* in Library of Congress.
[61] *Annals of Congress*, I: 495.

principle of the separation of powers as "another maxim which ought to direct us in expounding the Constitution." And when it was claimed that it would be officious for the legislature to expound the Constitution so far as the division of powers between the President and Senate is concerned, he replied, "it is incontrovertibly of as much importance to this branch of the government as to any other, that the Constitution should be preserved entire."[62] Continuing his argument, he said:

But the great objection drawn from the source to which the last arguments would lead us is, that the Legislature itself has no right to expound the Constitution; that wherever its meaning is doubtful, you must leave it to take its course, until the Judiciary is called upon to declare its meaning. I acknowledge, in the ordinary course of government, that the exposition of the laws and Constitution devolves upon the Judiciary. But I beg to know, upon what principle it can be contended, that any one department draws from the Constitution greater powers than another, in marking out the limits of the powers of the several departments? The Constitution is the charter of the people to the government: it specifies certain great powers as absolutely granted, and marks out the departments to exercise them. If the constitutional boundary of either be brought into question, I do not see that any one of these independent departments has more right than another to declare their sentiments on that point.

Perhaps this is an omitted case. There is not one government on the face of the earth, so far as I recollect, there is not one in the United States, in which provision is made for a particular authority to determine the limits of the constitutional division of power between the branches of the government. In all systems there are points which must be adjusted by the departments themselves, to which no one of them is competent. If it cannot be determined in this way, there is no recourse left but the will of the community, to be collected in some mode to be provided by the Constitution, or one dictated by the necessity of the case. It is therefore a fair question, whether this great point may not as well be decided, at least by the whole Legislature as by a part, by us as well as by the Executive or Judiciary? As I think it will be equally constitutional, I cannot imagine it will be less safe, that the exposition should issue from the Legislative authority than any other; and the more so, because it involves in the decision the opinions of both those departments, whose powers are supposed to be affected by it. Besides, I do not see in what way this question could come before the Judges, to obtain a fair and solemn decision; but even if it were the case it could, I should suppose, at least while the government is not led by passion, disturbed by faction, or deceived by any discolored medium of sight, but while there is a desire in all to see and be guided by the benignant ray of truth, that the decision may be made with the most advantage by the Legislature itself.[63]

Thus, in answering the argument that the Judiciary had the sole and exclusive authority to interpret the Constitution, Madison insisted that no such monopoly had been granted to the Judiciary and, that, so far as

[62] *Annals of Congress*, I: 500. If the question relates to a doubtful part of the Constitution, Madison observed, "I suppose an exposition of the Constitution may come with as much propriety from the Legislature, as any other department of the government." *Ibid.*, p. 461.

[63] *Annals of Congress*, I: 500, 501.

its own powers and those of the President having relation thereto were concerned, Congress had as much right to expound the Constitution as the courts. Later he formulated something in the nature of a principle for legislative construction of the Constitution. It was not to be the judgment or interpretation of a single Congress. "Let it, then, be left to the decision of every intelligent and candid judge," said Madison, "which, on the whole, is most relied on for the true and safe construction of the Constitution; that which has the uniform sanction of successive legislative bodies, through a period of years and under the varied ascendancy of parties; or that which depends upon the opinions of every new legislature heated as it may be by the spirit of party."[64] On this ground he justified his change of opinion regarding the constitutionality of a national bank and a protective tariff.[65] Regarding the Constitution as embodying in essence the people's will, Madison thought, as did Jefferson, that it was necessary to make a careful distinction between "cases where the general government opposes the will of its constituents, as happened when the Alien and Sedition laws were passed, and where the government has the States and the people on its side."[66]

Hamilton conceded that there should be a limit on the authority of the courts to review acts of Congress similar to that proposed by Madison and Jefferson. Discussing the process of amending the Constitution, he said: "The several departments being perfectly coordinate by the terms of their common commission, none of them, it is evident, can pretend to an exclusive or superior right of settling the boundaries between their respective powers; and how are the encroachments of the stronger to be prevented, or the wrongs of the weaker to be redressed, without an appeal to the people themselves, who, as grantors of the commission, can alone declare its true meaning, and enforce its observance?" He argued, however, that such proposed recurrences to the people as a means of keeping

---

[64] *Writings* (Cong. ed.), IV: 185, 186. Fearing the dominance of party spirit in Congress, Madison at one time expressed doubt whether the Judiciary is not "a safer expositor of the power of Congress than Congress will be when backed, and even pushed by their constituents, as in the canal and Missouri cases." *Ibid.*, III: 483.

[65] Relative to his change of opinion concerning the constitutionality of the establishment of a national bank, Madison noted that his assent was given in accordance with "my early and unchanged opinion, that, in the case of a Constitution as of a law, a course of authoritative expositions sufficiently deliberate, uniform, and settled, was an evidence of the public will necessarily overruling individual opinions." *Writings* (Hunt ed.), IX: 443, and *Writings* (Cong. ed.), IV: 232.

[66] *Writings* (Cong. ed.), III: 551.

For a misconstruction of the views of Madison relative to judicial review of legislative acts due to an incomplete examination of his views and also to a misinterpretation of some of the extracts quoted, see C. Perry Patterson, "James Madison and Judicial Review," 28 *Calif. Law Rev.* (Nov., 1939), 22. Changes in Madison's attitude toward judicial review will be considered further in subsequent chapters.

the departments within their constitutional limits was rather unwise and impractical. But he did not indicate any other procedure to deal with departmental conflicts concerning the meaning of the Constitution.[67]

Madison's views were not modified by the note which he added in a letter to Joseph Cabell on September 8, 1829, when he wrote of the need of "an arbiter or umpire in the constitutional authority provided for deciding questions concerning the boundaries of right and power." Such an arbiter, he thought, was provided by the Supreme Court of the United States as indicated in Number 39 of *The Federalist*.[68] Referring to this number of *The Federalist*, it is apparent that Madison was thinking of the duties of the Supreme Court in the review of state acts in order to uphold the supremacy of the federal government. This note, therefore, had no relation to the issue pertaining to the relative authority of Congress and the Supreme Court to pass on the constitutionality of Congressional acts. However, when individual states proposed to nullify acts of Congress, Madison supported the Federalist doctrine of national supremacy.[69]

Both Jefferson and Madison regarded agriculture as the stable and solid foundation for the American republic and viewed with misgivings the rapid development of commerce and industry. "Whenever commerce prevails," Madison wrote Randolph, "there will be an inequality of wealth, and wherever the latter does a simplicity of manners must decline."[70] Jefferson and Madison also were in agreement in the contention that there is a general tendency in all governments for power and authority to be augmented at the expense of liberty. It was necessary to keep a careful watch upon all public authorities for "wherever the real power in a government lies, there is danger of oppression."[71] For both of them the democratic state did not seek an ideal of efficiency or stability. Its primary purpose was to promote the happiness and the self-realization of the individual; and, in their opinion, democracy achieved this end better than any other form of government. The views of Jefferson and Madison on constitutional construction, after the Supreme Court under

---

[67] *Works* (Lodge ed.), IX: 314 ff.

[68] *Writings* (Hunt ed.), IX: 351.

[69] For Madison's views on the nullification of acts of Congress by the individual states, see below, pp. 573 ff.

[70] Smith, *James Madison: Builder*, p. 65. "Our governments will remain virtuous for many centuries; as long as they are chiefly agricultural." Jefferson, *Writings* (Ford ed.), IV: 480. For comments relating to the dangers inherent in an inequality of wealth, see letters of Jefferson and Madison, *Works* (Ford ed.), VIII: 194 and *Writings* (Hunt ed.), II: 246, 247.

[71] Smith, *op. cit.*, p. 99. "The natural progress of things," said Jefferson, "is for liberty to yield and government to gain ground." *Writings* (Mem. ed.), VII: 37.

the direction of Chief Justice Marshall had incorporated in its opinions some of the essential principles of Hamiltonian Federalism, will be presented in a subsequent chapter.

The political views and ideals of Hamilton and Jefferson have in a large measure determined the direction and trends of American political and economic affairs. And without doubt the success of the American experiment in government may be attributed to a considerable degree to the blending of apparently diametrically opposite attitudes and points of view in the strange admixture of philosophies and practices which have been characteristic of the growth of the American system of government. One of the significant facts in the development of American politics, observes James Truslow Adams, is that Hamilton's theories prevailed, but that citizens gave lip service with revolts about once a generation against Hamiltonianism, and turned in the direction of Jefferson's doctrines of the rights of man. But, continues Adams, "whether Jefferson was right or wrong yet remains an open question, for though in political life America's dream and ideal rest on the Jeffersonian faith in the common man, in her economic life she has developed along the lines of Hamiltonian special privilege and moneyed classes. As America grew she tried to serve, so to say, God and Mammon—that is, she insisted upon clinging to the ideal of Jeffersonianism while gathering in the money profits of Hamiltonianism."[72] In the gradual selection of the political and economic ideas which were to mold the state and federal governments in the United States, the Supreme Court assumed a prominent role and at times its decisions gave a decisive turn in the consideration and adjustment of public affairs.

---

[72] James Truslow Adams, *The Epic of America* (Boston, 1932), pp. 134, 135. "In the immediate conflict between the two," observes Charles Maurice Wiltse, "the democratic ideal won out because Jefferson had judged more soundly of the temper of the men with whom both had to deal. Yet after more than a century, the issue between them is not finally settled, and both theories still play an active role in our national life." *The Jeffersonian Tradition in American Democracy* (Chapel Hill, 1935), p. 101.

Part Three

A FEDERALIST SUPREME COURT UNDER REPUBLICAN ADMINISTRATIONS

CHAPTER VII

The Judiciary Repeal Act and
the Case of Marbury v. Madison

THE ATTEMPT of the Federalists to entrench themselves into power by an extension of the judicial system and the selection by President Adams of John Marshall as Chief Justice of the Supreme Court as well as the appointment of so-called "midnight judges" to the lower federal courts were particularly obnoxious to the Republicans. Jefferson rightly accused the Federalists of using the Judiciary as a means of perpetuating their power. "They have retired into the Judiciary as a stronghold," he wrote, and "there the remains of Federalism are to be preserved and fed from the Treasury, and from that battery all the works of Republicanism are to be beaten down and erased."[1] It is not surprising that the Republicans resented not only the reorganization of the Judiciary at the time a change of administration was about to take place but also the rewarding of faithful Federalists with judicial appointments. Richard Bassett, who voted for Adams as a presidential elector; Jeremiah Smith, who supported Federalist measures before Congress; Charles Lee, Adams' Attorney General; and Oliver Wolcott, who succeeded Hamilton as Secretary of the Treasury; as well as Jared Ingersoll and Philip Barton Key, all ardent Federalists, received commissions to new judgeships. To vacancies in the district judgeships created by promotions to the Circuit Bench, Senators Elijah Paine and Ray Greene, and Representatives William H. Hill and Jacob Read were appointed. Two other loyal Federalists in the House of Representatives, Harrison Gray Otis and John Wilkes Kittera, were commissioned as district attorneys.[2] Jefferson, showing his resentment at the effort to restrict the authority of the Republicans, pardoned the men who had been convicted under the Sedition Act; advised the repeal of the Judiciary Act of 1801, thus aiming to prevent the "midnight judges" from taking office; refused to deliver commissions to the justices of the peace appointed by Adams for the District of Columbia; and approved of the proposal to impeach Judges Pickering and Chase.

---

[1] *The Writings of Thomas Jefferson* (Mem. ed., Washington, 1905), X: 302.
[2] *Executive Journal (1789–1805)*, pp. 381–383; see also William S. Carpenter, "Repeal of the Judiciary Act of 1801," 9 *Amer. Pol. Sci. Rev.* (Aug., 1915), 520.

By a simple and direct method of requesting Congress to increase the number of Justices, the Republicans could have gained control of the Supreme Court. Commentators have commended Jefferson's moderation in refraining from such action. Thus, Edward S. Corwin writes, "when it came to legislation concerning the Supreme Court, the majority of the Republicans again displayed genuine moderation, for, thrusting aside an obvious temptation to swamp that tribunal with additional Judges of their own creed, they merely restored it to its original size under the act of 1789."[3]

The business of the Supreme Court increased very slowly. With the passage of the Eleventh Amendment, litigation between individuals and the states, with a few exceptions, was dropped. Cases arising out of the enforcement of debts due British creditors were referred by Jay's Treaty to a board of commissioners. The Sedition Act expired in March, 1801, and no more cases were tried under this statute. During the first term in which Marshall sat as Chief Justice, February, 1801, no cases were decided and only one case, *The Amelia,* was adjudicated at the August term. In June of this year it was stated in Congress that only eight cases were before the Court during this year.

Marshall hoped to be relieved of circuit duty with the passage of the Judiciary Act of 1801 and thought he would have ample time to devote to the biography of George Washington which he had agreed to write. Though he was obliged to take up circuit riding again after the passage of the Repeal Act of 1802, his judicial duties did not seriously interfere

---

[3] *John Marshall and the Constitution* (New Haven, 1921), p. 63. Edward Channing refers also to the moderate proposals of the Republicans as follows:

"One would have expected that the triumphant author of the Kentucky Resolutions and his chief adviser, who wrote the Virginia Resolutions, would have attacked the very bases of the system which had made those resolutions necessary. They did nothing of the sort. The key to the conflict between the nationalists like Hamilton and Marshall on the one side, and states-rights men like Jefferson and Madison on the other, was in the Supreme Court of the United States. At the moment that body was composed entirely of Federalists whose appointments would continue for life. The new Chief Justice, John Marshall, of Virginia, presumably had a long career before him, and his opinions on the Constitution were perfectly well known to Jefferson. The thing to do to carry out pre-election theories was to get rid of John Marshall and the other Judges of the Supreme Court, or to neutralize their power. The first could be done by the adoption of an amendment to the Constitution, changing the tenure of the Judges from life to four or six years; the second could be accomplished by the appointment of enough Judges to outvote Marshall and his Federalist companions, or by the alteration of the judiciary acts to impair seriously the activity of the Supreme Court. Jefferson advised none of these things. Instead of so doing, he merely suggested to Congress that the Judiciary as organized under the act of 1801 was out of all proportion to the business it had to perform." *The Jeffersonian System* (New York, 1906), pp. 22, 23. For a similar judgment see Henry Adams, *History of the United States During the Administration of Jefferson and Madison* (New York, 1921), I: 258, 259.

with his literary efforts.[4] During the years from 1801 to 1806 he wrote opinions in fifty-six cases tried on circuit and in twenty-seven cases tried before the Supreme Court. Most of these cases are of little historical interest and only one, that of *Marbury v. Madison,* is a significant precedent in the field of constitutional law.[5]

Jefferson claimed that the biography of Washington was written "principally with a view to electioneering purposes" and when it was completed called it a "five-volumed libel."[6] Though Marshall tried to be fair, he lauded Washington and Hamilton's nationalistic principles and policies and in praising the members of the Federalist party he inferentially condemned the attitude and program of the Democratic-Republicans. Men of "enlarged and liberal minds" and "far-seeing and upright persons" were contrasted with those dominated by narrow-minded local prejudices.[7] The volumes represented, indeed, history written from the conservative point of view and, though they were frequently criticized by the Republicans, appear to have had relatively slight political effect. When the second edition of the work appeared in 1832, Chancellor Kent commented on the partisan tenor and spirit of the biography as follows: "It may be truly said to constitute the only authentic record of the history of the principles and conduct of a party now . . . extinct, but which was illuminated by the wisdom of Washington, the brilliant and various talents of Hamilton, the impressive eloquence of Ames, the energetic zeal and forecast of Adams, the inflexible integrity and Roman firmness of Pickering, the accomplished elegance and various endowments of Morris and King, and the exalted learning and consummate judicial abilities of Jay, Ellsworth and Marshall."[8]

With the exception of some comments regarding the Republicans in his *Life of Washington,* Chief Justice Marshall was silent on current

---

[4] Marshall, in a circular letter to the Justices, said that he had come to the conclusion that the Judges of the Supreme Court could not constitutionally be required to hold other sessions than those of the Supreme Court. By their commissions, he said, they were appointed solely as Judges of the Supreme Court and could not be compelled to sit in any inferior court. In their replies the Associate Justices indicated that they agreed with the Chief Justice on the question of constitutionality but advised him that in their opinion the practice of holding courts on the circuits from 1789 to 1801 had settled the matter. Accepting their view Marshall decided to hold court in the Virginia circuit.

[5] Cf. Albert J. Beveridge, *The Life of John Marshall* (Boston, 1916), III: 273.

[6] *Works* (Ford ed.), IX: 372, and XII: 277, or (Mem. ed.), XI: 485.

[7] Beveridge, *op. cit.,* III: 259 ff.

[8] *New York Review* (Oct., 1938), III: 352, 353. "That Marshall's great work . . . was dominated by a political motive cannot be denied," is the opinion of Charles A. Beard, *Economic Origins of Jeffersonian Democracy* (New York, 1915), p. 242. For Marshall's method and technique in historical writing see William A. Foran, "John Marshall as a Historian," *Amer. Hist. Rev.* (Oct., 1937), XLIII: 51.

party issues, for, notes Beveridge, he was making ready to meet and over-come Republicanism "with the affirmative opinions of constructive judicial statesmanship."[9] Though his duties as Chief Justice were light, it is asserted he "quietly began to strengthen the Supreme Court." As a first step in this direction he decided to speak for the Court and to discontinue the practice, as heretofore, of having the Justices give their opinions *seriatim.* This leadership or domination of the Court became apparent in the first case decided by the Chief Justice.[10] The case involved the right of salvage for *The Amelia,* a vessel of the neutral city of Hamburg, captured by the French and recaptured by the American frigate *Constitution.* When one of the attorneys proposed to read a message of the President to Congress and certain despatches to the Department of State relating to the recapture of American vessels, as an indication of the Executive construction of the acts of Congress authorizing the capture of French vessels, the Court objected to hearing them on the ground that it would bring the Executive into the Court.[11] Thus, another step was taken toward judicial aloofness and independence.

In the opinion deciding this case the Chief Justice began to announce what were deemed to be the "universal principles" of international law applicable to the state of war, whether partial or general, and, following the established rules of exposition, to give a "sound construction of the law." The decree of the Circuit Court ordering the restoration of *The Amelia* without paying salvage was reversed and the captor was allowed one-sixth of the net value of the vessel. Since the Chief Justice had recently been transferred from the Department of State to the Supreme Court and, as this was the only case decided at the August term of the Court, it afforded an opportunity to prepare a twenty-page state paper on the laws and practices of war. Similar state papers in subsequent cases form the basis of the notable reputation of Chief Justice Marshall in the interpretation of the rules and principles of international law.

The validity of an Executive order was considered in a similar case, the *Schooner Peggy,*[12] involving proceedings for the condemnation of a captured French vessel. In accordance with the provision of the treaty with France negotiated by Ellsworth that captured ships not "definitely condemned" should be returned to the owners, President Jefferson directed that the proceeds of the sale of the vessel should be turned over to the French claimants. But the Judges in the Circuit Court of Connecticut

---

[9] *The Life of John Marshall,* III: 15.
[10] Talbot v. Seeman, 1 Cranch 1 (1801).
[11] *Ibid.,* p. 10.
[12] United States v. Schooner Peggy, 1 Cranch 103 (1801).

decided that the President's order was illegal and refused to obey it. Chief Justice Marshall sustained the position of the President and directed that the proceeds of the sale of the schooner be paid to the French claimants. Thus, the controversy between the Chief Justice and the President was merely deferred.[13]

With the debate over the Judiciary Repeal Act, the decision in the case of *Marbury v. Madison,* and the Chase impeachment trial, the Supreme Court became directly involved in political debate and partisan criticisms. The mingling of the Court in political affairs was largely due to the expression of the political views of the Justices both on and off the Bench. The foremost issue between the dominant parties of the day was thoroughly considered and discussed in the debate over the Judiciary Repeal Act of 1802. John Breckenridge of Kentucky and William G. Giles of Virginia advocated the advisability of repealing the Judiciary Act of 1801, and John Taylor of Caroline presented a forceful argument in support of such a plan.[14]

DEBATE ON THE JUDICIARY REPEAL ACT

The debate on the Judiciary Repeal Act of 1802 afforded an opportunity for both the Federalists and the Republicans to express publicly some of the fundamental tenets of their political philosophies. Defending the existing order as well as the program and policies which had prevailed during the two preceding administrations, the Federalist arguments may appropriately be considered first. Underlying all of the speeches of the members of this party was the assumption that something in the nature of a revolution in politics was taking place, that the very foundation of civil affairs was being undermined, and that heroic measures were necessary to save some of the remnants of the political order established to preserve the interests and control of "the wise, the rich and the good." The Judiciary Act of 1801, which was now being subjected to attack, was looked upon as a necessary and indispensable means to preserve at least some of the principles and ideas of the old order.

Federalist arguments.—The chief argument against the Repeal Act was in the nature of a defense of the popular conservative doctrine of checks and balances. Our government was described as "a system of salutary checks."[15] And it was insisted that the most important of these checks

---

[13] Despite this opinion reversing the decision of the Circuit Court, Charles Warren maintains that the action of the Circuit Court was "undoubtedly correct" and the President's order "utterly invalid." *The Supreme Court in United States History* (Boston, 1922), I: 199.

[14] Carpenter, *op. cit.,* pp. 522 ff.

[15] Senator Morris, *Annals,* 7th Cong., 1st sess., p. 83, and Senator Ogden, *ibid.,* p. 175.

must not be disturbed or weakened. The Judiciary, it was repeatedly asserted, was made an independent department not only to expound the laws but the Constitution as well; for, according to the American theory of the separation of powers, the Judges were expected to check the Legislature in case it should pass any laws in violation of the Constitution.[16] The familiar check argument was most effectively formulated by Gouverneur Morris of New York in language which the Republicans frequently referred in rebuttal.

"Governments are made," said Senator Morris, "to provide against the follies and vices of men. For to suppose that governments rest on reason is a pitiful solecism. . . . Hence, checks are required in the distribution of power among those who are to exercise it for the benefit of the people." And the Judges were characterized as "a check of the first necessity, to prevent an invasion of the Constitution by unconstitutional laws." For what purpose are we here, asked Morris, if not "to save the people from their most dangerous enemy; to save them from themselves."[17] Speaking of the necessity for the courts to check the wanton invasion of rights by the Legislative and Executive departments, Morris, who had been a member of the federal Convention, said, "it was partly for this purpose that they were established, and, I trust, that when properly called on, they will dare to act."[18]

By the passage of the Repeal Act, thought Representative Henderson, "the constitutional check which the Judges were to be on the legislature is completely done away" and "the monstrous and unheard of doctrine which has been lately advanced, that the Judges have not the right of declaring unconstitutional laws void, will be put into practice. . . . It is the very definition of tyranny, and wherever you find it, the people are slaves, whether they call their government a monarchy, republic or democracy."[19] Not only was a system of checks regarded necessary, with the Judiciary as the main check department, but such a system was also considered so indispensable that to disturb any of its essential features would certainly lead to the ruin of the system of government established

---

[16] Senator Mason of Massachusetts, *Annals, op. cit.,* pp. 31–32. An illuminating analysis of the arguments for and against the Repeal Act is given in Charles Kummer, *Congress and the Supreme Court, 1789–1860* (an unpublished dissertation, Los Angeles, University of California, 1939).

[17] *Annals, op. cit.,* p. 41. This postulate of Morris that it was the duty of the Judges to save the people from themselves became one of the historic principles of constitutional thought, often quoted and debated, but more frequently serving as an unexpressed dictum in support of the view that the courts should be the sole and authoritative interpreters of the words and phrases of written constitutions.

[18] *Ibid.,* p. 89. One of the chief objects of our government is to guard against man's "weakness and wickedness." See comments of Representative Stanley, *ibid.,* pp. 573 ff.

[19] *Ibid.,* p. 529.

by the Constitution. If either the federal government or the states should exceed their powers, thought Senator Tracy of Connecticut, "there is the utmost necessity that some timely checks, equal to every exigency, should be interposed. The Judiciary is established by the Constitution for that valuable purpose." Such powers must be exercised by the Judiciary to prevent a resort to "revolutionary principles" or possibly to a civil war.[20] By the "horrid doctrine" embodied in the Repeal Act, said Senator Bradley of Pennsylvania, "Congress erects itself into a complete tyranny."[21] The debate frequently brought forth expressions of alarm such as "the sealing of the death-warrant of the Constitution." In fact, the notion that the Constitution was sacred coupled with the fear that it was about to be destroyed was one of the main grounds of the opposition of the Federalists to the Repeal Act. "This Constitution is an invaluable inheritance," said Senator Tracy, "if we make inroads upon it and destroy it, no matter with what intentions, it cannot be replaced; we shall never have another." Portraying the nation on the brink of fate, Senator Morris of New York exclaimed: "For heaven's sake, pause."[22]

It is said that "the Judges have no right to declare a law to be unconstitutional; that no such power is given to that branch in the Constitution. . . . [But] the Judiciary, from the nature of their institution, are to judge of the law and what is the law. The Constitution is paramount and supreme. The Judge is bound by oath to support it. The Legislature have a right to exercise their judgment as to the constitutionality of a law on its passage; but the Judiciary decide at last, and their decision is final."[23] The Supreme Court was lauded and defended in language often repeated today, as "an impartial tribunal to decide on the fundamental principles of the government." An impartial tribunal to decide questions respecting the fundamental rights of the society and government was declared to be "an original principle of this country. . . . To have established this principle of constitutional security, is the peculiar glory of the American people."[24] Referring to the provisions of the Constitution and the twenty-fifth section of the Judiciary Act of 1789, Representative Bayard claimed that the doctrine of judicial review of acts of Congress was "not only clearly inferrible from the plain language of the Constitu-

---

[20] *Ibid.*, p. 56.

[21] *Ibid.*, p. 166.

[22] *Ibid.*, pp. 58, 92. "Subsequent history proved," says Charles Warren, "that the Federalist fears of the prostration of the Judiciary and the consolidation of the government were futile." *The Supreme Court in United States History*, I: 215.

[23] Representative Hemphill of Pennsylvania, *Annals, op. cit.*, p. 542; also Representative Stanley, *ibid.*, 574.

[24] *Ibid.*, p. 932.

tion, but by law has been expressly declared and established in practice since the existence of the government."[25]

Representative Dana, speaking for the Federalists near the conclusion of the extended debate on the Judiciary bill, reviewed the cases in which the issue of the validity of acts of Congress had been raised before the federal Judges, and, finding the opinions uniformly expressed on the issue favorable to the exercise of the power of review of legislative acts, declared: "The principle, therefore, which is now disputed, has been settled for years. It is the established principle of the Constitution."[26] It was Federalist Judges, however, who expressed these views, and, so far as the language and meaning of the Constitution was understood by the members of this party by the year 1802, the principle of judicial review of acts, both federal and state, was certainly regarded as settled. The Republicans, as a rule, did not so interpret the language of the Constitution.

The Democratic theory that one legislature cannot bind its successor or that the creature cannot be greater than the creator was answered by the Federalists with the contention that a legislature cannot abrogate its contracts. But, owing to the constitutional tenure of "good behavior," it was assumed that from the time of an appointment of a federal Justice to fill an office established by Congress, all the rights of independence and removal by impeachment only were regarded as attaching to him. The argument of patience and delay frequently made at later times under similar situations was advanced by Representative Bayard of Delaware. "I hope," he said, "there will be a little patience; these Judges are old and infirm men; they will die; they must die: wait but a short time their places will be vacant; they will be filled with the disciples of the new school, and gentlemen will not have to answer for the political murder which is now meditated."[27]

Republican arguments.—In his first message to Congress, Jefferson suggested that "the judiciary system . . . and especially that portion of it recently enacted, will of course, present itself to the contemplation of Congress." And as an aid to Congress, the President had secured from the states a statement of the cases decided since the establishment of the federal courts and the causes pending when the reorganization act was passed.[28] Jefferson's spokesman in the repeal of the Federalist Judiciary Act was Senator John Breckenridge of Kentucky. He contended that an

---

[25] *Annals, op. cit.,* p. 647.
[26] *Ibid.,* p. 926.
[27] *Ibid.,* p. 626.
[28] See comments of Senator Baldwin of Georgia on the President's report, *ibid.,* p. 104.

increase of courts was unnecessary when suits before the federal courts were decreasing and urged that litigation whenever possible should be taken care of in the state courts. The assertion that the office of a federal Judge could not be abolished did not impress Breckenridge, for he maintained that "sinecure offices" are not permitted by our laws.[29] To the Republicans it was necessary to make a clear distinction between the Supreme Court provided for in the Constitution and the inferior courts left to the discretion of Congress. For the latter it was assumed that Congress must have authority "to create, to annul, or to modify the courts, as the public good may require."[30] Breckenridge admitted that if the Judges were entitled to their salaries under the Constitution, the repealing act could not affect them. The Judges under such circumstances would resort to their proper remedy, "for where there is a constitutional right, there must be a constitutional remedy."[31] But summarizing the Democratic-Republican argument, Breckenridge maintained that the repealing act was both constitutional and expedient.

The Republicans replied to the check argument of the Federalists that, although it was taken for granted that the Judges were to be independent, they were not to be "independent of the Nation itself." Nor did they understand that the Judiciary was to have the constitutional authority "to control the other departments of the government."[32] The Justices of the Supreme Court, it was thought, from sheer want of employment may "hold the Constitution in one hand, and the law in the other, and say to the departments of government, so far shall you go and no farther. This independence of the Judiciary, so much desired, will, I fear sir, if encouraged or tolerated, soon become something like supremacy."[33] The objects of courts of law were declared to be "to settle questions of right between suitors; to enforce obedience to the laws, and to protect the citizens against the oppressive use of power in the executive offices. Not to protect them against the Legislature."[34] The familiar Federalist argument that checks are necessary, means, said Representative Davis, that the people "are incapable of governing themselves, your Representatives are incapable of doing it, [therefore], in the Judiciary alone you find a safe deposit for your liberties."[35]

---

[29] *Ibid.*, pp. 25 ff.

[30] *Ibid.*, p. 60. One of the main grounds of the Republican argument was tersely stated by Senator Mason of Virginia, "It is an axiom in politics that an ordaining power always embraces a repealing power." *Ibid.*, p. 547.

[31] *Ibid.*, p. 30.

[32] Senator Mason of Virginia, *ibid.*, p. 59.

[33] *Ibid.*, p. 63.

[34] Senator Stone of North Carolina, *ibid.*, p. 73.

[35] *Ibid.*, p. 558

The Judiciary, thought the Republicans, had no more right to control the acts of the other departments of the government, than the other departments had to direct those of the Judiciary.[36] If the doctrine for which the Federalists contend is adopted, said Representative Williams, "then is the sovereignty of the government to be swallowed up in the vortex of the Judiciary. Whatever the other departments of the government may do, they can undo. You may pass a law, but they can annul it. Will not the people be astonished to hear that their laws depend upon the will of the Judges, who are themselves independent of all law?"[37]

Speaking of the reputed calmness and thoroughness with which the proponents of judicial reorganization carried through the Federalist Act of 1801, Senator Mason pointed out that in committee all amendments proposed by the minority "were uniformly rejected, by a steady, inflexible, and undeviating majority." When the bill was presented to Congress there was no argument on the issues raised. Having reorganized the judicial system to suit their purposes, the Federalists now insisted that the system could be changed only by constitutional amendment. But the Republicans contended that the amending procedure was not only too slow and cumbersome to accomplish such ends, but that this method was utterly impracticable to secure the changes the people as creators of the Constitution desired.

Representative Thompson of Virginia could see no danger of usurpation in the acts of the Legislature or of the Executive, since both departments were regularly and periodically changed by the vote of the people. The real danger of usurpation came, he thought, from the desire "this check department of the government has to grasp at all power. Give the Judiciary this check upon the Legislature, allow them the power to declare your laws null and void; allow the common law, a system extending to all persons and to all things, to be attached to the Constitution, as I understand it is contended; and in vain have the people placed you upon this floor to legislate; your laws will be nullified, your proceedings will be checked."[38] "Where is the charter which places the sovereignty of this country in their hands," inquired Representative Nicholson of Virginia, and, he continued,

Give them the powers and the independence now contended for, and they will require nothing more; for your government becomes a despotism, and they become your rulers. They are to decide upon the lives, the liberties, and the property of your citizens; they have an absolute veto upon your laws by declaring them null and void at pleasure; they are to introduce at will the laws of a foreign country, differing essentially with

---

[36] John Bacon of Massachusetts, *Annals, op. cit.,* p. 983.

[37] *Annals, op. cit.,* p. 532.

[38] *Annals, op. cit.,* pp. 552, 553.

us upon the great principles of government; and after being clothed with this arbitrary power, they are beyond the control of the Nation, as they are not to be affected by any laws which the people by their representatives can pass. If all this be true; if this doctrine be established in the extent which is now contended for, the Constitution is not worth the time we are spending upon it. It is, as it has been called by its enemies, mere parchment. For these Judges, thus rendered omnipotent, may overleap the Constitution and trample on your laws; they may laugh the Legislature to scorn, and set the Nation at defiance.[39]

The Republicans raised strenuous objections to the continuance as unrepealable of a law which had been passed by the votes of men who had profited by the act by being appointed to vacancies created through the promotion of District Judges to the new Circuit judgeships.[40]

Representative Giles of Virginia ridiculed the claim of the Federalists that they had a "monopoly of all the intelligence and patriotism of the Nation." Instead of the spirit of the Constitution giving sanction to the notion of a superior or check department, he found "from the general character of the Constitution, that the general will was its basis, the general good its object, and the fundamental principle for effecting this object was the responsibility of all public agents, either mediately or immediately to the people."[41] The issue was declared to be "the doctrine of irresponsibility,—and the doctrine of despotism in opposition to the representative system." The Federalist position involved, as he saw it, an express avowal that the people were incompetent to govern themselves.[42] Giles, who was looked upon as the administration leader in the House, presented an able defense of the Jeffersonian political philosophy

---

[39] *Ibid.*, p. 823, 824.

[40] One of the peculiar results of the so-called "midnight appointments" was related by Representative Rutledge who cited the instance where "the District Judge in Rhode Island was appointed Circuit Judge, and Mr. Green was appointed District Judge. On the fourth day of March, Mr. Green took his seat in the Senate; the friends of the Administration objected to his keeping it; they said he was a Judge, as appeared by the journals of the Senate; they here made a complete recognition of his appointment as Judge, and he vacated his seat. After getting home he received his commission, in which the blanks had been filled up with the words Circuit Judge, instead of District Judge. Mr. Green enclosed his commission to the Executive, in a letter most profoundly respectful, and requested the errors of the clerk in the Department of State might be corrected, and his commission made to conform to the appointment, as recorded on the Senatorial journal. To this letter, which was in highly respectful terms, the President would not deign to have any answer given; he pocketed Mr. Green's commission, and placed another gentleman in his office. This is a history of the appointment of Mr. Green, and the manner in which the President 'corrected the procedure.' " *Ibid.*, p. 751.

[41] *Annals, op. cit.*, p. 584.

[42] Giles commented on the political activities of the Federalist Judges as follows: "It is sometime, Mr. Chairman, since a member of this House, and sundry printers throughout the United States, have been amerced and imprisoned to appease the vengeance of an unconstitutional sedition act, merely for publishing their own sentiments, which happened to be unpalatable to the then existing Administration! It is sometime, sir,

as related to the Judiciary. He was convinced that the Repeal Act was constitutional "upon the most fair and candid interpretation of the Constitution." For, said he,

believing that principles advanced in opposition, go directly to the destruction of the fundamental principle of the Constitution, the responsibility of all public agents to the people—that they go to the establishment of a permanent corporation of individuals invested with ultimate censorial and controlling power over all the departments of the government, over legislation, execution, and decision, and irresponsible to the people; believing that these principles are in direct hostility to the great principles of representative government; believing that the courts formerly established, were fully competent to the business they had to perform, and that the present courts are useless, unnecessary and expensive; believing that the Supreme Court has heretofore discharged all the duties assigned to it in less than one month in the year, and that its duties could be performed in half that time, . . . considering all the circumstances attending the substitution of the new system for the old one, by increasing the number of Judges, and compensations, and lessening their duties by the distribution of the business into a great number of hands. . . . I am obliged to support the Repeal Act.[43]

The whole argument of the Federalists, thought John Randolph, was founded on the assumption of "a total want of principle in the Legislature and Executive."[44] And he maintained,

if you pass the law, the Judges are to put their veto upon it, by declaring it unconstitutional. Here is a new power, of a dangerous and uncontrollable nature, contended for. The decision of a constitutional question must rest somewhere. Shall it be confided to men immediately responsible to the people, or to those who are irresponsible? for the responsibility by impeachment is little less than a name. From whom is a corrupt decision most to be feared? To me it appears that the power which has the right of passing, without appeal, on the validity of your laws, is your sovereign. . . . But, sir, are we not as deeply interested in the true exposition of the Constitution as the Judges can be? With all the deference to their talents, is not Congress as capable of forming a correct opinion as they are? Are not its members acting under a responsibility to public opinion, which can and will check their aberrations from duty?[45]

---

since we have seen Judges, who ought to have been independent, converted into political partisans, and like executive missionaries, pronouncing political harangues throughout the United States! It is sometime, sir, since we have seen the zealous Judge stoop from the Bench to look out for more victims for judicial vengeance! It is sometime since we have seen the same judicial impetuosity drive from the bar the most respectable counsel, who humanely proposed to interpose between a friendless and unprotected man and the judicial vengeance to which he was doomed! It is sometime, sir, since we have seen the same judicial zeal extending the provisions of the sedition act, by discovering that it had jurisdiction of the *lex non scripta,* or common law!" *Ibid.,* p. 583. The decisions and actions of the Judges, it was noted, were against practically every important doctrine of the Democratic-Republican party and supported in almost all cases the political principles of the Federalists. For a summary of the decisions involving partisan views, see Warren, *op. cit.,* I: 190.

[43] *Annals, op. cit.,* p. 602. Not only was the speech replied to by Bayard, the foremost member of the Federalist party in the House, but it called forth an essay by Hamilton. See *Works* (Const. ed.), VIII: 353–364.

[44] *Annals, op. cit.,* p. 658.

[45] *Ibid.,* p. 661.

Speaking for the omnipotent authority claimed for the Judges, Randolph observed: "Their humble pretensions extend only to a complete
exemption from Legislative control, to the exercise of an inquisitorial
authority over the cabinet of the Executive, and a veto of the Roman
Tribunate upon all your laws, together with the establishing any body
of laws which they may choose to declare a part of the Constitution."
Congress, he believed, may not erect in defiance of the spirit and letter
of the Constitution a judicial aristocracy over and above the people of
the United States.[46] "Alarm upon alarm, and threat upon threat, have
been sounded in our ears," said Representative Clopton, "the cry of
'unconstitutionality' has been reverberated again and again. In language
strong, positive, and unequivocal, we have been repeatedly told that we
are about to break down one of the main pillars of our Constitution, and
to unsettle the whole foundation of our government."[47] Senator Breckenridge urged the senators to confine the discussion to the merits of the
question and not to be led into the "regions of fancy and of terror" to
which the opponents were taking flight. Referring to the assertion of the
Federalists that there were only two ways of governing, one by the Judiciary and the other by the bayonet, Representative Mason replied that
the Republicans depended on better methods, namely, elections and
the good sense of the people.[48]

Federalist threats.—The proposal to nullify acts of Congress by state
action, when the constitutional grants to the federal government were
thought to be exceeded, was first formally and emphatically put forward
in the adoption of the Kentucky and Virginia Resolutions. But the threat
of secession and the dire prediction that civil war was likely to result
came from the Federalists in the famous judiciary debate of 1802. "There
are States in this Union," said Roger Griswold of Connecticut, "who will
never consent, and are not doomed to become humble provinces of
Virginia."[49] The attack on the Judiciary which the Republicans were
sponsoring, contended Bayard, involved "a doctrine which cannot be
practised without producing not discord only, but bloodshed. . . . There
are many now willing to spill their blood to defend that Constitution . . .
the moment is not far off when this fair country is to be desolated by civil
war."[50] Fisher Ames joined in the wail of the Federalists who had de-

---

[46] *Annals, op. cit.,* pp. 660–662.

[47] *Ibid.,* p. 970.

[48] *Ibid.,* p. 720.

[49] *Ibid.,* p. 793.

[50] *Ibid.,* pp. 642–650. The contention that the very foundation of the government of
the union was to be destroyed was made over and over again throughout the debate.
A few other comments of this nature may be cited. To Representative Griswold of

veloped as part of their program a rule or ruin policy by insisting that "the Federalists must entrench themselves in the state governments, and endeavor to make state justice and state power a shelter of the wise, and good, and rich, from the wild destroying rage of the Southern Jacobins."[51] Pickering began to visualize "a new confederacy" in which the northern states and the British provinces would join.[52] These and similar threats did not deter the Republicans from carrying out their design to restore the Judiciary to its former status and functions.

An instance of specious reasoning to confuse the issue is shown in the claim of the Federalists that they were the real champions of the rights of the people. When it was contended that the Legislature as well as the courts might interpret the Constitution and that when such interpretation was embodied in an act it was the duty of the courts to enforce it, the Federalists replied with Hamiltonian logic that "the sovereignty of America will no longer reside in the people, but in the Congress, and the Constitution is whatever they choose to make it."[53] But how does sovereignty reside in the people when a few appointed Judges alone have the authority to place a final interpretation on the Constitution—the people's fundamental law—and, by their decisions, to make it? The Federalists, maintaining that the Judiciary should be a coördinate branch of the government, asserted that the Republican point of view made of the Judiciary a subordinate or dependent branch of the government.[54] This objection was offset partly by Jefferson's concession that in relation

---

Connecticut there was no middle ground between a government of laws and a government of men. The former could only be supported by an independent Judiciary and, said he: "If by the passage of this bill you destroy this only barrier, the people of the country are left at the mercy of a host of despots, whose will is law, and whose enmity is death." *Annals, op. cit.*, p. 794.

Predicting dire consequences, Representative Tallmadge of Connecticut exclaimed: "Let this government and Constitution be prostrated, and I have no hesitation in declaring that a civil war must be our portion. For heaven's sake, for our country's sake, let everything tending to such an issue, be most carefully avoided." *Ibid.*, p. 947.

"Sir, I mean no threats, I have no expectation of appalling the stout hearts of my adversaries," said Bayard, "but if gentlemen are regardless of themselves, let them consider their wives and children, their neighbors and their friends. Will they risk civil dissension, will they hazard the welfare, will they jeopardize the peace of the country, to save a paltry sum of money—less than thirty thousand dollars? My feeble efforts can avail nothing, but it was my duty to make them. The mediated blow is mortal, and from the moment it is struck, we may bid a final adieu to the Constitution." *Ibid.*, p. 649.

[51] *Works*, ed. by Seth Ames (Boston, 1854), I: 310. The extinction of Federalism, Ames was sure, would result in "the ruin of the wise, rich, and good." *Ibid.*, p. 316.

[52] Henry Adams, *New England Federalism*, p. 338.

[53] Randolph inquired on several occasions whether the Judiciary as supported by the Federalists was to be a coördinate or a paramount department of government.

[54] *Ibid.*, p. 692. See argument of Representative Huger of South Carolina.

to the protection of their own powers and authority the courts might, in the first instance at least, refuse to enforce an act of Congress.

The system of circuit riding which the Act of 1801 eliminated was defended on the ground that it afforded an opportunity for the Judges to become acquainted with local laws and customs. To this argument the Federalists replied that they were not convinced that the best way to study law was to ride rapidly from one end of the country to another. They believed that knowledge of the law might be acquired more advantageously "in the closet than on the high road." It was also argued that most of the cases decided in the federal courts depended upon the common law, and knowledge of local conditions afforded no aid in this connection. But to the Republicans the use of the common law as a basis for decisions was especially objectionable.[55] Senator Breckenridge stated the view which became one of the main themes of the Democratic philosophy a few decades later. "I do not wish," said he, "to see all possible subjects drawn into the great vortex of federal legislation and adjudication. I do not, in short, wish, as some gentlemen may do, to see one mighty and consolidated sovereignty collected from and erected on the ruins of all the state sovereignties."[56]

Alternative proposals made by the Republicans.—Senator Wright of Maryland,[57] in stating the view of the Constitution regarding judicial powers to which the Republicans adhered, thought that the Judges, so far as questions constitutionally submitted to them were concerned, ought to be guardians of the Constitution; but he held the Legislature, Executive, and Judiciary, each severally, guardians of the Constitution, so far as they were called upon to carry out their duties. To the Republicans, the most satisfactory and effective corrective of violations of the Constitution was to be found in the Legislature itself. In case of misconstructions contrary to the wishes of the people, the election of members to Congress with instructions to adopt the appropriate remedy appeared to be an adequate mode of procedure to meet all conditions. To the Federalists, this argument meant that the Judiciary could not be a check on the Legislature, and that a legislative act expressing the public will must be carried into effect by the Judiciary whether the law carrying out this will was in accord with or in violation of the Constitution.[58]

Attorney General Levi Lincoln expressed the Republican attitude to-

---

[55] See objections to the exercise of common law jurisdiction by the federal courts presented by Representatives Randolph, Henderson, and Nicholson, below, pp. 240 ff.

[56] *Annals, op. cit.,* p. 99.

[57] *Ibid.,* p. 115.

[58] Cf. comments of Representative Hastings, *ibid.,* p. 884.

ward the review of acts of Congress in an opinion given to the President regarding the effect of the decision of the Supreme Court in the case of *United States v. Peggy*.[59] "The Supreme Court," said the Attorney General, "who were competent to decide this privilege have determined it in her case. It must, therefore, be considered as binding in this particular instance. Although they have fixed the principle for themselves, and thereby have bound others in reference to the case on which they have adjudicated, it can, I conceive, extend no further. In all other cases in which the Executive or other courts are obliged to act, they must decide for themselves; paying a great deference to the opinions of a court of so high an authority as the Supreme one of the United States, but still greater to their own convictions of the meaning of the laws and Constitution of the United States and of their oaths to support them."[60]

Senator Breckenridge, however, answered in most effective form the Federalist contentions regarding judicial review of acts of Congress with the alternative proposal suggested by the Republicans. "I did not expect," said Breckenridge,

to find the doctrine of the power of the courts to annul the laws of Congress as unconstitutional, so seriously insisted on. . . . It is said that the different departments of government are to be checks on each other, and that the courts are to check the Legislature. If this be true, I would ask where they got that power, and who checks the courts when they violate the Constitution? Would they not, by this doctrine, have the absolute direction of the government? To whom are they responsible? But I deny the power which is so pretended. If it is derived from the Constitution, I ask gentlemen to point out the clause which grants it. I can find no such grant. Is it not extraordinary, that if this high power was intended, it should nowhere appear? Is it not truly astonishing that the Constitution, in its abundant care to define the powers of each department, should have omitted so important a power as that of the courts to nullify all the acts of Congress, which, in their opinion, were contrary to the Constitution?

Never were such high and transcendent powers in any government (much less in one like ours, composed of powers specially given and defined) claimed or exercised by construction only. The doctrine of constructions, not warranted by the letter of an instrument, is dangerous in the extreme. Let men once loose upon constructions, and where will you stop them? Is the *astutia* of English judges, in discovering the latent meanings of law-makers, meanings not expressed in the letter of the laws, to be adopted here in the construction of the Constitution? Once admit the doctrine, that Judges are to be indulged in these astute and wire-drawn constructions, to enlarge their own power, and control that of others, and I will join gentlemen of the opposition, in declaring that the Constitution is in danger.

To make the Constitution a practical system, this pretended power of the courts to annul the laws of Congress cannot possibly exist. My idea of the subject, in a few words, is, that the Constitution intended a separation of the powers vested in the three great departments, giving to each exclusive authority on the subjects committed to it. That these departments are co-ordinate, to revolve each within the sphere of their own orbits, without being responsible for their own motion, and are not to direct or

---

[59] 1 Cranch 103 (1801).   [60] *Opinions of Attorneys-General*, I: 122.

control the course of others. That those who made the laws are presumed to have an equal attachment to, and interest in the Constitution; are equally bound by oath to support it, and have an equal right to give a construction to it. That the construction of one deparment of the powers vested in it, is of higher authority than the construction of any other department; and that, in fact, it is competent to that department to which powers are confided exclusively to decide upon the proper exercise of those powers: that therefore the Legislature have the exclusive right to interpret the Constitution, in what regards the law-making power, and the Judges are bound to execute the laws they make. For the Legislature would have at least an equal right to annul the decisions of the courts, founded on their construction of the Constitution, as the courts would have to annul the acts of the Legislature, founded on their construction.

Although, therefore, the courts may take upon them to give decisions which impeach the constitutionality of a law, and thereby, for a time, obstruct its operations, yet I contend that such a law is not the less obligatory because the organ through which it is to be executed has refused its aid. A pertinacious adherence of both departments to their opinions, would soon bring the question to issue, in whom the sovereign power of legislation resided, and whose construction of the law-making power should prevail.

If the courts have a right to examine into, and decide upon the constitutionality of laws, their decision ought to be final and effectual. I ask then, if gentlemen are prepared to admit, that in case the courts were to declare your revenue, impost and appropriation laws unconstitutional, that they would thereby be blotted out of your statute book, and the operations of government be arrested? It is making, in my opinion, a mockery of the high powers of legislation. I feel humbled by the doctrine, and enter my protest against it. Let gentlemen consider well before they insist on a power in the Judiciary which places the Legislature at their feet. Let not so humiliating a condition be admitted under an authority of resting merely on application (sic) and construction. It will invite a state of things which we are not justified by the Constitution in presuming will happen, and which (should it happen) all men of all parties must deplore.[61]

In place of a power of final and authoritative interpretation of the Constitution by the courts, Breckenridge's alternative proposal, to which all citizens and public officers must submit, was to permit each department to interpret the Constitution as it saw fit. In an irreconcilable conflict an appeal to the people as the ultimate authority might be made.

Senator Morris, replying to Breckenridge's concluding argument, inquired "if gentlemen are prepared to establish one consolidated government over this country? Sir, if the doctrine they advance prevails, if it be the true doctrine, there is no longer any legislature in America but that of the Union." Admitting that there was no clause in the Constitution which authorized the Judges to annul acts of Congress, Morris asserted that this did not worry him, for "I answer, they derived that power from authority higher than this Constitution. They derive it from the constitution of man, from the nature of things, from the necessary progress of human affairs."[62] Morris and his associates in the Senate were fearful that the proponents of the Repeal Act were moving in

---

[61] *Annals, op. cit.,* pp. 178–180.   [62] *Ibid.,* p. 180.

the direction of the establishment of legislative supremacy and this above all else they wished to prevent.[63]

Criticizing the language of Justice Paterson to the effect that the courts could declare an act of Congress void, Representative Davis of Kentucky said: "Never can I subscribe to that opinion. Never can I believe the Judiciary paramount to both branches of the Legislature. . . . I am willing to admit the Judiciary to be coordinate with the legislature in this respect, to wit: that Judges, thinking a law unconstitutional, are not bound to execute it; but not to declare it null and void. That power rests alone with the Legislature."[64]

Another contention of the Republicans was that the increase of the number of federal courts and Justices had a tendency to draw legal business away from the state courts when it was desirable to encourage the opposite trend. And the height of degradation and tyranny was depicted in the spectacle of a sovereign state "upon her knees before six venerable Judges, decorated in party-colored robes, as ours formerly were, or arrayed in more solemn black, such as they have lately assumed."[65] But the opinion of the Federalists that the federal courts were authorized to adopt the reasoning and principles of the common law aroused the most outspoken opposition and resentment. Refuting the arguments of Representative Henderson, Macon of North Carolina said:

He told us that the Judges only adopted such parts of the common law of England as suited the people, and that he apprehended no danger from this. Sir, I do apprehend danger from this, because I cannot find any authority given them in the Constitution to do it, and I suppose it is not an inherent right. Without pretending to know the extent of this common law, it has always appeared to me to be extremely dangerous to the rights of the people, for any person not elected by them, to undertake to exercise the power of legislating for them, and this adopting the common law is only another name for legislation. He has also told us, that the States had adopted it. If the States adopted it, it became a law of the State and not of the United States; but the adoption of it by the individual States, could not give the Judges a right to adopt it for the United States. The Judges have no powers but what are given by the Constitution or by statute, and this power cannot be found in either. He even told us, that the Constitution was a dead letter without it. I do not believe this was the opinion of the Convention that formed it, and by an examination of the debates of the state conventions that ratified it, it will not be found to be their opinion; nor is it, I believe, the opinion of all the Judges of the Supreme Court, that the Constitution would be a dead letter without the common law of England.[66]

And a similar sentiment was expressed by Nicholson of Virginia, who asked:

Have the people of this country ever consented to vest the Judges with this extensive discretionary power? Have they ever sanctioned the principle that the Judges should

[63] *Annals, op. cit.,* p. 180.
[64] *Ibid.,* p. 558.
[65] Senator Mason of Virginia, *ibid.,* p. 69.
[66] Senator Mason of Virginia, *ibid.,* p. 713.

make laws for them instead of their Representatives? Is it not legislation to all intents and purposes, when your Judges are authorized to introduce at pleasure the laws of a foreign country, to arm themselves with power? The American people never dreamed of such a principle in the Constitution, and never will submit to it. They never ought to submit to it. It is giving to the Judges a power infinitely more transcendent than that vested in any other branch of the Government. The legislature cannot recognize any principle of the common law having a monarchical tendency; yet this principle the Judges may recognize, if you leave it to their discretion to introduce any part of the common law which they think proper.[67]

The Federalist tendency to place around the Judge a halo of superior sanctity did not appeal to many members of Congress, for the query was raised: "Are not Judges men? Are they not subject to like passions and like feelings as other men?"[68] Brushing aside the Federalist arguments and their dire threats, the Republicans passed the Repeal Act and in other ways indicated their intention to control the Supreme Court. Seemingly, Republican theories of constitutional construction were in the ascendancy. But President Adams had by masterly partisan maneuvers placed a Federalist politician and statesman in the position of Chief Justice and, as Beveridge expresses it, the stage was set for Marshall's "performance of an imperative duty."[69] In fact, says Beveridge, "All the reasons for the opinion which John Marshall, exactly one year later, pronounced in *Marbury v. Madison* were given during the debate. Indeed, the legislative struggle now in progress and the result of it, created conditions which forced Marshall to execute that judicial *coup d'état*. It should be repeated that an understanding of *Marbury v. Madison* is impossible without a thorough knowledge of the debate in Congress which preceded and largely caused that epochal decision."[70]

The contention was made by the Federalists throughout the argument that the Judges of the Circuit Court held their offices during good behavior, and since their salaries could not be diminished during their continuance in office, Congress could not, by abolishing the offices, or by repealing the Judiciary Act of 1801, deprive them of their judgeships and salaries. Despite this and other arguments of the Federalists, the repealing act passed the Senate by a margin of one vote but by approximately a two to one majority in the House. Regardless of the reasons and arguments that Congress cannot abolish federal courts and thereby

---

[67] *Ibid.*, pp. 805, 806.

[68] *Ibid.*, p. 826.

[69] *The Life of John Marshall*, III: 100.

[70] *Ibid.*, p. 75. In the consideration of the repealing act Beveridge cannot conceal his partisanship. The Federalist act of 1801 is declared to be "one of the best considered and ablest measures ever devised by that constructive party." Admirable, excellent, and other adjectives are used in describing it, and the only objection to the act regarded as having any validity was the "alleged extravagance." See *ibid.*, III: 53.

remove from office Judges appointed to positions created by a previous act, it is now well settled, so far as the question of the power of Congress is concerned, that the tenure of good behavior in judicial office does not prevent the legislature from abolishing a federal court.

Some of the Judges removed by the Repealing Act petitioned Congress for relief, claiming that no provision had been made for the payment of salaries to which they were constitutionally entitled. They joined in sending a memorial to Congress protesting against their removal, claiming that rights secured to them by the Constitution, as members of the judicial department, had been impaired. Congress was required to define the duties which they should perform and provide for the compensation which was secured to them in accordance with the provisions of the Constitution. The committee of the Senate, to whom was referred the memorials of the Judges, regarded it improper to express opinions on the issues involved, but, in view of the serious import of the questions put forth, the committee requested the President, through the Attorney General, to file an information in the nature of a *quo warranto* on behalf of the petitioners for the purpose of securing a judicial determination of their claims.[71] After brief consideration in the House of Representatives the request of the petitioners was denied.[72] No further action was taken.

Chief Justice Marshall believed the Judiciary Repeal Act of 1802, so far as it deprived federal Judges of their offices and salaries, was unconstitutional.[73] No case arose, however, to test the validity of the act. The Justices did not deem their position secure enough to refuse to act under the law of 1789 which had now been restored. But an occasion soon arose for Marshall to assert doctrines of judicial independence and superiority. Through him the Judiciary was destined, as its proponents expected, to save the cause of Federalism through the process of constitutional interpretation.

The terms and jurisdiction of the Supreme Court were not affected by the original Judiciary Repeal Act, but the membership of the Court provided by the act of 1789 was restored. Because the Federalists looked to the Court to declare the Repeal Act void, the Republicans adopted a plan which rendered impossible immediate action of this kind. They changed the terms of the Supreme Court. The Judiciary Act of 1789 had

---

[71] *American State Papers*, Miscellaneous, I: 340.

[72] *Annals*, 7th Cong., 2d sess., pp. 427 ff.

[73] For Marshall's views on the validity of the Judiciary Repeal Act, see letters to Justice Paterson, April 6, 19, May 3, 1802, from which extracts are quoted, Warren, *op. cit.*, I: 269 ff. Cf. also James Kent, *New York Review* (1838), Vol. III, and Story, *Commentaries on the Constitution* (5th ed., 1891), p. 426.

provided for terms of the Court in February and August. The Federalist reorganization act changed the terms to June and December, but this act was quickly repealed, thus restoring the February and August arrangement. As the Judiciary debate progressed in the spring of 1802, the Congressional leaders decided to abolish the August session, except for the receipt of motions and other routine matters. The result of these enactments was that the Supreme Court sat in December, 1801, and did not meet again to hear cases until February, 1803.[74] With the passage of the law abolishing the sessions of the Supreme Court for fourteen months, claims Beveridge, the movement began "that finally developed into the plan for the secession of the New England States from the Union."[75]

The charge of political motives.—Advocates of the doctrine of judicial supremacy seek to minimize the opposition to judicial review of legislation at the time the practice was adopted by state and federal courts. Thus, Charles Warren claims that prior to the debate over the Judiciary Repeal Act of 1802 no prominent statesman other than Charles Pinckney of South Carolina publicly denied the Court's power to review acts of Congress.[76] Until this date, he asserts that the power of the Judiciary to review federal legislation "had been almost universally recognized, and even in 1802, it was attacked purely on political grounds and only by politicians from Kentucky, Virginia, North Carolina, and Georgia."[77] In defense of this contention Warren fails, as historians frequently do, to distinguish the doctrine of the supremacy of the federal Judiciary, so far as state enactments being in conflict with the powers or authority expressly granted to the federal government were concerned. Nor does he distinguish the right of the federal courts in the settlement of private controversies among citizens to pass in the first instance on the validity of acts of Congress. Not all of the Federalists and only a few Republicans supported the claim that the Judges had final and conclusive authority to interpret the Constitution in a manner which was binding on the states and on the coördinate departments of the federal government in the disputed fields of the interpretation of implied powers or of the settlement of political questions. Many who favored a limited type of

[74] James A. Bayard denounced these enactments "as a patchwork designed to cover one object, the postponement of the next session of the Supreme Court . . . to give the Repealing Act its full effect before the Judges are allowed to assemble." *Annals,* 7th Cong., 1st sess., p. 30.

[75] *The Life of John Marshall,* III: 97. See below, pp. 294 ff.

[76] "The Early History of the Supreme Court of the United States in Connection with Modern Attacks on the Judiciary," 8 *Mass. Law Jour.* (Dec., 1922), 15.

[77] *The Supreme Court in United States History,* I: 82, 256.

judicial review of state and federal acts, as did Madison and Jefferson, denied the high and commanding prerogative of the Judiciary to control the other departments which the Federalists usually defended.

Though more opinions were expressed favorable to the review of legislative acts by the courts than those expressed to the contrary, and though the members of the Democratic or Anti-Federalist groups occasionally joined in the defense of such review, it is apparent that the liberal or democratic groups usually doubted the wisdom of placing Judges in control of the fundamental law or vigorously opposed the adoption of a practice which would accord such a high prerogative to the courts. After a careful analysis of the debates in the state legislatures concerning the Virginia and Kentucky Resolutions, Frank M. Anderson concluded that the available evidence shows conclusively that many Anti-Federalists "did not accept the Federalist doctrine that the Supreme Court of the United States is the final arbiter of the differences between the federal government and the States."[78] When asserting the authority of the courts to review state acts, Chief Justice Kirkpatrick of New Jersey observed that the issue of judicial review enlisted "many champions on both sides."[79] And Justice Breckenridge of Pennsylvania discovered that opinions were rather evenly divided in that state. Arguing in favor of judicial review in the case of *John Towers,* he said:

I have enquired of a leading member of the state convention which framed the constitution, how it came to pass that, as this was a vexed question in the theory of government, even under the written constitution of the States, the power had not been expressly assigned to the judiciary, of testing a statute by the constitution; his answer was, that it was thought that if the principle had been brought broadly in view, it would have been rejected, and it was thought more advisable to leave it to be collected by construction.[80]

Much significançe is attached to a purported change of opinion in relation to judicial review by such opponents as Senator Breckenridge of Kentucky[81] and Thomas Jefferson.[82] The change is attributed to partisanship and is thereby thought to be discredited.

Following the same line of argument, John Marshall might be charged with partisanship in espousing the cause of judicial review in the *Mar-*

---

[78] Frank Maloy Anderson, "Contemporary Opinion of the Virginia and Kentucky Resolutions," *Amer. Hist. Rev.* (Oct., 1899), V: 54.

[79] State v. Parkhurst, 4 Halstead 444, 445 (1802).

[80] 2 Browne's Repts. (Court of Common Pleas, Phila., Dist., Pa., 1812), 195.

[81] John Breckenridge, in 1798, recognized in relation to acts of Congress that Judges might refuse to enforce an act because it was unconstitutional. Ethelbert D. Warfield, *The Kentucky Resolutions of 1798* (New York, 1887), pp. 93, 94.

[82] For Jefferson's opinions on judicial review, see above, pp. 206 ff.

bury Case. Marshall is on record both as approving and condemning the doctrine of review before rendering his famous pronouncement.[83] Gouverneur Morris also changed his views, first disapproving judicial review and then becoming an ardent advocate.[84]

By ignoring some of the most important facts of history of the previous decades, Warren claims that up to this time the Republicans had been the chief defenders of the right of judicial review, but in order to meet the Federalist arguments regarding the invalidity of the Judiciary Repeal Act they shifted their ground for the purpose of political expediency. The evidence of Republican views on judicial review has been made sufficiently clear to indicate the inaccuracy of such a claim.

This method of imputing political and selfish motives to those who espoused Republican doctrines is carried to an absurd extreme in the contention that the representatives of Virginia and Kentucky were led to oppose the review of legislative acts by the federal courts for fear of adverse holdings on the land laws of those states.[85] No doubt personal and private interests had their influence in the positions on public questions taken by the Republicans as well as by the Federalists. And it is obvious that those who declaimed loudest on behalf of an independent Judiciary with the right to veto acts of Congress were not thinking so much of the liberties of the people to which many references were made as they were of the property which they wished to have protected. This was an issue on which public men held divergent views from colonial times to date, and on which they were to continue to differ for many years to come. Why does it seem necessary to seek personal and political motives to justify the conduct of those who opposed judicial supremacy and assume that the proponents of such supremacy were necessarily highminded patriots who thought only of the public good and the general welfare?

POLITICAL ASPECTS OF THE CASE OF MARBURY V. MADISON

In the desire to keep the fountain of justice pure and uncontaminated by the waters of Republicanism, the Federalists passed a law in February, 1801, forming the District of Columbia into two counties and authorizing the President to appoint for each such number of justices of peace as he shall deem expedient, the incumbents to hold office for five years. Great importance was attached to the appointment of these justices of peace, since they were the only governing body for that part of the Dis-

[83] Elliot's *Debates*, III: 553, and Ware v. Hylton, 3 Dallas 199, 211 (1796).

[84] Jared Sparks, *Life of Gouverneur Morris* (Boston, 1832), III: 438, and *Annals*, 7th Cong., 1st sess., pp. 180, 181.

[85] Warren, *op. cit.*, I: 219 ff.

trict which was not included in the corporate limits of Alexandria and Georgetown.[86] Among his so-called "midnight appointments" President Adams designated twenty-three justices of peace for Washington County and nineteen for Alexandria County and they were confirmed by the Senate on March 3. Commissions for these positions were made out, signed, and sealed but remained in the office of the Secretary of State until after Jefferson assumed the presidency. Though Chief Justice Marshall insisted that the commissions for these officers were legally made out and should have been delivered by Jefferson's appointee, Secretary of State Madison, all of the commissions disappeared and none were received by the appointees. President Jefferson by a blanket commission later appointed fifteen justices for each county, including in his list twenty-three of those nominated by Adams.[87] Among those to whom commissions were refused were William Marbury, Dennis Ramsay, Robert Townsend Hooe, and William Harper. These men applied to the Supreme Court of the United States for a writ of mandamus to compel Secretary of State Madison to deliver the commissions, and an order was issued requiring him to show cause at the next term of the Court why the writ of mandamus should not be granted. It was this order to which the Republicans objected during the Judiciary debate, for they regarded the proceedings in the *Marbury Case*[88] as a political move on the part of the Federalists to prevent the repeal of the Judiciary Act.[89]

Chief Justice Marshall, who also served Adams as Secretary of State, had failed to deliver the commissions of Marbury and his associates who were now seeking a mandamus to compel the delivery of their commissions. He explained that the failure to deliver the commissions was due to "the extreme hurry of the time and the absence of Mr. Wagner (Clerk of the State Department) who had been called on by the President to act as his private secretary."[90] Because of his personal responsibility and interest in the case, it might have been expected that Marshall would decline to act as a Judge in passing upon the application for a mandamus.

---

[86] See acts of February 27 and March 3, 1801, 2 *U. S. Statutes at Large*, 103, 115.

[87] *National Intelligencer*, March 23, 1801, and Charles S. Bundy, "A History of the Office of Justice of Peace in the District of Columbia," *Records of the Columbia Historical Society*, V: 259 ff.

[88] 1 Cranch 137 (1803).

[89] See criticism of Senator Giles, *Annals*, 7th Cong., 1st sess., pp. 579 ff., and the reply of Senator Bayard, *ibid.*, pp. 603 ff. The Supreme Court Justices were lauded by Bayard for being "hardy enough to send their mandate into the Executive cabinet. . . . They have given a strong proof of the value of that constitutional provision which makes them independent. They are not terrified by the frowns of Executive power, and dare to judge between the rights of a citizen and the pretensions of a President."

[90] See letter quoted by Beveridge, *op. cit.*, III: 124, 125.

Though questions of judicial propriety, independence, and aloofness loomed strong when the relations with the coördinate departments were concerned, nice distinctions of this kind did not seem to have much weight when partisan feelings and inclinations were aroused.[91]

When the Supreme Court met in February, 1803, it was generally assumed that the Court would grant the mandamus sought by Marbury and his associates and that Madison on the instructions of the President would ignore the writ. The justices of peace appointed by President Jefferson were taking care of the business of the District, and there was little interest in the outcome of the case. "So far then, as practical results were concerned," observes Beveridge, "the case of *Marbury v. Madison* had now come to the point where it was of no consequence whatever to anyone. It presented only theoretical questions, and on the face of the record, even these were as simple as they were unimportant. This controversy, in fact, had degenerated into little more than 'a moot case' as Jefferson termed it twenty years later."[92] McLaughlin, also regarding the case as moot, condemns the unusual and extrajudicial attitude of the Chief Justice, for, he notes, "according to Marshall's own theories, the want of jurisdiction was plain on the very face of the pleadings."[93] Though there was no longer any real case before the Court and though Marshall, because of his personal interest in and relation to the proceedings, should have declined to act as a Judge in the case, he ignored these factors and used the controversy to announce some fundamental constitutional theories.

Marshall's opinion in the *Marbury Case* is subject to certain errors or misconstructions which would normally be discreditable in the action of a reviewing tribunal. In the first place, the legality of Marbury's claim to the office was considered *in extenso* before the question of the Court's jurisdiction in the case was discussed; that is, the usual order of the determination of issues was reversed; and second, the statute in question had been construed and could readily be interpreted so as to avoid the issue of constitutionality and, according to the generally accepted canon

---

[91] For consideration of the propriety of the action of Chief Justice Marshall in participating in and rendering the opinion in this case, see Andrew C. McLaughlin, "Marbury vs. Madison Again," 14 *Amer. Bar. Assn. Jour.* (Mar., 1928), 157, and J. A. C. Grant, "Marbury v. Madison Today," 23 *Amer. Pol. Sci. Rev.* (Aug., 1929), 678 ff.

[92] *The Life of John Marshall*, III: 125, and Jefferson, *Works* (Mem. ed.), XV: 447.

[93] Andrew C. McLaughlin, *Constitutional History of the United States* (New York, 1935), p. 306. "The learned Justice," says McLaughlin, "really manufactured an opportunity to declare an act void. . . . [He passed] upon a constitutional question involving the authority of a coordinate branch of the government, the Executive, in a case he had no right so much as to entertain if his own decision was correct." "Marbury vs. Madison Again," 14 *Amer. Bar. Assn. Jour.* (1928), 156, 157.

in controversies involving constitutional questions, should not have been
passed upon. It seems plain, thinks Warren,

that it would have been possible for Marshall, if he had been so inclined, to have
construed the language of the section of the Judiciary Act which authorized writs of
mandamus, in such a manner as to have enabled him to escape the necessity of declaring the section unconstitutional. . . . [But he] felt that in view of the recent attacks on
judicial power it was important to have the great principle firmly established, and
undoubtedly he welcomed the opportunity of fixing the precedent in a case in which
his action would necessitate a decision in favor of his political opponents.[94]

When Corwin, however, refers to Marshall's decision as "a political
pamphlet designed to irritate an enemy to the very limit of endurance"
and thinks the "decision bears many of the earmarks of a deliberate
partisan coup" because it was designed as a lecture to the President on
his duty to recent Federalist appointees to judicial office,[95] Warren protests that there is no basis for the imputation of "unjudicial motives."

Section 13 of the Judiciary Act of 1789, which was held void so far as
it related to the *Marbury Case,* provided that "the Supreme Court . . .
shall have power to issue writs of mandamus, in cases warranted by the
principles and usages of law, to any courts appointed, or persons holding
office, under the authority of the United States."[96] This section, which
had been drafted and approved by some of the leaders who participated
in the Philadelphia Convention, was regarded as constitutional from
1789 and applied as such in a number of cases.[97] Section 13 could have

---

[94] Warren, *op. cit.,* I: 242, 243. Differences of opinion on this point were expressed in
Myers v. United States, as follows: "The Court had, therefore nothing before it calling
for a judgment upon the merits of the question of issuing the mandamus. Notwithstanding this, the opinion considered preliminarily, first, whether the relator had the
right to the delivery of the commission, and, second, whether it was the duty of the
Secretary of State to deliver it to him and a duty which could be enforced in a court
of competent jurisdiction at common law by a writ of mandamus?" The whole statement of the Chief Justice, with reference to the issuance of a mandamus, "was certainly
obiter dictum with reference to the judgment actually reached." Chief Justice Taft in
majority opinion, 272 U. S. 52, 140 ff. But to Justice McReynolds, dissenting, "The point
thus decided was directly presented and essential to proper determination of the
cause. . . . The sometime suggestion that the Chief Justice indulged in an *obiter dictum,*
is without foundation." *Ibid.,* p. 217.

[95] *The Doctrine of Judicial Review* (Princeton, 1914), p. 9, and "Marbury v. Madison
and the Doctrine of Judicial Review," 12 *Mich. Law Rev.* (May, 1914), 538, 542.

[96] 1 *U. S. Statutes at Large,* 80, 81.

[97] United States v. Ravara, 2 Dallas 297 (1793); United States v. Judge Lawrence, 3
Dallas 42 (1795) and United States v. Peters, 3 Dallas 121 (1795); see also reference to
two other cases in the argument of Charles Lee in the Marbury Case, 1 Cranch 148, 149.
Section 342 of the Judicial Code now provides that the Supreme Court may issue
"writs of mandamus, in cases warranted by the principles and usage of law, or to
persons holding office under the authority of the United States, where a State or an
ambassador, or other public minister, or a consul, or vice consul is a party." This
is a reënactment of sec. 13, c. 20 of the Act of 1789 with little substantial change.

been construed in this, as in other cases, to uphold the validity, that is, as authorizing the Court to issue writs of mandamus, in cases arising under the original jurisdiction of the Court. But there was an emergency, an extraordinary need, for a decision political in its nature and implications. For "nothing but the emergency compelling the insistence at this particular time, that the Supreme Court had such power [that is, to declare void an act of Congress], can fully and satisfactorily explain the action of Marshall in holding this section void."[98]

Marshall, according to Beveridge, had prepared a constructive answer to the Kentucky and Virginia Resolutions and to the Republican arguments on the repeal of the Judiciary Act, the philosophy of which the Republicans generally approved, and which he had followed with great interest.[99] Believing that the nationalist majority on the Supreme Court might soon be changed by the appointment of new members to the Court and that the position of the Supreme Court as the guardian of the Constitution, according to Federalist standards, was none too secure, he "resolved to make use of this unimportant litigation to assert, at a critical hour when such a pronouncement was essential, the power of the Supreme Court to declare invalid acts of Congress that violate the Constitution."[100] As an "experienced politician" thoroughly familiar with the methods and arguments of the Republicans, he was prepared to take a "bold course" to preserve the ramparts of Federalism. "Thus," says Beveridge, "by a coup as bold in design and as daring in execution as that by which the Constitution had been framed, John Marshall set up a landmark in American history so high that all the future could take bearings from it, so enduring that all the shocks the Nation was to endure could not overturn it."[101] This was the "deed of a great man"—the act of a statesman of the first rank. Apparently this was not an instance of mechanical jurisprudence or the strict following of the letter of the law to which Marshall was wont to recur in subsequent decisions.

Early action was thought necessary, and in less than two weeks after the close of arguments in the case, Marshall's opinion, which no doubt had been in preparation for months as a Federalist pronunciamento, was announced. Marbury's appointment was held to be complete, and the

---

[98] Beveridge, *op. cit.*, III: 133.

[99] *Ibid.*, p. 104. There was, maintains Beveridge, an "absolute necessity of asserting that there was one department of government that could not be influenced by temporary public opinion. The value to a democracy of a steadying force was not then so well understood as it is at present but the Chief Justice appreciated it and determined at all hazards to make the national Judiciary the stabilizing power that it has become." *Ibid.*, p. 109.

[100] *Ibid.*, p. 111.

[101] *Ibid.*, p. 142.

President as well as his Secretary of State were declared to be derelict in the performance of their duties. Indicating a point of view to be developed with vigor and effectiveness in subsequent cases, Chief Justice Marshall maintained: "The government of the United States has been emphatically termed a government of laws, and not of men. It will certainly cease to deserve this high appellation, if the laws furnish no remedy for the violation of a vested legal right."[102] But here was a vested legal right for which the Chief Justice, desiring at this time to avoid a direct conflict with a hostile Executive department, held there was no remedy. Answering the charge frequently made during the debates in Congress in 1802 that the Supreme Court was attempting to intrude in the cabinet and to intermeddle with the powers of the Executive, Marshall disclaimed such pretensions for "an extravagance so absurd and excessive, could not have been entertained for a moment." He then proceeded to distinguish acts which were discretionary and necessarily political in nature and thus beyond judicial control, and acts based upon rights defined by law which might be asserted and protected in courts of justice no matter how exalted the position of the officer concerned.[103] The delivery of Marbury's commission being regarded in the latter category, the Chief Justice then turned to the nature of the remedy to enforce his right. Mandamus was held to be the appropriate remedy for this purpose. But could the Supreme Court issue the writ?

In the answer to this question the Chief Justice found a clue to present his argument on judicial review of acts of Congress. Adopting a narrow interpretation of the Constitution not required by its words, he held void section 13 of the Judiciary Act of 1789 so far as it authorized the Supreme Court to issue a mandamus in such a case. Marbury was entitled to a remedy, but there was no court to which he could go to secure judicial process for its enforcement. Because of its significance in the subsequent development of the political functions of the Judiciary, the pertinent parts of Marshall's opinion relating to the validity of section 13 of the Judiciary Act will be presented. After holding that Marbury was entitled to his commission and that mandamus was the appropriate remedy to secure its delivery, the Chief Justice continued:

The authority, therefore, given to the Supreme Court, by the act establishing the judicial courts of the United States, to issue writs of mandamus to public officers, appears not to be warranted by the Constitution; and it becomes necessary to inquire whether a jurisdiction, so conferred, can be exercised.

The question, whether an act, repugnant to the Constitution, can become the law of the land, is a question deeply interesting to the United States; but, happily, not of

---

[102] 1 Cranch 163.   [103] *Ibid.*, p. 170.

an intricacy proportioned to its interest. It seems only necessary to recognize certain principles, supposed to have been long and well established, to decide it.

That the people have an original right to establish, for their future government, such principles as, in their opinion, shall most conduce to their own happiness, is the basis on which the whole American fabric has been erected. The exercise of this original right is a very great exertion; nor can it, nor ought it to be frequently repeated. The principles, therefore, so established, are deemed fundamental. And as the authority, from which they proceed, is supreme, and can seldom act, they are designed to be permanent.

This original and supreme will organizes the government, and assigns, to different departments, their respective powers. It may either stop here; or establish certain limits not to be transcended by those departments.

The government of the United States is of the latter description. The powers of the legislature are defined, and limited; and that those limits may not be mistaken, or forgotten, the Constitution is written. To what purpose are powers limited, and to what purpose is that limitation committed to writing, if these limits may, at any time, be passed by those intended to be restrained? The distinction, between a government with limited and unlimited powers, is abolished, if those limits do not confine the persons on whom they are imposed, and if acts prohibited and acts allowed, are of equal obligation. It is a proposition too plain to be contested, that the Constitution controls any legislative act repugnant to it; or, that the legislature may alter the Constitution by an ordinary act. Between these alternatives there is no middle ground. The Constitution is either a superior, paramount law, unchangeable by ordinary means, or it is on a level with ordinary legislative acts and, like other acts is alterable when the legislature shall please to alter it. If the former part of the alternative be true, then a legislative act contrary to the Constitution is not law: if the latter part be true, then written constitutions are absurd attempts, on the part of the people, to limit a power, in its own nature illimitable.

Certainly all those who have framed written constitutions contemplate them as forming the fundamental and paramount law of the nation, and consequently the theory of every such government must be, that an act of the legislature, repugnant to the Constitution, is void. This theory is essentially attached to a written constitution, and is consequently to be considered, by this court, as one of the fundamental principles of our society. It is not therefore to be lost sight of in the further consideration of this subject. If an act of the legislature, repugnant to the Constitution, is void, does it, nothwithstanding its invalidity, bind the courts, and oblige them to give it effect? Or, in other words, though it be not law, does it constitute a rule as operative as if it was a law? This would be to overthrow in fact what was established in theory; and would seem, at first view, an absurdity too gross to be insisted on. It shall, however, receive a more attentive consideration.

It is emphatically the province and duty of the judicial department to say what the law is. Those who apply the rule to particular cases, must of necessity expound and interpret that rule. If two laws conflict with each other, the courts must decide on the operation of each. So if a law be in opposition to the Constitution; if both the law and the Constitution apply to a particular case, so that the court must either decide that case conformably to the law, disregarding the Constitution; or conformably to the Constitution, disregarding the law; the court must determine which of these conflicting rules governs the case. This is of the very essence of judicial duty. If then the courts are to regard the Constitution; and the Constitution is superior to any ordinary act of the legislature; the Constitution, and not such ordinary act, must govern the case to which they both apply.

Those then who controvert the principle that the Constitution is to be considered, in court, as a paramount law, are reduced to the necessity of maintaining that courts must close their eyes on the Constitution, and see only the law. This doctrine would subvert the very foundation of all written constitutions. It would declare that an act, which, according to the principles and theory of our government, is entirely void; is yet, in practice, completely obligatory. It would declare that if the legislature shall do what is expressly forbidden, such act, notwithstanding the express prohibition, is in reality effectual. It would be giving to the legislature a practical and real omnipotence, with the same breath which professes to restrict their powers within narrow limits. It is prescribing limits, and declaring that those limits may be passed at pleasure. That it thus reduces to nothing what we have deemed the greatest improvement on political institutions—a written Constitution—would of itself be sufficient, in America, where written Constitutions have been viewed with so much reverence, for rejecting the construction. But the peculiar expressions of the Constitution of the United States furnish additional arguments in favor of its rejection.

The judicial power of the United States is extended to all cases arising under the Constitution. Could it be the intention of those who gave this power, to say that, in using it, the Constitution should not be looked into? That a case arising under the Constitution should be decided without examining the instrument under which it arises? This is too extravagant to be maintained. In some cases then, the Constitution must be looked into by the Judges. And if they can open it at all, what part of it are they forbidden to read, or to obey?

There are many other parts of the Constitution which serve to illustrate this subject. It is declared that "no tax or duty shall be laid on articles exported from any state." Suppose a duty on the export of cotton, of tobacco, or of flour; and a suit instituted to recover it. Ought judgment to be rendered in such a case? Ought the Judges to close their eyes on the Constitution, and only see the law? The Constitution declares that "no bill of attainder or ex post facto law shall be passed." If, however, such a bill should be passed and a person should be prosecuted under it; must the Court condemn to death those victims whom the Constitution endeavors to preserve? "No person," says the Constitution, "shall be convicted of treason unless on the testimony of two witnesses to the same overt act, or on confession in open court." Here the language of the Constitution is addressed especially to the courts. It prescribes, directly for them, a rule of evidence not to be departed from. If the legislature should change that rule, and declare one witness, or a confession out of court, sufficient for conviction, must the constitutional principle yield to the legislative act?

From these, and many other selections which might be made, it is apparent, that the framers of the Constitution contemplated that instrument, as a rule for the government of courts, as well as of the legislature. Why otherwise does it direct the Judges to take an oath to support it? This oath certainly applies, in an especial manner, to their conduct in their official character. How immoral to impose it on them, if they were to be used as the instruments, and the knowing instruments, for violating what they swear to support! The oath of office, too, imposed by the Legislature, is completely demonstrative of the legislative opinion on this subject. It is in these words, "I do solemnly swear that I will administer justice without respect to persons, and do equal right to the poor and to the rich; and that I will faithfully and impartially discharge all the duties incumbent on me as ——————, according to the best of my abilities and understanding, agreeably to the Constitution, and laws of the United States." Why does a Judge swear to discharge his duties agreeably to the Constitution of the United States, if that Constitution forms no rule for his government—if it is closed upon him, and cannot be inspected by him? If such be the real state of things, this is worse than solemn mockery. To prescribe, or to take this oath, becomes equally a crime.

It is also not entirely unworthy of observation, that in declaring what shall be the supreme law of the land, the Constitution itself is first mentioned; and not the laws of the United States generally, but those only which shall be made in pursuance of the Constitution, have that rank. Thus, the particular phraseology of the Constitution of the United States confirms and strengthens the principle, supposed to be essential to all written constitutions, that a law repugnant to the Constitution is void; and that courts, as well as other departments, are bound by that instrument.[104]

In his opinion in the *Marbury Case* defending the authority of the Supreme Court to declare void an act of Congress, Chief Justice Marshall presented little in the way of argument that was new. The opinions of state justices, the views of the federal Judges in the Circuit and District Courts, and the Federalist speeches in the Judiciary debate of 1802 all tended to support and amplify the cogent argument of Hamilton in *The Federalist* that it was the duty of the courts to act as a check on Congress in order that private rights might be preserved. All that was necessary for Marshall to do was to reiterate, in language that had become current in legal thought, the doctrine of the supremacy of the Constitution as fundamental law and the presumed requirement that the Judges must compare the Constitution and the statute and hold void any conflicting provisions of the act. To supplement the main assumption that the Judges know better than anyone else what the Constitution means and what its language intends and that their views on the Constitution should be superior to all others, the Chief Justice contended that written constitutions with limitations on the exercise of governmental powers required the adoption of such a principle. The oath of Judges also rendered it necessary, thought Marshall, and, without citing any provisions expressly granting such authority, the Constitution was regarded as sanctioning the practice of judicial review.

Though the Chief Justice's opinion on the right of the Supreme Court to declare void an act of Congress has made the *Marbury Case* one of the most important pronouncements of the federal Judiciary in the performance of its functions of constitutional interpretation, it was the decision of the Court favoring the right to issue a mandamus to a member of the President's cabinet that caused the greatest irritation and resentment. This part of the opinion was regarded as an attempt to interfere with "the independence of the Executive and Senate within their peculiar

---

[104] 1 Cranch 176–180.

departments." Jefferson continued to refer to and criticize the contentions in this case as a "gratuitous opinion" and as an "obiter dissertation of the Chief Justice." His only immediate reference to the decision of Marshall was in a letter to Mrs. John Adams in September, 1804. "Nothing in the Constitution has given them [the Supreme Court Justices]," he wrote, "a right to decide for the Executive, more than the Executive to decide for them. . . . But the opinion which gives to the Judges the right to decide what laws are constitutional, and what not, not only for themselves in their own sphere of action, but for the Legislature and Executive also, in their spheres, would make the Judiciary a despotic branch."[105] Because of this and other expressions of opinion on the review of acts of Congress by the federal courts, Jefferson, it is maintained, changed his views on this issue for political purposes. Though Jefferson looked to the Judiciary for the protection of citizens from unauthorized acts of the government, he at no time approved the doctrine of final and authoritative interpretation of the Constitution by the courts which bound the coördinate departments. But when the Judiciary was manned by Federalists deliberately engaged in upholding party doctrines contrary to the clearly expressed will of the nation, it was scarcely to be expected that Jefferson would approve their theories of constitutional interpretation. If ever the principle of *sic rebus stantibus,* or changed conditions warrant new constructions, may be considered appropriate, it may be held to apply to the reversal of men's views on the developing doctrine of judicial supremacy.

The opinion of Marshall in the case of *Marbury v. Madison,* so far as it dealt with the right of the Judiciary to refuse to enforce an act of Congress which it deemed void, did not, however, differ or conflict substantially with the views expressed by both Madison and Jefferson. They agreed with Marshall that the coördinate departments of the government had the right to interpret the Constitution so far as their own powers were concerned. Jefferson's protest on this part of the opinion came from the impression which seemed to prevail that such a decision would bind not only the Judiciary but also the Legislative and Executive in their spheres. Such a doctrine, Jefferson declared, "would make the Judiciary a despotic branch." Jefferson later objected to the mode of procedure followed by Marshall which raised the issue of the validity of an act of Congress when such a decision was not necessary for the disposal of the case.

The main part of Marshall's opinion in the *Marbury Case* relating to the review of acts of Congress by the federal courts, which is one of the

---

[105] *Writings* (Mem. ed.), XI, 50, 51.

most important political pronunciamentos issued in the United States, is so well known and has been so frequently discussed in legal publications that it is unnecessary to consider the opinion in detail.[106]

The political aspects of this decision are obvious in any careful examination of the reasoning. Propositions and postulates involved in the judgment are:

1. A written constitution is a law of superior obligation and consequently any acts contrary thereto must be invalid.

There was almost universal agreement on this proposition, but its acceptance left the main issue of judicial review undetermined.

2. A written constitution with limitations on the powers of government necessitates the exercise of judicial review.

This is a postulate based on certain political theories which the adoption of many written constitutions has demonstrated may as well be determined otherwise, as for example, the French constitution of 1875 and the Belgian and Swiss constitutions of 1830 and 1874, respectively.

3. The oath of the Judges to support the Constitution requires that they follow the Constitution and disregard any conflicting statute.

This proposition fails to take into account that the officers of all three departments take the same oath and that by similar reasoning the members of Congress and the Executive could refuse to accept a decision of the Supreme Court with which they disagreed.

It is assumed that the determination of the validity of a law is a mechanical and necessitous matter in which personal or individual judgments do not enter, instead of a delicate and difficult question frequently with serious political implications on which lawyers and statesmen may well disagree.

4. Legislative acts contrary to the Constitution are *ipso facto* void, consequently the courts are obliged to disregard such statutes.

This proposition assumes that, constitutional provisions being laws of a superior order and statutes being laws of an inferior order, when a conflict arises the court whose duty it is to apply the laws and to resolve conflicts of law must enforce the superior law. In this assumption there is no recognition of the borderline cases where the judgments of the Judiciary, the Executive, and the Legislature may differ concerning whether there is a real conflict.

Moreover, this proposition fails to distinguish between the categories of *political laws* unenforceable by courts and ordinary *laws* which it is the duty of Judges to interpret and apply. This well-known distinction

---

[106] See Charles Grove Haines, *The American Doctrine of Judicial Supremacy* (Berkeley, 1932), pp. 199 ff., from which parts of the following pages are taken.

has resulted in placing all constitutional provisions outside of the pale of judicial authority in many European countries, and John Marshall himself was quick to recognize that certain parts of the federal Constitution were political in character and hence unenforceable by the Judiciary.[107] The real issue here is whether a conflict between a constitution and a statute can be regarded as a case within judicial cognizance. Prevailing theories and practice in foreign countries with constitutional forms of government have ruled that such a conflict is not a case for judicial action.

If certain provisions of the Constitution are political in nature and unenforceable, why are not all provisions in this category; and by what authority do courts accept cases under some provisions and refuse them under other provisions?

Why should a legislative act passed in due form and following all of the designated rules of procedure be considered as never having been passed or as *ipso facto* void? Is it not an unusual presumption for the officers of one department to consider the acts of the officers of another department of no avail? In fact, as indicated by Justices Bland and Gibson[108] and other opponents of judicial review, every argument in favor of judicial review was based on assumptions or postulates which assumed the whole ground of the dispute.

Marbury v. Madison was the first important case in which the principle of judicial review of an act of Congress was involved. Contrary to the general view, Jefferson and the other Republicans did not attack the decision because of its assertion of the power of the Supreme Court to declare null and void an act of Congress. The opposition to Marshall's decision in *Marbury v. Madison* was based chiefly on its alleged interference with the Executive department, not on its declaring unconstitutional the section of the Judiciary Act of 1789 which conferred the power on the Supreme Court to grant the writ of mandamus.

Both Warren and Beveridge comment on the failure of the Republicans to criticize the decision. Warren writes: "While the Federalist commendation of Marshall's opinion was profuse, it is surprising to note that the most bitterly partisan Republican newspapers . . . made no criti-

---

[107] See the distinction made between the political and ministerial acts of heads of departments in Marbury v. Madison, 1 Cranch 137, 165 (1803), and the application of the doctrine that political questions were beyond the jurisdiction of the federal courts in Foster v. Neilson, 2 Peters 253 (1829); Luther v. Borden, 7 Howard 1 (1849); Pacific States Tel. and Tel. Co. v. Oregon, 223 U. S. 118 (1912); and Oetjen v. Central Leather Co., 246 U. S. 297 (1918).

[108] For a summary of the opinions of Bland and Gibson, see *The American Doctrine of Judicial Supremacy*, pp. 261 ff.

cism of the decision, and contrary to the views advanced by opponents of the Court in later days these Republican papers show no antagonism whatever to Marshall's view of the right of the Court to pass upon the constitutionality of an act of Congress."[109] Beveridge ascribes Jefferson's silence to his desire to avoid political controversy at this time.[110] Though Jefferson, after he left the presidency, frequently criticized Marshall's opinion in *Marbury v. Madison,* it was always on the ground of the gratuitous assertion of the right of the judicial branch to compel the Executive to deliver a commission.

While the application of Marbury for a mandamus was pending before the Supreme Court, a case arose involving the validity of the Judiciary Act of 1802 and the provision of the law of 1789 requiring the Supreme Court Justices to act as Circuit Judges. Presented originally to Chief Justice Marshall in the Circuit Court of Virginia where the pleadings were held insufficient, the cause was taken on a writ of error to the Supreme Court. Marshall declined to sit in the case because of his participation in the trial in the Circuit Court and Cushing being ill, the decision was rendered by four Justices. Justice Paterson, answering the contention that a case could not be transferred from one inferior court to another, said, "Congress have constitutional authority to establish from time to time such inferior tribunals as they may think proper; and to transfer a cause from one such tribunal to another." To the objection that Congress could not require the Supreme Court Justices to sit as Circuit Judges, Paterson thought it sufficient to observe that practice and acquiescence under the Judiciary Act of 1789, for a period of years, "affords an irresistible answer, and has indeed fixed the construction. It is a contemporary interpretation of the most forcible nature. This practical exposition is too strong and obstinate to be shaken or controlled."[111] No further attempts were made to check the enforcement of the Judiciary Act of 1802, and the Republicans turned to the method of impeachment to remove from the Bench Judges who were acting in their judicial capacity as extreme partisans.

At no time were the lines more clearly drawn between the aristocratic-conservative factions and the democratic-liberal groups than during the

---

[109] Warren, *op. cit.,* I: 248.

[110] Beveridge, *op. cit.,* III: 144 ff.

[111] Stuart v. Laird, 1 Cranch 299, 309 (1803). Warren believes "no more striking example of the non-partisanship of the American Judiciary can be found than this decision by a Court composed wholly of Federalists, upholding, contrary to its personal and political views, a detested Republican measure." But was it an instance of non-partisanship or one in which the Court submitted to what Justice Holmes called "preponderant public opinion?" Warren, *op. cit.,* I: 272.

first term of Jefferson's Administration. Moreover, the basic political doctrines and legal theories, which inevitably led to a series of conflicts over federal and state supremacy, were taking form, the chief disputants being John Marshall and Joseph Story, on the one side, and Thomas Jefferson, Spencer Roane, and John Taylor, on the other.

CHAPTER VIII

Some of the Significant Interests and Activities of Federal Judges during Jefferson's Administration

THE REFUSAL to abide by the Court's opinion in the *Marbury Case* was merely a prelude to an attempt by the Republicans to check the political activities and the partisan invectives of the Supreme Court Justices. During the debate on the Repeal Act the method of impeachment was referred to as a means of removing Judges who were arbitrary, arrogant, and dictatorial and were using their official positions to enhance partisan interests. Resort to this method of procedure was, under the advice and approval of Jefferson, made a part of the program of the Republicans.

THE IMPEACHMENT OF JUDGES

The Republican doctrine regarding the use of impeachment to check the attempts to uphold Federalism through the Judiciary was stated by Senator Giles. "If the Judges of the Supreme Court should dare, as they had done," maintained Giles, "to declare an act of Congress unconstitutional, or to send a mandamus to the Secretary of State, as they had done, it was the undoubted right of the House of Representatives to impeach them, and of the Senate to remove them, for giving such opinions, however honest or sincere they may have been in entertaining them."[1]

Jefferson has often been criticized for his so-called "attack on the federal Judiciary." But the federal courts had been filled with Judges who were strong Federalist partisans and who were asserting their partisanship on and off the Bench sometimes in an assertive and overbearing manner. The Chief Justice actively participated in party affairs, for, as we have observed, while filling the offices of Chief Justice and Secretary

---

[1] John Quincy Adams, *Memoirs* (Philadelphia, 1874–1877), I: 322, 323. "The Judges of the Supreme Court are all Federalists. They stand in the way of the ruling power.... The Judges, therefore, are, if possible, to be removed. Their judicial opinions, if at all questionable, though *mere errors of judgment,* are interpreted into *crimes,* and to be grounds of impeachment." Pickering to Lyman in Henry Adams, *New England Federalism* (Boston, 1877), p. 344.

of State, he aided President Adams in selecting and securing the confirmation of Federalists for the judicial positions created during the closing hours of Adams' Administration.[2] Not only the Judges, but also the district attorneys, the clerks, and the marshals gave frequent indications of extreme partisanship in the enforcement of the Alien and Sedition Acts. Chief Justice Ellsworth had denounced the Republicans as "apostles of atheism, anarchy, bloodshed, and plunder." With the Judges participating in the party caucuses, delivering campaign speeches in their charges to grand juries, and using their authority as public prosecutors to silence the Republican press, there was ample evidence to convince Jefferson that something in the nature of a purge of the Judiciary was necessary for the preservation of the liberties of the people and the maintenance of democratic institutions.[3]

Jefferson's campaign to "wreck the Judiciary," as the Federalists referred to his action, consisted of two reports to the House of Representatives. When Judge Pickering conducted himself in a disgraceful and illegal manner in the case of *The Eliza,* Jefferson sent the reports which came to him regarding the case to the House with the suggestion that since he had no constitutional authority to remove a federal Judge, the House alone could take appropriate action. And when Justice Chase included in his charge to the grand jury in Baltimore a partisan tirade against democracy in general and the Republican policies in particular, Jefferson sent a clipping of this part of the charge to Representative Nicholson with the comment "ought this seditious and official attack on the principles of our Constitution, and on the proceedings of a State, go unpunished? And to whom more pointedly than yourself will the public look for the necessary measures?"

Judge John Pickering of the District Court for New Hampshire, who had been insane for some time, was impeached and removed from office.[4] About the same time the house of representatives of Pennsylvania brought charges against Judge Addison, who, like Chase, was using his official position as a vantage ground to condemn the Republicans. He delivered charges to juries on such subjects as the "horrors of revolution" and "the jealousy of the administration and government," pointing out the terrible things likely to happen if they did not respect and obey con-

---

[2] Four members of Marshall's family were appointed to office during the time he served as Secretary of State. See Albert J. Beveridge, *The Life of John Marshall* (Boston, 1919), II: 560, and III: 191.

[3] Claude G. Bowers, *Jefferson in Power* (Boston, 1936), pp. 268, 269.

[4] By the Federalists and those who have accepted their version of the history of this period, the removal of Pickering has been called "a shameful piece of business." John Bach McMaster, *History of the People of the United States* (New York, 1893), III: 172.

stituted authorities. Chief Justice Ellsworth expressed admiration for these charges and spoke of Judge Addison as "a light shining in the darkness though the darkness comprehends him not."[5] In defense of his conduct on the Bench, Judge Addison claimed that since there was no charge of corruption or dishonesty nor none conveying any stain of infamy against him, there could be no justifiable ground for impeachment.[6] One of the witnesses testified that Judge Addison had condemned the Jacobins from the Bench and had charged that they were daily making converts in this country. As evidence to this effect, he cited the Kentucky and Virginia Resolutions.[7] Though the evidence substantiated the charge that Judge Addison had acted illegally and unconstitutionally in the exercise of his duties as judge and had used his office as a forum to make partisan comments and criticisms, he could see nothing in his conduct worthy of blame; and nothing which on deliberation he would not do again. "I think it must now appear to the Senate," continued Addison in concluding his defense, "that in this accusation, there is no criminality, no fault, not even an error of judgment and that my conduct is not only innocent, but proper."[8] But the state senate did not consider the judge's official conduct so blameless and voted twenty to four that he should be removed from office and should not be permitted to serve as a judge in any court in the state.[9] The main effort, however, to check the partisan activities of federal Justices was made in the proceedings to impeach Justice Samuel Chase of the Supreme Court.

The articles of impeachment approved by the House of Representatives and submitted to the Senate charged Justice Chase with misconduct in the trials of Fries for treason and Callender for a violation of the Sedition Act, an improper attempt to induce a grand jury in Delaware to indict an editor of a Republican paper, and a perversion of his official position in a political address to the grand jury in Baltimore.[10]

Referring to the charges made by the House of Representatives for the impeachment of Chase, John Quincy Adams wrote, "these articles con-

---

[5] Henry Flanders, *The Lives and Times of the Chief Justices* (New York, 1875), II: 193.

[6] Thomas Lloyd, *The Trial of Alexander Addison on Impeachment Charges before the Senate of the Commonwealth of Pennsylvania* (Lancaster, 1803), p. 15.

[7] *Ibid.*, p. 50.

[8] *Ibid.*, pp. 119, 120.

[9] Alexander J. Dallas served as counsel to aid the managers of the house of representatives in bringing charges against Judge Addison. For an account of the argument against Addison, see George Mifflin Dallas, *Life and Writings of Alexander James Dallas* (Philadelphia, 1871), pp. 76–88.

[10] For a summary of the charges as presented by the managers representing the House of Representatives, see Roger Foster, *Commentaries on the Constitution of the United States* (Boston, 1895), I: 535 ff.

tained in themselves a virtual impeachment not only of Mr. Chase, but of the Judges of the Supreme Court from the first establishment of the national Judiciary." In view of the highhanded and partisan methods frequently employed by the Justices, this statement was correct. Granting that the standard of judicial decorum at this time was different from what it is today, the statement was scarcely as much of a reflection upon the Republican managers of the impeachment proceedings as it was on the conduct of the Judges themselves.

In the testimony of the Chase trial, William Marshall, John Marshall's brother, clerk of the federal court at Richmond, appointed under the Chief Justice's regime as Secretary of State, testified that none but Federalists had been selected for the jury in the trial of Callender. Of the three Democrats called on the panel, one was out of the city, another received no notice, and a third was excused through the efforts of John Marshall.[11] John Marshall, as a witness in the impeachment proceedings, disappointed and irritated the defenders of Chase when he admitted that it was unusual to refuse to hear the lawyers in the *Callender Case* on the question of the constitutionality of the Sedition Act, and when he said that the exclusion of the testimony of John Taylor and the refusal to hear counsel on the legal issues raised were contrary to the usual practice in courts.

The Federalists professed to agree that the Judges should not display their political prejudices or antipathies on the Bench. But they could see no evidence of partisanship in the attitude of the members of the federal Judiciary. All of the proceedings under the Sedition Act were defended as involving no more than the punishment of "malicious falsehoods, published with the wicked intention of destroying the government."[12] Chase admitted in his charge to the grand jury in Baltimore that he had expressed opinions concerning public measures of the government of Maryland and that of the United States,[13] but he denied that there was

[11] *Annals*, 8th Cong., 2d sess., pp. 262 ff.

[12] Representative Bayard, Delaware, *ibid.*, pp. 611–613.

[13] The pertinent part of Justice Chase's charge was as follows:

"You know, gentlemen, that our state and national institutions were framed to secure to every member of society, equal liberty and equal rights; but the late alteration of the federal Judiciary by the abolition of the office of the sixteen Circuit Judges, and the recent changes in our state constitution, by the establishment of universal suffrage, and the further alteration that is contemplated in our state judiciary (if adopted) will, in my judgment, take away all security for property and personal liberty. The independence of the national Judiciary is already shaken to its foundation, and the virtue of the people alone can restore it. The independence of the judges of this State will be entirely destroyed if the bill for the abolition of the two supreme courts should be ratified by the next general assembly. The change of the state constitution, by

anything unusual, improper, or unbecoming for a Judge to express such opinions, especially since he was speaking as a friend to his country and a firm supporter of both the state and federal governments.[14] The attorneys for Chase and the senators who supported him insisted that there could be no other constitutional ground for impeachment than the proof of acts in the nature of high crimes and misdemeanors—acts or offenses for which a Judge could be tried and convicted by a court and a jury. The Republicans, on the other hand, maintained that partisan activities whether on or off the Bench and conduct unbecoming a Judge in the course of a trial were sufficient grounds to warrant removal from office.

Through the whole tenor of Chase's judicial conduct, declared John Randolph, runs the spirit of party. In concluding his argument in support of Chase's impeachment, he declared: "We shall bring forward in proof such a specimen of judicial tyranny, as, I trust in God, will never be again exhibited in our country."[15] But the accusation against Chase, which Jefferson considered the most serious, and the one which he had brought to the attention of the House—the blatant and indiscreet charge to the Baltimore grand jury—was subordinated by the managers of his trial to the other articles of impeachment preferred by the House. Though little attention was paid to the Baltimore charge, the highest vote for conviction was cast on this charge. On two other charges—the forcing of Bassett on the jury when he admitted he had come to a conclusion adverse to Callender, and the exclusion of the evidence of John Taylor—a majority of votes was cast for conviction. The failure to secure the necessary two-thirds for conviction on the main charge was due, in part at least, to the mismanagement of the case by the majority leader, Randolph, and to the skillful efforts of the lawyers representing Chase.[16] Randolph and the other members of Congress who aided him were no match for Chase's attorneys—Luther Martin, Robert Goodloe Harper,

---

allowing universal suffrage, will, in my opinion, certainly and rapidly destroy all protection to property, and all security to personal liberty; and our republican constitution will sink into a mobocracy, the worst of all possible governments. I can only lament that the main pillar of our state constitution has already been thrown down by the establishment of universal suffrage. By this shock alone the whole building totters to its base and will crumble into ruin before many years elapse, unless it be restored to its original state." Simeon E. Baldwin, *The American Judiciary* (New York, 1905), pp. 45–46.

[14] *Annals, op. cit.*, p. 145.

[15] *Ibid.*, p. 165.

[16] The wrongs and grossly partisan conduct of Justice Chase while serving on the Bench, Morison and Commager maintain were "points of manners rather than justice." Samuel Eliot Morison and Henry Steele Commager, *The Growth of the American Republic* (Revised and enlarged ed., New York, 1940), p. 293.

Charles Lee, Philip Barton Key, and Joseph Hopkinson. The leadership of Randolph in presenting the charges against Chase was weakened not only by his ill health but also by a previous break with Jefferson and the Administration leaders over the methods of disposing of the Yazoo Frauds.

Whether Justice Chase should be removed from the Bench was not considered so important as whether the other Justices including Chief Justice Marshall ought to be removed and the federal Judiciary subjected to the type of control the Federalists had been exercising for nearly fifteen years. Chief Justice Marshall was alarmed, and while the Chase impeachment proceedings were under way, he suggested an alternative method of meeting the situation. "A reversal of those legal opinions deemed unsound by the Legislature," he said, "would certainly better comport with the mildness of our character than a removal of the Judge who has rendered them unknowing of his fault."[17] This has been called "the most radical method of correcting judicial decisions ever advanced" and declared to be "utterly destructive of the Federalist philosophy of judicial control over legislation."[18] It is interesting to note that this proposal of Marshall's is one of the measures which has frequently been suggested to check the extensive powers now exercised by the Supreme Court through the review of acts of the states and of Congress.

Immediately after Chase's acquittal, Randolph, feeling that his efforts had been largely in vain, proposed an amendment to the Constitution providing that "the Judges of the Supreme Court and all other courts of the United States shall be removed from office by the President on joint address of both Houses of Congress requesting the same." Though it may have appeared on the surface that Chase and the Federalists had won a notable victory, the results of the impeachment proceedings were on the whole favorable to the Republicans. The trial made clear that Judges might be removed for disreputable partisanship conduct on the Bench. Moreover, a definite restriction was placed upon the partisan activities of all federal judicial officers. It was necessary henceforth to manifest partisanship under the covert and unobtrusive method of judicial interpretation. Though the Judges were thereafter more cautious and circumspect in their political activities there were not infrequent indications of the influence of political or partisan views in the decisions

---

[17] Marshall to Chase, Jan. 23, 1804, Beveridge, *op. cit.*, III: 177. Marshall thought that he might be removed and replaced by Spencer Roane of Virginia who would have been appointed had not Chief Justice Ellsworth's timely resignation thwarted Jefferson's plans. Then the great principles of nationalism for which Marshall stood might never have been asserted by the national Judiciary. *Ibid.*, pp. 113, 114.

[18] *Ibid.*, p. 178.

of the Supreme Court. Some of the cases of Jefferson's Administration which involved the Court in politics or had political implications are worthy of analysis.

DECISIONS REGARDED AS HAVING POLITICAL SIGNIFICANCE

The case of *Wilson v. Mason*[19] concerned the validity of a grant of land to George Mason in the district of Kentucky while it was a part of the state of Virginia. Since the case involved the effect of cross caveats for the same tract of land, it was contended that in accordance with a law of Virginia the judgment of the state district court was final and that the Supreme Court could not entertain an appeal by writ of error. To this contention Chief Justice Marshall replied by giving his first interpretation of the clauses of the Constitution granting jurisdiction to the federal courts. The Constitution of the United States, to which the parties to the compact between Virginia and Kentucky had assented, he maintained,

gave jurisdiction to the federal courts in controversies between citizens of different States. The same Constitution vested in this Court an appellate jurisdiction in all cases where original jurisdiction was given to the inferior courts, with only "such exceptions, and under such regulations, as the Congress shall make." Congress, in pursuance to the Constitution, has passed a law on the subject, in which the appellate jurisdiction of this Court is described in general terms so as to comprehend this case, nor is there in that law any exception or regulation which would exclude the case of a caveat from its general provisions. If then, the compact between Virginia and Kentucky was even susceptible of the construction contended for, that construction could only be maintained on the principle that the legislatures of any two States might, by agreement between themselves, annul the Constitution of the United States.[20]

In upholding the jurisdiction of the Court, it was decided that Wilson had the better title because Mason's title was based upon a survey alone, whereas a survey in Kentucky without a previous legal entry gave no basis whatever for title. A decision of a case in a similar issue nearly two decades later resulted in one of the most prolonged and formidable attacks on the jurisdiction of the Supreme Court.[21]

The fear that the federal courts by means of their jurisdiction under the diversity of citizenship provision might overthrow the established system of land titles in the West—a fear commonly expressed during the early years of the nineteenth century—was partially dispelled by another decision affecting Kentucky land titles. In deciding the case in accordance with the settled principles of the Kentucky court of chancery, Chief Justice Marshall observed:

The Court is compelled to believe that the principle is really settled in a manner different from that which this Court would deem correct. It is impossible to say how

[19] 1 Cranch 45 (1803). [20] 1 Cranch 91, 92. [21] Cf. *Green v. Biddle*, below, pp. 464 ff.

many titles would be shaken by shaking the principle. The very extraordinary state of land titles in that country has compelled its judges, in a series of decisions, to rear up an artificial pile from which no piece can be taken, by hands not intimately acquainted with the building, without endangering the structure, and producing a mischief to those holding under it, the extent of which may not be perceived. The rule as adopted must be pursued.[22]

The tendency of the Supreme Court to limit the Executive authority in the issuance of ordinances to the strict letter of the law was noticeable in the case of *Little v. Barreme*.[23] Congress, in placing restrictions on the trade with France, authorized the President to instruct commanders to seize vessels of the United States which were bound or sailing to any port within the confines of France. An order of President Adams instructed commanders to seize vessels bound to or from French ports. Captain Little, carrying out the President's directions, was held answerable in damages to the owner of a neutral vessel which was captured on a voyage from and not to a French port. The Chief Justice said that his original opinion had been favorable to the commander acting under a presidential order but that he now acquiesced in the opinion of his brethren. Originally argued in the last term under the Administration of John Adams, it was not decided until the February term, 1804. It may be surmised that the change in presidency was one of the factors which occasioned a reversal of former views, though it was an order of a Federalist President to which exception was taken.

The Federalist theory of judicial independence was applied also to the justices of peace of the District of Columbia by a decision of the Circuit Court for the district in the case of the *United States v. Benjamin More*. A justice of peace was held to be a judicial officer of the United States under the Constitution, and, therefore, the act of Congress of May 23, 1802, so far as it abolished the fees of the justices, was declared void.[24]

When an attempt was made to sustain the priority prescribed by act of Congress for debts due the United States as against the claims of the state of Pennsylvania, the state supreme court intervened, claiming that the federal law was not intended to apply to cases where an individual state was a creditor and had a lien on the debtor's property. Upholding the rights of the state, Judge Yeates thought "the Constitution of the United States, considered as federal, is to be construed strictly in all cases, when the antecedent rights of a State may be drawn in question; and it is a maxim of political law, that sovereign States cannot be deprived of any

---

[22] Bodley v. Taylor, 5 Cranch 191, 234 (1809).

[23] 2 Cranch 170 (1804).

[24] *National Intelligencer*, Aug. 5, 1805; also Charles Warren, *The Supreme Court in United States History* (Boston, 1922), I: 255.

of their rights by implication, nor in any manner whatever but by their own voluntary consent, or by submission to a conqueror."[25] He maintained that no part of the act of Congress of March 3, 1797, directing that in the disposal of the property or estates of insolvent persons debts due the United States shall be satisfied first, related to the states in their political and corporate capacities, as competitors with the United States. Judge Brackenridge, who regretted that he did not have available the opinion in *United States v. Fisher*,[26] believed that priority was intended to apply to revenue officers only and that it could not dissolve "a lien existing in a sovereign independent State."

Four years later the case was appealed to the Supreme Court of the United States and the governor and attorney general were cited to appear and defend, if they saw fit, the rights of the state. In answer to this citation, the legislature, maintaining that it was inexpedient for the commonwealth to appear or "become a party to the said suit or in such manner to permit her right aforesaid to be questioned," directed the clerk of the court to pay the money into the state treasury.

At the first available opportunity Marshall criticized and condemned the Jeffersonian theory of strict construction of the Constitution. In deciding the issue whether under the federal bankruptcy law a debtor of the United States was entitled to priority of payment from the property and credits of the bankrupt, the Chief Justice held, contrary to the opinion of the Pennsylvania justices, that the provisions of the act of 1797 applied to debtors generally and not merely to revenue officers. The Hamiltonian view of the "necessary and proper" phrase in the so-called elastic clause of the Constitution was approved in this opinion. The preference claimed by the United States, said Marshall, is not prohibited, "but it has been truly said that under a constitution conferring specific powers, the power contended for must be granted, or it cannot be exercised." In construing the elastic clause, however, "it would be incorrect, and would produce endless difficulties, if the opinion should be maintained that no law was authorized which was not indispensably necessary to give effect to a specified power.... Congress must possess the choice of means, and must be empowered to use any means which are in fact conducive to the exercise of a power granted by the Constitution."[27] This

---

[25] United States v. Nicholls, 4 Yeates 258 (1805).

[26] 2 Cranch 358 (1805).

[27] United States v. Fisher, 2 Cranch 358, 395. In this case Marshall stated a canon of interpretation which was followed in subsequent cases involving interference with private rights, "Where rights are infringed, where fundamental principles are overthrown, where the general system of the laws is departed from, the legislative intention must be expressed with irresistible clearness to induce a court of justice to suppose

adoption of Hamilton's theory of constitutional construction was not necessary for the decision of the case, but, as Beveridge notes, "it presented an opportunity for a judicial statement of liberal construction which might not soon come again."[28] In fact, nearly fifteen years elapsed before Marshall had an opportunity to declare as a principle of constitutional construction the Hamiltonian theory of interpretation of implied powers.[29] The obiter dictum of the Chief Justice had its repercussions in Congress where Representative Clopton of Virginia introduced a constitutional amendment to define the phrase "necessary and proper" to include "only such laws as shall have a rational connection with and immediate relation to the powers enumerated." Clopton deplored the trend toward the usurpation of powers by the federal government through the process of constitutional construction and as a consequence the weaving around state institutions of "the web of destruction."[30]

The Chief Justice soon began to render decisions which were irritating to the states and caused resentment not only against the Court but also against the federal government. In 1805 an issue arose concerning the interpretation of acts of Pennsylvania providing for the settlement of vacant lands on which the Circuit Judges were divided. Discovering uncertainties and inconsistencies in the language of the state acts, the Chief Justice undertook to change the words of the law so as to make the intention of the legislature intelligible. Thus, following the suggestion of the counsel for the plaintiff, the phrase "and residing, or causing a family to reside thereon" was changed to "and shall reside, etc." Such judicial legislation might not have been objectionable had it not been necessary to reverse the supreme court of Pennsylvania. Adopting the characteristic attitude of the Federalists to humiliate the states, Marshall noted that "the State is in the situation of a person who holds forth to the world the conditions on which he is willing to sell his property." Though a contract to which the state is a party is involved, "it ought to be construed according to those well-established principles, which regulate contracts generally." The principles of equality and fair dealing, it was held, re-

---

a design to effect such objects. But where only a political regulation is made, which is inconvenient, if the intention of the legislature be expressed in terms which are sufficiently intelligible to leave no doubt in the mind when the words are taken in their ordinary sense, it would be going a great way to say that a constrained interpretation must be put upon them, to avoid an inconvenience which ought to have been contemplated in the legislature when the act was passed, and which, in their opinion was probably overbalanced by the particular advantages it was calculated to produce." *Ibid.*, p. 390.

[28] *The Life of John Marshall*, III: 163.

[29] See above, pp. 203 ff.

[30] *Annals*, 9th Cong., 2d sess. (Dec. 11, 1806), pp. 131–148.

quired that the courts should disapprove a construction which would allow the states to get back the land and retain the purchase money.[31]

The legislature was indignant at this interference with state affairs. A resolution was passed insisting that the state was the real party to the suits affecting these lands and denying "the right of any court of the United States to take cognizance of or exercise any jurisdiction touching any suit or action" that may be brought. Governor McKean thought the legislative action was hasty and vetoed the resolution. But the Republicans who disagreed with the governor protested vigorously against the unconstitutional exercise of authority by the federal Judiciary. And there was good ground for the resentment against the decision, for the Court had adopted "an exceedingly strained construction of the statute."[32]

As foreign affairs began to absorb the primary attention and interests of the nation, the Supreme Court again rendered a decision which appeared to approve the Federalist bias toward England. The capture and condemnation of American ships under the illegal orders of France and Great Britain raised the issue whether the doctrine of conclusiveness of the decisions of the English prize courts should be followed. In a decision in which Chief Justice Marshall, and Justices Cushing, Washington, and Johnson concurred, and Justices Livingston and Chase dissented, it was held that the sentence of a foreign court of admiralty condemning a vessel for breach of blockade is conclusive evidence of that fact in an action on the policy of insurance.[33] The decision resulted in an advantage to England at a time when the Administration was enacting and enforcing measures of embargo and nonintercourse against this country. The Republicans looked upon the decision as another attempt to embarrass the Administration. But the foremost objections to the decisions of the federal courts frequently arose over controversies which involved the

[31] Huidekoper's Lessee v. Douglas, 3 Cranch 1, 66 ff. (1805). Thus the way was being prepared for the adoption of the doctrine that there was a general commercial law which might be applied by the federal courts when passing upon the validity of state rules and regulations. See Justice Story's opinion in Swift v. Tyson, 16 Peters 1 (1842).

[32] Warren, *op. cit.*, I: 370.

[33] Croudson v. Leonard, 4 Cranch 434 (1808); see also Rose v. Himely, 4 Cranch 241; and Hudson v. Guestier, 4 Cranch 293 involving the illegal acts of French privateers.

These cases show Chief Justice Marshall's policy and practice of speaking for the Court and at times deciding cases whether or not the other Justices fully agreed with him. When the case of *Hudson and Smith v. Guestier* again came to the Supreme Court during the February, 1810, term Chief Justice Marshall, dissenting from an opinion and judgment delivered by Justice Livingston, observed "that he had supposed that the former opinion delivered in these cases upon this point had been concurred in by four Judges. But in this he was mistaken. The opinion was concurred in by one Judge [Washington]. He was still of opinion that the construction then given was correct." The Chief Justice conceded, however, that the principle of *Rose v. Himely* was now overruled. 6 Cranch 285.

alleged sovereign rights and authority of the states. Because of the belief that her position and powers as an independent state in the period of the Revolution was not duly respected, Pennsylvania, for nearly thirty years, resisted the attempted exercise of national authority over her own tribunals in prize cases.

THE CASE OF THE SLOOP ACTIVE AND THE DOCTRINE OF STATE RIGHTS

The closing years of Jefferson's second Administration were marked by serious conflicts with the states, bordering on the range of civil war. Not only were forcible methods of resistance employed to prevent the enforcement of the Embargo Acts, but Pennsylvania was preparing to resist the execution of a decree of the Committee on Appeals of the Continental Congress awarded in 1779. The Pennsylvania court of admiralty, established upon the recommendation of Congress, decided that the proceeds of the capture of the sloop *Active* should be awarded to the captors who brought the vessel into the port of Philadelphia for condemnation. Gideon Olmsted and others, the owners of the sloop, appealed to Congress, and, through its Committee on Appeals, the decree of the state court was reversed. Contrary to the decision of the committee, Judge Ross of the state court directed that the funds from the sale of the ship should be paid to the state treasurer, who, for thirty years, became responsible for a considerable sum of money involved in litigation. After futile efforts to prevail upon Judge Ross to enforce the decree of the committee, it was declared that "this court being unwilling to enter upon any proceedings of contempt, lest consequences might ensue at this juncture dangerous to the public peace of the United States, will not proceed further in this affair, nor hear any appeal until the authority of this court shall be so settled as to give full efficacy to their decrees and processes."[34] The matter was then laid before Congress and a committee was appointed to investigate the controversy and to report to Congress. This committee presented the report together with resolutions declaring in effect that the Committee on Appeals of Congress had authority to review the facts and the law in this case and to give a final decree thereon. It was further resolved:

> That no act of any State can, or ought to, destroy the right of appeal to Congress, in the sense above declared. That Congress is by these United States invested with the supreme sovereign power of war and peace.
>
> That the power of executing the law of nations is essential to the sovereign supreme power of war and peace.

---

[34] "The Whole Proceedings in the Case of Olmsted and Others versus Rittenhouse Executrices," collected and arranged by Richard Peters, Jun. (Philadelphia, 1809), p. 40.

That the legality of all captures on the high seas must be determined by the law of nations.

That the authority, ultimately and finally to decide on all matters and questions touching the law of nations, does reside and is rested in the sovereign supreme power of war and peace.[85]

To these resolutions the legislature of Pennsylvania responded by directing the judge of admiralty to ignore the authority of Congress and to turn the proceeds of the sale of the sloop over to the state treasurer, David Rittenhouse. Being thus thwarted in securing judgment, the plaintiffs again appealed to the state courts. Judgment being rendered in their favor by default in the county court, an appeal was taken to the state supreme court. Chief Justice McKean, who, because of his dual capacity as chief justice of the state and a member of the committee, had failed to participate in the proceedings before the Committee of Congress of which he was chairman, now rendered the opinion of the state supreme court. After a recital of the facts of the case, he said: "I am sorry to be obliged to say, that, in my judgment, the decree of the Committee of Appeals was contrary to the provisions of the act of Congress, and of the general assembly, extra-judicial, erroneous and void." The chief objection was that the trial before the committee had been conducted without a jury.[36] The other Judges differed on the question whether the Committee of Congress had jurisdiction to give a final award in the case, but agreed with the Chief Justice that the case should be dismissed on procedural grounds.

On the authority of *Penhallow v. Doane*,[37] holding that the District Courts of the United States had authority to execute the decrees of the Committee on Appeals, Olmsted applied to the federal courts for a remedy. In January, 1803, District Judge Peters, stating that the federal courts had authority to carry into effect the decrees of the Committee on Appeals in prize cases, issued a decree that the certificates and the interest money be paid by the respondents to the libelants in accordance with the decision of the Committee of Congress. This decree remained unenforced.

By an act of February 26, 1801, the Pennsylvania legislature had directed the state treasurer to secure the proceeds of the ship from the heirs of David Rittenhouse, but they had refused to comply with this requisition. After Judge Peters' decree had been awarded, Governor McKean sent a message to the legislature objecting to the proceedings

---

[85] Peters, Jun., *op. cit.*, p. 43.

[36] Ross v. Rittenhouse, 2 Dallas 160, 163 (1792), and Peters, Jun., *op. cit.*, pp. 45 ff.

[37] 3 Dallas 54 (1795).

in the case because the state, a real party in the case, had had no notice or opportunity to appear and because, according to the Eleventh Amendment recently adopted, the state could not be made a party to the suit. The legislature on April 2, 1803, passed a law reviewing the essential facts of the case and declaring that the jurisdiction entertained by the Committee on Appeals over the state admiralty court "was illegally usurped and exercised in contradiction to the just rights of Pennsylvania,"[38] and, hence, was null and void. The governor was also instructed to protect the just rights of the state by any further means and measures that he might deem necessary for the purpose and to protect the Rittenhouse heirs from any process whatever issued out of any federal court in consequence of their obedience to the requisition.

No further proceedings were taken in the case until 1808, when an application was made to the Supreme Court of the United States to issue a mandamus to Judge Peters to compel him to enforce obedience to his sentence of 1802. Judge Peters declined to issue the writ because he deemed it best to avoid embroiling the government of the United States and that of Pennsylvania "on a question which was rested on my single opinion." The case being then appealed to the Supreme Court, an opportunity was afforded for Chief Justice Marshall to defend, in his opinion, the Federalist doctrine of nationalism against the Jeffersonian doctrine of State rights. Reciting the language of the state act passed in defiance of the order of Judge Peters, he declared:

If the legislatures of the several States may, at will, annul the judgments of the courts of United States, and destroy the rights acquired under those judgments, the Constitution itself becomes a solemn mockery; and the Nation is deprived of the means of enforcing its laws by the instrumentality of its own tribunals. So fatal a result must be deprecated by all; and the people of Pennsylvania, not less than the citizens of every other State, must feel a deep interest in resisting principles so destructive of the Union, and in averting consequences so fatal to themselves.[39]

It was held that the jurisdiction of the courts of the United States was not to be determined by the state legislatures, but by the "supreme judicial tribunal of the Nation." The real issue, however, was whether, before the federal Constitution was adopted, the Committee on Appeals of the Continental Congress had such authority and jurisdiction over the state admiralty courts, that a decree of the committee could be enforced against a recalcitrant and sovereign state.

Consideration of the issue of state versus national sovereignty prior to 1789 has made it clear that the question of supremacy at this time was

---

[38] Richard Peters, Jun., *op. cit.*, p. 81.
[39] United States v. Peters, 5 Cranch 115, 136 (1809).

much in doubt and that a number of states had resisted the attempts to enforce the decrees of the Confederate tribunal over those of the state courts. Ignoring the doubts and uncertainties which prevailed at the time this controversy arose—doubts and uncertainties which caused a number of federal and state Judges to hold that federal supremacy during this period should not be insisted upon—Marshall dogmatically asserted the doctrine of national supremacy. "By the highest judicial authority of the Nation," he maintained, "it has been long since decided, that the court of appeals erected by Congress had full authority to revise and correct the sentences of the courts of admiralty of the several States, in prize causes. That question, therefore, is at rest. . . . The full right to that property was immediately vested in the claimants, who might rightly pursue it, into whosesoever hands it might come."[40] A peremptory writ of mandamus was awarded to carry into effect the District Judge's decree. That the fundamental political question here involved was not so completely "at rest" as the Chief Justice intimated is apparent not only from the proceedings which immediately followed, but also from a long chain of circumstances similar in nature.

As soon as Marshall's decision was announced, the governor sent a message to the legislature with a notice that he proposed to call out the militia to prevent the enforcement of the Court's decree. Since serious difficulties might arise between the state government and the federal authorities, he thought it advisable to inform the legislature of his action.

The senate committee to which the governor's message was referred contended that during the period of the Revolution and under the Articles of Confederation the government of the union could act, so far as its decisions were acquiesced in by the states, but that when a state legislated on a subject, Congress could assume no power in contravention of the state act. And from this point of view the decision of the Committee of Congress was illegal. On April 3, 1809, the Pennsylvania legislature resolved that, as a member of the federal union, they acknowledge

the supremacy, and will cheerfully submit to the authority of the general government, as far as that authority is delegated by the Constitution of the United States. But, whilst they yield to this authority, when exercised within constitutional limits, they trust they will not be considered as acting hostile to the general government, when, as *guardians of the state rights,* they cannot permit an infringement of those rights by an unconstitutional exercise of power in the United States' courts.

When a collision arises between state and federal authorities, they thought it a misfortune "that no provision is made in the Constitution for determining disputes between the general and state governments by

---

[40] 5 Cranch 140.

an impartial tribunal." And it was further resolved that "to suffer the United States' courts to decide on state rights will, from a bias in favor of power, necessarily destroy the federal part of the government: And whenever the government of the United States becomes consolidated, we may learn from the history of nations what will be the event."[41] This contention that the federal Judges could not serve in the capacity of impartial arbiters in controversies involving the powers and jurisdiction of the federal and state governments was to be asserted with increasing frequency until the outbreak of the Civil War.

The governor, enclosing a copy of the resolutions adopted by the legislature, appealed to President Madison, and said he trusted that he would "discriminate between opposition to the Constitution and laws of the United States and that of resisting the decree of a judge founded, as it is conceived, on a usurpation of power." Madison replied that, as the federal Executive, he was "not only unauthorized to prevent the execution of a decree sanctioned by the Supreme Court of the United States, but is expressly enjoined by statute, to carry into effect any such decree, where opposition may be made to it." Massachusetts was resisting the enforcement of federal laws and was threatening secession, with the result that many Republicans, who would under normal circumstances have applauded Pennsylvania's action, now came to the support of the federal government. It was necessary under the circumstances for the state to seek an honorable retreat.

Mrs. Sergeant, who was under arrest for refusal to obey the decree of the federal court, applied to the chief justice of the state supreme court for a writ of habeas corpus. The chief justice, disapproving of the action of the governor and the legislature, dismissed the petition and expressed the hope that the long-continued controversy might be terminated "without any material interruption of that harmony between this State and the United States so essential to the prosperity of both." The state troops were withdrawn from the Rittenhouse residence and the legislature in a conciliatory move appropriated sufficient money to comply with the order of the Court. And President Madison was pleased to report that "the affair of Olmsted has passed off without the threatened collision of force."

The legislatures of eleven states passed resolutions disapproving the resistance of Pennsylvania to the enforcement of the federal decree. To the proposal to establish an impartial tribunal to decide disputes between the state and federal Judiciary, Virginia replied, "a tribunal is already

---

[41] Herman V. Ames, *State Documents on Federal Relations* (Philadelphia, 1906), pp. 46–49.

provided by the Constitution of the United States, to wit: the Supreme Court, more eminently qualified from their habits and duties, from the mode of their selection, and from the tenure of their offices, to decide the disputes aforesaid in an enlightened and impartial manner, than any other tribunal which could be erected."[42] Virginia was soon to regret her espousal of the doctrines of Federalism and nationalism and to find that in the settlement of her controversies her sister states gave her no more support and encouragement than she accorded to Pennsylvania.

The federal government not only secured the enforcement of the District Judge's decree but also brought further humiliation to the state by the trial and conviction of Michael Bright, and others who carried out the orders of the governor and legislature, for forcibly resisting the federal marshal in executing the decree. Alexander J. Dallas, arguing the case on behalf of the federal government, recognized the political nature of the controversy by stating the real question at issue, "whether a free government, established and administered by the people themselves, can possess sufficient energy for its own preservation."[43] As a Republican official appointed by Jefferson and acting under the direction of him and his successor, Madison, Dallas defended the theory and policy of nationalism. The federal government was declared to be based on a compact with sovereignty residing in the people. It was regarded as a perversion of language to speak of the states as sovereign and independent. The theory of divided sovereignty was then advanced that the federal and state governments alike were possessed of sovereign powers. A typical nationalist view of the formation of the state and federal governments was presented in order to justify the delegation of truly sovereign powers to the central government. Moreover, the doctrine of federal supremacy in carrying out the purposes of the union was strongly defended. Differing from the views of both Madison and Jefferson, an extreme conception of judicial independence and superiority was announced that "a combination of all the powers of the federal government, the President, the Senate, and the House of Representatives, could not reverse, or impair the obligation of a judicial decision, made by a court of the United States."[44]

To sustain the jurisdiction of the federal courts in the case, Dallas found it necessary to assert, contrary to well-known facts and circumstances, that the states had only such authority in relation to the settlement of prize cases as was granted to them by Congress. Upon this

[42] *Acts of General Assembly of Virginia, 1809–10,* pp. 102, 103; also Ames, *op. cit.,* p. 49.
[43] Thomas Lloyd, "A Report of the Whole Trial of General Michael Bright and Others" (Philadelphia, 1809), p. 19.
[44] Lloyd, *op. cit.,* p. 61.

assumption the nationalist superstructure leading to federal judicial supremacy was readily constructed. Pennsylvania's only recourse for what she considered illegal or unconstitutional action by federal Judges then, according to this interpretation, was withdrawal from the Confederacy or the union. Nationalism was further buttressed by the assertion that no state could maintain a military force in time of peace except with the consent of Congress and could not employ such force in opposition to the judicial power of the United States.

On behalf of the defendants, it was argued by the attorney general for the state, Walter Franklin, that at the time of the Declaration of Independence the states became sovereign and independent states and that, so far as the trial of prize cases was concerned, Pennsylvania had not parted with her rights as an independent state. The federal court, therefore, had no authority to take jurisdiction of the appeal of Olmsted, and the continued proceedings in these courts were rendered doubly illegal because of the inhibitions of the Eleventh Amendment on suits against a state—this, in effect, being a suit against Pennsylvania. When Dallas objected to the reading of the act of the legislature authorizing General Bright to resist the marshal in carrying out Judge Peters' decree, it was replied that "if the federal Judges assumed unconstitutional power, and exercised authority over the property of the State in violation of the Constitution, the State had a right to oppose the unconstitutional exercise of authority, not merely as an individual, but as an organized sovereign, independent power, by legislative and executive acts."[45]

Attorney General Franklin, defending the procedure of the state, built his argument on the assumption that prior to the adoption of the federal Constitution "the several States had absolute and unlimited sovereignty within their respective boundaries" and that they still possess those powers, except so far as they have expressly granted them to the federal government. Where differences of opinion arise concerning such grants of power "there is no common umpire but the people, who should adjust the affair by making amendments in the constitutional way, or suffer from the defect.... There is no provision in the Constitution, that in such a case the Judges of the Supreme Court of the United States shall control and be conclusive; neither can the Congress of the United States confer that power."[46]

Jared Ingersoll, speaking on behalf of the state of Pennsylvania, contended that, "on general principles, it is inconsistent with the idea of our remaining States, independent sovereignties, that we should be amenable

[45] Lloyd, op. cit., pp. 64, 65.
[46] Ibid., p. 76.

in federal courts of justice by compulsory means; it would reduce us to the rank of common corporations."[47]

An extreme nationalistic view was assumed throughout the charge to the jury as delivered by Justice Washington. On the crucial issue of the case, whether the decrees of the Committee on Appeals of Congress were supreme and took precedence over any state action to the contrary, Washington maintained: "The jurisdiction of that court to reëxamine the whole cause, as to both law and fact, was considered as resulting from the national character of the appellate prize court, and not from any grant of power by the State, from whose court the appeal had been taken. The right of the State to limit the Court of Appeals in the exercise of its jurisdiction, was determined to be totally inadmissable."[48] To the contention that because the money had been paid into the state treasury it was a suit against the state and was not permissible under the Eleventh Amendment, Washington replied that the decree of the Committee on Appeals extinguished the interest of Pennsylvania in any share of *The Active* and her cargo and vested full right to the whole in Olmsted and his associates, who might rightfully claim that part of the proceeds which came into the hands of the representatives of Rittenhouse, who, up to this time, held them as stakeholders only.

A singular argument that the Eleventh Amendment applied only to cases in law and equity, and not to proceedings in an admiralty court was then indulged in. And, then, adherence was given to the fundamental principle of Federalism that "it is a truth, not to be questioned, that the power to declare the judgment of your courts void, can never be safely lodged with a body, who may enforce its decisions by the physical force of the people. This power necessarily resides in the judicial tribunals, and can safely reside nowhere else."[49] After having taken an unmistakable position as a partisan in one of the greatest political controversies of the day, Judge Washington admonished the jury to discard from their minds "all political considerations."[50]

From the discussions which took place between the Judge and the jury, the jury was directed to render a verdict of guilty regardless of their feeling that no crime had been committed. And to make an example of those who, in obedience to the orders of the state authorities, opposed the laws of the United States, Bright and his associates were given sentences of fine and imprisonment. But, owing to the mistaken sense of

[47] Lloyd, *op. cit.*, p. 131.
[48] Penhallow v. Doane, 3 Dallas 54 (1795), and Thomas Lloyd, *op. cit.*, p. 186.
[49] United States v. Bright, 24 Fed. Cases 1237 (1809).
[50] *Ibid.*, p. 1238.

duty under which they acted, the President voluntarily pardoned Bright and his associates. The state of Pennsylvania was humiliated and the cause of federal supremacy was victorious, but the victory was not regarded as settling the basic question whether the states or the nation possessed real sovereignty with respect to the issue involved in this case. The conflict over this question was merely in its early stages.

State resentment against the Bank of the United States was manifested by Georgia in 1805 by the passage of a law to tax the branch in Savannah. On refusal by the bank to pay the tax, state officers took two thousand dollars, for which the Bank of the United States brought an action in trespass in the Circuit Court of the United States. Not only was the right of a state to tax the national bank involved, but there was also embraced what seemed for the time being a more fundamental question, that is, whether a corporation created by the law of the United States could sue in the federal courts on the ground of diversity of citizenship.

Chief Justice Marshall, speaking for the Court, held that the jurisdiction of the Circuit Court with respect to the character of the parties being limited to controversies between citizens of different states, both parties must be citizens and that the "invisible, intangible, and artificial being, that mere legal entity, a corporation aggregate, is certainly not a citizen; and, consequently, cannot sue or be sued in the courts of the United States."[51] Having gone out of his way to assert the jurisdiction of the federal courts where there was no need to do so, Marshall thought this an appropriate occasion to announce that it was the duty of the Supreme Court "to exercise jurisdiction where it is conferred, and not to usurp it where it is not conferred." A way around the difficulty was found by the suggestion that the corporators, by virtue of their own citizenship, could sue in their corporate name.

By declining to accept jurisdiction the Court in this case failed to pass judgment on the real issue—the validity of a state tax on a national bank. It is probable that the political aspects of the case caused Chief Justice Marshall to defer the settlement of this knotty constitutional question until a more propitious occasion.[52] Despite the probable embarrassment to the bank and similar institutions there was a general belief that to ascribe citizenship to a corporation would give it rights under the privileges and immunities clause, which would thereby place corporations above the state. Corporations were detested in the South, and these states would have resented the placing of such an artificial entity on the same plane as individuals, especially with relation to the privileges of trade

---

[51] Bank of United States v. Deveaux, 5 Cranch 61, 86 (1809).

[52] See *McCulloch v. Maryland*, below, pp. 353 ff.

and commerce. To have declared that corporations were citizens would have enabled the North to force its corporations on the South, and "to persons familiar with the political passions which the bank controversies had aroused, it must have been apparent that such a doctrine would have seriously imperilled the Union."[53] But the Chief Justice was soon to become embroiled in a case of great political significance.

THE TRIAL OF AARON BURR

The extreme limits to which men in high judicial positions may be led by the exigencies of party strife is exemplified in Chief Justice Marshall's conduct of the trial of Aaron Burr. Marshall's conduct in this trial has been called "the one serious blemish in his judicial career."[54] But the blemish is merely more obvious because of the bitterness of the party conflict over the trial and the necessary mingling of law and politics throughout the proceedings. The Chief Justice was again applying his favorite political principles on the Bench as he did in the case of *Marbury v. Madison*. The fact that John Marshall was to preside, Claude G. Bowers maintains, gave the trial a political coloring, for "no man in America hated Jefferson and his democracy more bitterly." Moreover, as a politician on the Bench he was a consummate politician "wearing a mask of impartial benevolence."[55]

The long and involved story of Burr's conspiracy and of the train of events leading to his arrest and trial need not be retold.[56] From the stand-

---

[53] Gerard Carl Henderson, *The Position of Foreign Corporations in American Constitutional Law* (Cambridge, 1918), p. 62. For the development of a fiction to sustain jurisdiction in such cases because of "a strong conviction that the spirit and purpose of the Constitution required them to give corporations the rights of citizens in the federal courts; and a profound aversion to reaching such a result by the simple and direct method of calling a corporation a citizen," see *ibid.*, chaps iv, v.

[54] But to Corwin the Chief Justice's conduct was not "without a measure of extenuation," for the President had behaved deplorably and the charge of political persecution raised by Burr's attorneys was not groundless. Edward S. Corwin, *John Marshall and The Constitution* (New Haven, 1921), p. 111.

[55] *Jefferson in Power*, p. 399. "The moment Burr was turned over to the authorities," claims Bowers, "the Federalist party determined that Jefferson should be tried instead of Burr." *Idem*. To Corwin "the real defendants before the bar of opinion were Thomas Jefferson and his precious ally James Wilkinson, not their harried and unfortunate victim, Aaron Burr!" *John Marshall and the Constitution*, p. 91.

[56] The well-known historical facts relating to the *Burr Case* are summarized from a point of view friendly to Jefferson in Claude G. Bowers, *Jefferson in Power*, chaps. xviii, xix and from a point of view favorable to Marshall in Beveridge, *op. cit.*, III, chaps. vi–ix.

In the four-volume *Life of Marshall* by Beveridge, less than two volumes are devoted to Marshall's career as a Judge. And approximately one-half of the part of one of these volumes concerned with the work of the Chief Justice deals with the apprehension and trial of Aaron Burr for treason. The account of the conspiracy and trial is pre-

point of the federal Judiciary, the first step in the proceedings to punish the Burr conspirators was the trial of Bollman and Swartout on charges of treason. Beveridge, overlooking the notorious partisanship of the Judges during the Federalist Administrations, observes in this case what he regards as the first evidence of a court dividing on political grounds. Judge Cranch, a Federalist, appointed by President Adams, favored discharge of the plaintiffs. On the contrary, Judges Fitzhugh and Duckett, Jefferson appointees, opposed the discharge. Dissenting from the opinion of his associates in committing Bollman and Swartout for treason, Cranch maintained that "in times like these, when the public mind is agitated, when wars and rumors of wars, plots, conspiracies and treasons excite alarm, it is the duty of a court to be particularly watchful lest the public feeling should reach the seat of justice, and thereby precedents be established which may become the ready tools of faction in times more disastrous."[57] When the judgment of the Supreme Court was rendered in the case of Bollman and Swartout which in part at least approved his dissenting opinion, Cranch gave further indications of his partisan feelings by

---

sented with more than the usual anti-Jeffersonian bias which characterizes this author's *The Life of John Marshall*. It paints Burr as a man of fine spirit and heroic qualities being persecuted by the wily and designing Republicans who were moved by selfish and partisan motives only in apprehending Burr and bringing him to trial. The case is described in such a way as to add glory to and to enhance the reputation of Marshall, for, were not the two men, Marshall and Burr, despite their many differences, intellectually similar, since "clear, cold logic was the outstanding element of their minds!" And it is admitted that both were "subtle and astute." Beveridge, *op. cit.*, III, chaps. vi, vii, and pp. 371, 372.

Claude G. Bowers, in his volume on *Beveridge and the Progressive Era*, characterizes Beveridge as "fundamentally a Hamiltonian, temperamentally 'a champion of a strongly centralized government, and a bit skeptical of democracy." In Bowers' opinion Beveridge was using Jefferson as a foil for Marshall throughout his biography of the Chief Justice. "Accepting suggestions freely as to method and facts, [Beveridge] was immovable in regard to his theories or interpretations; and this brought him into numerous conflicts with his friends among the historians in his treatment of Jefferson." *Beveridge and the Progressive Era* (New York, 1932), pp. 554 ff. In a comment shortly before his death, Beveridge said, "If I were rewriting the 'Life of Marshall' today I should not be quite so positive in my criticisms of Jefferson." *Ibid.*

"From the first step toward commitment March 30, to the last day of the tedious trials, October 20," says Henry Adams, "Burr and his counsel never ceased their effort to convict Jefferson.... Over this tournament the Chief Justice presided as arbiter.... That he held Federalist prejudices and nourished a personal dislike to Jefferson was notorious." *History of the United States of America during the Second Administration of Thomas Jefferson* (New York, 1890), I: 442, 443.

James Truslow Adams refers to Beveridge's "unrestrained prejudice which did so much to mar that author's otherwise great book and to reflect upon his intellectual integrity." *The Living Jefferson* (New York, 1936), p. 44.

[57] See Allen C. Clark, *Greenleaf and Law in the Federal City* (Washington, 1901); from letter of Cranch, Feb. 2, 1807.

congratulating the country "upon this triumph of reason and law over popular passion and injustice—upon the final triumph of civil over the military authority, and of the practical principles of substantial personal liberty over the theoretic doctrine of philosophic civil liberty."[58] Beveridge regards it fortunate, that when Bollman and Swartout were held for trial on the charge of treason, that John Marshall and the Supreme Court had yet to be reckoned with.[59]

When it was argued, in the application to the federal Judges for the issuance of a writ of habeas corpus, that the federal courts could not issue the writ because it was customary for the common law courts to issue such writs, Chief Justice Marshall indicated the position which the federal courts were soon to announce denying common law jurisdiction for the federal courts. This Court, said he, "disclaims all jurisdiction not given by the Constitution, or by the laws of the United States."[60] Therefore, the power to award the writ of habeas corpus by any of the courts of the United States must be given by written law. Holding that the awarding of the writ in this case was under the appellate jurisdiction, Marshall, presenting the opinion in which Justices Washington and Livingston concurred,[61] regarded the granting of the writ as proper. Justice Johnson, dissenting, thought that according to the reasoning of *Marbury v. Madison* the writ should not have been granted. Referring to *Ex parte Burford*,[62] in which he had acquiesced in the granting of such a writ, Johnson pointed out that he had objected to the issuance of the writ, but since the gentleman who had argued that cause confined himself strictly to those considerations which ought alone to influence the decisions of this Court, there was no necessity for vindicating his opinion. Popular observations on the necessity of protecting the citizens from Executive oppression and an animated address calculated to enlist the passions or prejudices of an audience in defense of his motion were fortunately lacking.[63] This was a criticism of the tendency to inject politics into the argument and consideration of cases.

In rendering the decision that Bollman and Swartout could not be held and tried for the offenses charged in the District of Columbia, Marshall took occasion to criticize President Jefferson who had sought authority to suspend the writ of habeas corpus and had been denied this

---

[58] Warren, *op. cit.*, I: 308.

[59] Beveridge, *op. cit.*, III: 346.

[60] *Ex parte* Bollman and Swartout, 4 Cranch 75, 93 (1807).

[61] Justices Chase and Cushing did not hear the case on account of illness.

[62] 3 Cranch 447 (1806).

[63] 4 Cranch 107. Justice Johnson stated that one of the absent members of the Court agreed with him in his opinion.

request by an adverse vote in the House of Representatives. The framers of the Constitution, contended Marshall,

must have conceived it more safe that punishment in such cases should be ordained by general laws, formed upon deliberation, under the influence of no resentments, and without knowing on whom they were to operate, than that it should be inflicted under the influence of those passions which the occasion seldom fails to excite, and which a flexible definition of the crime, or a construction which would render it flexible, might bring into operation. It is, therefore, more safe as well as more consonant to the principles of our Constitution, that the crime of treason should not be extended by construction to doubtful cases.[64]

It was the opinion of the majority of the Court[65] that in the case of Swartout there was not sufficient evidence of his levying war against the United States to justify his commitment on the charge of treason and that there was still less evidence against Bollman. All of the Justices agreed that the men could not be tried in the District of Columbia. Objecting to the proceedings instituted under the authority and direction of the President, Marshall said: "It would too, be extremely dangerous to say, that because the prisoners were apprehended, not by a civil magistrate, but by the military power, there could be given by law a right to try the persons so seized in any place which the general might select."[66]

In defining the crime of treason under the Constitution, Marshall declared that an individual may be guilty of treason "who has not appeared in arms against his country. On the contrary, if war be actually levied, that is, if a body of men be actually assembled for the purpose of effecting by force a treasonable purpose, all those who perform any part, however minute, or however remote from the scene of action, and who are actually leagued in the general conspiracy, are to be considered as traitors."[67] It was necessary for Marshall to repudiate this reasoning in order to set Aaron Burr free.

Beveridge depicts in glowing terms the patience, consideration, and prudence of Marshall as he moves with courage and astute statesmanship to counteract the efforts of the President, who was seeking "to inflame the passions of the people against the Judiciary." An impartial account of the trial does not warrant such a favorable estimate of the procedure and opinions of the Chief Justice. In the first place, Blackstone was quoted to the effect that a prisoner may be discharged only when it appears that

[64] 4 Cranch 127.
[65] Chief Justice Marshall, Justices Chase, Washington, and Johnson being present.
[66] 4 Cranch 136.
[67] 4 Cranch 126. For an account of the efforts of the Marshalls of Kentucky with the aid of the Chief Justice to discredit Wilkinson, one of the chief witnesses against Burr, for his alleged treasonable transactions with Spain, see Charles H. Ambler, *Thomas Ritchie: A Study in Virginia Politics* (Richmond, 1913), p. 38.

the suspicion against him is "wholly groundless." With Jefferson's conduct in mind, Marshall made it clear that he did not propose to have this statement mean that "the hand of malignity may grasp any individual against whom its hate may be directed or whom it may capriciously seize, charge him with some secret crime and put him on the proof of his innocence." When Jefferson's friends expressed their indignation at the uncalled for insinuations regarding the conduct of the President, Marshall hastened to assure the press that he did not allude to the Administration's conduct in his remarks, but merely intended to elucidate Blackstone.[68]

Again, after the attorneys of Burr had indulged in uncalled for invectives against the Administration without any admonition from the presiding judge, Wirt, speaking to Marshall, inquired, "do they flatter themselves that this court feels political prejudices which will supply the place of argument and innocence on the part of the prisoner. Their conduct amounts to an insinuation of the sort."[69] Marshall's mild admonition to the attorneys to confine themselves to the issues before the Court were thought insincere and were disregarded.

The worst offense of Marshall, from the standpoint of the Republicans and one which seriously reflected upon his conduct as the presiding Judge in the case, was his participation as a guest in a dinner given in Burr's honor by the chief counsel of the defense, John Wickham. The Richmond *Enquirer* reported that the Judge, the accused, and his attorney were fellow guests at a "treason rejoicing dinner,"[70] and regarded Marshall's conduct as "grossly indecent." In defense of Marshall's action, which has been severely criticized, Beveridge insists that it was merely an ordinary dinner given by his neighbor Wickham, that Marshall did not know that Burr was to be present, and that he could not leave when he found Burr was there. Judge Tucker, however, notes that Wickham had informed the Chief Justice that Burr was expected to be at the dinner.[71]

---

[68] Beveridge, *op. cit.,* III: 376, 377. Marshall had irritated the President by making John Randolph, one of his political enemies, foreman of the grand jury.

[69] David Robertson, *Reports of the Trial of Colonel Aaron Burr* (New York, 1875), I: 144.

[70] *Enquirer,* April 10, 28, 1807. Marshall's dining with Burr was regarded by the editor of the *Enquirer,* Thomas Ritchie, as "a wilful prostration of his own dignity and a wanton insult to his country." Ambler, *op. cit.,* p. 40.

[71] Tucker's *Blackstone,* II: 254, cited in Bowers, *Jefferson in Power,* p. 402. "Even had he been ungraciously trapped into the acceptance of the invitation" thinks Bowers, "the wonder grows that when he found himself confronted by Burr in Wickham's house, his own sense of propriety did not impel him indignantly to rebuke his host and take his instant departure." *Idem.*

Regarding Marshall's participation in the dinner given by Wickham, one of Burr's counsel, James Bradley Thayer observes, "Marshall had accepted the invitation before he knew that Burr was to be of the company. I have been informed by one of his de-

Despite his indiscreet and unjustifiable behavior in this incident, Marshall did not hesitate to preside over the trial of Aaron Burr. With the trial beginning, observes Beveridge, "the whole bar understood the strength and limitations of the Chief Justice, the power of his intellect no less than his unfamiliarity with precedents and the learning of the law."[72] Though this appears to be an unfair insinuation regarding Marshall's ability as a lawyer and a Judge, it is undeniable that his political feelings and views were displayed at every stage in the trial.

Beveridge describes fully the contentions of Burr, the arguments of counsel, and the political maneuvers which led Marshall to issue a *subpoena duces tecum* to President Jefferson. Disavowing any disrespect for the President in the exercise of his official duties, Marshall, as on similar occasions, hid behind what he declared to be the compulsions of the law, observing "if it be a duty the court can have no choice." The order was sent to the President to come to Court and to bring certain designated papers with him. The President, however, wrote an answer in which Beveridge admits that "Jefferson the lawyer shines brilliantly forth." Jefferson maintained that Marshall enlarged upon small objections to his appearance as a witness and passed over those which are solid. The Judges, Jefferson observed, had persistently maintained the independence of the Judiciary in their relations with the other two coördinate branches of the government, but what would become of the independence of the President "if the several courts could bandy him from pillar to post, keeping him constantly trudging from north to south and east to west, and withdraw him entirely from his constitutional duties."[73]

Despite the apparent evidence of partiality on the part of the Court and the bitter invectives against Jefferson and the Republican Administration by the counsel for Burr, the grand jury returned indictments against Burr for treason and misdemeanor. At the beginning of the trial for treason the political forces were lined up on both sides—to mold public opinion and to determine Burr's guilt.[74]

True to Jefferson's prophecy, Marshall found a mode of procedure for the escape of Burr from conviction for treason: first by a strict and

scendants that his wife advised him not to go; but he thought it best not to seem too fastidious, or to appear to censure his friend, by staying away. It is said that he sat at the opposite end of the table, had no communication with Burr, and went away early. But we must still wonder at his action; and he himself, it is said, afterwards much regretted it." From address of Thayer in *John Marshall: Life, Character and Judicial Services,* ed., with an introduction, by John F. Dillon (Chicago, 1903), I: 233, 234.

[72] Beveridge, *op. cit.,* III: 408.

[73] *The Writings of Thomas Jefferson,* ed. by Paul Leicester Ford (New York, 1892), IX: 60.

[74] As the trial began, Jefferson, writing to Du Pont de Nemours, indicated his per-

formal method of defining treason, as well as of the establishment of the evidence to prove guilt; and, second, by excluding much of the most important and relevant testimony. Concerning the definition of treason, Marshall held: "It is then the opinion of the court, that this indictment can be supported only by testimony which proves the accused to have been actually or constructively present when the assemblage took place on Blennerhasset's island," and that "there is no testimony whatever which tends to prove that the accused was actually, or constructively present when that assemblage did take place. Indeed, the contrary is most apparent." The overt act of levying war "must be proved, according to the mandates of the Constitution and of the act of Congress, by two witnesses. It is not proved by a single witness."[75]

Though Marshall differed from most of his Federalist brethren in holding that the courts of the United States had no common law jurisdiction, he adopted an attitude of subservience to the common law in interpreting the words of the Constitution relating to treason, which was considered unwarranted by many Republican lawyers. In defining the term "levying war" in the trial of Burr, he said: "It is a technical term. It is used in a very old statute of that country, whose language is our language, and whose laws form the substratum of our laws. It is scarcely conceivable that the term was not employed by the framers of the Constitution in the sense which had been affixed to it by those from whom we borrowed it."[76] Marshall's opinion on the definition of treason was one of his longest and the only one that contains extensive citations from judicial decisions and other authorities on the subject. It was, Beveridge asserts, "a state paper of first importance and marked a critical phase in the development of the American Nation."[77]

The Constitution of the United States confines the crime of treason to the levying of war against the United States and to the giving of aid and comfort to her enemies. In providing for the punishment of this crime, the words of the statute of treason of Edward the Third were regarded by Marshall as adopted for the American federal system, and by implication it was thought the definition of these phrases was intended which had prevailed in England for centuries.[78] Story believed that judges in the United States uniformly adhered to the established doctrines, even when Executive influence was exerted to secure convictions. But the best

---

sonal conviction of Burr's guilt but admitted that "although there is not a man in the United States who is not satisfied of the depth of his guilt, such are the jealous provisions of our laws in favor of the accused that I question if he can be convicted." *Writings* (Ford ed.), II: 274.

[75] 4 Cranch 520, 525.   [77] Beveridge, *op. cit.*, III: 504.
[76] 4 Cranch 475.   [78] *Blackstone's Comm.*, pp. 81–84.

definition of treason, according to Story, was Marshall's statement in *Ex parte Bollman* which was repudiated in his opinion in the *Burr Case*.[79]

Soon after the trial began the attorneys for Burr moved that Marshall exclude all further testimony because no direct evidence had been presented connecting Burr with the treasonable plot on Blennerhassett's Island. Ten days of argument ensued in the presentation of the case. The attorneys for the prosecution tried to show that they were not only following the long established rules of evidence according to the English law but also according to the decision by Chief Justice Marshall in the case of *Bollman and Swartout*.

Marshall objected to the construction of his own language in the case of *Bollman and Swartout* so far as it was considered "to mean that any assemblage whatever for a treasonable purpose, whether in force, or not in force, whether in a condition to use violence, or not in that condition, is a levying of war." Justices Iredell, Paterson, Chase, and Judge Peters were cited as confining the term levying war to the actual use of force or violence. By an ingenious process of interpretation, Marshall construed his language in the case of *Bollman and Swartout* to mean exactly the opposite of what both the friends and foes of Burr had understood it to mean. The indictment of Burr was formulated on the basis of this opinion and was stated in part in the exact words of the Chief Justice. The attorneys for Burr took it for granted that it was necessary to overrule this opinion to acquit their client. Marshall alone seemed able to defend his language as still good law and to find a method of evading its actual meaning and application in *Burr's Case*. The convenient device of avoiding the consequences of the earlier case as a precedent was found in the usual common law method of escaping the rigidity of *stare decisis*. In explaining that opinion, Marshall declared that the language of the Court must be considered in reference to the particular case being tried.[80]

After Marshall had overruled himself, as his language in the case of *Bollman and Swartout* had been understood and interpreted, or had, as he thought, explained away the effect of this case so far as the presentation of evidence against Burr was concerned, Hay, the chief counsel for the prosecution announced that he had nothing further to offer to the Court in the way of evidence or argument. And the jury soon reported to the Court that "Aaron Burr is not proved guilty under this indictment by any evidence submitted to us."

It was the tricks of legal legerdemain which brought the trial of Burr to an abrupt close and on which John Quincy Adams commented in Congress. In presenting the report of a Senate committee to expel Senator

---

[79] See 4 Cranch 125, 126, 474 ff.   [80] See 4 Cranch 490.

Smith of Ohio, who was under indictment for treason, John Quincy Adams criticized Marshall for withholding from the jury a great part of the evidence essential to Burr's conviction similar to the evidence resulting in Smith's indictment. Though Burr was acquitted because of a technical interpretation of the language and intent of the Constitution relating to treason, Adams maintained that "but for the vigilance and energy of the government, and of faithful citizens under its directions, in arresting their progress and in crushing his designs, they would, in a very short lapse of time have terminated, not only in a war, but in a war of the most horrible description, in a war at once foreign and domestic ... if the daylight of evidence combining one vast complicated intention, with overt acts innumerable, be not excluded from the mind by the curtain of artificial rules, the simplest understanding cannot but see what the subtlest understanding cannot disguise, crimes before which ordinary treason whitens into virtue."[81]

When Jefferson found Marshall favorably inclined to Burr and critical of every move the Administration was making to secure his conviction, he wrote: "The fact is that the Federalists make Burr's cause their own, and exert their whole influence to shield him,"[82] and to him it was unfortunate that Federalism was still predominant in the Judiciary and that the Judges were doing all in their power to obstruct the Administration. Marshall insisted that evidence be presented by actual witnesses of overt acts amounting to the levying of war, but Jefferson raised the query whether such evidence was not presented to the Court in letters, newspapers, and public documents. With the law being interpreted to aid the men whom Jefferson regarded as enemies of the Republic and actively seeking its destruction, it can be readily understood why Jefferson urged Randolph to take steps to secure the approval of the amendment to the Constitution proposed at the time of the Chase impeachment providing for the removal of federal Judges by the President on the address of both houses of Congress. Something must be done, urged Jefferson, to prevent a recurrence of the situation where one of the great coördinate branches of the government sets itself in opposition to the other two, and to the common sense of the nation and "proclaims impunity to that class of

[81] *Annals,* 10th Cong., 1st sess., pp. 61, 62. For similar views see speech of Senator Giles—"You have seen your Judiciary publicly held up to the world as a spectacle of disgrace. You have seen a jury sworn to try an issue in a criminal case, and excluded from the privilege of hearing the most material evidence, upon which the trial of the issue depended. You have seen treason go unpunished. And you have seen the character of imbecility given to our government, calculated to excite distrust at home, and invite contempt and attacks from abroad." Giles, commenting on the Burr trial, *Annals,* 10th Cong., 2d sess., p. 274.

[82] *Writings* (Ford ed.), IX: 41.

offenders which endeavors to overturn the Constitution, and are themselves protected in it by the Constitution itself."[83]

When, in accordance with Marshall's charge, the petit jury acquitted Burr, Jefferson was indignant and proposed to lay the whole proceedings before Congress in the hope that it might provide the proper remedy. After Burr had been acquitted also of the charge of committing a misdemeanor and had been held over for trial for a similar offense in Ohio, the prosecution for which was dropped, Jefferson transmitted the record to Congress with the observation that "you will be enabled to judge whether the defect was in the testimony, or in the laws, or whether there is not a radical defect in the administration of the law? And wherever it shall be found the Legislature alone can apply or originate the remedy."[84] There was, as the New York *Evening Post* suggested, "no acquittal, for there has been no trial, no evidence having been given."[85]

After being nearly mobbed in Baltimore, Burr hastened to Philadelphia, and, regardless of his freedom under bail for trial in Ohio, at the earliest opportunity sailed for Europe to continue his political intrigues in France. Marshall hastened to the mountains to escape the excitement and the odium to which he was subjected because of his conduct of the trial. Fortunately for the future career of the Chief Justice as the expounder of constitutional Federalism, Jefferson and the nation became entangled in foreign affairs which were verging in the direction of war.

---

[83] *Writings* (Ford ed.), IX: 46. The extract relating to Burr from the letter of Jefferson to William B. Giles, Apr. 20, 1807, is as follows:

"The Nation will judge both the offender and the Judges for themselves. If a member of the Executive or Legislature does wrong, the day is never far distant when the people will remove him. They will see then and amend the error in our Constitution which makes any branch independent of the Nation. They will see that one of the great coordinate branches of the government, setting itself in opposition to the other two and to the common sense of the Nation, proclaims impunity to that class of offenders which endeavors to overturn the Constitution, and are protected in it by the Constitution itself; for impeachment is a farce which will not be tried again. If their protection of Burr produces this amendment, it will do more good than his condemnation would have done." *Writings* (Ford ed.), IX: 45, 46. When Jefferson was informed that the attorneys for the prosecution were citing, as authority, *Marbury v. Madison,* he wrote: "I have long wished for a proper occasion to have the gratuitous opinion in Marbury v. Madison brought before the public and denounced as not law; and I think the present a fortunate one, because it occupies such a place in the public attention." *Writings* (Ford ed.), IX: 54.

[84] *Writings* (Ford ed.), IX: 163–164. The political machinations of the Federalists during the trial were frequently condemned by Jefferson and at one time, when he considered the Chief Justice as displaying more than his ordinary political leanings, he exclaimed: "If there ever had been an instance in this and the preceding administrations, of federal Judges so applying principles of law as to condemn a federal or acquit a republican offender, I should have judged them in the present case with more charity." *Writings* (Ford ed.), IX: 45.

[85] *Evening Post,* Oct. 3, 1807.

CHAPTER IX

New England's Espousal of the Cause of State Rights and Chief Justice Marshall's Interpretation of the Contract Clause

T̲HE FEDERALISTS, who had called a nation into being and who had erected the barriers which were designed to check and keep under control the imprudences of an ignorant and unscrupulous electorate, found it difficult to become reconciled to the election of Jefferson to the presidency and to what appeared to many to be his successful administration of the government. Members of this party hated Jefferson "with no common political hatred, but rather with the vindictiveness of men toward a deadly foe who, as they firmly believed sought the ruin of all they most prized and cherished."[1] It was to be expected, therefore, that the Federalists would fail to coöperate with Jefferson as the leader of the Republican party and would take steps to thwart the administration of the federal government even though these steps might lead them into the direction of nullification and secession. Disaffection among the leaders of the Federalists came near to culminating in a disunion movement in the early years of Jefferson's Administration. It was Jefferson's embargo policy and the declaration and conduct of the War of 1812, however, which furnished the occasion for the development of an organized and aggressive policy of opposition to the federal Administration and of the public espousal of disunion doctrines.

OPPOSITION TO THE EMBARGO ACTS

Following the disheartening results of the Burr trial, the Administration became absorbed in the protection of the rights of American citizens engaged in commerce and trade. The European wars instigated by Napoleon led to various attempts to establish a blockade of French ports and to the issuance of retaliatory decrees by France and England which

---

[1] Henry Cabot Lodge, *Life and Letters of George Cabot* (Boston, 1877), p. 426. Lodge thinks there was only one man of real ability in the Republican party, namely, Madison.

placed serious restrictions on American commerce. To make matters worse England insisted on taking American citizens from both English and American vessels and impressing them into her naval service. The unwarranted attack on the *Chesapeake* by the *Leopard* aroused such indignation that the President and Congress were forced to act. A form of nonintercourse act was first tried but proved ineffective, and to the Administration leaders more drastic measures seemed imperative. Albert Gallatin favored a declaration of war, but Jefferson and Madison preferred to employ the method of economic reprisals and recommended the passage of embargo acts.[2]

The acts passed in 1807 and 1808 prohibited sending out of the United States any goods either the produce of the United States or those shipped through American ports. Unexpected difficulties arose when the collectors of customs attempted to enforce the acts, the result being that the President and his subordinates were required to exercise powers which many men regarded as unauthorized by the Constitution and the laws.[3] In January, 1809, a new and more drastic act was passed. This act authorized collectors to seize goods which were on the way to the frontier, to refuse permits to load merchandise on vessels, and to detain vessels in American ports. It was the passage and enforcement of these acts which was the occasion of the first serious constitutional crisis since the establishment of the new government. From the time of their enactment, the Embargo Acts were challenged on the ground of unconstitutionality.

District Judge Davis, a member of the Federalist party, answering the contention that the Embargo Acts were unconstitutional, found that they contravened none of the exceptions or restrictions expressed in the Constitution nor were they repugnant to any of its affirmative declarations.[4] In confining judicial review to the enforcement of the express language of the Constitution, Judge Davis differed from most of his Federalist associates on the Bench. Moreover, in upholding a law enacted by the Republicans, a method of interpretation was adopted which was soon to be approved by Chief Justice Marshall. A national sovereignty has

---

[2] Louis Martin Sears is of the opinion that "one cannot understand Jefferson's initiation of the embargo and his subsequent relation to its enforcement without examining his point of view as it ripened into pacifism. For the embargo was the practical outcome of a philosophy long maturing. It was the projection into foreign affairs of the peace ideals of a democracy, the contribution to international polity of one of the world's greatest democrats." *Jefferson and the Embargo* (Durham, 1927), p. 4.

[3] According to Sears the odds were against Jefferson when "he embarked upon an era of personal government which called for the arbitrary enforcement of a most inquisitorial act, for a tampering with what men regarded as their dearest rights, and which put in jeopardy both his popularity and his fame, the cherished rewards of a long career." *Ibid.,* p. 74.

[4] United States v. The William, 28 Federal Cases 614 (1808).

been created, said Judge Davis, not an unlimited sovereignty, but a
sovereignty confined to the objects surrendered and specified. In relation
to commercial intercourse, the federal government is sovereign. Commerce was given a broad definition including shipping, navigation, and
fisheries. The necessary and proper clause was then called to the aid of
the commerce clause to sanction such commercial regulations or prohibitions as Congress might consider necessary for the purpose of carrying
out general national policies.

Ezekiel Bacon, referring to this decision, was surprised to hear the constitutionality of the act attacked after this question had once been submitted to the decision of that tribunal, whose judgment the Federalists
had been heretofore in the habit of respecting. A judgment had been
rendered sanctioning the constitutionality of the law "by a judge of great
legal weight and personal respectability and whose opinion, from his
known political character, could not be suspected of any party views."
These opinions appeared to Bacon all the more indefensible because
they came "from a quarter where we have been accustomed to hear the
doctrine that the judicial power was supreme, controlling not only the
exercise of individual rights but also the power of every other branch of
the government."[5] The issue of the constitutionality of the Embargo Acts
was by no means settled by Judge Davis' decision. Though the act was
held valid, juries failed to sustain convictions even when the evidence
of the violation of the act was clear beyond doubt. And many eminent
men regarded the Embargo and Enforcement Acts as unwarranted by
the Constitution.

To carry out the purposes of the Embargo Acts it was provided that collectors of customs were authorized "to detain any vessel ostensibly bound
with a cargo to some other port of the United States, whenever, in their
opinion, the intention is to violate or evade any provisions of the acts
laying an embargo." Because of difficulties in the enforcement of this
provision, the President directed the Secretary of the Treasury to see
that all vessels suspected of intention to evade the Embargo Acts should
be detained. It was this order which led to a rebuke of the national Administration by Justice Johnson, the first appointee of President Jefferson to the federal Bench. In issuing a mandamus to the collector of the
port of Charleston, Johnson declared that the President's order was un-
supported by the act of Congress and hence was invalid. Justifying his
conduct in the case, the Justice said: "The officers of our government,
from the highest to the lowest, are equally subjected to legal restraint;
and it is confidently believed that all of them feel themselves equally

<hr>

[5] *Annals of Congress*, 10th Cong., 2d sess., p. 564.

incapable, as well from law as inclination, to attempt an unsanctioned encroachment upon individual liberty."⁶ Because the act granted a discretion to the collector in the clearance of vessels, the right remained with him and a contrary order by the Secretary of the Treasury was held to have no effect.

Jefferson considered the decision of Justice Johnson such a serious interference with the administrative policies and practices of the government that he requested Attorney General Rodney to prepare and to publish a reply to the opinion. Because the act organizing the Circuit Courts made no provision for the issuance of writs of mandamus, the Attorney General contended these courts had no authority to issue such writs. Nor could such power be regarded as inherent or necessarily incidental to a court of justice even of general jurisdiction. And it was claimed that the King's Bench, the only court which could issue such a writ in England, would not have awarded the writ in such a case.

The publication of this opinion elicited a prompt reply from Justice Johnson. He regarded the act of the President in directing its publication as "so unprecedented in the history of executive conduct" that it could be "intended for no other purpose than to secure the public opinion on the side of the Executive and in opposition to the Judiciary." Hence it seemed necessary to attempt a vindication of that decision. In language which pleased the Federalists, Johnson protested against the effort to bias public opinion "by the overbearing influence of high office." It was pointed out that when the case was argued in court the federal District Attorney, basing his argument on the validity of the presidential order, did not contest the authority to issue a mandamus. A distinction was then noted between a question of jurisdiction concerning which there was no doubt in the case and the awarding of the appropriate writs to make such jurisdiction effective. For the latter purpose the issuance of a mandamus was "a mere incident to the judicial power." Concerning such an incident, said Johnson, "I see no reason why it should not follow with the principal jurisdiction, when vested by Congress in its courts." The Justice then indulged in a method of interpretation almost as broad in scope as the claim of common law jurisdiction in the federal courts which the Federalists approved and the Republicans abhorred. Speaking of the act granting jurisdiction to the inferior federal courts by the Judiciary Act of 1789, Johnson maintained "the correct, legal and received construction of this act therefore is, that the forms and modes of administering justice, the remedies to be applied to the rights which are committed to our juris-

---

⁶ Gilchrist v. Collector, 10 Federal Cases 355, 356 (1808).

diction shall be such as are used and allowed in the supreme courts of the States over which we respectively preside.'"[7] Since the state courts of South Carolina could, in accordance with common law and equity processes, issue a mandamus in a case of this kind, it was consequently entirely appropriate, according to Johnson, for a remedy to be granted by the Circuit Court. To the Attorney General's contention that the writ of mandamus should not be applied to the order of the Secretary of the Treasury, since he was merely a ministerial officer, Justice Johnson responded that:

The courts do not pretend to impose any restraint upon any officer of government, but what results from a just construction of the laws of the United States. Of these laws the courts are the constitutional expositors; and every department of government must submit to their exposition; for laws have no legal meaning but what is given them by the courts to whose exposition they are submitted. It is against the law, therefore, and not the courts, that the Executive should urge the charge of usurpation and restraint; a restraint which may at times be productive of inconveniences, but which is certainly very consistent with the nature of our government.[8]

The Judge's extrajudicial defense of his opinion was concluded by insisting on the illegality of the President's order and by objecting to the Attorney General's assumption that the Judiciary has no power to prevent the unlawful acts of the Executive.

In a letter to Jefferson, commenting on Justice Johnson's reply, Attorney General Rodney thought that the Justice now "stands forth the champion of all the *high-church* doctrines so fashionable on the Bench. . . . The judicial power, if permitted, will swallow all the rest. They will become omnipotent."[9] A few years later the Supreme Court sustained the position of the Attorney General that the Circuit Courts did not have authority to issue a mandamus in a case of this nature.[10] Though for the time being the President directed the collectors of customs to disregard Johnson's opinion, this judicial obstacle seriously interfered with the enforcement of the Embargo Acts.

The controversy over this decision demonstrated that, though Justice Johnson at the time of his appointment to the Supreme Court was a friend of Jefferson and was considered to be in accord with his political views, he had by this time gone a long way, so far as constitutional interpretation was concerned, toward the acceptance of the main tenets of Federalism. And for the remaining years of a long judicial career he supported the views of Marshall and Story, though at times objecting to the

---

[7] 10 Federal Cases 363.
[8] 10 Federal Cases 364.
[9] Jefferson Papers MSS, letter of Rodney, Oct. 31, 1808.
[10] M'Intyre v. Wood, 7 Cranch 504 (1813).

extreme nationalist notions of his associates. It was in New England, however, that the challenge of unconstitutionality of the Embargo Acts and of the presidential orders issued thereunder led to obstructive and drastic methods of resistance which bordered on the verge of treason.[11]

NEW ENGLAND'S DEFENSE OF STATE RIGHTS AND APPROVAL OF DOCTRINES OF NULLIFICATION AND SECESSION

The alarm and disgust of the New England Federalists concerning the anti-Judiciary doctrines of Jefferson, John Quincy Adams believed, were the cause which led the Federalists in these states in the first instance to favor a project for the separation of the states and the establishment of a northern confederacy.[12] But earlier than this, Timothy Dwight, President of Yale College, wrote, "I sincerely declare that I wish the Northern States would separate from the Southern, the moment that event [the election of Jefferson] shall take effect."[13] The passage of the Judiciary Repeal Act, the purchase of Louisiana, as well as the enforcement of the Embargo Acts tended to foster views favorable to secession and the formation of "a separate and independent empire." Early in Jefferson's Administration something in the nature of a plot to take steps to secede from the union was frequently discussed among a small group of Federalists. No serious attempt, however, was made to carry the proposal into effect.

Referring to the collection of the sentiments of public men on secession from 1790 to 1804 to be found in William Plumer's life of his father,[14] McMaster notes that particularly in 1803 and 1804 many public men in New England favored separation from the union, for "Virginia influence, Virginia politics, Virginia men ruled everywhere. The influence of New England in the affairs of the Nation seemed gone forever. She was, they thought, fast becoming no better than a Virginia colony.

---

[11] The only practical result of the embargo, thinks Samuel Eliot Morison, was the revival of the Federalist ascendancy in New England. *The Life and Letters of Harrison Gray Otis* (Boston, 1913), II: 1.

[12] Henry Adams, *Documents Relating to New England Federalism* (Boston, 1877), pp. 160–162.

[13] William Plumer, Jr., *Life of William Plumer,* ed. by A. P. Peabody (Boston, 1857), p. 825. To the great dismay of the Federalist leaders, many of their own party had "much of the Democratic taint." For, reflected George Cabot, "we are altogether Democratic in our principles and these principles of necessity place power in the worst hands." Adams, *op. cit.,* p. 362. On the other hand, he thought that no government could be maintained that did not have "a material portion of the democratic mixture in its composition" and that it was necessary for the time being "to bear the evils which the delusion of democracy is bringing upon us." *Ibid.,* pp. 346, 347.

[14] Plumer, *op. cit.,* pp. 277–284.

From such a fate she must, at all hazards, be saved.[15] The idea of separation was an old one.... Long before the Constitution was framed, the secession of the country beyond the mountains and the formation of a Western Republic in the valley of the Mississippi was the dream of such scheming politicians as Wilkinson, and the ever present dread of such earnest patriots as Washington."[16] The separation sentiment in 1803 was fostered chiefly in Congress and especially by Timothy Pickering, Roger Griswold, Uriah Tracy, and William Plumer who secured the active interest and participation of Aaron Burr. The wildness of the plan arranged by these men, McMaster observes, "was conclusive proof of the depth of their despair and the intemperance of their political zeal." Most of the men who participated in the secession schemes of 1803–1804 later denied that they had anything to do with Pickering's fantastic proposals, but contemporary correspondence clearly demonstrates their active participation in the consideration of the plans. The only immediate result of the movement was the proposal by the general assembly of Massachusetts of an amendment designed to secure the apportionment of representatives and direct taxes among the states according to free population.

With the purchase of Louisiana the Federalists became aware that the popular will was arrayed against them, and they knew of but one method of relief—a dissolution of the union.[17] It was not, however, the acquisition of Louisiana that they feared, but rather the inevitable supremacy of democratic ideas and political philosophy. New England Federalists "were men of one idea and one object: to suppress democracy. Their political theories were founded on the fallacy that the masses in America had the same passions as the Paris mob. Democracy to them meant atheism, destruction of property, and mob rule."[18] Aroused again by the extreme measures adopted to enforce the Embargo Acts, political leaders of New England began to agitate for separation and regarded the time for such a move most favorable. A confederacy was to be formed with New England as its nucleus, the British provinces as adherents, and with New York as a barrier against the South.

Edward Channing points out that to the men who formed and set into operation the federal government under the Constitution the institu-

---

[15] Fisher Ames believed that "the Federalists must entrench themselves in the state governments, and endeavor to make state justice and state power a shelter of the wise, and good, and rich, from the wild destroying rage of the southern Jacobins," *Works of Fisher Ames,* ed. by Seth Ames (Boston, 1854), I: 310.

[16] John Bach McMaster, *A History of the People of the United States from the Revolution to the Civil War* (New York, 1900), III: 43.

[17] Lodge, *op. cit.,* p. 435.

[18] Morison, *op. cit.,* I: 265.

tions thereby established were in the nature of an experiment. For decades after 1789 not a year passed in which groups of men did not condemn the experiment and consider ways and methods of establishing a better form of government for the union.[19] Writing to Washington on May 23, 1793, Jefferson observed "that opposition to the Union was originally so extensive in the South, and had been recently so much increased, that a small number only was wanting to place the majority on the other side." Usually these groups were aroused and led to discuss the weakness of the existing system because of a conflict in which one state was primarily concerned with the other states taking an indifferent or hostile attitude. With the passage and the enforcement of the Alien and Sedition Laws, there was active coöperation between Kentucky and Virginia and an attempt was made to enlist the interest and support of the other states. The states of the north condemned the proposals made in these resolutions and, though a majority in most of the southern states approved the ideas contained in the resolutions, few were willing to take concerted action to prevent the enforcement of the acts.

It was the New England states as a group which first joined in approving measures which tended in the direction of nullification and secession. The Federalists, who, during the time they were in charge of the administration of the government, sought to give the terms and provisions of the Constitution the broadest kind of interpretation to carry out their aims for the enlargement and strengthening of the federal authority, were now filled with alarm—for to them the Republicans treated the Constitution as "mere paper, to be folded into any shape to suit the view of the dominant party."[20]

It was distressing to conservative-minded people to observe Jefferson replacing men of "property and integrity," as Timothy Pickering called the Federalist officeholders, with citizens of the type who comprised the

---

[19] "In justice to those men who wrote about and talked about secession, it should be said that during the first thirty-five years of the federal government under the Constitution it was a possibility often suggested." Kendrick C. Babcock, *The Rise of American Nationality, 1811–1819* (New York, 1906), p. 161, and *The Works of John Adams* (Boston, 1851), VI: 629.

See account of a conference of Rufus King and Oliver Ellsworth with John Taylor of Caroline in May, 1794, relating to the possible separation of the union into a northern and southern confederacy. "Disunion Sentiment in Congress in 1794. A Confidential Memorandum written by John Taylor of Caroline for James Madison," ed., with an introduction, by Gaillard Hunt (Washington, 1905).

[20] Letter of Pickering to Lyman, Adams, *op. cit.*, p. 358. Henceforth, "the Federal party in Massachusetts was anti-federal and anti-national, gaining its ends by methods, sheltering itself under theories that were finally used to justify secession from the Union." Morison, *op. cit.*, II: 15.

mainstay of the Republican party.[21] As the control of political affairs by the Federalists declined, Pickering looked to a new confederacy for an escape from the "corrupting influence and oppression of the aristocratic Democrats of the South." He could see nothing in the Jeffersonian policies but "innovations which threaten the subversion of the Constitution, and the prostration of every barrier erected by it for the protection of the *best*."[22] The unity and congeniality of the New England states together with New York and New Jersey was contrasted with the designing and dominant slave states which now had the political advantage over the other members of the union. Leaders of the Federalist party appealed to Aaron Burr to carry out their plans and aimed, by securing his election as governor of New York, to unite the states of the north against those of the south. Pickering thought this extreme measure essential, for, said he: "I have no hesitation myself in saying, that there can be no safety for the Northern States without a separation from the Confederacy."[23] Hamilton, however, discouraged his New England party associates by writing that "dismemberment of our empire will be a clear sacrifice of great positive advantages, without any counterbalancing good; administering no relief to our real disease, which is Democracy."[24] The plot of the Federalists with Aaron Burr to aid his candidacy for governor with the understanding that he should lead the secession movement failed because of Burr's defeat and was the immediate cause of the duel which led to Hamilton's death.

The strongest opposition to the Embargo Acts was expressed in Massachusetts and the other New England states.[25] Doctrines similar to those embodied in the Kentucky and Virginia Resolutions were approved by the Massachusetts legislature when Louisiana was admitted into the union as a state. The power of Congress to admit states in territories acquired beyond the limits of the original United States was declared to be "nothing less than the power to create in foreign countries, new po-

---

[21] "Timothy Pickering was the fanatic of the Federal party. With him, politics and religion seemed one and the same thing—a struggle between Good which must be defended, and Evil which must be crushed. The social structure of eighteenth-century New England and the principles of Federalism were the Good; French philosophy and Democracy the Evil." Cf. Morison, *op. cit.*, I: 183.

[22] Adams, *op. cit.*, pp. 338, 339.

[23] Adams, *op. cit.*, p. 356.

[24] *Ibid.*, p. 365. Quoted from the last political letter written by Hamilton. Calling attention to the Tenth Amendment, however, Pickering asked, "How are the powers reserved to the States respectively, or to the people, to be maintained, *but by the respective States judging for themselves and putting their negative on the usurpations of the general government.*" Thus Pickering approved the underlying principles of the Kentucky and Virginia Resolutions.

[25] See Sears, *op. cit.*, chap. vi.

litical sovereignties, and to divest the old United States of a proportion of their political sovereignty, in favor of such foreigner. It is a power, which, in the opinion of your Committee, no wise people ever would have delegated, and which they are persuaded, the people of the United States, and certainly, the people of Massachusetts, never did delegate."[26] The act admitting Louisiana was characterized as a usurpation of a power not granted to Congress by the federal Constitution.[27] My father, wrote William Plumer, Jr., regarded the treaty acquiring Louisiana "as a virtual dissolution of the Union, and held that it was optional with any of the old States to say whether they would longer remain in the present Confederacy, or form new ones more to their liking."[28] But the resentment against the measures employed to carry into effect the embargo policy and the declaration of war against England brought matters to a crisis.

Theophilus Parsons, the chief justice of the supreme court of Massachusetts, insisted that the Embargo Acts were unconstitutional.[29] Having failed to secure redress from Congress, the Massachusetts protestants against the enforcement of the Embargo Acts turned to the state legislature. In what were known as "patriotic proceedings" the legislature on January 9, 1809, declared the Force Act, which was designed to render more effective the administration of the Embargo Acts, "unjust, oppressive, and unconstitutional, and not legally binding on the citizens of this State." But the people were advised to abstain from forcible resistance. And it was resolved that the commonwealth will "zealously cooperate with any of the other States, in all legal and constitutional measures, for procuring such amendments to the Constitution of the United States, as shall be judged necessary to obtain protection and defence for commerce, and to give to the commercial States their fair and just considera-

---

[26] Resolves of Massachusetts on the Extension of Territorial Limits, June 16, 1813. On the Louisiana Purchase, John Taylor of Caroline admitted that "the treaty was a violation of the Constitution, but declared that he would ratify it, and throw himself on the people for pardon, and on Heaven to absolve him from the violation of a trust he had sworn to maintain." Plumer, op. cit., p. 262. For Jefferson's views on the Louisiana Purchase, see above, pp. 209 ff.

[27] See Resolves of Massachusetts (1812–15), pp. 310–318; also Niles' Register, IV: 285–287. In the argument over the third article of the treaty with France providing for the purchase of Louisiana, Timothy Pickering contended that, so far as the treaty provided for the admission of new states to the union to be carved out of the newly acquired territory, it was unconstitutional. The addition of such new states to the union, Pickering maintained, could not be validated by the President and Congress nor by an amendment to the Constitution. The assent of every state was declared to be necessary to add such foreign territory to the union. McMaster, op. cit., III: 8.

[28] Plumer, op. cit., p. 265.

[29] The Writings of John Quincy Adams, ed. by W. C. Ford (New York, 1913–1917), III, Nov. 17, 1808.

tion in the government of the Union; and for affording permanent security, as well as present relief, from the oppressive measures under which they now suffer."

Had the embargo remained after March, 1809, notes Morison, "there is every probability that Massachusetts would have called a New England or Northern convention with the object of securing a concerted nullification of the embargo by the disaffected States, and amendments to the Constitution protecting commercial interests in the future."[30] Delaware also protested that the Force Act was "an invasion of the liberty of the people, and the constitutional sovereignty of the state governments."[31] And Rhode Island again reaffirmed the doctrine of state sovereignty.

Governor Trumbull in a message to the Rhode Island legislature said: "Whenever our national legislature is led to overleap the prescribed bounds of their constitutional powers, on the state legislatures, in great emergencies, devolves the arduous task—it is their right—it becomes their duty, to interpose their protecting shield between the right and liberty of the people, and the assumed power of the general government."[32] The legislature approved the conduct of the governor in declining to designate persons to aid in carrying the Embargo Acts into effect and lauded this action "as an example to persons, who may hold places of distinguished trust, in this free and independent republic." It was regarded as a "paramount public duty to assert the unquestionable right of this State to abstain from any agency in the execution of measures, which are unconstitutional and despotic." The doctrine of the Kentucky and Virginia Resolutions was reaffirmed when the legislature adopted a resolution containing the provision "that the people of this State, as one of the parties to the federal compact, have a right to express their sense of any violation of its provisions and that it is the duty of this general assembly as the organ of their sentiments and the depository of their authority, to interpose for the purpose of protecting them from the ruinous inflections of usurped and unconstitutional power."[33]

The clause to which special exception was taken empowered the President to employ the land and naval forces of the United States as well as

---

[30] Otis, op. cit., II: 81. See proposals for a similar convention by Gouverneur Morris of New York, Morison, op. cit., pp. 82 ff. To the end of the war Morris continued to urge secession in letters to Otis, Rufus King, and others, and he was disgusted at the moderation of the Hartford Convention.

[31] Herman V. Ames, State Documents on Federal Relations (Philadelphia, 1906), p. 37.

[32] From message of Governor Trumbull, Feb. 23, 1809, American Register, 1809, pt. ii, p. 177, and Ames, op. cit., p. 40.

[33] Ames, op. cit., pp. 43, 44.

the state militia to enforce the provisions of the Embargo Act and to prevent or suppress "any armed or riotous assemblage of persons resisting the custom-house officers in the exercise of their duties, or in any manner opposing the execution of the laws laying an embargo." The proposal to use the state militia to aid in the enforcement of the Embargo Acts aroused the ire of New England Federalists. An opinion was sought from the judges of the supreme court of Massachusetts whether the governors of the states had a right to determine when such an exigency existed as to require them, at the request of the President, to place the militia in the service of the United States. The judges replied that no power was given either to the President or to Congress, and, since the power was not delegated to the United States by the federal Constitution, nor prohibited by it to the states, it was reserved to the states.[34] Connecticut also objected to the use of the militia by the President of the United States. Claiming that the state of Connecticut "is a *free, sovereign* and *independent* State; that the United States are a *Confederacy* of States; that we are a confederated and not a consolidated Republic," the legislature asserted that "it would be not only the height of injustice to the militia, to be ordered into the service of the United States, to do such duty, but a violation of the Constitution and laws of this State, and of the United States."[35] At the same time that Governor Griswold declined to place the state militia under the command of a federal army officer, the Connecticut legislature authorized the raising of an army to defend the state. "We spurn the idea," declared the Massachusetts legislature, "that the free, sovereign and independent State of Massachusetts is reduced to a mere municipal corporation, without power to protect its people, and to defend them from oppression, from whatever quarter it comes. Whenever the national compact is violated, and the citizens of this State are oppressed by cruel and unauthorized laws, this legislature is bound to interpose its power, and wrest from the oppressor his victim."[36]

Madison informed Congress that the refusal to turn the state militia over to the army of the United States was founded on "a novel and unfortunate exposition of the provisions of the Constitution relating to the militia" and that such an interpretation meant that there was not "one Nation for the purpose most of all requiring it." The views of Madison were later sustained by a decision of the Supreme Court. Justice

---

[34] 13th Cong., 3d sess., Senate Doc., Feb. 28, 1815, pp. 278–281.

[35] *Niles' Register*, III: 23.

[36] The General Court of Massachusetts on the Embargo, Feb. 22, 1814. *Legislative Documents, 1807–14, No. 19*, pp. 381–392; also *Niles' Register*, VI: 7.

Story, speaking for the Court, maintained that "the authority to decide whether the exigency [of calling out the militia] has arisen belongs exclusively to the President, and that his decision is conclusive upon all other persons."[37] But for the time being the authority of the national government was being successfully defied.

STEPS LEADING TOWARD NULLIFICATION AND SECESSION

New England refused to give financial support to "Mr. Madison's War," as it was called. Though the larger part of the fluid capital of the country was in the New England states, they subscribed less than three million dollars to loans, whereas the middle states subscribed thirty-five millions. And what was more reprehensible, Babcock notes, than that "the moneyed interests of the east were not content with passive resistance, they bought British drafts at a discount with specie sent to Canada; they supplied beef to the British armies in Canada, and furnished subsistence to British fleets off the eastern coasts—all for highly profitable considerations."[38]

The passage of an act of Congress in April, 1812, admitting Louisiana to the union as a state called forth strong disunion sentiments. Josiah Quincy of Massachusetts, in the debate on the bill to admit Louisiana into the union, set forth the position which the New England Federalists were to make a part of their creed until the end of the War of 1812. "If this bill passes," said Quincy, "it is my deliberate opinion that it is virtually a dissolution of the Union; that it will free the States from their moral obligation; and as it will be the right of all so it will be the duty of some, definitely to prepare for a separation,—amicably if they can, violently if they must."[39] The Speaker declared this language disorderly, but the House overruled the Speaker. A committee of the Massachusetts legislature on June 4, 1813, presented a report relating to the extension of territorial limits and the formation of new states within the territorial limits of the United States. The committee declared that "on occasions of this kind the duty of a people is as plain, as it is imperious. The beginnings of manifest usurpations are never to be neglected; since silence, on the part of the people is, always, taken as an acquiescence by the advocates of usurpation. What power seizes, without right, today, it holds tomorrow by precedent; and the day after by prescription." The act of April 8, 1812, admitting Louisiana to the union as a state was condemned as "a manifest usurpation by the Congress of the United

---

[37] See James D. Richardson, *A Compilation of the Messages and Papers of the Presidents* (Washington, 1911), I: 516, and Martin v. Mott, 12 Wheaton 19, 30 (1827).

[38] *The Rise of American Nationality*, p. 158.

[39] *Annals*, 11th Cong., 2d sess., p. 524.

States of a power not granted to that body by the federal Constitution."
Congress was denied this authority, in the opinion of the committee,
because Louisiana was formed out of territory situated beyond the limits
of the original United States. The power assumed by Congress in this
instance, "if acquiesced in, is plainly a power to admit new States into
this Union at their discretion, without limit of place or country." And
no such power is deemed to be granted by the Constitution, because such
authority was neither considered nor contemplated by the framers of
the Constitution.

The effect of the creation of new states in what was formerly foreign
country was thought to be particularly alarming because it involved not
only the establishment of new political sovereignties in this territory,
but also the original states were divested of a part of their political sovereignty. These new states, it was feared, might become "one of the destinies of the Nation." In the resolutions proposed by the committee, the
act of Congress was declared not merely to be unauthorized by the constitution, but also to be "a measure tending to the dissolution of the
Confederacy."[40]

There were frequent expressions of opinion in the public press that
the federal Constitution is nothing more than a treaty between independent sovereignties and that the Constitution was formed as a result
of a compact among the states and that it is for the states to decide
whether the terms of the compact have been violated. If the terms of the
compact were violated, its validity was annihilated and the parties to it
were released from their obligations.[41] The possibility of secession was
broached as early as April, 1813, in a letter from Gouverneur Morris to

[40] *Niles' Register*, IV: 285–287. See especially the efforts of Gouverneur Morris and
others in the federal Convention to maintain the control and the predominance of the
commercial and propertied interests of the Atlantic seaboard. Morris wished to limit
the authority of Congress to admit new states, and, failing to secure an express provision to this effect, he maintained that the clause "new states may be admitted by the
Congress into this Union" did not grant authority to Congress to admit as a new state,
territory which did not belong to the United States when the Constitution was made.
Max Farrand, "Compromises of the Constitution," *Amer. Hist. Rev.* (Apr., 1904), IX:
483, 484.

[41] Frank Maloy Anderson, "A Forgotten Phase of the New England Opposition to
the War of 1812," *Proceedings*, Mississippi Valley Hist. Soc. (1913), VI: 176 ff. The
compact theory in the formation of the union was forcefully defended by the Federalist, Roger Griswold of Connecticut. "The Union of the States," said Griswold, "is
formed on the principle of a co-partnership, and it would be absurd to suppose that
the agents of the parties, the general government, who have been appointed to execute
the business of the compact, in behalf of the principals, the States, could admit a new
partner, without the consent of the parties themselves. The treaty for the acquisition
of Louisiana, therefore, so far as it stipulates for such an incorporation, is void."
Plumer, *op. cit.*, p. 263.

Harrison Gray Otis in which the question was raised whether it was for the interest or the happiness of the "Northern and Eastern States to continue in Union with the owners of slaves."[42]

In February, 1814, the Massachusetts house of representatives favored the passage of laws designed to nullify the Embargo Acts and suggested the calling of a convention to secure amendments to the Constitution which would protect the citizens of the northern states against similar abuses of power. Eight months later the Massachusetts legislature adopted a resolution providing for the appointment of delegates to confer with the representatives of other New England states on the best means of conserving their resources and on ways and means to secure a convention of delegates from all the United States to revise the federal Constitution.[43] Representatives from five states met at Hartford, Connecticut. Among the resolutions adopted by the Hartford Convention were the following:

> Resolved, That the following amendments of the Constitution of the United States, be recommended to the States represented as aforesaid, to be proposed by them for adoption by the state legislatures, and in such cases as may be deemed expedient, by a convention chosen by the people of each State.
>
> And it is further recommended, that the said States shall persevere in their efforts to obtain such amendments, until the same shall be effected.
>
> First. Representatives and direct taxes shall be apportioned among the several States which may be included within this Union, according to their respective numbers of free persons, including those bound to serve for a term of years, and excluding Indians not taxed, and all other persons.
>
> Second. No new State shall be admitted into the Union by Congress in virtue of the power granted by the Constitution, without the concurrence of two-thirds of both Houses.
>
> Third. Congress shall not have power to lay any embargo on the ships or vessels of the citizens of the United States, in the ports or harbors thereof, for more than sixty days.
>
> Fourth. Congress shall not have power, without the concurrence of two-thirds of

---

[42] Morison, op. cit., II: 84; also Edward Channing, A History of the United States (New York, 1926), IV: 559 ff. See letter of Otis to Josiah Quincy, Dec. 15, 1808, suggesting the calling of a convention in Hartford, "for the purpose of providing some mode of relief that may not be inconsistent with the union of these States, to which we should adhere as long as possible." As a result of this letter, Otis is credited with originating the scheme of the Hartford Convention, though Morison believes the idea may properly be attributed to Timothy Pickering. Harrison Gray Otis, II: 4–6.

[43] Prior to the call of the Hartford Convention a circular letter had been sent to the selectmen of certain towns in New England inviting them to consider whether a convention of the commercial states should be called to procure "such alterations in the federal Constitution as will give to the Northern States a due proportion of representation, and secure them from the future exercise of powers injurious to their commercial interests." See A Letter of Noah Webster to Daniel Webster, Sept. 6, 1834; reprinted in Amer. Hist. Rev. (Oct., 1903), IX: 102.

both Houses, to interdict the commercial intercourse between the United States and any foreign nation or the dependencies thereof.

Fifth. Congress shall not make or declare war, or authorize acts of hostility against any foreign nation, without the concurrence of two-thirds of both Houses, except such acts of hostility be in defence of the territories of the United States, when actually invaded.

Sixth. No person who shall hereafter be naturalized, shall be eligible as a member of the Senate or House of Representatives of the United States, nor capable of holding any civil office under the authority of the United States.

Seventh. The same person shall not be elected President of the United States a second time; nor shall the President be elected from the same State two terms in succession.

Resolved, That if the application of these States to the government of the United States, recommended in a foregoing Resolution, should be unsuccessful, and peace should not be concluded, and the defence of these States should be neglected, as it has been since the commencement of the war, it will in the opinion of the Convention be expedient for the legislatures of the several States to appoint delegates to another Convention, to meet at Boston, in the State of Massachusetts, on the third Thursday of June next, with such powers and instructions as the exigency of a crisis so momentous may require.[44]

These amendments were endorsed by the legislatures of Connecticut and Massachusetts but were disapproved by the legislatures of nine states. The legislature of New Jersey declared that:

The favorite master principle pervading all the propositions in question, is to reduce within a narrower sphere the power and influence of the general government, and thereby to weaken its arm, at a time when, above all others, it requires to be strengthened. Their obvious tendency also is, to throw amongst the States of the Union the apple of discord—to increase those jealousies and suspicions, which have been already too far excited, and to give new life, activity and nurture to those seeds of dissension and disunion which have been recently sown with an unsparing hand by insidious combinations and associations, all of them professing to promote the general good, but acting in direct opposition to their professions.

And the legislature of New York conceived it to be their duty, in the language of Washington, to "frown indignantly upon the first dawning of every attempt to alienate any portion of our country from the rest, or to enfeeble the sacred ties which now holds together the various parts."[45]

In the opinion of Morison, the "New England Federalists did everything short of actual treason to bring disaster on their own flag; hoping by this means Madison would be forced to a speedy peace, and trusting 'British magnanimity' to prevent the peace from being disastrous."[46] But K. C. Babcock maintains that the conduct of the New England Federalists from 1812 to 1815 "was marked by a fine Puritan consistency and resourcefulness."[47]

---

[44] Ames, *op. cit.*, pp. 84, 85.
[45] *Ibid.*, pp. 86, 87, and *Niles' Register*, VII: 313.
[46] Otis, *op. cit.*, II: 53.
[47] *The Rise of American Nationality*, p. 150.

When the committee of the Hartford Convention came to Washington to negotiate with the national government regarding the above resolutions and proposals, the news of peace changed the whole situation and the committee returned "amid the jeers of Republicans and the reproaches of conservative Federalists." With the signing of the treaty of peace, the cause of the union was greatly strengthened and the Federalist party, unable to disassociate itself from the odium cast upon it by the participation of its leaders in the Hartford Convention, gradually declined in importance and prestige. Henceforth the party ceased to be a potent factor in national affairs.

The report of the Hartford Convention, which Morison thinks should take a high rank among American state papers, was "an attempt both to satisfy enraged New England, and to persuade or frighten the rest of the country into bringing the war to a close, and treating New England more justly in the future." Moreover, the work of this convention must be considered in the light of the well-known historical facts that the statesmen of all parties in the ante-bellum period at some time regarded secession as a measure of ultimate resort against sectional oppression.[48]

Timothy Pickering, who had for years been plotting for the secession of the New England states and who was trying to enlist the coöperation of England in carrying out his designs, sent his vitriolic speeches against the Administration's embargo policy to John Marshall. Commending him for his excellent speeches, Marshall thought that "if sound argument and correct reasoning could save the country it would be saved. Nothing can be more completely demonstrated than the inefficacy of the embargo, yet that demonstration seems to be of no avail. I fear most seriously that the same spirit which so tenaciously maintains this measure will impel us to a war with the only power which protects any part of the civilized world from the despotism of that tyrant with whom we shall then be ravaged."[49]

Marshall shared with the New England Federalists the feeling and resentment against President Madison and the Republican Administration for declaring war against England. In a letter to Robert Smith, who had been dismissed as Secretary of State by Madison and was trying to vindicate himself, Marshall joined the disloyal Federalists in calling on

---

[48] *Harrison Gray Otis*, II: 156, 158. To the *Richmond Enquirer*, which later led the movement for the assertion of state sovereignty, the proposals of the New England Federalists for nullification or secession were treasonable and it recommended that the leaders of the movement be treated as traitors. See issues for Nov. 1, 19, 1814. For a similar opinion by John Quincy Adams, see *Otis, op. cit.*, pp. 79, 80.

[49] Letter of Marshall to Pickering, Dec. 19, 1808, Pickering MSS, *Mass. Hist. Soc.* Marshall and Pickering apparently held frequent conferences. Albert J. Beveridge, *The Life of John Marshall* (Boston, 1919), IV: 14 ff.

peace advocates and British partisans to combine to end the war by overthrowing the Administration.[50] At this time Federalist politicians were urging Marshall to assume the leadership of the party and to become a candidate for President. In correspondence with Pickering and other Federalists, Marshall gave his sanction to and aided the anti-Administration measures designed to oppose and interfere with the conduct of the war. When the Administration defended the doctrine of free and unrestricted expatriation, it was answered by the Federalist John Lowell in an argument warmly commended by Marshall.[51] "Thus the record shows," says Beveridge, "that John Marshall was as bitterly opposed to the War of 1812 as was Pickering or Otis or Lowell. So entirely had he become one of the 'aristocracy of talents, of reputation, and of property,' as Plumer, in 1804, had so accurately styled the class of which he himself was then a member, that Marshall looked upon all but one subject then before the people with the eyes of confirmed reaction. That subject was nationalism."[52] But to many Republicans, Marshall's views on nationalism were also an indication of undue conservatism, for they ran counter to the frequently expressed public will of the people of most of the states.

The signing of the treaty of peace with England and the establishment of normal conditions throughout the country brought an end to the designs and procedure of the New England Federalists to dissolve the union and to take steps to form a new confederacy. But as we shall see, the nationalistic theories and principles of the Federalist party were destined to survive and, under Marshall's direction, to acquire new vitality and force.

Despite the opposition of Jefferson and Madison to the exercise of common law jurisdiction by the federal courts—a view in which Justice Johnson concurred—a number of criminal indictments were sustained in the federal courts from 1803 to 1809.[53] A group of these indictments were directed against Federalists in Connecticut for libels on President Jefferson. As soon as the indictments were brought to the attention of Jefferson, he ordered the dismissal of the charges, but not in time to prevent some partisan attacks in Congress.[54] One of these cases was finally brought to the Supreme Court. As the members of both the Federalist

---

[50] *The Life of John Marshall* (Boston, 1919), IV: 34–36.

[51] *Ibid.*, p. 54.

[52] Beveridge, *op. cit.*, IV: 55.

[53] See Charles Warren, *The Supreme Court in United States History* (Boston, 1922), I: 435.

[54] See *Annals*, 9th Cong., 2d sess., p. 247; 10th Cong., 2d sess., Feb. 2, 1809, p. 1303; and 11th Cong., 1st sess., May 25, 1809, p. 74.

and Republican parties now opposed the exercise of such jurisdiction by the federal courts, attorneys declined to argue the case.

Hence the sequel of the prolonged controversy whether the inferior federal courts could exercise a type of common law jurisdiction, especially in matters of a criminal nature, was presented to the Supreme Court without argument in the case of *United States v. Hudson and Goodwin*.[55] On an indictment for libel brought against the publishers of the *Connecticut Courant* for charging the President and Congress with having voted in secret two million dollars as a present to Napoleon Bonaparte for leave to make a treaty with Spain, the Judges of the Circuit Court were divided on the question whether the Circuit Court had common law jurisdiction in cases of libel. Justice Johnson, rendering judgment for the Supreme Court, said that:

Although this question is brought up now for the first time to be decided by this Court, we consider it as having been long since settled in public opinion. In no other case for many years has this jurisdiction been asserted; and the general acquiescence of legal men shows the prevalence of opinion in favor of the negative of the proposition.... Certain implied powers must necessarily result to our courts of justice from the nature of their institution. But jurisdiction of crimes against the State is not among those powers. To fine for contempt—imprison for contumacy—inforce the observance of order, etc., are powers which cannot be dispensed with in a court, because they are necessary to the exercise of all others; and so far our courts no doubt possess powers not immediately derived from statutes; but all exercise of criminal law cases we are of opinion is not within their implied powers.[56]

Evidently for reasons of politics and expediency the Justices deemed it no longer good policy to insist upon general and extensive powers as belonging to the federal courts under common law principles and practices.

The decision that there was no common law jurisdiction in the federal courts was, however, thought by some of the Judges and political leaders to be unwise. John Quincy Adams believed that it not only crippled the powers of the Judiciary but also of all the departments of the national government. And when resistance to federal authority was generally espoused by the Federalists of New England, Justice Story urged Con-

---

[55] 7 Cranch 32 (1812); see also United States v. Coolidge, 1 Wheaton 415 (1816), wherein it was held that the Court would not review its decision in the *Hudson Case* because counsel declined to argue the cause. Chief Justice Marshall anticipated this decision by his comment in 1811 that: "I am decidedly of opinion that the jurisdiction of the Courts of the United States depends, exclusively, on the Constitution and laws of the United States." Livingston v. Jefferson, 1 Brockenbrough 211 (1811). In this case he expressed regret that Livingston had rights for which on jurisdictional grounds there was no remedy. Had the law not been so clearly to the contrary nothing would have pleased the Chief Justice more than to have rendered a decision which would have embarrassed and perhaps financially ruined his arch political opponent, Jefferson.

[56] *Ibid.*, pp. 32, 33.

gress to grant the federal courts authority to punish all crimes and offenses against the government at common law. He thought conspiracies to destroy the union should not be permitted to be formed without any laws to punish them.[57] Story continued his efforts to secure what he deemed to be necessary legislation to meet the situation caused by the Hudson decision. A bill drafted by him and approved by all of the Justices except Johnson was intended to give jurisdiction to the Circuit Courts in all cases in law and equity arising under the Constitution, the laws of the United States, and under treaties made under its authority. But Congress did not heed Story's warnings and the bill failed to pass. In 1825, however, another act drafted by Story and supported by Daniel Webster gave to the federal courts some of the jurisdiction over crimes which Story thought they should be permitted to exercise.[58]

The War of 1812 marked a great change in American political ideas and alignments. Hitherto statesmen had looked to Europe, and the destinies of America seemed to be inextricably intertwined with the alliances, wars, and diplomacy of the great European nations. Now statesmen began to turn their attention to the West and the frontier. And it was the consciousness of nationality which was the chief political result of the war. The Republicans had come into power emphasizing democratic principles, State rights, and a strict construction of the Constitution. But fourteen years of practical administration had required a number of deviations from the principles of 1801. Most of these deviations, such as the purchase of Louisiana, the embargo, and the seizure of West Florida, tended in the direction of nationalism. By 1815 the party had absorbed some of the Federalist principles, and nationalism and democracy were to develop together—with nationalism, however, in the ascendancy. It was the Supreme Court, however, that was to become the champion of some of the fundamental principles of the Federalist party. Two of the foremost of these principles were the necessity of protecting property rights and contractual obligations from what were deemed to be unreasonable interferences by state legislation, and the subordination of the rights and privileges of the states to the authority of the national government, so far as it was considered necessary to carry out national policies. Decisions of the Supreme Court gave effective sanction and significance to the carrying out of these principles as part of the program of the national government. Though the most important decisions up-

---

[57] *Life and Letters of Joseph Story*, ed. by William W. Story (Boston, 1851), I: 243 ff. "In my opinion," wrote Story, "the government will be completely prostrated unless they give jurisdiction to their courts and a common law authority to punish crimes against the United States." 7 Cranch 247.

[58] 4 *U. S. Statutes at Large* 115.

holding the policy of nationalism were rendered by the Supreme Court
after 1815, one of the far-reaching precedents tending to favor the protection of vested rights was announced at the beginning of the Administration of James Madison. Like *Marbury v. Madison,* the case of *Fletcher
v. Peck*—because it involved an attempt to settle a question involving
serious political issues—became the object of partisan criticisms and de-
nunciations.

THE CASE OF FLETCHER V. PECK

During the 1810 term of the Court an important case was decided. In
fact, it ranks as one of the foremost constitutional pronouncements of
Chief Justice Marshall. It was the first case involving an interpretation
of the contract clause of the federal Constitution[59] and it arose out of one
of the largest and most extensive land frauds perpetrated during the
early years of the American republic. The title to a large part of the
territory now comprised in the states of Alabama and Mississippi was at
stake in the controversy. Ownership and control over this territory was
very uncertain. Spain had not relinquished her claim of sovereignty over
this section; much of the land included in the grants made by the state
of Georgia belonged to the Indians and their rights and authority remained to be determined; and the United States also insisted on its
sovereignty and control over the disputed area. In this condition of uncertainty Georgia undertook in 1789 to sell a large part of this section
to three land companies known as the South Carolina, Virginia, and
Tennessee Yazoo companies. From the long and notorious series of transactions involved in the sale of these lands the proceedings have come to
be designated the "Yazoo Frauds." This attempt to sell the lands was
unsuccessful, owing to the failure of the companies to pay the price in
currency demanded by the state.[60] A suit against the state for refusal to
transfer title in accordance with the terms of the grant was dismissed for
lack of jurisdiction after the adoption of the Eleventh Amendment to
the federal Constitution.

Six years later a group of land companies, by means of wholesale bribery in which it was found every member of the legislature but one participated,[61] secured a legislative grant for more extensive tracts of land.
Many prominent men were interested in the grant. Among these were

[59] No state shall pass any "law impairing the obligation of contracts," Art. I, sec. 10.

[60] President Washington took a vigorous and decisive stand against the first Yazoo
sale by forbidding intrusions on the Indian lands under any claims by the Yazoo purchasers or other persons.

[61] See statement of Absalom H. Chappell, *Miscellanies of Georgia* (Atlanta, 1874),
p. 91, and William Cabell Bruce, *John Randolph of Roanoke, 1773–1833* (New York,
1922), I: 180 ff.

Wade Hampton of South Carolina, District Judge Nathaniel Pendleton, and Associate Justice of the Supreme Court James Wilson,[62] who had $25,000 to invest. Robert Goodloe Harper of Baltimore and Robert Morris of Philadelphia were also reputed to be interested. Judge William Smith of Georgia received $13,000 for his services as lobbyist. But General James Gunn, senator-elect from Georgia, appeared to be in charge of the proceedings to secure the passage of the bill and was prepared to use any measures necessary to attain his object. A veto by the governor of the first bill to make a grant to the interested land companies did not discourage Senator Gunn and a second bill was passed and approved.

The law was responsible for the disposal of more than thirty-five million acres of fertile, well-watered, heavily wooded land at less than one and one-half cents an acre.[63] The purchasers were four land companies named The Georgia Company, The Georgia Mississippi Company, The Tennessee Company, and The Upper Mississippi Company. The total purchase price was five hundred thousand dollars in specie or approved currency. On the day of the passage of the law, The Georgia Company sold eleven million acres of land, the sale yielding a net profit of about a million dollars. Despite the fraudulent aspects of the transaction, the sale of lands may be considered for a number of reasons advantageous to the state. In the first place, the title to these tracts was disputed by Spain, by the Indian tribes, and by the federal government. In 1797 a Senate committee had rendered an adverse report on Georgia's claims.[64] And, second, the measure was designed to relieve the pressure on the frontier, to encourage settlement, to open up the back country, with which, owing to the unfriendliness of Indians, the state was unable to very well cope, and to provide some funds for the state government as well.

William H. Crawford, who presented a petition to the governor to veto the second bill, and Senator James Jackson undertook to arouse the people of Georgia. Public resentment against the legislators who voted for the grant—all but one of whom had shares of stock in the purchasing companies—was intense. A newly elected legislature quickly repealed the obnoxious law. In a long and clumsily drawn measure the sovereign rights and independent authority of the states were asserted and the

[62] Though the evidence does not appear to implicate Wilson in the corrupt proceedings to secure the passage of the act, his presence in Georgia at the time with a considerable sum of money to engage in the speculative venture and his purchase of a large amount of the lands in dispute—approximately 750,000 acres—may be considered "a grave blemish on his character." See Horace H. Hagan, "Fletcher v. Peck," 16 *Georgetown Law Jour.* (Nov., 1927), 3.

[63] Charles H. Haskins, "The Yazoo Land Companies," Amer. Hist. Assn., *Papers* (1891), pp. 395, 416 ff.

[64] *American State Papers, Public Lands,* I: 79, 80.

"atrocious peculation, corruption, and collusion by which the said usurped act and grants were obtained" were severely condemned. The previous act was therefore "declared null and void; and the grants, right or rights, claim or claims, issuing, deduced, or derived therefrom, or from any clause, letter, or spirit of the same is hereby annulled, rendered void and of no effect; and, as the same was made without constitutional authority, and fraudulently obtained, it is hereby declared of no binding force, or effect, on this State, or the people thereof."[65] To dramatize the proceedings the previous act was publicly burned on the Statehouse steps.[66]

The land companies refused to accept as final the Rescinding Act and continued to sell stock, though the governments of both Georgia and the United States proceeded as if this act restored the status existing prior to January, 1795. Speculation in Georgia lands became popular despite the reputed fraudulent character of the original grant. Pamphlets were issued for and against the validity of the grant.

While Georgia was repealing her fraudulently secured grant, the agents of the land companies were hastily disposing of their lands to so-called "innocent purchasers" and, more frequently no doubt, to those who were familiar with the fraudulent methods used. Speculation was rife in New England, especially in Boston, where millions of acres were purchased netting inordinate returns to the speculators. On the passage of the Rescinding Act, the New England–Mississippi Company was formed to protect the interests of the "innocent purchasers." It was this company which secured an opinion from Alexander Hamilton on the validity of the titles of the land companies. In his opinion the Rescinding Act was invalid because it violated the contract clause of the Constitution. "Every grant," said Hamilton, "whether from a State or an individual, is virtually a contract." He thought the Rescinding Act void and advised that "the courts of the United States ... will be likely to pronounce it so."[67]

Robert Goodloe Harper, an attorney for several of the land companies, also prepared an argument denying the authority of the state of Georgia to repeal the grant made to the companies. "The force, validity, or meaning of a legislative act," he maintained, "is purely a judicial question,

<hr />

[65] *American State Papers, Public Lands,* I:156–158.

[66] For an interesting account of the enactment of the Repealing Act and subsequent proceedings, see Beveridge, *op. cit.,* III: 546 ff., and Bruce, *op. cit.,* pp. 183 ff.

[67] Beveridge, *op. cit.,* III: 569. The nationalist attitude of Chief Justice Marshall, says Phillips, was well known and "his action could be foretold regarding the claims, if any litigation should bring them within his province," "Georgia and State Rights," **Amer. Hist. Assn.,** *Reports,* 1901, II: 36.

and altogether beyond the province of the legislature. It is the province of the legislative power to make laws, to give them their existence; but to expound and enforce them, belongs to the judiciary. . . . This is a fundamental principle of all our constitutions which declare, that the judicial and legislative powers shall be distinct and separate. It results also from the very existence of a written constitution; which, by its necessary operation, prescribes limits to the legislative body, and confides the protection and maintenance of those limits, to the judicial power." Because the sales of land to the four companies was a contract for valuable consideration and was carried into execution, it was declared to be an "unvariable maxim of law, and of natural justice, that one of the parties to a contract cannot by his own act, exempt himself, from its obligation." This principle is held to apply to governments as well as to individuals and, therefore, the repealing of the act by Georgia could have no legal effect. Harper also contended that "a legislative act can never be invalidated on account of the motives from which it may have been agreed to by individual members of a legislative chamber." "If motives could be inquired into," said he, "the very foundations of legislative authority would be shaken." No mention was made in Harper's argument of the contract clause as a basis for declaring Georgia's Repealing Act void.[68]

During the time that the validity of the act granting title to the lands and Georgia's effort to repeal its grant were being extensively debated and the speculators were busily engaged in disposing of as much of their grants as possible, a proposal was made in Congress for the appointment of commissioners to settle the disputes between Georgia and the government and to secure, if possible, the cession of the lands to the nation.

Three members of the cabinet, James Madison, Albert Gallatin, and Levi Lincoln, presented a report on the basis of which Congress passed a law with the proviso that Georgia cede her rights over the disputed territory to the United States for $1,250,000. Five million acres were reserved to constitute a fund from which indemnity should be paid to those who had bona fide claims upon the lands which could not otherwise be adjusted. As to the payment of the claims of the various Yazoo companies and those who had purchased from them, the commissioners thought their claims inadmissible and reported that "without pretending to affirm that the legislature of the State of Georgia was competent to make the decision, they feel no hesitation in declaring it as their opinion, that, under the circumstances which may affect the case, as they

---

[68] Robert Goodloe Harper, "The Case of the Georgia Sales on the Mississippi Considered with a Reference to Law Authorities and Public Acts," *Amer. Law Jour.* (1814), V: 354, 394 ff.

have come within their knowledge, and as herein stated, the title of the claimants cannot be supported."[69] But they nevertheless believed that the interest of the United States, the tranquillity of those who might hereafter inhabit the territory, and various equitable considerations which might be urged in favor of most of the present claimants rendered it expedient to enter into a compromise on reasonable terms. To accomplish the purpose proposed involving "the expenditure of five million dollars from the sale of the reserved five million acres," the commissioners were authorized by Congress, in providing for the disposal of the lands ceded by Georgia, to investigate and report upon the claims of individuals and companies within the ceded territory.[70] In accordance with the acts of Congress and agreements entered into with the state of Georgia, title to the lands covered by the grants of 1795 and of April, 1802, became vested in the United States.

When the bill came before Congress to carry out the recommendations of the commissioners regarding the Yazoo claimants, John Randolph, who had been in Georgia while the corrupt proceedings of the legislature of 1795 were under consideration, offered a resolution that no part of the five million acres reserved for satisfying and quieting claims should be used to compensate any claims derived from the act of 1795.[71] Randolph argued that a subsequent legislature had an undoubted right both legally and constitutionally to repeal the 1795 act and that there was no provision in the federal or state constitutions to interfere with such action. Despite the able arguments of the agents of the Yazoo companies and the lobbying of the Postmaster General, Gideon Granger, who sponsored the cause of the New England–Mississippi Company, Randolph prevented the enactment of the bill to compromise with the Yazoo claimants.[72]

Randolph contended that Georgia had no right to make the sale; and that even if she had, the contract being laid in corruption and fraud, was null and void, *ab initio*. Consequently, the question of notice to innocent purchasers, provided there were any persons totally ignorant of the fraud, was not material to the question of title in the hands of third persons. He further held that because the original grant was obtained

---

[69] *American State Papers, Public Lands*, I: 134.

[70] 2 *U. S. Statutes at Large* 229 ff.

[71] Randolph attempted to discredit Madison for his joining in the report to Congress because he believed he had forfeited his claim to public esteem by recommending a shameful bargain with unprincipled speculators.

[72] See *Annals*, 8th Cong., 2d sess., p. 1024. Randolph claimed that the plot to swindle Georgia out of her lands was planned in Philadelphia, New York, and Boston, and that the funds by which it was effected were largely furnished by the capitalists in these cities. *Ibid.*, pp. 1100, 1108.

by bribery and fraud, no right could vest under it, and the grantees of 1795 could not sell a better title than they themselves possessed.[73] Engaging in vitriolic attacks on Granger and the other Republicans, who were, he thought, led astray by the astute and misleading arguments of the claimants, Randolph could see in this monstrous fraud and corruption the very "spirit of Federalism! That spirit which considers the many as made only for the few.... When I behold a certain party supporting and clinging to such a measure almost to a man, I see only men faithful to their own principles; pursuing, with steady step and untired zeal, the uniform tenor of their political life."[74]

After repeated efforts to secure favorable action from Congress had ended in failure, the Yazoo claimants turned to the courts, though it seemed that judicial recourse had been prevented by the provision of the Rescinding Act against suits to enforce claims against the state and by the prohibition in the Eleventh Amendment of suits against the state by citizens of other states. But Hamilton's suggestion that the federal courts would probably declare the Rescinding Act void had not been forgotten, and the attorneys and agents of the claimants had persisted in the hope that a judicial determination of their rights could be secured. Eminent attorneys, such as John Quincy Adams, Joseph Story, Luther Martin, and Robert G. Harper, representing the land companies were leaving no stones unturned in the efforts to satisfy their clients. A "friendly suit," begun no doubt on the advice of counsel and other interested parties, was heard in the federal court for the district of Massachusetts.

John Peck of Boston, one of the large speculators in Georgia lands,[75] pretended to sell, among his minor transactions, a small tract of Georgia lands to Robert Fletcher of Amherst, New Hampshire, thereby predicating the necessary diversity of citizenship for the bringing of a suit in the federal courts. Fletcher brought suit for the recovery of his purchase money, but so unsubstantial was the matter in controversy that the case was continued by consent in the United States Circuit Court at Boston from June, 1803, to October, 1807, at which time a jury rendered a special verdict respecting the rights of the state to the disputed lands. Associate Justice Cushing decided, in October, 1807, in Peck's favor all of the questions raised by the pleadings. In the elaborate pleadings and briefs the attorneys for the claimants carefully planned to bring before the Supreme Court all the controverted questions relative to the Yazoo grants, to wit:

---

[73] *Annals*, 8th Cong., 2d sess., p. 1029.

[74] *Ibid.*, p. 1032.

[75] *American State Papers, Public Lands*, I: 220 ff.

whether Georgia had good title to the lands in question and had authority to make the grants to the Yazoo companies, whether Peck's title had been acquired from this grant, and whether if legally made the grants could be rescinded by a subsequent act of the legislature. Owing to a defect in the pleadings, the case was twice argued before the Supreme Court. Luther Martin, in arguing for Peck, referred to the Declaration of Independence as declaring the states to be free, sovereign, and independent, "and the sovereignty of *each,* not of the whole, was the principle of the Revolution; there was no connection between them but that of necessity and self-defence." But Chief Justice Marshall, refusing to accept this reasoning, rendered an epoch-making decision sustaining the contentions of the Yazoo claimants and declaring void the Georgia Rescinding Act.[76] Prior to the decision in the case of *Fletcher v. Peck* there were a few cases in which the Justices regarded legislative acts in the nature of grants under which private rights had become vested so as not to be subject to revocation in such a way as to destroy or divest such rights.[77]

Fletcher v. Peck not only afforded Marshall another opportunity to expound his Federalist theories of law and of the function of the Judiciary as an equilibrator in the American federal system, but also to predicate a basis for the protection of his own personal interests. Beveridge notes that Marshall was personally profoundly interested in the "stability of contractual obligations." The title to the Fairfax estate in which he and his brother had an important stake had been put in jeopardy by acts of the Virginia legislature. At this time a suit affecting the title of his brother to some Fairfax lands was pending in the Virginia courts. This case[78] was destined to become a landmark in the development of the doctrine of federal supremacy. "No man in America, therefore," says

---

[76] Fletcher v. Peck, 6 Cranch 87, 118 (1810). According to Edward Channing, "while Randolph proposed that Congress should lend its authority to a declaration that a State could annul contracts which it had entered into, in another part of the Capitol John Marshall and his Federalist colleagues in the Supreme Court were eagerly awaiting the opportunity to declare that under the Constitution of the United States no state could pass any law impairing the obligation of contracts." *Jeffersonian System,* American Nation Series, p. 132. And see comment of Henry Adams that, "no one who knew Chief Justice Marshall could doubt that he, and the Supreme Bench with him, would hold that the State of Georgia was bound by its contract with the land companies." *History of the United States During the First Administration of Thomas Jefferson* (New York, 1889), II: 212.

[77] See *Champion and Dickason v. Casey,* discussed in Warren, *Supreme Court in United States History,* I: 67; Justice Paterson's opinion in Vanhorne's Lessee v. Dorrance, 2 Dallas 304 (1795); and Chief Justice Parson's opinion in Wales v. Stetson, 2 Mass. 143 (1806).

[78] *Martin v. Hunter's Lessee,* see below, pp. 340 ff.

Beveridge, "could have followed with deeper anxiety the Yazoo controversy than John Marshall."[79]

Marshall took up the four questions presented in the declaration and decided each against the plaintiff. First, he found that the Georgia legislature, in passing the act of January 7, 1795, had not transgressed the constitution of that state, for "the legislature of Georgia, unless restrained by its own constitution, possesses the power of disposing of the unappropriated lands within its own limits, in such a manner as its own judgment shall dictate."[80]

On the second point, that of whether fraud could invalidate the contract, Marshall said:

How far a court of justice would, in any case, be competent, on proceedings instituted by the State itself, to vacate a contract thus formed, and to annul rights acquired, under that contract, by third persons having no notice of the improper means by which it was obtained, is a question which the court would approach with much circumspection. It may well be doubted how far the validity of a law depends upon the motives of its framers, and how far the particular inducements, operating on the members of the supreme sovereign power of a State, to the formation of a contract by that power, are examinable in a court of justice. If the principle be conceded, that an act of the supreme sovereign power might be declared null by the court, in consequence of the means which procured it, still there would be much difficulty in saying to what extent those means must be applied to produce this effect. Must it be direct corruption, or would interest or undue influence of any kind be sufficient? Must the vitiating cause operate on a majority, or on what number of the members? Would the act be null, whatever might be the wish of the Nation, or would its obligation or nullity depend upon the public sentiment?[81]

It was admitted that Georgia would not be bound by the grant made to the four companies if the transaction was shown to be affected by fraud, duress, or mistake. But why was Georgia not permitted to rescind the grant when notorious fraud in its procurement was discovered? The answer to this query was evaded by the contention that the legislature could not pass on the validity of titles—such matters must be determined by courts. Marshall was formulating a new version of the separation of powers theory.

Since Georgia was not seeking annulment of the contract, the issue was whether private citizens could contest an act of the legislature on the ground of fraud. Marshall thought that if the title be plainly deduced from a legislative act which the legislature might constitutionally pass and if the act be clothed with all the requisite forms of a law, a court, sitting as a court of law, cannot sustain a suit brought by one individual against another founded on the allegation that the act is a nullity, in

[79] *The Life of John Marshall,* III: 582.
[80] 6 Cranch 128.
[81] *Ibid.,* p. 130.

consequence of the impure motives which influenced certain members of the legislature who passed the law.[82]

Posing as a defender of State rights, Marshall declared that "it would be indecent, in the extreme, upon a private contract between two individuals, to enter into an inquiry respecting the corruption of a sovereign power of the State." Georgia's Rescinding Act was considered to be in the nature of a decision and, as such, beyond the scope of the legislative authority. A beginning at least was made toward the construction of the theory of separation of powers as a prolific source for limitations on legislative actions. Not merely the rights of the present litigants were at stake, but there was involved a principle which loomed especially important in the opinion of the leading Federalists, namely, whether "a legislature may, by its own act, divest the vested estate of any man whatever, for reasons which shall, by itself, be deemed sufficient." Moreover, a pregnant idea for the judicial construction of legislative restrictions was thrown out in the comment: "To the legislature all legislative power is granted; but the question, whether the act of transferring the property of an individual to the public, be in the nature of the legislative power, is well worthy of serious reflection."[83] It was not long before the lawyers took up the notion that a legislative act interfering with property or acquired rights was not true legislation and hence was void.[84]

In disposing of the third count, that of whether the Repeal Act rescinded any rights or title granted by the act of 1795, Marshall granted that a legislature may repeal any act which a former legislature was competent to pass, but "if an act be done under a law, a succeeding legislature cannot undo it." The past cannot be recalled by the most absolute power. And, hence, said Marshall: "the parties to this case cannot be affected by such a subsequent act. They did not participate in the fraud; they were merely innocent purchasers." In such a case, when

a law is in its nature a contract, when absolute rights have vested under that contract, a repeal of the law cannot divest those rights; and the act of annulling them, if legitimate, is rendered so by a power applicable to the case of every individual in the community. It may well be doubted whether the nature of society and of government does not prescribe some limits to the legislative power; and, if any be prescribed, where are they to be found, if the property of an individual, fairly and honestly acquired, may be seized without compensation.[85]

It was assumed, therefore, that the Rescinding Act was invalid because it violated some of the fundamental or natural law principles which surround and control the exercise of legislative powers. And, even if a state

---

[82] 6 Cranch 131.   [83] *Ibid.*, p. 136.
[84] See Webster's argument in the *Dartmouth College Case*, below, pp. 391–398.
[85] 6 Cranch 135.

may be conceded to have authority to judge its own case, yet "there are certain great principles of justice that ought not to be entirely disregarded." Among the foremost of these principles is the requirement that an innocent purchaser shall not suffer from the illegal or fraudulent acts of others. Thus, there were limitations to which Georgia must submit even if the state might be regarded as an independent and a sovereign nation. But Georgia was a member of the union, and Marshall's chief duty was to find what limitations the federal Constitution imposed on the state, so far as the rescinding of contracts was concerned.

Before the Chief Justice considered the contract clause and the bearing of the Constitution on the case in hand, he discoursed at length on the privileges of innocent purchasers, the propriety of inquiring into the motives of legislators, and the fact that the state of Georgia did not file a bill in equity, but that the suit was between two private citizens and that the record did not show that the state of Georgia had an interest in it. In view of the legal grounds on which he finally based his decision, all this discussion appears to be irrelevant and, indeed, weakens the opinion from a legal point of view. "Indeed, much of Marshall's opinion up to the point where he commences to discuss the constitutional question," says Hagan, "can hardly bear close analysis."[86]

The Constitution of the United States does not say that no state shall impair the *effect* of contracts or divest *rights* vested through contracts; those safeguards of property rights are left to the states. The states are only inhibited from impairing the obligation of contracts. What is the obligation of a contract? It is merely the duty which either of the contracting parties has assumed toward the other for the consideration named.[87] This duty exists only so long as the contract remains *executory*. When the contract is performed on either side, the obligation of the contract assumed by that party is discharged and at an end. But Marshall did not hesitate over such a trifling difficulty of interpretation. His fertile mind discovered an implied obligation in an executed contract.[88]

The opinion of Marshall on the validity of the Rescinding Act to the point where he bases his reasoning on the express language of the Con-

---

[86] Hagan, *op. cit.*, p. 26. "In refusing to permit courts to inquire into legislative motives," Hagan thinks, "Marshall's position is wholly sound, both from a legal and a practical standpoint, but one cannot escape the conclusion that his opinion would be greatly strengthened, so far as the legal mind is concerned, had he omitted all references to bills in equity, innocent purchasers, etc., thus seemingly holding out promises which other parts of his opinion sweep away." *Ibid.*

[87] For a brief analysis of the meaning of the phrase obligation of contract, see below, pp. 323 ff.

[88] Seymour D. Thompson, "Abuses of Corporate Privileges," 26 *Amer. Law Rev.* (Mar., Apr., 1892), 175, 176.

stitution is called "mere camouflage, designed to give moral sanction to the sound constitutional principle about to be announced," and it is assumed that he knew the limitations on legislatures suggested by him were not supported by legal precedents.[89] But it is apparent, not only from the opinion itself, but also from Marshall's political ideas and faith, that the argument predicated on general principles and on implied limitations on legislative powers was the primary and fundamental part of his opinion and that the reasoning founded on the constitutional inhibition was secondary. In the *Bank of the United States v. Deveaux*,[90] Marshall noted that the Constitution deals in general terms, not in detail, and that since the framers could not perceive the minute distinctions which arise in the progress of the nation, they had therefore confined its language "to the establishment of broad and general principles." These broad and general principles were now being interpreted to carry into effect one of the important purposes of Federalism—the preservation of the sacredness of contractual rights against legislative interference. It is obvious that such rights were to be preserved whether or not constitutional provisions so declared.

With relatively little argument, citation, or discussion, Marshall assumed that an executed contract in the nature of a legislative grant was a contract, and thus the case was brought within the purview of the Constitution. But because the grant made by Georgia to the land companies was an executed contract, how could the transaction be brought within the scope of the contract clause? Does not the obligation of contract cease when the grant is made and the purchasers make their payment in accordance with its terms?[91] Justice Johnson thought there could be no obligation beyond the time the contract was executed, for a contract of this kind "is *functus officio* the moment it is executed, and continues afterward to be nothing more than the evidence that a certain act was done."[92]

Turning to the constitutional issue, Marshall quoted Blackstone to the effect that a contract executed does not differ from a grant. A contract executed, such as that made between Georgia and the purchasers, con-

---

[89] Hagan, *op. cit.*, p. 26.

[90] 5 Cranch 61, 87 (1809).

[91] On this point the opinion of the foremost modern authorities on the law of contracts may well be cited, as follows: "If a transaction is fully executed on both sides, it is not properly described as a contract. . . . All contracts to a greater or less extent are executory. When they cease to be so, they cease to be contracts." Samuel Williston and George J. Thompson, *A Treatise on the Law of Contracts* (Rev. ed., New York, 1936), I, sec. 14.

[92] 6 Cranch 145. For confirmation of this view, see William Trickett, "Is a Grant a Contract? A Review of Fletcher v. Peck," 54 *Amer. Law Rev.* (Sept., Oct., 1920), 728. "It is idle to talk of the subsistence of the contract, or of its obligation," says Dean Trickett, "after full discharge of it by both parties." *Ibid.*

tains obligations which are binding on the parties. Since the general term contract is used in the Constitution, Marshall contended that it must be regarded as including executed as well as executory contracts. If, then, a grant is a contract, is it the sort of contract included in the constitutional restriction? Is a contract of a state prohibited by the Constitution from being impaired by the state? Marshall thought so. Employing the familiar check argument of the Federalists that the framers of the Constitution feared the acts of state legislatures and intentionally placed restrictions on them, including the prohibition against bills of attainder and *ex post facto* laws, he said they viewed with some apprehension the violent acts which might grow out of the feelings of the moment; and, hence, in adopting the Constitution the people had manifested a determination to shield themselves and their property from the effects of the sudden and strong passions to which men are exposed. Hence, it was also provided that no state shall pass a law impairing the obligation of contracts. These limitations, Marshall maintained, constituted a bill of rights for each state.

Unfortunately for his purpose, the Supreme Court had limited the *ex post facto* phrase of the Constitution to acts affecting criminal conduct.[93] But, said Marshall, "the legislature is then prohibited from passing a law by which a man's estate, or any part of it, shall be seized for a crime which was not declared, by some previous law, to render him liable to punishment. Why, then, should violence be done to the natural meaning of words for the purpose of leaving to the legislature the power of seizing, for public use, the estate of an individual in the form of a law annulling the title by which he holds that estate?"[94]

It was then announced as the unanimous opinion of the Court that, in this case, "the estate having passed into the hands of a purchaser for a valuable consideration, without notice, the State of Georgia was restrained, either by general principles which are common to our free institutions, or by the particular provisions of the Constitution of the United States, from passing a law whereby the estate of a plaintiff in the premises so purchased could be constitutionally and legally impaired and rendered null and void."[95] On the last point, that of whether the title to the lands in question was in the United States and not in Georgia, Marshall considered briefly the special verdict in the lower court and concluded that Georgia had a good title and had power to make the grant of 1795.[96]

[93] Calder v. Bull, 3 Dallas 398 (1798).
[94] 6 Cranch 138.
[95] *Ibid.*, p. 139.
[96] The Federalist point of view which Marshall had adopted in his decision was stated

Justice Johnson, dissenting in part, agreed with the other Justices that a state could not revoke its grants, but he did not base this limitation on the contract clause of the Constitution. It was founded, he thought, "on a general principle, on the reason and nature of things: a principle which will impose laws even on the diety."[97] He wanted it distinctly understood, however, that his opinion on this point was not based on the provision of the Constitution relating to laws impairing the obligation of contracts.

On the meaning of the contract clause, Justice Johnson regretted that "words of less equivocal signification" had not been adopted in that article of the Constitution. The letters of Publius, as found in *The Federalist*, were cited as confirming the view that it was the object of the federal Convention to afford a general protection to individual rights against the acts of the state legislatures. To give the clause the effect of a general restriction in favor of private rights, Johnson thought, would be going far beyond the obvious and necessary import of the words. Johnson also disagreed with Marshall's views on the nature of Georgia's title to the lands. The interest of Georgia in the lands, he conceived, amounted to nothing more than a "mere possibility."[98]

In regard to the contention that there was no *bona fide* controversy involved and that the suit had been framed to secure the opinion of the Supreme Court on behalf of the claimants, John Quincy Adams noted that the Chief Justice and Judge Livingston had indicated "the reluctance of the Court to decide the case at all, as it appeared manifestly made up for the purpose of getting the Court's judgment upon all the points."[99] Judge Johnson expressed his doubts on this matter in his dissenting opinion. "I have been very unwilling," said he, "to proceed to the decision of this cause at all. It appears to me to bear strong evidence on the face of it, of being a mere feigned case. It is our duty to decide on the rights but not on the speculations of parties. My confidence, however, in the respectable gentlemen who have been engaged for the parties, has

by Representative Findley of Pennsylvania as follows: "As long as we pay respect to constitutional obligations and the distribution of the powers of government, and as long as we respect the federal Constitution, which expressly asserts that no *ex post facto* law, or law impairing the obligation of contracts, shall be made, we must agree that one session of a legislature cannot annul the contracts made by the preceding session." *Annals,* 8th Cong., 2d sess., p. 1083, Jan. 31, 1805.

[97] 6 Cranch 143.

[98] Regarding the political implications of the case, Beveridge, who strongly approves Marshall's reasoning, thinks the conclusion inescapable that "had not Jefferson, who placed Johnson on the Supreme Bench, and Jefferson's Secretary of State and political legatee, James Madison, ardently desired the disposition which Marshall made of the case, Justice Johnson would have placed on record a stronger statement of the nature of this litigation." *The Life of John Marshall,* III: 592, 593.

[99] *The Diary of John Quincy Adams,* ed. by Allan Nevins (New York, 1928), I: 546.

induced me to abandon my scruples, in the belief they would never consent to impose a mere feigned case upon this Court."[100]

The New England–Mississippi Land Company, taking advantage of the decision of the Supreme Court in *Fletcher v. Peck,* pressed its claims for adjustment of the rights of its clients upon Congress; but Randolph and other Republicans again intervened. Representative Troup of Georgia thought the decision was one "which the mind of every man attached to Republican principles must revolt at."[101] Randolph's motion, which would have involved a legislative condemnation of the decision of the Supreme Court, was defeated by a narrow margin of votes. Since the title to the lands was now in the United States and the Court had decided in favor of the Yazoo claimants, Troup urged that the national government should resist by military force if necessary the enforcement of the federal court's decree.

The decision of the Supreme Court had no effect on the status of the Yazoo claimants. Georgia had ceded the lands to the United States on April 24, 1802. The claimants, most of whom were speculators, turned to Congress for the settlement of their claims. Finally, on March 31, 1814, after John Randolph had failed of reëlection to Congress, provision was made for the settlement of the Yazoo claims by an appropriation of five million dollars. Francis Scott Key, John Law, and Thomas Swann, as commissioners, adjusted the claims of the "innocent purchasers" for an expenditure of $4,282,151.12. When Congress voted to appropriate funds to reimburse the Yazoo claimants, Daniel Webster, a supporter of the bill, characterized the closing scene in this bitterly fought partisan controversy as follows: "The Yazoo bill is through, passed by eight majority. It excited a great deal of feeling. All the Federalists supported the bill, and some Democrats. Georgians, and some Virginians and Carolinans, opposed it with great heat. . . . Our feeling was to get the Democratic support of it."[102] The "Federalist-Jeffersonian coalition," as Beveridge

---

[100] 6 Cranch 147, 148. Haskins, however, asserts that "a feigned issue was arranged and a favorable decision obtained from the Circuit Court." *op. cit.,* p. 433.

Failing to secure redress from Congress, the speculators turned to the Judiciary, where "they presented precisely those points for the decision of the Court which they wished the Court to decide, and the Court did actually decide them as the speculators themselves would have decided them if they had been in the place of the Supreme Court. . . . The case of Fletcher v. Peck was a decision of a feigned case, made up by two speculators, to decide certain points, in the decision of which they were interested. Will any man, in his senses, say that the right of the United States to the public property could be affected by such decision." Representative Troup, *Annals,* 12th Cong., 2d sess., p. 857, and 13th Cong., 2d sess., p. 1848.

[101] See *Annals,* 11th Cong., 2d sess., p. 1882, and *Annals,* 11th Cong., 3d sess., p. 415, Apr. 17 and Dec. 17, 1810.

[102] *Private Correspondence of Daniel Webster,* ed. by Fletcher Webster (Boston, 1857), p. 244. "The huge villainy," as Chappell called it, was "distent with odious interest

calls it, was too strong for the rising Republican strength of the South and West. Because the case of *Fletcher v. Peck* involved the first attempt to define the phrase "obligation of contract" as used in the Constitution, there was considerable discussion concerning the purpose of the inclusion of this prohibition on state authority.

THE MEANING OF THE PHRASE "OBLIGATION OF CONTRACT"

The limitation on the states with respect to legislation impairing the obligation of contracts was inserted in the federal Constitution on the motion of Rufus King to add "a prohibition on the States to interfere with private contracts." King wished to have included a clause similar to one adopted as a part of the Ordinance of Congress for the Northwest Territory to the effect that "no law ought ever to be made or have force in the said territory, that shall, in any manner whatever interfere with or affect private contracts or engagements, bona fide, and without fraud previously formed."[103] In place of the provision suggested by King, Rutledge made a motion that the states should not "pass bills of attainder nor retrospective laws." This motion was adopted with three states voting in the negative. The Committee on Style[104] was responsible for the wording of the limitation in its present form, but King probably prepared the draft which was adopted by the committee.[105] When the draft of the Constitution was presented to the Convention, that body refused to insert the word "previous" before "obligation" in the clause relating to the impairment of contracts. Pointing out that the provision in the Constitution relating to the impairment of contracts was not introduced until the latter days of the Convention sessions, that its introduction occasioned very little dissension, and that the final form of the language with one exception was prepared by the Committee on Style, Benjamin Fletcher Wright observes that "about all that can be asserted with confidence is that the Framers showed surprisingly little interest in the problem, that the clause as we have it was prepared in committee, and that

---

and energy at every turn, making its way over all obstacles, discouragements and delays, first through the state legislature, next through the cabinet, courts and Congress of the United States, and in the end, after near twenty years of unholy striving and perseverance, triumphing at last and plunging its felonious hands deep into the national treasury." *Miscellanies of Georgia*, p. 56.

[103] The original form of the contract clause was opposed by Gouverneur Morris, George Mason, and James Madison. The prohibition was favored by Elbridge Gerry who wished to have it apply also to acts of Congress. Farrand, *op. cit.*, I: 170, II: 439, 440.

[104] The members of this committee were Hamilton, Johnson, King, Madison, and Morris.

[105] *The Records of the Federal Convention of 1787*, ed. by Max Farrand (New Haven, 1923), II: 596, 597.

the records of the Convention throw very little light upon the meaning to be attached to 'impairing the obligation of contracts.'"[106]

Few references to this phrase were made in the debates on the Constitution. Quoting this provision, William R. Davie of North Carolina agreed that without such restrictions and a controlling Judiciary "laws might be made in particular States, to enable citizens to defraud the citizens of other States."[107] But Davie thought the contract clause referred merely to contracts between individuals. In *The Federalist*, Madison, commenting on the phrase, said: "very properly, therefore, have the Convention added this constitutional bulwark in favor of private rights. . . . The sober people of America are weary of the fluctuating policy which has directed the public councils. They have seen with regret, and with indignation, that sudden changes and legislative interference, in cases affecting personal rights, become jobs in the hands of enterprizing and influential speculators, and snares to the more industrious and less informed part of the community."[108] Luther Martin expressed his views regarding the reasons for the adoption of the contract clause as follows:

I considered, Sir, that there might be times of such great public calamities and distress, and of such extreme scarcity of specie, as should render it the duty of a government, for the preservation of the most valuable part of its citizens, in some measure to interfere in their favor, by passing laws totally or partially stopping the courts of justice, or authorizing the debtor to pay in installments, or by delivering up his property to his creditors at a reasonable and honest valuation. The times have been such as to render regulations of this kind necessary in most all of the States, to prevent the wealthy creditor and the moneyed man from totally destroying the poor, though even industrious debtor. Such times may again arrive.[109]

The framers of the Constitution, so far as any definite intent was expressed, apparently desired to avoid the danger of interference with contracts through the medium of depreciated currency rather than the invalidation of agreements by legislative acts.[110] On the other hand, Patrick Henry, speaking of *ex post facto* laws and laws impairing the obligation of contracts, said: "The expression includes public contracts, as well as private contracts between individuals. Notwithstanding the sagacity of the gentleman, he cannot prove its exclusive relation to pri-

---

[106] *The Contract Clause of the Constitution* (Cambridge, 1938), p. 11.

[107] Elliot's *Debates* (2d ed.), IV: 157, and Farrand, *op. cit.*, III: 349, 350.

[108] No. 44 (Ford ed.), pp. 296, 297.

[109] Elliot's *Debates* (2d ed., 1888), III: 244, 245.

[110] The framers of the Constitution, Beveridge thinks, had in mind "the danger of the violations of contracts through depreciated paper money rather than the invalidation of agreements by the direct action of state legislatures." *The Life of John Marshall*, III: 558, footnote. For an account of the uncertainty and confusion of ideas relating to the meaning of this clause of the Constitution, see Wright, *op. cit.*, pp. 8 ff.

vate contracts."[111] Answering Henry's argument, Governor Randolph, a
member of the federal Convention, maintained that the clause was included because of the "frequent interferences of the state legislatures
with private contracts."

The term "obligation of contracts" was in general use in Roman and
civil law countries but not in jurisdictions where the common law prevailed. Summarizing the views of English and Continental jurists on the
meaning of obligation, Warren B. Hunting concludes that "although
these jurists differ upon the question whether or not a conveyance
should properly be termed a contract, they all agree that a conveyance,
whether contract or not, does not give rise to obligation."[112] So far as
there were differences between the Roman and common law usage of
the term "obligation," there is no indication in the Constitution debates
of a recognition of these differences.[113]

In the first case in which John Marshall was called upon to interpret
the contract clause, he followed the reasoning of Hamilton that a grant
is a contract executed and that the grant involves an implied contract
that the grantor will not reassert his right over the thing granted.[114] But

---

[111] Elliot's *Debates*, II: 474. But see comment of Justice Miller: "It has seemed probable to many judges and lawyers who have considered this clause of the Constitution
that it was not designed by the framers of that instrument to do anything more than
protect private contracts, those between individuals and those between individuals and
private corporations, that is, not municipal corporations, but those organized for purposes of profit; and if it were now an original question, it is by no means certain but
that this would be held to be the sound view of it. But those eminent men who at an
early day had the duty of defining the meaning of this provision thought otherwise.
They held it to apply very largely to contracts made by the State and not only to
those made by it, but to contracts arising out of state statutes and legislation." Samuel
Freeman Miller, *Lectures on the Constitution of the United States* (New York, 1891),
p. 555.
   "It is very plain," says Hunting, "that the Convention had in mind only retrospective
laws as impairing the obligation of contracts, and it is almost equally plain that they
had in mind only the contracts of private individuals." *The Obligation of Contracts
Clause of the United States Constitution*, Johns Hopkins University Studies in Historical and Political Science (1919), XXXVII: 120.

[112] Hunting, *op. cit.*, pp. 21, 22. See also Pufendorf, *Law of Nature and of Nations*,
trans. by Kennett (4th ed., 1729), p. 259.

[113] Nathan Isaacs, "John Marshall on Contracts: A Study in Early American Juristic
Theory," 7 *Virginia Law Rev.* (Mar., 1921), 418, 419.

[114] Called upon to give advice regarding the meaning of the phrase "obligation of
contract" used in the Constitution, Hamilton replied: "When a government enters into
a contract with an individual, it deposes, as to the matter of the contract, its constitutional authority, and exchanges the character of legislator for that of a moral agent
with the same rights and obligations as an individual. Its promises may be justly considered as excepted out of its power to legislate, unless in aid of them. It is in theory
impossible to reconcile the idea of a promise which obliges, with a power to make a
law which can vary the effect of it." *The Works of Alexander Hamilton*, ed. by John
C. Hamilton (New York, 1850), III: 518, 519.

such an interpretation did not accord with the customary understanding of the phrase obligation of contract.

In his opinion in *Fletcher v. Peck*,[115] Marshall starts by showing that according to the inherent nature of governmental institutions, natural law and justice, and the attributes of a just society, there was a contract which the state could not abrogate. Assuming from the point of view of natural justice that there was a contract the conditions of which must be protected, Marshall maintains that the provision in the Constitution merely serves to strengthen and support a position he would not have hesitated to take, even though no express provision could be found to support his theory of the impotency of a state to revoke a contract. This reading of the natural law philosophy into the Constitution tended to give a permanent sanction for Marshall's ideas of natural law and justice. If the contract clause could be stretched both extensively and intensively to include what Marshall and other conservative thinkers thought necessary for the protection of vested or acquired rights, the protection of property would be more secure than if such protection were predicated merely on principles of natural justice. To Marshall and many others the prime duty of the government was to protect vested rights. The Constitution, he thought, was established for this purpose. It was, therefore, the duty of the Supreme Court to find the constitutional sanction effectively to accomplish this end. Predicting the future course of constitutional interpretation with respect to the protection of vested rights, Marshall approved "the new course of thinking which had been inspired by the adoption of a Constitution that was understood to prohibit all laws impairing the obligation of contracts," because it had "in a great measure restored that confidence which is essential to the internal prosperity of nations."[116]

The natural law theory of the obligation of a contract then was looked to as furnishing the test of the obligation of contracts entered into by a state. Upon this theory an obligation existed irrespective of the legal omnipotence or sovereignty of one of the contracting parties. This view of the contract clause was an outgrowth of the tendency of the eighteenth century natural law philosophers to exalt principles of reason and natural justice and to place them above the state. From this point of view it was not the state that gave force and validity to contracts but the obli-

---

[115] 6 Cranch 87 (1810). James Wilson had contended, as early as 1782, that a legislative act granting a charter to a corporation was in the nature of a compact, and when the terms of the compact were observed by one of the parties it could not consistently, with the rules of good faith, be departed from by the other party. Wilson, *Works*, ed. by James DeWitt Andrews (Chicago, 1896) I: 565, 566.

[116] *The Life of George Washington* (Philadelphia, 1804–1807), V: 178, 179.

gation inhered in the contractual relation itself. Adopting the natural law philosophy, Chief Justice Marshall in *Ogden v. Saunders* asserted that the existence of the obligation of a contract was independent of the acts or authority of the state.[117] The notion inherited from the eighteenth century political thought that a contract is beyond the control of ordinary legislation, Nathan Isaacs thinks, gives the clue to Marshall's decisions in *Fletcher v. Peck, Sturges v. Crowninshield,* and *Dartmouth College v. Woodward.*[118]

Marshall predicted that if the majority opinion in the case of *Ogden v. Saunders* prevailed, the states could nullify this important clause of the Constitution by merely declaring that all contracts shall be made subject to the existing laws of the states. But the attempts of the states to evade by this device the effect of the contract clause was checked by the inclusion through judicial interpretation of a liberty of contract provision as a part of the Fourteenth Amendment.

It is apparent that one of the most important constitutional decisions in our history and one which greatly affected the states in their authority over the relations to the corporations which they created was rendered in a feigned case.[119] "It seems clear," says Haskins, "that *Fletcher v. Peck,* rather than the more famous *Dartmouth College Case,* lies at the root

---

[117] The defendants maintain, said Marshall, "that an error lies at the very foundation of this argument. It assumes, that contract is the mere creature of society, and derives all its obligation from human legislation. That it is not the stipulation an individual makes which binds him but some declaration of the supreme power of a state to which he belongs, that he shall perform what he has undertaken to perform. That though this original declaration may be lost in remote antiquity, it must be presumed as the origin of the obligation of contracts. This postulate the defendants deny, and, we think, with great reason."

"It is an argument of no inconsiderable weight against it, that we find no trace of such an agreement. So far back as human research carries us we find ... no allusion, from the earliest time, to any supposed act of the governing power giving obligation to contracts. On the contrary, the proceedings respecting them of which we know anything, evince the idea of a pre-existing intrinsic obligation which human law enforces. If, on tracing the right to contract, and the obligation created by contract, to their source, we find them to exist anterior to, and independent of society, we may reasonably conclude that those original and pre-existing principles are, like many other natural rights, brought with man into society; and, although they may be controlled, are not given by human legislation." Commenting on this extract, Nathan Isaacs observes that Marshall, like most thinkers at this time, was making not only his own law, but also his history, *a priori*, in accordance with what he believed must have happened. 12 Wheaton 213, 344 (1827).

[118] "John Marshall on Contracts," 7 *Virginia Law Rev.*, p. 423. For consideration of the cases of *Sturges v. Crowninshield, Dartmouth College v. Woodward,* and *Ogden v. Saunders,* see below, pp. 368–369, 379–423, and 526–532.

[119] Marshall's defenders, however, resent Beveridge's intimation that he deliberately rendered one of his most cogent and most far-reaching opinions in a case that he knew to be a sham. Hagan, *op. cit.*, p. 34.

of the law of public contracts."[120] In a decision supporting the supremacy of nationalism over localism, Marshall gave legal sanction to many land speculations that were at least doubtful and to some that were corrupt, and his reasoning furnished the basis for many questionable grants in the future.

Beveridge assumes that throughout his opinion in *Fletcher v. Peck,* Marshall is speaking as a legislator and a politician. Deprecating the claim by Justice Johnson that the Chief Justice was using "a feigned case" to announce what he deemed as great constitutional principles, Beveridge thinks "the fact that Marshall rendered an opinion, under the circumstances, is one of the firmest proofs of his greatness. As in *Marbury v. Madison,* the supremacy of the national Judiciary had to be asserted or its inferiority conceded, so in *Fletcher v. Peck,* it was necessary that the nation's highest court should plainly lay down the law of public contract, notify every State of its place in the American system, and announce the limitations which the national Constitution places upon each State. Marshall's opinion did more than affect the controversy in Congress over the Yazoo lands. It announced the fundamental principles for the guidance of the States and the stabilizing of American business."[121] The Court was thus performing some of the broadest and most significant functions of a legislative body.

Marshall's strength lay in the fields where law impinges on politics, namely, constitutional and international law. "Where special learning, or the examination of the technicalities and nice distinctions of the law were required," Beveridge finds that "Marshall did not shine. Of admiralty law in particular he knew little." Though he might depend on Story for advice in admiralty cases or on intricate points in the law of real estate, in expositions of the Constitution, Marshall took "supreme command."[122]

In March, 1804, Jefferson presented to the Senate his first nomination for a vacancy on the Supreme Court. William Johnson of South Carolina was chosen. He was a man described by his contemporaries as of irreproachable character and of Republican connections. Henry Brockholst Livingston, appointed in November, 1806, was the second made by Jefferson. The following year Congress created a new Associate Judgeship to take care of the increasing business in the districts of Kentucky, Tennessee, and Ohio, and Jefferson nominated for this new position Thomas Todd of Kentucky, a lawyer who had been strongly recom-

---

[120] Haskins, *op. cit.,* p. 434. See also New Jersey v. Wilson, 7 Cranch 164 (1812).
[121] *The Life of John Marshall,* III: 593.
[122] *The Life of John Marshall,* IV: 119–121.

mended to the President by the members of Congress from these states. The majority of the members of the Court comprising Justices Cushing, Chase, and Washington together with Chief Justice Marshall were Federalists, and the change in the personnel of the Court on the appointment of three Republicans had only a slight effect on the trend of judicial decisions. During Jefferson's Administration the Supreme Court was inextricably involved in the political controversies of the time through the argument over and the enactment of the Repeal Act, the impeachment of Justice Chase, and the Burr trial. Despite control by the Republicans of the Legislative and Executive branches of the government, the Supreme Court continued to give its sanction and approval to the doctrines of the Federalist party. The decision of Chief Justice Marshall in the case of *Fletcher v. Peck* had relatively little effect in disposing of the interests and claims of the speculators in Georgia lands, but it afforded an opportunity to give an interpretation of the contract clause in accordance with the well-known Federalist policy of limiting state legislatures to as great an extent as possible. In the year following the decision in the Georgia land case, two more Justices were appointed, giving for the first time a majority of the members of the Court to the Republican party. But, as we shall see, this change in the political affiliations of Justices did not secure the anticipated results in changing constitutional interpretation. The main principles and hypotheses which Chief Justice Jay announced and applied and which were developed and extended by Chief Justice Marshall were continued in the decisions rendered during and immediately after the War of 1812. The way was being prepared for the adoption of definite and decisive nationalist principles by the Supreme Court.

CHAPTER X

The Supreme Court Adopts
the Nationalistic Theory
of Interpretation

FEDERALISM did not disappear, however, with the overthrow of the Federalist party. The denomination of parties may be
altered, said Robert Goodloe Harper, but the principles on which the
Federalists acted must be adopted, or the government will fall to pieces.
Those narrow maxims, he thought, which apply properly to small communities will prove in practice wholly inadequate to the government of
a great nation. The principles of Federalism were destined to survive.
By deliberate design, John Marshall was expected to save the government from falling to pieces, and upon him devolved a large share of the
responsibility to preserve some of the salient principles of Federalism.

During the first fourteen years of John Marshall's service as Chief Justice, only three important constitutional decisions came to the Court for
decision. And in two of these there was strong opposition to the Court's
judgment. Georgia refused to accede to the decision in *Fletcher v. Peck*,
and Pennsylvania for a long time prevented the enforcement of the decree in the *Olmsted Case*. But Kendrick C. Babcock believes good use
was made of this time, for "Marshall was moulding to his views of the
Constitution and the federal government the men who were serving with
him as Associate Justices." It was said that by 1811 the Supreme Court
was "Federalized, or perhaps Marshallized."[1] From 1811 to 1816 the way
was being prepared for the announcement by the Court of its first great
decision sustaining federal supremacy.

DECISIONS FROM 1811 TO 1816

During the February, 1811, term only three Justices, Marshall, Livingston, and Washington were present. No one had been appointed to take
Cushing's place, Chase was ill, and Todd and Johnson were unable to
attend. By law it was necessary for four Justices to be present to transact
business. An attempt to change the requirement that a majority of the

[1] *Rise of American Nationality, 1811–1819* (New York, 1906), p. 292.

Justices must be present to transact business, so that cases could be heard by a Court of three, failed of passage in the House of Representatives owing to the resentment caused by the decision in the Georgia land case. Representative Troup said that "five members of the Court had, as far as they could, given away eighty millions of the public property (in the *Yazoo Case*), and he would not confide such powers to a smaller number of Judges."[2] Before the time of the meeting of the Court in the year following, Joseph Story had been confirmed for Cushing's place; and Gabriel Duval, for the vacancy caused by the death of Chase.

Warren thinks it fortunate that Levi Lincoln declined the appointment to the Court, for he was a strong partisan Republican and would have been "a thorn in the flesh of Marshall," and that it was even more fortunate that the Senate rejected Alexander Wolcott, for he regarded the authority to review legislative acts as a usurped power. Determined and assertive Republicans, along with stubborn and dogmatic Federalists, might not have permitted the smooth and undisturbed announcement of the political doctrines of Federalism in rendering Supreme Court decisions. John Quincy Adams, who was nominated and promptly confirmed, declined the appointment with a frank recognition of a lack of qualifications, as being "conscious of too little law," and being "too much of a political partisan"—grounds which might well have deterred a number of previous and subsequent appointees to the Supreme Bench from acceptance of appointments.

Commenting on the appointment of members of the Supreme Court at this time, Jefferson referred to "the cunning and sophistry" with which Marshall was able to enshroud himself and that "it will be difficult to find a character of firmness enough to preserve his independence on the same bench with Marshall. . . . His twistifications in the case of Marbury, in that of Burr, and the late Yazoo case show how dexterously he can reconcile law to his personal biases."[3] The next day he wrote to Judge Tyler, whose cause he favored, as follows:

we have long enough suffered under the base prostitution of law to party passions in one Judge, and the imbecility of another. In the hands of one the law is nothing more than an ambiguous text, to be explained by his sophistry into any meaning which may subserve his personal malice. Nor can any milk-and-water Associate maintain his own dependence, and by a firm pursuance of what the law really is, extend its protection to the citizens or the public.[4]

At another time Jefferson objected to the practice of the Judiciary in "erecting themselves into a political body to correct what they deem the errors of the Nation."

[2] *Annals,* 11th Cong., 3d sess., p. 962.   [4] *Writings* (Mem. ed.), XII: 392.
[3] *Writings* (Ford ed.), IX: 275, 276.

On Cushing's death, September 13, 1810, the Court from a political standpoint was thought to be evenly divided—with three Federalists, Marshall, Chase, and Washington—and three Republicans, Johnson, Todd, and Livingston. At length, wrote Jefferson to Gallatin, "we have a chance of getting a Republican majority in the Supreme Judiciary. For ten years that Branch has braved the spirit and will of the Nation after the Nation has manifested its will by a complete reform in every branch depending on them."[5] But the expected change in the political views of Justices to which Jefferson referred was not accomplished. Although with the appointment to the Court of Justices Duval and Story the majority of the Court was Republican in politics, Marshall continued to dominate the tribunal as fully as when the members were of his own political faith. Owing, no doubt, to their own personal views and predilections as well as to the steady and directing influence of the Chief Justice, the Republican members of the Court gradually espoused the cause of nationalism—Justices Johnson and Story at times exceeding Marshall in urging the expansion of the powers of the federal government and the consequent diminution of the authority of the states.[6]

In the case of *Schooner Exchange v. McFaddon*,[7] Marshall's political and diplomatic background and his particular bent in deciding cases on general principles were applied to good purpose. It was decided that a public armed vessel of a state at peace with the United States coming within this nation's territory is exempt from the jurisdiction of the courts. The decision ran counter to the personal and political feelings of the Chief Justice who shared the opinion of the Federalists favorable to England and in opposition to France. The schooner *Exchange*, an American vessel, had been captured by the French under the orders of Emperor Napoleon and was sailing as a public vessel under the Emperor's directions. Though Marshall declared that the jurisdiction of the nation within its own territory is necessarily exclusive and absolute and is susceptible of no limitation not imposed by itself, he found plausible reasons for refusing to assert jurisdiction over a public armed vessel which had been permitted to enter American ports.

The clause of the Constitution prohibiting the states from passing laws impairing the obligation of contracts was again applied by the Court in the case of *New Jersey v. Wilson*.[8] An act of the state legislature passed

---

[5] Jefferson Papers MSS, Library of Congress.

[6] See Albert J. Beveridge, *The Life of John Marshall* (Boston, 1919), IV: 59, 60.

[7] 7 Cranch 116 (1812).

[8] 7 Cranch 164 (1812). See the decision of the New Jersey supreme court holding that under the facts of this case the contract clause of the federal Constitution was not involved, State v. Wilson, 1 Pennington 300 (1807).

in 1758 had provided that certain lands which were purchased for the Indians should not thereafter be subject to any tax. A subsequent act repealed the provision exempting these lands from taxation and the act was sustained by the state supreme court. Referring to the case of *Fletcher v. Peck*,[9] the Chief Justice noted that it was there held that the contract clause of the Constitution extends to contracts to which a state is a party, as well as to contracts between individuals. Every requisite to a contract being present in the proceedings between the colony of New Jersey and the Indians, the state was held bound by its agreement which could not be impaired by a subsequent act. Since the New Jersey law limiting the power of taxation had been enacted several decades before the federal Constitution was adopted, the contract clause applying to this case was given retroactive force. The Court's opinion was based upon a doctrine expressed by the Chief Justice on a number of occasions that the sanctity of contracts and the inhibition against their impairment had a natural law as well as a constitutional background.

Marshall frequently indicated his belief in the acceptance of natural law principles, especially as applied to the settlement of questions relating to international law. When the Court upheld as lawful prize the capture of goods of a citizen of the United States, with domicile in England, shipped to the United States before war was declared, Marshall, dissenting, maintained:

> The law of nations is a law founded on the great and immutable principles of equity and natural justice. To draw an inference against all probability, whereby a citizen, for the purpose of confiscating his goods, is clothed, against his inclination, with the character of an enemy, in consequence of an act which, when committed, was innocent in itself, was entirely compatible with his political character as a citizen, and with the political views of his government, would seem to me to subvert those principles. The rule which, for obvious reasons, applies to the merchant in time of peace or in time of war, the national commercial character of the country in which he resides, cannot, in my opinion, without subverting those principles, apply a hostile character to his trade carried on during peace.[10]

In consideration of the question of the common law jurisdiction of the federal courts on which the Federalists and the Republicans differed, Justice Story conceded that the courts of the United States are tribunals of limited jurisdiction and can exercise only such powers as are confided to them, but he contended "when once an authority is lawfully given, the nature and extent of that authority, and the mode, in which it shall be exercised, must be regulated by the rules of the common law."[11] The

---

[9] 6 Cranch 87 (1810).
[10] The Venus, 8 Cranch 297, 298 (1814).
[11] United States v. Coolidge, 1 Gallison 488 (1813).

Constitution as well as the laws of the United States were regarded as necessarily predicated upon the existence of the common law. The general grant of jurisdiction to the inferior federal courts authorized them to try all cases involving "crimes and offenses cognizable under the authority of the United States." For the interpretation of the nature and extent of this jurisdiction, Story maintained, recourse must be had to the principles of the common law. Though many common law offenses against the public rights and powers of the United States are cognizable by the state courts, it was held that, independent of any statute, "whenever the offence is directed against the sovereignty or powers confided to the United States, it is cognizable under its authority."[12] Story thought the decision of the Supreme Court in *United States v. Hudson and Goodwin*[13] was entitled to the most respectful consideration, "but having been made without argument, and by a majority only of the Court, I hope it is not an improper course to bring the subject again in review for a more solemn decision."[14] But no case arose before the Supreme Court in which this issue was raised and Story's Associates were not inclined to agree with him regarding his views on the case of *Hudson and Goodwin*.

The years 1815 and 1816 were significant in the history of the Court for the emphatic assertion of the authority to prohibit legislatures from repealing grants when vested rights were at stake and for the insistence that the federal courts by writs of error could control and review the judgments of state courts. Justice Story rendered the judgments in some of the leading cases during these terms.

The Virginia legislature having granted lands to the towns in the state for the support of religious worship undertook later to repeal these grants. Story, speaking for the Supreme Court, held the repealing acts, so far as they divested the church of property acquired previous to the Revolution, contrary to the Constitution and hence void.[15] "If the legislature possessed the authority to make such a grant and confirmation," he said, "it is very clear to our minds that it vested an indefeasible and irrevocable title. We have no knowledge of any authority or principle which could support the doctrine that a legislative grant is revocable in its own nature, and held only *durante bene placito*. Such a doctrine would uproot the very foundations of almost all the land titles in Virginia, and is utterly inconsistent with a great and fundamental principle of a republican government, the right of the citizens to the free enjoy-

---

[12] *Ibid.*, pp. 491, 494.
[13] 7 Cranch 32 (1812).
[14] 1 Gallison 494, 495 (1813).
[15] Terrett v. Taylor, 9 Cranch 43 (1815).

ment of their property legally acquired.''[16] In his opinion the legislature, under proper limitations, might modify or restrain public corporations, but

that the legislature can repeal statutes creating private corporations, or confirming to them property already acquired under the faith of previous laws, and by such repeal can vest the property of such corporations exclusively in the State, or dispose of the same to such purposes as they may please, without the consent or default of the corporators, we are not prepared to admit; and we think ourselves standing upon the principles of natural justice, upon the fundamental laws of every free government, upon the spirit and the letter of the Constitution of the United States, and upon the decisions of most respectable judicial tribunals, in resisting such a doctrine.[17]

Justices Johnson and Todd were absent and Story indicated that he was speaking for a majority of the Court only. Once more the doctrines of higher law, such as the principles of natural justice and the fundamentals of free government, were appealed to as a sanction for the protection of private rights, rather than the specific language of the Constitution. Moreover, the Federalists strongly insisted that vested or acquired rights were placed beyond the reach of legislative interference. No reference was made to the provision of the Constitution on which this decision was based.

By 1815 Story had become a confirmed nationalist. The associations with and the well-directed efforts of the leading Federalists, including Marshall and the other members of this party on the Court, as well as the nationalist tendencies which were prevalent following the War of 1812, all combined to carry Story over to the Federalist cause. Not only did he try to secure common law jurisdiction for the federal courts and to extend their authority by interpretation, but he also became an advocate of a rampant nationalism. Writing to Judge Williams, he expressed the view that the Republicans had a "glorious opportunity" to place themselves permanently in power. All that was necessary was for the party to adopt the essential policies of Federalism. "Let us extend," he said,

the national authority over the whole extent of power given by the Constitution. Let us have great military and naval schools; an adequate regular army; the broad foundations laid of a permanent navy; a national bank; a nationl system of bankruptcy; a great navigation act; a general survey of our ports, and appointments of port-wardens and pilots; judicial courts which shall embrace the whole constitutional powers; national notaries; public and national justices of peace, for the commercial and national concerns of the United States. By such enlarged and liberal institutions, the govern-

---

[16] 9 Cranch 50, 51 (1815).

[17] *Ibid.*, p. 52. For another decision holding that a state could not repeal an act granting lands to towns so as to divest the rights of the towns under the grant, see Town of Paylet v. Clark, 9 Cranch 292 (1815).

ment of the United States will be endeared to the people, and the factions of the great States will be rendered harmless. Let us prevent the possibility of a division by creating great national interests which shall bind us in an indissoluble chain.[18]

In the case of *Martin v. Hunter's Lessee*,[19] Justice Story was afforded an opportunity to give effect to a part of this philosophy in announcing a nationalistic interpretation of the provisions of the federal Constitution.

The decisions of the Supreme Court in the cases of *Martin v. Hunter's Lessee, McCulloch v. Maryland*,[20] and *Dartmouth College v. Woodward*[21] brought to the forefront the issue of nationalism versus State rights which was smouldering from the time of the adoption of the Constitution and which had led to occasional resistance to the exercise of federal authority by the states.[22] Just as Hamilton and Jefferson differed over this issue soon after the adoption of the Constitution, and as Virginia and Kentucky issued their defiance to the federal government in 1798, so, after the War of 1812, Marshall espoused the cause of nationalism, and Spencer Roane and John Taylor of Caroline championed the rights of the states. Roane, as judge of the Virginia court of appeals, did all he could through his opinions and his writings to check the power of the Supreme Court which he believed was gradually transforming a confederate form of government into a federal or consolidated form.

Roane was an Anti-Federalist and a great admirer of Thomas Jefferson. He opposed the adoption of the federal Constitution. In his opinion, some powers were given by the Constitution which should have been withheld and he believed that important powers belonging to the states and to the people were not reserved with sufficient explicitness. His foremost political principle was "that the federal government was *limited* in its powers, that it possessed only those which were *expressly granted* by the terms of the compact or were *fairly incidental* to them."[23] Roane expressed his agreement with and supported the Virginia Resolutions. In 1804 he established the *Richmond Enquirer* with his cousin, Thomas Ritchie, as editor. Ritchie, Taylor, Roane, and John W. Brockenbrough controlled Virginia politics for several decades. Though Henry Adams and other historians of this period have little to say of Roane and his protests against the decisions of the Supreme Court, it is well known that he "fought long and strenuously against a construction of the United States Constitution which he and his co-workers thought would lead to

---

[18] *Life and Letters of Joseph Story*, ed. by William W. Story (Boston, 1851), I: 254.

[19] 1 Wheaton 304 (1815).

[20] 4 Wheaton 316 (1819).

[21] 4 Wheaton 519 (1819).

[22] See especially the Virginia and Kentucky Resolutions and the contests with New Hampshire and Pennsylvania, above, pp. 165 ff., 139 ff., and 270 ff.

[23] *Richmond Enquirer*, Sept. 17, 1822.

monarchy."[24] It was Taylor, however, who was the most vigorous and persistent opponent of the nationalistic tendencies which were sanctioned by the Supreme Court.

Taylor, who was an orphan adopted by Edmund Pendleton, approved in his early years the democratic and radical views of such men as Richard Henry Lee and Patrick Henry. From 1776 to 1781 he opposed measures designed to establish a union of the states. He was opposed to Washington and joined the popular party in Virginia in its attack on the Constitution.[25] In treatises published in 1794 entitled "A Definition of Parties, or the Political effects of the Paper System Considered" and "An Enquiry into the Principles and the Tendency of Certain Public Measures," Hamilton's financial program and especially his plan for a national bank and his debt funding system were attacked. At this early date Taylor predicted that the usurpation of constitutional authority involved in these measures, if not checked, would lead to the dreadful remedy of civil war.[26] He foresaw grave dangers in the development of a new kind of property—stocks and bonds—a form of credit or "paper interest" which was capable of indefinite expansion. The paper or capitalistic aristocracy of the United States, Taylor thought, was founded on exploitation sanctioned and fostered by the federal government and tended inevitably to divide the nation into two great classes. To offset the influence of the stock-jobbing security holders, he advised excluding them from the suffrage and from the legislative halls.[27]

Taylor joined in the protest against the Alien and Sedition Acts. Considering possible measures against these laws, he suggested that *the right of the state governments to expound the Constitution might possibly be made the basis of a movement towards its amendment. If this is insufficient the people in state conventions are incontrovertibly the contracting parties and, possessing the infringing rights, may proceed by orderly steps to attain the object.*[28] It was the agitation against the Alien and Sedition Laws which led to the meeting in Jefferson's home to which William E. Dodd refers as "setting in motion a movement that was to have a far-reaching effect on the history of the United States." At this meeting resolutions were drafted declaring that laws of Congress

---

[24] Edwin J. Smith, "Spencer Roane," *Branch Historical Papers* (June, 1905), II: 4.

[25] William E. Dodd, "John Taylor of Caroline, Prophet of Secession," *Branch Historical Papers* (June, 1908), II: 215 ff.

[26] Jefferson, *Writings* (Ford ed.), VI: 511; also Henry H. Simms, *Life of John Taylor* (Richmond, 1932), pp. 52–55.

[27] Eugene Tenbroeck Mudge, *The Social Philosophy of John Taylor of Caroline* (New York, 1939), p. 7.

[28] Letter to Jefferson, June 25, 1798, *Branch Historical Papers* (June, 1908), II: 225, and Simms, *op. cit.*, p. 72.

which were deemed unconstitutional could be set aside by the states. Breckenridge, a member of the party, presented a copy of the resolutions to the Kentucky legislature. Taylor introduced similar resolutions, drawn by Madison, in the Virginia assembly.[29] Though Taylor sponsored the Virginia Resolutions, he desired to have a law passed formally declaring the obnoxious acts unconstitutional; but, because Jefferson disapproved such a plan, Taylor withdrew his proposal.[30]

By the close of the War of 1812 the leaders in Congress, such as Henry Clay and John C. Calhoun, who were now espousing doctrines of nationalism similar to those sponsored by Hamilton, embarked upon a policy which was intended to enhance the importance and powers of the nation.[31] They began to champion a broad construction of the Constitution and, under this impetus, a second charter was granted to the Bank of the United States, thus preparing the way for one of Chief Justice Marshall's greatest decisions. They favored the adoption of a liberal protective tariff policy to aid industries suffering from British competition, and they desired to use the surplus income which might accrue from such a tariff to carry out a program of extensive public improvements. When the Supreme Court, under the influence of Marshall, began in constitutional opinions to endorse the nationalistic trends of the time, Taylor set about to refute the arguments of Marshall and to counteract the growing trends toward centralization.[32]

In a book published in 1814, Taylor attempted to reply to the conservative doctrines of John Adams in his "defense of the American Constitution." A follower of Rousseau, Taylor expounded the radical democratic philosophy of 1776. He advocated the doctrine of rotation in office as an essentially democratic doctrine. The Supreme Court, he thought, ought to be directly responsible to the people and ought not to be permitted to interfere with the popular will by their interpretations of the law and the Constitution. And he opposed the Hamiltonian idea of developing a privileged class which would be attached to the government by financial ties.[33] After the War of 1812, Roane and Taylor

---

[29] See Virginia and Kentucky Resolutions, above, pp. 165 ff.

[30] Dodd, *op. cit.*, p. 226.

[31] Speaking of Henry Clay and his enthusiastic support of the national bank, a protective tariff, internal improvements, and, above all, the expansion and development of the West, Babcock observes that he represented "not merely the aggressive, optimistic spirit of Kentucky and the west, but also the positive, exuberant nationalism of a new generation." *The Rise of American Nationality, 1811–1819*, p. 210. On all the great questions which before 1817 had divided the Federalists from the Republicans, Calhoun had supported the Federalist policies. See William MacDonald, *Jacksonian Democracy* (New York, 1906), p. 80.

[32] *Branch Historical Papers* (June, 1908), II: 239, 240.

[33] For analyses of the arguments in Taylor's "Inquiry into the Principles and Policy

began to take issue with Chief Justice Marshall who, according to Dodd, "made little pretense to legal lore, but whose decisions were doing more to establish the ideas of Hamilton than all the laws of the Federalist regime could possibly have done."[34] Roane's doctrines will be presented in connection with the cases of *Martin v. Hunter's Lessee* and *McCulloch v. Maryland;* Taylor's, which were published later, will be considered in the next chapter.

The first decision of the Supreme Court to affirm the doctrines and philosophy of nationalism, which the Court steadily and persistently asserted for the next two decades, was rendered by Justice Story in *Martin v. Hunter's Lessee.* Because of his personal interest in the cause, Chief Justice Marshall did not participate in the decision, though it is generally understood that he consulted with Story in the writing of the opinion which Story delivered.

MARTIN V. HUNTER'S LESSEE AND THE FIRST GREAT CONFLICT WITH VIRGINIA

Only a brief sketch can be given of the long and involved controversy through which the case of *Martin v. Hunter's Lessee* came to the Supreme Court. The case arose over the title to approximately three hundred thousand acres of land—one of the most valuable tracts of land in the so-called "Northern Neck" of Virginia. These lands belonged to Lord Fairfax, who, upon his death in England in 1781, provided for their transfer to his nephew Denny Fairfax.

The first suit in an extended course of litigation arose when Denny Fairfax, the heir of the Fairfax grant, moved to eject Hite who had taken out a patent from the state for a section of the Fairfax lands. The state claimed possession of the land under an act of 1782 declaring void the Fairfax grant from the English Crown. The local court having decided against him, Fairfax appealed to the general court of Virginia and engaged John Marshall as his attorney. Marshall at this early date formed a judgment with respect to the validity of the Fairfax claim. He thought it should be unnecessary to defend the title of Lord Fairfax, for "the long and quiet possession of himself and his predecessors; the acqui-

---

of the Government of the United States," see Simms, *op. cit.,* pp. 134 ff., Charles A. Beard, *Economic Origins of Jeffersonian Democracy* (New York, 1915), pp. 197 ff., and Benjamin F. Wright, Jr., "The Philosopher of Jeffersonian Democracy," 22 *Amer. Pol. Sci. Rev.* (Nov., 1928), pp. 875 ff. Beard thinks this volume of Taylor deserves to rank among the two or three really historic contributions to political science which have been produced in the United States. *Ibid.,* p. 323. A useful summary of Taylor's economic and political doctrines is given in Mudge, *op. cit.,* pp. 27 ff.

[34] *Branch Historical Papers* (June, 1908), II: 242, 243.

escence of the country; the several grants of the Crown, together with
the various acts of the assembly recognizing, and, in the most explicit
terms, admitting his right, seemed to have fixed it on a foundation, not
only not to be shaken, but even not to be attempted to be shaken."[35] John
Marshall's brother Thomas already had an interest in part of the Fairfax
tract and the Chief Justice himself, as a member of the Marshall syndi-
cate, was soon to become a joint purchaser. The court decided in favor
of Hite and ordered that the Fairfax heirs convey legal title to Hite for
the land included in his patent.

Virginia, under its laws, denied the right of an alien to inherit property and, claiming title to the Fairfax lands in accordance with the confiscation acts passed during the period of the Revolution, granted a
tract of land in the "Northern Neck" to David Hunter. In 1791 Hunter
brought an action of ejectment against Fairfax in the county court at
Winchester. The court decided against Hunter, and he appealed to the
state supreme court. In the meantime, John Marshall, then a member
of the Virginia legislature, secured the passage of an act confirming a
compromise of the Fairfax claims entered into between the state and the
Fairfax purchasers, each party relinquishing certain lands. The act
stated that Marshall had become one of the purchasers of the lands of
Mr. Fairfax and was authorized to act for them all.[36] The supreme court
held that the act of compromise passed by the legislature in 1796 at the
request of John Marshall and his brother, who now claimed a substantial
interest in the Fairfax lands, had extinguished the title of Fairfax and
of those who claimed under him such lands in the "Northern Neck" as
were waste and unappropriated at the time of the death of Lord Fairfax.
Consequently the decision of the county court was reversed and the
claim of Hunter sustained. Judge Roane criticised the Marshalls for
agreeing to a compromise and in effect repudiating it because they
thought Jay's Treaty had strengthened and affirmed their title to the
Fairfax lands.[37] An appeal was taken to the Supreme Court of the United
States. The governor recommended that the appeal of the case be prosecuted by the state. When the legislature declined to authorize the ex-

---

[35] Hite v. Fairfax, 4 Call 42, 69 (1786).

[36] *Statutes at Large of Virginia*, II: 22, 23.

[37] Said Judge Roane: "I consider the compromise as having been deposited with the
court for the purpose of settling all the causes embraced thereby, according to the
provisions thereof: and I can never consent that the appellees, after having got the
benefit thereof, should refuse to submit thereto, or pay the equivalent." Hunter v.
Fairfax's Devisee, 1 Mumford 218, 232 (1810). Beveridge contends that the Marshalls
agreed in the compromise to execute deeds extinguishing the Fairfax title as soon as
conveyance should be made to him by Fairfax and that the Fairfax deed was not
executed until ten years after the compromise. *The Life of John Marshall*, IV: 149.

penditure of funds for this purpose and Hunter's counsel died, an effort was made to secure the postponement of the trial of the case. On granting this request, Justice Chase remarked: "It is a matter of great moment and ought to be deliberately and finally settled."[38]

The case came before the Supreme Court again in February, 1812, on a writ of error from the supreme court of Virginia which had now taken a decided stand against the Fairfax heirs. Chief Justice Marshall and Justice Washington were absent during the argument, and when, in March, 1813, Justice Story rendered an opinion for the Court, Chief Justice Marshall and Justice Todd were absent. In an elaborately documented opinion, Story concluded that Fairfax held fee simple in his own right to the tract in dispute and at the commencement of the original suit by Hunter had complete possession of the land and that Jay's Treaty confirmed the title to him and his heirs and protected him from any forfeiture by reason of alienage. Though it was conceded that Virginia could have vested the title in itself by an inquest of office, or its equivalent, no such proceedings had been taken. To this view Justice Johnson dissented. An alien did not in his opinion have such rights to property that they could not be taken away by legislative action. Hunter claimed title under a law expressly relating to the lands of Lord Fairfax authorizing them to be entered, surveyed, and granted. Such grants could be made by act of Parliament, and Johnson could not see any reason why similar authority could not be exercised by the legislature of Virginia.

Despite the fact that only three Justices, Story, Livingston, and Duval, concurred in the opinion and judgment—unless Washington who had not heard the argument voted with the majority—Story rendered a judgment which ran counter to the laws of Virginia, both with respect to the interpretation and effect of the confiscation acts and to the decision of the state courts that an alien could not acquire land by devise; and an order was entered requiring the Virginia court of appeals to enter judgment for Philip Martin, the Fairfax devisee.

The judges of the Virginia court consulted Jefferson and Monroe and also many members of the Virginia bar. In addition to the attorneys who argued the case for the interested parties, several members of the bar spoke on behalf of Hunter as *amicus curiae*. It was finally decided not to obey the mandamus of the Supreme Court, the Judges rendering their opinions *seriatim*.

In the opinion of Judge Cabell,

neither government nor any of its departments, can act *compulsively*, on the other or on any of its organs in their political or official capacities. . . . The Constitution of the

---

[38] 3 Dallas 305 (1796).

United States contemplates the independence of both governments, and regards the *residuary* sovereignty of the states, as not less inviolable, than the delegated sovereignty of the United States. It must have been foreseen that controversies would sometimes arise as to the boundaries of the two jurisdictions. Yet the Constitution has provided no umpire ... to give to the general government or any of its departments a direct and controlling operation upon the state departments, *as such,* would be to change at once, the whole character of our system.[39]

To Judge Cabell, it was the supremacy of the Constitution, laws, and treaties which were established by the Constitution, not the supremacy of the federal judges and courts, and it was the conclusive authority of these courts, to which exception was taken. It was admitted, said he, that the appellate power claimed for the federal courts was not given by the Constitution in express terms and that it must be deduced by inference and implication and by such inference and implication it was concluded that the federal courts might determine finally and conclusively the extent of their own jurisdiction. The claim that the federal courts were supreme, he maintained, thus rested on a weak and indefensible foundation.

Defending the doctrine of divided sovereignty, Judge Cabell insisted that "the two governments, therefore, possessing, each its portion of the divided sovereignty, although embracing the same territory, and operating on the same persons and frequently on the same subjects, are nevertheless separate from, and independent of, each other. From this position, believed to be incontrovertible, it necessarily results that each government must act by *its own* organs; from no other can it expect, command, or enforce obedience, even as to objects coming within the range of its powers." But despite the independence of the two sets of courts, by the terms of the mandamus, said Judge Cabell, "we are required as state judges to enter upon a judgment, not our own, but dictated and prescribed to us by another court."

Counsel, said Judge Roane, have warned us of the consequences of a decision contrary to the enforcement of national decrees because of the anarchical principles prevalent in New England at the time of the argument. They ought to have remembered that it is not for this court to regard political consequences in rendering its judgments and "they should also have recollected, that there is a Charybdis to be avoided, as well as a Scylla; that a centripetal, as well as a centrifugal principle, exists in the government; and that no calamity would be more to be deplored by the American people, than a vortex in the general government, which should ingulph and sweep away, every vestige of the state constitutions."[40] According to Roane the state had a right to confiscate

---

[39] Hunter v. Martin, 4 Mumford 8, 9 (1814).   [40] 4 Mumford 26.

property belonging to an alien enemy. This was done by the act of 1782 whereby quit rents were to be paid to the state instead of to Fairfax. It was his opinion that the title of the state to the land in question having been perfected under the act of 1782, the treaty of 1783 could not affect any subsequent transfer of the property authorized by the state. Since the title given by the governor in 1789 was good, there was no legal basis on which Hunter's rights could be attacked. Under such circumstances, the assertion of appellate jurisdiction over the Virginia courts on a matter touching the validity of titles to land was deemed particularly objectionable.

In reply to the citations from *The Federalist* favorable to the exercise of the appellate power contended for, Judge Roane noted that these papers were written in the heat and hurry of the contest to secure the ratification of the Constitution and that "its principal reputed author was, an active partisan of the Constitution, and a supposed favorer of a consolidated government." In opposition to the nationalist views of the authors of *The Federalist*, Roane quoted and made extensive use of Madison's report to the Virginia legislature on the Virginia Resolutions of 1798 upholding the rights and duties of the states in defining their relations to the federal compact. Summarizing the arguments of the Republicans in defense of the Resolutions of 1798, Roane raised the query, "What, then, do the gentlemen contend for, but a power neither expressly granted to the general government, nor taken from the States, nor forming a part of the judicial power of the United States?"

When counsel called attention to the fact that the Supreme Court had assumed jurisdiction in a number of cases of this kind,[41] Judge Roane claimed that the question did not receive the deliberate consideration which it deserved and that this jurisdiction had been attained under a piecemeal process involving "a latitude of construction and discretion in the Court, which is at war with the idea of limited and specified powers in the general government." These decisions, said he, were rendered at the same time that sundry acts of the national Legislature were passed expanding federal authority. Though the acts in dispute have been repealed or dropped by general consent, under a more correct view of the Constitution some of the corresponding decisions of the federal courts have remained to be followed as precedents.

---

[41] From 1789 to 1813 the Supreme Court had taken jurisdiction of writs of error to state courts in sixteen cases. The first case appealed to the Court on a writ of error to a state court was Olney v. Arnold, 3 Dallas 308 (1796), which involved the construction of an act of Congress. The first case in such a proceeding in which a state law relating to British debts was declared void, because in conflict with the treaty of 1783, was Clerke v. Harwood, *ibid.*, p. 342.

Quoting the Virginia Resolution that, in an instance of a deliberate and palpable exercise of powers not granted to the federal government, the states, as parties to the compact, "have the right and are in duty bound to arrest the progress of the evil," Roane maintained that "while the States in their legislative, or even original, character, are authorized to interfere, in cases of the palpable nature just mentioned, the courts of the States are also authorized to check the evil when it occurs, in the exercise of their ordinary jurisdiction." The case of *Respublica v. Cobbett*[42] was cited as an instance in which the supreme court of Pennsylvania refused to permit the removal of a case to the federal courts. Upon the whole, thought Roane, the Constitution confers no power upon the Supreme Court of the United States to meddle with the judgments of this court in a case of this kind.[43]

Counsel for Martin based much of their argument on the ground of expediency. If the appellate power of the federal courts be denied, said they, the general government will be deprived of an effective means of executing its laws and treaties; there would be no uniformity in the decisions relating to federal powers; and hence the power was necessary for the preservation of the union. To these arguments the judges replied that the weakness in federal law enforcement and dangers to the peace and tranquillity of the union were not sufficient to warrant the extension of federal judicial powers to fields not specifically granted by the Constitution.

Following the separate opinions of the judges, it was declared that:

The court is unanimously of opinion, that the appellate power of the Supreme Court of the United States does not extend to this court, under a sound construction of the Constitution of the United States;—that so much of the 25th section of the act of Congress, to establish the judicial courts of the United States, as extends the appellate

---

[42] 3 Dallas 467 (1798)

[43] William E. Dodd regards Roane's paper as "a political manifesto designed to advance the cause of state sovereignty and to arouse hostility towards Marshall, who seemed still to dominate the Court. Public discussion was at once aroused and the local court was fully sustained in its refusal to honor the mandamus. John Taylor of Caroline took up his pen once more on behalf of state rights and the Enquirer 'thundered' against the great Chief Justice who was again proving false to the 'ancient dominion.' " "Chief Justice Marshall and Virginia, 1813–1821," *Amer. Hist. Rev.* (July, 1907), XII: 776, 779.

Roane wrote to Jefferson about submitting his opinion in *Martin v. Hunter's Lessee* to James Monroe, and said, "He seemed entirely to concur in my conclusion, it strengthened the claim of his paper to your inspection. I was, therefore, highly satisfied, when, on my return, he offered to send it to you." When Jefferson commended Roane's opinion, he wrote: "I am much flattered and gratified by the result of your letter: flattered by the very civil manner in which you are pleased to speak of my humble labors; and gratified to find that I have not erred, in the great principles at least, on which the question seems to turn." *Branch Historical Papers* (June, 1905), II: 131, 132.

jurisdiction of the Supreme Court to this court, is not in pursuance of the Constitution of the United States; that the writ of error in this case was improvidently allowed under the authority of that act; that the proceedings thereon in the Supreme Court were *coram non judice* in relation to this court; and that obedience to its mandate be declined by this court.[44]

This has been called "the first 'pass at arms' between the Virginia school of states-rights advocates and the great Chief Justice,"—Marshall and Story sought to sustain the position that a state was subordinate to the union; whereas Roane and the other state judges supported the view that a state could refuse obedience to the national authority.[45]

Judge Tucker, arguing on behalf of Hunter on his third appeal to the Supreme Court, agreed that the Supreme Court had all the incidental authority necessary to carry into effect the powers expressly given by the Constitution, but believed that this authority could not extend to the exercise of any power inconsistent with the whole genius, spirit, and tenor of the Constitution. The whole scheme of the Constitution aims to secure action on the citizens of the United States at large, and not on the state authorities.[46]

Justice Story delivered the opinion of the Court which has been called "the keystone of the whole arch of federal judicial power."[47] The questions involved were, he admitted, of great importance and delicacy— "perhaps it is not too much to affirm, that, upon their right decision, rest some of the most solid principles which have hitherto been supposed to sustain and protect the Constitution itself." He commented on the great learning and ability of the members of the state supreme court whose judgment was under review and then turned to what were called "some preliminary considerations." The Constitution of the United States, in his opinion,

was ordained and established, not by the States in their sovereign capacities, but emphatically, as the preamble of the Constitution declares, by "the people of the United States." There can be no doubt, that it was competent to the people to invest the general government with all the powers which they might deem proper and necessary; to extend or restrain these powers according to their own good pleasure, and to give them a paramount and supreme authority. As little doubt can there be, that the people had a right to prohibit to the States the exercise of any powers which were, in their judgment, incompatible with the objects of the general compact; to make the powers of the state governments, in given cases, subordinate to those of the Nation, or to reserve to themselves those sovereign authorities which they might not choose to delegate to either. The Constitution was not, therefore, necessarily carved out of the

---

[44] 4 Mumford 58, 59.

[45] Dodd, *op. cit.*, p. 779.

[46] Martin v. Hunter's Lessee, 1 Wheaton 304, 316 (1816).

[47] Charles Warren, *The Supreme Court in United States History* (Boston, 1922), I: 449.

existing state sovereignties, nor a surrender of powers already existing in state institutions. . . .

The government, then, of the United States can claim no powers which are not granted to it by the Constitution, and the powers actually granted must be such as are expressly given, or given by necessary implication. On the other hand, this instrument, like every other grant, is to have a reasonable construction, according to the import of its terms; and where a power is expressly given in general terms, it is not to be restrained to particular cases, unless that construction grows out of the context expressly, or by necessary implication. The words are to be taken in their natural and obvious sense, and not in a sense unreasonably restricted or enlarged.[48]

Quoting the sections of the Constitution defining the jurisdiction of the federal courts, Story said this "is the voice of the whole American people, solemnly declared, in establishing one great department of that government which was, in many respects, national, and in all, supreme. It is a part of the same instrument which was to act not merely upon individuals, but upon States; and to deprive them altogether of the exercise of some powers of sovereignty, and to restrain and regulate them in the exercise of others."[49]

Without lower courts, some of the express provisions of the Constitution could not be carried into effect, as, for example, punishment of crimes against the United States and suits between citizens of different states. Hence, Story declared: "The judicial power must, therefore, be vested in some court by Congress; and to suppose that it was not an obligation, binding on them, but might, at their pleasure, be omitted or declined, is to suppose that, under the sanction of the Constitution, they might defeat the Constitution itself; a construction which would lead to such a result cannot be sound."

The jurisdiction of the federal courts, Story insisted, includes cases arising under the Constitution, laws, and treaties of the United States and does not depend upon the nature of the parties to the suits. It is the case—not the court—that predicates a basis for the appellate jurisdiction. Referring to the reasoning of the state judges, Story observed:

It has been argued, that such an appellate jurisdiction over state courts is inconsistent with the genius of our governments, and the spirit of the Constitution. That the latter was never designed to act upon state sovereignties, but only upon the people, and that if the power exists, it will materially impair the sovereignty of the States, and the independence of their courts. We cannot yield to the force of this reasoning. . . . It is a mistake, that the Constitution was not designed to operate upon the States, in their corporate capacities. It is crowded with provisions which restrain or annul the sovereignty of the States in some of the highest branches of their prerogatives. . . . The courts of the United States, can, without question, revise the proceedings of the executive and legislative authorities of the States, and if they are found to be contrary to

[48] 1 Wheaton 324–326.
[49] *Ibid.*, p. 328.

the Constitution, may declare them to be of no legal validity. Surely, the exercise of the same right over judicial tribunals is not a higher or more dangerous act of sovereign power.[50]

The arguments of policy and expediency which were urged by counsel on behalf of Martin in the state court were cogently stated and approved by Story. Appellate power claimed by the Supreme Court was necessary to assure uniformity in the decisions relating to federal laws and treaties, for the purposes of the Constitution would be carried out inadequately if the federal courts could act only on parties and not on the states. On the whole, Story concluded "that the appellate power of the United States does extend to cases pending in the state courts; and that the 25th section of the Judiciary Act, which authorizes the exercise of this jurisdiction in the specified cases, by a writ of error, is supported by the letter and spirit of the Constitution. We find no clause in that instrument which limits this power; and we dare not interpose a limitation where the people have not been disposed to create one."[51] The judgment of the court of appeals of Virginia was reversed and the judgment of the district court at Winchester affirmed.

Justice Johnson, concurring, observed that "the Court disavows all intention to decide on the right to issue compulsory process to the state courts; thus leaving us, in my opinion, where the Constitution and laws place us—supreme over persons and cases, as far as our judicial powers extend, but not asserting any compulsory control over the state tribunals."[52]

He conceded that "the general government must cease to exist whenever it loses the power of protecting itself in the exercise of its constitutional powers," but, on the other hand, he was "persuaded that the American people can no longer enjoy the blessings of a free government, whenever the state sovereignties shall be prostrated at the feet of the general government, nor the proud consciousness of equality and security, any longer than the independence of judicial power shall be maintained consecrated and intangible, that I could borrow the language of a celebrated orator, and exclaim, 'I rejoice that Virginia has resisted.' "[53]

Deprecating the extreme position taken by the Virginia court, Johnson raised the query, "are then, the judgments of this Court to be reviewed in every court of our Union?" The authority of the Supreme Court of the United States, he thought, should rest, not upon supremacy over state tribunals, but as "a superior claim upon the comity of the state tribunals."

---

[50] 1 Wheaton 324–344.

[51] *Ibid.*, p. 351.

[52] *Ibid.*, p. 362.

[53] *Ibid.*, p. 363.

"It is enough, at present," Johnson thought,

to have shown that Congress has not asserted, and this Court has not attempted, to exercise that kind of authority *in personam*, over the state courts, which would place them in the relation of an inferior responsible body, without their own acquiescence. And I have too much confidence in the state tribunals, to believe that a case ever will occur in which it will be necessary for the general government to assume a controlling power over these tribunals. . . . I flatter myself that the full extent of the constitutional revising power may be secured to the United States, and the benefits of it to the individual, without ever resorting to compulsory or restrictive process upon the state tribunals.[54]

The language of the two opinions of Story in the Fairfax controversy follows so closely the main lines of Marshall's reasoning that it has been claimed that Marshall wrote the opinions. Whether or not there is any truth in this contention, Story wrote in 1831 that Marshall "concurred in every word" of his second opinion.[55] In the minds of the Federalists this opinion was as necessary and as appropriate an answer to the New England doctrines of State rights and secession as was Marshall's reply to the Republican attack on the Judiciary in 1802.

The Republicans condemned Story for his nationalist principles of constitutional interpretation. William E. Dodd calls Judge Roane's opinion in the Virginia court "a political manifesto to advance the cause of state sovereignty." On the other hand, Story's opinion was a political manifesto under the cloak of constitutional interpretation, the purpose of which was to advance the cause of federalism and nationalism. It is true, of course, that with certain Federalist assumptions or presuppositions, such as the presumed design of the Constitution to establish a sovereign nation with federal supremacy over the states and the proposed superiority of the Judiciary in interpreting the Constitution, the language of the document could be construed to grant the authority to the federal courts for which Story and Marshall were contending. But starting with different assumptions and interpreting the course of American history to date, together with the express provisions of the Constitution and its amendments, the decision of the Virginia supreme court could just as readily be sustained. At bottom the issue was one of politics and expediency rather than law. Was it preferable to have a federation or a confederation of states?

The Republicans rallied around Roane and made a political issue of

---

[54] 1 Wheaton 376, 382.

[55] Story, *Life and Letters*, II: 49. Warren thinks that Story's opinion was entirely in accord with the nationalist views he had espoused and that "it was the Federalist law breakers and traitors of New England who produced the decision in Martin v. Hunter's Lessee, and not the pressure of Marshall's influence." *The Supreme Court in United States History*, I: 453.

his opinion. The Federalists as strongly supported Story, defending, they insisted, the patriotic cause of national unity. It was a Court predominantly Republican—five Republicans and one Federalist—that decided against Hunter and the state of Virginia, but the Republican members of the Bench had given evidence in previous cases that on the issue of nationalism versus State rights they were ready to follow in the footsteps of Marshall, even though they did so with some hesitation and, as Johnson expressed it, with misgivings about the meddling of the Court in such grave political controversies. Men were beginning to catch a glimpse of the fact that the conflict between the Supreme Court and the court of appeals of Virginia was a phase of an underlying issue which judicial pronouncements alone could not settle. When the Supreme Court attempted to settle a grave political question—the status of slaves—in the *Dred Scott Case* it was severely criticized, but was it not as clearly participating in the settlement of a political controversy in the efforts to resolve the conflicting claims over the location of sovereignty between the states and the nation?

When it was held, in an opinion delivered by Chief Justice Marshall,[56] that the phrase, "any person or persons on the high seas," in the Piracy Act of 1790, was intended not to apply to persons on board any vessel belonging exclusively to subjects of a foreign state, John Quincy Adams thought that the Supreme Court, by a decision founded upon captious subtleties, cast away the jurisdiction which a law of Congress had given. "Their reasoning," he maintained, "is a sample of judicial logic—disingenuous, false, and hollow—a logic so abhorrent to my nature that it gave me an early disgust to the practice of law, and led me to the unalterable determination never to accept a judicial office. In this case, if human language means anything, Congress had made general piracy, by whomsoever and wheresoever upon the high seas committed, cognizable by the Circuit Court."[57]

The interpretation of the twenty-fifth section of the Judiciary Act of 1789 was involved again in the case of *Gelston v. Hoyt*.[58] Revenue officers were being sued for damages for seizing a vessel by the order of President Madison in the enforcement of the federal neutrality laws. The case, it was contended, could not be removed to the Supreme Court of the United States, because it had been decided in the state court in favor of

---

[56] United States v. Palmer, 3 Wheaton 610 (1818). For a different interpretation of this phrase by Justice Story, speaking for the Court, see United States v. Smith, 5 Wheaton 153 (1820).

[57] *Memoirs of John Quincy Adams*, ed. by Charles Francis Adams (Philadelphia, 1875), IV: 363.

[58] 3 Wheaton 246 (1818).

Hoyt, affirmed by the court of errors, and transmitted to the Supreme Court to enforce the decree, and the record was no longer in the possession of the court of last resort.

The Judiciary Act, said Story in rendering the opinion of the Court, allows the person who thinks himself aggrieved by the decision of any inferior court five years, within which time he may sue out his writ of error, and bring his cause into this Court. The same time limit applies to judgments and decrees of a state court in cases within the jurisdiction of the Supreme Court. The constitutional jurisdiction of the Courts of the union cannot be affected by any regulation which a state may make for its own judicial system.

The writ being properly granted, Story held that the Courts of the United States have exclusive jurisdiction over questions of forfeiture in the application of federal laws. Since the statute under which the revenue officers acted provided only that the President may employ the land and naval forces in the detention and the taking possession of ships, the presidential instructions to civil officers to accomplish the same purpose was unauthorized by law. The argument of the Attorney General that the policy of the law is "to throw its shield over officers while acting under fair and honest convictions" did not seem to warrant, said the Court, giving protection to the officers who, in following the instructions of the President, had acted illegally. Having demonstrated, in certain respects at least, its superiority over the Legislative branch of the government, the Court was asserting a similar superiority over the Executive branch, particularly in the way of requiring the President and his subordinates to act in accord with its interpretation of the letter of the Constitution and statutes. But the act reëstablishing a national bank brought to the Court the greatest constitutional issue since the establishment of the federal government in 1789.

THE CONTEST WITH MARYLAND OVER THE TAXATION OF THE NATIONAL BANK

The national bank's charter, having expired in 1811, was not renewed because of the objections raised on constitutional grounds—objections in which Jefferson and Madison concurred. Madison, agreeing with the views expressed by Jefferson, had opposed Hamilton's proposal to establish a national bank on the ground that Congress was not granted the authority to charter such an institution. But Congress and President Washington ignored their objections and a national bank was organized and set into operation. The Republicans frequently objected to the establishment of the bank on practical and political as well as constitutional grounds.[59] But financial difficulties during the War of 1812 and thereafter led the President and Congress to establish a second national bank in 1816.[60] The Republicans now regarded the consideration of the constitutional question as a "useless consumption of time," whereas the Federalists, led by Daniel Webster, opposed the bank bill. It was freely admitted that the force of circumstances had led to the change of opinions on the bank issue. President Madison declared that he regarded the constitutional issue as settled "by repeated recognitions . . . of the legislative, executive, and judicial branches of the government, accompanied by indications . . . of a concurrence of the general will of the nation." Such evidence of the public judgment, he thought, necessarily superseded individual opinions.[61]

The second Bank of the United States had an inauspicious beginning. Established to check bank inflation, the new institution became the center of spectacular inflation in its own stock. In August, 1818, the bank

---

[59] The sentiment which had become widespread is indicated by the resolutions adopted by the legislatures of Pennsylvania and Virginia. It was resolved by the legislature of Pennsylvania that "the people of the United States by the adoption of the federal Constitution established a general government for special purposes, reserving to themselves respectively, the rights and authorities not delegated in that instrument. To the compact thereby created, each State acceded in its character as a State, and is a party. The act of union thus entered into being to all intents and purposes a treaty between sovereign States, the general government by this treaty was not constituted the exclusive or final judge of the powers it was to exercise; for if it were so to judge then its judgment and not the Constitution would be the measure of its authority.

"Should the general government in any of its departments violate the provisions of the Constitution, it rests with the States, and with the people, to apply suitable remedies." Resolutions against the Bank, January 11, 1811. *Senate Journal of Pennsylvania, 1810–11*, pp. 92, 93, 104, 105. See *Amer. State Papers, Finance*, II: 467.

The legislature of Virginia resolved on January 22, 1811, that "this assembly are deeply impressed with the conviction that the original grant of that charter was unconstitutional; that Congress have no power whatever to renew it; and that the exercise of such a power would be not only unconstitutional, but a dangerous encroachment on the sovereignty of the States." *Acts of Virginia, 1811–12*, pp. 143–152.

[60] In his veto of a bank bill passed in 1814, Madison indicated his willingness to waive the question of the constitutional authority of the legislature to establish a bank "as being precluded in my judgment by repeated recognitions, under varied circumstances, of the validity of such an institution in acts of the legislative, executive, and judicial branches of the government, accompanied by indications in different modes, of a recurrence of the general will of the nation." James D. Richardson, *A Compilation of the Messages and Papers* (Washington, 1911), I: 555.

[61] *Letters and other Writings of James Madison* (Cong. ed., 1865), IV: 211. Madison explained in 1831 his change of opinion on the constitutionality of the national bank bill. My abstract opinion of the text of the Constitution had not changed, said he, but my assent was given "in pursuance of my early and unchanged opinion, that, in the case of a Constitution as of a law, a course of authoritative expositions sufficiently deliberate, uniform, and settled, was an evidence, of the public will necessarily overruling individual opinions." *Writings* (Hunt ed.), IX: 442, 443.

decided upon a policy of contraction which resulted in the suspension of specie payments by many banks. Agitation against the bank led to a Congressional investigation which revealed mismanagement and dishonest practices. About the time the case of *McCulloch v. Maryland* was on its way to the Supreme Court, a movement was under way to repeal the bank charter.[62] Through mismanagement and the exercise of undue control over state banks, the new national bank faced a hostile public sentiment, particularly in the states of the West and the South. Legislation was enacted to prevent the effective operation of the bank in Georgia, Indiana, Illinois, Kentucky, Maryland, North Carolina, and Ohio. The acts of Maryland and Ohio finally came to the Supreme Court for adjudication. It was the Maryland act levying a stamp tax on all notes issued by banks chartered outside the state that raised the constitutional issue of *McCulloch v. Maryland*.[63]

Arguing for the bank, Webster thought that since all branches of the government had been, for nearly thirty years, acting on the view that the federal government had authority to establish a national bank, it would seem to be too late to question the exercise of this authority. Hamilton's argument in support of a national bank was cited in detail in accordance with which Congress was warranted in using "all proper and suitable means, not specially prohibited" in carrying out the express grants of power made in the Constitution. Hopkinson, for the state, contended that whereas the first national bank act was probably unwarranted by the Constitution, the conditions which were regarded as rendering necessary at that time the establishment of a national bank institution no longer existed. It was claimed also on behalf of the state that even if the authority to establish a national bank was conceded, both the state and federal governments had concurrent power to tax such agency. Luther Martin, also supporting the cause of the state, said the real question before the Court was whether by interpretation powers now could be engrafted upon the Constitution which were disclaimed by the makers and which, "if they had been fairly avowed at the time, would have prevented its adoption."

Chief Justice Marshall, who was expected to take up the work of "administering" the Constitution along the lines laid down by Hamilton,[64] rendered the opinion of the Court,[65] in which all of the justices including

---

[62] Samuel Rezneck, "The Depression of 1819–22, A Social History," *Amer. Hist. Rev.* (Oct., 1933), XXXIX: 29.

[63] 4 Wheaton 316 (1819).

[64] Cf. James Truslow Adams, *The Living Jefferson* (New York, 1936), p. 301.

[65] This opinion, thinks William Draper Lewis, was perhaps "the most celebrated judicial utterance in the annals of the English speaking world." *Great American Lawyers* (Philadelphia, 1907), II: 363.

the five Republican members concurred. The opinion was delivered three days after the extensive arguments of counsel had been concluded. It is not unlikely, therefore, that much of this political state paper was written before the argument took place before the Court. Beveridge regards it as reasonably probable that at least the framework of the opinion was written in Richmond during the summer, autumn, and winter of 1818–1819.[66]

As was his custom when issues of grave political import were involved, Marshall began by the making of assumptions on seriously contested points which resolved the questions in dispute in favor of the federal government. The contention frequently asserted by the states, particularly from 1810 to 1816, that the Supreme Court did not have jurisdiction in such a case was denied with the following comment:

The Constitution of our country, in its most interesting and vital parts, is to be considered; the conflicting powers of the government of the Union and of its members, as marked in that Constitution, are to be discussed; and an opinion given, which may essentially influence the great operations of the government. No tribunal can approach such a question without a deep sense of its importance, and of the awful responsibility involved in its decision. But it must be decided peacefully, or remain a source of hostile legislation, perhaps of a hostility of a still more serious nature; and if it is to be so decided, by this tribunal alone can the decision be made. On the Supreme Court of the United States has the Constitution of our country devolved this important duty.[67]

Those defending the rights of the states had repeatedly asserted before the courts and in Congress that the Constitution as an instrument of government did not emanate from the people but resulted from the acts of sovereign and independent states. This may be regarded as the fundamental assumption of the State rights party. Asserting the primary assumption to the contrary, Marshall admitted that the members of the federal Convention were elected by state legislatures and that the completed document was referred back to the legislatures and then under their auspices adopted by conventions called in the states.[68] But, regardless of this procedure, said Marshall,

the government of the Union, then, . . . is, emphatically, and truly, a government of the people. In form and in substance it emanates from them. Its powers are granted by them, and are to be exercised directly on them, and for their benefit.

This government is acknowledged by all to be one of enumerated powers. . . . That

---

[66] *The Life of John Marshall,* IV: 290. According to Beveridge, John Marshall in this case, "rose to the loftiest heights of judicial statesmanship. . . . It is . . . among the very first of the greatest judicial utterances of all time." *Ibid.,* pp. 280, 289.

[67] 4 Wheaton 400, 401 (1819).

[68] "They [the people, Marshall maintained] acted upon it, in the only manner in which they can act safely, effectively, and wisely on such a subject, by assembling in

principle is now universally admitted. But the question respecting the extent of the powers actually granted, is perpetually arising, and will probably continue to arise, as long as our system shall exist. . . . If any one proposition could command the universal assent of mankind, we might expect it would be this—that the government of the Union, though limited in its powers, is supreme within its sphere of action. This would seem to result necessarily from its nature. It is the government of all, its powers are delegated by all, it represents all, and acts for all.[69]

The discouraging situation, so far as those defending State rights are concerned, was commented upon by Marshall when he noted that though any one state may be willing to control the operations of the federal government, no state is willing to allow others to control them. "The government of the United States, then," he asserted, "though limited in its powers, is supreme; and its laws, when made in pursuance of the Constitution form the supreme law of the land 'anything in the Constitution or laws of any state to the contrary notwithstanding.' "[70]

Though the power to establish a national bank was not expressly granted to the federal government, Marshall pointed out the broad and significant grants of power to Congress, and then observed that "a government, entrusted with such ample powers, on the due execution of which the happiness and prosperity of the Nation so vitally depends, must also be entrusted with ample means for their execution. The power being given, it is the interest of the Nation to facilitate its execution. It can never be their interest, and cannot be presumed to have been their intention, to clog and embarrass its execution by withholding the most appropriate means."[71]

When it was argued that the creation of a corporation appertains to sovereignty and that the power necessarily belonged to the states, Marshall answered with the familiar dual or divided sovereignty theory prevalent during the days when the Constitution was being drafted. In America, he said, "the powers of sovereignty are divided between the government of the Union and those of the States. They are each sovereign, with respect to the objects committed to it, and neither sovereign with respect to the objects committed to the other."[72]

The attorneys for the state adopted the Jeffersonian interpretation of the clause authorizing Congress to enact laws "which shall be necessary

---

convention. It is true, they assembled in their several States—and where else should they have assembled? No political dreamer was ever wild enough to think of breaking down the lines which separate States, and of compounding the people into one common mass. Of consequence when they act, they act in their States. But the measures they adopt do not, on that account, cease to be the measures of the people themselves, or become the measures of state governments." 4 Wheaton 403 (1819).

[69] *Ibid.*, pp. 404, 405.   [71] *Ibid.*, p. 408.
[70] *Ibid.*, pp. 405, 406.   [72] *Ibid.*, p. 410.

and proper for carrying into execution the foregoing powers," namely, that only such additional powers were conferred by this provision as were "absolutely" necessary for the execution of the powers expressly granted to Congress. This interpretation could not be adopted, insisted Marshall, without "confiding the choice of means to such narrow limits as not to leave it in the power of Congress to adopt any which might be appropriate, and which were conducive to the end. This provision is made in a Constitution intended to endure for ages to come, and, consequently, to be adapted to the various crises of human affairs."[73]

Then, adopting outright the Hamiltonian method of interpreting federal powers and using Hamilton's language when he argued in defense of the first national bank act, Marshall concluded:

The result of the most careful and attentive consideration bestowed on this clause is, that if it does not enlarge, it cannot be construed to restrain the powers of Congress. . . . If no other motive for its insertion can be suggested, a sufficient one is found in the desire to remove all doubts respecting the right to legislate on that vast mass of incidental powers which must be involved in the Constitution, if that instrument be not a splendid bauble.

We admit, as all must admit, that the powers of the government are limited, and that its limits are not to be transcended. But we think the sound construction of the Constitution must allow to the national legislation that discretion, which will enable that body to perform the high duties assigned to it, in the manner most beneficial to the people. Let the end be legitimate, let it be within the scope of the Constitution, and all means which are appropriate, which are plainly adapted to that end, which are not prohibited, but consist with the letter and spirit of the Constitution, are constitutional.[74]

The famous doctrine of implied prohibitions as an essential feature of the federal system of the United States was then announced, as follows:

That the power to tax involves the power to destroy; that the power to destroy may defeat and render useless the power to create; that there is a plain repugnance, in conferring on one government the power to control the constitutional measures of another. . . .

The Court has bestowed on this subject its most deliberate consideration. The result is a conviction that the States have no power, by taxation or otherwise, to retard, impede, burden, or in any manner control, the operations of the constitutional laws enacted by Congress to carry into execution the powers vested in the general government. This is, we think, the unavoidable consequence of that supremacy which the Constitution has declared.[75]

Conceding that the exemption of a federal instrumentality from state taxation was not expressly provided for in the Constitution, Marshall found that the prohibition was sustained "on a principle which so en-

[73] 4 Wheaton 415.
[74] Ibid., pp. 420, 421.
[75] Ibid., pp. 431, 436.

tirely pervades the Constitution, is so intermixed with the materials which compose it, so interwoven with its web, so blended with its texture, as to be incapable of being separated from it without rending it into shreds."[76]

Recognizing the political nature and significance of Marshall's opinion, Beveridge maintains that the cause before the Supreme Court was not merely a controversy between McCulloch and the state of Maryland but that it was primarily the cause of nationalism versus localism. From this standpoint Marshall's opinion was regarded in the nature of a reply to the challenge of the Virginia Republicans as manifested in the case of *Martin v. Hunter's Lessee*. "In effect," says Beveridge, "John Marshall thus rewrote the fundamental law of the Nation; or, perhaps it may be more accurate to say that he made a written instrument a living thing, capable of growth, capable of keeping pace with the advancement of the American people and ministering to their changing necessities."[77] Indicating his bias toward nationalistic doctrines, Justice Story commended in the highest terms the argument of William Pinkney for the bank. Writing to Pinkney, he praised him for speaking "like a great statesman and patriot, and a sound constitutional lawyer. All the cobwebs of sophistry and metaphysics about state rights and state sovereignty he brushed away with a mighty besom."[78]

The reaction to the decision was along sectional and political lines. The North and East applauded; the South and the West denounced it bitterly. Niles in his *Weekly Register* and Spencer Roane led the attack in Virginia.[79] Niles thought a deadly blow had been struck at the sovereignty of the states "from a quarter so far removed from the people as to be hardly accessible to public opinion."[80] In communications to the *Richmond Enquirer*, Roane, again basing his argument on the principles formulated in the Kentucky and Virginia Resolutions, declared that if Marshall's view was sustained, the "rights and freedom of the people of the States" were lost and that to prevent the tendencies toward consolidation Virginia might have to appeal to force. Roane complained that a Supreme Court which was supposed to be Republican had become the

---

[76] *Ibid.*, pp. 425, 426.

[77] *The Life of John Marshall*, IV: 304, 308.

[78] *Life and Letters*, I: 324, 325.

[79] Roane has been criticized for his purported change of opinion relating to judicial review. In 1793 Roane said: "I now think the judiciary may and ought not only to refuse to execute a law expressly repugnant to the constitution; but also one which is, by plain and natural construction, in opposition to the fundamental principles thereof." Kamper v. Hawkins, 1 Va. Cases 35, 36. But Roane's argument was directed against the finality which the Federalists usually claimed for such decisions.

[80] *Weekly Register*, XVI: 41, 44.

bulwark of "a New Federalism."[81] He presented in cogent and effective form the State rights doctrines as opposed to the political principles of federalism and nationalism and, since these doctrines are often inadequately considered by historians, a summary of his argument with appropriate extracts appears indispensable to an understanding of subsequent developments in the process of constitutional interpretation.

Referring to the announcement that the decision of the Supreme Court was unanimous, Roane observed: "We are not informed whether this whole Court united in the course of reasoning adopted by the Chief Justice, nor whether they all accorded in the various positions and principles which he advanced. . . . I confess, that as a citizen, I should have been better pleased to have seen the separate opinions of the Judges. The occasion called for *seriatim* opinions."[82]

Roane's position was well stated in the following extract:

There are two principles advocated and decided on by the Supreme Court, which appear to me to endanger the very existence of states rights. The first is the denial that the powers of the federal government were delegated by the States; and the second is, that the grant of powers to that government, and particularly the grant of powers "necessary and proper" to carry the other powers into effect, ought to be construed in a liberal, rather than a restricted sense. Both of these principles tend directly to consolidation of the States, and to strip them of some of the most important attributes of their sovereignty. If the Congress of the United States should think proper to legislate to the full extent upon the principles now adjudicated by the Supreme Court, it is difficult to say how small would be the remnant of power left in the hands of the state authorities.[83]

Marshall's opinion on the first point was then declared to be erroneous, for the several states delegated to the federal government the powers which it possesses, and they are parties to the compact. Each state, he maintained, was an independent political society. The Constitution was not binding on any state without its own free and voluntary consent. The states "gave birth to the Constitution; they support its existence, and they alone are capable of reforming or changing its form and substance, and yet we are informed by a solemn adjudication that its powers are not derived from that source, and consequently, that they are not parties to it."[84]

With reference to the contention that the Supreme Court was the ulti-

---

[81] Dodd, *op. cit.*, pp. 780, 781, and *Branch Historical Papers* (June, 1905), II: 1, 76, 118.

[82] *Branch Historical Papers* (June, 1905), II: 51, 52. Marshall's opinion, thought Roane, "is very able everyone must admit. This was to have been expected, proceeding as it does from a man of the most profound legal attainments, and upon a subject which has employed his thoughts, his tongue, and his pen, as a politician, and an historian for more than thirty years."

[83] *Ibid.*, p. 53.

[84] *Ibid.*, p. 55.

mate authority or umpire to decide controversies between the states and the United States, Roane replied that it was impossible to conceive

that the right of the state governments to protest against, or to resist encroachments on their authority is taken away, and transferred to the federal Judiciary, whose power extends to all cases arising under the Constitution; that the Supreme Court is the umpire to decide between the States on the one side, and the United States on the other, in all questions touching the constitutionality of laws, or acts of the Executive. There are many cases which can never be brought before that tribunal, and I do humbly conceive that the States never could have committed an act of such egregious folly as to agree that their umpire should be altogether appointed and paid by the other party. The Supreme Court may be a perfectly impartial tribunal to decide between two States, but cannot be considered in that point of view when the contest lies between the United States and one of its members.[85]

Roane then cited the decisions of the Pennsylvania supreme court in *Respublica v. Cobbett*[86] and of the Virginia court of appeals in *Hunter v. Martin*[87] as approving his views. He also quoted freely from Madison's report to the legislature of Virginia in 1799 on the constitutionality of the Alien and Sedition Acts.[88]

Turning to the second of Marshall's principles, that the federal government might exercise implied as well as express powers, Roane argued,

The danger arising from the implied powers has always been seen and felt by the people of the States. Those who opposed the Constitution always apprehended, that the powers of the federal government would be enlarged so much by the force of implication as to sweep off every design of power from the state governments. The progress of the government from the commencement of it to this day, proves that their fears are not without foundation. To counteract this irresistible tendency in the federal government to enlarge their own dominion, the vigilance of the people and state governments should constantly be exerted. . . .

Although every one admits that the government of the United States is one of limited powers; that it cannot exercise any, but such as are actually granted; yet so wide is the latitude given to the words *"general welfare,"* in one of these clauses, and to the word *"necessary,"* in the other, that it will (if the construction be persisted in), really become a government of almost unlimited powers. If such a consequence will necessarily result from the liberal construction which has been contended for, ought we not to recur to first principles, and change the Constitution?[89]

Roane then contended that the use of the word "necessary" in the Constitution was not intended in the Hamiltonian sense as meaning "convenient, useful, or conducive to." He thought it was clear that the intention of the Constitution was to confer on Congress the power of resorting to such means as were incidental to the express powers, that is,

[85] *Branch Historical Papers* (June, 1905), II: 56, 57.
[86] 3 Dallas 473 (1798).
[87] 4 Mumford 3 (1813).
[88] See above, pp. 169 ff.
[89] *Branch Historical Papers* (June, 1905), II: 63, 64.

to such means as directly and necessarily tend to produce the desired effect. It was pointed out that the opponents of the Constitution foretold that this clause would be construed into an unlimited commission to exercise every power which might be alleged to be necessary to the general welfare. But Madison treated that prophecy with contempt. He asked: "For what purpose could the enumeration of particular powers be inserted, if these and all others were meant to be included in the preceding general power?"[90] Notwithstanding this opinion, the prophecy of the opponents of the Constitution has turned out to be true. Two interpretations of the necessary and proper clause were then noted, first, that Congress had a right to pass any law the purpose of which was to provide for the general welfare, and, second, Congress might provide for the general welfare in all cases in which there might be an application of the money to be raised by taxes. Hamilton, as we have noted,[91] adopted the latter view and maintained that there were no limitations on the powers of Congress so far as the appropriation of money was concerned. The effect of either of these constructions was, according to Roane, to render nugatory the particular enumeration of powers. And since the decision of the Supreme Court in the bank case amounted in effect to the adoption of both of the above modes of enlarging federal powers by construction, Roane considered the result most unfortunate. As he saw it, a new method of amending the Constitution had been added to the ample ones provided in that instrument. He could see no substantial difference "between an unlimited grant of power and a grant limited in its terms, but accompanied with unlimited means of carrying it into execution."[92]

In another paper the principle of the grant of express powers to the federal government and the reservation of residuary powers to the states was examined. According to this principle, Roane insisted that it is incumbent upon those who seek to justify the exercise of a power by the federal government to prove that the power is granted or, to use Madison's phrase, is fairly incident to a granted power. And the incidental powers must be confined, as Jefferson contended, by the touchstone of "sheer necessity" or, as stated in *The Federalist*, "all powers *indispensably necessary* are granted by the Constitution." In this sense the "necessary and proper" phrase added nothing to the powers before given to the general government. Marshall's trick of reasoning by which he sanctioned the interpretation which he regarded as politically desirable was then criticized. When Congress selects a means to carry out a granted or

[90] *The Federalist* (Ford ed.), pp. 268, 269.
[91] See above, p. 242.
[92] *Branch Historical Papers* (June, 1905), II: 70–80.

implied power, the means selected, asserted Marshall, must be deemed appropriate and valid unless they are specifically prohibited by the Constitution. The burden of proof was thus placed upon those who attacked the validity of federal action. But such a method of interpretation was in direct contradiction to the view advanced in Madison's report that "it is incumbent on the general government to *prove* that the Constitution grants the *particular* power."[93]

The argument of policy and expediency as a justifiable basis for the extension of the powers of the federal government was not controverted, but Roane repeatedly argued that such extension should be made by amendments to the Constitution, and not by strained or loose interpretation of the general phrases of the written document. Roane disapproved the attitude which regarded the Constitution as a perfect instrument of government and then proposed to warp its language to accomplish the desired political ends. The men who made the Constitution, he observed, did not consider it such a perfect instrument, as the amendments which they added indicated, and there was no reason why additional amendments could not be adopted if it appeared desirable that more extensive powers should be given to the national government.

Taking the generally recognized and accepted meaning of "necessary and proper," Roane asserted that the establishment of a bank is not peculiar or necessary to the execution of any of the granted powers. But the Supreme Court, adopting the Hamiltonian construction which had not been heard of since the time of the Alien and Sedition Laws, declared that "necessary" frequently means "convenient or useful" and that it sometimes means "conducive to." Such a construction, Roane insisted, opened too wide a door to the powers of the national government.

The most significant issue in the whole argument was, according to Roane, whether by the Constitution a federal or consolidated government was established. Though the general intention and language of the Constitution at the time of adoption was to set up a federal type of government, the Supreme Court, Roane thought, had misinterpreted this design and now declared that a national or consolidated government had been formed through the adoption of the Constitution by the people and not by the states. Such reasoning had been refuted by Madison in the report of 1799 wherein it was asserted that the powers allotted to the general government were the result of a compact to which the states as sovereign entities were parties. Marshall's reference to "We, the people" in the preamble to the Constitution was regarded as preposterous so far as an extension of federal powers was concerned. Roane doubted whether

---

[93] *Ibid.*, p. 92–96.

the preamble was a part of the Constitution, but if it was a part of the document, he thought that the idea was long since exploded that such general language invested Congress with all powers conducive to the "general welfare." The conclusion was arrived at by Roane that "our general government then, with due submission to the opinion of the Supreme Court, is as much a federal government, or a 'league,' as was the former Confederation. The only difference is, that the powers of the government are much *extended*."[94]

Facing the possibility of disagreements over the interpretations of the terms of the compact, Roane observed that: "If the founders of our Constitution did not foresee the clashings between the respective governments, nor provide an impartial tribunal to decide them, it only affords another instance of the imperfection of the instrument; of which imperfection its authors themselves were most sensible." The ground was laid for nullification by adopting the language of the report of 1799 which held that in instances of infractions of the Constitution the states have a right to interpose to arrest the progress of the evil; for it is essential to the nature of compacts, that when resort can be had to no tribunal superior to the authority of the parties, the parties themselves must be the rightful judges whether the compact has been violated. Adopting Madison's views, it was contended that certain cases of usurpation could not be brought before the Judiciary and, even if they could, a subordinate department in one division of a federal government could not be "an impartial and competent judge." Roane's views in this respect were well stated in a resolution of the Pennsylvania legislature relating to a national bank approved January 11, 1811. Pertinent extracts were quoted as follows:

The people of the United States, by the adoption of the federal Constitution, established the general government, for specified purposes, *reserving* to themselves, respectively, the rights and authorities not delegated in that instrument. To the *compact* thereby created, *each State* acceded in its character as a State, and is a party, the United States forming as to it, the other party. The act of union thus entered into, being to *all* intents and purposes a *treaty* between sovereign States, the general government, by this treaty, was *not* constituted the *exclusive* or final judge of the powers it was to exercise; for if it were to so judge, then *its judgment*, and not the Constitution, would be the measure of its authority. Should the general government, in any of its departments, violate the provisions of the Constitution, it rests with the States and with the people to apply suitable remedies. . . .

From a careful review of the powers vested in the general government, they have the most positive conviction that the authority to grant charters of incorporation, within the jurisdiction of any State, without the consent thereof, is not recognized in that instrument, either expressly or by any *warrantable implication*. Therefore, resolved, by the said house of representatives, of the said commonwealth of Pennsyl-

[94] *Branch Historical Papers* (June, 1905), II: 113.

vania, in general assembly met, that the senators of this State in the Senate of the United States, be and they are hereby, instructed, and the representatives of this State, in the House of Representatives of the United States, be and they are hereby, requested, to use every exertion in their power, to prevent the charter of the bank of the United States from being renewed, or any other bank from being chartered by Congress, designed to have operation within the jurisdiction of any State, without first having obtained the consent of the legislature of such State.[95]

Some of the Justices who joined in the opinion in the *McCulloch Case* were considered Republicans, but Roane noted that "if so, their works would lead me to believe that they have changed their politics, in thus changing, they have undergone the common fate attending the possession of power." The Supreme Court claimed the right, in effect, to change the government from a federal to a consolidated form and asserted that this important right and duty had been devolved upon it by the Constitution; but Roane raised the query:

If there be a clause to that effect in the Constitution, I wish the Supreme Court had placed their finger upon it. I should be glad to see it set out *haec verba....* When a right is claimed by one of the contracting parties to pass finally upon the rights or powers of another, we ought at least to expect to see an *express* provision for it. That necessity is increased, when the right is claimed for a *deputy* or department of such contracting party. The Supreme Court is but a department of the general government. A department is not competent to do that to which the whole government is inadequate. The general government cannot decide this controversy, and much less can one of its departments. They cannot do it, unless we tread under foot the principle which forbids a party to decide his own cause.[96]

Following a summary of the points emphasized, Roane put his case before the people; he did not invoke "revolutionary or insurrectionary measures." If the people could be made to understand the question, the force of public opinion, he thought, would rectify the evil.

In Judge Roane's opinion the Supreme Court had no jurisdiction or authority to determine the bank case, but, having assumed jurisdiction, the Court decided the case wrongly. He admitted somewhat reluctantly that so far as the decision was concerned, there was nothing to do but to submit to the Court's construction of the Constitution, but he wished principally to "make war against the declaratory decision of the Supreme Court, giving Congress power to 'bind us in all cases whatsoever.' ... I differ entirely from the Supreme Court when they say, that by *that tribunal*, alone, can the decision which they have made be made."

Roane sent copies of his articles to Jefferson, Madison, and Monroe. Madison and Monroe declined to express their opinions on the issues raised. Jefferson, however, strongly endorsed Roane's views character-

---

[95] *Branch Historical Papers* (June, 1905), II: 117, 118.   [96] *Ibid.*, p. 119.

izing the decision in the case of *McCulloch v. Maryland* as a usurpation.[97] Thomas Ritchie contended that if Congress can select any means which it considers convenient, useful, or conducive to the execution of the specified powers, and if the word "necessary" can thus be frittered away, then "we may bid adieu to the sovereignty of the States."[98] He commended Roane's articles as an exposure "of the alarming errors of the Supreme Court" and prophesied "whenever state rights are threatened or invaded, Virginia will not be the last to sound the tocsin."

Similar sentiments to those of Roane were presented by Mr. Stevenson of Richmond to the lower house of the Virginia legislature in the form of instructions which were to be forwarded to James Barbour and James Pleasants, Jr., the Virginia senators in Congress. Whatever diversity of opinion may have existed in the United States, Stevenson maintained

that there were some principles of government, so sacred in themselves, and so sanctified by public sentiment, that they were not now to be brought into question. They had supposed, that of this character are the propositions, that the government of the United States is a government of limited and defined powers; that it has no authorities, except those expressly given, or such as are *indispensable* to carry into effect powers expressly delegated; and that all other rights and authorities are retained to the States respectively, or to the people. That this is the real character of the government of the Union, results not only from the express declarations of the Constitution itself; the avowed sentiment of those engaged in framing it; but also from the circumstances, under which it was established.[99]

It was pointed out that the dangers of consolidation were foreseen by the opponents of the Constitution and were disavowed by its advocates when it was submitted in the state conventions. Without such emphatic disavowals the Constitution would not have been adopted. But in the decision in *McCulloch v. Maryland*, the Supreme Court was undermining the pillars of the Constitution and sapping the foundations and rights of the state governments.[100] Stevenson, in referring to this decision, said the general assembly of Virginia does not concede that the opinions

---

[97] *Writings* (Ford ed.), X: 140–142; also XII, Sept. 6, 1819. In the judgment of Charles Maurice Wiltse, there is a marked difference between Jefferson's treatment of the Constitution in the proceedings for the purchase of Louisiana and Marshall's decisions giving a broad interpretation of the Constitution, for "Jefferson was not construing, but transcending, the Constitution for the public good, and the means were at hand for the public to accept or reject his judgment. Marshall was subverting the Constitution for an end, which he knew in advance, the people would reject, were they given the opportunity." *The Jeffersonian Tradition in American Democracy* (Chapel Hill, 1935), p. 173.

[98] Cf. *Richmond Enquirer*, March 26, 30; April 2, 13, 16, 23, 26, 30; June 11, 15, 18, 22, 1819.

[99] *Journal of the House of Delegates*, Virginia, 1819, p. 56, and *Niles' Register*, XVII: 311 ff. These resolutions were not adopted, but they presented views in which many Republicans concurred.

[100] *Journal of the House of Delegates*, p. 57.

of the Supreme Court are conclusively binding on the states, since, in questions relating

to the extent of the powers delegated to the general government, or retained to the States, in those great and important contests, which may arise upon the true construction of the compact, it must devolve on the parties, themselves, to judge of the infractions of it, whether occasioned by the legislature, the executive, or the judiciary. . . . This results from the plain consideration, that the parties to the federal compact were sovereign States, and that, with respect to the powers retained, the States are as sovereign as the United States are, as to those granted. It could never therefore have been the intention of the States to submit the extent of their authorities, and rights, to courts created by one party to the compact, which party has the appointment of judges; who, however enlightened and honest, could not be presumed, in a contest between rival authorities, to be exempt from that esprit de corps, to which all men may be, more or less, subject; and, who in relation to the diminution of duties, and increase of compensation, at least, are dependent on the very body whose acts, or authority, may be brought in question: Nor does the provision in the Constitution, that the judicial power shall extend to all cases arising under the Constitution, impair the force of the construction which is contended for. . . . However, this may relate to questions to be decided, as to the different departments of the government, it does not, and cannot, as this assembly believe, extend to questions which would amount to a subversion of the Constitution itself, by the usurpation of one contracting party or another. . . . The words are . . . "all cases arising under the Constitution," plainly referring to the power of construction in cases which would be presented by the exercise of powers transferred by the Constitution, and not to those great and paramount considerations which, in their effects, may be subversive of all law, and all Constitutions. These general words, which also may be thus abundantly satisfied, ought not to receive a construction which violates great principles, and permits a party to be judge in its own cause. It would, moreover, be unreasonable and unjust to suppose, that if the framers of that glorious instrument intended to confer a power, so infinitely more transcendent than that vested in any other department of the government, it would not have been given by an express and unequivocal delegation, rather than left to rest on doubtful or arbitrary implication. The change in the Constitution which took away, by an amendment, the power to sue a state in the courts of the United States, serves to mark, in a striking manner, the well-founded jealousy of the States, as to any infringement of their sovereign character, through the medium of the federal Judiciary; and to show that they have never meant to allow the courts of the United States to decide conclusively on their rights, under the compact, in cases of conflicting claims to power, then it may do, incidentally and collaterally, what it has been forbidden to do directly; and may arraign before it, and subject to its control, those very sovereignties which the amendment to the Constitution intended to place beyond its reach. And therefore, the general assembly denies to the Supreme Court of the United States the right to impair, or construe away the sovereign authorities reserved to the States or the people; and as that Court, in the decision alluded to, has attributed to itself, the sole power of deciding on the high questions, supposed to arise between the government of the Union and its members . . . it is deemed highly important to communicate to you the sentiments of this assembly upon the subject.

And the general assembly are more particularly induced to do so, because in their best and most deliberate judgment, the construction adopted by the Supreme Court is not only calculated to break down and destroy those barriers which the illustrious framers of the Constitution were so solicitous to erect for the security of the people, and the preservation of the state sovereignties, but to change the whole character of the government itself; and to convert it from a limited and defined Constitution operating among sovereign States, united by a general compact into one great consolidated government of undefined and unlimited powers.[101]

With a number of Supreme Court decisions in mind, the query was raised whether these opinions do not

give to Congress a most alarming latitude of authority, to which no practical limits can be assigned? And do they not lay a foundation for administering government upon principles unacknowledged by the Constitution and unknown to the States and the people, at the time of its adoption? . . . Instead of conforming to the Constitution, may not Congress conform the Constitution to their own designs: and does not their power become unlimited and uncontrolled, if they are the only judges of its extent, and the only restrainers of its excess? In its exercise under the plea, that a law may be conducive to some one of the specified powers of the government, it may exercise what authority it pleases, which has the most remote tendency to promote the alleged object.[102]

Recurring to the resolution adopted by the state of Virginia at the time of the ratification of the Constitution, that "every power not granted remains with the people, and at their will," Stevenson maintained:

This was the opinion of Virginia when called upon to ratify or reject the Constitution: Not only, therefore, is the construction now given sanctioned by opinions, contemporaneous with the original discussion of the Constitution in Virginia, but it has since been regarded as sacred by the most enlightened statesmen and patriots in our country; and as affording the only security against consolidation, and the only safeguard to the rights of the States. Thus we find this construction contended for, both before and after the adoption of the general government, by men who had been most concerned in the formation of the Constitution and persisted in since, it is believed, by a large majority of the people of this State.[103]

The general assembly was then urged to approve a resolution memorializing the members of Congress:

1st. To procure an amendment to the Constitution of the United States, creating a tribunal for the decision of all questions, in which the powers and authorities of the general government and those of the States, where they are in conflict, shall be decided.

2nd. To resist on every occasion all acts of legislation in the Congress of the United States, which attempt to exercise any power or authority, which is not either expressly given to Congress by the Constitution, or which is not "necessary and proper"

---

[101] *Journal of House of Delegates*, pp. 57, 58. It was frequently asserted that "the extension of the federal judicial power to cases in law and equity, arising under the federal Constitution and laws, did not deprive the States of the inherent attribute of sovereignty to dispense justice to their people in these cases, nor expose their decisions in cases of law and equity to be annulled by the federal Judiciary." Though it was admitted that under the Constitution controversies might arise between the political departments in relation to their powers, those controversies were regarded as not comprehended within the authority to try suits in law and equity. Daniel R. Goodloe, *Federalism Unmasked*, pp. 131 ff.

[102] *Journal of the House of Delegates*, p. 58.   [103] *Ibid.*, pp. 58, 59.

to carry into effect the powers so expressly given; or any other powers vested by the Constitution in the government of the United States or any department, or officer thereof; and that, in construing the words "necessary and proper," they be regulated by the construction herein before put on them, and also that given by the resolutions and report adopted by the general assembly of Virginia, at their sessions of 1798 and 1799, which have been considered and are fully and entirely approved of by this assembly.[104]

An amendment to the preamble proposed by Mr. Morris and resolutions offered by Mr. Henderson having been defeated, the first resolution of Mr. Henderson, adopted by the vote of 138 to 16, was amended as follows:

And they renew the expression of their opinion that the general government have no rightful authority, under the Constitution, to grant a charter of incorporation to a Bank of the United States:

The General Assembly, therefore, influenced by these considerations, instruct you, as their Senators, and request the Representatives from this State in the Congress of the United States, to use their best efforts:

1st. In procuring a declaratory amendment to the Constitution of the United States, which shall prohibit Congress from erecting or incorporating any bank, or other monied institution, except within the District of Columbia; and that every bank, or other monied institution, which shall be established by the authority of Congress, shall, together with its branches and offices of discount and deposit, be confined to the District of Columbia.

The other resolutions were carried by large majorities.[105] A similar set of resolutions relating to the Missouri question was presented and adopted. In these sets of resolutions, claims Beveridge, "ran the intimation of forcible resistance to national authority."[106] Fortunately for Marshall and the Federalist cause, General Jackson's extreme measures in Florida turned the public interest away from the bank and the Court.

For the Federalists, Justice Story, admitting that the Court was dealing with a political issue, expressed the prevailing sentiment. The case, he said, "excites great interest, and in a political view is of the deepest consequence to the Nation. It goes to establish the Constitution upon its great original principles."[107] Webster thought the decision "admirable" and heard only universal praise. Republican papers throughout the West and South, however, continued to denounce the decision and the representatives in Congress from these states attempted to secure a constitutional amendment to confine the operations of the national bank to the District of Columbia.

---

[104] *Journal of the House of Delegates*, Virginia, p. 59. See also preamble and resolutions proposed by Mr. Archer and Mr. Baldwin, *ibid.*, pp. 59–65, 85, 86.

[105] *Ibid.*, pp. 178–180.

[106] *The Life of John Marshall*, IV: 326.

[107] *Life and Letters*, I: 325.

Chief Justice Marshall was alarmed at the attacks on his decision and commented to Story that "our opinion in the bank case has aroused the sleeping spirit of Virginia, if indeed it ever sleeps." He later observed: "The opinion in the bank case continues to be denounced by the democracy in Virginia. An effort is certainly being made to induce the legislature which will meet in December to take up the subject and to pass resolutions not very unlike those which were called forth by the Alien and Sedition laws in 1799." Marshall urged his friends to secure, if possible, counter resolutions endorsing the opinion of the Supreme Court, for he thought if Roane's principles should prevail, "the Constitution would be converted into the old confederation."[108] About the same time the decision was rendered in the bank case, Chief Justice Marshall also interpreted the federal grant of authority over bankruptcy in a manner which irritated the states.

THE VALIDITY OF STATE ACTS REGULATING BANKRUPTCY

In the case of *Sturges v. Crowninshield*[109] it was argued that from the time of the adoption of the Constitution the power to enact a bankruptcy law was vested exclusively in Congress. The exclusive nature of this grant was deemed so specific that Massachusetts did not pass any bankruptcy laws. An attempt was made, however, to distinguish between insolvency laws of the nature of the New York act in question and bankruptcy laws, authority concerning which was expressly granted to Congress. Chief Justice Marshall, holding the New York law void because of impairing the obligation of contracts, thus discussed the relations between federal and state authority on this subject:

The mere grant of a power to Congress did not imply a prohibition on the States to exercise the same power. But it has never been supposed, that this concurrent power of legislation extended to every possible case in which its exercise by the States has not been expressly prohibited. The confusion resulting from such a practise would be endless. . . . Whenever the terms in which a power is granted to Congress, or the nature of the power, require that it should be exercised exclusively by Congress, the subject is as completely taken from the state legislatures, as if they had been expressly forbidden to act on it.[110]

But the power of Congress to establish uniform bankruptcy laws was held not to be of this description.

Marshall recognized that there was a distinction between a bankruptcy and an insolvency law, but admitted that the line is difficult to draw

---

[108] *Proceedings of the Massachusetts Historical Society*, 2d ser., XIV: 324, and John Edward Oster, *The Political and Economic Doctrines of John Marshall* (New York, 1914), p. 107.
[109] 4 Wheaton 122 (1819).
[110] *Ibid.*, p. 193 (1819).

and that for the purpose of this case it was not necessary to distinguish between the two. He thought it was sufficient to hold that until the power to pass uniform bankruptcy laws was exercised by Congress, the states, so far as they did not violate the contract clause of the federal Constitution, might pass such acts.

Marshall, in discussing whether the New York law impaired the obligation of contracts, thought that the meaning of the phrase obligation of contract was clear. In fact, he held that it would be

difficult to substitute words which are more intelligible, or less liable to misconstruction than those which are to be explained. A contract is an agreement in which a party undertakes to do, or not to do, a particular thing. The law binds him to perform his undertaking, and this is, of course, the obligation of his contract. In the case at bar, the defendant has given his promissory note to pay the plaintiff a sum of money on or before a certain day. The contract binds him to pay that sum on that day; and this is the obligation. Any law which releases a part of this obligation, must, in the literal sense of the word, impair it. Much more must a law impair it which makes it totally invalid, and entirely discharges it.[111]

Marshall noted that the prevailing evil which produced the contract clause in the Constitution was the practice of issuing paper money, of making property which was useless to the creditor a discharge of his debt, and of changing the time of payment by authorizing distant installments; but the intention of the makers of the Constitution was, he thought, also to inscribe the principle of the inviolability of contracts and to afford protection to contracts from all kinds of attack. The fact that colonial and state legislatures had for many years passed insolvent laws and that this authority had not been questioned did not, according to Marshall, militate against the construction that by the Constitution such acts were now inhibited so far as they changed the terms of existing contracts, for "the Convention appears to have intended to establish a great principle, that contracts should be inviolable."

Justice Washington in 1814[112] had held that the power of Congress over the subject of bankruptcy was exclusive. In 1817 Justices Livingston and Johnson held to the contrary.[113] Referring to the *Sturges Case,* Justice Johnson noted that "the Court was greatly divided, in their views of the doctrine, and the judgment partakes as much of a compromise as a legal adjudication."[114] So cautiously did Marshall word his judgment and decree that it was understood to mean that no state could pass a bankruptcy law.

---

[111] 4 Wheaton 197, 198.

[112] Golden v. Prince, 3 Wash. C. C. 313.

[113] Adams v. Storey, 1 Paine 79, and Farmers and Mechanics Bank v. Smith, *Hall's Amer. Law Jour.*, VI.

[114] Ogden v. Saunders, 12 Wheaton 272 (1827).

It was at this time that the Marshall policy of asserting nationalistic doctrines through the decisions of the Supreme Court was beginning to be considered in relation to the question of the control over slavery.[115] In the argument on a resolution condemning the restrictions which were to be placed on the introduction of slavery in the territory of Missouri, it was suggested that such action would be hostile to the fraternal affection and prudent forbearance which ought to pervade the confederate union. And it was maintained that unless State rights, which Marshall's reasoning condemned, were upheld, the union could not be preserved, for "no government can long exist which lies at the mercy of another." With action by Congress imminent on the prohibition of slavery in Missouri, the threat of secession which was soon to become more ominous was made. It was resolved that "Virginia will support the good people of Missouri in their just rights ... and will cooperate with them in resisting with manly fortitude any attempt which Congress may make to impose restraints or restriction as the price of the admission" to the union. The people of Virginia and others in the South saw in Marshall's decisions the threat of control over slavery in the states and the exclusion of slavery from the territories and new states. The criticisms of the Supreme Court by Niles, Roane, and Taylor and the defiant attitude of Virginia, Ohio, and Pennsylvania are characterized by Beveridge as "militant localism."[116] But these criticisms were mild in comparison with the outburst of indignation and alarm occasioned by the proposal to prohibit slavery within the new state of Missouri. The right of a state to secede and the division of the union were freely discussed, and in ominous tones the threat of civil war was sounded.[117]

THE MISSOURI COMPROMISE

Negro slavery existed in Louisiana while under French and Spanish control. When the territory was purchased by the United States, it was taken for granted that property in slaves would be recognized and protected by the United States. As no action to the contrary was taken, slaves were held both in Lower and Upper Louisiana, though there were not many slaves in either area. When the people of Missouri applied to Congress for admission to the union, Representative James Tallmadge of New York moved to amend the enabling act by prohibiting the further introduction of slaves into Missouri and by providing that all children of slaves born after the admission of Missouri as a state should become free

---

[115] *The Life of John Marshall*, IV: 327.
[116] Beveridge, *op. cit.*, p. 340.
[117] *Annals*, 16th Cong., 1st sess., pp. 107 ff.

at the age of twenty-five years.[118] The precise meaning of the amendment was not clear, but it was regarded by many of the people of the North as a necessary move to check the extension of slavery and by the people of the South as a vicious blow intended to hasten the abolition of slavery.

The Missouri controversy was in fact "a contest between two antagonistic social systems which moved westward along parallel lines until both sought to possess the same region west of the Mississippi."[119] Much of the bitterness of feeling in the South was caused by the espousal of the cause of antislavery by Rufus King who had twice been the Federalist candidate for Vice-president. To King, the real issue of the Missouri question was the danger and injustice of extending and perpetuating the political power of the slave states. If slavery is not checked, maintained King, we "shall continue to be ruled by men in the name of liberty and who by the permission of power are ordained to be our masters, as they are the masters of the black men on whose labor they live."[120]

Since the proposal to admit Maine, which was before Congress at the same time, furnished a possible offset to the political significance of admitting Missouri as a slave state, an arrangement was agreed upon which was designed to maintain the equality of power in the Senate between the North and the South. In the Maine-Missouri bill for the admission of both states a compromise amendment was agreed upon as follows: "That in all that territory ceded by France to the United States, under the name of Louisiana, which lies north of thirty-six degrees thirty minutes north latitude, excepting only such part thereof as is included within the limits of the State contemplated by this act, slavery and involuntary servitude, otherwise than in the punishment of crimes whereof the party shall have been duly convicted, shall be and is hereby forever prohibited." The original Tallmadge amendment and the later substitute amendment aroused such a furor in feeling and debate that men feared the permanence and security of the union was in danger. In fact it was admitted that the proposed compromise was agreed to as a lesser evil than dividing the union or throwing it into confusion.

Historians have noted that in the first two decades of the nineteenth century the national spirit was greater in the South than in the other parts of the country. At this time Virginia could not arouse vigorous opposition to what appeared to be encroachments by the federal government through judicial decisions upon the reserved rights of the states.

[118] *Ibid.*, 15th Cong., 2d sess., p. 272.

[119] Homer C. Hockett, "Rufus King and the Missouri Compromise," *Missouri Hist. Rev.* (Oct., 1907–July, 1908), p. 211.

[120] *The Life and Correspondence of Rufus King*, ed. by Charles R. King (New York, 1894), VI: 267.

A number of southern states joined with Maryland in its opposition to the views of Chief Justice Marshall as expressed in *McCulloch v. Maryland,* but, again, little in the nature of vigorous opposition or definite action could be secured in the southern states to counteract the nationalist doctrines of Chief Justice Marshall. But the Missouri Compromise marked the end of the second period of emerging nationalism. For forty years the tendencies were against the assertion of greater national powers and in the direction of assertive doctrines of State rights.

The Missouri Compromise, which had been approved by both the abolitionists and the proslavery group, is supposed to have put off the "irrepressible conflict" for more than a generation; but, on the other hand, it may be looked upon as the beginning of a chain of events which led the nation on the way to civil war. There was begun at this time the consolidation of opinion among the southern states to defend the institution of slavery, and it was thought necessary, henceforth, not only to encourage a form of social solidarity in the South but also to maintain and strengthen the grip of these states upon the government of the country.[121]

While the discussion of the Missouri Compromise was under way, John Quincy Adams made a note in his diary that secession for the cause of slavery would be combined with a war between the two parts of the union and that "its result must be the extirpation of slavery from this whole continent."[122] Jefferson also sounded a note of warning when he said: "This momentous question like a fire bell in the night, awakened and filled me with terror. I considered it at once as the knell of the Union. It is hushed, indeed, for the moment. But this is a reprieve only, not a final sentence. A geographical line, coinciding with a marked principle, moral and political, once conceived and held up to the angry passions of men, will never be obliterated; and every new irritation will mark it deeper and deeper."[123] To many, the Missouri issue raised anew the question whether the New England states, now aided by some middle Atlantic and western members of the union, or the southern states under the leadership of Virginia should control the government of the union. Samuel E. Morison thinks that "Virginia had ruled the Union so long that her statesmen, like the deposed Essex junto in 1804, were willing to break it up rather than relinquish her power."[124] But more than ques-

[121] See Edward Channing, *History of the United States* (New York, 1927), V: 307, 326, 405 ff.

[122] *Memoirs of John Quincy Adams,* ed. by Charles Francis Adams (Philadelphia, 1865), IV: 503, 531, and V: 210; see also Channing, *op. cit.,* p. 147.

[123] *Writings* (Ford ed.), X: 157.

[124] *The Life and Letters of Harrison Gray Otis* (Boston, 1913), II: 228.

tions of political power were concerned. There were fundamental differences in economic conditions, in social philosophy, in social practices, and, above all, there was a divergence in the theories of constitutional construction which was quite irreconcilable.

At the time that the decision was rendered in *McCulloch v. Maryland* there was a marked reaction, particularly in certain sections of the country, against the nationalistic trends prevalent during and after the War of 1812. The arguments of the proponents and opponents of the extension of the powers of the national government centered not only around the issue of the establishment and the dominant control of the Bank of the United States over financial matters but also over the proposal to have the federal government render aid to internal improvements within the states. Madison and Jefferson recognized the growing sentiment among the representatives of the western states in agitating for federal aid for internal improvements and realized the inherent dangers involved in the consequent extension of the powers of the federal government by the mere process of construction. Because of this they became advocates of the theory which had occasional adherents during the years of the Federalist control of the government, namely, that Congress could collect and spend money only for the purposes enumerated in the Constitution. In his veto of the Bonus Bill in aid of internal improvements, Madison expressed his views as follows:

Seeing that such a power is not expressly given by the Constitution, and believing that it cannot be deduced from any part of it without an inadmissible latitude of construction and a reliance upon insufficient precedents; believing also that the permanent success of the Constitution depends on a definite partition of powers between the general and state governments, and that no adequate landmarks would be left by the constructive extension of the powers of Congress as proposed in the bill, I have no option but to withhold my signature from it, . . . cherishing the hope that its beneficial objects may be attained by a resort for the necessary powers to the same wisdom and virtue in the nation which established the Constitution in its actual form and providently marked out in the instrument itself a safe and practicable mode of improving it as experience might suggest.[125]

The nationalistic doctrines of constitutional construction of Hamilton and Marshall, which had an appropriate background and sanction during the Federalist Administrations, were now clearly not in accord with the prevailing opinions of the people or of their representatives. Under Marshall's leadership the Supreme Court was placing itself definitely in opposition to the prevailing public sentiment on some of the foremost political controversies of the time. The constitutional basis for the Court's exercise of jurisdiction over these questions was on the insecure

[125] Richardson, *op. cit.,* I: 584.

ground of implied powers or related legal doctrines. It was to be expected that there would be vigorous opposition to the efforts of the Court to assert federal supremacy over the state courts, despite the Eleventh Amendment and to enlarge and strengthen the federal powers over finance and banking.[126] But it was the emergence of a new issue—the continuance and the extension of slavery—which gave increased zest and bitterness to the arguments over the extension of federal authority. The Federalist and nationalist theories of constitutional interpretation which had been a fruitful source of conflict between the nation and the states during the decades from 1800 to 1820 were henceforth to be associated with the efforts to extend national powers over what were deemed to be the most vital interests of the southern states. And in an atmosphere surcharged with political feelings and resentments, decisions especially irritating to the states were rendered by the Supreme Court.

---

[126] When the Supreme Court declared invalid certain of the stay laws enacted by the states and then denied the right of the state of Maryland to tax the Bank of the United States, the issue was carried into the realm of constitutional interpretation. Thus, remarks Rezneck, it "was the logic of the depression of 1819 carried to a climax. What had begun as a contraction of money and credit accompanied by a general decline of prices and property values, led finally, by an unbroken chain of economic circumstance and political agitation, to a questioning of the Constitution itself, particularly in reference to the newly developed power of judicial interpretation." Samuel Rezneck, "The Depression of 1819–22, A Social History," *Amer. Hist. Rev.* (Oct., 1933), XXXIX: 46.

APPENDIX

MADISON'S LETTER *of September 2, 1819, to Spencer Roane is reprinted here to show the views of a moderately conservative member of the Republican party regarding Marshall's method of construing the Constitution in the case of McCulloch v. Maryland.*

DEAR SIR: I have received your favor of the 22d Ult. inclosing a copy of your observations on the judgment of the Supreme Court of the United States in the case of McCulloch against the State of Maryland; and I have found their latitudinary mode of expounding the Constitution, combated in them with the ability and the force which were to be expected.

It appears to me as it does to you that the occasion did not call for the general and abstract doctrine interwoven with the decision of the particular case. I have always supposed that the meaning of a law, and for a like reason, of a Constitution, so far as it depends on judicial interpretation, was to result from a course of particular decisions, and not these from a previous and abstract comment on the subject. The example in this instance tends to reverse the rule and to forego the illustration to be derived from a series of cases actually occurring for adjudication.

I could have wished also that the Judges had delivered their opinions *seriatim*. The case was of such magnitude, in the scope given to it, as to call, if any case could do so, for the views of the subject separately taken by them. This might either by the harmony of their reasoning have produced a greater conviction in the public mind; or by its discordance have impaired the force of the precedent now ostensibly supported by a unanimous and perfect concurrence in every argument and dictum in the judgment pronounced.

But what is of most importance is the high sanction given to a latitude in expounding the Constitution which seems to break down the landmarks intended by a specification of the powers of Congress, and to substitute for a definite connection between means and ends, a legislative discretion as to the former to which no practical limit can be assigned. In the great system of Political Economy having for its general object the national welfare, everything is related immediately or remotely to every other thing; and consequently a power over any one thing, if not limited by some obvious and precise affinity, may amount to a power over every other. Ends and means may shift their character at the will and according to the ingenuity of the legislative body. What is an end in one case may be a means in another; nay in the same case, may be either an end or a means at the legislative option. The British Parliament in collecting a revenue from the commerce of America found no difficulty in calling it either a tax for the regulation of trade, or a regulation of trade with a view to the tax, as it suited the argument or the policy of the moment.

Is there a legislative power in fact, not expressly prohibited by the Constitution, which might not, according to the doctrine of the Court, be exercised as a means of carrying into effect some specified power?

Does not the Court also relinquish by their doctrine, all control on the legislative exercise of unconstitutional powers? According to that doctrine, the expediency and constitutionality of means for carrying into effect a specified power are convertible terms; and Congress are admitted to be judges of the expediency. The Court certainly cannot be so; a question, the moment it assumes the character of mere expediency or policy, being evidently beyond the reach of judicial cognizance.

It is true, the Court are disposed to retain a guardianship of the Constitution against legislative encroachments. "Should Congress," say they, "under the pretext of executing its powers, pass laws for the accomplishment of objects not entrusted to the government, it would become the painful duty of this Tribunal to say that such an act was not the law of the land." But suppose Congress should, as would doubtless happen, pass unconstitutional laws not to accomplish objects not specified in the Constitution, but the same laws as means expedient, convenient or conducive to the accomplishment of objects entrusted to the government; by what handle could the Court take hold of the case? We are told that it was the policy of the old government of France to grant monopolies, such as that of tobacco, in order to create funds in particular hands from which loans could be made to the public, adequate capitalists not being formed in that country in the ordinary course of commerce. Were Congress to grant a like monopoly merely to aggrandize those enjoying it, the Court might consistently say, that this not being an object entrusted to the government the grant was unconstitutional and void. Should Congress however grant the monopoly according to the French policy as a means judged by them to be necessary, expedient or conducive to the borrowing of money, which is an object entrusted to them by the Constitution, it seems clear that the Court, adhering to its doctrine, could not interfere without stepping on legislative ground, to do which they justly disclaim all pretension.

It could not but happen, and was foreseen at the birth of the Constitution, that difficulties and differences of opinion might occasionally arise in expounding terms and phrases necessarily used in such a charter; more especially those which divide legislation between the general and local governments; and that it might require a regular course of practice to liquidate and settle the meaning of some of them. But it was anticipated I believe by few if any of the friends of the Constitution, that a rule of construction would be introduced as broad and as pliant as what has occurred. And those who recollect, and still more those who shared in what passed in the State Conventions, through which the people ratified the Constitution, with respect to the extent of the powers vested in Congress, cannot easily be persuaded that the avowal of such a rule would not have prevented its ratification. It has been the misfortune, if not the reproach, of other nations, that their governments have not been freely and deliberately established by themselves. It is the boast of ours that such has been its source and that it can be altered by the same authority only which established it. It is a further boast that a regular mode of making proper alterations has been providently inserted in the Constitution itself. It is anxiously to be wished therefore, that no innovations may take place in other modes, one of which would be a constructive assumption of powers never meant to be granted. If the powers be deficient, the legitimate source of additional ones is always open, and ought to be resorted to.

Much of the error in expounding the Constitution has its origin in the use made of the species of sovereignty implied in the nature of government. The specified powers vested in Congress, it is said, are sovereign powers, and that as such they carry with them an unlimited discretion as to the means of executing them. It may surely be remarked that a limited government may be limited in its sovereignty as well with respect to the means as to the objects of his powers; and that to give an extent to the former, superseding the limits to the latter, is in effect to convert a limited into an unlimited government. There is certainly a reasonable medium between expounding the Constitution with the strictness of a penal law, or other ordinary statute, and expounding it with a laxity which may vary its essential character, and encroach on the local sovereignties with which it was meant to be reconcilable.

The very existence of these local sovereignties is a control on the pleas for a constructive amplification of the powers of the general government. Within a single State possessing the entire sovereignty, the powers given to the government by the people are understood to extend to all the acts whether as means or ends required for the welfare of the community, and falling within the range of just government. To withhold from such a government any particular power necessary or useful in itself, would be to deprive the people of the good dependent on its exercise; since the power must be there or not exist at all. In the government of the United States the case is obviously different. In establishing that government the people retained other governments capable of exercising such necessary and useful powers as were not to be exercised by the general government. No necessary presumption therefore arises from the importance of any particular power in itself, that it has been vested in that government because though not vested there, it may exist elsewhere, and the exercise of it elsewhere might be preferred by those who alone had a right to make the distribution. The presumption which ought to be indulged is that any improvement of this distribution sufficiently pointed out by experience would not be withheld. . . .[127]

---

[127] *Writings* (Hunt ed.), VIII: 447–453.

CHAPTER XI

The Dartmouth College Case

THE CASE of *Dartmouth College v. Woodward,* considered
in many respects to be the foremost case in American constitutional law,
arose out of religious as well as political differences prevalent in New
England during the first decades of the nineteenth century. The immediate clash originated in a controversy between John Wheelock, President of Dartmouth College, and members of his faculty with respect to
the control over and the doctrines preached in local churches. The issue
gradually took a form in which Presbyterians, who were inclined toward
the Calvinistic faith in theology and who were partisans of Jeffersonianism in politics, were on one side and the Congregationalists, who were
deemed to be more rigid and bigoted in their religious views and who had
adopted Federalist principles of politics, were on the other. When Nathaniel Niles, who was a friend of Thomas Jefferson, was chosen a trustee
of the college and gained control of the board, he sought to limit Wheelock's authority as president and to secure his removal. At the time the
controversy began the board of trustees of the college was composed
mainly of Federalists.[1] The friends of the president regarded him as liberal in his religious views and the trustees as religious bigots. Though a
contest for the control of the college had been under way for some time
between President Wheelock and the trustees, under the leadership of
Judge Niles, open hostilities broke out in April, 1815, with the publication of a series of pamphlets and articles stating the views of the rival
factions.[2]

[1] Lord notes that "President Wheelock, himself, and his immediate friends, as well
as all of his opponents in the Board, save one, were Federalists, of the old school, and
some of them of great prominence in their party, while Judge Niles, whom the president viewed with unmitigated rancor as the leader of his foes, was equally prominent
as a Democrat." John King Lord, *A History of Dartmouth College: 1815–1909* (Concord, 1913), p. 65; for an account of the early years of the history of the college, see
Frederick Chase, *A History of Dartmouth College and the Town of Hanover, New
Hampshire,* ed. by John K. Lord (Cambridge, 1891).

[2] The controversy was precipitated by the publication and distribution of two
pamphlets: "Sketches of the History of Dartmouth College and Moor's Charity School"
and "A Candid and Analytical Review of Sketches." The trustees presented their case
in "A Vindication of the Official Conduct of the Trustees," published after the college
commencement, 1815, and prepared largely by Charles Marsh and signed by eight
members of the board.

THE ORIGIN OF THE CASE

As it was likely that legal proceedings would be necessary to settle some of the issues in which the college was becoming involved, Wheelock consulted Daniel Webster, who was regarded as in sympathy with his views. Having lost the support of the faculty and the trustees, largely as a result of acrimonious religious disputes, President Wheelock proposed that the board make application to the legislature to examine the management and government of the college and Moor's Charity School. As a result of this, a committee was appointed to investigate the college. When Wheelock applied to Webster, whom he considered his counsel and to whom a retaining fee had been sent, for aid in preparing his report to this committee, Webster failed to appear. By this time Webster had decided to join the anti-Wheelock faction.[3] As the contest between the factions took on more of a political cast, the Federalists supported the trustees and the Republicans favored Wheelock.[4]

In August, 1815, when the removal of President Wheelock was contemplated by the trustees, Jeremiah Mason, their attorney, advised delay because of the effect it might have on the legislative investigation under way, for, said he, "the legislature, I think, for certain purposes, have a right to inquire into an alleged mismanagement of such an institution, a visitorial power rests in the State, and I do not deem it important for my present view to determine in what department or how to be exercised."[5] But contrary to Mason's advice and before the committee had completed its investigation the board removed Wheelock and appointed Reverend Francis Brown to the presidency. Up to this point the contro-

---

[3] Of Webster's change of interest and affiliation, Fuess thinks, there may be some question how far Webster was ethically bound, especially since it does not appear that he returned the fee paid to him by Wheelock. Fuess comments, however, "that it would have been both injudicious and inconsistent for him to let himself be the tool of the Wheelock faction, which was drawing its support from the Republicans, his political foes. Furthermore, [Thomas W.] Thompson, Jeremiah Mason, and Jeremiah Smith, all of whom were Federalists, were involved, and Webster was inclined to follow where they led." Claude Moore Fuess, *Daniel Webster* (Boston, 1930), I: 221.

The explanation of Webster's shift of position and interest, according to Shirley, was due to the fact that Webster's closest personal and political friends were opposed to Wheelock and that he was detached from Wheelock against his convictions. See John M. Shirley, *Dartmouth College Causes and the Supreme Court of the United States* (St. Louis, 1879), p. 94. Shirley was for some time reporter of the supreme court of New Hampshire.

[4] Charles Marsh and Daniel Webster were members of the House of Representatives, Jeremiah Mason and Thomas W. Thompson were in the United States Senate and, asserts Lord, "all were Federalists and together with Jeremiah Smith, were, with the exception of Marsh who was a citizen of Vermont, the leaders of the Federal party in New Hampshire." Lord, *op. cit.*, p. 83.

[5] Shirley, *op. cit.*, p. 95.

versy was mainly among the Federalists who controlled the trustees and the legislature which was in control of the Democratic-Republican party. In religious as well as in political faith, Lord observes, "the antecedents of Wheelock and of [Isaac] Hill and Plumer were as wide apart as the poles. The last two stood, above everything else, for the fullest freedom of religious thought and action, as opposed to the dominance of orthodoxy; while the starting point of Wheelock's complaints was the countenance given by the trustees to those 'who dared to encroach on Presbyterian ground,' and to subvert the ancient order of things."[6] When the Anti-Federalists elected William Plumer to the governorship and secured a majority in the legislature the efforts to control the college took a new political turn. Webster, sensing trouble ahead, hoped that it would be possible to soften the irritated feelings of democracy toward the college. He was willing to have the legislature establish a new college and suggested the name "University of New Hampshire."

Governor Plumer, in his message to the legislature, noted that a charter emanating from the King naturally contained principles congenial to monarchy and hence provided for a self-perpetuating board.[7] This principle, he thought, was hostile to the spirit and genius of a free government. Sound policy required that the trustees in the future should be elected by some other body of men. The college, he said, "was founded for the public good, not for the benefit or emolument of its trustees"; and he contended that the right to amend and improve acts of incorporation of this nature had been exercised by all governments, both monarchial and republican.[8] This message, Jefferson commended as

replete with sound principles, and truly Republican. . . . The idea that institutions established for the use of the Nation cannot be touched nor modified, even to make them answer their end, because of rights gratuitously supposed in those employed to manage them in trust for the public, may, perhaps, be a salutary provision against the abuses of a monarch, but it is most absurd against the Nation itself. Yet our lawyers and priests generally inculcate this doctrine; and suppose that preceding generations held the earth more freely than we do; had a right to impose laws on us, unalterable by ourselves; and that we, in like manner, can make laws, and impose burdens on future generations, which they will have no right to alter; in fine, that the earth belongs to the dead, and not to the living.[9]

Following the recommendation of the governor, the legislature passed an act changing the name of the college to Dartmouth University, increasing the number of trustees from twelve to twenty-one, and providing for a board of twenty-five overseers with a veto power over the acts

[6] Lord, *op. cit.*, p. 66.
[7] For a copy of the charter establishing Dartmouth College, see 4 Wheaton 519 (1819).
[8] Lord, *op. cit.*, p. 85.
[9] William Plumer, Jr., *Life of William Plumer* (Boston, 1857), pp. 440, 441.

of the trustees. The governor and council of state were to appoint the overseers, fill all vacancies on the board of trustees, inspect the university, and present regular reports to the legislature.[10] With the old trustees refusing to accept the provisions of the law, the governor and council set up a new university and an attempt was made to conduct two institutions.[11] While the bill to reorganize Dartmouth College was being considered by the legislature, two of the trustees of the college, Thomas W. Thompson and Asa McFarland, prepared a remonstrance which foreshadowed Webster's argument before the Supreme Court and John Marshall's decision. According to these trustees, the charter of Dartmouth College was a contract made by the state with the twelve persons named as trustees and "certain rights and privileges were vested in them and their successors for the guarantee of which the faith of government was pledged by necessary implication." It was further asserted that the new corporation "will be deemed by the courts of law altogether diverse and distinct from the corporation to which all the grants of property have hitherto been made."[12]

When William H. Woodward, the secretary and treasurer of the college, declined to recognize the college trustees and served as the officer of the university, the trustees removed him from his position and brought suit to recover the charter, record books, and college seal. This was the beginning of the *Dartmouth College Case*. By consent of the parties the case was taken directly to the state court of appeals.[13] It was argued for the college by Jeremiah Mason, Jeremiah Smith, and Daniel Webster and for the university by George Sullivan and Ichabod Bartlett. Because of the extraordinary significance of the case in the political and economic development of the United States, the arguments of the attorneys, both in the trial in the state court and before the federal Supreme Court, deserve consideration.

ARGUMENTS BEFORE THE STATE COURT

"Parchment barriers," as Jeremiah Mason called them, were considered to have little effect "unless carefully guarded, and firmly defended by the judiciary."[14] And, defending the cause of the college, he thought the courts in exercising this function should be bold, and not be guided by

---

[10] Copies of the act amending the charter are included in the report of the case, 4 Wheaton 539 ff.

[11] For the difficulties encountered by the governor and his newly appointed boards to take official action and to operate the new institution, see Lord, *op. cit.*, pp. 94 ff.

[12] *Ibid.*, pp. 88, 89.

[13] If the hearing had been conducted in the court of first instance the case would have been tried by William H. Woodward, who was the justice of peace for the district.

[14] Dartmouth College v. Woodward, 65 New Hampshire Reports 478 (1817).

an attitude of "cautious timidity" to keep the legislature from drawing all power into its vortex. With prophetic insight, so far as the development of implied constitutional restrictions is concerned, he said: "If therefore the passing of the acts, in question, be not within the general scope of the legislative power, they cannot be valid."[15] The attempt, which was made by the acts in dispute, to take away the college's property and privileges, it was asserted, "cannot be done by the exercise of the legislature. . . . A legislature can never, by virtue of its general power interfere in questions of private rights."[16] And it was declared to be a general principle that no vested right can be taken away from one and transferred to another except through the agency of a court of justice. A college devoted to the promotion of learning was considered to be an eleemosynary institution or private corporation which was not subject to control by the state as a public corporation. The rights of such a corporation, though arising by virtue of a grant from the state, were regarded as entitled to the same protection as were those of individuals.

The main conclusion of Mason was that, in England, though the King granted charters, he could not revoke them except by writ of *quo warranto*. Attempts of the legislature to interfere with the college and to change its charter were regarded as a violation of vested rights which the plaintiffs had acquired under existing laws and were hence void. Justice Chase's opinion in *Calder v. Bull*[17] was cited as authority for the doctrine that legislatures may not destroy or interfere with vested rights. The "law of the land" provision of the bill of rights of the state constitution was regarded as providing additional security for private rights. This provision, it was contended, was unquestionably designed to restrain the legislature, as well as the other branches of government, from all arbitrary interference with private rights. Lord Coke was quoted as holding that the "law of the land" clause bound Parliament. And finally the contract clause of the federal Constitution was declared to be a means of affording "an additional and uniform security for private rights throughout the United States."[18] The essential lines of defense on which Webster elaborated in his argument before the Supreme Court of the United States are to be found in Mason's argument.

Counsel for the college objected strenuously to the efforts to establish the public control of education. "If these acts are held to be valid," they

---

[15] 65 N. H. 479.

[16] 65 N. H. 480. See also Timothy Farrar, *Report of the Case of the Trustees of Dartmouth College against William H. Woodward* (Portsmouth, 1819), pp. 36 ff., for Mason's argument.

[17] 3 Dallas 386, 387 (1798).

[18] 65 N. H. 497, and Farrar, *op. cit.*, pp. 56, 64.

declared, "not only this College, but every other literary and charitable institution must become subject to the varying, and often capricious will, of the legislatures. Their revenues will be blended with the public revenues, and liable to be applied to any use, which the emergency of occasions may, in the opinion of the legislatures, require."[19] It was predicted that if New Hampshire's "bold experiment" were carried into effect it would lead to the final destruction of New England colleges.

Jeremiah Smith, arguing on behalf of the college, attempted to distinguish types of corporations such as *public,* counties and towns; *civil,* such as banks; and *eleemosynary,* established for charitable or educational purposes. The power of visitation and control exercised by the King or his agents over the third type of corporation was somewhat troublesome to dispose of, but the ingenuity of the attorney was not lacking, and it was contended that for the charitable and educational institutions of New England such powers of visitation and control belonged to the trustees alone. All outside control or inquiry over charitable or educational corporations was thus to be removed.

Smith assumed, as did all those who defended the rights and privileges of the old college, that by means of the charter a private corporation was formed and that the funds of the college must be considered as private property. He admitted that the state might establish a university of its own and govern it as it saw fit, but that it could not alter an existing endowed institution, because such an institution was under the control and jurisdiction of the courts alone. It belonged to the judiciary, then, "to keep this corporation within the limits, prescribed by the charter, and the law of the land."[20] The legislature could not pass any acts altering the charter or in any way interfering with the organization or management of the corporation without its consent.

The typical attitude of disrespect for popular government, which was one of the main tenets of the Federalist party, was shown in the comment that "no body of men can be imagined in every way worse qualified for the exercise of the powers now claimed for the legislature."[21] The political nature of the underlying issues was recognized by Smith when he noted that the primary objection to the charitable institutions established in this country was that they retained the monarchical principles enumerated in charters granted by the King and were therefore hostile to the spirit and genius of a free government. Webster, in a concluding argument, added little that was new, since the contentions of the college

---

[19] 65 N. H. 501, and Farrar, *op. cit.,* p. 69.
[20] 65 N. H. 548, and Farrar, *op. cit.,* p. 138.
[21] 65 N. H. 551, and Farrar, *op. cit.,* p. 143.

trustees had been fully considered by Mason and Smith. It is especially significant that the attorneys for the college gave a minor place in their arguments to the contract clause of the federal Constitution as a ground for an attack upon the New Hampshire acts.[22] The main contention of the attorneys for the college was that the primary purpose of a written constitution, as interpreted and applied by the Judiciary, was to define and to protect private rights such as were involved in this case.

George Sullivan, arguing on behalf of the state, assumed that the college, as stated in the charter, was not a private but a public corporation created for the public interest or "for the benefit of said Province." As a public corporation, the right of the legislature to alter or amend its charter must be clear. It was pointed out that the legislatures frequently took away the rights and privileges of private corporations. The idea, said Sullivan, that when a charter is granted to a corporation, whether public or private, that there is an implied contract on the part of the government not to alter or amend its charter without its consent is wholly unfounded as well as visionary.[23] And if a charter granted by the legislature is a contract, it certainly is not such a contract as comes within the spirit and meaning of the contract clause of the federal Constitution. The object of the contract clause was to guard against paper money, stay laws, and the like, and not to interfere with the public control of educational institutions. It was agreed that the King could not change the charters of corporations, but Sullivan insisted that Parliament had such authority. The separation of powers argument urged by counsel for the college was regarded as inapplicable because of the public nature of the college corporation.

The assertion that the legislature was an improper body to superintend literary institutions was considered as running counter to the plain requirements of the state constitution which provided that "it shall be the duty of legislators, in all future periods of this government, to cherish the interest of literature and the sciences, and all seminaries and public schools."

Sullivan noted that those defending the cause of the state found themselves in opposition to strong and inveterate prejudices favoring the sanctity of the rights and privileges of corporations. He then stated a principle that was later to become an important feature in the applica-

---

[22] Lodge notes that in the argument in the state court Webster spoke with great force and, going beyond the limits of legal argument, wound up with "a splendid sentimental appeal which drew tears from the crowd in the Exeter court room, and which he afterwards used in an elaborated form and with similar effect before the Supreme Court at Washington." Henry Cabot Lodge, *Daniel Webster* (Boston, 1898), p. 80.

[23] 65 N. H. 508, and Farrar, *op. cit.*, p. 80.

tion of the due process of law clause in the federal Constitution, namely, that a corporation created for the purpose of promoting the public interest may be altered in such a manner as the public interest may require.[24]

Ichabod Bartlett, representing the state, thought that the chief arguments for making corporations independent of the legislature were based on the sacredness of the character of corporations and the unfitness of legislatures, because of their weakness and wickedness, to govern them properly. The attempt of the counsel for the college to defend their position by referring to English precedents was answered by quoting Blackstone's comment on the legislative powers of Parliament as follows: "It hath sovereign and uncontrollable authority in making, confirming, enlarging, restraining, abrogating, repealing, reviving and expounding the laws concerning matters of all possible denominations, ecclesiastical or temporal, civil or military, maritime or criminal."[25]

Instances were cited in which the legislature of Connecticut changed the charter of Yale College and the legislature of Massachusetts amended the charter of Harvard College without the consent of the trustees. The Massachusetts constitution of 1780 provided for the continuance of Harvard College under its established form of government and expressly provided "that nothing herein shall be construed to prevent the legislature of this commonwealth from making such alterations in the government of said University as shall be conducive to its advantage, and the interest of the republic of letters, in as full a manner as might have been done by the legislature of the late Province of Massachusetts Bay."[26] At this time Harvard College was definitely considered as subject to control by the state legislature. Changes were made in the charter affecting the governing boards of the institution in 1810, 1812, and 1814.[27]

The trustees of Dartmouth College, Bartlett observed, say to the supreme power of the state "we are mightier than thou."[28] And the attempt to secure sanction from the "law of the land" provision to protect vested

---

[24] 65 N. H. 523, and Farrar, *op. cit.*, p. 102. Cf. also Munn v. Illinois, 94 U. S. 113 (1876).

[25] 4 *Comm.* 481.

[26] Chap. v, art. iii.

[27] See Samuel Eliot Morison, *The Life and Letters of Harrison Gray Otis* (Boston, 1913), I: 252, 253, and Edward Channing, *History of the United States* (New York, 1927), V: 256, 257. In 1779 the Pennsylvania legislature revoked the charter of the College of Philadelphia and vested the control of the institution in a new corporation to be known as the "University of the State of Pennsylvania." By this act the university was placed under the control of the people of Pennsylvania. Though by a subsequent act the older corporation was revived, it was taken for granted that the legislature had the power to grant and revoke the charters of educational institutions. Elmer Ellsworth Brown, *The Origin of American State Universities* (Berkeley, 1903), pp. 27, 28.

[28] Farrar, *op. cit.*, p. 190.

rights was answered by the comment that "the history of Magna Carta must be too familiar to need at this time the introduction of proofs to show that its provisions were to guard against the arbitrary proceedings of the Crown and were not intended as a restraint upon Parliament."[29] Bartlett could not conceive that the contract clause of the federal Constitution by any mode of interpretation could be "so distorted as to extend its shadow to a purpose so oblique and distant from its original intent." The attorneys for the college were considered as the "first discoverers" of a new meaning for this clause.[30]

CHIEF JUSTICE RICHARDSON'S OPINION

The mingling of politics and judicial affairs had become the accepted practice in New Hampshire. Originally the judicial positions were in the hands of the Federalists, but when the Republicans gained control of state affairs Republicans were appointed in their place. The Federalists, who insisted in the debate of 1802 on the independence and permanence in office of judges appointed and, by the Constitution, holding their offices "during good behavior," when they came into power in New Hampshire in 1813, abolished the inferior courts and the superior court or court of last resort, turned out all of the judges, and established a new judicial system. These proceedings, which were approved by Webster and most of the Federalists, led to frequent complications and disturbances. Following the election of a Republican governor and legislature, this law was repealed, the Federalist judges were removed upon the ground that the former law was unconstitutional, and the old system was restored. Webster, in his attack on the legislature of 1816, maintained a "guarded silence" on the proceedings of his political associates in 1813. According to Beveridge, the *Dartmouth College Case* came before a court consisting of three Republicans appointed by Governor Plumer. But Shirley maintains that Chief Justice Richardson was a Federalist and that his associates, Bell and Woodbury, were Anti-Federalists.[31] Chief Justice Richardson, delivering the opinion for the superior court of appeals of New Hampshire, deemed it unnecessary to decide how far the legislature had a constitutional right to interfere in the concerns of private corporations.[32] "All public interests," he held, "are proper

[29] Farrar, *op. cit.*, p. 193.

[30] *Ibid.*, p. 196.

[31] Cf. William Plumer, Jr., *op. cit.*, pp. 411, 412.

[32] See Albert J. Beveridge, *The Life of John Marshall* (Boston, 1919), IV: 234, and Shirley, *op. cit.*, p. 150. Webster observed: "It would be a queer thing if Governor Plumer's court should refuse to execute his laws." Lord, *op. cit.*, p. 124. "Although Judge Woodbury joined in the decision," Lord states that, "it would appear from

objects of legislation; and it is peculiarly the province of the legislature, to determine by what law those interests shall be regulated."[33]

The language of Lord Ashurst in *King v. Passmore*[34] was quoted as describing the status of the old trustees as follows: "the members of the old body, have no injury or injustice to complain of, for they are all included in the new charter of incorporation, and if any of them do not become members of the new incorporation, but refuse to accept it, it is their own fault." The plaintiffs, Richardson thought, had failed to recognize a distinction between the rights and faculties relating to corporations, which can exist only in the corporators as natural persons, and the corporate rights and faculties, which can exist only in the corporation. It is not the corporators, as natural persons, but the artificial entity—the corporation—which has legal title to the property, and the natural persons who compose "this artificial, immortal individual," in which the property is vested, must, in the nature of things, be continually fluctuating.[35] The addition of new members by a legislative act, even to a private corporation, does not, he observed, necessarily divest the old corporators of any private beneficial interest.

The court held that the New Hampshire acts did not dissolve the old corporation, nor create a new one; nor did they operate in such a manner as to change or transfer any legal title or beneficial interest in the corporate property, but the legal title remained in the corporation, and the beneficial interest in the public, unaffected.[36] The issue was not, the plaintiffs had contended, whether the legislature could compel the old members to become members of the corporation, but whether it had the constitutional right to make a new organization of the corporation by adding new members.

The chief justice agreed with the attorneys for the state that the acts were not in violation of the law of the land provision of the state constitution, for this clause was intended as a limitation on the Crown and not on Parliament.[37] Recognizing the far-reaching effect of the interpretation of the "law of the land" or its equivalent "due process of law," as contended by the friends of the college, Richardson observed: "If we decide that these acts are not 'the law of the land' because they interfere

---

the dockets that he did not sit in the case, as would, indeed, be expected, since he had been himself one of the first Trustees of the University and very active in its behalf." *Ibid.*, p. 130.

[33] 65 N. H. 631, and Farrar, *op. cit.*, p. 216.

[34] 3 Durnford and East 244 (1789).

[35] 65 N. H. 633, and Farrar, *op. cit.*, p. 218.

[36] 65 N. H. 634, and Farrar, *op. cit.*, p. 219.

[37] As sustaining this view, Sullivan's *Lectures*, pp. 383–408, 2 Coke's *Institutes*, 45, and 4 Blackstone's *Comm.*, 423, were cited.

with private rights, all other acts, interfering with private rights, may, for ought we see, fall within the same principle; and what statute does not either directly or indirectly interfere with private rights."[38]

To the contention that the acts were void because in conflict with the contract clause of the federal Constitution, Richardson replied that such a charter was not a contract within the meaning of the Constitution. In his opinion this clause was not intended to limit the power of the states in relation to their public officers and servants or to their own civil institutions. Nor could it be construed to embrace contracts or grants of power by a state to individuals to be exercised for public purposes. If the charter of a public institution like that of Dartmouth College, said he, is to be construed as a contract within the intent of the Constitution of the United States, it will be difficult to say what powers, in relation to their public institutions, if any, are left to the states. This construction, in our view, is repugnant to the very principles of all government.[39]

Continuing his defense of the cause of the state, Richardson observed that:

No man prizes more highly than I do, the literary institutions of our country, or would go farther to maintain their just rights and privileges. But I cannot bring myself to believe, that it would be consistent with sound policy, or ultimately with the true interests of literature itself, to place the great public institutions, in which all the young men, destined for the liberal professions, are to be educated, within the absolute control of a few individuals, and out of the control of the sovereign power—not consistent with sound policy, because it is a matter of too great moment, too intimately connected with the public welfare and prosperity, to be thus entrusted in the hands of a few. The education of the rising generation is a matter of the highest public concern, and is worthy of the best attention of every legislature. The immediate care of these institutions must be committed to individuals, and the trust will be faithfully executed so long as it is recollected to be a mere public trust, and that there is a superintending power, that can and will correct every abuse of it. But make the trustees independent, and they will ultimately forget that their office is a public trust—will at length consider these institutions as their own—will overlook the great purposes for which their powers were originally given, and will exercise them only to gratify their own private views and wishes, or to promote the narrow purposes of a sect or a party. It is idle to suppose that courts of law can correct every abuse of such a trust. Courts of law cannot legislate. There may be many abuses, which can be corrected by the sovereign power alone. Nor would such exemption from legislative control be consistent with the true interests of literature itself, because these institutions must stand in constant need of the aid and patronage of the legislature and the public; and without such aid and patronage, they can never flourish. Their prosperity depends entirely upon the public estimation in which they are held. It is of the highest importance that they should be fondly cherished by the best affections of the people, that every citizen should feel that he has an interest in them, and that they constitute a part

---

[38] 65 N. H. 639, and Farrar, *op. cit.*, p. 228.

[39] 65 N. H. 639–641, and Farrar, *op. cit.*, pp. 229, 230.

of that inestimable inheritance, which he is to transmit to his posterity in the institutions of his country. But these institutions, if placed in a situation to dispute the public will, would eventually fall into the hands of men, who would be disposed to dispute it; and contests would inevitably arise, in which the great interests of literature would be forgotten. Those who resisted that will, would become at once the object of popular jealousy and distrust: their motives, however pure, would be called in question, and their resistance would be believed to have originated in private and interested views, and not in regard to the public welfare. It would avail these institutions nothing that the public will was wrong, and that their right could be maintained in opposition to it, in a court of law. A triumph there might be infinitely more ruinous than defeat. Whoever knows the nature of a popular government, knows that such a contest could not be thus settled by one engagement. Such a triumph would only protract the destructive contest. The last misfortune which can befall one of these institutions, is to become the subject of popular contention.

I am aware that this power in the hands of the legislature may, like every other power, at times be unwisely exercised; but where can it be more securely lodged? If those, whom the people annually elect to manage their public affairs, cannot be trusted, who can? The people have most emphatically enjoined it in the constitution, as a duty upon "the legislators and magistrates, in all future periods of the government, to cherish the interests of literature and the sciences and all seminaries and public schools." And those interests will be cherished, both by the legislature and the people so long as there is virtue enough left to maintain the rest of our institutions. Whenever the people and their rulers shall become corrupt enough to wage war with the sciences and liberal arts, we may be assured that the time will have arrived, when all our institutions, our laws, our liberties must pass away,—when all that can be dear to freedom, or that can make their country dear to them, must be lost, and when a government and institutions must be established, of a very different character from those under which it is our pride and happiness to live.[40]

Webster thought Chief Justice Richardson's opinion was "able, ingenious and plausible."[41] Chancellor Kent also strongly commended the opinion. It is one of the strongest statements in our legal literature in support of the public control of educational institutions. The states of the South and of the Middle West carried into effect Chief Justice Richardson's doctrine in the establishment of educational corporations which have become large and well-supported state universities. Encouragement was given to the movement to establish state universities through Thomas Jefferson's aid and assistance in the establishment of the University of Virginia. The foundation was laid in 1816 in the constitution of Indiana for a general system of public education "ascending in a regular graduation from township schools to a state university, wherein tuition shall be gratis, and equally open to all."[42]

[40] 65 N. H. 641–643, and Farrar, *op. cit.*, pp. 232–234. See decision in Virginia sustaining the view of the New Hampshire justices, Currie's Admr's v. Mutual Assurance Co., 4 Hen. and M. 315 (1809).

[41] See letter to Justice Story, Sept. 9, 1818, *The Private Correspondence of Daniel Webster*, ed. by Fletcher Webster (Boston, 1857), I: 287.

[42] Art. XI, sec. 2.

ARGUMENT BEFORE THE SUPREME COURT

The Dartmouth College trustees at the earliest opportunity appealed from the decision of the superior court of New Hampshire to the Supreme Court of the United States.[43] When Mason and Smith, the attorneys who defended the college cause in the state court, were unable to go to Washington, the burden of the defense fell upon Webster, who had now irrevocably shifted his allegiance to the old board. Moreover, because he had raised money in Boston to defray the expenses of the suit, he had a personal interest in it. Webster predicated his attack on the legislative acts on the familiar conservative assumption that if such alterations in charters, as those provided in the New Hampshire acts, could be made in the rights and privileges of the plaintiffs, all their rights and privileges could be abolished.

Webster admitted that the Supreme Court could not decide the case on general or fundamental principles, but he thought a discussion of such principles might aid in forming a correct judgment, and he devoted more than thirty pages to this part of his argument.[44] At the outset he contended that the New Hampshire acts were void because they "are not the exercise of a power properly legislative. Their object and effect is to take away, from one, rights, property, and franchises, and to grant them to another. This is not the exercise of a legislative power." This interference with property rights, he argued, could be declared only by the Judiciary. Following the reasoning of Justice Chase in *Calder v. Bull*,[45] and of Justice Story in *Terrett v. Taylor*,[46] as well as Chief Justice Marshall in *Fletcher v. Peck*,[47] Webster aimed to place the cause of the college upon the fundamental principle that private property must be protected from confiscation. This principle, he claimed, was as old as Magna Carta and was inscribed in the general terms of the state constitution. He saw no reason to change the plan of Smith and Mason who,

---

[43] "The opinion of the state court was based upon a statement of facts, which was, by previous agreement, to be turned into a special verdict at the request of either party, in order to carry the cause to the United States Supreme Court." See Lord, *op. cit.*, p. 138.

[44] "I am aware," said he, "of the limits which bound the jurisdiction of the Court in this case; and that on this record, nothing can be decided, but the single question, whether these acts are repugnant to the Constitution of the United States. Yet it may assist in forming an opinion on their true nature and character, to compare them with those fundamental principles, introduced into the state governments for the purpose of limiting the exercise of the legislative power, and which the Constitution of New Hampshire expressed with great fullness and accuracy." 4 Wheaton 557–558.

[45] 3 Dallas 386 (1798).

[46] 9 Cranch 42 (1815).

[47] 6 Cranch 87 (1810).

in their argument for the college in the state court, gave a minor place to the contention that the state acts violated the contract clause.[48]

The omnipotent power claimed for the British Parliament whereby the charters to corporations might be dissolved, Webster asserted, "does not belong to any legislature in the United States." "A corporation," said Blackstone, "may be dissolved by act of Parliament, which is boundless in its operations."[49] But Webster met this proposition by the contention that only the regal, and not the parliamentary power relating to charters passed to the legislature of New Hampshire. The King granted charters, only Parliament could revoke them. No such authority, Webster claimed, belonged to the state legislature. To counteract the view of the attorneys for the state and the reasoning of Chief Justice Richardson that Dartmouth College was a public corporation and, as such, subject to the changes that the state legislature might choose to make, Webster adopted the classification of corporations presented by Jeremiah Smith which placed the college in the category of eleemosynary corporations. Much of his argument was based on the proposition that what was concerned here was merely "a private charity"—a part of his argument which was contrary to well-known facts regarding the establishment and development of the college. As the board of directors of such an eleemosynary corporation, the trustees were regarded as having liberties, privileges, and immunities which "being once lawfully obtained and vested, are as inviolable as any vested rights of property whatever."[50]

Chancellor Kent and civilian authorities were quoted as saying that statutes which impair vested rights acquired under existing laws must be deemed retrospective and hence void.[51] Assuming, contrary to the facts, that the legislature had destroyed property rights, Webster insisted that it had thereby exercised judicial power and hence had violated the principle of the separation of powers.[52] If the constitution be not altogether waste paper, exclaimed he, the legislature must be inhibited from passing acts "directly and manifestly impairing private property and private privileges." Sanctioning an early form of the doctrine of academic tenure, Webster claimed that both "the president and profes-

---

[48] Only four of the forty-two pages in Mason's argument were devoted to the contract clause. Cf. Farrar's *Report*, pp. 28 ff., and Beveridge, *op. cit.*, IV: 234, 244.

[49] *Comm.*, I: 485.

[50] Dartmouth College v. Woodward, 4 Wheaton 568–576, and Farrar, *op. cit.*, p. 263.

[51] See Dash v. Van Kleeck, 7 Johns Rep. 477 (1811).

[52] "Who ever heard, before," asked Webster, "that a gift to a college, or hospital, or an asylum, was, in reality, nothing but a gift to the State?" See 4 Wheaton 574. This question is based on the assumption that the legislature had destroyed the college corporation, whereas it had only changed the board of control.

sors have freeholds in their offices; subject only to be removed, by the trustees, as their legal visitors, for good cause."[53]

Disagreeing with Chief Justice Richardson, Webster regarded the state acts as in violation of the "law of the land" clause of the state constitution, for, by "law of the land," is most clearly intended the general law; a law which hears before it condemns; which proceeds upon inquiry, and renders judgment only after trial. The meaning is that every citizen shall hold his life, liberty, property, and immunities under the protection of the general rules which govern society. Agreeing with Justice Chase in *Calder v. Bull,* Webster observed that: "everything which may pass under the form of enactment, is not, therefore, to be considered the law of the land. If this were so, acts of attainder, bills of pains and penalties, acts of confiscation, acts reversing judgments, and acts directly transferring one man's estate to another, legislative judgments, decrees and forfeitures, in all possible forms, would be the law of the land. Such a strange construction would render constitutional provisions, of the highest importance, completely inoperative and void. It would tend directly to establish the union of all powers in the legislature."[54] Thomas M. Cooley regarded this statement as the best definition of "due process of law." It has frequently been considered as authority for the doctrine that acts not legislative in nature are, in accordance with the separation of powers theory and the due process of law provision, necessarily void.

Having based his argument chiefly upon general and fundamental principles and the denial of the authority to interfere with private rights granted under a charter, Webster briefly considered the application to the case of the contract clause of the federal Constitution.[55] Citing the cases of *Fletcher v. Peck*[56] and *Terrett v. Taylor,*[57] he maintained that the college case fell within the true meaning of the contract clause of the Constitution expounded in the decisions of the Supreme Court and that the acts in question impaired this contract. Referring to other institutions which were in a similar situation to Dartmouth College, he insisted "it will be . . ., a most dangerous experiment to hold these institutions subject to the rise and fall of popular parties and the fluctuation of political opinions."[58] Painting a dark picture of the dire consequences which

---

[53] 4 Wheaton 583, and Farrar, *op. cit.,* p. 269.

[54] 4 Wheaton 581, 582.

[55] Only few pages of Webster's argument were devoted to the issue before the Supreme Court. See 4 Wheaton 588–596.

[56] 6 Cranch 87 (1810).

[57] 9 Cranch 43 (1815).

[58] 4 Wheaton 598–599, and Farrar, *op. cit.,* pp. 282, 283.

would follow if acts such as those of New Hampshire were upheld, Webster minimized the abuses that might arise if there were no public control over such educational and literary institutions. But it was not Webster's legal argument which made the greatest impression at the time.

"No skilled performer," claims Shirley, "ever handled the keys of his instrument with anything like the consummate skill and art with which Webster, when hard pressed, played upon the prejudices, passions and sympathies, as well as the understanding, of men."[59] He undoubtedly realized that on this occasion he could not rely on legal argument and pure reason alone. Without appearing to overstep the line of propriety, he felt it necessary to go beyond the legal argument in the case and to appeal to the members of the Court as men, subject as other individuals are to emotions and prejudices. Webster boldly and successfully adopted this procedure in the part of his argument to the Court which was not included in the printed copy prepared and distributed to aid the college cause while the case remained undecided.

In the printed brief and in the reporter's notes "something was left out," said Webster. That something, notes Lodge,

which must have occupied in its delivery nearly an hour was the most conspicuous example of the generalship by which Mr. Webster achieved victory, and which was wholly apart from his law. . . .[60]

Mr. Webster was fully aware that he could rely, in any aspect of the case, upon the sympathy of Marshall and Washington. He was equally certain of the unyielding opposition of Duval and Todd; the other three Judges, Johnson, Livingston, and Story, were known to be adverse to the College, but were possible converts. The first point was to increase the sympathy of the Chief Justice to an eager and even passionate support. Mr. Webster knew the chord to strike, and he touched it with a master hand. This was the "something left out," of which we know the general drift, and we can easily imagine the effect. In the midst of all the legal and constitutional arguments, relevant and irrelevant, even in the pathetic appeal which he used so well in behalf of his alma mater, Mr. Webster boldly and yet skilfully introduced the political view of the case. So delicately did he do it that an attentive listener did not realize that he was straying from the field of "mere reason" into that of political passion. Here no man could equal him or help him for here his eloquence had full scope, and on this he relied to arouse Marshall, whom he thoroughly understood. In occasional sentences he pictured his beloved College under the wise rule of Federalists and of the church. He depicted the party assault that was made upon her. He showed the citadel of learning threatened with unholy invasion and falling helplessly into the hands of Jacobins and free-thinkers. As the tide of his resistless and solemn eloquence, mingled with his masterly argument, flowed on, we can imagine how the great Chief Justice roused like an old warhorse at the sound of the trumpet. The words of the speaker carried him back to the early years of the century, when, in the full flush of manhood, at the head of his Court, the last stronghold of Federalism, the last bulwark of sound government, he had faced the power of the triumphant Democrats. Once more it was

[59] *Dartmouth College Causes*, p. 4.   [60] *Daniel Webster*, p. 87.

Marshall against Jefferson—the Judge against the President. Then he had preserved the ark of the Constitution. Then he had seen the angry waves of popular feeling breaking vainly at his feet. Now, in his old age, the conflict was revived. Jacobinism was raising its sacrilegious hand against the temples of learning, against the friends of order and good government. The joy of battle must have glowed once more in the old man's breast as he grasped anew his weapons and prepared with all the forces of his indomitable will to raise yet another constitutional barrier across the path of his ancient enemies.

We cannot but feel that Mr. Webster's lost passages, embodying this political appeal, did the work, and that the result was settled when the political passions of the Chief Justice were fairly aroused. Marshall would probably have brought about the decision by the sole force of his imperious will. But Mr. Webster did a good deal of effective work after the arguments were all finished, and no account of the case would be complete without a glance at the famous peroration with which he concluded his speech and in which he boldly flung aside all vestige of legal reasoning, and spoke directly to the passions and emotions of his hearers.[61]

Webster's argument, its political appeal, and his emotional peroration represents a notable instance of the *ad hominem* method of advocacy.[62] It has been pointed out that except for these features there was little new in Webster's argument. There is in fact a remarkable case of identity between Mason's argument before the state court and Webster's defense of the cause of the college in Washington.[63] After showing the striking identity of material, method, and phraseology in Mason's and Webster's arguments, Noyes concludes that "to Webster's knowledge of men in general, and of the Judges before him in particular, to his consequent daring introduction of nearly an hour's discussion of the political side of the case and of his splendid peroration, was no doubt largely, perhaps principally due to the effect of his argument upon the judges and the public." Webster at various times recognized his debt to Mason and Smith.

Because the appeal of the college to the Supreme Court was considered a forlorn hope,[64] the state officials and the university trustees thought it a needless expense to send the original counsel, Sullivan and Bartlett, to Washington. John Holmes, a representative in Congress, and William Wirt, recently appointed Attorney General, were selected to defend the cause of the state. Holmes, it is claimed, delivered a political speech

---

[61] Lodge, *op. cit.*, pp. 87–89.

[62] For a firsthand impression of a part of this political and personal appeal, see the account of Channing A. Goodrich in Samuel Gilman Brown's *The Works of Rufus Choate with a Memoir of His Life* (Boston, 1862), I: 515 ff.; also Lord, *op. cit.*, pp. 147–149.

[63] W. S. G. Noyes, "Webster's Debt to Mason in the Dartmouth College Case," 28 *Amer. Law Rev.* (May–June, 1894), 356.

[64] Webster said he had never allowed himself to indulge any great hope of success. C. H. Van Tyne, *The Letters of Daniel Webster* (New York, 1902), p. 77.

rather than a logical and sustained legal argument.[65] Wirt, not being familiar with the facts of the case, was unprepared to meet the contentions of the counsel for the college and broke down in the midst of his argument. But Daniel Webster and Joseph Hopkinson, whom Webster had prevailed upon to serve as associate counsel,[66] were familiar with the facts and the issues involved and presented effective arguments.

Holmes, for the state, contended that the prohibition in the Constitution which alone gives the Court jurisdiction in the case did not extend to grants of political power, nor to contracts concerning the internal government and policy of a sovereign state. The education of youth was declared to be one of the most important objects of civil government, the regulation of which belonged, with few exceptions, such as copyrights, to the states. It was also noted that where a private proprietary interest was coupled with the exercise of political power or a public trust, the charters of corporations had frequently been amended by legislative authority. Hopkinson in reply insisted that the whole argument for the state proceeded on an unwarranted assumption, namely, that the corporation created by the charter was a public corporation. He then proceeded to demonstrate that this assumption was contrary to the facts as he conceived them.

On the morning after the conclusion of the argument Chief Justice Marshall announced that some of the Judges were of different opinions, that some had not formed an opinion, and consequently the cause must be continued. Beveridge thinks that Marshall, Washington, and Story were for the college, Duval and Todd against it, and that Livingston and Johnson had not made up their minds. This surmise of the attitudes of the Justices, with the exception of that of Story, appears from the evidence to be correct. Webster believed,[67] that following argument, only

---

[65] Holmes, says Shirley, "was a scheming, busy, restless, rollicking politician . . . he was as much out of place before Judge Marshall's court and pitted against such a man as Webster as it was possible to be . . . he had neither taste, time, inclination, nor the mental qualities to grasp, prepare, and argue a cause like this." *Dartmouth College Causes,* p. 231.

[66] To President Brown, Webster wrote that if he was expected to argue the college case, "I should choose to associate with me some distinguished Counsel. Mr. Thompson and myself have mentioned Mr. Hopkinson of Philadelphia. He is well known to us, and I think him capable of arguing this cause as well as any man in the United States. . . . I think I would undertake, for a thousand dollars, to go to Washington, and argue the case, and get Mr. Hopkinson's assistance also. I doubt whether I could do it for a much less sum." Lord, *op. cit.,* p. 138.

It is thought that Webster sought the aid of Hopkinson in arguing the case because of his friendship with Marshall. Hopkinson had been counsel for Justice Chase on his impeachment trial. For an historical note dealing with the attorneys in the *Dartmouth College Case,* see Charles Warren, 46 *Amer. Law Rev.* (Sept.–Oct., 1912), 665.

[67] Writing to Chief Justice Smith, Webster observed, "I have no accurate knowledge of the manner in which the Judges are divided. The Chief and Washington I have

two Justices supported the college, and, on the review of the evidence, Shirley is of the opinion that Webster's prediction was correct.

Webster did not regard the attack on the acts of the legislature as based on the contract clause as a particularly strong argument. His main hope rested on the contention that the acts were not "within the general scope of legislative power and were contrary to general principles"—a mode of attack on which he felt sure the Court at Washington would be favorable. He encouraged the friends of the college to bring cases before the Circuit Court in New Hampshire the purpose of which, he hoped, was to raise before the Supreme Court at Washington the question whether by the general principles of our governments and independent of the constitutional provisions respecting contracts the state legislature can be restrained from divesting vested rights. Lord notes that through the efforts of Webster and Marsh and with the advice and concurrence of Justice Story a method of procedure was adopted which was calculated to try all of the rights of the parties.[68] Webster's plan involved the turn-

---

no doubt are with us. Duval and Todd perhaps against us; the other three holding up. I cannot much doubt but that Story will be with us in the end, and I think we have much more than an even chance for one of the others. I think we shall finally succeed." *Private Correspondence*, I: 276.

[68] On the progress of the cases, which were brought by the officers of the college at Webster's solicitation, Marsh wrote to President Brown as follows:

"I have just returned from Portsmouth where I have been two days past. The actions are all continued, but the court made the most positive injunction on the defendants to plead in season and be prepared for trial early the next term, and it was suggested that an adjourned term would be holden for their trial, if necessary in order that some one or more of them might be entered in the Supreme Court at next term. The Judge [Justice Story] intimated that this was of great importance as the action now there did not perhaps present all of the questions that would naturally arise out of the controversy and as it was time the controversy should be finished, the Judge assured the parties that nothing should be wanting on the part of the Court to place the actions in such train as would insure their final decision." Lord, *op. cit.*, p. 154.

After considerable acquaintance with Justice Story, Marsh observed, "an impartial decision is all that we ought to desire and this I think without doubt we shall have." By this time Justice Story had apparently decided to aid the cause of the college in every way within his power. Webster, following the course of these cases, let it be known that he had given the Supreme Court "reason to expect that a case would be presented at the Circuit Court raising the question in its amplest form" and said he would be "mortified if it were not so." Webster, *Private Correspondence*, I: 278, and Lord, *op. cit.*, p. 154.

In a letter to Mason, April 28, 1818, Webster wrote, "I saw Judge Story as I came along. He is evidently expecting a case which shall present all the questions. . . . The question which we must raise in one of these actions, is, 'whether by the general principles of our governments, the state legislatures be not restrained from divesting vested rights'? This of course, independent of the constitutional provision respecting contracts. The particular provisions in the New Hampshire constitution no doubt strengthen this general proposition in our case; but on general principles, I am very confident the Court at Washington would be with us." *Private Correspondence*, I: 282, 283; also Lord, *op. cit.*, pp. 141 ff.

ing of an agreement drawn by counsel into a special verdict, whereupon Justice Story and the District Judge were to disagree *pro forma,* without argument or decision. Then the cause could be taken immediately to the Supreme Court of the United States upon the certificate of the disagreement of the Judges.[69] At the instigation of Webster, three such suits were brought before the federal court in New Hampshire, any one of which, as Beveridge notes, would have afforded Story the opportunity which he probably by this time desired, namely, to declare the New Hampshire acts void as contrary to natural rights and justice.[70] But the original case presented to the Supreme Court was decided before any of these cases could be brought to trial.

It is well known that influences other than strict legal arguments not infrequently affect the decisions of judges. On the contrary, it is rather unusual to take steps to change the tentative judgments which may have been formed by the judges after a case has been argued and prior to the announcement of the court's decision. That such steps were taken before Chief Justice Marshall rendered his opinion in the *Dartmouth College Case* is apparent from the available historical records relating to the case.

ATTEMPTS TO INFLUENCE THE OPINIONS OF THE JUDGES

It is difficult to extricate the actual facts of the *Dartmouth College Case* from the religious, political, and emotional setting surrounding the case. Beveridge, following the footsteps of other historians of the Supreme Court, attempts to place the decision of the case on the high plane of legal logic and wise judicial statemanship.[71] It is customary to condemn

---

[69] Lord, *op. cit.,* pp. 154, 155, 159.

[70] On the difficulties of preparing and presenting an appropriate case to the federal courts, see Shirley, *op. cit.,* pp. 277 ff., and appendix, below, p. 420.

[71] Beveridge defends the activities of the friends of the college to influence the Judges by saying: "Although the efforts of the College to get its case before Kent were praiseworthy rather than reprehensible, and although no smallest item of testimony had been adduced by eager searches for something unethical, nevertheless out of the circumstances just related has been woven, from the materials of eager imaginations, a network of suspicion involving the integrity of the Supreme Court in the Dartmouth decision." In a footnote he continues: "This is principally the work of John M. Shirley. ... [His] volume is crammed with the results of extensive research, strange conglomeration of facts, suppositions, inferences, and insinuations, so inextricably mingled that it is with utmost difficulty that the painstaking student can find his way." Beveridge, *op. cit.,* IV: 258, 259.

"Before us, as we write," says Shirley, "lies the written statement of one of the great actors in this controversy, showing that on February 28, 1824, he 'destroyed many letters to and from F. Brown and D. Webster, and letters to and from J. Mason, T. Farrar, M. Olcott, B. J. Gilbert, T. W. Thompson, C. Marsh, A. Livermore, R. Fletcher,' etc., relating to this controversy. But enough remains to show what was done, though it does not disclose every step of the actors." From the available records and cor-

Shirley's *Dartmouth College Causes and the Supreme Court* for its "inferences and insinuations" regarding the political methods used to secure a favorable decision for the college. Lord refers to Shirley as "betraying a strong bias against the College in the controversy, and drawing some unwarrantable conclusions from distorted facts," but as "crammed with learning and information."[72] Lord, on the contrary, aims in every way to place the cause of the college in the best light. An illustration of Lord's failure to treat both sides fairly is shown when, in the consideration of the case in the New Hampshire superior court, the decision against the college and the opinion of Chief Justice Richardson are practically ignored.[73]

Both parties to the dispute resorted to political and extralegal influences to win their cause. Chief Justice Richardson's opinion was printed and circulated. But the efforts on behalf of the state to secure support were scarcely comparable to the adroitly planned and systematically executed schemes of Webster and the college group. Without depending upon inferences or insinuations, it is evident that a persistent and somewhat indecorous campaign was waged to win over to the college side the doubtful members of the Supreme Court as well as those who supported the action of the state. Webster submitted a copy of his argument at Washington to Judge Parker, the chief justice of the supreme court of Massachusetts, who advised the printing and circulation of the argument, for, said he: "Public sentiment has a great deal to do in affairs of this sort, and it ought to be well formed. That sentiment may even reach and affect a court, at least if there be any members who wish to do right, but are a little afraid, it will be a great help to know that all the world expects they will do right." And in due course Webster's brief was revised and printed to be used as a campaign document.[74] Commenting on the printing of his argument, Webster said: "The opinion of the New Hampshire court had been a good deal circulated, and I was urged to exhibit in print our view of the case. A few copies only were printed,

respondence, Shirley presents an interesting and illuminating account of the proceedings relating to this case.

Hagan thinks that Shirley failed to prove that the decision of the Supreme Court was obtained by improper influences, but concedes that "he abundantly demonstrated that important facts relative to the foundation of Dartmouth College were misstated both in Webster's argument and in Marshall's opinion." Horace H. Hagan, "Dartmouth College Case," 19 *Georgetown Law Jour.* (May, 1931), 416.

[72] Lord, *op. cit.*, p. 69.

[73] *Ibid.*, p. 130. For unfavorable comments on President Wheelock, see *ibid.*, pp. 116 ff.

[74] For an account of the efforts to create public sentiment favorable to the college after the case had been argued and submitted in a court of last resort, see Shirley, *op. cit.*, pp. 249 ff., and address by Ephriam A. Otis, "The Dartmouth College Case," 27 *Amer. Law Rev.* (July–Aug., 1893), 525.

and they have been used rather cautiously. A respect for the Court, as well as general decorum, seem to prohibit the publishing of an argument while the cause is pending. I have no objection to your showing this to any professional friend in your discretion, I only wish to guard against its becoming too public."[75] Copies of the argument were furnished to Justice Story to be distributed as he saw fit. Webster wrote to Story regarding these copies that "if you send one of them to each of such of the Judges as you think proper, you will of course do it in the manner least likely to lead to a feeling that any indecorum has been committed by the plaintiffs."[76]

Because the friends of the university had entertained Chancellor Kent, had placed in his hands documents relating to the controversy, and had secured an expression of opinion from him favorable to the cause of the state, Webster, Charles Marsh, and President Brown took prompt and effective measures to counteract the impressions Kent had formed on his visit to Hanover. Marsh, one of the trustees of the college, sent Kent a copy of Webster's argument. Under the direction of Marsh and President Brown, conferences were held in Albany, New York, with Kent and Governor Clinton and, through Kent, information favorable to the college was placed in the hands of Justices Johnson and Livingston. Doubtless as a result of these conferences, Chancellor Kent changed his opinion regarding the case and agreed to present his views to Justice Johnson who finally joined Justices Livingston and Story in supporting the views of Justices Marshall and Washington.[77] Justice Johnson, who

---

[75] See Lord, *op. cit.*, p. 152.

[76] See letter to Justice Story in *Private Correspondence*, I: 287.

[77] See Shirley, *op. cit.*, pp. 262 ff., for comments and extracts from correspondence.

Kent, who was known to be a strong and active Federalist, was reported to have based his change of view upon a decision of the Council of Revision, of which he was a member, holding that the charter of the city of New York could not be altered without the consent of the corporation. See letter of Francis Brown, President of Old College, to Daniel Webster regarding conversations of Brown with Chancellor Kent. Shirley, *op. cit.*, pp. 268–270. It is apparent from this letter that Kent had shown Brown the copy of his record of the proceedings of the Council of Revision which had considered the validity of an act of the New York legislature passed in 1804. According to this record this bill, designed to change the charter of the city of New York to increase the number of wards without any application from or consent of the officials of the city, was turned over to Kent for his recommendation to the Council. He reported objections which included the following: "It has been considered and treated as a salutary principle in our government that charters of incorporation were not to be essentially affected without due process of law, or without consent of the parties concerned. Nothing but a strong *public necessity* would justify such an interference."

Kent's objections were overruled by the other judges, but Governor Clinton criticized the measure on the same grounds as those advanced by Kent, using, however, the phrase "ordinary process of law" instead of "due process of law." Kent explained to Brown that he had made his objections to the bill "as a politician, not as a judge; and

vigorously dissented from the broad doctrines approved by the Chief Justice on the interpretation of the contract clause in *Fletcher v. Peck*, concurred in the opinion and judgment in the *Dartmouth College Case* "for the reasons stated by the Chief Justice." The conferences with Chancellor Kent and the discussions over the contract clause in *Sturges v. Crowninshield* probably had some influence in determining Johnson's final vote.[78] A representative of the college party, B. J. Gilbert, visited Richmond and attempted to see Chief Justice Marshall. "Unable finally to meet Judge Marshall," notes Lord, "he yet managed to get into his hands a copy of the charter and newspapers giving accounts of the case."[79]

Personal and political factors were no doubt of some significance in securing a favorable decision for the college, though the influence of these factors in securing the final determination may at times have been exaggerated. Without doubt it was the adroit political skill as well as the eloquence of Webster[80] which finally brought victory to the college cause. The case had assumed, under Webster's direction, a strong political tinge, so that, like *Marbury v. Madison*, it was looked upon as a "judico-political wager of battle between John Marshall and Thomas Jefferson, the two great Virginians, whose political and personal hate descended with them into the tomb."[81] Webster made good use of this personal and political hatred in his effort to secure the ardent championship of the college cause by Chief Justice Marshall.[82]

The cause of the state had been poorly presented to the Supreme Court at Washington, partly, no doubt, because a decision favorable to

---

he was not clear that the doctrine laid down was correct, as applied to corporations for the purposes of governments, etc." By 1807, however, Kent regarded it as "a sound principle of free government . . . that charters of incorporation, whether granted for private or local, or charitable, or literary or religious purposes were not to be affected without due process of law, or without the consent of the parties concerned." Shirley, *ibid.*; and Mark De Wolfe Howe, "A Footnote to the Conspiracy Theory," 48 *Yale Law Jour.* (Apr., 1939), 1007 ff. For the official record of the Council of Revision, see A. B. Street, *Council of Revision of the State of New York* (Albany, 1859).

[78] Otis thinks the published correspondence "conclusively shows that the learned Chancellor was visited by friends of the College and supplied with arguments in its favor, for the sole purpose of securing his influence upon Judges Johnson and Livingston, who were still undecided, and who, it was learned, had asked Chancellor Kent for his opinion on the subject." "The Dartmouth College Case," 27 *Amer. Law Rev.* 536. A copy of the letters of President Brown to Webster on his visit to Albany is included in the appendix, below, pp. 420–422.

[79] Lord, *op. cit.*, p. 153.

[80] Lodge, *op. cit.*, pp. 87–89, and above, p. 394.

[81] Otis, "The Dartmouth College Case," 27 *Amer. Law Rev.*, 532.

[82] Fuess regards the *Dartmouth College Case* as "a phase of the historic conflict during the formative days of the Republic between conservatives and liberals, Federalists and Democrats, John Marshall and Thomas Jefferson. It need hardly be said that Daniel Webster was on the side of established order," *Daniel Webster*, I: 216.

the state was taken for granted.[83] In fact, the friends of the university were so confident of the success of their cause that they expected a unanimous decision in their favor.[84] When the likelihood of an adverse decision appeared imminent, William Pinkney of Maryland was employed, because it was thought he could most effectively meet the arguments of Webster. Though Pinkney had thoroughly familiarized himself with the facts and issues of the case and had notified the Justices and opposing counsel that he would move for a reargument, Chief Justice Marshall, on the convening of the Court, refused to recognize him and began the reading of his opinion.[85]

CHIEF JUSTICE MARSHALL'S OPINION

In rendering the decision of the Supreme Court which reversed the unanimous and carefully reasoned opinion of the New Hampshire court in the *Dartmouth College Case,* Chief Justice Marshall took sides on a bitterly contested political and social issue of the day and emphasized the detached or mechanical approach to constitutional interpretation. In the first place, he maintained, the Court will not pronounce an act of the legislature void in a doubtful case. Adverting to the contract clause and the jurisdiction granted to the federal courts, it was declared to be the high and solemn duty of the Court to protect the legislative violation of those contracts which the Constitution has placed beyond legislative control. However irksome this task may be, observed Marshall, it is "a duty from which we dare not shrink." One of the main issues of the case, that is, whether the charter was a contract, was disposed of in a short paragraph introduced by the sentence: "it can require no argument to prove that the circumstances of this case constitute a con-

---

[83] Holmes was a Jeffersonian Democrat and was despised by Marshall. Wirt's argument was weak because he was not familiar with the facts of the case.

[84] Lord, *op. cit.,* p. 151.

[85] Justice Story apparently believed that the college case would be reargued. On December 9, 1818, he wrote: "The next term of the Supreme Court will probably be the most interesting ever known. Several great constitutional questions, the constitutionality of the insolvent laws, the taxing of the bank of the United States, and of the Dartmouth College new charter, will probably be splendidly argued. Mr. Pinkney is engaged in these and in several other very important questions sent from my circuit." *Life and Letters of Joseph Story,* ed. by William W. Story (Boston, 1851), I: 313. And Webster thought "it is most probable, perhaps, that Pinkney will succeed in his motion, although I do not think it by any means certain." Lord, *op. cit.,* p. 160.

Speaking of the efforts of the friends of the university to have another argument of the case upon the ground of new facts, Webster referred to "the echoes of the clamor in New Hampshire"—that the cause had not been heard on its true facts and observed: "In truth I did not want a second argument here, upon an assumption of facts. If I do not misjudge we shall have no difficulty in the Circuit Court." Letter to Jeremiah Smith, Feb. 28, 1819, Van Tyne, *op. cit.,* p. 80.

tract."[86] Having without argument or rational justification assumed that the charter in the case had every ingredient of a complete and legitimate contract,[87] it was only necessary to adopt the reasoning of the attorneys for the plaintiffs that the college was a private eleemosynary institution and not a public corporation to resolve the cause in its favor. Such a corporation as "an artificial being, invisible, intangible, and existing only in contemplation of law" was held to be "no more a state institution than a natural person exercising the same powers would be." Chief Justice Richardson's decision that such a corporation as that establishing Dartmouth College as an educational institution was a public corporation was summarily discarded.[88]

Admitting that Parliament could have repealed the charter after it was granted by the Crown and claiming that such an act would have been perfidious, Marshall, gradually, and by steps that are neither clear nor logical, arrived at the conclusion that when a private eleemosynary corporation is created, it is no longer subject to its creator for visitation, alteration, or control—in short, a self-perpetuating and politically and legally independent entity had come into being. Then recurring to the contract to which, according to the fictions of the law, the donors, the trustees, and the Crown were the original parties, Marshall conceded that it is likely that "the preservation of rights of this description was not particularly in the view of the framers of the Constitution, when the clause under consideration was introduced into that instrument."[89] But adopting the rule of interpretation that every effort must be made to give a meaning to the Constitution favorable to the protection of private rights, he said:

It is not enough to say, that this particular case was not in the mind of the Convention, when the article was framed, nor of the American people, when it was adopted. It is necessary to go further, and to say that, had this particular case been suggested, the language would have been so varied, as to exclude it, or it would have been made a special exception. The case being within the words of the rule, must be within its operation likewise, unless there be something in the literal construction so obviously absurd, or mischievous, or repugnant to the general spirit of the instrument, as to justify those, who expound the Constitution in making it an exception.[90]

With a different outlook or perspective from that of Chief Justice Richardson of New Hampshire relating to the development of public

---

[86] 4 Wheaton 627 (1819).

[87] "It should be noted that 'contract' was given a wider meaning in the Constitution and in general use in 1789 than it has in this treatise, or in the Restatement of Contracts, e.g., the corporate charter, as held in Dartmouth College v. Woodward, 4 Wheaton 518 (1819)." *Williston on Contracts*, rev. ed. by Samuel Williston and George J. Thompson (New York, 1936), I, sec. 1, note 2.

[88] 4 Wheaton 632–639.   [89] *Ibid.*, p. 644.   [90] *Ibid.*, pp. 644, 645.

education, Marshall thought "it is probable, that no man ever was, and that no man ever will be, the founder of a college, believing at the time, that an act of incorporation constitutes no security for the institution; believing, that it is immediately to be deemed a public institution, whose funds are to be governed, and applied, not by the will of the donor, but by the will of the legislature."[91] Before Marshall's opinion was rendered substantial beginnings had been made toward the establishment of state colleges or universities in other states as well as New Hampshire. Following the trend indicated in the acts relating to educational institutions in New England and in the middle Atlantic states, state institutions, which later became universities, were established in North Carolina in 1795, South Carolina in 1805, Michigan in 1817, Virginia in 1819, and Indiana in 1820. Though the decision in the *Dartmouth College Case* put an end to the attempts to reorganize or to control the close corporations which were formed by the charters of certain educational institutions in the South and the West, it encouraged the establishment and maintenance of colleges and universities under state control and direction.

Assuming that the funds secured for the support of Dartmouth College consisted entirely of private donations[92] and that education supported by endowment from private funds should be private and not public, Marshall concluded that the charter of Dartmouth College was plainly a contract to which the donors, the trustees, and the Crown were the original parties and that the acts of the New Hampshire legislature reorganizing the college, as founded under the charter of 1769, so far as they interfered with the rights of the trustees and donors, were void. The Chief Justice thus based his reasoning on a principle which the leading Federalist lawyers regarded as uncertain and insecure ground for invalidating the state laws.[93]

The opinion of Chief Justice Marshall in the *Dartmouth College Case*

---

[91] 4 Wheaton 647.

[92] As a matter of fact, a large part of the funds secured for Dartmouth College was in the nature of public grants.

[93] According to Lodge, "this doctrine of 'impairing the obligation of contracts,' which produced a decision in its effects more far-reaching and of more general interest than perhaps any other ever made in this country, was imported into the case at the suggestion of laymen, was little esteemed by counsel, and was comparatively neglected in every argument." *Daniel Webster*, p. 83.

Commenting on Marshall's method of arriving at a conclusion and of writing opinions without consulting his associates, Beveridge thinks Marshall prepared his opinion in Virginia and "had barely time to read it to his associates before the opening of Court." The opinion was later submitted to Justice Story who suggested a few alterations. The other Justices wrote opinions later which were published in the reports. See *Proc.* Mass. Hist. Soc., 2d ser., XIV: 324–325; and Story, *Life and Letters*, I: 323, 324.

is a good illustration of the method of the Chief Justice in construing and stating facts which give a plausible basis for the legal and political theories he wished to announce, without adhering closely to the actual evidence in the case. Marshall referred to an application which was made to the Crown for a charter to incorporate a religious and literary institution.[94] But the charter was granted by the royal governor of New Hampshire, nominally in the name of the sovereign, to place on a more secure basis Moor's Charity School for the education of Indians, funds for which had been solicited in England. He also noted that large contributions were made which were to be turned over to the corporation as soon as it was created. Most of these contributions, however, were made to Moor's Charity School, which was designed primarily to educate Indians as teachers or missionaries, without any relation to the incorporation of the school.[95] The charter for the school, which was given the name of Dartmouth College in the act of incorporation, was apparently secured without the knowledge and consent of the trustees, most of whom resided in England, to expand the educational and missionary work of the charity school, particularly for students from American families. The trustees, to whom the funds solicited in England had been committed for distribution, insisted that the funds secured in England should be used as agreed—for the Indian charity school, that regular accounts be kept of the money expended, and that the work of the charity school be not blended with the college. Contrary to this stipulation, some of the funds secured in England were used to erect buildings for the use

[94] On the assertion that the charter of the college was defective for lack of power to make such a grant, Lord says: "It is true that Governor Wentworth's commission nowhere conferred upon him the power to erect a corporation of this description. The charter never having been confirmed by the Crown may perhaps have been open to question at the beginning, but it is hard to believe that the infirmity, if any, was not cured subsequent to the Revolution, by the repeated recognition of the College as a legal body in numerous acts of the state legislature, by the acts of 1789 and 1807, which changed the constitution of the corporation as to lands given by the State, and even by the controverted acts of 1816 themselves." An original defective charter was thus made legal by action of the state which was now denied the right to change the board of control of the corporation. See Lord, op. cit., pp. 167, 168.

"It would gratify curiosity to be informed how the Chief Justice knew that 'an application was made to the Crown for a charter,' or the contents of that application. The probability is that George III died without even knowing that a charter had been granted to Dartmouth College. It is a historical fact that no formal application was made even to Governor Wentworth, who granted the charter in the name of the King. . . . This is of no particular importance except to exemplify the haste and recklessness with which great judges sometimes come to conclusions of fact as well as law." From comments of James C. Jenkins, "Should the Dartmouth College Decision be Recalled," 51 Amer. Law Rev. (Sept.–Oct., 1917), 720.

[95] See Frederick Chase, A History of Dartmouth College and the Town of Hanover, ed. by John K. Lord (Cambridge, 1891), pp. 8 ff.

of the college and to meet other expenses not attributable to the charity school.[96] The funds of the college, Marshall asserted, consisted entirely of private donations. The first endowment of the college, however, came in the nature of a grant of public lands made by Governor Wentworth at the time the charter was granted. Other donations were made by the states of Connecticut, Massachusetts, New Hampshire, and Vermont.[97] In fact, Webster in his argument referred to a grant of land to the college by the state of Vermont which he maintained could not have been intended as a grant to the state of New Hampshire.[98]

The Constitution did not deal with the moral obligations of state governments. And what relation did the disappointment of the donors, or the perfidy, or the ethics of the transaction have to do with the legality of it? As a matter of policy, it should have been a matter for the legislature to decide. Marshall really conceded the whole argument for the opponents of the college when he admitted that the power of Parliament to repeal the charter was unquestioned and that the nature of the situation was in reason, in justice, and in law what it was in 1769.[99] These two admissions leave relatively little basis for the existence of a contract or for any obligation arising thereunder. If the King originally was not under any obligation, and if the nature of the transaction was not changed by the Revolution or by the adoption of the federal Constitution, then how could an obligation arise where there was none before?

It is not difficult to demonstrate the converse of the main proposition by which Chief Justice Marshall brings the case within the meaning of the words of the Constitution. This particular case, the Chief Justice admitted, is not within the meaning of the constitutional prohibition by the normal and usual interpretation of the language used. If by a fair and reasonable construction of the provision of the Constitution this case is excluded, it devolved upon the attorneys for the college and the Justices to show why an exception would be made. But this plain and obvious duty was declined, and the burden of proving an exclusion of the case was by a trick of legal logic turned back upon the university and its adherents.

It is a remarkable fact, noted James C. Jenkins, that Chief Justice Marshall, in deciding that the charter to Dartmouth College was a contract, resorted neither to rational discussion nor the citation of authority

---

[96] Chase, *op. cit.*, pp. 150, 243 ff.

[97] Chase, *op. cit.*, pp. 23, 29, 37, 277, 575. See especially the grant of 23,000 acres of land by the legislature of Vermont, one-half to be devoted to the charity school and one-half to the college; also the Landoff grant of more than 25,000 acres, made in 1764 and granted anew in 1770. *Ibid.*, pp. 588 ff.

[98] 4 Wheaton 574.   [99] *Ibid.*, p. 643.

except to make two references to Blackstone which cover universally conceded points.[100] According to Mr. Jenkins, the complete and legitimate ingredients of a contract were not present in the granting of a charter to Dartmouth College. These ingredients are: (1) parties—competent, intending, and willing; (2) a sufficient consideration; (3) an actual agreement in the form prescribed by law engendering mutual legal relations and obligations; (4) a legal subject matter. But by common law the King could not enter into a contract. And the charters granted in the name of the King were subject to revocation, hence, if there was a contract one of the parties to the agreement was not bound. There were, indeed, some important ingredients of a contract absent in the transactions leading to the grant of a charter to the college.[101]

When Marshall applied the contract clause to executed as well as executory contracts, he refused to follow the ordinary understanding and significance of contractual obligations. In prohibiting the impairment of the obligation of contracts, the makers of the Constitution, it is believed, intended the inhibition to apply to executory contracts only. If the obligation of contract is, as Marshall stated, its legal bond or binding force, the obligation could only look to the future and could not apply to a past act. Hence, "in an executed contract, there is no outstanding contractual obligation; and, therefore, no obligation of contract to be impaired."[102] How could a charter which was in the nature of a license subject to revocation at any time become a binding and irrevocable contract?

According to the established principles of the common law no obligation inheres in a contract which is executed. Rights may have become

---

[100] Jenkins, *op. cit.*, p. 718. Joseph P. Cotton thinks that "there can be little question that, by the influence of counsel, by some subtle influence of politics or friendships, there seems to have crept into the consideration of the *Dartmouth College Case,* a distinct bias in favor of the College. It is not easy to support such an assertion; but it is the inference from Marshall's opinion. It is characteristic of Marshall's opinions to be argumentative, combative, to state logically, cogently, but one rises from this opinion dissatisfied. There is bias in the statement of facts, a bias in the statement of premises; and surely, what seems now to us the main issue of the case, the assumption that the charter of the college was a 'contract,' as that term is used in the Constitution, is too hasty and too barely supported." *The Constitutional Decisions of John Marshall* (New York, 1905), I: 347.

[101] Jenkins, *op. cit.*, pp. 719 ff.

[102] *Ibid.*, pp. 736, 737. See also William Trickett, "The Dartmouth College Paralogism," 40 *Amer. Law Rev.* (Mar.–Apr., 1906), 183. For the claim that the contract arising from the grant of a charter to a corporation is not an executed but a continuous contract, see R. N. Denham, Jr., "An Historical Development of the Contract Theory in the Dartmouth College Case," 7 *Mich. Law Rev.* (Jan., 1909), 219. Of the failure to recognize or appreciate the difference between an executory and executed contract, Denham says Marshall did not hesitate over such "a trifling difficulty of interpretation."

vested through such a contract, but those rights are no more sacred than rights which have become vested in any other manner. The federal Constitution did not provide that no state shall pass any law impairing vested rights; it merely inhibited the passage of laws impairing the obligation of contracts. Only executory contracts can be said to have an obligation inhering in them, that is, contracts in which one of the parties, by virtue of the agreement, is under the obligation to do something which is still undone. The purpose of the constitutional provision was to prevent states from releasing contracting parties from such obligations. Summarizing the views prevailing at the time, Shirley thinks that an interpretation which would have restricted the contract provision to executory contracts would have been more natural and reasonable than the construction adopted by Chief Justice Marshall.[103] But there are sustainable grounds for the view that Marshall, like others who were associated with him during the early decades of the nineteenth century, looked upon the "obligation of contract" as something dictated by reason or nature which transcends the lawmaking power of the state. And, as Nathan Isaacs observes, Marshall, like most thinkers of the eighteenth and early nineteenth centuries, "is quite willing to make not only his law but also his history *a priori*, out of that which the human mind figures out must have happened."[104]

Another feature of Marshall's reasoning was the division of corporations into two classes—public and private. But this division, it is claimed, was unknown to English law wherein all chartered rights were political privileges over the exercise of which Parliament had plenary power. The charter to Dartmouth College was granted on this implied condition.[105]

Neither the arguments of the attorneys nor the opinions of the Justices give a satisfactory definition of a contract, nor do they indicate clearly what was meant by the phrase "obligation of contracts." The term "obligation of contracts" did not arise from English law. A similar expression was in use in the Roman law and is to be found in the Spanish civil code. The word "obligation" is defined in the Code of Justinian as a chain which binds a person to the performance of something in accordance with the law of the land.[106]

---

[103] *Dartmouth College Causes*, p. 227.

[104] "John Marshall on Contracts: A Study in Early American Juristic Theory," 7 *Virginia Law Rev.* (Mar., 1921), 423.

[105] C. H. Hill, "The Dartmouth College Case," 8 *Amer. Law Rev.* (Jan., 1874), 216.

[106] R. N. Denham, Jr., tracing the law relative to corporations in the Roman law, concludes that "the corporate franchise was a valuable right, regarded as property vested absolutely in the incorporators, who could only be deprived of it if they abused or misused their privilege." The practice with regard to the protection of corporations, it is noted, was somewhat uncertain and did not seem to fit into any of the accepted theories

Though the Chief Justice ostensibly refused to accept the reasoning of Mason at Exeter, which was elaborated upon by Webster in Washington, that, regardless of the state and federal constitutions, the legislative acts were void because they were judicial, and not legislative in nature, in effect he adopted this proposition. The so-called "mathematical demonstration" and the "pure reasoning" of Marshall in the case consisted primarily in stating the facts to accord with the judgment which he desired to render and in steering away from the crucial questions at issue.

Marshall was accustomed to insist that he was following rules of construction which offered no opportunity for choice and that the words of the Constitution compelled the rendering of the one and only decision which he was announcing.[107] But to the leading exponents of Federalism in his day as well as to many historians of later years, the Chief Justice was giving life and vigor to the Constitution by injecting new meaning into the general phrases of the inert document.[108] While professing to follow only the will of the law and to be guided by the compulsions of the language of the Constitution, Marshall, as politician and diplomat, Beveridge observes, "rewrote the fundamental law of the Nation; or, perhaps, it may be more accurate to say that he made the instrument a living thing, capable of growth, capable of keeping pace with the advancement of the American people and ministering to their changing necessities."[109]

---

for the protection of legal rights, but Denham thinks, "it is natural justice that such things should be so" and, hence, from Roman theories of natural law there arose, he believes, the doctrine of corporate independence and irresponsibility. "An Historical Development of the Contract Theory in the Dartmouth College Case," 7 *Mich. Law Rev.* (Jan., 1909), 205.

[107] "Those rules of construction, which have been consecrated by the wisdom of ages, compel us to say that these words prohibit the passage of any law discharging a contract without performance." Sturges v. Crowninshield, 4 Wheaton 206 (1819).

[108] William Wirt, an admirer of Marshall, described his method as follows: "In a bad cause his art consisted in laying premises so remotely from the point directly in debate, or else in terms so general and so spacious, that the hearer, seeing no consequence which could be drawn from them, was just as willing to admit them as not; but his premises once admitted, the demonstration, however distant, followed as certainly, as cogently, as inevitably, as any demonstration in Euclid." Beveridge, *op. cit.*, II: 196.

[109] *Ibid.*, IV: 308. According to Beveridge, "Marshall's economic and political views formed as a young man, had been strengthened by every event that had since occurred until, in his sixty-fifth year, those early ideas had become convictions so deep as to pervade his very being. The sacredness of contract, the stability of institutions, and, above all, nationalism in government, were to John Marshall, articles of a creed as holy as any that ever inspired a religious enthusiast." *Ibid.*, p. 221.

From a less sympathetic point of view James Truslow Adams observes that "gradually Marshall's inordinate love of money, and reverence both for it and those who possessed it, changed the frontier boy into the leader of the Federalist Party in Virginia,

In a summary of the obvious objections to the opinion of the Chief Justice the following may be noted: He assumed that there was a contract between the Crown and the donors and trustees, when in fact no such contract was made; if at any time a contractual relationship had been established, it was an executed contract and, according to well established legal usage, there could be no obligation involved in such a contract. He also assumed that Dartmouth College was a private eleemosynary institution, whereas the major part of the funds secured for the college, separate from those which were diverted from their intended purpose to assist the Indian charity school, were donated by the states or were subscribed under state assistance and patronage. The college was, therefore, more in the nature of a public than a private institution. Finally, another one of Marshall's assumptions and one on which the entire case for the college was predicated was that the old corporation was destroyed and its property was dispersed. No such action had been taken. The corporate entity remained, and the property rights of the corporation were not in any way interfered with, but the former trustees—a self-perpetuating board—became members of an enlarged board over which the overseers were to exercise a supervisory authority. The college was to operate for the future under these changed boards of control with periodic reports to the legislature. All of these assumptions are essential to the Court's opinion and all could be refuted by facts familiar to those who were acquainted with the history of the college. Webster, no doubt, had good grounds for opposing a reargument with the presentation to the Court of a new statement of facts.

In accordance with his political views, Marshall thought it was necessary to give steadiness to American business and vitality to the national government. It was, therefore, the function and duty of the Supreme Court to aid in preserving the union according to Federalist ideals and notions.[110] Speaking of the advantage of Marshall's decision to corporations now being rapidly formed for the economic development of the country, Beveridge maintains "it reassured investors in corporate securities and gave confidence and steadiness to the business world. It is undeniable and undenied that America could not have been developed so

---

a complete reactionary, and a close colleague of the most reactionary Federalists of all, the members of the Essex Junto in Massachusetts. There was never the slightest blemish on his financial honor, but in studying his mind we must, as even Beveridge allows, take the above facts into consideration. There was not a spark of liberalism in John Marshall." *The Living Jefferson* (New York, 1936), p. 299.

It is contended, however, that "one never finds in Marshall's decision any theory of government, or natural rights, or of sovereignty." Francis Newton Thorpe, "Hamilton's Ideas in Marshall's Decision," 1 *Boston Univ. Law Rev.* (1921), 10.

[110] Beveridge, *op. cit.*, pp. 169 ff., 208.

rapidly and solidly without the power which the law as announced by Marshall gave to industrial organization." And more important, however, as Beveridge thinks, "it aligned on the side of nationalism all powerful economic forces operating through corporate organization."[111] Expressed in the language of the Federalists of Jefferson's time and since, Marshall's decisions stand for "order, power and progress," whereas the Republican notions lead to "strife, decay and chaos."[112] But these views were to be challenged by Republican leaders in a campaign which made the Supreme Court the center of attack and which embittered the closing years of the life of the Chief Justice. Justice Story, however, asserted views which were subject to even stronger condemnation than those of Marshall.

JUSTICE STORY'S CHANGE OF OPINION

Justice Story, who had now shifted his position in relation to the rival educational institutions, indicated that he favored placing upon legislatures the broadest limits possible, both express and implied. He thought that contracts concerning the salaries of public officers for fixed terms could not be changed by the legislatures—a doctrine in which few Judges and other public men concurred. And even such public corporations as counties, towns, and cities must be, he insisted, free from public control so far as their private property is concerned. Such rights, Story maintained, could be changed only through "judicial enquiry, construction and abrogation."[113] Nor did he agree with Chief Justice Marshall that marriage contracts were not within the reach of the prohibitory clause of the Constitution. It was admitted that executory contracts could not be enforced unless there was a valuable consideration to sustain them. The consideration for which they stipulated, according to Marshall, "was the perpetual application of the fund to its object."

To Justice Story the consideration was the valuable rights relinquished by Dr. Wheelock and the laborious office which he undertook in accordance with the grant of incorporation. The most significant part of his opinion, however, related to the independent and impregnable position accorded to corporations such as Dartmouth College. When a donation was made to such a corporation, Justice Story maintained that there was an implied contract that the Crown would not revoke or alter the charter

---

[111] *The Life of John Marshall*, IV: 276. Claiming that Marshall's decision was necessary at the time to save the country, Beveridge regards it highly probable that if the question were to arise today free from the complications and alterations of more than a century the Supreme Court would not give such a broad protection to corporate franchises.

[112] Cf. F. N. Thorpe, "Hamilton's Ideas in Marshall's Decisions," 1 *Boston Univ. Law Rev.* (1921), 60, 61.

[113] 4 Wheaton 695.

or change its administration without the consent of the corporation.[114] To support this contention Justice Story found it advantageous to fall back on the higher law doctrine. "It is a principle of the common law," said he, "which has been recognized as well in this as in other countries, that the division of an empire works no forfeiture of previously vested rights of property. And this maxim is equally consonant with the common sense of mankind and the maxims of eternal justice."[115] Speaking of the delicate, difficult, and ungracious task which devolved upon the Court and of the necessity that under such circumstances the Justices must be guided only by authority and principle, Story concluded: "It is not for judges to listen to the voice of persuasive eloquence or popular appeal. We have nothing to do but to pronounce the law as we find it; and having done this, our justification must be left to the impartial judgment of our country."[116]

It is well known that Story's first opinion was favorable to the changes made in the college charter. Referring to the report that Justice Story was one of the framers of the law establishing Dartmouth University, Lord says "it was now ascertained that, even if he did not draft the act, he had, at all events, advised about it and with his usual industry and discretion examined it at an early stage and vouched its legality, and the University people felt secure."[117] His views had been communicated to Ichabod Bartlett, one of the counsel for the state, and through him to the friends of President Wheelock. After the legislature had passed the act reorganizing the college, Governor Plumer appointed Story, his friend and neighbor, to the position of overseer of the university, though there is no indication that he accepted the appointment. While he did not participate actively in the controversy, the friends of the university had good reasons to be "dumbfounded, thunderstruck, when they found Story had gone against them."[118]

---

[114] 4 Wheaton 689.

[115] *Ibid.*, p. 706.

[116] *Ibid.*, p. 713.

[117] Lord, *op. cit.*, pp. 142, 143.

[118] Webster to Mason, Oct. 6, 1819. The original views and conduct of Justice Story in relation to the college controversy having been brought to the attention of Joseph Hopkinson, he wrote:

"The situation in which, if you are not misinformed, Judge Story has placed himself is much more alarming to us—and so disreputable to him should he sit in the case—that I confess I am inclined to believe that your information in this respect, must be mistaken, should it however be otherwise and he is about to sit as judge in a cause in which he has been a feed counsellor, I should have no hesitation in resorting to any legal and proper means to prevent such an abuse of power and office. The influence of the judge with the court in general cases, is I think, considerable; and will probably be very great in one like the present. If, therefore, the judge has committed himself

With Story, observes Lodge, who was "a Democrat by circumstances and a Federalist by nature," there was little difficulty in securing a reversal of opinion relating to the college controversy. Indications of a change in views favorable to Federalist doctrines were apparent early in Story's public career. "Though I was a decided member of what was called the Republican party, and of course a supporter of the administration of Mr. Jefferson and Mr. Madison," said Justice Story, "you are not to imagine that I was a mere slave to the opinions of either or that I did not exercise an independent judgment upon public affairs. . . . I was at all times a firm believer in the doctrines of General Washington, an admirer of his conduct, measures and principles during his whole administration."[119] Noting the difference between a Virginia and Massachusetts Republican, Story wrote of his disapproval of the antifederal doctrines of the former state, for, said he, "I was and always have been a lover, devoted lover of the Constitution of the United States, and a friend to the union of the States. I never wished to bring the government to a mere confederacy of States; but to preserve the power of the general government given by all the States, in full exercise and sovereignty for the protection and preservation of all of the States."[120]

Jefferson regarded Story as a "pseudo-Republican" because of his opposition to the Embargo Acts. And the change in his political point of view and outlook was commented upon by the Massachusetts Federalists. "Though he is a man whom the Democrats support," wrote George Cabot, "I have seldom if ever met with one of sounder mind on the principal points of national policy. He is well worthy the civil attention of the most respectable Federalists."[121] A similar sentiment was expressed by Harrison Gray Otis who spoke of Story as a young man of talents "who commenced Democrat a few years since and was much fondled by his party. He discovered however too much sentiment and honor to go *all lengths,* and acted on several occasions with a very salutary spirit of independence, and in fact did so much *good* that his party have de-

---

in the way you mention, it will never do to hazard so important a case on a question of delicacy to him." Joseph Hopkinson to Marsh, Dec. 31, 1817, Shirley, *op. cit.,* pp. 274–275.

With regard to this letter, Lord states that "it is evident that means were found to convey to Judge Story in a friendly way (apparently through Mr. Mason whom the Judge held in high esteem) the sentiments of Mr. Hopkinson's letter, and to obtain assurances of impartiality." And though doubts and fears regarding Story's views harassed the college group to the last, Lord thinks he "faithfully preserved a judicial temper." Lord, *op. cit.,* p. 143. Judicial temper in this instance apparently meant an attitude which was favorable to the college.

[119] *Life and Letters,* I: 128.
[120] *Life and Letters,* I: 128.
[121] Henry Cabot Lodge, *Life and Letters of George Cabot* (Boston, 1877), p. 377.

nounced him, and a little attention from the right sort of people will be very useful to him and to us."[122]

It was apparent that by the time of the preparation of his opinion in the *Dartmouth College Case,* Justice Story had adopted the broad interpretation of the contract clause favored by Daniel Webster. To both of them the prime object of this clause was not only to protect private rights but also to accomplish certain definite political objectives. Webster stated the position in his argument in *Ogden v. Saunders* with which Story agreed. In answering the inquiry whether the legislature of New York could pass a law such as that involved in the controversy, he said:

> The question is general. We differ from our learned adversaries, on general principles. We differ as to the main scope and end of this constitutional provision. They think it entirely remedial: we regard it as preventive. They think it adopted to procure redress for violated private rights; to us it seems intended to guard against great public mischiefs. They argue it, as if it were designed as an indemnity or protection for injured private rights in individual cases of *meum* and *tuum:* we look upon it as a great political provision, favorable to the commerce and credit of the whole country. Certainly, we do not deny its application to cases of violated private right. Such cases are clearly and unquestionably within its operation. Still, we think its main scope to be general and political.

And he concluded that upon any other construction of the Constitution one great political object of the Constitution would fail of its accomplishment.[123] Story not only turned away from the doctrines, which, after careful deliberation, he had accepted in the college controversy, but he also became a stronger and more persistent advocate than the Chief Justice for the protection of chartered privileges and vested rights.[124]

Webster's energy and ingenuity in developing a favorable view in the public mind toward the college was evident not only in his arguments as an attorney in the case but also in his efforts to secure the publication of the college's side of the controversy. Notes of the argument in the state court at Exeter were taken by Webster, and he conceived the plan of publishing the record of the case in the state and federal courts. Timothy Farrar, Jr., son of one of the college trustees, was selected as the editor of

---

[122] Morison, *The Life and Letters of Harrison Gray Otis,* I: 263.

[123] Ogden v. Saunders, 12 Wheaton 247, 248 (1827), and Shirley, *op. cit.,* p. 345. Story's son, referring to the decision in *Martin v. Hunter's Lessee,* said of his father: "Upon taking his seat on the bench, my father devoted himself to this branch of the law [constitutional law], and the result was a cordial adherence to the views of Marshall, whom he considered, then and ever afterwards, as the expounder of the true principles of the Constitution." *Life and Letters,* I: 277.

[124] In a letter to Jeremiah Mason, Oct. 6, 1819, Story wrote: "I am exceedingly pleased with your argument in the Dartmouth College case. I always had a desire that the question should be put upon the broad basis you have stated; and it was a matter of regret that we were so stinted in jurisdiction in the Supreme Court, that half the argument could not be met and enforced." *Life and Letters,* I: 323.

the work, and the volume was issued in his name. Webster, however, not only planned the publication but did a large share of the editorial work.[125]

Issued for definite propaganda purposes, the volume by Webster and Farrar does not give an unbiased report of the arguments for the college and for the state. Care was taken to present as complete a report as possible of the arguments for the college, and for this purpose Webster wrote Hopkinson's argument from notes furnished to him.[126] Farrar's report, on the contrary, devotes only four and one-half pages to the argument of Holmes, attorney for the state before the Supreme Court. This is evidence, Beveridge thinks, of the contempt of the legal profession for Holmes. It is more likely that it represented the contempt of Webster and of the college partisans for a Republican lawyer and politician who was defending the cause of the popular party.[127]

By an arrangement among Webster, Chief Justice Marshall, Justices Washington and Story, and Supreme Court Reporter Wheaton,[128] it was agreed that the opinions of the Justices would be published first in Farrar's Report. Justice Story favored the publication of Farrar's volume because he thought it would be a useful work[129] and he agreed to correct the proof sheets. Webster was very much concerned at the delay in printing the book and at the likelihood of inaccurate printing of the opinions of the Justices, for, said he, "I made myself answerable for that both to the Chief Justice and Judge Washington."[130] Webster and his associates who participated in arguing the case, as well as others who aided the college cause, were cognizant of the fact that fundamental political and legal issues were at stake and that a favorable judgment would have far-reaching effects, not only so far as educational developments were concerned, but also with respect to the development of future legal principles and doctrines. But no one could have realized the extent to which the decision in this cause would affect the growth of American law.

---

[125] It is interesting to note that the copy of Webster's argument as printed in Farrar's work and in Wheaton's Reports was prepared with the arguments of opposing counsel in hand.

[126] Lord, *op. cit.*, p. 168.

[127] In a letter to Jeremiah Mason, Webster referred to the Farrar Report as follows: "My own interest would be promoted by *preventing* the Book. I shall strut well enough in the Washington Report, and if the "Book" should not be published the world would not know where I borrowed my plumes— But I am still inclined to have the Book— One reason is, that you and Judge Smith may have the credit which belongs to you— Another is, I believe, Judge Story is strongly of opinion it would be a useful work, that Wheaton's Reports go only into the hands of Professional men, but this Book might be read by other classes." Van Tyne, *op. cit.*, pp. 80, 81.

[128] Wheaton was paid $100 by Webster for the loss of sales due to the separate publication of the opinions in the *Dartmouth College Case.*

[129] Letter of Webster to Mason, Apr. 10, 1819, Shirley, *op. cit.*, p. 211.

[130] *Ibid.*, p. 298.

The Effect of the Court's Decision

Webster's peroration which was widely disseminated gave the impression that the Supreme Court's decision in the college case was a victory for the forces of liberalism and educational freedom. The result, however, was a victory for the forces of political and religious bigotry and intolerance.[131] It was generally believed by the people of New Hampshire that Governor Plumer had tried to change a sectarian seminary into a liberal and broad-gauged university.[132] The decision was so unpopular that New Hampshire became a Democratic stronghold and Webster was regarded as an enemy of the state.

Federalists, on the other hand, and those favoring the extension of national powers and the restriction of state action enthusiastically lauded Marshall's decision. Chancellor Kent thought the decision "did more than any other single act, proceeding from the authority of the United States, to throw an impregnable barrier around all rights and franchises derived from the grant of government; and to give solidity and inviolability to the literary, charitable, religious and commercial institutions of our country."[133] Unless I am very much mistaken, wrote Justice Story, the principles on which that decision rested "will be found to apply with an extensive reach to all the great concerns of the people, and will check any undue encroachments upon civil rights, which the passions or the popular doctrines of the day may stimulate our state legislatures to adopt.[134] Sir Henry Maine commended the decision as "the bulwark of American individualism against democratic impatience and Socialistic phantasy."[135] And it has been frequently asserted that no action was taken by the federal government which had a greater effect in extending federal powers and limiting the authority of the states.[136]

A few men foresaw the far-reaching effect of the sweeping language of the decision. Arguing the cause of the state, Bartlett, in prophetic language observed that "there is no other alternative, the government must control these institutions or they shall control the government!"[137] And Niles saw in the condemnation of the New Hampshire acts a deadly blow

---

[131] Horace H. Hagan, "Dartmouth College Case," 19 *Georgetown Law Jour.*, 421.

[132] "Whether good or bad policy for the country at large," says Frank B. Sanborn, Marshall's decision "seems to have delayed for half a century that cordial interest of the state in the affairs of its sole College, which it was the intention of Plumer and his friends to promote." *New Hampshire: An Epitome of Popular Government* (Boston, 1904), p. 252.

[133] James Kent, *Commentaries on American Law* (5th ed., New York, 1844), I: 418.

[134] Letter to Chancellor Kent, Aug. 21, 1819, *Life and Letters*, I: 331.

[135] *Popular Government* (New York, 1886), p. 248.

[136] See John Fiske, *Essays, Historical and Literary* (New York, 1902), I: 379.

[137] Farrar, *op. cit.*, p. 186.

at the sovereignty of the states "from a quarter so far removed from the people as to be hardly accessible to public opinion."[138] Joseph Hopkinson rejoiced, not only because the decision was in favor of the college, but also because it was placed "upon principles broad and deep, and which secure corporations of this description from legislative despotism and party violence for the future."[139] In the opinion of Joseph P. Cotton, "The *Dartmouth College Case* is one of the greatest of Marshall's cases, great in its daring, great in its results. The bare legal proposition for which it stands, that a corporate franchise is a contract, and so inviolate, and beyond the control of the State, has woven itself into the tissue of our law as has, perhaps, no other paper-made doctrine of constitutional law."[140]

It was soon discovered that Marshall's decision gave encouragement to self-seeking organizations and private interests to secure charters through fraudulent and corrupt means and to defy any control through public agencies. Some of the baneful effects upon the regulative authority of the states were removed by laws and constitutional provisions reserving to the legislature the right to alter or repeal charters granted to corporations and the development by legislative and judicial construction of the doctrine of the police power whereby the state, despite contractual grants of power to corporations, may enact the necessary regulations for the protection of the public peace, health, morals, and general welfare.

Except for the limitations placed on the doctrines of the *Dartmouth College Case* by subsequent decisions of the Supreme Court, such as the *Charles River Bridge Case*[141] and those relating to the police power, Chief Justice Marshall and Justice Story's interpretation of the contract clause would have been an insuperable obstacle to the development of any reasonable and effective methods of the regulation of commercial and industrial undertakings by the states. But these modifications of the principles announced at this time and other limitations which were gradually evolved by judicial interpretation affected only to a minor degree the doctrine of political *laissez faire* with respect to corporate organizations which was now laid down as a fundamental tenet of federal constitutional law.

Opinions at the time and since have differed whether Marshall's opinion was correct and defensible from a legal point of view and whether it

---

[138] *Niles' Register*, XVI: 41–44.
[139] Webster, *Private Correspondence*, I: 301.
[140] *The Constitutional Decisions of John Marshall*, I: 347.
[141] 11 Peters 420 (1837).

was justifiable as a matter of sound and rational governmental policy.[142] But regardless of the diverse views of the correctness of the opinion, there can be little doubt of the great significance of the case in the development of American legal thought. It carried one step farther the progressive exposition of the Federalist doctrines of nationalism and the use of the provisions of written constitutions to preserve and protect vested rights.[143] The legal basis was thus laid for the extension of the protection to private property against the authority of the government—a principle which became the cornerstone of the American doctrine of constitutional government. The two leading events which weakened the government and correspondingly expanded the rights and immunities of property holders were the *Dartmouth College Case* and the adoption of the "due process clause" of the Fourteenth Amendment in 1868.[144] But it is doubtful whether due process of law would have had such a potent effect in limiting governmental powers if the groundwork for the development of a doctrine of political *laissez faire* had not been so ably prepared by Chief Justice Marshall.

The opinions of the Justices in the case should, no doubt, be judged by the conditions and standards at the time the case was decided, and these standards condoned a rather free and unconcealed mixture of law and politics. But approval of the political nature and implications of the decision does not justify the mistakes of fact and the legal misconceptions involved in the Court's reasoning. To allow these mistakes and misconceptions "to reach down through the decades and make law for us in regard to some of our most vital interests," Jesse F. Orton thinks, "is hard to explain on the theory that we are an intelligent, self-governing people."[145]

Another significant step had been taken to incorporate, by means of judicial interpretation, the doctrines of Federalism into our constitutional law. The principle of federal supremacy over the state courts, as announced in *Martin v. Hunter's Lessee*,[146] and the denial of the right of a state to tax an instrumentality of the federal government, for the establishment of which there was no express warrant in the Constitution

---

[142] The decision, said Lodge, "brought within the scope of the Constitution of the United States every charter granted by a State, limited the action of the States in a most important attribute of sovereignty, and extended the jurisdiction of the highest court more than any other judgment ever rendered by them." *Daniel Webster,* p. 96.

[143] Few lawyers and judges have openly and avowedly defended Marshall's reasoning and decision in the *Dartmouth College Case.*

[144] See Arthur Twining Hadley, "The Constitutional Position of Property in America," *The Independent* (Apr. 16, 1908), Vol. 64, pp. 834–838.

[145] "Confusion of Property with Privilege; the Dartmouth College Case," 15 *Virginia Law Rev.* (Oct., 1909), 427.

[146] 1 Wheaton 394 (1816).

in *McCulloch v. Maryland*,[147] were now supplemented by a rule which laid a heavy hand upon the exercise of state powers. The complexities of social and industrial life brought about a great increase in the number and types of corporations established by the state legislatures or by agencies authorized to grant charters, and in accordance with the wishes of the Federalists, old and new, a large part of the control over social and economic affairs had been taken from the people and their elected representatives. The well-known device of reserving the right of cancellation of charters and the control over corporations by constitutional provisions and by charter restrictions, as well as the decisions favorable to the public rather than private interests, only modified to a slight degree the perdurance of ideas of independence, irresponsibility, and inviolability of corporate organizations. But the Democratic-Republicans who still favored popular control and direction of all of the affairs of the people were to engage in a titanic struggle which, by one of the strange turns in the course of human affairs, was to be waged over slavery, with state sovereignty and the ultimate principle of democratic control as side issues. When the war over slavery and state sovereignty was ended, however, the victory of those who sought to entrench special privileges beyond the range of harmful or destructive public regulation was secured with only occasional delays and discouragements.

---

[147] 4 Wheaton 316 (1819).

APPENDIX

LETTERS *of Daniel Webster relating to the bringing of new actions to raise the general issue of legislative powers with respect to the interference with vested rights:*

To Judge Smith, on December 8, 1817, Webster wrote: It is our misfortune that our cause goes to Washington on a single point. I wish we had it in such shape as to raise all the other objections, as well as the repugnancy of these acts to the Constitution of the United States. I have been thinking whether it would not be advisable to bring a suit, if we can get such parties as will give jurisdiction, in the Circuit Court of New Hampshire. I have thought of this the more, from hearing of sundry sayings of a great personage. Suppose the corporation of Dartmouth College should lease to some man of Vermont (e.g., C. Marsh) one of their New Hampshire farms, and that the lessee should bring ejectment for it. Or suppose the trustees of Dartmouth College should bring ejectment in the Circuit Court for some of the Wheelock lands. In either of these modes the whole question might get before the Court at Washington.[148]

In a letter of the same date to Jeremiah Mason, he said: I am sorry our College case goes to Washington on *one* point only. What do you think of an action in some court of the United States that shall raise all the objections to the act in question? Such a suit could easily be brought, that is jurisdiction could easily be given to the court of the United States by bringing in a Vermont party.[149]

You are aware that in the College cause, the only question that can be argued at Washington, is whether the recent acts of the legislature of New Hampshire do not violate the Constitution of the United States. This point, though we trust a strong one, is not perhaps stronger than that derived from the character of these acts, compared with the constitution of New Hampshire. It has occurred to me whether it would not be well to bring an action, which should present both and all our points to the Supreme Court. This could be done by bringing the action originally in the Circuit Court.[150]

After the completion of his argument in Washington, Webster wrote to President Brown: I am glad a suit is to be brought—I am very much inclined to think the Court *will not* give a judgment this term. It is therefore most essential to have an action in which all the questions arise. Pray, therefore take care, that a *proper* action *be properly* commenced, and in the earliest season—in the Circuit Court of New Hampshire.[151]

Letters relating to the efforts to secure a favorable opinion from Chancellor Kent and through him to influence the opinions of Justices Livingston and Johnson:

I have seen Chancellor Kent, and am to dine with him today. The Chancellor was in our quarter about the last of July—saw Judge Richardson's opinion—was pleased with it—and spoke in approbation of it before the great men of Windsor. The story of

---

[148] *Private Correspondence,* I: 267–268.

[149] C. H. Van Tyne, *The Letters of Daniel Webster* (New York, 1902), p. 75.

[150] Daniel Webster to Charles Marsh and Francis Brown, Dec. 8, 1817, Shirley, *Dartmouth College Causes,* p. 5.

[151] Van Tyne, *op. cit.,* p. 76.

course went through the country, that Chancellor Kent had, after examination of the case, given a decided opinion in favor of the University. Mr. Marsh sent him your argument.

As soon as I saw him, he began to express his regret at what he had said at Windsor—he really had not examined the subject at all—gave a hasty perusal of Judge Richardson's pamphlet—was disappointed to find in it so much legal talent—and, although he was careful to state that his opinion was not to be relied on, yet, *if the premises assumed* by the court were correct, he did not see but the conclusion would follow. This is substantially the account he gives of his remarks at Windsor. He told me he had replied to Mr. Marsh's letter accompanying the argument, and had said to him that this argument gave a very different complexion to the case.

I think it may be of some importance to the right decision of the case, that the Chancellor should not only have a correct opinion, but should be induced to declare it. Judge Johnson has been here. This the Chancellor mentioned, and he also said that the judge conversed on our case, and remarked that the court had a cause of 'awful' magnitude to decide. From what I learned from other sources the judge has formally requested the Chancellor's opinion. This opinion, if given, will also have great influence on Judge Livingston. Now I think the Chancellor on examination of the case, cannot fail to be right. He had, he said, great pleasure in reading your argument, and spoke in terms sufficiently flattering of the legal ability and logical power displayed in it, and added he should probably, if he had time to examine all the facts, agree fully with you. But still there was some reserve, which perhaps arose altogether from an apprehension that I should imprudently report what he might say,—but possibly it may be otherwise.

I have thought it best to communicate these facts to you, that you may consider whether anything is to be done. Does Judge Parker know the Chancellor, and would he be inclined to write him on the subject?

Evening.—I have been with the Chancellor. He has read the charter, and it is evident to me that he is satisfied. I asked him if the corporation of D. C. did not appear to be a private eleemosynary corporation. He smiled and said he believed he must express no more opinions till the cause should be decided.

I have also been presented to Governor Clinton today, who kindly inquired respecting our cause, and expressed a desire to see our charter and the argument. These, of course, I did not hesitate to furnish him. I shall have opportunity of calling on him again before I leave Albany, and hope he will incline to favour us rather than our competitors.

The following statement, which I have had from the best authority, will show the leaning of three great men in New York: In 1803, the legislature of this State attempted to change the charter of New York City without consent of the corporation. The present Governor and Chancellor and Judge Livingston were of the Council of Revision (if that be the name), that year—the Chancellor objected to the bill, and assigned his reasons, which embrace some of the main points of your argument. The objection was overruled. The next year a still further attempt was made by the legislature, a similar objection was made, and it prevailed. Both Governor Clinton and Judge Livingston sided with the Chancellor.

Judge Johnson expressed to Chancellor Kent a strong desire to have a copy of the printed argument. I wish you would forward one to him. I have none to spare.[152]

---

[152] Brown to Webster, Sept. 8, 1818. This letter was sent by Webster to Judge Farrar. Farrar preserved it and it is now in the archives of the New Hampshire Historical Society.

I am so far on my way from Albany. After I wrote you I had repeated opportunities with the Chancellor. There is no doubt that, by the argument and the charter, he is brought completely over to our side; and he has a full impression of the importance of the question. I believe he will take every proper and prudent measure to import correct views to others. While I remained in Albany another copy of your argument fell into his hands, which, he said, agreeably to the strong wish of Judge Johnson, he should transmit to him. You will judge of the expediency of requesting any Massachusetts jurist to write a line to the Chancellor, as hinted in my last. A little delay, however, I should think be advisable, should any communication be made.[153]

Letter of Kent to Story, August 3, 1819: Our friend Mr. Webster has favored me with a short and flattering visit, and I hope to see you and him together in some future time. He will mention to you the reasons which weigh with me against giving a review of the Dartmouth question, and I have no doubt you will be perfectly satisfied.[154]

Extracts from comments on the Dartmouth College Case:

It was not stated in the charter that it was an agreement; it was not stated that the corporators gave anything to the King or to Governor Wentworth for it; and the fact was that they gave nothing for it. Nor did the charter say that it was a contract; nor did it contain any provision that the Parliament should not revoke it. Indeed, neither the King nor Governor Wentworth could have inserted in it such a provision, because neither could bind the Parliament of England.[155]

Marshall's decision, in the opinion of Shirley, made "what the parties to the charter and the 'laws of England' never did, a contract which no human external power could ever modify or change."[156]

The most reasonable and natural construction, therefore, would be that the obligation clause has reference solely to the legal obligations of private executory contracts or engagements, and not to delictual or to moral obligations or to grants and executed contracts; and certainly not to the grant of a charter of incorporation to a literary institution by a British king ex mero motu, without petition, without capacity to contract, without consideration, without intent to contract, without a contractual tie, or a subsisting outstanding obligation in law; but with the reserved right to revoke the charter at the will and pleasure of Parliament; and where there is also no legal obligation resting on the grantees to execute the object of the creation of the corporation.[157]

As a matter of law and a matter of fact, an exemption is not proved. It is as certain that it never existed in the intention and understanding of the parties, as that it was never signed or written or spoken by them or by any one of them. The subject is one on which public opinion, in England and America, has been so unanimous and vehement since 1688, that no successor of James II would have dared to grant, and no grantee would have dared to accept, a dispensation *non obstante;* and the grant that would have been unavailing if it had been put in writing, would not be effectual if it were implied. The law does not infer and enforce a contractual violation of itself. . . .

---

[153] Brown to Webster, Sept. 15, 1818, Shirley, *op. cit.,* pp. 268, 269.

[154] Mass. Hist. Soc., *Proceedings,* XIV (2d ser.), p. 413.

[155] S. D. Thompson, "Abuse of Corporate Privileges," 26 *Amer. Law Rev.* (Mar.–Apr., 1892), 172.

[156] *Dartmouth College Causes,* p. 16.

[157] James C. Jenkins, "Should the Dartmouth College Decision Be Recalled," 51 *Amer. Law Rev.* (Sept.–Oct., 1917), 744, 745.

Upon a true view of the state constitution, the charter, and the effect of corporate dissolution, the constructive suspension of repealing power is an effort to avert a danger that does not exist, by setting up a void contract that was not made.[158]

Opinion of James A. Garfield on the Dartmouth College Case:

In the famous *Dartmouth College Case* it was decided, in 1819, by the Supreme Court of the United States, that the charter of Dartmouth College is a contract between the State and the corporation, which the legislature cannot alter without the consent of the corporation; and that any such alteration is void, being in conflict with that clause of the Constitution of the United States which forbids a State to make any law impairing the obligation of contracts. This decision has stood for more than half a century as a monument of judicial learning, and the great safeguard of vested rights. But Chief Justice Marshall pronounced this decision ten years before the steam railway was born, and it is clear he did not contemplate the class of corporations that have since come into being. But, year by year, the doctrine of that case has been extended to the whole class of private corporations, including railroad and telegraph companies. But few of the States, in their early charters to railroads, reserved any effectual control of the operations of the corporations they created. In many instances, like that of the Illinois Central charter, the right to amend was not reserved. In most States each legislature has narrowed and abridged the powers of its successors, and enlarged the powers of the corporations; and these by the strong grip of the law, and in the name of private property and vested rights, hold fast all they have received. By these means, not only the corporations, but the vast railroad and telegraph systems, have virtually passed from the control of the State. It is painfully evident, from the experience of the last few years, that the efforts of the States to regulate their railroads have amounted to but little more than such feeble annoyance. In many cases the corporations have treated such efforts as impertinent intermeddling, and have brushed away legislative restrictions as easily as Gulliver broke the cords with which the Liliputians attempted to bind him. In these contests the corporations have become conscious of their strength, and have entered upon the work of controlling the States. Already they have captured several of the oldest and strongest of them; and these discrowned sovereigns now follow in chains the triumphal chariot of their conquerors. And this does not imply that merely the officers and representatives of States have been subjected to the railways, but that the corporations have grasped the sources and fountains of power, and control the choice of both officers and representatives.

The private corporation has another great advantage over the municipal corporation. The jurisdiction of the latter is confined to its own territory; but by the recent constructions and devices of the law, a private corporation, though it has no soul, no conscience, and can commit no crime, is yet a citizen of the State that creates it, and can make and execute contracts with individuals and corporations of other States. Thus, the way has been opened to those vast consolidations which have placed the control of the whole system in the hands of a few, and have developed the Charlemagnes and the Caesars of our internal commerce.[159]

---

[158] Charles Doe, "A New View of the Dartmouth College Case," 6 *Harvard Law Rev.* (Nov.–Dec., 1892), 180, 181. Chief Justice Doe of the supreme court of New Hampshire came to the conclusion that a corporate charter is not a contract within the meaning of the federal Constitution and is revocable; but he believed that the state court should have held the acts of 1816 in violation of the state constitution.

[159] *The Works of James Abram Garfield,* ed. by B. A. Hinsdale (Boston, 1883), II: 61, 62.

Part Four

FOREMOST NATIONALISTIC DECISIONS
OF THE SUPREME COURT AND THE
CONTINUANCE OF ATTACKS
UPON THE COURT

CHAPTER XII

The Second Conflict with the State of Virginia

Iᴛ ʜᴀs frequently been noted that the proposal to make the Supreme Court the final arbiter of the constitutionality of both state and federal laws presented certain difficulties which inevitably led to serious controversies. In the first place, the Court in passing on acts of Congress was transcending its own express constitutional sphere; in the second place, in the process of reviewing state acts it was assuming the role of final judge of its own acts. From 1820 to 1830 the nullification of state acts by the federal Judiciary aroused persistent attacks on the federal courts by the states and eventual resistance to the enforcement of the judgments of these tribunals. The feelings aroused and the opposition engendered by the bold and daring method of construction adopted in the case of *McCulloch v. Maryland*[1] had scarcely subsided when Virginia again deemed it imperative to defend the cause of State rights against encroachments resulting from judicial construction.

It was in the midst of the excitement over the Missouri question that Chief Justice Marshall's decision was rendered in the case of *Cohens v. Virginia*.[2] "The noble passages of that remarkable state paper," says Beveridge, "were inspired by, and can be understood only in the light of, the crisis that produced them." And though Beveridge thinks it likely that it was a "feigned case," in which technicalities were waived in order to enable Marshall to assert once more the supremacy of the nation, he lauds Marshall's opinion as an "immortal nationalist address" and "one of the strongest and most enduring strands of that mighty cable woven by him to hold the American people together as a united and imperishable Nation."[3] But the states were unwilling to have that cable woven and to have their rights and prerogatives permanently curtailed by the process of judicial construction without a struggle.

The act of Congress of May 3, 1802, incorporating the District of Columbia authorized "the drawing of lotteries for effecting any im-

---

[1] 4 Wheaton 316 (1819).

[2] 6 Wheaton 266 (1821).

[3] Albert J. Beveridge, *The Life of John Marshall* (Boston, 1919), IV: 343.

portant improvements in the city which the ordinary funds or revenue thereof will not accomplish." Under this act the city passed an ordinance creating a national lottery. A statute of Virginia prohibited the sale of lottery tickets within the state except for lotteries authorized by the laws of Virginia. It was the sale of a few of the national lottery tickets contrary to the state act which marked the beginning of the proceedings in *Cohens v. Virginia*. In accordance with the provisions of the Virginia law, the Cohens were found guilty of violating the act and were assessed a fine of one hundred dollars, the minimum sentence prescribed. From the decision of the borough court of Norfolk the case was taken directly to the Supreme Court of the United States on a writ of error. Though the case could have been taken on appeal to the state supreme court at Richmond, counsel for the state did not object to the direct appeal to the federal courts because they thought the case afforded a good opportunity to test the right and authority of the Supreme Court to assert jurisdiction over a sovereign state. The situation which arose from the attempt to appeal this case to the Supreme Court of the United States appeared so dangerous and alarming that the governor submitted a message to the legislature on the political issues at stake in the controversy, and a report concerning the case was presented to the legislature.

REPORT ON THE CASE OF COHENS V. VIRGINIA

The committee of the legislature to which was referred the governor's message relating to the controversy before the Supreme Court in the *Cohens Case* offered a report and resolutions from which a few extracts are quoted, as follows:

The committee are unwilling to believe, that the Congress of the United States, representing as they always should, the justice, the wisdom and the interests of the people, could so far forget the sacred obligations under which they were convened to legislate, as to delegate to the corporation of the city of Washington authority to vend and distribute these tickets through the Union, in open defiance of the constituted authorities of the respective States; because, it is believed that such a delegation of authority is new and unheard of; supported by no experience; justified by no analogy; without example of our ancestors, or root in the Constitution.

Since the power of the commonwealth to enforce its penal laws was questioned, the committee conceived it to be its duty to sustain "the balance of the Constitution, the integrity of the Union, and the dearest sovereign rights of the people." The committee then defended the rights of the state in these emphatic terms:

When it is remembered that the power of taxation indirectly affects all the moral, political and intellectual relations of mankind, it ceases to be matter of wonder that the exercise of such a power, by the natural and rightful possessors of it, should be dearly valued and pertinaciously maintained against every encroachment directed against it: or, that the rivalry of opposing governments should frequently infringe the rules of public justice to acquire and monopolize it. But, as motives are the governing principles of national actions; and as human reasoning can discover no visible motive why the States, being perfect, sovereign and independent nations, should surrender to the general government the power of taxation over persons and property within their territorial limits; so, arguments to prove the actual surrender of this power ought to be fairly and reasonably deduced from the positive provisions of the federal compact. It cannot be expected, that arguments deduced from the latitudinous and undefined doctrine of implied powers, and from the equally fertile sources of pretended necessity in the general government, will ever prove satisfactory to the people of the United States. The power is too precious; it cannot pass so; whatever the policy for getting it may be.[4]

Referring to the concurrent power of taxation in both the federal and state governments and the possibility of conflicts in the exercise of this authority, the committee observed that: "If this occasional conflict of authority in the different governments of the Union may be justly regarded as a dangerous consequence of our federative system, the wise framers of the Constitution have prescribed no antidote against its possible and foreseen occurrence. It is highly probable they greatly preferred it to that fearful and absolute supremacy, which could alone invest one government with power to abrogate the rightful laws of another; and the exercise of which by the general government would directly affect the existence of the state governments, the balance of the Constitution, and the integrity of the Union." After quoting the clauses of the Constitution defining the appellate jurisdiction of the federal courts, the committee maintained that:

From these plain provisions of the Constitution, it is apparent, that the framers of that instrument never intended to distribute legislative power between a supreme and subordinate legislature; as they considered the federal and state legislatures wholly independent of each other, within their respective spheres. Had they considered the state legislatures subordinate to the federal legislatures, the subordination of the former and the supremacy of the latter, would have been explicitly declared by a positive provision in the federal Constitution. The federal legislative power bears the same relation to the state legislative power, that the federal judicial power bears to the state judicial power; and, if either be independent of the other, whilst acting within its own sphere, both must be also independent of the other. And, if the federal legislature cannot abrogate state laws, the federal judiciary cannot abrogate state judgments. The word "supreme," as descriptive of the federal tribunal, is relative, not absolute; and evidently implies that the supremacy bestowed upon the Supreme Court is *over the inferior courts*, to be *ordained and established* by Congress, and not *over the state courts*. This becomes more apparent from the apportionment of jurisdiction between the supreme and inferior courts, which immediately follows in the 2d clause in the 2d section of the same article, where it is declared that, "in all cases affecting ambassadors, other public ministers and consuls, and those in which a State shall be a party, the Supreme Court shall have original jurisdiction." This clearly shows an intention

[4] *Journal of the House of Delegates, Virginia*, 1820, pp. 102–104.

to limit the jurisdiction of the Supreme Court to the specified cases in the preceding article. But, a limited jurisdiction, with an absolute supremacy over the state tribunals, would be no limitation at all: as the power of that supremacy would annihilate every means in the state governments to enforce the limitation, and make the extent of jurisdiction commensurate with the pleasure of the Supreme Court. What more fully fortifies this conclusion is, that if the word *supreme* had conferred upon the Supreme Court a control over the state courts, it would have been wholly unnecessary to enlarge the jurisdiction of the Supreme Court, by a positive provision for that purpose, in a subsequent clause. This subsequent clause declares that, "in all cases affecting ambassadors, other public ministers and consuls, and those in which a state shall be a party, the supreme court shall have original jurisdiction." In all the other specified cases, the appellate jurisdiction of the Supreme Court is bottomed upon the power of the *inferior* courts. Hence, it follows, that if the word *supreme* does not extend the jurisdiction of the inferior courts, it does not extend the jurisdiction of the Supreme Court, the latter deriving its powers altogether from the former. But, the word *supreme,* cannot possibly extend the jurisdiction of the *inferior* courts over the courts of the State, because the word *supreme* is not applicable to the *inferior* courts. And, as the power of the *inferior* courts is made the basis of the appellate jurisdiction of the Supreme Court (except in the few specified cases), and the power of the inferior courts reaches not to the state courts, it seems to be a reasonable conclusion that the Supreme Court has no jurisdiction over the state courts.[5]

The twenty-fifth section of the Judiciary Act of 1789 was then declared not to have changed the relations between the state and federal courts.

The principles of the Virginia and Kentucky Resolutions were summarized and approved, and the cases of *Respublica v. Cobbett*[6] and *Hunter v. Martin*[7] were cited as confirming these doctrines. In the light of past history and experience the committtee thought themselves entitled to conclude "that there is no rightful power in the federal legislature to abrogate taxes imposed under the authority of a State; nor in the federal Judiciary, to arraign the sovereignty of a Commonwealth before any tribunal, but that which resides in the majesty of the people."[8] And the following resolutions were proposed:

Resolved, therefore, That the Supreme Court of the United States have no rightful authority under the Constitution to examine and correct the judgment for which the commonwealth of Virginia has been "cited and admonished to be and appear at the Supreme Court of the United States": and that the general assembly do hereby enter their most solemn protest against the jurisdiction of that Court over the matter.

Resolved, That the executive department of the government transmit a copy of this report and resolutions to each of the counsel employed to appear before the Supreme Court on behalf of this Commonwealth; and also a copy to each of the Senators and Representatives of this State in the Congress of the United States.[9]

[5] *Journal of the House of Delegates,* p. 105.
[6] 3 Dallas 467 (1798).
[7] 4 Mumf. 3 (1813).
[8] *Journal of the House of Delegates,* p. 108.
[9] *Journal of the House of Delegates,* p. 108.

On February 9, 1821, the Virginia senate passed a resolution that the counsel engaged by the executive to appear before the Supreme Court in the case of *Cohens v. Virginia* in sustaining the rights of the state should confine their argument to the question of jurisdiction alone. If the jurisdiction of the Court should be sustained, they were to consider their duties at an end. Senator Barbour, arguing for the state, said it seemed strange that a lottery authorized by the municipal corporation of the city of Washington for the local purpose of the city should be regarded as a law of the United States so as to give the federal courts jurisdiction for its enforcement beyond the confines of the District of Columbia. The absurdity of the local ordinances of the city being considered laws of the United States and having effect in the adjoining states was clearly pointed out. Because a state was a party in the case, it was contended that the Supreme Court could have neither original nor appellate jurisdiction. The Eleventh Amendment was declared to mean that "a State can never be subjected, at the suit of any individual, to any judicial tribunal, without its own consent."[10] Defending the cause of the state, Mr. Smyth insisted that "there is not a word in the Constitution that goes to set up the federal Judiciary above the state Judiciary."[11] If the ordinance enacted in accordance with the acts of Congress relating to the District has no application to the state of Virginia, then the Supreme Court has no basis for its claim of jurisdiction.

D. B. Ogden, supporting the claim of the Cohens, maintained that the District of Columbia, with all its subordinate agencies, was a creature of the Constitution and that all regulations relating thereto were laws of the United States. The contention that Virginia, as a sovereign state, was exempt from suit was denied on the ground that "since the establishment of the national Constitution, there is no such thing as a sovereign State, independent of the Union. The people of the United States are the sole sovereign authority of this country."[12] To William Pinkney, also counsel for the Cohens, the supremacy of the national Constitution was a fundamental principle of the federal system which would be rendered abortive by state action if Congress could not invest the courts of the union with either exclusive or appellate jurisdiction over such cases as the one before the Supreme Court. "It is the case, then," said he, "and not the *forum* in which it arises, that is to determine whether the judicial authority of the Union shall be exercised over it."[13] In reply to the argument that the Constitution reposes confidence in the state judges who take an oath to support the Constitution, laws, and treaties of the United States as the supreme law, Pinkney, accepting one of the primary doc-

---

[10] 6 Wheaton 308.   [11] *Ibid.*, p. 318.   [12] *Ibid.*, p. 347.   [13] *Ibid.*, p. 355.

trines of the Federalist party, contended that "the actual Constitution of this country is not a government of confidence; it is a scheme of government conceived in a spirit of jealousy."[14] Reference was made to the inconsistency of the state of Virginia, for, when Pennsylvania sought support against the assertion of federal authority over its tribunals, a resolution was adopted declaring that "a tribunal is already provided by the Constitution of the United States, to wit, the Supreme Court, more eminently qualified from their habits and duties, from the mode of their selection, and from the tenure of their offices, to decide the disputes aforesaid, in an enlightened and impartial manner, than any other tribunal which could be created."[15] The argument for the Cohens was predicated to a considerable extent upon the decision and reasoning in *Martin v. Hunter's Lessee.*[16] Moreover, the reasoning in this case was not only adopted but was also given a more extensive application in Chief Justice Marshall's opinion sustaining the Cohens contention.

CHIEF JUSTICE MARSHALL'S OPINION

In rendering the Court's opinion, Chief Justice Marshall said that those who oppose the jurisdiction of the Supreme Court in this case

maintain that the Nation does not possess a department capable of restraining, peaceably, and by the authority of law, any attempts which may be made by a part, against the legitimate powers of the whole; and the government is reduced to the alternative of submitting to such attempts, or of resisting them by force. They maintain that the Constitution of the United States has provided no tribunal for the final construction of itself, or of the laws or treaties of the Nation; but that this power may be exercised in the last resort by the courts of every State in the Union. That the Constitution, laws, and treaties, may receive as many constructions as there are States, and that this is not a mischief, or, if a mischief, is irremediable. . . .

If such be the Constitution, it is the duty of the Court to bow with respectful submission to its provisions. If such be not the Constitution, it is equally the duty of this Court to say so; and to perform that task which the American people have assigned to the judicial department.[17]

The first question, whether the jurisdiction of the Supreme Court was excluded by the parties, one of them being a state and the other a citizen of that state, was disposed of by accepting the argument of counsel that the jurisdiction of the federal courts depended, first, on the character of the cause, when the courts must decide cases regardless of the parties and, second, when the jurisdiction arises from the character of the parties. Jurisdiction over the case was then defended as follows:

The jurisdiction of the Court, then, being extended by the letter of the Constitution to all cases arising under it, or under the laws of the United States, it follows that those

---

[14] 6 Wheaton 356.

[15] *Ibid.,* p. 358, note (a).

[16] 1 Wheaton 304 (1815).

[17] 6 Wheaton 377.

who would withdraw any case of this description from that jurisdiction, must sustain the exemption they claim on the spirit and true meaning of the Constitution, which spirit and true meaning must be so apparent as to overrule the words which its framers have employed.

The counsel for the defendant in error have undertaken to do this; and have laid down the general proposition, that a sovereign independent State is not suable, except by its own consent.

This general proposition will not be controverted. But its consent is not requisite in each particular case. It may be given in a general law. And if a State has surrendered any portion of its sovereignty, the question whether a liability to suit be a part of this portion, depends on the instrument by which the surrender is made. If upon a just construction of that instrument, it shall appear that the State has submitted to be sued, then it has parted with this sovereign right of judging in every case on the justice of its own pretensions, and has intrusted that power to a tribunal in whose impartiality it confides.

The American States, as well as the American people, have believed a close and firm Union to be essential to their liberty and to their happiness. They have been taught by experience, that this Union cannot exist without a government for the whole; and they have been taught by the same experience that this government would be a mere shadow, that must disappoint all their hopes, unless invested with a large portion of that sovereignty which belongs to independent States. Under the influence of this opinion, and thus instructed by experience, the American people in the conventions of their respective States, adopted the present Constitution.

If it could be doubted whether, from its nature, it were not supreme in all cases where it is empowered to act, that doubt would be removed by the declaration that "this Constitution, and the laws of the United States which shall be made in pursuance thereof, and all treaties made, or which shall be made, under the authority of the United States, shall be the supreme law of the land; and the judges in every State shall be bound thereby, anything in the constitution or laws of any State to the contrary notwithstanding."

This is the authoritative language of the American people; and, if gentlemen please, of the American States. It marks with lines too strong to be mistaken, the characteristic distinction between the government of the Union and those of the States. The general government, though limited as to its objects, is supreme with respect to those objects. This principle is a part of the Constitution; and if there be any who deny its necessity, none can deny its authority.

To this supreme government ample powers are confided; and if it were possible to doubt the great purposes for which they were so confided, the people of the United States have declared that they are given "in order to form a more perfect union, establish justice, insure domestic tranquillity, provide for the common defence, promote the general welfare, and secure the blessings of liberty to themselves and their posterity."

With the ample powers confided to this supreme government, for these interesting purposes, are connected many express and important limitations on the sovereignty of the States, which are made for the same purposes. The powers of the Union, on the great subjects of war, peace, and commerce, and on many others, are in themselves limitations of the sovereignty of the States; but in addition to these, the sovereignty of the States is surrendered in many instances where the surrender can only operate to the benefit of the people, and where, perhaps, no other power is conferred on Congress than a conservative power to maintain the principles established in the Constitution.

The maintenance of these principles in their purity, is certainly among the great duties of the government. One of the instruments by which this duty may be peaceably performed, is the judicial department. It is authorized to decide all cases, of every description, arising under the Constitution or laws of the United States. From this general grant of jurisdiction, no exception is made of those cases in which a State may be a party. When we consider the situation of the government of the Union and of a State, in relation to each other; the nature of our Constitution, the subordination of the state governments to that Constitution; the great purpose for which jurisdiction over all cases arising under the Constitution and laws of the United States, is confided to the judicial department, are we at liberty to insert in this general grant, an exception of those cases in which a State may be a party? Will the spirit of the Constitution justify this attempt to control its words? We think it will not. We think a case arising under the Constitution or laws of the United States, is cognizable in the courts of the Union, whoever may be the parties to that case.[18]

Marshall then referred to what he regarded as the "mischievous consequences" which might result from an interpretation of the national laws by the state courts. It would, he thought, be hazarding too much to assert that the courts of the states would be exempt from the prejudices by which the legislatures and people are influenced and might be regarded as impartial tribunals for the settlement of federal questions. Collisions between the federal and state authorities, he observed,

may take place in times of no extraordinary commotion. But a Constitution is framed for ages to come, and is designed to approach immortality as nearly as human institutions can approach it. Its course cannot always be tranquil. It is exposed to storms and tempests, and its framers must be unwise statesmen indeed, if they have not provided it, as far as its nature will permit, with the means of self-preservation from the perils it may be destined to encounter. No government ought to be so defective in its organization, as not to contain within itself the means of securing the execution of its own laws against other dangers than those which occur every day. Courts of justice are the means most usually employed; and it is reasonable to expect that a government should repose on its own courts, rather than on others.[19]

On the assertion that the states might check effective operation of the federal system by refusing to perform their duties as prescribed by the Constitution, Marshall said, "it is very true, that, whenever hostility to the existing system shall become universal, it will be also irresistible. The people made the Constitution, and the people can unmake it. It is the creature of their will, and lives only by their will. But this supreme and irresistible power to make or unmake, resides only in the whole body of the people; not in any subdivision of them. The attempt of any of the parts to exercise it is usurpation, and ought to be repelled by those to whom the people have delegated their power of repelling it."[20]

In answer to the contention that the appellate power of the Supreme Court cannot be exercised over the judgment of a state court, Marshall

---

[18] 6 Wheaton 380–383.   [19] *Ibid.*, pp. 387, 388.   [20] *Ibid.*, p. 389.

replied that for some very important purposes the united states form a single nation and that for a government acknowledged to be supreme "with respect to objects of vital interest to the Nation, there is nothing inconsistent with sound reason, nothing incompatible with the nature of government, in making all its departments supreme, so far as respects those objects."[21] The contention of counsel for the state of Virginia that the federal and state courts must from the nature of the Constitution be considered independent of each other, then, was emphatically rejected, because, said Marshall, it is founded, not on the words of the Constitution, but on its spirit extracted, not from the words of the instrument, but from views regarding the nature of the union.[22]

Much of Marshall's opinion was predicated on the hypothesis that the provisions of the Constitution granting jurisdiction to the federal courts must be interpreted so as to permit the courts to uphold the Constitution and laws regardless of the Eleventh Amendment. But so far as amendments were in conflict with the provisions of the Constitution, the former should have been given effect in preference to the original words. Adopting Marshall's favorite method of reasoning, no exception of cases relating to the interpretation of the Constitution and laws was made in the amendment; hence, why import such language to warrant the construction which the Chief Justice deemed politically desirable. But it is obvious that those defending state powers must show the express language of the Constitution to sustain their contentions, whereas those who support federal authority need only find sanction for their views sustaining the dominance of federal over state authorities in the inferences, implications, and general purposes of the document. For, said the great exponent of nationalism: "Let the nature and objects of our Union be considered; let the great fundamental principles, on which the fabric stands, be examined; and we think, the result must be, that there is nothing so extravagantly absurd, in giving to the Court of the Nation the power of revising the decisions of local tribunals on questions which affect the Nation."[23] How different the great fundamental principles on which the fabric stands appear when they are conceived as supporting the essential features of state sovereignty out of which an emerging nation was grudgingly carved! On fundamental principles requiring a nationalistic interpretation of the written instrument, it was concluded that a defendant, who appeals from a state court to the Supreme Court for the purpose of determining whether the judgment of the state court violates the Constitution or laws of the United States, does not prosecute a suit against a state.

---

[21] 6 Wheaton 415.   [22] *Ibid.*, pp. 413 ff.   [23] *Ibid.*, pp. 422, 423.

The assertion that the ordinance of the District was an act of a local legislature, and, as such, not a law of the United States to be deemed enforcible in an adjoining state, was apparently the most difficult contention to meet. Moreover, as was customary for the Chief Justice when he was treading on weak ground, he dealt with the issue very briefly and followed the familiar method of assuming without argument that the lottery ordinance was, like other acts of Congress, a law of the United States. But having assumed jurisdiction and having read his "immortal state paper," the Chief Justice suggested that a way out of an embarrassing situation might be found in the determination whether any particular law was designed to operate without the District or not. This issue, said Marshall, depends upon the words of the law, and under the direction of the Court there was another argument. The case was then argued on the merits of the controversy, with new attorneys participating. It was again contended that neither the Congressional act nor the ordinance limited the operation of the ordinance to the District of Columbia and that the lottery tickets must be salable throughout the union despite any laws prohibiting such sale. But, having answered the State rights arguments which were growing louder and more persistent, Chief Justice Marshall adopted the reasoning of the attorneys for the state, and decided that the federal act was applicable only to the District of Columbia, that the decision of the Norfolk court was a local affair, and that its judgment must be affirmed. The practical result of the appeal, notes Beveridge, amounted to nothing, "but it afforded John Marshall the opportunity to tell the Nation its duty in a crowning national emergency." For "the Chief Justice is exerting to the utmost his tremendous powers, not to protect two furtive peddlers of lottery tickets, but to check a powerful movement, which, if not arrested, must destroy the Republic. . . . In *Cohens v. Virginia,* John Marshall stamped upon the brow of Localism the brand of illegality. . . . With savage relish the Chief Justice attacks and demolishes the State Rights theory that the Supreme Court cannot review the judgment of a state court, 'in any case.' "[24] With such an objective in the mind of the Chief Justice it could scarcely be expected that the people of Virginia would submit to the decision without vigorous protests.

Governor Randolph made the Supreme Court the chief item of his message to the legislature in December, 1821. The commonwealth, he said, "has undergone the humiliation of having endeavored in vain to vindicate and assert her rights and sovereignty at the bar of the Supreme Court of the United States, and now endures the mortification, of having

[24] *The Life of John Marshall,* IV: 353, 355, 357.

altogether failed to procure a disavowal of the right, or the intention, to violate that sovereignty." The Supreme Court, he continued, "arrogates to itself, always, the high authority to judge exclusively in the last resort how far the federal compact is violated, and to arraign before it, not only the decisions of the state courts, but the States themselves."[25] Roane's surmise, however, was correct, for no action was taken by the legislature. The extreme position of the State rights party in opposition to the nationalistic leanings of the Court was stated in a set of resolutions rejected by a close vote in the legislature proposing to instruct the senators and representatives from the state in Congress to procure amendments to the Constitution, as follows:

1. That the legislative authority of the United States shall not be construed to extend to, or embrace, any power which is not expressly granted to Congress by the Constitution, or *absolutely* necessary and proper for carrying the same into execution.

2. That neither the government of the United States, nor any department thereof, shall be construed to have the power to bind, *conclusively*, the claims of the States composing the Union, to rights contested between the general and state governments, under the Constitution.

3. That the judicial power of the United States shall not be construed to extend to *any* case in which a State shall be a party, except in controversies between two or more States nor to any other controversies involving the rights of a State, and to which such a State shall claim to become a party.

4. That no appeal shall be construed to lie to any court of the United States from any decision rendered in the courts of a State.

5. That no law made for the District of Columbia, or for any State, district, or territory, shall be construed to have force within any other State, which shall conflict with justice, with the principles of morality, with rights claimed under such States, or with the systems of policy or revenue of such a State.[26]

The decision in the *Cohens Case* came at the time that Jefferson and others were warning the people against the consolidating tendency of the decisions of the Supreme Court. The part of the opinion relating to the jurisdiction of the Court seemed to the Republicans a climax in the continual round of encroachments of the Court on the sovereignty of the states, and many believed the fundamental doctrines of the union

---

[25] *Virginia House Journals*, Dec. 3, 1821. Regarding this message, Roane wrote to Archibald Thweatt that "the governor's patriotic message on the subject of the Supreme Court has been very well received by the Republicans here, in consequence of the public mind having been somewhat prepared on the subject. But such is the apathy of the times, and the dearth of talents in the legislature, that I doubt whether anything will be done by that body. Certainly not, I expect, unless they should be aided by some of our veteran statesmen. I shall write to Colonel Taylor today and touch on that subject. If you could do likewise with Mr. Jefferson (as I cannot take the liberty to do), his name would settle the controversy. The career of this high Court must be stopped or the liberties of our country are annihilated." *Branch Historical Papers* (June, 1905), II: 140, 141.

[26] *Niles' Register*, XXI: 404.

were in peril. The most emphatic and disturbing attacks on the opinion came from Virginia and in particular from Judge Spencer Roane of that state, writing under the pseudonym of Algernon Sydney.[27]

THE ARGUMENTS OF SPENCER ROANE

"I ask from you," said Spencer Roane, "no revolution, but what consists in the preservation of an excellent Constitution. I require from you no insurrection, but that of a frequent recurrence to fundamental principles."[28] The Cohens decision, he thought, "negatives the idea that the American States have a real existence, or are to be considered, in any sense, as sovereign and independent States. . . . If this power of decision is once conceded to either party, the equilibrium established by the Constitution is destroyed, and the compact exists thereafter, but in name."

Such a decision, to Roane, was equivalent to an amendment to the Constitution by the process of judicial construction, and it was deemed especially objectionable, since an act of the state of Virginia was considered inferior to an ordinance of the city of Washington. Judge Roane condemned the arrogance of the Court in assuming authority in contempt of the sovereign power of the people and in claiming the authority to define its own powers as well as those of the other departments of government. Having been appointed in one generation, the Court claims to make laws and constitutions for another, and "it acts always upon the foundation of its own precedents, and progresses, 'with a noiseless foot and unalarming advance,' until it reaches the zenith of despotic power."[29]

Describing Marshall's method of interpretation, Roane finds "the opinion, besides being unusually tedious and tautologous abounds in defects which are more important. It often adopts premises which cannot be conceded, and takes for granted the very points which are to be proved." Roane objected also to the haste with which the decision was rendered and the seeming unanimity of opinion among the Judges. It is to be regretted, said Roane, "that these high Judges, have abandoned the practice of giving, each, their own opinions. That is well known to

---

[27] Concerning these papers, Jefferson wrote to Roane on June 25, 1821, "I have now to thank you for the papers of Algernon Sydney, which I had before read with great approbation successively, as they came out. I had hoped Mr. Ritchie would publish them in pamphlet form, in which case I would have taken half a dozen or a dozen myself, and enclosed them to some of my friends in the different States, in the hope of exciting others to attend to this case, whose stepping forward in opposition would be more auspicious than for Virginia to do it. I should expect that New York, Ohio, and perhaps Maryland might agree to bring it forward, and the two former being anti-Missourians, might recommend it to that party." *Branch Historical Papers* (June, 1905), II: 138, 139.

[28] *Ibid.* (June, 1906), II: 79, 80.

[29] *Ibid.* (June, 1906), II: 79, 80.

be one of the chief guarantees of the integrity and independence of the Judges." But, commenting on the somewhat hopeless effort in which he was engaged, Roane exclaimed: "Yet, REPUBLICANS! I greatly fear that your sins have overtaken you. I deeply regret that you are found sleeping at your posts, and 'that you could not watch one hour.' I greatly fear, that the day of retribution is at hand. The sceptre of power, is, I fear, about to depart 'from beneath your feet.' "[30]

Roane adverted to the dictum of George Clinton of New York who, casting the deciding vote in the Senate against the second bank bill, said that as a result of his experience "government is not to be strengthened by an assumption of doubtful powers, but by a wise and energetic execution of those which are incontestable; the former never fails to produce suspicion and distrust while the latter inspires respect and confidence."[31] And the query was raised whether, when there are two sovereign governments joined by a league or treaty, the courts of either are competent to bind the constitutional rights of the other. One of the Kentucky Resolutions of 1798 approved, if not drafted, by Jefferson was also quoted.[32] According to the doctrines therein announced, in a contest over rights between the two parties to the federal compact, neither is competent to bind the other or to act as a judge in its own cause, but the matter is to be referred to their common superior, the people, who will settle the dispute between them.

Objection was raised to the contention that the powers of the federal government and of the Supreme Court were supreme. The word supremacy does not appropriately apply to the national government, for even the sovereignty of the people is limited by the principles of reason and justice. The Court, however, assumed that a case was before it and that it was its duty to render a judgment, when, as a matter of fact, there is only one party before the court—the other, a sovereign state, having, according to the Eleventh Amendment, declined to appear.

Marshall foresaw great evils resulting from the different constructions which might be adopted by the several states. But such a result, Roane observed, followed from our being a group of free and independent governments. The only effective remedy for this difficulty would be to wipe out the state governments altogether and to establish one great consolidated empire. The Supreme Court feared that state authorities would manifest improper prejudices against the general government. But prejudices will not be confined to state officers. Federal judges are

---

[30] *Ibid.*, p. 85.
[31] 22 *Annals of Congress*, 346–347 (Feb. 20, 1811).
[32] See above, pp. 166–167.

not exempt from their prejudices and "their prejudices will be on the side of power and of the government which feeds them." The attitude of the Judges in enforcing the infamous sedition law were cited as an illustration of such prejudices on the part of federal Judges. The interpretation of the Constitution, Marshall believed, could not safely be entrusted to state judges dependent for office and salary upon the will of the legislature. Most of the state judges, however, were independent of the legislature both with respect to office and to salary, and it was regarded as an unfair imputation that on vital issues and principles of constitutional construction state judges would be guided primarily by personal and financial considerations.

The Supreme Court was pleased to say that a Constitution, "which was designed to approach immortality," ought not to be so defective as to lack power to secure the execution of its own laws against all dangers. But, said Roane, "if that Constitution was designed for immortality, it was certainly not so intended in its original form. It is admitted to have been eminently defective by the very provision contained in it for its amendment; and it has been accordingly, actually and greatly amended."[33]

It was charged that although Marshall referred to the history of the formation of the Constitution, he ignored the most fundamental fact of that history, namely, that the idea of "one great consolidated government" was abhorrent to a large majority of the people who participated in the making and adoption of the Constitution. Attention was directed to the sovereignty of the states which was expressly recognized under the Articles of Confederation and was never expressly repudiated in the making of the Constitution.

Roane found that the Supreme Court throughout its opinion indulged in groundless jealousy of the state governments and supposed that they would arrest the constitutional course of the general government, for it was only when unconstitutional and ungranted powers were exercised that the state governments attempted to interfere. He then asserted: "I boldly deny therefore that the Judiciary of the general government has any greater interest in the system of the federal government than have those of the States, or any greater inducement to preserve it. Nor are they the exclusive judges of a matter."[34]

Exceptions were also taken to Marshall's explanation of the cause of the adoption of the Eleventh Amendment which he attributed to the fear that the states would have to pay their debts. Only three suits were

---

[33] *Branch Historical Papers* (June, 1906), p. 133.
[34] *Ibid.*, p. 145.

brought against states in the federal courts by citizens of other states before the adoption of the Eleventh Amendment. These suits were against Massachusetts,[35] Georgia, and Virginia. Roane continued:

On the third of December, 1793 the legislature of Virginia had resolved, "that a State cannot, under the Constitution of the United States, be made a defendant at the suit of any individual, and that the decision of the supreme federal court, that a State may be placed in that situation, is *inconsistent with*, and *dangerous to, the sovereignty and independence of the individual States,* as the same tends to a *general consolidation* of these *confederate* republics." It was, at the same time, resolved, that our Senators and Representatives in Congress be instructed to obtain such amendments to the Constitution "as will remove or explain any clause or article of the said Constitution, which can be construed to imply or justify a decision that a State is compellable to *answer*, in any suit, by an individual or individuals, in any court of the United States." It was because the States claimed to be *sovereign* and independent States, although they had entered into a federal compact and because one sovereign State has no right to set itself up as the judge of another that this alarm took place; and not on the sordid ground of unwillingness in the States to pay debts which are not shown to have had an existence.[36]

Roane referred again to "the artful manner in which the pretensions of the Supreme Court are almost always stated. Everything which makes against their side of the question is greatly distorted and aggravated, and everything in its favor is very much palliated and softened. They often assume premises which cannot be conceded and take for granted what ought to be proved. These are arts, I had almost said artifices, scarcely to be excused in an advocate and which are surely unworthy of the high character of the Supreme Court."[37]

According to Roane, the supremacy bestowed by the judiciary article was over the inferior courts established by Congress, and not over the state courts. But, as George Mason argued in the Virginia convention, the power to be extended over ten miles square was a dangerous power which might be extended "by implication to overthrow the rights of the States." Now, said Roane: "It has been so extended, and that by the most remote and unwarrantable implication."

Jefferson's opinion was sought in the *Cohens Case,* and in a letter to William Johnson in June, 1823, he reviewed the history of the contest between the Federalists and Anti-Federalists. Regarding the request to examine the question whether the Supreme Court had advanced beyond its constitutional limits, he replied that age disqualified him for the task and that this examination had already been very well done. He then

---

[35] In Massachusetts, John Hancock, who was summoned as governor to answer the prosecution, resisted the process and maintained inviolate the sovereignty of the commonwealth.

[36] *Branch Historical Papers, op. cit.,* p. 154.

[37] *Ibid.,* p. 163.

referred to certain papers which appeared in the *Enquirer* prepared by Judge Roane under the name of Algernon Sydney, and said:

I considered these papers maturely as they came out, and confess that they appeared to me to pulverize every word which had been delivered by Judge Marshall, of the extra-judicial part of his opinion; and all was extra-judicial, except the decision that the act of Congress had not purported to give to the corporation of Washington the authority claimed by their lottery law, of controlling the laws of the States within the States themselves. But unable to claim that case, he could not let it go entirely, but went on gratuitously to prove, that notwithstanding the Eleventh Amendment of the Constitution, a State *could* be brought as a defendant, to the bar of his Court; and again, that Congress might authorize a corporation of its territory to exercise legislation within a State, and paramount to the laws of that State.[38]

This doctrine of Marshall, Jefferson thought, "was so completely refuted by Roane, that if he can be answered, I surrender human reason as a vain and useless faculty, given to bewilder, and not to guide us."[39] The practice of Judge Marshall "of travelling out of his case to prescribe what the law would be in a moot case not before the Court" was regarded as very irregular and censurable.[40] To bear out these criticisms, *Marbury v. Madison* was cited. In this case the Court determined at once that, being an original process, they did not have cognizance of it, and therefore the question before them was ended. But the Chief Justice went on to expound what the law would be if they had jurisdiction over the case, when "the object was clearly to instruct any other court having the jurisdiction, what they should do if Marbury should apply to them."[41] Although the Court could not issue a mandamus to the President or to the Legislature, said Jefferson, "this case of *Marbury v. Madison* is continually cited by bench and bar as if it were settled law." As a partial remedy to meet the situation, Jefferson advocated an amendment that each Judge should give his individual opinion on all issues concerning the constitutionality of laws. An attempt was made also to secure the views of Madison.

In expressing to Spencer Roane his opinion relative to the decision of the Supreme Court in the case of *Cohens v. Virginia,* Madison thought it was "to be regretted that the Court is so much in the practice of mingling with their judgments pronounced, comments and reasonings of a scope beyond them; and that there is often an apparent disposition to amplify the authorities of the Union at the expense of those of the States. It is of great importance as well as an indispensable obligation that the con-

---

[38] *The Writings of Thomas Jefferson,* ed. by Paul Leicester Ford (New York, 1892), X: 229.

[39] *Ibid.*

[40] *Writings* (Ford ed.), X: 230.

[41] *Ibid.*

stitutional boundary between them should be impartially maintained."[42] But Madison believed there were as great dangers from misinterpretations of the Constitution by Congress as by the Courts and that infractions of the fundamental law by any department should be carefully watched.

In another letter to Spencer Roane, Madison said that he had "always thought that a construction of the instrument ought to be favored, as far as the text would warrant, which would obviate the dilemma of a judicial rencounter or a mutual paralysis; and that on the abstract question whether the federal or state decisions ought to prevail, the sounder policy would yield to the claims of the former."[43] He again recurred to the compact philosophy in the statement that "our governmental system is established by a compact, not between the government of the United States, and the state governments; but between the States, as sovereign communities, stipulating each with the others, a surrender of certain portions, of their respective authorities, to be exercised by a common government and a reservation, for their own exercise, of all their other authorities."[44] Madison admitted that the Gordian knot of the Constitution appeared to lie in the problem of collisions between the federal and state powers, but he thought, "if the knot cannot be untied by the text of the Constitution it ought not, certainly, to be cut by any Political Alexander." In looking at the matter abstractly and separately from Marshall's tendency to extend federal judicial powers through the process of interpretation, Madison was inclined to favor the decisions of the federal tribunals on doubtful points of jurisdiction between the nation and the states. It was in the works of John Taylor of Caroline, however, that the reasoning of Chief Justice Marshall and the decisions of the Supreme Court relating to state authority were thoroughly analyzed and severely condemned.

---

[42] *The Writings of James Madison*, ed. by Gaillard Hunt (New York, 1910), IX: 56. How far those who were responsible for the official action of the government, and in particular the federal courts, had strayed from the general lines and purposes drawn by the framers was indicated by Madison in the observation that: "It could not but happen, and was foreseen at the birth of the Constitution, that difficulties and differences of opinion might occasionally arise in expounding terms and phrases necessarily used in such a charter; more especially those which divide legislation between the general and local governments; and that it might require a regular course or practice to liquidate and settle the meaning of some of them. But it was anticipated, I believe, by few, if any, of the friends of the Constitution, that a rule of construction would be introduced as broad and pliant as what has occurred. And those who recollect, and, still more, those who shared in what passed in the state conventions, through which the people ratified the Constitution, with respect to the extent of the powers vested in Congress, cannot easily be persuaded that the avowal of such a rule would not have prevented its ratification." Madison to Judge Roane, Max Farrand, *The Records of the Federal Convention* (New Haven, 1923), III: 435.

[43] *Writings* (Hunt ed.), IX: 66.   [44] *Ibid.*

THE DOCTRINES OF JOHN TAYLOR

When Henry Clay and John C. Calhoun espoused nationalistic doctrines and the Supreme Court under the dominance of Chief Justice Marshall strongly endorsed centralizing tendencies in constitutional construction, John Taylor set to work to refute their arguments. Colonel Taylor, who was considered one of the strongest intellectual leaders of the Republican party, and of whom Jefferson wrote, we "have rarely, if ever, differed in any political principle of importance,"[45] took up the defense of the Republican theories of constitutional interpretation in such extensive treatises as *Construction Construed and Constitutions Vindicated,*[46] *Tyranny Unmasked,* and *New Views on the Constitution of the United States.* Taylor's early espousal of democratic principles has been briefly treated elsewhere,[47] but his doctrines of constitutional construction are worthy of careful consideration. In fact, these doctrines have not received the consideration they deserve in the evolution of the principles of constitutional interpretation during the first three decades of the nineteenth century.

Thomas Ritchie, presenting Taylor's *Construction Construed*[48] to the public, charged that as bad as the second bank charter was, it "has been justified by the Supreme Court of the United States on principles so bold and alarming, that no man who loves the Constitution can fold his arms in apathy upon the subject. Those principles, so boldly uttered from the highest judicial tribunal in the United States, are calculated to give the tone to an acquiescent people, to change the whole face of our government and to generate a thousand measures, which the framers of the Constitution never anticipated." Taylor maintained that the national bank was unconstitutional because Congress could not lawfully create a corporation. Yet, a corporation established in violation of the fundamental law was by Marshall's reasoning permitted to defy a sovereign state. Taylor believed that the formation of the national government had been a reaction from the Revolution, that the election of 1800 had been a restoration, and that in 1820 a second reaction was taking

---

[45] *Writings* (Ford ed.), X: 170.

[46] Jefferson strongly endorsed this work as "the most logical retraction of our governments to the original and true principles of the Constitution creating them, which has appeared since the adoption of that instrument. . . . It should be put into the hands of all our functionaries, authoritatively, as a standing instruction, and true exposition of our Constitution, as understood at the time we agreed to it. It is a fatal heresy to suppose that either our state governments are superior to the federal, or the federal to the States." *Writings* (Ford ed.), X: 190.

[47] See above, p. 337.

[48] For a summary of Taylor's doctrines in his *Construction Construed,* see Henry H. Simms, *Life of John Taylor* (Richmond, 1932), pp. 181 ff.

place. He regarded Marshall and the Supreme Court as the champions of the cause of privilege and a moneyed aristocracy.

At the outset Taylor expressed his disapproval of "the habit of corrupting our political system, by the instrumentality of inference, convenience and necessity, with the endless series of consequences attached to them."[49] He resented the use by Marshall of the "science of verbality," whereby the Constitution was turned into a reservoir of every meaning for which its expounder might have occasion.[50] The doctrines of "limited powers" and "unlimited inferences" were regarded as irreconcilable. Referring to the broad construction of the phrase, "general welfare," and of the elastic clause of the Constitution, Taylor contended that "no construction of particular words or phrases can change or abolish the division of power between the state and federal governments, without changing or abolishing an essential principle of the Constitution itself."[51] The necessary and proper clause was held to be no basis for the assumption of powers not delegated to the federal government. On the contrary, the jurisdiction of the federal courts was declared to be limited to laws passed by Congress in conformity with the delegated powers.

In speaking of sovereignty, Taylor said: "I do not know how it has happened, that this word has crept into our political dialect, unless it be that mankind prefer mystery to knowledge; and that governments love obscurity better than specification."[52] He could not take seriously Marshall's contention that each unit of the federal system was sovereign within its sphere of action. According to Taylor sovereignty is incapable of division; it must reside in one or the other of the divisions of the government of the United States. The real division of powers, in his opinion, was between the people and their governments, not between the state and federal governments. Taylor contended that since the states as states adopted the Constitution and they alone are authorized to amend the document, they, not the people, are the real source and authority for the Constitution. In following this line of reasoning, he comes to the conclusion that "the federal is not a national government: it is a league between nations. By this league, a limited power only over persons and property was given to the representatives of the united nations. This power cannot be further extended under the pretext of national good, because the league does not create a national government."[53]

---

[49] *Construction Construed and Constitutions Vindicated* (Richmond, 1820), p. 2.

[50] *Ibid.*, p. 161. Later, he observed: "To me this new notion of a Constitution by implication is, I confess, exactly like no Constitution at all; nor has it been proved to my satisfaction, that principles ought to be lost in verbal definitions, or property crushed in the jaws of sovereignty." *Ibid.*, p. 284.

[51] *Ibid.*, pp. 164 ff.   [52] *Ibid.*, pp. 25 ff.   [53] *Ibid.*, pp. 234 ff.

In condemning the capitalistic sect who had acquired a hundred millions of dollars of capital artificially created by the authority of the federal government and who sought special advantages and favors to maintain their hold upon the capital and monetary system of the country, Taylor said: "The secret, as to the distresses of the United States, lies in the difference between republican and aristocratical legislation upon the important subject of money." The chief methods of maintaining this control were the legislative measures organizing and controlling banks and the establishing of protective duties. As he saw it, the protective system invested "a combination of capitalists with a legislative power over manufactures and exchanges."[54] To Taylor, a monopoly of intelligence, if it could be effected by any class or combination, would be a tyranny; but a monopoly of any means for obtaining wealth from a community, by a class or combination unpossessed of an unnatural superiority of intelligence, prevents the increase and diminishes the stock of national intelligence because it is only cunning, associated with avarice, which resorts to means for the gratification of self-interest unfavorable to the increase of intelligence itself. It is freedom which makes both religion and civil government more productive of benefits to mankind than it is intelligence when monopolized by combinations and exerted by exclusive privileges.[55] Taylor believed that the American system of government was devised to combat all forms of monopoly, and to this end the governments set up were not sovereign, but were trustees of the sovereignty of the people. Hence they were invested with limited powers only and composed of coördinate departments established to discharge specified duties.[56]

Taylor then raised the query which was the crux of the argument between the Federalists and the Anti-Federalists with respect to the authority to construe the Constitution. Recognizing that the Constitution distributes rights and powers among the legislative, executive, and judicial departments, and between the federal and state governments, and that one department or division of the federal system may interfere with or attempt to control another, he inquired, "where does the authority lie for removing the inconvenience, admitting it to be one; in the people, or in the implied supremacy of one of these departments, intended by the people to be controlled?"[57]

Though the Constitution declares that its provisions and the laws of Congress are to be the supreme law of the land, it is, in the opinion of Taylor, a supremacy of law that is established, and not a supremacy of the

---

[54] *Construction Construed,* pp. 231 ff.   [56] *Ibid.,* p. 264.
[55] *Ibid.,* pp. 250, 251.   [57] *Ibid.,* p. 174.

officers or departments of the federal government. For, he maintained, "the supremacy of the Constitution is not confined to any particular department or functionary, but extends to our entire system of political law. Under its protection, the federal Senate has a right to defend itself against the House of Representatives; and the federal judicial power against the federal legislative power; and if so, it seems impossible to doubt, that the same sanction invests the state and federal judicial powers with a mutual right of self defence, against the aggressions of each other."[58] The argument of the Supreme Court, he thought, might be thus condensed:

The federal and state governments have limited powers under the federal constitution. The powers of both are attended by such a portion of spherical sovereignty, as is necessary or convenient for their execution. Sovereignty can legitimately use the means it may choose, for the execution of the powers it legitimately possesses. So far nothing is gained; because the sovereignty bestowed, and the means it may use, are limited by the spheres of action bestowed upon each government. But the difficulty is gotten over, and the Court's own argument overthrown, by thrusting the word "paramount" into the Constitution. The mutuality and equivalence of the spherical sovereignties allowed to the state and federal sovereignties is revoked; and one is made an absolute sovereign over the other, by a construction of the word "supreme" and an interpolation of the word "paramount"; which must be unconstitutional, if the limited spherical sovereignties, previously assigned to each, are sustainable by a correct construction.[59]

The only supremacy bestowed by the language of the Constitution is over the persons and things specifically subjected to the limited power of each. No supremacy is given to one department over another, and sovereignty, if there is any such thing in the federal system, is applicable only to the relations of the people to these departments. Taylor does not approve of the reasoning of the Supreme Court whereby the sovereignty of the people of each state is to be transferred to the people of the United States by whom it has not and cannot legally be exercised.[60]

---

[58] *Ibid.*, p. 143.

[59] *Ibid.*, p. 139.

[60] *Ibid.*, pp. 60, 121. The Supreme Court's theory of constructive supremacy was characterized by Taylor, as follows: "If the inconvenience of collisions between coordinate political departments begets a *necessity* for the supremacy of one, and this necessity will justify its assumption, the scheme of checks and balances is entirely chimerical, and a political fabric built upon that theory must fall. Necessity, inference and expediency never fail to beget an endless successive progeny. Roads are necessary in war; therefore Congress may legislate locally concerning roads. Victuals, manufactures, and a certain state of national manners, are more necessary in war; therefore Congress may legislate locally, concerning agriculture, manufactures and manners. The favour of the Deity is more necessary than either; therefore Congress may provide salaries for priests of all denominations, in order to obtain it, without infringing the constitutional prohibition against an establishment; or they may incorporate sects, and exempt them from taxation. Roads are more necessary for collecting taxes than even banks. Taverns are very necessary or convenient for the offices of the army, Congress themselves, the conveyance

Throughout this volume Taylor expressed grave fears regarding the antagonism aroused by the Missouri Compromise. He thought the controversy resulted from an effort to maintain a balance of power between two combinations of states, rather than the desire to limit or extend slavery. In the Missouri Compromise lurked the germ of destruction of the confederation of states, for the inevitable result was to change Congress into a diplomatic body whose chief purpose would be to adjust controversies between rival sectional interests.[61] He looked upon a balance of power as "the most complete invention imaginable for involving one combination of States, in a war with another." And as the arguments over the Compromise indicated that an attempt might be made to control, through the federal government, the institution of slavery contrary to the prevailing opinions and interests in the South, Taylor made the prophetic statement that:

There remains a right, anterior to every political power whatsoever, and alone sufficient to put the subject of slavery at rest; the natural right of self-defence. Under this right, societies imprison and put to death. By this right, nations are justified in attacking other nations, which may league with their foes to do them an injury. And by this right, they are justified, if they see danger at a distance, to anticipate it by precautions. It is allowed on all hands, that danger to the slave-holding States lurks in their existing situation, however it has been produced; and it must be admitted, that the right of self-defence applies to that situation, of the necessity for which the parties exposed to the danger are the natural judges. Otherwise this right, the most sacred of all possessed by men, would be no right at all. I leave to the reader the application of these observations.[62]

Thomas Ritchie, in an editorial on Taylor's book, *Construction Construed,* declared: "The crisis has come." The Missouri question, the tariff question, and the bank question, he thought, made it necessary to come to a decision whether the national government shall be permitted to go on with its usurpations.[63]

---

of the mail, and the accommodation of judges. But horses are undoubtedly more necessary for the conveyance of the mail and for war, than roads, which may be as convenient to assailants as defenders; and therefore the principle of implied power of legislation, will certainly invest Congress with a legislative power over horses. In short, this mode of construction completely establishes the position, that Congress may pass any internal law whatsoever in relation to things, because there is nothing with which war, commerce and taxation may not be closely or remotely connected; and the Constitution does not contain any prohibited degrees of consanguinity. The several departments established by the state constitutions seem indeed to be without the scope of this mode of construction, which can only strip them of their whole wardrobe of rights, and reduce them to a sort of naked political skeletons." *Ibid.*, p. 170.

[61] *Construction Construed,* pp. 291, 292.

[62] *Ibid.*, p. 314.

[63] Beveridge, *op. cit.*, IV: 335. Regarding this work of Taylor, Roane wrote to Jefferson: "Colonel Taylor will be highly gratified by your just and strong testimony in

Taylor's next book, *Tyranny Unmasked,* published in 1822, was an attack on the system of protective tariffs, the reasoning being based upon the model of Adam Smith and the *laissez-faire* school.[64] The greatest danger on the political horizon, as Taylor viewed the situation, was the possibility of an alliance between the government and the special interests desiring public favors, whereby the mechanism of government is utilized to increase the personal wealth of those exercising public authority. Hence, his chief aversions were Hamilton's fiscal policies, Marshall's nationalistic construction of the Constitution, and the depredations made on agriculture by the protective tariff. He joined with many of the southern leaders in opposing, not only the general policy of protective tariffs, but also their constitutionality. Much of the material in *Tyranny Unmasked* had no particular bearing on constitutional interpretation, but the author took occasion to criticize the Supreme Court's practice of nullifying state acts and its solicitude for the protection of special interests. The veto over state acts having been rejected by the federal Convention, Chief Justice Marshall was asserting a national power which Taylor regarded "infinitely more objectionable" and one which amounted to an unwarranted restraining power over the state governments.[65] In interpreting the Constitution so as to secure and protect special interests, Taylor, moreover, characterized Marshall's method as a "mode of construction, which considers the Constitution as a lump of fine gold, a small portion of which is so malleable as to cover the whole mass. By this golden rule for manufacturing the Constitution, a particular power given to the federal government may be made to cover all the rights reserved to the people and the States; a limited jurisdiction given to the federal courts is made to cover all the state courts; and a legislative power over ten miles square is malleated over the whole of the United States, as a single guinea may be beaten out so as to cover a whole house."[66]

Marshall's mode of interpretation, Taylor thought, was equivalent to the insertion of the following amendment to the Constitution: "Congress shall have power to exercise or usurp, and to prohibit the States from exercising, any or all of the powers reserved to the States, whenever they shall deem it convenient, or for the general welfare." Such a doctrine, it

---

favor of his inestimable work. To that work may already, in a measure, be ascribed the revival which has taken place in the subject of state rights." *Branch Historical Papers* (June, 1905), p. 138.

[64] See Simms, *op. cit.,* pp. 192 ff., and Eugene Tenbroeck Mudge, *The Social Philosophy of John Taylor of Caroline* (New York, 1939), pp. 7 ff.

[65] *Tyranny Unmasked,* p. 33.

[66] *Tyranny Unmasked,* pp. 260, 285, 305, 341.

was charged, leads inevitably to civil war. By such a method of judicial construction, Taylor believed, the Supreme Court became the agent of special interests and the people were made the prey of exclusive privileges. In November, 1823, *New Views on the Constitution* came from the press.[67] Taylor's main object in this volume was to bring the Supreme Court into contempt by showing how far afield from its original purpose or design that institution had wandered under the leadership of Chief Justice Marshall.

The point of departure for the conflict, which was becoming a menace to the safety and security of the nation, was considered to be the federal Convention of 1787. According to Taylor, there had been three parties in that body—those who, with Hamilton, desired to create a monarchy; the advocates of a national government; and the friends of the Confederation who, like Luther Martin and others, continually reminded the members of the Convention of the limitations of their powers as contained in their credentials. The monarchists failed, but, adding their strength to the nationalists, were able to deadlock the body. Out of this balancing of parties and interests came a federal, not a national Constitution. Reviewing the instructions given by the legislatures to the delegates appointed to the Philadelphia Convention, Taylor observed that the states "unanimously rejected the recommendation of a *national* government, and by excluding the word national from all their credentials, demonstrated that they well understood the wide difference between *federal* and a *national* union."[68] The rejection of the word "national," as used in the Randolph plan for a Constitution, was to Taylor conclusive evidence that the constructive supremacy now claimed for the federal government was rejected by the Convention. There were in the Convention advocates of a national government invested with supreme power to construe the articles of union, but this plan was replaced by a limited judiciary with defined powers. The right of alteration was, therefore, placed in the states because they made the Constitution, and the right of construction was attached to the altering power, and not given to a national government.[69]

As in his *Construction Construed,* Taylor directed his attack strongly against Marshall's claim of the supremacy of the Judiciary in the interpretation of the Constitution. The supremacy clause of the Constitution, he asserted, neither enlarges nor abridges the powers delegated or reserved, and "it is enforced, not by an oath to be faithful to the supreme constructions of the federal departments, but by an oath to be faithful

---

[67] Simms, *op. cit.,* pp. 197 ff.
[68] *New Views on the Constitution of the United States,* p. 15.
[69] *Ibid.,* p. 23.

to the supremacy of the Constitution."[70] Express provision is made in the Constitution for the supremacy only of the Supreme Court over the inferior courts established by Congress. Cases in law and equity would naturally arise under the Constitution, but the judicial power was extended to such cases only, and not to the principles of the compact, nor to the mechanism of our governmental system. Controversies, continued Taylor,

may arise under the Constitution between political departments, in relation to their powers; between the Senate and the House of Representatives; between the President and the Senate; or between the state and federal departments; but they would not be cases in law and equity, nor is any power to decide them given to the federal Judiciary. One species of controversy relates to the form of government; the other flows from its operation. The power by which a government is formed or altered, is not the power by which the law-suits of individuals are tried; and therefore a power to try suits in law and equity, was never supposed to comprise the former power.[71]

Thus, the primary basis for Taylor's attack on the broad powers Marshall claimed for the Supreme Court was that the Court was in effect exercising political powers. If it had been intended that the Court should decide controversies concerning the extent of the powers of the federal government and the states, this power, Taylor maintained, would have been specified in the Constitution. Taylor believed that the type of Supreme Court conceived by Madison and developed by Marshall destroyed the independence of the departments of the federal government and of the two spheres of government, state and federal, and established a supreme national government contrary to the avowed purposes of the makers of the Constitution. Above all, Taylor objected to the exercise of the power by Judges of declaring laws void, for such decisions, said he: "may affect the lives and properties of citizens, and may implicate the peace of the nation. Opinion may be divided on them. A great majority of Congress, the President, and the people may consider them constitutional; the Judges alone may pronounce them unconstitutional. It is as probable, nay more probable that the Judges should err on this point, than the Legislature, elected for the special purpose of passing laws. Their decision, supported by that of another department of the government and by the people, greatly multiplies the probability on their side."[72] Taylor prophesied that courts with the power of judicial review of legislation would become superlegislatures. And he had little respect for the notion that it was necessary to have the Judges act as sentinels or guardians of the Constitution. The Declaration of Independence, the

[70] *New Views on the Constitution*, pp. 23, 24.
[71] *Ibid.*, p. 134.
[72] Mudge, *op. cit.*, pp. 120–123.

Articles of Confederation, and the Constitution agree upon the principle "that the guardianship of each belonged to the people as organized into States, and they have never surrendered a power, essential for the preservation of liberty, to a chamber of men, inducted, like bishops, for life, by executive selection."[73] In his opinion the Constitution was not turned afloat to be carried hither and thither by the winds and waves of forensic and geographical constructions, without the concurrence in making amendments required to give it stability.

According to Taylor, certain principles were deemed fundamental to the political system of the United States. The first of these is the supremacy of both the state and federal constitutions over the repositories of power created by their articles. This is a limited supremacy, however, subject, in the one instance, to the authority of the people in each state, and in the other, to the control of the people in three-fourths of the states. The second principle is that no power or authority created by these constitutions can violate the articles or evade the supremacies to which the constitutions are themselves subject. From these principles it results "that neither laws nor judgments are valid, which do not conform to constitutions; and that a mutual control of political departments, is the only mode of enforcing this doctrine, necessary to sustain both the supremacy of constitutions, and of those who make them."[74]

One of Taylor's fundamental assumptions was that every species of concentrated sovereignty over extensive territories, whether monarchial, aristocratical, democratical, or mixed, must be despotic. It seemed impossible to him that politicians, whether acting in the capacity of judges or in the legislative halls, could extend the intellectual powers of men beyond their natural limits.[75] "Every body of men invested with supreme power," said he, "whether collected together by the single principle of representation, or by the mixed principles of monarchy, aristocracy, and democracy, is influenced by a secret or an avowed spirit of avarice or ambition." As a consequence, he was as fearful of a concentrated supremacy in Congress as he was of such supremacy in the Supreme Court, except that the unwarranted acts of Congress were more likely to be detected and to be prevented by an aroused public sentiment. But the Court moved silently and stealthily in assuming its supreme censorial functions. On this ground Taylor found objections to the Senate acting as a supreme court of appeal between the nation and the states. He held that only the people, acting through three-fourths of the states by the process of amendment, could perform such a function. Thus, "the security

---

[73] *New Views on the Constitution*, pp. 126, 138 ff.

[74] *Ibid.*, p. 163.

[75] *Ibid.*, pp. 237, 240.

against unconstitutional or inconvenient state acts, is deposited in two-thirds of Congress and three-fourths of the States, as provision for settling collisions between the state and federal governments amicably, and for avoiding the more dangerous conflicts which a supremacy of geographical majorities would produce, if invested with a supremacy liable to geographic fluctuations."[76]

In the formation of the federal government the states endeavored "by limitations and prohibitions, to reserve and secure as many of their individual rights as might be retained without defeating the end of providing for their common interest. The two principles of division or a concentration of power, are the adversaries contending for preference. Every government must be of one or the other description." As Taylor saw it, concentrated power is ever active and ingenious in repairing its defeats and inventing new expedients for the gratification of its desires. And, assuming the role of a prophet, Taylor observed that this same power "proposes that we should renounce our progress in political science, recede by the road of construction, dissolve our new and soundest division of power, and revive a concentrated supremacy, which ultimately will maintain itself by a standing army."[77]

Vigorous objections were raised to Madison's theory of constitutional construction which, by this time, and so far as most questions relating to the division of powers between the nation and the states were concerned, sanctioned the supremacy of the Judiciary. Hamilton contended that the Convention had divided sovereignty between the federal government and the states, but one, namely, the federal, was supreme over the other. Hamilton's supremacy, however, was bestowed on a national government under the control of the people, whereas Madison's was confided to a court not under the control of the people.[78]

"Judge Construction," as Marshall was called, was held up to ridicule, for it was possible for the Chief Justice to find some word or omission in the Constitution to sanction all of his nationalistic designs. Taylor thought, however, that:

The delegations, reservations, and prohibitions of the Constitution, combined with the rejection of powers proposed in the Convention, constitute a mass of evidence, more coherent and irrefragable for ascertaining the principles of our political system, than can be exhibited by any other country; and if it cannot resist the arts of construction, constitutions are feeble obstacles to ambition, and ineffectual barriers against tyranny. Delegations are limitations; reservations are repetitions of these limitations; prohibitions expound the extent of reservations; and rejections of powers proposed in the Convention, are constructions forbidding their assumption. This mass of evidence stands opposed to those constructions which are laboring to invest the federal government

[76] *Ibid.*, p. 256.   [77] *Ibid.*, pp. 238, 239, 243.   [78] *Ibid.*, p. 76.

with powers to abridge the state right of taxation; to control States by a power to legislate for ten miles square; to expend the money belonging to the United States without
control; to enrich a local capitalist interest at the expense of the people; to create corporations for abridging state rights; to make roads and canals; and finally to empower
the Supreme Court to exercise a complete negative power over state laws and judgments, and an affirmative power as to federal laws.[79]

Starting with the proposition that the states were recognized as free
and independent in the Declaration of Independence and that each state
retained its sovereignty under the Articles of Confederation and that
no express language in the federal Constitution provided for a consolidation of the states, Taylor concluded that the states remain sovereign
and possessed of all powers they have not expressly granted to a general
government. Since the states, in creating the federal government, exercised the highest act of sovereignty, they may, if they please, repeat the
proof of their sovereignty by annihilating it.[80] The fact that the states
adopted the Constitution by means of conventions did not mean, as
Marshall insisted, that the people adopted the instrument. Adoption was
by states, as states. Despite such unimpeachable evidence, the Supreme
Court, comprised of "refined politicians," was engaged in destroying the
sovereignty of twenty-four states by the acuteness of construction. Taylor
deemed it a mockery to speak of the sovereignty of the states and the
supremacy of the federal Judiciary. Marshall's contention that the state
governments might obstruct federal measures, unless they were subordinate to some federal agency, was only equivalent to the claim that the
federal government might obstruct state measures, unless it was subordinate to state supremacy. Neither contention was deemed valid, since
the Constitution provided no method of adjustment for the conflicts
between the nation and the states except by mutual concessions, agreement, and compromise.

Agreeing with Jefferson, Taylor thought that each department had
the unlimited authority to determine the limits of their own respective
rights and powers. Minor conflicts would not, in his opinion, disturb the
proper functioning of the governmental system. Major conflicts would
have to be referred to the original source of power—the people. Upon the
contention which was repeated many times in the arguments over the
adoption of the Constitution and was often referred to later, namely,
that in cases of usurpation of powers by the federal government the
natural and effective agencies for protection were the individual states,
Taylor commented as follows:

It may safely be received as an axiom in our political system, that the state governments will, in all possible contingencies, afford complete security against invasions of

[79] *New Views on the Constitution,* pp. 155, 156.   [80] *Ibid.,* p. 37.

the public liberty by the *national* authority. Projects of usurpation cannot be masked under pretences so likely to escape the penetration of select bodies of men, as of the people at large. The legislature will have better means of information; they can discover the danger at a distance; and possessing all the organs of civil power, and the confidence of the people, they can at once adopt a regular plan of opposition, in which they can combine all the resources of the community. They can readily communicate with each other in the different States; and unite their common forces for the protection of their common liberty. If the federal army should be able to quell the resistance in one State, the distant States would have it in their power to make head with fresh forces. The people are in a situation, through the medium of their state governments, to take measures for their own defence, with all the celerity, regularity, and system, of *independent nations*.

But of what use is this eulogised capacity in state legislatures to discover usurpations, if they cannot constitutionally resist them; and how can they resist usurpations, if they are subjected by a Constitution to a sovereignty or supremacy in the usurper? The people of each State are recognized as independent nations; and the state governments not as judicial, but as political departments, intended to watch over the constitutional rights of these nations, and invested with a power to resist federal usurpations. They are recognized as possessing all the organs of power necessary to discharge the important duty of breaking the snares of tyranny, by which the people are frequently caught, for want of the means of discovering the danger, which these select bodies of men possess. It is even admitted that the state governments may form regular plans of opposition, and appeal to arms for the defence of their rights. But what becomes of this whole fabric intended by the Constitution to preserve the rights and liberty of the people, if the federal government is sovereign, or the federal court supreme? What becomes of the essential right in these independent nations to control their governments for the preservation of the Union, if these governments cannot control a sovereignty or supremacy, usurped for the purpose of destroying the Union by a consolidated national government? Of what value is the responsibility of state governments to the people, when it is liable to be rendered inefficient by a supremacy in a federal court? How can the people cherish or preserve the Union, if its preservation depends on this Court, and not on their state governments? What good can the people reap from the intelligence and foresight of their state governments, if the supreme mandate of this Court can forbid them from seeing or resisting usurpations? Where lies the mutual check between the two governments, if a supreme power to expound the articles of the Union, is thrown into the scale of one by construction? By this contrivance, the influence of the people over their state governments, urged as necessary for the preservation of their rights, both state and federal, is transferred from them to a federal Court. The state governments may still "adopt regular plans of opposition." Opposition must therefore be constitutional. They may even oppose armies to armies. Why then may they not array laws against laws, and judgments against judgments?[81]

The fact was deplored that a superiority of talents has appeared and is likely to continue to appear on the side of "a high-toned system of government." Alluding to the propaganda of the nationalists, Taylor notes that many pamphlets and essays have appeared for the purpose of proving that a supreme national government was, or ought to have

---

[81] *New Views on the Constitution*, pp. 70, 71.

been, established by the Constitution, and that the newspapers contained frequent expressions of opinion favorable to such a government. Caricaturing some of the reasoning of the nationalists, Taylor says: "The natural right of a government to supremacy is completely sustained by the natural supremacy of construction, as it could not be a government, if this supremacy of construction belonged to the people who wished to control it." The caricature of the supposed reasoning of the nationalists was concluded by comparing their methods of construction to Swift's allegorical implications in "A Tale of a Tub."

Taylor's state sovereignty doctrine was summed up as follows:

By these political individual entities, called States, the Constitution was framed; by these individual entities it was ratified; and by these entities it can only be altered. It was made by them and for them, and not by or for a nation of Americans. The people of each State, or each State as constituted by a people, conveyed to a federal authority, organized by States, a portion of state sovereign powers, and retained another portion. In this division, all the details of the Constitution are comprised, one dividend consisting of the special powers conferred upon a federal government, and the other, of the powers reserved by the States which conferred these special powers. The deputation and reservation are both bottomed upon the sovereignty of the States, and must both fall or both stand with that principle. If each State, or the people of each State, did not possess a separate sovereignty, they had no right to convey or retain powers. If they had a right both to convey and to retain powers, it could only be in virtue of state sovereignty. Admitting the utmost which can be asked, and more than ought to be conceded, by supposing that these sovereignties, in conveying limited powers to the federal government, conveyed also a portion of sovereignty, it must also be allowed, that by retaining powers, they retained also a portion of sovereignty. If sovereignty was attached to the ceded powers, it was also attached to the powers not ceded, because all or none of the powers of the States must have proceeded from this principle.

Having proved that state sovereignties were established by the Declaration of Independence; that their existence was asserted by the Confederation of 1777; that they are recognized by the Constitution of 1787, in the modes of its formation, ratification, and amendment; that this Constitution employs the same words to describe the United States, used by the two preceding instruments; that the word State implies a sovereign community; that each State contained an associated people; that an American people never existed; that the Constitution was ordained and established, for such States situated in America, as might accede to a Union; that its limited powers was a partial and voluntary endowment of state sovereignties, to be exercised by a Congress of the States which should unite; that the word Congress implies a deputation from sovereignties, and was so expounded by the Confederation; and that a reservation of sovereign powers cannot be executed without sovereignty; the reader will consider, whether all these principles, essential for the preservation both of the federal and state governments, were intended to be destroyed by the details of the Constitution.[82]

There was, therefore, to be no superior department in the American political system—no final authority. Unappropriated powers were to be

[82] *New Views on the Constitution*, pp. 173–176.

state powers, whereas specified powers only were to be exercised by the federal government. If states encroached upon the general government, there was to be no redress; neither was there recourse if the federal authority transcended its bounds.

Taylor's books, *Construction Construed and Constitutions Vindicated, Tyranny Unmasked,* and *New Views on the Constitution,* presented the most elaborate and effective arguments against the proposals and designs of Alexander Hamilton and of those who agreed with his ideas of a federal form of government by the substitution of a centralized system, which would shift the balance of power from the states to the national government. To Taylor, the nationalistic program of the federal government, including Hamilton's funding measures, the national bank acts, as well as tariff and internal improvement acts, were unconstitutional.[83]

Indicating how serious men regarded the situation relating to the conflict between state and federal powers, Jefferson, expressing his approval of the views of Roane and Taylor, said: "The Judiciary branch is the instrument which, working like gravity, without intermission, is to press us at last into one consolidated mass. Against this I know no one who, equally with Judge Roane himself, possesses the power and the courage to make resistance; and to him I look, and have long looked, as our strongest bulwark. If Congress fails to shield the States from dangers so palpable and so imminent, the States must shield themselves, and meet the invader foot to foot. This is already half done by Colonel Taylor's book [*Construction Construed*]. . . . This book is the most effective retraction of our government to its original principles which has ever yet been sent by heaven to our aid."[84]

And in a letter to Nathaniel Macon, commenting on John Taylor's *Construction Construed,* Jefferson wrote, on August 18, 1821, "it has long, however, been my opinion, and I have never shrunk from its expression . . . that the germ of dissolution of our federal government is in the constitution of the federal Judiciary; an irresponsible body (for impeachment is scarcely a scare-crow) working, like gravity, by day and night, gaining a little today and a little tomorrow, and advancing its noiseless step, like a thief over the fields of jurisdiction, until all shall be usurped from the States, the government of all becoming a consolidated one. To this I am opposed; because whenever all government, domestic and foreign, in little as in great things shall be drawn to Washington as the center of all power, it will render powerless the checks provided, of one government on another and will become as venal and oppressive

[83] Mudge, *op. cit.,* pp. 60, 61.
[84] *Writings* (Foid ed)., X: 184.

as the government from which we departed."[85] Roane and Taylor followed the practice of Jefferson and Madison, as well as many others who were in the habit of asserting the doctrine of state sovereignty, that is, they referred to the government of the United States as a "general government." They strenuously objected to the use of the words "national" or "supreme" in relation to the authority granted to federal authorities by the Constitution.[86]

Marshall was alarmed and confided to Story that "the opinion of the Supreme Court in the Lottery Case has been assaulted with a degree of virulence transcending what has appeared on any former occasion. . . . I think for coarseness and malignity of invention Algernon Sydney surpasses all party writers who have ever made pretensions to any decency of character. There is on this subject no such thing as a free press in Virginia, and of consequence the calumnies and misrepresentations of this gentleman will remain uncontradicted and will by many be believed to be true. He will be supposed to be the champion of state rights, instead of being what he really is, the champion of dismemberment."[87] A month later he wrote in a pessimistic mood that things in Virginia were verging rapidly "to the destruction of the government and the re-establishment of a league of sovereign States. I look elsewhere for safety." Marshall's views had definitely and finally been repudiated by his own state and it was in the North and West that support for his doctrines of nationalism had to be found.

The situation, as Marshall saw it, was so threatening that he thought the friends of the Constitution should take active and aggressive measures, for, said he,

a deep sign to convert our government into a mere league of States has taken a strong hold of a powerful and violent party in Virginia. The attack upon the Judiciary is in fact an attack upon the Union. The judicial department is well understood to be that through which the government may be attacked most successfully, because it is without patronage, and of course without power. And it is equally well understood that every subtraction from its jurisdiction is a vital wound to the government itself. The whole attack, if not originating with Mr. Jefferson, is obviously approved and guided by him. It is therefore formidable in other States as well as in this, and it behooves the friends of the Union to be more on the alert than they have been. An effort will certainly be made to repeal the 25th section of the Judiciary Act.[88]

---

[85] Letter submitted to the editor of *The Nation* by Professor William E. Dodd and published Apr. 15, 1909.

[86] For a similar characterization of the federal government, see dissenting opinion of Justice Johnson in Brown v. Maryland, 12 Wheaton 452 (1827).

[87] Letter of June 15, 1821, *Proceedings*, Mass. Hist. Soc., 2d ser., XIV: 327, 328; and John Edward Oster, *The Political and Economic Doctrines of John Marshall* (New York, 1914), pp. 111, 112.

[88] *Proceedings*, Mass. Hist. Soc., 2d ser., XIV: 330, 331; and Oster, *op. cit.*, pp. 115, 116.

The case of *Cohens v. Virginia* is one of the best examples of Marshall's method of interpreting the language of the Constitution—in accordance with his own political hypotheses or assumptions. These are essentially the hypotheses or assumptions of the nationalist or "organic" viewpoint in considering the facts and events of American historical development to which attention was directed in a previous chapter.[89] It has been noted that if the jurisdictional question had first been considered, there would have been no occasion or justification for a lengthy opinion on the relations between the nation and the states in the American federal system. But the repetition and the growing insistence upon what were to Marshall the Republican heresies regarding the rights, powers, and sovereignty of the states prompted him to step aside from the strict line of his judicial duties and to write one more state paper on what should be the federal relationships established by the Constitution.

In the first place, Article III, section 2 of the Constitution was considered and applied separate from and independent of the necessary modifications and implications resulting from the adoption of the Tenth and Eleventh Amendments. These amendments, designed to check the nationalistic tendencies of the Constitution and the decisions of the Supreme Court, might have been interpreted as a mandate subsequent to the adoption of the article granting jurisdiction to the federal courts directing them not to enlarge the powers of the federal Judiciary by the process of judicial construction. On the other hand, it was assumed throughout Marshall's opinion that in the framing and adoption of the Constitution a nation or a federation was called into being and that it was the duty of all those connected with the federal government to see that this nation was not only to be preserved but also that its powers were to be enlarged. Not finding the intention to form a national government with the desired supremacy over the states written out in express language in the Constitution, Marshall turned to the preamble for support for his nationalistic doctrines. Because, in his opinion, the decisions of the state tribunals on constitutional questions would not be impartial, and because "mischievious consequences" would follow from the exercise of a state veto on powers assumed by the federal government, it was concluded that it was not only expedient but also absolutely necessary for the federal government to have supreme powers. If the federal government was to endure "for ages to come," it must possess the authority to execute its own laws, and the courts, it was assumed, were not only the most appropriate but also the most effective agency to secure such execution. But, as John Taylor observed, there is no indication in the Consti-

---

[89] See above, chap. iii.

tution that a greater responsibility was placed in the hands of the federal Judges than the state judges in seeing that the Constitution was enforced and preserved. With but few exceptions, the provisions of the Constitution were predicated upon confidence rather than a distrust in public men, whether in the state or federal governments.

Assuming, however, on grounds of convenience and of necessity, that the Supreme Court was authorized to decide all cases of every description arising under the Constitution and laws of the United States, though no such broad powers of review had been sanctioned by Congress whose duty it was to regulate the appellate jurisdiction of the Court, it was held that the authority to decide such cases belonged to the Court, unless there was an express prohibition against the exercise of such jurisdiction. In the case of *McCulloch v. Maryland* the principle that powers not expressly granted to the federal government belong to the states was turned about so that with a grant of jurisdiction in general terms the limitations and restrictions on this grant must be explicit in the Constitution. The fact that it was almost universally conceded by the Federalists or nationalists, as well as by practically all of the Anti-Federalists, when the Constitution containing these particular jurisdiction provisions was adopted, that a state might not be sued without its consent was ignored, and it was asserted that such consent may be given by a surrender of a part of sovereignty. But when was such a vital phase of sovereignty, such as the grant of permission to be sued without their consent, surrendered by the states?

Marshall claimed that the argument for the state of Virginia was founded, not on the words of the Constitution, but on its spirit, and was based on a particular view of the nature of the union, and of the great fundamental principles on which the fabric stands. But did not Marshall's conclusions also arise from the spirit and fundamental principles of the document as he saw them? To him the great and overruling need was a uniformity in the decisions concerning and a "correctness in expounding the Constitution and laws of the United States." This uniformity and correctness could, he thought, be secured only with a single tribunal which had final and authoritative power to determine the meaning of the Constitution. But was this mode of interpreting the fundamental law not one of the main principles of the Federalist party, rather than a rule or principle which was explicitly provided for in the Constitution? And was not the Supreme Court giving its support and prestige to one of the political groups which were engaged in the contests for political preferment in the nation and to the group which was then in a minority?

The Constitution provided that the Constitution itself was the supreme law of the land and judges in every state were to be bound thereby, anything in the constitution or laws of a state to the contrary notwithstanding. But was the binding obligation of the federal Constitution a legal obligation subject to enforcement by federal agencies or a moral obligation rather of the type that obligated all officers, state and federal, to regard the Constitution as the standard by which their public conduct was to be guided? And was it not the latter view which was prevalent at the time the Constitution was adopted? The fact that Marshall was construing the Constitution in the direction of a growing nationalist sentiment and feeling, which prevented a repudiation of the Court's constitutional doctrines and which checked both the movements to reorganize the Court and to repeal the twenty-fifth section of the Judiciary Act, may well be lauded today as the political development of a century and a half is surveyed, but it was the political significance of these decisions which called forth some vitriolic attacks upon the Supreme Court in the halls of Congress and in the state legislatures.

CHAPTER XIII

Attacks upon the Jurisdiction and Authority of the Supreme Court by Kentucky, Ohio, and New York

FREDERICK JACKSON TURNER commented on "the joyous outburst of nationalism" which followed the War of 1812—a nationalism which was expressed in measures passed by Congress and in the decisions of the Supreme Court.[1] But it was not long before a reaction came against this outburst of nationalism. The reaction took the form of protests against the loose-construction tendencies of Congress and criticisms of the decisions of the Supreme Court. By 1820 men were beginning to think primarily in terms of the protection of interests and the adjustment of relations among the several sections of the country, and by 1830 American politics had become essentially a struggle for power among these sections.

The chief objections to the decisions of the Supreme Court, which gradually became more general and more persistent after the decision in the case of *Cohens v. Virginia*,[2] were directed against the broad interpretation of the Constitution. Marshall and Story were considered to be primarily responsible for this situation which was thought to be leading toward a consolidated government and as involving an interference with the rights of the states by declaring state acts invalid.

Though five out of the seven Supreme Court Justices were Democrats appointed by Democratic Presidents, the decisions of the Court were considered as opposed to the principles of democracy and of republicanism. On constitutional issues all of the Justices except Johnson were regarded as ultra-Federalists.[3] To the Democrats John Marshall appeared as the supreme politician masquerading under the cloak of a Justice, and Joseph Story as the tool of Daniel Webster. On the other hand, the necessity of a broad construction of the Constitution to prevent the control of the government by the South was defended by the Federalists. Though they

---

[1] Frederick Jackson Turner, *Rise of the New West, 1819–1829* (New York, 1906), p. 4.
[2] 6 Wheaton 266 (1821).
[3] See opinion of Thomas Cooper of South Carolina, *Amer. Hist. Rev.* (July, 1901), VI: 729.

were mostly from the northern states, they anticipated that all departments of government would soon be dominated by the slave states.[4]

Opposition to the Supreme Court and the criticisms of its decisions aroused by the case of *Cohens v. Virginia* had scarcely subsided when another decision irritated and aroused public resentment in Kentucky. By the ordinance of separation between Virginia and Kentucky it was agreed that all private rights and interests in Kentucky lands derived from the laws of Virginia shall be determined by the laws then in force in Virginia. To settle many disputed claims to lands, Kentucky passed an act in 1797 which provided that persons occupying lands in the state who could show a clear and connected title could not, without notice of adverse title, be held liable for rents and profits during such occupancy. All permanent improvements made on the land must, in the instance of eviction, be deducted from the value of the land as against the successful claimant. In 1812 the legislature amended the so-called "occupant-claimant" law by providing that when any improvements were made on lands which a person believed to be his own, because of a then valid and recorded claim, such person was to receive payment for these improvements from anyone who was later declared to be the legal owner of the lands.[5] Virginia and Kentucky agreed, under the compact of separation, to submit to commissioners the adjustment of differences which would arise between the states. On the occupant-claimant dispute Kentucky agreed to arbitrate and appointed commissioners.[6] But Virginia, declining to be bound by the terms of the compact, refused to appoint commissioners and made it clear that the state preferred to have the validity of the claimant laws determined by the Supreme Court of the United States. A case soon arose to bring about the result which Virginia desired.

GREEN V. BIDDLE AND THE CONFLICT WITH KENTUCKY

Green and Biddle, both claiming title to the same land, brought a case in the lower federal courts to test the validity of the Kentucky occupant-claimant laws, which, owing to a division of opinion among the judges, was brought to the Supreme Court on a writ of error. The case was first argued in February, 1821, and reargued in March, 1822. Justice Story

---

[4] *The Life and Correspondence of Rufus King*, ed. by Charles R. King (New York, 1894), VI: 267.

[5] This law was held valid by the state supreme court in Fowler v. Halbert, 4 Bibb. 52 (1815).

[6] See *Niles' Register*, XXI: 404, 405. This sets forth a copy of the resolutions adopted by the Kentucky legislature instructing the commissioners representing the state to arbitrate the matters in dispute, if possible, and if the arbitration was unsuccessful, to oppose any decision procured from the Supreme Court that the claimant laws were void.

rendered the first opinion of the Court and stated the general rule that in a transfer of sovereignty titles to land are determined in accordance with the laws under which they were acquired and that the compact between Virginia and Kentucky, so far as land titles were concerned, merely gave declaratory effect to this principle.[7] The acts of Kentucky, Story thought, materially impaired the rights and interests of the rightful owner in the land, and as such they are parts of a system whose object is to compel the owner, without his consent, to relinquish his lands or to pay for lasting improvements made upon them. Since the compact affirming general legal principles aimed to secure all the private rights and interests derived from the laws of Virginia as valid under the laws of Kentucky, Justice Story stated that it was the unanimous opinion of the Court that the Kentucky acts of 1797 and 1812 were invalid.

No attorney having appeared for the tenants, Henry Clay, as *amicus curiae,* sought a rehearing because of the disastrous effect of the decision upon the rights and claims of numerous occupants of land in Kentucky. The decree was deferred and reargument permitted. Supporting the claims of the Kentucky tenants, Clay contended that the compact between Virginia and Kentucky had never been expressly approved by Congress, as required by the Constitution, and was therefore invalid so far as it affected the rights of land ownership in Kentucky. The terms of the compact, in his opinion, constituted a marked restriction upon the sovereign rights of Kentucky and, as such, was contrary to the true theory of our government which is predicated upon the principle of perfect equality among the states. Speaking with prophetic wisdom, Clay asserted: "This Court is not a mere court of justice applying ordinary laws. It is a political tribunal, and may look to political considerations and consequences. If there be doubt, ought the settled policy of a State, and its rules of property, to be disturbed?"[8] In a move favorable to the original owners, it was pointed out that the compact between Virginia and Kentucky was in effect approved by Congress in the act admitting Kentucky to the union and that the validity of the compact had been officially recognized by the authorities of both states.

An entire week was given to the reargument of the case, and, as the Court was aware of the seriousness of the adverse sentiments already aroused in Ohio, Virginia, Maryland, Kentucky, and other states, the case was held under consideration for a year. Thus, it had first arisen in 1819, reached the Supreme Court in 1821 for the first time, was reargued in 1822, and the final decision was given in 1823. But in spite of the

---

[7] Green v. Biddle, 8 Wheaton 15 (1823).
[8] 8 Wheaton 57.

seriousness of the situation, the Court adhered to its former views. Realizing the resentment which decisions of the Supreme Court had aroused, Justice Washington, speaking for the Court, said: "We hold ourselves answerable to God, our consciences, and our country, to decide this question according to the dictates of our best judgment, be the consequences of the decision what they may."[9] It was obvious, thought Washington, that the Kentucky acts interfered with the rights and interests of the owners of property in Kentucky who had acquired title under the laws of Virginia and hence were an unjustifiable and invalid interference with such rights. The rights of the parties were held to be determined by a compact to which both states agreed and which had been approved by Congress, and Kentucky could not legally violate these rights. Both Justices Story and Washington based their opinions upon general principles of right and justice rather than upon the express language of the federal Constitution.

Justice Johnson, dissenting, charged that the majority opinion cut deep into the sovereign powers of Kentucky and irrevocably fastened the land laws of Virginia upon two-thirds of the territory of Kentucky. "I cannot admit," said he, "that it was ever the intention of the framers of this Constitution, or of the parties to this compact, or of the United States, in sanctioning that compact, that Kentucky should be forever chained down to a state of hopeless imbecility."[10] Since the laws of Virginia had created a state of confusion relative to land titles in this country, Johnson regarded it as well within the authority of Kentucky to provide some security for those who had bestowed labor and expense in developing the country and to assure to the tenant in charge that where the successful claimant recovered his land, enhanced in value by the labors of another, he should be required to make compensation for the enhanced value.

When the decision was announced, the people of Kentucky strongly opposed such interference with their local affairs. Governor Adair, in his message to the legislature, warned the people of the dire results which would follow from the decisions of the Supreme Court. "I need not be told," he continued, "that the general government is authorized to use physical force to put down insurrection and enforce the execution of its laws, I know it; but I know too, with equal certainty, that the day when the government shall be compelled to resort to the bayonet, to compel a State to submit to its law, will not long precede an event of all others to be deprecated." Referring to the effect of the Court's decision on the property and pecuniary relations of the community, Gov-

---

[9] 8 Wheaton 93.   [10] *Ibid.*, p. 104.

ernor Adair said: "The principles they would establish, and the effects they would produce, sink much deeper, and would produce infinitely more permanent evils. They strike at the sovereignty of the State, and the right of the people to govern themselves. It is in this view that they have been contemplated, and justly excited the apprehensions of the most intelligent and sober minded members of the community."[11]

The legislature passed a series of resolutions protesting against "the erroneous, injurious and degrading doctrines of the opinion of the Supreme Court," and it was resolved to present to the Congress "a temperate but firm remonstrance against its doctrines, and therein to call upon the Nation to guarantee to the State its co-equal sovereignty with the States which compose the Union, and also to request Congress therein, so to organize the Supreme Court of the United States that no constitutional question growing out of the Constitution of the United States, or the constitution of either of the States, involving the validity of state laws, shall be decided by said Court unless two-thirds of all the members belonging to said Court shall concur in such decision."[12] This proposal was made because it was asserted that the decision was rendered by only three Justices—three being absent and one dissenting. Warren notes, however, that the records of the Supreme Court substantiate the fact that six Justices, all except Washington, were present at the time of the argument in *Green v. Biddle* and that five Justices were present, with Johnson dissenting, when the opinion was rendered. This record, Warren thinks, bears out the statement of Justice Washington that in rendering his opinion he was speaking for a majority of the Court.[13] Whether Warren's analysis is correct or not, the general impression was that it was a three-Judge decision. This impression was based upon the fact that Justices Todd and Livingston were ill; Chief Justice Marshall did not sit; and Justice Johnson dissented. The explanation that Todd and Livingston agreed with the decision did not prevent attacks upon what was generally regarded to be a minority opinion.[14] In view of the cir-

[11] Herman V. Ames, *State Documents on Federal Relations* (Philadelphia, 1906), p. 106, and *Niles' Register*, XXV: 205.

[12] Ames, *op. cit.*, pp. 107, 108.

[13] Charles Warren, "Legislative and Judicial Attacks on the Supreme Court of the United States—A History of the Twenty-Fifth Section of the Judiciary Act," 47 *Amer. Law Rev.* (Jan., Feb., 1913), 23. For the opposite view see speech of Representative Wickliffe in Congress on Jan. 11, 1826, *Cong. Debates*, II, pt. 1, and statement of Judge Mills in Fisher v. Cockerill, 5 T. B. Monroe 129, 133 (1829).

[14] In *Bodley v. Garther* the Kentucky court of appeals refused to accept the binding authority of the decision of the Supreme Court. Said the court: "For the case of Green v. Biddle, was decided by three only of the seven Judges that compose the Supreme Court of the United States; and being the opinion of less than a majority of the Judges,

cumstances and conditions the Kentucky assembly declared that they consider the decision of the Supreme Court incompatible with the constitutional powers of the state and highly injurious to the best interests of the people.[15] A year later the legislature again protested that

the injury inflicted upon the people, great and extensive as it is, and much as it is deplored, weighs but comparatively little with these remonstrants. It is the *principle* which that decision establishes at which they *shudder,* and with which they can never be reconciled. The people of Kentucky ... can bear anything but degradation and disfranchisement. They can not bear to be construed out of their right of self-government; they value their freedom above everything else, and are as little inclined to be *reasoned* out of it as they would be to surrender it to *foreign force.*[16]

To counteract the decision of the Supreme Court, the Kentucky legislature passed an act in 1824 forfeiting the title of all persons owning a hundred acres or more of land, unless they cleared and fenced a part of the tract within a year, and granting title to the person in possession. This act was held void by the Kentucky court of appeals.[17] Securing no favorable action on their remonstrance, the house of representatives of the state requested the governor to inform them of "the mode deemed most advisable in the opinion of the executive to refuse obedience to the decisions and mandates of the Supreme Court of the United States, considered erroneous and unconstitutional, and whether, in the opinion of the executive, it may be advisable to call forth the physical power of the State to resist the execution of the decisions of the Court, or in what manner the mandates of said Court should be met by disobedience."[18] The governor refused to comply with the request and suggested the continuance of "pacific measures" through appeals to Congress. Governor

cannot be considered as having settled any constitutional principle." T. B. Monroe 57, 59 (1825).

Representative Buckner referred to the decision as follows: "The validity of those laws had, to be sure, been tested in the crucible of judicial investigation, in both the inferior and superior courts of that State, and had been uniformly supported, both by the judges of that State, and by a very large majority of its ablest lawyers; and, when decided upon in the Supreme Court of the United States, of the four Judges on the bench, one was in favor of them. But the opinion of the three determined the principles, and Kentucky was thus bound to abandon a policy which she regarded as essential to the improvement of the State and the security and repose of her citizens." *Cong. Debates,* II, pt. 1, 19th Cong., 1st sess. (1825–1826), p. 1003.

[15] *Niles' Register,* XXI: 404, 405.

[16] *Acts of Kentucky,* 1823–1824, 520–527, and Ames, *op. cit.,* p. 110.

[17] Gaines v. Buford, 1 Dana 481 (1833). See reference in this case to "the sinister operation of the decision of the Supreme Court against our occupant laws."

[18] Ames, *op. cit.,* pp. 108 ff., and *Niles' Register,* XXIX: 228, 229. Commenting on the fact that the majority of the members of the Kentucky house of representatives agreed with the governor in his objection to certain decisions of the state supreme court and of the Supreme Court of the United States, the editor of *Niles' Register* observed that

Desha in his message to the legislature on November 7, 1825, referring to the failure to secure redress in the case, said:

in fact, most of the encroachments made by the general government flow through the Supreme Court itself, the very tribunal which claims to be the final arbiter of all such disputes. What chance for justice have the States when the usurpers of their rights are made their Judges? Just as much as individuals when judged by their oppressors. It is therefore believed to be the right, as it may hereafter become the duty of the state governments, to protect themselves from encroachments, and their citizens from oppression, by refusing obedience to the unconstitutional mandates of the federal Judges.[19]

As the governor was not inclined to assume the responsibility for the use of physical force, a feeble resistance was continued until 1831, when a second decision of the Supreme Court was accepted as final by the state authorities.[20]

To Senator Johnson of Kentucky, who was arguing in Congress in favor of proposals to limit the jurisdiction of the federal courts, the decision of the Supreme Court in this case set aside the policy which the state had pursued in relation to land titles for several decades. The effect is, said he, "to legislate for the people, to regulate the interior policy of that community, and to establish their municipal code as to real estate."[21]

For a number of years attacks on the Court continued in the legislature and bills were introduced in Congress and supported by the members of Congress designed to restrict the powers of the Court, either through the repeal of the twenty-fifth section of the Judiciary Act, or the requirement of more than a majority of the Justices to annul state acts. Because of the personal interests of many of her citizens, Virginia supported the exercise of jurisdiction by the Supreme Court in spite of the opposition to the exercise of such jurisdiction in the *Cohens Case.* "Again," remarks Charles Warren, "it was made plain that state opposition to judicial action depended, not so much on the political theory held by the States, as on the particular interest aided or injured."[22]

Kentucky also protested vigorously against the interference of the federal courts with the enforcement of her stay laws. In *Wayman v. South-*

"there must be a power in every country from whose judgment there cannot safely be any appeal—that power, in the United States, belongs to its sovereign citizens! But they have seemingly delegated it to the Supreme Court, if more fully or firmly than they designed that it should be (as, in my opinion, they have), they have a right to recall it by amendments to the Constitution—not by a *juggle,* as proposed by holding a caucus to make a president, or by *force of arms,* as some seem almost willing to resort to in Kentucky." XXV: 195.

[19] *Ibid.,* p. 113.
[20] Hawkins v. Barney's Lessee, 5 Peters 457.
[21] 38 *Annals,* 17th Cong., 1st sess., p. 104.
[22] *The Supreme Court in United States History* (Boston, 1922), II: 102.

ard[23] the question was raised whether the common law, as modified by acts of Congress and the rules of the federal courts, must govern the officer in all the proceedings upon executions involving the contested land laws of Kentucky. The assertion that proceedings in such cases must be governed solely by state laws is rejected. Referring to the clause of the Constitution granting jurisdiction to the federal courts, Marshall said: "That a power to make laws for carrying into execution all the judgments which the judicial department has power to pronounce, is expressly conferred by this clause, seems to me one of those plain propositions which reasoning cannot render plainer."[24] The practice of the federal courts and the conduct of their officers, he maintained, cannot be regulated either directly or indirectly by the state.

Three cases were brought to test the power of the inferior federal courts to require the levying of executions in a manner other than that prescribed by the laws of Kentucky. They were the *Wayman Case, Bank of United States v. Halstead,*[25] and *Bank of United States v. January.*[26] The state was anxious to obtain a decision on the point involving the levying of executions, and the bank desired to test the constitutionality of the state stay and replevin laws. This was the first opportunity for having a high court examination of these laws, because the state court of appeals had hitherto held the laws invalid, precluding bringing the case up for an opinion of the Supreme Court of the United States. When the opinion was announced it avoided the issue of the constitutionality of the state laws but dealt a blow to the debtor interests of Kentucky which was almost as serious, since it held in effect that no state laws in regard to levying executions or replevy of property sold to satisfy judgment were binding upon the courts. The result was that any creditor who was not a citizen of Kentucky could escape the restrictions of the state laws by suing in the federal courts; thus, the state law, which had been enacted mainly to attack the obnoxious Bank of the United States, was of no avail. Citizens of Kentucky again protested vigorously, believing "that a judicial tyranny was secretly creeping in upon us." Kentucky was brought to the verge of open rebellion against the Court; other states with similar stay laws viewed the opinions with alarm; and the movement for judiciary reform in Congress waxed stronger.

When the Kentucky courts held the stay laws void, being in violation of the contract clause of the Constitution, the legislature abolished the court of appeals and set up a new court to which judges known to be

---

[23] 10 Wheaton 1 (1825).
[24] 10 Wheaton 22 (1825).
[25] *Ibid.,* p. 51.
[26] *Ibid.,* p. 66.

favorable to these acts were appointed. But when the legislative attempt
to interfere with the authority of the supreme court was brought before
the court of appeals, it was held ineffectual for want of legislative power.
The judges appointed to the new positions were held to be neither officers
de jure nor *de facto*.[27]

In *Elmendorf v. Taylor*,[28] a case involving the construction of laws
relating to Kentucky land titles, the Chief Justice attempted to allay some
of the feeling aroused by previous decisions by declaring that it was the
duty of the federal courts to accept the decisions of the state courts relative to the interpretation of local laws. This Court, observed Marshall,
"has uniformly professed its disposition, in cases depending on the laws
of a particular State, to adopt the construction which the courts of the
State have given to those laws. This course is founded on the principle,
supposed to be universally recognized, that the judicial department of
every government, where such department exists, is the appropriate
organ for construing the legislative acts of that government. . . . On this
principle, the construction given by this Court to the Constitution and
laws of the United States is received by all as the true construction; and
on the same principle, the construction given by the courts of the several
States to the legislative acts of those States, is received as true, unless they
come in conflict with the Constitution, laws, or treaties of the United
States. If, then, this question has been settled in Kentucky, we must suppose it to be rightly settled."[29]

The resentment against and resistance to the decisions of the federal
courts in Kentucky were duplicated in the contest of Ohio to tax a branch
of the Bank of the United States despite the decision of the Supreme
Court in *McCulloch v. Maryland*.[30] It was the western states, and not
Maryland and Virginia, that were now carrying the brunt of the attack
against what appeared to be encroachments on state powers by judicial
construction.

Ohio's Attack on the National Bank

The controversy over the establishment of branches of the Bank of the
United States in Ohio was at first largely an issue economic and financial
in nature. At this time the banks of Ohio supplied a circulating medium
greatly in excess of the needs of the people. When branches of the Bank
of the United States were established at Cincinnati and Chillicothe a

[27] Hildreth's Heirs v. McIntire's Devisee, 1 J. J. Marshall 206 (1829).

[28] 10 Wheaton 152 (1825).

[29] 10 Wheaton 159, 160. See also opinion of Justice Johnson in Shelby v. Guy, 11
Wheaton 367 (1826).

[30] Cf. above, pp. 351 ff.

large amount of notes was issued which displaced the issues of the local bank. A method of taxation was resorted to as a means of saving the situation for the local banks. It was contended that the right to tax the branches of the Bank of the United States could be sustained on the ground that the charter of the bank did not include exemption from taxation, that such immunity did not generally attach to incorporated companies, and that since the state banks had paid bonuses for their charters the establishment of branches of the Bank of the United States would result in an impairment of the state's contracts with the local banks.[31] Commenting on the mismanagement in the operation of the branches of the Bank of the United States in Ohio and on the methods used during the depression of 1819 in foreclosing its mortgages as a consequence of which the bank owned a large part of Cincinnati, Ernest L. Bogart concludes "that the people of Ohio had a very good case against the Bank, that they were convinced of the justice of their position, and that they proceeded to test their rights in constitutional, legal, and peaceful ways."[32]

Owing to mismanagement the branches of the Bank of the United States in Ohio were on the verge of bankruptcy in 1818 when measures were taken by the directors to assure solvency. This policy of the directors resulted in the closing of some of the largest banks in Ohio and in arousing sentiment against the national bank. Moved by this sentiment, the legislature on February 8, 1819, passed a law taxing the branches of the Bank of the United States established in Ohio. The law was not to become effective until September, thus giving the bank time to arrange its affairs or to withdraw from the state. In the meantime the decision of the Supreme Court in the case of *McCulloch v. Maryland*[33] had been rendered. Before proceeding to levy the tax the state auditor secured legal advice whether papers which had been served on him operated as an injunction. On receiving information that no injunction had been issued, an order was given to John L. Harper to collect the tax. On the bank's refusal to pay the tax, Harper took money and notes amounting to more than $120,000. The excess over $100,000 was restored to the bank. Harper retained $2000 as his fee and turned over to the state treasurer $98,000. After the tax had been collected and paid into the state treasury an in-

---

[31] Ernest L. Bogart, "Taxation of the Second Bank of the United States by Ohio," *Amer. Hist. Rev.* (Jan., 1912), XVII: 315.

[32] Bogart, *op. cit.*, p. 322. Bogart corrects the impression sometimes given that the action of Ohio was prompted by and followed the decision of the Supreme Court in the case of *McCulloch v. Maryland*. See also John Bach McMaster, *A History of the People of the United States* (New York, 1914), III: 119, 246, and James Schouler, *History of the United States of America* (Washington, 1889), IV: 498.

[33] 4 Wheaton 316 (1819).

junction was served on Osborn, the state auditor, directing him not to collect the tax nor to pay it out if collected. He refused to obey this order because the matter had passed out of his control. A few days later, on September 22, 1819, an injunction was granted by the United States District Judge restraining the auditor, the treasurer, and the depository bank from making any disposition of the moneys collected as a tax from the bank. About one month later Chief Justice Marshall granted an injunction against Osborn, Curry, and others, to restrain them from disposing of the moneys collected as a tax from the Bank of the United States.[34] A supplemental order was then given that the defendants turn over to the bank the amount of money unlawfully seized. The state treasurer refused to comply, and an attachment for contempt was issued against him. He was committed to prison. But before being incarcerated the key to the state treasury was taken from him by the commissioner of the court who entered and removed about $98,000. The defendants appealed to the Supreme Court of the United States.

The case of *Osborn v. Bank of the United States* was twice argued before the Supreme Court by eminent counsel on both sides. Attorneys for Osborn contended that the circumstances of the case were not such as to warrant the issuance of an injunction and that the proceeding was in effect a suit against the state. Being a suit against the state, it was maintained that the Supreme Court alone, under its original jurisdiction, could take jurisdiction of the case. The Supreme Court was requested to reconsider as much of its opinion in *McCulloch v. Maryland*[35] as applied to the decision that a state may not tax the Bank of the United States. The bank was declared to be a private corporation, not a governmental agency, and as such ordinarily immune from taxation.

Henry Clay, representing the bank, declined to argue the question of the authority of Ohio to tax the bank on the ground that this issue had been determined by the *McCulloch Case*. Ohio's act was regarded as a confiscatory measure, and not a tax. Moreover, the query was raised whether "our jurisprudence should be so defective that the law of the whole may be defeated in its operation by a single part?"[36]

In response to the claim of the immunity of suit of a state, Clay observed that "the Constitution merely ordains, that a State, in its sovereign capacity, shall not be sued. It does not ordain, that a citizen shall not have justice done him, because a State may happen to be collaterally

---

[34] Bogart, *op. cit.*, pp. 324, 325. Bogart does not detect in any of these proceedings an intention to resist the orders of the federal courts but rather to insist upon the technical correctness of each step.

[35] 4 Wheaton 316 (1819).

[36] Osborn v. Bank of the United States, 9 Wheaton 796 (1824).

interested."[37] At the request of the Court, and together with a similar case from the state of Georgia, the case was reargued, particularly on the provision of the bank's charter authorizing it to bring suits in the Circuit Courts. To strengthen the cause of the bank it was then argued that all its powers were conferred solely for the purpose of facilitating the fiscal operations of the national government. The varied and extensive operations of the bank which brought it into conflict with similar activities in the states apparently did not accord with this contention.[38]

Chief Justice Marshall, in delivering the opinion of the Court, again reaffirmed the mechanical doctrine of judicial construction as he was inclined to do when the decisions of the Supreme Court bordered on the realm of public policy and political expediency. "Judicial power, as contra-distinguished from the power of the laws," said he,

has no existence. Courts are the mere instruments of the law, and can will nothing. When they are said to exercise a discretion, it is a mere legal discretion, a discretion to be exercised in discerning the course prescribed by law; and, when that is discerned, it is the duty of the Court to follow it. Judicial power is never exercised for the purpose of giving effect to the will of the judge; always for the purpose of giving effect to the will of the legislature; or in other words, to the will of the law.[39]

Finding that the right to sue in the federal courts had been expressly granted in the act of incorporation, Marshall first considered the constitutionality of this clause. The provision defining the judicial power as extending to all cases in law and equity arising under the federal Constitution and laws was then declared to enable "the judicial department to receive jurisdiction to the full extent of the Constitution, laws, and treaties of the United States, when any question respecting them shall assume such a form that the judicial power is capable of acting on it. That power is capable of acting only when the subject is submitted to it by a party who asserts his rights in the form prescribed by law."[40] Thus a broad principle was formulated the elucidation of which has been only partially clarified in subsequent cases. Marshall then went on to say:

The Constitution establishes the Supreme Court, and defines its jurisdiction. It enumerates cases in which its jurisdiction is original and exclusive; and then defines that which is appellate, but does not insinuate, that in any such case, the power cannot be exercised in its original form by courts of original jurisdiction. It is not insinuated, that the judicial power, in cases depending on the character of the cause, cannot be exercised, in the first instance, in the courts of the Union, but must first be exercised in the

---

[37] 9 Wheaton 798.
[38] A committee of the legislature of Ohio reported that *McCulloch v. Maryland* was an agreed case prepared for the purpose of securing an early decision from the Supreme Court; and state officers were advised to ignore the decision.
[39] 9 Wheaton 866.
[40] *Ibid.*, p. 819.

tribunals of the State; tribunals over which the government of the Union has no adequate control, and which may be closed to any claim asserted under a law of the United States. We perceive, then, no ground on which the proposition can be maintained, that Congress is incapable of giving the Circuit Courts original jurisdiction, in any case to which the appellate jurisdiction extends.[41]

The argument that an entire case must depend upon the Constitution or federal acts for the courts of the nation to have jurisdiction was rejected, and it was held that the issue concerning federal authority need be only "an ingredient of the original cause." Marshall, who on occasion could refuse to recognize and consider obvious facts which might bear detrimentally on the opinion he was determined to render, now cut across legal lots, reviewed some of the well-known proceedings in the case, and held Sullivan, the state treasurer to whom the funds taken from the bank had been transferred, responsible for the illegal detention of the money of the bank.

The real issue of the case was then stated to be whether "an injunction can be issued to restrain a person, who is a state officer, from performing any official act, enjoined by statute; and whether a court of equity can decree restitution, if the act be performed."[42] In determining this issue it was assumed to be the avowed purpose of Ohio, by its tax upon the bank, to expel it from the state. The issuance of the injunction was justified on the ground that the state officers were acting illegally and that a court of equity will always interpose to prevent the transfer of a specific article, which, if transferred, will be lost to the owner.

With regard to the contention that the federal courts did not have jurisdiction because the state was a party, Marshall admitted the direct interest of the state in the suit and thought that if the law had permitted it the bank would have brought suit against the state. But assuming that the suit was against the state, Marshall turned to the argument of expediency by which he could place other alternatives than judicial intervention in an unfavorable light. Ohio's contention, as Marshall phrased it, was that

each member of the Union is capable, at its will, of attacking the Nation, of arresting its progress at every step, of acting vigorously and effectually in the execution of its designs, while the Nation stands naked, stripped of the defensive armour, and incapable of shielding its agent or executing its laws, otherwise than by proceedings which are to take place after the mischief is perpetrated, and which must often be ineffectual, from the inability of the agents to make compensation.... The question, then, is, whether the Constitution of the United States had provided a tribunal which can peacefully and rightfully protect those who are employed in carrying into execution the laws of the Union, from the attempts of a particular state to resist the execution of those laws.[43]

---

[41] *Ibid.*, p. 821.   [42] *Ibid.*, p. 838.   [43] *Ibid.*, pp. 848, 849.

But the bank replied that the suit was not against the state since it was directed merely to the officers of the state and hence that the Eleventh Amendment was not applicable. By circuitous and inapposite reasoning it was concluded that the Eleventh Amendment could apply only to those suits in which a state is a party on the record. The validity of the Ohio act was then considered, and Marshall pointed out that the opinion in the *McCulloch Case* was based on the assumption that the bank, though a private corporation, was an instrument created by the federal government for carrying into effect the powers vested in that government. The act of Ohio being more objectionable than the Maryland act, so far as it interfered with the execution of a law of Congress made in pursuance of the Constitution, was therefore held void, and a void act could afford no protection to the officers who executed it. Marshall's opinion was concluded by affirming the Circuit Court's decree requiring the restitution of the funds taken from the bank.[44]

Justice Johnson, dissenting, conceded that "a state of things has now grown up, in some of the States, which renders all the protection necessary, that the general government can give to this bank."[45] But he did not believe that the Constitution and laws sanctioned such a right of action as sought by the bank in this case. Disagreeing with the majority on the issue of jurisdiction, Johnson declined to consider the main issues raised in the arguments.

This case had been pending for three years. The action of the Court in upholding the bank was expected, but the ruling that a state official might be sued for committing a trespass while relying on an unconstitutional state statute, even in the face of the Eleventh Amendment, aroused intense antagonism at a time when the attacks in Congress upon the Court and its jurisdiction were becoming increasingly frequent. The proponents of State rights claimed the decision repealed the Eleventh Amendment, and the decision only served to add fuel to their opposition to the Court.

In a report and resolutions on the case of *Osborn v. Bank of the United*

---

[44] The argument on the point of jurisdiction was concluded on March 11, and Marshall's opinion was rendered on March 19. Since the opinion in the official report extends over fifty-five pages, it is likely that the larger part of the opinion was written prior to the argument. On Marshall's preparatory work for his legal-state papers, see Albert J. Beveridge, *The Life of John Marshall* (Boston, 1919), IV: 221, 261, 290.

Charles Warren believes that "the mighty reasoning of the Chief Justice in his insistence upon the supremacy of the powers of the national government, gave the death blow to the bills pending in Congress for the amendment and repeal of the 25th section of the Judiciary Act." See "Legislative and Judicial Attacks on the Supreme Court of the United States—A History of the Twenty-Fifth Section of the Judiciary Act," 47 *Amer. Law Rev.* (Jan., Feb., 1913), 30.

[45] 9 Wheaton 871, 872.

States prepared by a committee and approved by the legislature of Ohio, it was contended that the suit was to every substantial purpose a suit against the state and that the federal courts were asserting a jurisdiction which a just construction of the Constitution did not warrant. Pointing out that before the adoption of the Eleventh Amendment the Circuit Court could not entertain a suit to enjoin state officers from executing state laws, it was declared to be a strange doctrine to maintain that an amendment to the Constitution expressly forbidding the Judges so to construe the Constitution as to call states before the Supreme Court as defendants, at the suit of individuals, operates as vesting the Circuit Courts with power to do indirectly that which they never had any direct power to do. It was declared to be evident that the principle of the proceeding secures to the federal tribunals every power supposed to be taken from them by the amendment. If the auditor of the state can be enjoined from acting officially and if the treasurer can be compelled to pay back money received as revenue upon the doctrine that the Court considers them wrong-doers, there is no case of the exercise of state power that may not be completely controlled.[46]

Following the citation of extracts from the Kentucky and Virginia Resolutions, it was affirmed that:

The resolutions of Kentucky and Virginia, and of Massachusetts, Rhode Island, the senate of New York, New Hampshire and Vermont, in reply, and the answer to these replies by the legislature of Virginia, were a direct and constitutional appeal to the States and to the people, upon the great question at issue. The appeal was decided by the presidential and other elections of 1800. The States and the people recognized and affirmed the doctrines of Kentucky and Virginia, by effecting a total change in the administration of the federal government. In the pardon of Callender, convicted under the sedition law, and in the remittance of his fine, the new administration unequivocally recognized the decision and the authority of the States, and of the people. Thus has the question, whether the federal courts are the sole expositors of the Constitution of the United States in the last resort, or whether the States, "as in all other cases, of compact among parties having no common judge," have an equal right to interpret that Constitution for themselves, where their sovereign rights are involved, been decided against the pretension of the federal Judges by the people themselves, the true source of all legitimate power.[47]

After the Ohio legislature passed the law taxing the branches of the national bank in the state, and before the time of its taking effect, it was noted the Supreme Court of the United States decided that the states were debarred by the Constitution of the United States from levying

---

[46] 37 *Annals of Congress*, pp. 1690 ff.; *Journal of the House of Representatives of Ohio*, 1820–1821, pp. 98–132; and *Journal of the House of Delegates of Virginia*, 1820–1821, pp. 166–178.

[47] *Virginia House Journal*, 1820–1821, p. 170, and Ames, *op. cit.*, pp. 95, 96.

such a tax. And upon the promulgation of this decision it was maintained that it became the duty of the state and its officers to acquiesce and treat the act of the legislature as a dead letter. The committee considered this position and became satisfied that it is not a correct one. It has been already shown that since the passage of Eleventh Amendment to the Constitution the separate states, as parties to the compact of union, are not subject to the jurisdiction of the federal courts upon questions involving their power and authority as sovereign states. Not being subject to their jurisdiction, no state can be concluded by the opinions of these tribunals; these are questions in respect to which there is no common judge, and therefore the state has a right to judge for itself. Citing the cases of *Marbury v. Madison*,[48] in which Marbury did not obtain his commission, and *Fletcher v. Peck*,[49] which was merely a "make-weight in effecting a compromise," the committee contended that "these cases are evidence that in great questions of political rights and political powers a decision of the Supreme Court of the United States is not conclusive of the rights decided by it."

Since the bank received its chartered privileges from the government of the United States, it was claimed that it must be exempt from state taxation. The reasoning of the Supreme Court, the committee finds, is based upon the following propositions:

First—The government of the Union, though limited in its powers, is supreme within its sphere of action.

Second—It is of the very essence of supremacy, to remove all obstacles to its action within its own sphere, and so to modify every power vested in subordinate governments, as to exempt its own operations from their influence.

Third—A power to create, implies a power to preserve.

Fourth—A power to destroy, if wielded by a different hand, is hostile to, and incompatible with these powers to create and to preserve.

Fifth—Where this repugnancy exists, that authority which is supreme must control, not yield to that over which it is supreme.

On the significance of this reasoning the committee commented:

It is important to glance at the train of implications with which this doctrine is connected. The power to create the bank implies the power to preserve it. This power to create is, itself, derived by implication. It is found among the subsidiary powers, as incident to the choice of means for the administration of the government. This implied power to create is made the foundation for further implication; it implies the power to preserve; and again, of necessity the power to preserve implies a choice in selecting the means of preservation; and upon the doctrine of the Court, all these powers are supreme, to the operations of which, the constitutions and laws of the States, can oppose no obstacle. It is certainly difficult to see the point where these implications terminate, or to name the power which they leave to the States unimpaired.[50]

---

[48] 1 Cranch 137 (1803).   [49] 6 Cranch 87 (1810).

[50] *Virginia House Journal*, 1820–1821, p. 174.

The committee disposed of the argument founded upon a supposed abuse of power by the states by the answer that every argument of this sort is inadmissible, because it might be urged with equal force against the exercise of any power by either government and thus would lead to the destruction of all authority. A compromise was proposed in which the bank was to withdraw from the state and the amount of tax collected would be returned. But if the compromise were accepted the committee thought that it was necessary to awaken the attention of the states to the consequences that might result from the doctrines of the federal courts upon the questions that have arisen. On the other hand, if the compromise were not accepted, it was declared to be "the duty of the general assembly to take ulterior measures for asserting and maintaining the rights of the States by all constitutional means within their power." Since the exemptions claimed by the bank were sustained upon the proposition that the power that created it must have the power to preserve it, it appeared to be appropriate to the committee to put the matter to a test and to ascertain whether the Executive and Legislative departments of the government of the union would attempt to enforce the doctrines of the judicial department. To secure such a test the committee recommended

that provision be made by law, forbidding the keepers of our jails from receiving into their custody, any person committed at the suit of the Bank of the United States, or for any injury done to them: prohibiting our judicial officers from taking acknowledgments of conveyances, where the bank is a party, or when made for their use, and our recorders from receiving or recording such conveyances; forbidding our courts, justices of the peace, judges and grand juries, from taking any cognizance of any wrong, alleged to have been committed upon any species of property, owned by the bank, or upon any of its corporate rights or privileges, and prohibiting our notaries public from protesting any notes or bills, held by the bank or their agents, or made payable to them.

The adoption of these measures will leave the bank exclusively, to the protection of the federal government; and its constitutional power to preserve it in the sense maintained by the Supreme Court, may thus be fairly, peaceably and constitutionally tested. Congress must be called to provide a criminal code, to punish wrongs committed upon it, and to devise a system of conveyances, to enable it to receive and transmit estates; and being thus called to act, the national legislature must be drawn to the serious consideration of a subject, which the committee believe demands much more attention than it has excited. The measures proposed are peaceable and constitutional; conceived in no spirit of hostility to the government of the Union, but intended to bring fairly before the Nation great and important questions, which must one day be discussed, and which may now be very safely investigated.[51]

The committee concluded its report with a series of resolutions, the most important of which was: *"Resolved further,* That this general assembly do protest against the doctrine that the political rights of the

[51] *Virginia House Journal,* 1820–1821, pp. 177, 178.

separate States, that compose the American Union, and their powers as sovereign States, may be settled and determined in the Supreme Court of the United States, so as to conclude and bind them, in cases contrived between individuals, and where they are, no one of them, parties direct."[52]

When these resolutions and the report were sent to the states, only a few replied. Massachusetts, still being under the control of the Federalist party, resolved that the construction given to the constitutional questions, having been solemnly determined by the Supreme Court, appears to be final and binding on the states. If the operation of this decision proved to be injurious to the best interests of the states, the remedy was to be found in an amendment to the Constitution. Massachusetts apparently had repented from its doctrines of nullification and secession preceding and during the War of 1812 and was prepared to defend the construction of the Constitution after the Hamiltonian model.[53]

The people of Ohio continued to express their disapproval of the decision of the Court in the newspapers and the legislative chambers. "From the formation of the Constitution of the United States until the present time," it was maintained, "there have been frequent contests between the legislative power and the courts and judges, in almost all of which the judges, contrary to the wishes of large majorities of the people, have succeeded in maintaining not only all the power respecting the grant of which there remained doubts, but have also arrogated to themselves an authority as well above the laws as above the Constitution itself."[54] It was the Kentucky and Ohio cases which called forth an attempt to revive the plan of granting to the Senate jurisdiction over disputes arising between the states and the nation.

THE PROPOSAL TO AUTHORIZE THE SENATE TO ACT AS A FINAL COURT OF APPEAL IN DETERMINING POLITICAL QUESTIONS ARISING BETWEEN THE STATES AND THE NATION

Since the Supreme Court continued to exercise its asserted authority to review acts of Congress and state legislatures in order to require their conformity to the express language of the Constitution and to judicially construed implied limitations, it became apparent that the Court, to a certain extent at least, was exercising political powers. To the Republicans the exercise of such authority, unless the courts were responsible to the people, was incompatible with American ideas of government. The

[52] For these resolutions and other extracts from the report of the committee, see Ames, *op. cit.*, pp. 93–101.

[53] *Resolves of Massachusetts*, 1819–1824, pp. 417–419; *Niles' Register*, XXI: 404.

[54] *Western Herald and Steubenville Gazette*, Sept. 29, 1829.

cases of *Cohens v. Virginia,*[55] *Green v. Biddle,*[56] and *Osborn v. Bank of United States*[57] brought the issue of judicial supremacy over the state courts into national prominence. The proposal to authorize the Senate to review the decisions of the Supreme Court when questions of State rights were concerned was again brought forward for public discussion.

A plan which had been considered at the time of the adoption of the Constitution[58] was presented by Senator Johnson of Kentucky on December 12, 1821, as a resolution proposing an amendment to the Constitution. It was as follows:

> That in' all controversies where the judicial power of the United States shall be so construed as to extend to any case in law or equity, arising under this Constitution, the laws of the United States, or treaties made, or which shall be made, under their authority, and to which a State may desire to become a party; and in all controversies in which a State may desire to become a party, in consequence of having the Constitution or laws of such State questioned, the Senate of the United States shall have appellate jurisdiction.[59]

[55] 6 Wheaton 266 (1821).

[56] 8 Wheaton 15 (1823).

[57] 9 Wheaton 738 (1824).

[58] For the efforts to secure the establishment of a commission to review the decisions of the Supreme Court, see the resolutions of the New York and Massachusetts ratifying conventions. Elliot's *Debates,* I: 331; II: 409. In the federal Convention, James Wilson suggested a plan for giving the Senate jurisdiction in disputes between the states in boundary controversies. Later Wilson thought his plan unnecessary because of the establishment of the national Judiciary. *The Records of the Federal Convention,* ed. by Max Farrand (New Haven. 1923), II: 172, 173, 400, 401.

Speaking for the supreme court of Pennsylvania regarding the division of power between the federal and the state governments in *Respublica v. Cobbett,* Chief Justice M'Kean said:

"Should there be any defect in this form of government, or any collision occur, it cannot be remedied by the sole act of the Congress, or of a State; the people must be resorted to, for enlargement or modification. If a State should differ with the United States about the construction of them, there is no common umpire but the people, who should adjust the affair by making amendments in the constitutional way, or suffer from the defect. In such a case, the Constitution of the United States is federal; it is a league or treaty made by the individual States as one party, and all the States as another party. When two nations differ about the meaning of any clause, sentence, or word, in a treaty, neither has an exclusive right to decide it; they endeavor to adjust the matter by negotiation; but if it cannot be thus accomplished, each has a right to retain its own interpretation, until a reference be had to the mediation of other nations, and arbitration, or the fate of war. There is no provision in the Constitution that in such a case the Judges of the Supreme Court of the United States shall control and be conclusive; neither can Congress by law confer that power. There appears to be a defect in this matter, it is a *casus omissus,* which ought in some way to be remedied. Perhaps the Vice-President and Senate of the United States; or commissioners appointed, say one by each State, would be a more proper tribunal than the Supreme Court. Be that as it may, I rather think the remedy must be found in an amendment of the Constitution." 3 Dallas 473, 474 (1798).

[59] 38 *Annals,* 17th Cong., 1st sess., Dec. 12, 1821, pp. 23, 24. Concerning this amendment Judge Spencer Roane wrote to Archibald Thweatt that "the subject of amending

This amendment, Johnson said, was introduced because of the serious consequences which had lately taken place between the several states and the federal Judiciary. The immediate reason was the decision of the Supreme Court in which the Occupant Claimant Law of Kentucky had been declared invalid. This decision, in Johnson's opinion, overturned "the deliberate policy of the State for upwards of ten years past, the object of which was the settlement of conflicting land claims, which had been a serious evil to the prosperity of the State." "Unfortunately," he said, "the doctrine of federal supremacy is the basis of encroachment— and the principle is established by a tribunal which knows no change. Its decisions are predicated upon the principle of perfection, and assume the character of immutability. Like the laws of the Medes and the Persians, they live forever, and operate through all time."[60]

Senator Johnson, arguing in support of this resolution, contended that:

The States claim authority which the federal Judiciary denies and the federal Judiciary exercises powers which the States do not acknowledge to be legitimate. There is no umpire to decide between them; and the difficulty is, to determine which shall submit. It is contended on the one part, that, as the general government was instituted for national purposes, its claims to the highest supremacy must be superior to those of the States; and that it is an essential attribute of national sovereignty, that its Judiciary shall be the judge of its own powers, and shall have authority to overrule every other tribunal, according to its own sovereign will and pleasure. But this argument cuts like the two-edged sword, and furnishes a position quite as strong in favor of the States. It is not denied, that all power not delegated to Congress; nor prohibited to the States, is reserved to the States respectively, or to the people; that the States are also supreme and independent within the orbit of their powers. If, then, it is the attribute of sovereignty to judge of its own powers, where is the sovereignty of the States, if that judgment must be submitted to the federal Judiciary? The argument is precisely the same in both cases, and may be called an argument in a circle.[61]

The contention of Virginia that the states created the general government and delegated certain powers to it and that they had a superior claim to an exclusive decision in all cases of conflicting power would, Johnson thought, lead to confusion. Hence, the proposal of Pennsyl-

---

the Constitution, in relation to decisions of the federal courts, has been taken up in the Senate, as you will see, on the resolution of Mr. Johnson of Kentucky, supported by Barbour. With a view to aid them, or rather to lead, on this important subject, I have prepared some amendments to the Constitution to be adopted by our Assembly. They are very mild, but go the full length of the wishes of the Republicans on this subject. They will be copied by another hand and circulated among the members. I would not wish to injure the great cause by being known as the author. My name would damn them, as I believe, nay hope with the Tories. . . . Jefferson, and Madison hang back too much in this great crisis." *Branch Historical Papers* (June, 1905), II: 141, 142.

[60] 38 *Annals*, pp. 23, 24.   [61] *Ibid.,* p. 70.

vania which claimed an equal right with the general government to decide constitutional cases affecting her sovereignty was accepted, namely, that in serious collisions an umpire was necessary and that for this purpose the Senate of the United States was the appropriate body. It was maintained that the purpose of the amendment was to restore confidence in the system of government established under the Constitution, for

at this time there is, unfortunately, a want of confidence in the federal Judiciary, in cases that involve political power; and this distrust may be carried to other cases, such as the lawyers call, *meum et tuum*. It is the opinion of many eminent statesmen that there is a manifest disposition, on the part of the federal Judiciary, to enlarge, to the utmost stretch of constitutional construction, the powers of the general government, at least in that branch, and by consequence to abridge the jurisdiction of state tribunals. I do not assert this to be the fact; but, if it is not, we should adopt some method, if practicable, to remove these ill-founded suspicions.[62]

It was deemed essential to adopt some such provision, because, thought Johnson, it is a principle of our government both in theory and in practice that every department which exercises political power should be responsible to the people. The people control every department except the Judiciary and since the Judges have arrogated to themselves political powers it is urgently necessary that some form of popular control be exercised over them. Continuing this line of argument, Johnson said:

If a judge can repeal a law of Congress, by declaring it unconstitutional, is not this the exercise of political power? If he can declare the laws of a State unconstitutional and void, and, in one moment, subvert the deliberate policy of that State for twenty-four years, as in Kentucky, affecting its whole landed property, even to the mutilation of the tenure upon which it is held, and on which every paternal inheritance is founded; is not this the exercise of political power? All this they have done, and no earthly power can investigate or revoke their decisions. If this is not the exercise of political power, I would be gratified to learn the definition of the term, as contra-distinguished from judicial power. If the exercise of such tremendous powers be legitimate, their acts, like those of all other trustees of power, should be subject to the sanction of revocation by the people; if not by a direct responsibility, yet by an appeal to a tribunal that is responsible. If, on the contrary, this exercise of power is an act of usurpation, the case is yet more alarming; for the Judges hold their offices during good behaviour, and bad opinion is not bad behaviour, and the opinion of the court is a law, and above all other law. A Judge can be removed by impeachment for treason and other high crimes and misdemeanors; and, in case of impeachment by the other House, two-thirds of this body must concur to effect his removal. The difficulty of removing a Judge in this way is such that it will seldom be attempted; and experience tells us it will more rarely succeed.[63]

Referring to the division of opinion among the Judges in the case of *Green v. Biddle*,[64] Johnson said it may happen that a single individual may be responsible for the decision which overturns the deliberate act

---

[62] 38 *Annals*, pp. 72, 73.   [63] 38 *Annals*, p. 75.   [64] 8 Wheaton 15 (1823).

of a whole state, and "we are admonished to receive their opinions as the ancients did the responses of the Delphic oracle."

Some instances of judicial oppression and arrogance in England were cited with the observation that "no truth is more universally established in history and no proposition can be more plainly demonstrated than this, that judges may oppress the people—that power cannot be safely confided anywhere without the guarantee of responsibility." We have given such transcendent powers to the Judiciary, Johnson believed, because we fear that we may enslave ourselves. Thus we transfer the power to them, because we fear the consequences of holding it ourselves; and surrender our liberties, our lives, the disposition of our property, to the Judiciary to escape the danger of oppressing ourselves. But whereas in this country the government and the people are one, "we ask not the guardian care of our superiors to bind our hands so that we cannot wound ourselves."[65]

It is maintained that Judges assumed the right of deciding upon the constitutionality of the laws of the union and of the states and of setting them aside at pleasure. Though many have acquiesced in the exercise of this power, Johnson asserted that it has not been approved by the great body of the people. And the query was raised:

from what source is the power which they exercise derived? From the Constitution? No; that is as silent as death on the subject; and it is doubtful whether one man in a thousand in the Nation would vote so as to amend the Constitution to confer this power. Is it in the theory of our government? No; it is in direct hostility to the theory of our government. . . . The Senators and Representatives in Congress, the members of the several state legislatures, and all executive and judicial officers, both of the United States and the State, shall be bound, by oath, or affirmation, to support the Constitution. Judges, in common with other officers, being bound by oath a duty is said to be created in them to decide upon the constitutionality of the laws of Congress, state laws, and state constitutions; and when, in their opinion, repugnant to the federal Constitution, to declare them null and void. Would it not be equally the duty of Congress to declare the opinion of the federal Judiciary null and void, in every case where a majority of Congress might deem it repugnant to the Constitution? For instance: the legislature, after full discussion upon the constitutionality of the measure, shall pass a law involving the best interest of the country in peace or in war. The court shall express a different opinion; and, upon every question arising under it, act in conformity to their own opinion, that the law is unconstitutional and void. . . . I know of no clause in the federal Constitution that gives the power to the Judiciary of declaring laws and constitution of a State repugnant to the Constitution of the United States, and, therefore, null and void. No express grant, nor fair construction, contains it; and, I presume, every gentleman, in and out of Congress, will agree with me, that the States never designed so to impair their sovereignty as to delegate this power to the federal Judiciary. But they have assumed it, and, to counteract the evils which must result from this assumption, a responsible tribunal of appeal should be provided.[66]

---

[65] 38 *Annals*, p. 78.   [66] 38 *Annals*, pp. 79–81.

Senator Johnson did not look with favor upon the federal Judiciary as a safe depository of individual liberties. For, when the freedom of speech and of the press was seriously threatened by aggressive federal action, the courts not only failed to arrest the progress but rather were the willing instruments of federal usurpation. Similar powers, in Johnson's opinion, were usurped when the federal Judiciary extended the implied powers of the general government so as to humiliate the states of New Jersey, Pennsylvania, and Maryland, as well as Kentucky and Virginia. Adverting to the decision of the Supreme Court in the case of *Osborn v. Bank of the United States*,[67] Johnson said that the decision was an unwarranted breach of Ohio's sovereignty and a violation of her rights as a state. "She was prosecuted," he continued, "and placed into the custody of the marshal. She was imprisoned and bound in chains by the federal Judiciary. Her treasurer was taken by a process from the United States court; the keys of the treasury taken from him; the doors of the strong box opened, and money taken from the coffers." It was due, Johnson maintained, in this and other similar cases, "more to the patriotic forbearance of the States, that intestine commotions have not been the result, than to a conviction in the minds of those States that these proceedings were sanctioned by justice or by the spirit of the Constitution."[68]

Another method of attack on the Court was directed at the procedure in rendering decisions on issues involving crucial constitutional questions. On February 20, 1823, the Senate received the remonstrance from Kentucky against the decision in *Green v. Biddle*[69] asking their Representatives in Congress to use their best exertions to procure the passage of a law requiring the concurrence of two-thirds of the Judges of that Court in all cases involving the validity of a law of any state. If this proposal was not adopted, the Kentucky legislature suggested that an increase in the number of the Judges be made. Senator Johnson of Kentucky offered a resolution in the first session of the Eighteenth Congress instructing the Committee on the Judiciary to inquire into the expediency of forming three additional circuits, of requiring a concurrence of at least seven Judges in any opinion which would involve the validity of the laws of the United States or of the states, and of requiring the Judges to have spread on the record their respective opinions.[70] In accordance

[67] 9 Wheaton 796 (1824).

[68] 38 *Annals*, p. 91. On January 15 Senator Johnson discussed in detail what he regarded as the extraordinary and unwarranted features of the Court's decision in *Green v. Biddle*. *Ibid.*, pp. 96–114.

[69] 8 Wheaton 15 (1823).

[70] 41 *Annals*, Dec. 10, 1823, p. 28.

with the above resolution, Senator Van Buren of New York reported from the Committee on the Judiciary a bill providing that no law of any state should be rendered invalid without the concurrence of at least five Judges with their opinions expressed *seriatim*. The bill was laid on the table. Representatives from Kentucky in the House also attacked the decision of *Green v. Biddle* and presented resolutions designed to require the concurrence of more than a majority of the Justices to declare any law invalid.[71] Webster wrote to Story in April, 1824, that he was about to call up some bills approved by the Judiciary Committee of the House and remarked that "the gentlemen of the West will propose a clause requiring the assent of a majority of all the Judges to a judgment which pronounces a state law void as being in violation of the Constitution or laws of the United States. Do you see any great evil in such a proposition? Judge Todd told me he thought it would give great satisfaction in the West."[72]

In the consideration of the policy of the federal government of rendering aid for improvements within the states and of the validity of a protective tariff policy, frequent opinions were expressed that it was necessary to establish a special tribunal to adjudicate controversies between the national government and the states. Governor Troup of Georgia, in a letter to the representatives of the state in Congress on February 21, 1827, stated the view in which many Republicans concurred. "I consider all questions of mere sovereignty," said the governor, "as matter for negotiation between the States and the United States, until the proper tribunal shall be assigned by the Constitution itself for the adjustment of them. . . . The States cannot consent to refer to the Supreme Court, as of right and obligation, questions of sovereignty between them and the United States, because that Court, being of exclusive appointment by the government of the United States, will make the United States the judge in their own cause; this reason is equally applicable to a state tribunal."[73]

While the debate over the jurisdiction asserted by the Supreme Court over state acts was growing in significance and intensity, Chief Justice Marshall rendered one of the few important decisions during his service on the bench which received popular support and acclaim. At the time of the adoption of the Constitution, the fear was expressed that the clause giving Congress authority to control commerce might readily lead to dis-

---

[71] 42 *Annals*, pp. 2514, 2527, 2635.

[72] *The Private Correspondence of Daniel Webster*, ed. by Fletcher Webster (Boston, 1857), I: 349.

[73] *Niles' Register*, XXXII: 20.

crimination between various sections of the country. Richard Henry Lee presented the view in which many concurred. His observation was that

> it seems to me clear, beyond doubt, that the giving Congress a power to legislate over the trade of the Union would be dangerous in the extreme to the five Southern or Staple States, whose want of ships and seamen would expose their freightage and their produce to a most pernicious and destructive monopoly. . . . The spirit of commerce throughout the world is a spirit of avarice and could not fail to act as above stated. . . . In truth it demands most careful circumspection that the remedy be not worse than the disease.[74]

Some of the prophecies came true when certain states, New York in particular, attempted, both in state and foreign commerce, to secure a monopoly of navigation by steam. Much criticism resulted from these efforts and in some instances retaliatory legislation was enacted. The issue of the validity of such state monopolies came before the Supreme Court of the United States in the case of *Gibbons v. Ogden*.[75]

Five state acts, passed in the years 1798, 1803, 1807, 1808, and 1811, were involved in the controversy. In all of these the appellants were granted the exclusive privilege of using steamboats upon the navigable waters of the state of New York. Before the passage of the acts Congress took steps to provide for the licensing of vessels employed in the coasting trade and fisheries.[76] New York not only claimed jurisdiction over navigable waters within the state but also over the coasting trade along and adjacent to the shores of the state.

When the New York laws were contested in the state courts, it was first contended that the matter was not one of judicial determination. Justice Thompson in *Livingston v. Van Ingen* asserted that

> all the arguments which have been urged against the policy or expediency of granting exclusive privileges in general, or the particular privilege which forms the present subject of inquiry have been addressed to the wrong forum. They are arguments for legislative, not for judicial consideration. We are called upon to pronounce what the law is, not what it ought to be. . . . It certainly affords a strong and powerful argument in favor of the constitutionality of a law, that it has passed not only that branch of the legislature which constitutes the greater portion of our court of *dernier resort,* but also of the Council of Revision, which is composed of the governor and the two highest judicial tribunals of the State (next to this court), and whose peculiar province it is to examine and make all constitutional objections to bills, before they become laws.[77]

At the same time, Chancellor Kent maintained that Congress does not have by the grant of authority over commerce any direct jurisdiction over interior commerce or waters.[78] Later Chancellor Kent approved the

---

[74] *The Letters of Richard Henry Lee,* ed. by J. C. Ballagh (New York, 1911–1914), II: 383.

[75] 9 Wheaton 1 (1823).

[76] 1 *U. S. Statutes at Large,* 305.

[77] 9 Johnson 507, 564 (1812).

[78] 9 Johnson 579.

grant of an injunction to restrain citizens of another state from navigating the waters of New York by vessels propelled by steam without the consent of Livingston and Fulton, or their assigns, although such vessels may have been licensed under the laws of the United States, as coasting vessels.[79] It was the appeal from the decision upholding this injunction which gave Chief Justice Marshall his first opportunity to define the term "interstate commerce."

GIBBONS V. OGDEN AND THE COMMERCE CLAUSE

The case of *Gibbons v. Ogden,* involving the New York steamboat monopoly, resulted in one of Marshall's greatest and most decisive opinions which, Beveridge asserts, have "vitalized the Constitution." Vitalizing the Constitution means, of course, reading into the indefinite language of the document the political views and doctrines of which Beveridge approved. The political implications of the decision, Beveridge believes, reveals Marshall the statesman- rather than the Judge. Because of its great importance the case was ably argued on both sides before the Supreme Court of the United States.

In arguing for Gibbons, Daniel Webster referred to the New York monopoly, originally granted in 1787 and extended at different times, which had resulted in hostile and retaliatory acts by the adjoining states. New Jersey attempted to afford protection in the use of the waters between New Jersey and New York by providing for an action of damages with treble costs against anyone acting under the authority of the New York law who interfered with the rights of her citizens. "Nothing was more complex than commerce," said Webster, "and in such an age as this no words embraced a wider field than commercial regulation. Almost all the business and intercourse of life may be connected, incidentally, more or less, with commercial regulations."[80] He thought the power of granting monopolies either for trade or navigation rested exclusively with Congress, for he did not find in the adoption of the Constitution any reference to a concurrent power in the states over interstate commerce. Because of the broad scope of the term "commerce," Webster believed that only such phases of the power should be exclusively regulated by Congress as the conditions of business and trade required.

Thomas J. Oakley in reply maintained that by the Declaration of Independence the states became free and independent, with the full power to levy war, conclude peace, contract alliances, establish commerce, and to do all other acts and things which independent states have

---

[79] Ogden v. Gibbons, 4 Johnson Ch. 150 (1819). This decision was affirmed by the state supreme court in Gibbons v. Ogden, 17 Johnson 488 (1820).

[80] Gibbons v. Ogden, 9 Wheaton 1, 9.

the right to do. The national Constitution, being in a measure a derogation of state sovereignty, must be construed strictly and every share of power not granted to the federal government remained with the states.[81] It was declared to be well settled by this time that an affirmative grant of power to the United States does not divest the states of a like power. And by the accepted rule of construction all powers not expressly made exclusive or which are clearly exclusive in their nature ought to be deemed concurrent. All implied powers must of necessity be concurrent, for any other doctrine "would deprive the States almost entirely of sovereignty, as these implied powers must inevitably be very numerous, and must embrace a wide field of legislation."[82] The grounds which make a power exclusive to the federal government, insisted Oakley, must be clear, direct, and positive. They cannot be based on speculation or theory.

By the practically uniform course of interpretation, Oakley observed, it has been decided that: first, a state may legislate in all cases of concurrent power, even though Congress has acted under the same power and upon the same subject; second, the question of supremacy cannot arise, except in the case of actual collision, but such collision must operate to limit or defeat the effect of an act of Congress; and, third, in such a case the state law yields only so far as the actual collision arises and remains valid in all other respects.[83] The state monopoly over navigation was then defended upon the concurrent authority of the state to encourage inventors and to protect patent rights and on its general authority to regulate and control the use of property. And by the accepted principles of interpretation, it was maintained that the regulation of commerce is a concurrent power. It was possessed by the states as one of the attributes of sovereignty prior to the adoption of the Constitution; it was not granted in exclusive terms to Congress; and, its regulation by the states was not prohibited. It was pointed out that New York, and other states as well, had passed numerous laws regulating commerce with foreign nations, with other states, and with Indian tribes. On the other hand, it was contended that the power of Congress over commerce did not extend to the internal commerce of a state. New York's control over the land and waters within its domain was regarded as that of a sovereign over his domain. Commerce, instead of being given the broad significance attached to it by Webster, was defined as the transportation and the sale of commodities.

Thomas Addis Emmet, arguing on the same side, noted that at six different times the acts of New York granting the special privileges involved in the controversy were approved by the Council of Revision,

---

[81] *Ibid.*, pp. 33, 34.　　[82] *Ibid.*, pp. 37–40.　　[83] *Ibid.*, pp. 40, 41.

which comprised some of the most eminent lawyers and judges in the state. Congress had no authority to regulate the internal commerce of the states, and it does not have the power to regulate the transportation of passengers which, according to the usual meaning of these terms, is not trade and commerce. Numerous state acts granting exclusive privileges for state and interstate traffic of ferries, bridges, and stages were cited. Then a summary was given of the state acts regulating or prohibiting traffic in or importation of slaves together with the quarantine and pilotage laws which were applied to foreign as well as interstate traffic.

Chancellor Kent's doctrine of interpretation of the Constitution was then approved as follows: "If any given power was originally vested in this State, if it has not been exclusively ceded to Congress, or if the exercise of it has not been prohibited to the States, we may then go on in the exercise of the power, until it comes practically in collision with the actual exercise of some congressional power. When that happens to be the case, the state authority will so far be controlled; but it will be good in all those respects, in which it does not absolutely contravene the provision of the paramount law."[84] According to Emmet the right to enter a state is primarily under the control of Congress; the right to trade is under the concurrent regulation of Congress and the state legislatures; but the control over navigation is almost exclusively under the control of the states.

Marshall, speaking for the Court, again made law in *Gibbons v. Ogden*—an opinion which Beveridge declares "has done more to knit the American people into an indivisible Nation than any other one force in our history, excepting only war. In *Marbury v. Madison*[85] he established that fundamental principle of liberty that a permanent written constitution controls a temporary Congress; in *Fletcher.v. Peck*,[86] in *Sturges v. Crowninshield*,[87] and in the *Dartmouth College Case*[88] he asserted the sanctity of good faith; in *McCulloch v. Maryland*[89] and *Cohens v. Virginia*[90] he made the government of the American people a living thing; but in *Gibbons v. Odgen*[91] he welded that people into a unit by the force of their mutual interests."[92]

---

[84] 9 Wheaton 130.
[85] 1 Cranch 137 (1803).
[86] 6 Cranch 87 (1810).
[87] 4 Wheaton 122 (1819).
[88] 4 Wheaton 518 (1819).
[89] 4 Wheaton 316 (1819).
[90] 6 Wheaton 264 (1821).
[91] 9 Wheaton 1 (1824).
[92] *The Life of John Marshall*, IV: 429, 430.

Referring to the claim of the attorneys for the state, that, prior to the adoption of the Constitution, the states were sovereign, were completely independent, and were connected with each other only by a league; Marshall said this is true, but by the adoption of the Constitution "these allied sovereigns converted their league into a government" and therefore the situation was changed. The Constitution, maintained Marshall,

contains an enumeration of powers expressly granted by the people to their government. It has been said, that these powers ought to be construed strictly. But why ought they to be so construed? Is there one sentence in the Constitution which gives countenance to this rule? In the last of the enumerated powers, that which grants expressly, the means of carrying all others into execution, Congress is authorized "to make all laws which shall be necessary and proper for the purpose." But this limitation on the means which may be used, is not extended to the powers which are conferred; nor is there one sentence in the Constitution, which has been pointed out by the gentlemen of the bar, or which we have been able to discern, that prescribes this rule. We do not, therefore, think ourselves justified in adopting it. What do gentlemen mean, by a strict construction? If they contend only against that enlarged construction, which would extend words beyond their natural and obvious import, we might question the application of the term, but should not controvert the principle. If they contend for that narrow construction which, in support of some theory not to be found in the Constitution, would deny to the government those powers which the words of the grant, as usually understood, import, and which are consistent with the general views and objects of the instrument; for that narrow construction, which would cripple the government, and render it unequal to the objects for which it is declared to be instituted, and to which the powers given, as fairly understood, render it competent; then we cannot perceive the propriety of this strict construction, nor adopt it as the rule by which the Constitution is to be expounded. . . . If, from the imperfection of human language, there should be serious doubts respecting the extent of any given power, it is a well-settled rule, that the objects for which it was given, especially when those objects are expressed in the instrument itself, should have great influence in the construction. We know of no reason for excluding this rule from the present case.[93]

Adverting to the authority granted to Congress to regulate commerce, Marshall then proceeded to define commerce. To the assertion of counsel for Ogden that the term "commerce" must be limited, in accordance with the language and general purport of the Constitution, to traffic, that is, to buying, selling, and interchange of commodities, Marshall replied, "commerce is undoubtedly traffic, but it is more; it is intercourse." The word "commerce" was understood at the time of the formation of the Constitution as involving a broader meaning than traffic. "All America," said he, "understands, and has uniformly understood, the word 'commerce' to comprehend navigation." The words of the Constitution were then cited to confirm the Court's interpretation, but, like the term "commerce," the pertinent phrases of the document required interpolation to

---

[93] 9 Wheaton 187, 188.

give support to Marshall's doctrines.[94] The attempts to impose embargoes were also cited as indicative of the broader meaning of commerce. It was therefore concluded that the term "commerce," as used in the Constitution, comprehends "navigation within its meaning; and a power to regulate navigation, is as expressly granted, as if that term had been added to the word 'commerce.'"[95]

Turning to the explanatory words, with foreign nations, among the several states, and with the Indian tribes, Marshall observed that every species of commercial intercourse with foreign nations is thus brought within the federal authority, and the phrase "among the several States" was held to mean that "commerce among the States, cannot stop at the external boundary line of each State, but may be introduced into the interior." Commerce among the states may properly be restricted to that commerce which concerns more states than one, for, said Marshall: "The genius and character of the whole government seem to be, that its action is to be applied to all the external concerns of the Nation, and to those internal concerns which affect the States generally; but not to those which are completely within a particular State, which do not affect other States, and with which it is not necessary to interfere, for the purpose of executing some of the general powers of the government. . . . The power of Congress, then, whatever it may be, must be exercised within the territorial jurisdiction of the several States."[96]

Having defined the scope of the term "commerce," the inquiry was raised concerning what is meant by the power to regulate. "This power," continued Marshall, "like others vested in Congress, is complete in itself, may be exercised to its utmost extent, and acknowledges no limitations, other than are prescribed in the Constitution. These are expressed in plain terms, and do not affect the question which arises in this case."[97] In considering the contention of counsel that granting the power of Congress over commerce may be exercised within a state, so far as interstate traffic is concerned such authority is concurrent between the states and the nation, and therefore, in the absence of Congressional acts the states may control commerce as they see fit, Marshall attempted to distinguish the fields of taxation in which concurrent authority could clearly be exercised and that of commerce in which the concurrent power doctrine

---

[94] Art. 1, sec. 9, provides as follows: "No preference shall be given, by any regulation of commerce or revenue, to the ports of one State over another." "Nor shall vessels bound to or from one State, be obliged to enter, clear, or pay duties, in another."

[95] 9 Wheaton 189–193. For confirmation of Marshall's interpretation of the word "commerce," see Walton H. Hamilton and Douglass Adair, *The Power to Govern: The Constitution—Then and Now* (New York, 1937), especially p. 181.

[96] 9 Wheaton 195, 196.

[97] 9 Wheaton 196, 197.

was inapplicable. The states, agreed Marshall, undoubtedly retain a limited authority to enact inspection, pilotage, and health laws and such acts as relate solely to the internal commerce of the state.[98] But even in this field Congress may enter with such regulations as may be deemed necessary to carry out national purposes. In order to avoid conflicts in the field in which concurrent power may be exercised, Marshall announced the principle that "although Congress cannot enable a State to legislate Congress may adopt the provisions of a State on any subject."[99]

Interpreting the act of Congress regulating the coasting trade, Marshall refused to accept the contention of counsel that the carrying of passengers was not commerce and held that such transportation was obviously a part of commerce as much as was the carrying of cargo. The act of Congress of March, 1819, regulating passenger ships was cited as supporting the construction adopted by the Court. Justifying a somewhat extended train of reasoning which attempted "to demonstrate propositions which may have been thought axioms," Marshall concluded that:

Powerful and ingenious minds, taking, as postulates, that the powers expressly granted to the Union, are to be contracted, by construction, into the narrowest possible compass, and that the original powers of the States are retained, if any possible construction will retain them, may, by a course of well-digested, but refined and metaphysical reasoning, founded on these premises, explain away the Constitution of our country, and leave it, a magnificent structure, indeed, to look at, but totally unfit for use. They may so entangle and perplex the understanding, as to obscure principles, which were before thought quite plain, and induce doubts where, if the mind were to pursue its own course, none would be perceived. In such a case, it is peculiarly necessary to recur to safe and fundamental principles to sustain those principles, and, when sustained, to make them the tests of the arguments to be examined.[100]

Thus, Marshall admitted that in the interpretation of the phrases of the Constitution much depended upon the postulates accepted and applied. His own postulates were in the nature of "safe and fundamental principles to sustain the authority of the national government."

Justice Johnson in a concurring opinion indicated his complete agreement with the reasoning of the Chief Justice. As he saw it, the grant of power to Congress over commerce among the states to meet the existing evils had to be commensurate with the authority over the subject which belonged to the separate and sovereign states. This power, which for-

---

[98] See acts of Congress, 2 *U. S. Statutes at Large*, 545, and 3 *U. S. Statutes at Large*, 126, directing the officers of the federal government to conform to and assist in the execution of the quarantine and health laws of the states. Also see act of 1803, 2 *U. S. Statutes at Large*, 205, prohibiting the importation of slaves into any state which shall itself prohibit importation. This was regarded as an admission that the states possessed the power to exclude or admit slaves.

[99] 9 Wheaton 207.

[100] 9 Wheaton 222.

merly belonged to the states and was transferred to Congress by the constitutional grant, involved the power to limit and restrain commerce at pleasure whether within or without the states. Marshall's reasoning had veered in the direction of an exclusive grant of authority over commerce to the federal government; but Johnson asserted that "the power must be exclusive; it can reside in one potentate; and hence, the grant of this power carries with it the whole subject, leaving nothing for the State to act upon."[101] In differing with the Chief Justice, Johnson did not deem it necessary to cite or refer to the act of Congress regulating the coasting trade, because state authority was inhibited from such transactions whether or not Congress had passed any laws.[102] A member of the Court appointed by a Democratic President to counteract the nationalistic views of Chief Justice Marshall had now become a more emphatic and insistent nationalist than the Chief Justice.

The decision had important economic results throughout the union and it aided in building up New York as a commercial center. But the political results were of even greater importance. Marshall's opinion, says Warren, "marked another step in the broad construction of the Constitution, and became at once a mighty weapon in the hands of those statesmen who favored prospects requiring the extension of federal authority. . . . While the actual decision of the case was based on the conflict between the New York and the federal statutes, the language used by the Chief Justice in his opinion as to the extent of the power of Congress was directly contrary to the contentions of the Republican party, and could be used in support of every political measure favored by its opponents."[103]

Despite its political implications, this has been called the "only popular opinion" which Marshall rendered. The complainants, observes Beveridge, were merely the owners of the steamboat monopoly, the theorists of localism, and the slave autocracy. In the argument of counsel for the monopoly, it was insisted that the states had authority to regulate commerce, especially so far as the prohibition of the importation of slaves was concerned. A number of states had passed such prohibitory acts. But Marshall noted that the power of the states over the importation of slaves did not extend beyond the year 1808 and that, by implication at least, state laws enacted after that date would be void. It was this phase of the

---

[101] 9 Wheaton 227. See Beveridge's comment that "Johnson's astonishing opinion in Gibbons v. Ogden is conclusive proof of the mastery the Chief Justice had acquired over his Republican associate, or else the conquest by Nationalism of the mind of the South Carolina Republican," *The Life of John Marshall*, IV: 444, 445.

[102] Thompson, a recently appointed Justice, did not participate in the case, because he was the brother-in-law of Robert Livingston, one of the former owners of the monopoly.

[103] Warren, *op. cit.*, II: 76, 77.

decision which particularly aroused the opposition of the statesmen of the South. Alarmed at the implications of the decision, Robert S. Garnett exclaimed in Congress: "Sir, we must look very little to consequences if we do not perceive in the spirit of this construction, combined with the political fanaticism of the period, reason to anticipate, at no distant day, the usurption, on the part of Congress of the right to legislate on a subject which, if you once touch, will inevitably throw this country into revolution—I mean that of slavery."[104]

The discussions in Congress and in the public press from 1819 to 1825 gave a clear and emphatic indication that the prevailing sentiment in a considerable number, if not in most, of the states strongly disapproved of the constructions which the Supreme Court was rendering concerning both the doctrine of implied powers and the jurisdiction to be exercised under the twenty-fifth section of the Judiciary Act. There was, however, if the methods and procedure adopted by Chief Justice Marshall were to be condemned, a marked lack of agreement among the states relating to the issues deemed most vital for the assertion of State rights or state authority and to a practical method of dealing with controversial constitutional questions. The alternatives to federal supremacy exercised under the grants of power given to the federal departments by the Constitution with the surveillance and control of the Supreme Court were usually suggested to be: the repeal of the twenty-fifth section of the Judiciary Act; the establishment of the Senate or some specially created tribunal as a final court of appeal; a referendum on specially significant or vital issues to the people of the states; or, the development of some practicable means for arbitration, conciliation, or the peaceable adjustment of matters between sovereign states. Each of these alternative proposals had obvious or readily discoverable defects which militated against its acceptance by most of those who opposed Marshall's method of construction and his mode of asserting federal authority.

The repeal of the twenty-fifth section of the Judiciary Act would not only have prevented the Supreme Court from passing upon constitutional questions in which the powers of the states were concerned, but it would also have taken from the Court some of the necessary and indispensable powers to deal with other questions whereby a measure of unity and uniformity was being established by the Supreme Court in the interpretation of federal treaties and statutes. Chief Justice Marshall was correct in his insistence that the repeal of section twenty-five would have deprived the Court of its most valuable and essential function as the umpire or equilibrator of the American federal system. The Senate was regarded

---

[104] 42 *Annals of Congress*, 18th Cong., 1st sess., p. 2097.

as too large and too much of a political tribunal to serve as a desirable and appropriate court of appeal on constitutional questions. Few of those who were most critical of the work of the Supreme Court were willing to have controversial constitutional questions turned over to the Senate for final determination. With the prospect of the admission of new states to the union there were also grave apprehensions that the balance of power between the chief contending sections, the North and the South, might readily be changed. And no feasible plan was offered to establish a similar body to perform the function of a final reviewing tribunal. Though from the time of the debate over the Judiciary Repeal Act of 1802, the proposal of a referendum for the final determination of crucial constitutional questions, particularly of the division of power in the federal system, was made a number of times by the leaders of the Democratic-Republican party, this proposal, which would have meant the introduction into the United States of one of the chief features of the parliamentary system of government of England, was at no time given either serious consideration or effective support. Neither the leaders of the Federalist party nor those of the Democratic-Republican party wished to turn the American form of government too definitely in the direction of a pure democracy. And the rank and file of the voters, though becoming increasingly democratic in political feeling and outlook, would probably not have given their sanction to such an extreme departure from the customary practices and procedure of the time.

Spencer Roane, John Taylor, and others deplored the fact that a strict and literal interpretation of the language of the Constitution led them to the conclusion that no means had been provided by the document to decide controversial questions affecting the political powers of the state and of the nation. But assuming that the states were sovereign during the Revolutionary and critical periods and that they at no time expressly renounced their sovereignty, these men believed that until a separate, independent, and impartial umpire could be established, and such an umpire could not be directly connected with either the state governments or the national government, the only practical and legal way to settle disputes relating to the division of power between the nation and the states was to have recourse, as sovereign states were accustomed, to arbitration, conciliation, or mutual adjustment. In the background of this reasoning there also lurked the belief that in the failure of arbitration there remained the appeal to the people of the states through the process of amendment. But the procedure of the submission of doubtful questions of power and jurisdiction to arbitral boards was seldom resorted to by sovereign states and was generally regarded as too slow and cumbersome as well as too ineffective to be considered a practical mode of procedure to settle controversies arising in the field of interstate relations. The situation in this respect was regarded so serious by those defending the sovereignty of the states that amendments to the Constitution were frequently proposed, and at other times the calling of a convention of the states similar to the Philadelphia assembly was suggested. The opponents of Chief Justice Marshall and the Supreme Court could not agree to sponsor and carry into effect any of these proposals. Moreover, the growing sentiment of nationalism both in the North and in the West gave support to the essential principles and doctrines which were being formulated in the decisions of the Supreme Court. And the Chief Justice and his Associates began to temper their decisions to accord more nearly to the prevailing public sentiment of the country. The change in judicial decisions which is particularly noticeable in the decade from 1825 to 1835 came in time to ward off attempts to reform or to reorganize the Court, to require more than a majority of the Judges to declare void either an act of Congress or of a state legislature, or to prevent further efforts to restrict its authority and jurisdiction. In the background, however, loomed the threats and the danger of sectional strife.

CHAPTER XIV

The Supreme Court and Constitutional Construction as the Center of Political Debates in the Nation and States

IN REFERRING to the decision of the Supreme Court in the case of *Gibbons v. Ogden,* Thomas Addis Emmet said that "enlightened men have viewed the progress of the Union towards consolidation with a fearful solicitude. . . ." He further maintained that:

If the liberties of this country are to be long preserved it must be done by upholding the rights of the States; and, with the utmost respect, I say it, if some of the principles laid down by the Chief Justice in the case of *Gibbons v. Ogden* are not overruled within twenty years the Constitution will before then have verged towards a form of government which many good men dread, and which assuredly the people never chose.

There is a pretty general impression that the decisions of that Court on constitutional law tend to such a result. . . . It is upon state rights we stand and state rights are state liberty. They are more—they are in this land the bulwarks of individual and personal liberty; they are the outposts of the Constitution. While they are preserved entire, our federative Union will stand against the shocks of time and the approaches of despotism; but let them be broken down or suffered to moulder away, and a consolidated power must succeed in governing this mighty empire.[1]

In these words there was a forecast of the issue which was uppermost in the minds of political leaders for the next decade. The arguments, which were waged with the fear of a centralized or consolidated nation in the background, involved the questions of federal aid to the states for internal improvements, a protective tariff, and the review of acts of the states as provided in the twenty-fifth section of the Judiciary Act of 1789. Behind the arguments was a belief growing more prevalent that unless the movement toward centralization was checked the institution of slavery was endangered, if not eventually doomed. Opposing an internal improvement bill, John Randolph warned those living south of Mason and Dixon's line "to oppose to it associations, and every other

[1] North River Steamboat Co. v. Livingston, 2 Hopkins Ch. 189, 197 (1824); and see opinion of Chief Justice Savage in this case, 3 Cow. 941 (1824).

means short of actual insurrection ... we shall keep on the windward side of treason—but we must combine to resist, and that effectually, these encroachments, or the little upon which we now barely subsist will be taken from us."[2] There was a widespread belief that the Supreme Court was largely responsible for the centralization movement and that by judicial construction a consolidation of public affairs was to be accomplished which the people had not approved and which, so far as they realized what was going on, they did not now sanction.

Albert J. Beveridge notes that at the time the tariff act of 1824 was under debate in Congress, seven states were in revolt against the Supreme Court. In the debate over the tariff, which John Taylor had called "the plundering device of nationalism," threats of forcible resistance were again made and the probability of nullification of such a Congressional act was suggested.[3] "Time and again," Beveridge continues, "Marshall's nationalist construction of the Constitution was condemned. To the application of his theory of government was laid most of the abuses of which the South complained; most of the dangers the South apprehended."[4] It was this belief which gave an impetus to the efforts to reorganize the Court and to restrict its jurisdiction. This belief was also responsible for the decline in authority and prestige of the Court which embittered the closing years of the term of Chief Justice Marshall. The relation of the Supreme Court to State rights and state sovereignty centered for a period of twenty years around the twenty-fifth section of the Judiciary Act, providing for appeals from the state courts to the Supreme Court.[5]

ATTEMPTS TO REPEAL THE TWENTY-FIFTH SECTION
OF THE JUDICIARY ACT OF 1789

Despite the significance of section twenty-five of the Judiciary Act in the legal and political history of the United States, it is noteworthy that there was relatively little debate on the section when the Judiciary Act was before Congress in 1789 and that for more than twenty-five years no case arose in which this provision was directly contested. Nathaniel Macon, in a speech before the House of Representatives in 1802, referred to a North Carolina case in which the state judges refused to obey the summons of a federal court. In 1798 Chief Justice McKean of Pennsylvania refused to allow the removal of a case to the federal Circuit Court.[6] Pennsylvania also challenged the jurisdiction of the federal courts in the

---

[2] *Annals*, 18th Cong., 1st sess., p. 1311.
[3] *Ibid.*, p. 2097.
[4] *The Life of John Marshall* (Boston, 1919), IV: 384.
[5] See above, pp. 21 ff.
[6] Respublica v. Cobbett, 3 Dallas 462.

Olmsted Case.[7] By the time the first direct attack was made on the validity of the Court's interpretation of the twenty-fifth section, the Supreme Court had taken jurisdiction upon writs of error in sixteen cases in which appeals were taken from state courts.[8] Warren notes that the acquiescence of the state authorities in this exercise of power by the Supreme Court was probably due to the fact that only two of the cases involved a conflict between provisions of the federal Constitution and a statute and in only one of these—*New Jersey v. Wilson*[9]—was a state enactment invalidated.

The challenge to the federal courts under this section by Virginia has been considered elsewhere.[10] In this case the issue was clearly drawn, and the arguments on the part of the Federalists and Anti-Federalists were ably and fully presented. The standard was set at this time for the arguments of two decades. *McCulloch v. Maryland*[11] and *Dartmouth College v. Woodward*,[12] two important cases concerning state acts which were deemed to be invalid, were discussed largely on other than jurisdictional grounds, but the advocates of State rights took occasion again to reaffirm the Republican doctrines announced in *Martin v. Hunter's Lessee*. It was not until the decisions against Virginia and Ohio in *Cohens v. Virginia*[13] and *Osborn v. Bank of the United States*[14] that the appeal of cases from the state to the federal courts was crystallized into an open and avowed attack upon the twenty-fifth section of the Judiciary Act. Attempts had been made at various times to secure an amendment to the Constitution to secure the establishment of a special tribunal to decide questions in which the powers of the general government and of the states were concerned.[15] But the attack upon the decision of the Supreme Court in the *Cohens Case* was so serious that Chief Justice Marshall predicted that an attempt would be made to repeal section twenty-five.

In April, 1822, a bill was introduced in Congress by Representative Stevenson of Virginia designed to repeal this section of the Judiciary Act.[16] Representative Wickliffe of Kentucky on January 2, 1824, proposed to have the Judiciary Committee inquire into the expediency of either repealing section twenty-five entirely or modifying it so as to permit the

---

[7] See above, pp. 270 ff.

[8] See Charles Warren, "Legislative and Judicial Attacks on the Supreme Court of the United States—A History of the Twenty-Fifth Section of the Judiciary Act," 47 *Amer. Law Rev.* (Jan., Feb., 1913), 36, for a list of these cases.

[9] 7 Cranch 164 (1812).

[10] Martin v. Hunter's Lessee, 8 Cranch 305, above, pp. 340 ff.

[11] 4 Wheaton 316 (1819).

[12] *Ibid.*, p. 518.

[13] 6 Wheaton 266 (1821).

[14] 9 Wheaton 796 (1824).

[15] *Niles' Register*, XVII: 314.

[16] See *Annals*, 17th Cong., 1st sess., p. 1681.

awarding of a writ of error to either party without reference to the manner in which the question shall have been decided by the state supreme court. But owing to the antagonism already aroused by the exercise of the limited jurisdiction then granted to the Court, the efforts to increase its powers were not at all favorably received.[17]

The failure to make any progress in curtailing the authority and jurisdiction of the Supreme Court, according to William Wirt, was due to the prevailing sentiment of the people. In urging the appointment to the Court of the staunch Federalist Chancellor Kent, Wirt wrote: "If there are a few exasperated portions of our people who would be narrowing the sphere of action of that Court and subduing its energies to gratify popular clamour, there is a far greater number of our countrymen who would wish to see it in the free and independent exercise of its constitutional powers, as the best means of preserving the Constitution itself."[18] Warren agrees with this judgment. That none of these attempts to restrict the powers of the Court succeeded, he thinks, "was an amazing tribute to the popular confidence in that tribunal; and that Jefferson and his followers in Virginia, Kentucky and Georgia failed so completely to convince the American people of the need of reform in the judiciary system can only be explained by the assumption that the country at large was convinced of the Court's integrity, of its freedom from partisan bias, and of its infinite value in the maintenance of the American Union."[19]

But immediately following this explanation of the presumed popularity of the federal Judiciary, Warren observes that despite the need of reform in the Judiciary system and the necessity of additional circuits in the West, measures recommended by Presidents Madison and Monroe for judicial reform were rejected by Congress. The Federalists opposed the bills because they wished to prevent the appointment of new Republican Judges and the Republicans did not wish to extend the jurisdiction of the federal courts.[20] A survey of the discussions and controversies which arose with respect to the exercise of authority over the states by the Supreme Court and the proposals to revise the judicial system from 1825 to 1835 do not indicate general approval of the work of the Court.

Part of the difficulty in connection with the delay in the administration of justice in the lower federal courts arose from the requirement that in the establishment of new circuits a Justice of the Supreme Court was

---

[17] Representative Wickliffe's proposal was not adopted until 1914.

[18] John Kennedy, *Memoirs of the Life of William Wirt* (Philadelphia, 1850), II: 184.

[19] Charles Warren, *The Supreme Court in United States History* (Boston, 1922), II: 131, 132.

[20] See *Life and Letters of Joseph Story,* ed. by William W. Story (Boston, 1851), I: 326, 327.

expected to preside in the circuits. The establishment of new circuits, therefore, seemed to demand the addition of new Justices to the Supreme Court. When the circuit comprising the states of Kentucky, Tennessee, and Ohio was established in 1807, it was taken for granted that a new Associate Justice would be appointed to serve the new circuit. Justice Thomas Todd, who was appointed to this position, found it impossible to cover the entire circuit, with the result that he eliminated Tennessee from his circuit attendance. Representative Claiborne of Tennessee, in protesting to the House of Representatives against the failure to hold circuit sessions in Tennessee, said that "unless some remedy was provided, there was in that State an operative denial of justice as to the laws of the United States."[21] Other new states were admitted to the union without out adequate provision being made for District or Circuit Courts. Various proposals to remedy the situation were ignored by Congress.[22] But

---

[21] 31 *Annals*, p. 419. See also Felix Frankfurter and James M. Landis, *The Business of the Supreme Court: A Study in the Federal Judicial System* (New York, 1927), pp. 34 ff.

[22] See especially the "Judges Bill" prepared by Justice Story providing for a radical reorganization of the circuit system. *Life and Letters*, I: 300. William Plumer of New Hampshire reported for the Judiciary Committee of the House of Representatives on March 3, 1823, as follows: "The Judiciary system of the United States, as originally established, consisted of one Supreme Court, six Circuit Courts, and thirteen District Courts. The District Court was held by one Judge in each district; the Circuit Court was formed by the union of the District Judge with one or more of the Judges of the Supreme Court; and the Supreme Court itself was composed of a Chief Justice and five associate Judges. The number of the District Courts has since been increased to twenty-seven, by the admission of new States into the Union, or the division of the old ones into separate districts; there being two District Courts in New York, two in Pennsylvania, two in Virginia, and one in each of the other States. By an act of Congress, passed February 13, 1801, the United States were divided into six circuits, with a Circuit Court in each, consisting of three Judges, who were to hold two terms a year in each district, and were invested with the same general powers and jurisdiction as the former courts possessed. By the same act, the sessions of the Supreme Court were, in future, to be holden twice a year at the city of Washington, the Judges were no longer required to sit in the Circuit Courts; and their number, on the death or resignation of the Judges then on the bench, was to be reduced to five. On the 8th of March, 1802, this act was repealed, and the former system was restored. On the 24th of February, 1807, a new circuit was formed in the Western country, embracing the States of Kentucky, Tennessee, and Ohio; and the number of Judges of the Supreme Court was increased to seven. Since that time, six new States have been admitted into the Union from the West alone; and one has been created in the East, by the separation of Maine from Massachusetts. From the extent of the country, the number of the States, and the increasing mass of business constantly depending in the Circuit Courts, it was obviously impossible for seven Judges to hold two courts annually in each of the twenty-seven judicial districts, into which the United States (exclusive of the territories) are now divided. The Judges of the Supreme Court have not, therefore, been required by law to go into the new Western States; and there are, accordingly, no Circuit Courts holden in Louisiana, Indiana, Mississippi, Illinois, Alabama, and Missouri, nor in the territories of Michigan, Arkansas, and Florida. In each of these States and Territories, the District Court is vested with, and exercises, the jurisdiction of a Circuit Court of the United States." 40 *Annals*, pp. 1173, 1174.

by 1824 the situation had become so desperate that Congressional consideration of the matter could be delayed no longer. In this session of Congress bills were presented to discontinue circuit riding after the model of the Federalist scheme of 1801, to provide separate Circuit Judges for the western circuits, and to increase the membership of the Supreme Court. No action was taken on these bills. They paved the way, however, for the measure introduced by Daniel Webster on December 22, 1825, providing for three new circuits and three new Associate Justices. This resulted in the great Judiciary Debate of 1826.

THE JUDICIARY DEBATE OF 1826

The second great debate on the judiciary system of the federal government, which was similar to the extensive discussions of 1802, came in 1826. It arose over a bill presented by Daniel Webster for the Judiciary Committee of the House of Representatives which proposed to add three new Justices to the Supreme Court, making a total of ten Justices, and to provide additional Circuit Courts for the states of the South and the West. The primary purpose of the bill was to provide a more satisfactory system for the administration of federal justice in the states to which the circuit system of the Atlantic seaboard states had not been extended. In certain states the District Judges were required to perform the duties usually allotted to the Circuit Courts, and in others the dockets were crowded with untried cases. Nine states—Kentucky, Ohio, Tennessee, Missouri, Alabama, Illinois, Mississippi, Indiana, and Louisiana—were seeking better facilities for the handling of cases which came within the jurisdiction of the federal courts; some of them had repeatedly requested Congress to consider and provide more effectively for their needs. The revision of the Circuit Court system was, therefore, a matter which received primary consideration.[23]

Another issue of the debate and one which had been a matter of controversy from the time of the establishment of the Supreme Court was whether the practice of circuit riding should be continued. Webster believed that circuit riding, because it established a direct contact with the communities affected by the Judges' decisions, rendered the Judges less

---

[23] Speaking of the acrimonious debate over the Repeal Act of 1802, Senator Van Buren of New York said: "Strong as the feelings then produced were, time and experience have demonstrated the wisdom of the act of 1802, by which the system of 1789 was restored and improved. Men who saw, or thought they saw, the prostration of the fairest and firmest pillar in the edifice, have been enabled by observation and more dispassionate reflection, to see the error of impressions made by the excitements of the moment, and, what is of equal value, have had the wisdom and the honesty to acknowledge their conversion to better and sounder opinions." *Cong. Debates*, II, pt. 1, p. 414.

theoretical and kept them closer to the will of the people. It was also contended that if they were confined to appellate duties only they would lose their familiarity and contacts with the common law and the peculiar laws of the states.[24] When it was asserted that the Judges were physically incapable of circuit riding, it was contended that physical incapacity for work of this kind would involve the loss of mental power and energy to perform the duties of a Justice. To James Buchanan it was necessary to "preserve the country from suffering all the evils which flow from the administration of justice by an incompetent and a superannuated Judge."[25] The knowledge of the law, said the opponents of circuit riding, was acquired from books and not from travel or the trial of cases in widely separated sections of the country. What the Judges needed was leisure and ample opportunity to increase their store of legal knowledge. Daniel Webster expressed the prevailing sentiment regarding the circuit riding when he said:

In the first place, it appears to me that such an intercourse as the Judges of the Supreme Court are enabled to have with the profession, and with the people, in their respective circuits, is itself an object of no inconsiderable importance. It naturally inspires respect and confidence, and it communicates and reciprocates information through all the branches of the judicial department. This leads to a harmony of opinion and of action. The Supreme Court is, itself, in some measure insulated; it has not frequent occasions of contact with the community. The Bar that attends it is neither numerous, nor regular in its attendance. The gentlemen who appear before it, in the character of counsel, come for the occasion, and depart with the occasion. The profession is occupied mainly in the objects which engage it in its own domestic forums; it belongs to the States; and their tribunals furnish its constant and principal theatre. If the Judges of the Supreme Court, therefore, are wholly withdrawn from the circuits, it appears to me there is danger of leaving them without the means of useful intercourse with other judicial characters, with the profession of which they are members, and with the public. But, without pursuing these general reflections, I would say, in the second place, that I think it useful that Judges should see in practice the operation and effect of their own decisions. This will prevent theory from running too far, or refining too much. We find, in legislation, that general provisions of law, however cautiously expressed, often require limitation and modifications; something of the same sort takes place in judicature; however beautiful may be the theory of general principles, such is the infinite variety of human affairs, that those most practised in them, and conversant with them, see at every turn a necessity of imposing restraints and qualifications on such principles. The daily application of their own doctrines will necessarily inspire courts with caution; and, with a knowledge of what takes place upon the circuits, and occurs in constant practice, they will be able to decide finally, without the imputation of having overlooked, or not understood any of the important elements and ingredients of a just decision.[26]

---

[24] Cf. speech of Representative Buchanan of Pennsylvania and Senator Reed of Mississippi, *Cong. Debates*, II, pt. 1, 1825–1826, pp. 562, 931 ff.

[25] *Ibid.*, p. 925. See also comments of Senator Robbins of Rhode Island, *ibid.*, p. 505.

[26] *Ibid.*, pp. 877, 878.

Ten Justices serving in circuits throughout all sections of the country were deemed less likely to be under the immediate influence of party and patronage than a smaller number of Justices.[27] Behind this argument was the belief that without the benefit of circuit riding and with the centralization of the administration of federal justice in Washington, the decisions of the Supreme Court would, as had been the tendency of recent years, uniformly favor the authority of the federal government as against the states.

A third issue of the debate centered around the provision of the bill which was designed to increase the number of Justices to ten. The fear was frequently expressed that to enlarge the Supreme Court would make of it a political tribunal. Proponents of the bill replied that it was already to a large extent a political tribunal and that the more it was concentrated in Washington the more political it would become.

Those opposing the increase in the number of Judges asserted that the proposal would create a "judicial assembly" rather than a court and that such a body would lessen individual responsibility, would increase the influence of prejudice and political feelings in judicial decisions, and that such a large number of Justices would be likely to result in frequent disagreements between the majority and minority, with a consequent undermining of the public confidence in the Court. The plan of increasing the size of the Court was opposed also on the ground that it was an attempt to adopt the principle of political representation on the Court. To Representative Mangum and others "the very idea of representation, in matters of judicial character, is not only very strange, it is more. It is alarming."[28] Many contended the real danger was not so much that new sections would be represented, but the fear that men opposed to the extension of the authority and jurisdiction of the Court would be appointed—men, in fact, who might seriously limit or curtail that jurisdiction. On the other hand, it was not political representation as usually understood that was being urged, but rather a representation of the knowledge of the law as affected by local conditions and interests. An important assumption in the 1826 debate by those who desired to secure a change in the federal court system was that both the law and the courts should be made to respond to and be guided by the wishes of the people. To the objections raised concerning the increase in the number of Justices on the Supreme Court, Webster replied:

I admit that, for some causes, it will be inconveniently large: for such, especially, as required investigation into matters of fact, such as those of Equity and Admiralty: and, perhaps, for all private causes, generally. But the great and leading character of

[27] *Cong. Debates, op. cit.,* Jan. 10, 17, 19, pp. 932, 1017, 1050.
[28] *Ibid.,* p. 942.

the Supreme Court, its most important duties, and its highest functions, have not yet been alluded to. It is its peculiar relation to this government, and the state governments. It is the power which it rightfully holds and exercises, of revising the opinions of other tribunals on constitutional questions, as the great practical expounder of the powers of the government; which attaches to this tribunal the greatest attention, and makes it worthy of the most deliberate consideration. Duties at once so important and so delicate, impose no common responsibility and require no common talent and weight of character. A very small court seems unfit for these high functions. These duties, though essentially judicial, partake something of a political character. The Judges are called on to sit in judgment on the acts of independent States; they control the will of sovereigns: they are liable to be exposed, therefore, to the resentment of wounded sovereign pride; and from the very nature of our system, they are called on, also, sometimes, to decide whether Congress has not exceeded its constitutional limits. Sir, there exists not upon the earth, and there never did exist, a judicial tribunal clothed with powers so various, and so important. I doubt the safety of rendering it small in number.[29]

Behind the sentiment to have a larger number of Justices on the Supreme Court was the belief that for such important issues as those affecting the sovereignty of the states, a greater number of Justices concurring in an opinion would be likely to gain better public support.

Throughout the debate two different concepts of the method and technique by which judicial decisions are arrived at were contrasted. The ideal of the "just judge" acting as a judicial automaton was beginning to find its way into the popular imagination. Senator Harper of South Carolina thought that the members of the Supreme Court "ought to possess, in a high degree, talent, firmness, and integrity; and more than these; the individuals discharging duties on the Bench should . . . all be statesmen . . . they should be without the manner, party, or passions, and views of politicians; they should be perfectly acquainted with men, with the workings of human passions without being subject to the influence of passions."[30] In a legal adjudication Senator Eaton of Tennessee could conceive of no place for motive, feeling, or bias, for "it would indeed be a miserable system of judicial hazard, if the random notions of individuals, selected to the Bench, apart from what is termed previous decisions and authority are to be made the test, the standard of adjudication."[31] Representative Powell of Virginia thought it a startling reflection that the courts of our country were influenced by political or sectional feelings, for, said he, "a greater curse could not be inflicted upon our country by a benign Providence."[32]

[29] *Cong. Debates, op. cit.*, pp. 879, 880.
[30] *Ibid.*, pp. 549, 550.
[31] *Ibid.*, p. 493.
[32] *Ibid.*, p. 976. Representative Livingston of Louisiana spoke of Judges as "vaccinated by honor, integrity and truth." *Ibid.*, p. 1013.

On the other hand, a Judge on the Bench, said Representative Kerr of Maryland, "can only represent the majesty of the law. He decides by the lights of his own mind, and on the words of the Constitution, and on the laws, with the aid of proper rules of construction." As he saw it, if men should be appointed to the Supreme Court who were infected with the atmosphere of local prejudice, they would soon throw aside their sectional notions and opinions and adopt nobler and loftier views.[33] So marked in the minds of some members of Congress was this detachment, aloofness, and superiority of the Justices that Senator Rowan of Kentucky exclaimed: "There has been, and is at this moment, in this country, a judicial idolatry—a judicial superstition—which encircles the Judges with infallibility."[34] Viewing the development of these ideas, Van Buren observed a sentiment of idolatry for the Supreme Court which claims for its members an almost entire exemption from the fallibilities of human nature, and so powerful had this sentiment become that public men hesitated to express views in conflict with it.[35]

To offset the mechanistic conception of the interpretation of federal laws and the Constitution which was beginning to be expressed in Congress, there were a few at least who viewed the judicial function from a more realistic angle. Representative Powell of Virginia, opposing the increase of the number of Supreme Court Justices, thought the greater the number of men the greater the weakness, for "they are but men, after all: they are liable to all the infirmities of men."[36] Recognizing that the federal Justices were inclined to adopt the doctrines of Federalism in their decisions, Representative Wickliffe of Kentucky said he did not believe that association of the Judges with the Republicans of the country would "taint the judicial ermine," for "it is by intercourse with man we learn the nature of man; and a knowledge of human nature will never make a man the worse Judge."[37]

Finally, the most important objection raised against the practice and procedure of the Supreme Court concerned the review of the decisions of the state supreme courts. And there was a firm conviction that the extent of the review, as exercised, was not sanctioned by any express mandate of the Constitution and that the chief difficulties which had arisen were due to misconstructions of that document.

Though it was usually claimed that the Judges could not exercise powers not expressly accorded to them in the Constitution, Senator

---

[33] *Cong. Debates, op. cit.,* p. 1102.
[34] *Ibid.,* p. 442.
[35] *Ibid.,* pp. 420, 421.
[36] *Ibid.,* p. 980.
[37] *Ibid.,* p. 931.

Rowan found it difficult to depict either the extent or the magnitude of the evils inflicted upon the states by the Judges in the exercise of implied powers.[38] Aware of the fact that the Supreme Court was gaining authority by the process of interpretation, Senator Rowan described "judicial construction" as "a new and mighty agent,—boundless in its strength, indefinable in its structure, and terrible in its operations. It has the faculty of enveloping certainty in doubt, and eventually substituting judicial discretion for law—for rule."[39] With deep feeling of resentment, he said: "If the object had been to destroy the liberty of the people of the States, and human ingenuity had been tortured to devise a plan, more effectual for that purpose, than any other, the one which is now, and for some time past has been, in operation, is the one which, in my opinion, would have been adopted as the most effectual."[40]

From the Democratic point of view, Senator Van Buren analyzed the situation relating to the Supreme Court's review of state acts as follows:

Not only are the acts of the national legislature subject to its review, but it stands as the umpire between the conflicting powers of the general and state governments. That wide field of debatable ground between those rival powers is claimed to be subject to the exclusive and absolute dominion of the Supreme Court. The discharge of this solemn duty has not been unfrequent, and, certainly, not uninteresting. In virtue of this power, we have seen it holding for naught the statutes of powerful States, which had received the deliberate sanction, not only of their legislatures, but of their highest judicatories, composed of men venerable in years, of unsullied purity, and unrivaled talents—statutes, on the faith of which immense estates had been invested, and the inheritance of the widow and the orphans were suspended. You have seen such statutes abrogated by the decision of this Court, and those who had confided in the wisdom and power of the state authorities, plunged in irremediable ruin. Decisions—final in their effect, and ruinous in their consequences. I speak of the power of the Court, not of the correctness or incorrectness of its decisions. With that we have here nothing to do.

But this is not all. It not only sits in final judgment upon our acts, as the highest legislative body known to the country—it not only claims to be the absolute arbiter between the federal and state governments—but it exercises the same great power between the respective *States* forming this great Confederacy, and *their own citizens*. By the Constitution of the United States, the States are prohibited from pasing "any law *impairing the obligation of contract*." This brief provision has given to the jurisdiction of the Supreme Court a tremendous sweep. . . .

There are few States in the Union, upon whose acts the seal of condemnation has not, from time to time, been placed by the Supreme Court. The sovereign authorities of Vermont, New Hampshire, New York, New Jersey, Pennsylvania, Maryland, Virginia, North Carolina, Missouri, Kentucky, and Ohio, have, in turn, been rebuked and silenced, by the overruling authority of this Court. I must not be understood, sir, as complaining of the exercise of this jurisdiction by the Supreme Court, or to pass upon the correctness of their decisions. The authority has been given to them, and this is

[38] *Ibid.*, p. 428.
[39] *Ibid.*, p. 437.
[40] *Ibid.*, p. 442.

not the place to question its exercise. But this I will say, that, if the question of conferring it was now presented for the first time, I should unhesitatingly say, that the
people of the States might, with safety, be left to their own legislatures, and the protection of their own courts. . . .

It is true, as has elsewhere been said, with apparent triumph, that the States, whose
legislative acts have successively fallen under the interdiction of the Court, have excited
little or no sympathy on the part of their sister States, and, after struggling with the
giant strength of the Court, have submitted to their fate. . . .

There are those, sir, and they are neither small in number, nor light in character,
who think that the uniform tendency of the political decisions of the Supreme Court
has been to strengthen the arm of the general government, and to weaken those of
the States. Such men think that danger to the state governments is to be apprehended
from permanently fixing the Judges of the Supreme Court at the seat of the federal
government. They fear (to use an expression, though not literally applicable here,
still so well conveys the idea) that it would be "establishing a power behind the throne
stronger than the throne itself." Thus thinking, they commenced, as far back as the
now vindicated, but formerly much abused, act of 1802, to confine the Justices of the
Supreme Court to their respective circuits, and that course has been persevered in to
the present day. They think the inevitable tendency of a change would be for the
worse—that, if the Judges come here under the eye of the government, prominent
parties as they always must be to all collisions between the respective governments,
they could not fail to embark more strongly in the feelings of men in power here,
than they now do. . . .

That this uncommon man who now presides over the Court, and who I hope may
long continue to do so, is, in all human probability, the ablest judge now sitting upon
any judicial bench in the world, I sincerely believe. But to the sentiment, which claims
for the judges so great a share of exemption from the feelings that govern the conduct
of other men, and for the Court the character of being the safest depository of *political
power*, I do not subscribe. I have been brought up in an opposite faith, and all my
experience has confirmed me in its correctness. In my legislation upon this subject,
I will act in conformity to those opinions. I believe the Judges of the Supreme Court
(great and good men as I cheerfully concede them to be) are subject to the same infirmities, influenced by the same passions, and operated upon by the same causes
that good and great men are in other situations. I believe they have as much of the
esprit de corps as other men: those who act otherwise, form an erroneous estimate of
human nature; and if they act upon that estimate, will, soon or late, become sensible of
their delusions.[41]

Senator Rowan observed that it seemed not to have occurred to the
people that the Judges might as readily enlarge the Constitution of the
United States by construction as the states might violate it by legislation.
And I do believe, said he, "that the federal Judges have erred more
frequently, and much more injuriously, in pronouncing state laws unconstitutional, than the States have erred in enacting laws of that character."[42] He could not understand why the people did not trust their

[41] *Cong. Debates, op. cit.*, pp. 417–419
[42] *Cong. Debates, op. cit.*, p. 444. In Senator Rowan's judgment the sovereign power
of a state should not be submitted to any judicial tribunal. He thought the situation

legislators as did the people of England. It was apparent to a certain extent that the issue in the debate was one between judicial and legislative supremacy. "If we can send into the Supreme Court an overruling majority," said Representative Burgess of Rhode Island, "whenever the united ambition of Congress and the Executive may choose to do it, we place the Constitution and laws of the States, in the power of two branches of the government, and thus erect ourselves into a complete tyranny; and, that too, as the advocates of the bill contend, upon perfectly constitutional principles."[43] The Constitution, it was contended by those who supported one of the main tenets of Federalism, did not thus place the Judiciary at the good will and pleasure of the other departments.

Among the proposals discussed to meet the persistent objections to the decisions of the Supreme Court were plans to abolish the circuit riding of the Supreme Court Justices, the requirement that a majority or more than a majority of all of the Justices of the Court should be necessary to declare invalid either a law of Congress or a law of a state, and the insistence that a more satisfactory and effective system of judicial administration be provided for the West and the Southwest. But despite the prevailing sentiment favorable to judicial reform in Congress and throughout the country, nothing was accomplished by the debate of 1826. The bill of 1826, which added three additional Judges to the Supreme Court and required more than a majority of the Judges to declare legislative acts void, passed the House of Representatives after a protracted discussion. In the Senate the bill was passed with an amendment providing certain changes in the two northwestern circuits. This bill, as passed in the House, placed Ohio and Kentucky in the seventh circuit, and constituted Indiana, Illinois, and Missouri into a separate circuit. By the Senate amendment Kentucky and Missouri were to comprise the seventh circuit and Ohio, Indiana, and Illinois were placed in another circuit. Upon the bill's passage in both the Senate and the House, Tennessee and Alabama were placed in one circuit, and Mississippi and Louisiana in another. Owing to this slight difference of opinion between the two houses in the arrangement of the two northwestern circuits, the bill was not enacted into law.[44] Effective judicial reform to meet some of the per-

intolerable when three Judges could paralyze the sovereign power of a state, and much worse when one Judge, as happened in the instance of a division of opinion among the Judges, could do it. It was regarded as a discouraging outlook when people were willing to resort to force to preserve their rights but patiently submitted to the loss of these same rights by judicial fiat. *Ibid.,* p. 445.

[43] *Ibid.,* p. 1092.

[44] See comments of Representative Polk of Tennessee on January 20, 1830, 21st Cong., 1st sess., *Cong. Debates,* VI, pt. 1, p. 548.

sistent objections of the Republican majorities in the states was thus deferred until the advent of the Democratic regime of Andrew Jackson rendered some of the important changes urged during the decade from 1820 to 1830 unnecessary and inappropriate.

In the Judiciary Debate of 1826 a number of proposals were made in the House of Representatives requiring the concurrence of a majority of the Justices, including the Chief Justice, in all cases involving the validity of legislative acts; but all failed to receive the approval of the House.[45] Continuing the efforts to reform the Judiciary, Representative Wickliffe introduced in the second session of the Nineteenth Congress a bill which he asserted would bring permanency into the decisions of the Supreme Court by requiring the joint opinion of at least five of seven Judges to invalidate the law of any state and stipulating that the opinions of the Justices be delivered *seriatim*.[46] In the second session of the Twentieth Congress the Committee on the Judiciary submitted a favorable report on a bill prescribing the concurrence of five Justices to declare a state law unconstitutional. The committee concluded that: "The concurrence, then, of a greater number than a bare majority of that tribunal will tend to produce a greater spirit of acquiescence, to quiet heart-burnings, and thus add a strong cement to that Union which we all desire to be indissoluble and perpetual."[47] The bill was postponed. Having failed in these attempts, those favoring judicial reform turned to another type of measure, such as Representative Le Compte's proposed constitutional amendment in the Twenty-second Congress prescribing that the Judges of the federal superior and inferior courts should hold their offices for a period of years.[48] This proposal was also defeated.

At the same time that the Supreme Court was being subjected to persistent criticisms regarding its decisions affecting the powers of the states and attempts were being made to restrict the jurisdiction of the Court as well as to reorganize the federal Judiciary, other difficulties tended to

---

[45] See resolutions of Representatives Forsyth of Georgia, Moore of Kentucky, and Wickliffe of Kentucky, *Cong. Debates, op. cit.*, pp. 884, 1122, 1124, 1125. Mr. Wickliffe's proposal was as follows: "That in all cases brought before the Supreme Court, in which shall be drawn in question the validity of any act of Congress or treaty of the United States, or any part of the constitution of a State, six Justices of the Supreme Court shall concur in pronouncing such act of Congress, treaty of the United States, part of a constitution, or act of the legislature of any State, to be invalid; and that, without the concurrence of that number of Justices, no act of Congress, treaty of the United States, part of a constitution, or any act of the legislature of a State (as the case may be) so drawn in question, shall be deemed or holden invalid." *Ibid.*, p. 1124.

[46] *Cong. Debates*, III: 775.

[47] *Op. cit.*, Jan. 2, 1829, V, appendix, p. 24.

[48] See *Cong. Debates*, VIII: 1856.

undermine public confidence in the administration of justice by the federal courts. Owing to the increase in cases appealed to the Supreme Court, its docket became overcrowded and cases were no longer expeditiously handled.

In the 1825 term the Supreme Court was in session for six weeks. Thirty-eight cases from a docket of one hundred and sixty-four were decided. It was observed in *Niles' Register* that the Court had enough cases on hand to occupy all of the spare time of the Judges for nearly five years and that, in view of the fact that the number of cases would surely increase, "it appears absolutely necessary that a remedy should be applied to relieve the Judges of this Court of some part of their present duties, else justice must be, in effect, refused by delay."[49] The following term it was reported that forty-nine cases were disposed of from a docket of one hundred and ninety, and it was charged that "the laws are not administered, under the present organization of the courts of the United States, as promptly or efficaciously as they ought to be."[50] More serious objections were raised, however, to the arrangement which required a District Judge to preside both in the District and Circuit Courts in some of the western states. As new states were admitted to the union from western or southern territories, Congress failed to provide Circuit Courts for them. Senator Berrien, reporting to the Judiciary Committee of the Senate in January, 1829, expressed the almost universal objection that no matter how important the controversy, the single opinion of the District Judge was decisive in the controversy on almost every issue presented to the Court. Owing to the great distances from Washington and the long time and expense involved in appeals to the Supreme Court, these decisions were usually final. According to the committee report "the evil is more striking in criminal cases. The fiat of an individual, which dooms the accused to imprisonment, or to death is irresistible, irreversible. No appeal is allowed—no writ of error provided by law; and, from the constitution of the court, no disagreement can arise to invoke the protective interposition of the supreme tribunal."[51]

It was during this decade, however, that new issues of constitutional construction were taking shape which severely strained the relations between the nation and the states and which led, in the beginning of Jackson's Administration, to the carrying out of the threat of the nullification of a federal act by South Carolina. Historians, who have approached the analysis of the events of this period from a nationalistic point of view, have been inclined to place a larger share of the responsibility for such drastic action by the states upon Thomas Jefferson than

[49] XXVIII: 49.   [50] XXX: 83.   [51] 20th Cong., 2d sess., ser. no. 181, *Sen. Doc.*, 50, 5.

the facts warrant. But before the stage was set for a conflict over federal versus state powers which brought the nation to the verge of war, Jefferson expressed views, which, supporting those of Spencer Roane and John Taylor, strengthened the Republican sentiment against the encroachments on state powers by the enlargement of federal authority through judicial construction. In any analysis which aims to present both sides of the argument on the great underlying issue of the day, the views of Jefferson cannot be ignored.

JEFFERSON'S CRITICISMS OF MARSHALL AND HIS NATIONALISTIC INTERPRETATION OF THE CONSTITUTION

The differences in method of constitutional interpretation between Alexander Hamilton and Thomas Jefferson have been analyzed in a previous chapter.[52] And the objections of Jefferson to the display of partisanship by the Chief Justice on the Bench in the Burr trial and on other occasions have been noted.[53] In the struggle between Jefferson and the Judiciary, which occupied his entire Administration and, indeed, continued in one form or another for the rest of his life, Jefferson received the worst of the battle. He and his associates failed in the attempt to remove Justice Chase by impeachment; his attempt to convict Burr of treason proved ineffectual; he tried unsuccessfully to have the Constitution amended so as to make the removal of Judges easier; he saw his appointees to the Supreme Court, and those of Madison for the most part, accept the views of Chief Justice Marshall with respect to nationalism and the protection of the vested rights of property; and he witnessed the gradual establishment of a constitutional doctrine of the distribution of state and federal powers at variance with his own. But his views in opposition to John Marshall's nationalistic theories of construction deserve more attention than is usually accorded to them.

On his return to private life, Jefferson became an uncompromising foe of Marshall and a persistent critic of the practice of the review of federal and state acts by the federal courts. On this hypothesis the Constitution became, he thought, a mere thing of wax in the hands of the Judiciary which might twist and shape it into any form desired.

Jefferson's view of the proper use of the power of impeachment was a natural outgrowth of his doctrine that the people themselves were the ultimate authority in interpreting the Constitution.[54] If the President or Congress erred in such interpretation, the fault could speedily be cor-

---

[52] See chap. vi.
[53] See above, pp. 287–288.
[54] In a letter to William Jarvis on September 28, 1820, Jefferson wrote: "I know no safe depository of the ultimate powers of the society but the people themselves; and

rected by an election. But if the Supreme Court misinterpreted the Constitution, there was no effective means other than the indirect one of impeachment whereby the Judges could be held accountable to the people, for the amending process of the Constitution was so hedged about by restrictions as to render popular control impracticable through this channel. Accordingly, Jefferson and the other Republican leaders favored the use of impeachment, not merely as a method of removing incompetent and corrupt Judges, but also as a means of requiring a type of political responsibility for the Court in the determination of constitutional questions.

The failure to convict Justice Chase convinced Jefferson of the futility of this method of removal, and he repeatedly referred to impeachment as a farce and a scarecrow which would not be tried again. Immediately following the Chase acquittal a constitutional amendment was introduced in Congress, presumably at Jefferson's instigation, providing for the removal of the Judges of the Supreme Court and of the other federal Judges by the President on address of both houses of Congress. This would have provided a method of removal similar to the English system. The need for such an amendment was again asserted by Jefferson during the Burr trial when, in a letter to William B. Giles, he stated that if the protection of Burr by the Judiciary "produces this amendment, it will do more good than his condemnation would have done." In later writings Jefferson reverted to the problem of devising some method of curbing the Judiciary. He referred at various times to the advisability of the adoption of the English method of removal of Judges by the King on an address by a simple majority in both houses of Parliament. "Our Judiciary," said Jefferson, "should be submitted to some practical and impartial control."

In a letter to James Pleasants, Jefferson discussed in some detail the problem of controlling the Judiciary. He considered the proposal of erecting the Senate into an appellate court on constitutional questions but rejected it on the ground that the Senate was not properly representative of the people. He thought a six-year term for Judges, with eligibility for reappointment by the President upon the approval of both houses, was a better remedy. A third, and more immediate remedy, said Jefferson in referring particularly to the *Cohens Case*, would be a joint protestation of both houses of Congress that the doctrines expressed in

---

if we think them not enlightened enough to exercise their control with a wholesome discretion, the remedy is not to take it from them, but to inform their discretion by education. This is the true corrective of abuses of constitutional power." *The Writings of Thomas Jefferson*, ed. by Paul Leicester Ford (New York, 1892), X: 160, 161.

such a case are contrary to the Constitution. An avowal such as this, would, he thought, effectively prevent the execution of the judgment within the states.[55]

Another reform which Jefferson favored as a means of curbing the Judiciary was to return to the original practice of rendering opinions *seriatim* instead of almost exclusively by the Chief Justice. In the first decade following the establishment of the Supreme Court, the majority of its opinions were rendered *seriatim,* but with the accession to the Bench of John Marshall as Chief Justice in 1801 the practice of delivering opinions *seriatim* was abandoned.[56] In the letter to James Pleasants,

---

[55] A part of Jefferson's letter to Pleasants, dated December 26, 1821, follows:

"But you will have a more difficult task in curbing the Judiciary in their enterprises on the Constitution. I doubt whether the erection of the Senate into an appellate court on constitutional questions would be deemed an unexceptionable reliance; because it would enable the Judiciary, with the representatives in Senate of one-third only of our citizens, and that in a single house, to make *by construction* what they should please of the Constitution, and thus bind in a double knot the other two-thirds, for I believe that one-third of our citizens choose a majority of the Senate, and these too of the smaller States whose interests lead to lessen state influence, and strengthen that of the general government. A better remedy I think, and indeed the best I can devise would be to give future commissions to judges for six years (the Senatorial term) with a re-appointmentability by the President with the approbation of *both* houses. That of the H. of Repr. imports a majority of citizens, that of the Senate a majority of States and that of both a majority of the three sovereign departments of the existing government, to wit, of its executive and legislative branches. If this would not be independence enough, I know not what would be such, short of the total irresponsibility under which we are acting and sinning now. The independence of the judges in England on the King alone is good; but even there they are not independent on the Parliament; being removable on the joint address of both houses, by a vote of a majority of each, but we require a majority of one house and two-thirds of the other, a concurrence which, in practice, has been and ever will be found impossible; for the judiciary perversions of the Constitution will forever be protected under the pretext of errors of judgment, which by principle are exempt from punishment. Impeachment therefore is a bugbear which they fear not at all. But they would be under some awe of the canvass of their conduct which would be open to both houses regularly every 6th year. It is a misnomer to call a government republican in which a branch of the supreme power is independent of the Nation. By this change of tenure a remedy would be held up to the States, which, although very distant, would probably keep them quiet. In aid of this a more immediate effect would be produced by a joint protestation of both Houses of Congress, that the doctrines of the Judges in the case of Cohens, adjudging a State amenable to their tribunal, and that Congress can authorize a corporation of the District of Columbia to pass any act which shall have the force of law within a State, are contrary to the provisions of the Constitution of the U.S. This would be effectual; as with such an avowal of Congress, no State would permit such a sentence to be carried into execution, within its limits. If, by the distribution of the sovereign powers among three branches, they were intended to be checks on one another, the present case calls loudly for the exercise of that duty, and such a counter declaration, while proper in form, would be most salutary as a precedent." *Writings* (Ford ed.), X: 198, 199. See also letter to Nathaniel Macon, Aug. 19, 1821, *Writings* (Ford ed.), X: 192, 193.

[56] See *The American Doctrine of Judicial Supremacy* (Berkeley, 1932), pp. 352 ff.

cited in footnote 55, Jefferson referred to the practice of "cooking up a decision in Caucus" and asserted that this defeated "the possibility of impeachment by smothering evidence." A constitutional amendment requiring *seriatim* opinions would place responsibility on the individual Judges for their opinions, would improve the quality of the opinions, and give us reports "unswelled by the arguments of counsel and within the compass of our reading and bookshelves."

Writing to Justice Johnson on October 27, 1822, Jefferson urged the return to the practice of rendering opinions *seriatim* and argued that this practice was supported by the custom of England and by the valuable results that would follow its adoption. He said:

> Some of these [United States Supreme Court] cases too have been of such importance, of such difficulty, and the decisions so grating to a portion of the public as to have merited the fullest explanation from every judge *seriatim*, of the reasons which had produced such convictions on his mind. It was interesting to the public to know whether these decisions were really unanimous, or might not perhaps be of 4 against 3 and consequently prevailing by the preponderance of one voice only. The judges holding their offices for life are under two responsibilities only. 1. Impeachment. 2. Individual reputation. But this practice completely withdraws them from both. For nobody knows what opinion any individual member gave in any case, nor even that he who delivers the opinion, concurred in it himself. Be the opinion therefore ever so impeachable, having been done in the dark it can be proved on no one. As to the 2nd guarantee, personal reputation, it is shielded completely. The practice is certainly convenient for the lazy, the modest and the incompetent. It saves them the trouble of developing their opinion methodically and even of making up an opinion at all. That of *seriatim* argument shows whether every judge has taken the trouble of understanding the case, of investigating it minutely, and of forming an opinion for himself, instead of pinning it on another's sleeve. It would certainly be right to abandon this practice in order to give to our citizens one and all, that confidence in their Judges which must be so desirable to the Judges themselves, and so important to the cement of the union.[57]

In reply to this letter, Justice Johnson wrote to Jefferson from Charleston on December 10, 1822:

> When I was on our state bench I was accustomed to delivering *seriatim* opinions in our appellate court, and was not a little surprised to find our Chief Justice in the Supreme Court delivering all the opinions in cases in which he sat, even in some instances when contrary to his own judgment and vote. But I remonstrated in vain; the answer was, he is willing to take the trouble, and it is a mark of respect to him. I soon, however, found out the real cause. Cushing was incompetent, Chase could not be got to think or write, Paterson was a slow man and willingly declined the trouble, and the other two judges (Marshall and Bushrod Washington) you know are commonly estimated as one Judge.

---

[57] *Writings* (Ford ed.), X: 223–225. At another time Jefferson referred to Judge Roane's efforts in doing away with the method of Lord Mansfield and Marshall, namely, "of making opinions in secret and delivering them as the oracles of the court in mass." Roane, when he came to the bench, said Jefferson, "refused to hatch judgments in conclave, or to let others deliver opinions for him." *Ibid.*, X: 224.

The real trouble, Johnson thought, was that there were too many Justices on the Court. "Among seven men," he said, "you will always find at least one intriguer, and probably more than one who may be acted upon only by intrigue." Four Judges were enough. He would have the country divided into a southern, a western, a middle, and an eastern division and a Judge appointed from each.[58]

Again writing to Justice Johnson in the following year, Jefferson commended the Justice for attempting to restore the *seriatim* method of delivering opinions and suggested that some of the other Judges be encouraged to follow his example.[59] Jefferson urged Madison to aid in securing a change in the practice whereby one Justice serves as the mouthpiece for the Court. He thought that Madison's friendship with Justices Todd and Duval might justify him in speaking to them on the subject and in urging them to join Justice Johnson in the practice of preparing separate opinions. In this manner, it was believed that "this dangerous engine of consolidation would feel a proper restraint by their being compelled to explain publicly the grounds of their opinions."[60]

Madison replied that he was pleased to read Justice Johnson's letter and to know that Jefferson was urging upon him a change in the Court's method of delivering opinions. "I have taken frequent occasions to impress the necessity of the *seriatim* mode," said Madison, "but the contrary practice is too deeply rooted to be changed without the injunction of a law, or some very cogent manifestation of the public discontent."[61] From these expressions of opinion it is apparent that both Madison and Jefferson approved the proposals made in Congress to require the Justices to render separate opinions.

In a number of his letters, Jefferson recurred to the doctrine which he had expressed at the time of Chief Justice Marshall's decision in the case of *Marbury v. Madison,* namely, that each of the branches of the general government is coördinate with the others, that each may inter-

---

[58] From Jefferson MSS in Library of Congress.

[59] *Writings* (Ford ed.), X: 232, 248–249. Referring to Chief Justice Marshall's practice of rendering the opinion in all important cases, Jefferson wrote to Thomas Ritchie:

"An opinion is huddled up in conclave, perhaps by a majority of one, delivered as if unanimous, and with the silent acquiescence of lazy or timid associates, by a crafty Chief Judge, who sophisticates the law to his mind, by the turn of his own reasoning. A judiciary law was once reported by the Attorney General to Congress, requiring each Judge to deliver his opinion *seriatim* and openly, and then to give it in writing to the clerk to be entered in the record. A judiciary independent of a king or executive alone is a good thing; but independence of the will of the Nation is a solecism, at least in a republican government." *Writings* (Ford ed.), X: 171.

[60] *Writings* (Ford ed.), X: 260.

[61] *Writings* (Ford ed.), IX: 115, 116. See also Jefferson's letter in *Writings* (Ford ed.), X: 169–171.

pret the Constitution in its own way, and that in cases of conflict an appeal to the people affords the proper method of determining whose interpretation shall prevail. On September 8, 1819, Jefferson wrote to Judge Spencer Roane: "My construction of the Constitution is . . . that each department is truly independent of the others, and has an equal right to decide for itself what is the meaning of the Constitution in the cases submitted to its action; and especially, where it is to act ultimately and without appeal."[62] Jefferson denied the right of the Judiciary to finally and exclusively interpret the Constitution. He did not deny its equal right with the other departments to determine its meaning.

Citing the pardon of those who had been convicted under the Sedition Act because he deemed the act unauthorized by the Constitution, and his refusal to deliver Marbury's commission, and his decision not to present a treaty to the Senate which he regarded unsatisfactory—Jefferson referred to these as examples of his position that "each of the three departments has equally the right to decide for itself what is its duty under the Constitution, without any regard to what the others may have decided for themselves under a similar question."[63] According to this view, Jefferson realized that the Judiciary would have more frequent occasions to act on constitutional questions than the other departments, and he deplored the fact that the Judges were not, like the executive and legislative officers, responsible directly to the people.[64]

The most important criticism made by Jefferson of the Supreme Court under Chief Justice Marshall's direction is contained in his repeated attacks on the assertion by the Court of the doctrine of federal supremacy over the states. His views were expressed with great force and effectiveness in letters to friends following the decisions of the Supreme Court which interpreted broadly the grants of power to the federal government and which thereby limited the authority of the states. His feelings grew in intensity with every decision from the Court which affected the fundamental rights claimed by the states. When the opinions favoring national authority, such as *McCulloch v. Maryland, Dartmouth College v. Woodward,* and *Cohens v. Virginia,* followed in close succession, his letters contain frequent references to the Supreme Court. To Judge Spencer Roane, Jefferson wrote on September 6, 1819, relative to the decision of the Supreme Court in the bank case:

I had read in the *Enquirer,* and with great approbation, the pieces signed Hampden, and have read them again with redoubled approbation, in the copies you have been so kind as to send me. I subscribe to every tittle of them. They contain the true principles of the revolution of 1800, for that was as real a revolution in the principles of our gov-

[62] *Writings* (Ford ed.), X: 141.   [63] *Ibid.,* p. 142.
[64] See letter to Wm. C. Jarvis, Sept. 28, 1820, *Writings* (Ford ed.), X: 160, 161.

ernment as that of 1776 was in its form; not effected indeed by the sword, as that, but by the rational and peaceable instrument of reform, the suffrage of the people. The Nation declared its will by dismissing functionaries of one principle, and electing those of another, in the two branches, executive and legislative, submitted to their election. Over the Judiciary department the Constitution had deprived them of their control. That, therefore, has continued the reprobated system, and although new matter has been occasionally incorporated into the old, yet the leaven of the old mass seems to assimilate to itself the new, and after twenty years' confirmation of the federal system by the voice of the Nation, declared through the medium of elections, we find the Judiciary on every occasion, still driving us into consolidation.

In denying the right they usurp of exclusively explaining the Constitution, I go further than you do, if I understand rightly your quotation from *The Federalist*, of an opinion that "the Judiciary is the last resort in relation *to the other departments* of the government, but not in relation to the rights of the parties to the compact under which the Judiciary is derived." If this opinion be sound, then indeed is our Constitution a complete *felo de se*. For intending to establish three departments, co-ordinate and independent, that they might check and balance one another, it has given, according to this opinion, to one of them alone, the right to prescribe rules for the government of the others, and to that one too, which is unelected by, and independent of the Nation. For experience has already shown that the impeachment it has provided is not even a scarecrow; that such opinions as the one you combat, sent cautiously out, as you observe also, by detachment, not belonging to the case often, but sought for out of it, as if to rally the public opinion beforehand to their views, and to indicate the line they are to walk in, have been so quietly passed over as never to have excited animadversion, even in a speech of any one of the body intrusted with impeachment. The Constitution, on this hypothesis, is a mere thing of wax in the hands of the Judiciary, which they may twist and shape into any form they please. It should be remembered, as an axiom of eternal truth in politics, that whatever power in any government is independent, is absolute also; in theory only, at first, while the spirit of the people is up, but in practice, as fast as that relaxes. Independence can be trusted nowhere but with the people in mass. They are inherently independent of all but moral law. My construction of the Constitution is very different from that you quote. It is that each department is truly independent of the others, and has an equal right to decide for itself what is the meaning of the Constitution in the cases submitted to its action; and especially, where it is to act ultimately and without appeal.[65]

In 1820 a work by William C. Jarvis entitled "The Republicans," in which the Judges were considered as the ultimate arbiters of all constitutional questions, was submitted to Jefferson. This, Jefferson held, was a "very dangerous doctrine indeed, and one which would place us under the despotism of an oligarchy. Our Judges are as honest as other men, and not more so. They have, with others, the same passions for party, for power, and the privilege of their corps. The Constitution has erected no such single tribunal, knowing that to whatever hands confided, with the corruptions of time and party, its members would become despots."[66] Their power, he thought, is the more dangerous because they are in

---

[65] *Writings* (Ford ed.), X: 140, 141.   [66] *Ibid.*, p. 160.

office for life, and they are not responsible, as are those in the Legislative and Executive departments, to the people through the elective control. It is respectfully submitted that the Constitution restrains the authority of the Judges to judicial duties as it does the Executive and Legislative to their respective duties. But regardless of this principle, the Judges have undertaken to dictate to the Executive in the discharge of his duties.

Jefferson regularly expressed the fear that the courts of the United States were attempting to break down the constitutional barriers between the coördinate powers of the states and the union. In his autobiography, which was prepared in 1821, he discussed the draft of the Constitution submitted to the Philadelphia Convention together with certain amendments thereto. He then referred to an amendment which was overlooked at the time and in the omission of which lurked the danger that was leading to the destruction of the combination of national powers in a general government and independent powers in the states.[67] This amendment, which was intended to submit the federal Judiciary to a practical and impartial control, Jefferson regarded as indispensable to the continuance of federal government in the United States.[68] He wrote:

It is not enough that honest men are appointed judges. All know the influence of interest on the mind of man, and how unconsciously his judgment is warped by that influence. To this bias add that the *esprit de corps,* of their peculiar maxim and creed that "it is the office of a good judge to enlarge his jurisdiction," and the absence of responsibility, and how can we expect impartial decision between the general government, of which they are themselves so eminent a part, and an individual State from which they have nothing to hope or fear. We have seen too, that, contrary to all correct example, they are in the habit of going out of the question before them, to throw an anchor ahead and grapple further hold for future advances of power. They are then in fact the corps of sappers and miners, steadily working to undermine the independent rights of the states, and to consolidate all power in the hands of that government in which they have so important a freehold estate.[69]

He became more and more convinced, as decision after decision was announced defining the powers and duties of the various departments of government in the calm and commanding logic of Marshall, that the Judges would soon be in a position "to lay all things at their feet."[70]

Though Madison agreed with Jefferson that the Supreme Court under Marshall's direction had gone beyond the constitutional mandates and requirements to support the centralization of authority in the general

---

[67] *Writings* (Ford ed.), X: 160.

[68] *Ibid.,* I: 111–113.

[69] *Ibid.*

[70] See C. G. Haines, "The Conflict over Judicial Powers in the United States to 1870," *Columbia University Studies in History, Economics, and Public Law,* XXXV (1909), pp. 65–68, from which a few extracts have been used in the preceding pages.

government, he did not approve the views of Roane, Taylor, and Jefferson to meet the situation. Regarding the necessity of the review of state acts by the federal courts, he wrote to Jefferson as follows:

In tracing the boundary between the general and state governments the problem remains for maintaining it in practice; particularly in cases of judicial cognizance. To refer every point of disagreement to the people in conventions would be a process too tardy, too troublesome, and too expensive; besides its tendency to lessen a salutary veneration for an instrument so often calling for such explanatory interpositions. A paramount or even a definitive authority in the individual States, would soon make the Constitution and laws different in different States, and thus destroy that equality and uniformity of rights and duties which form the essence of the compact; to say nothing of the opportunity given to the States individually of involving by their decisions the whole Union in foreign contests. To leave conflicting decisions to be settled between the judicial parties could not promise a happy result. The end must be a trial of strength between the Posse headed by the Marshal and Posse headed by the Sheriff. Nor would the issue be safe if left to a compromise between the two governments the case of a disagreement between different governments being essentially different from a disagreement between branches of the same government. In the latter case neither party being able to consummate its will without the concurrence of the other, there is a necessity on both to consult and to accommodate. Not so, with different governments each possessing every branch of power necessary to carry its purpose into complete effect. It here becomes a question between independent nations, with no other *dernier* resort than physical force. Negotiation might indeed in some instances avoid this extremity; but how often would it happen, among so many States, that an unaccommodating spirit in some would render that source unavailing.

We arrive at the agitated question whether the judicial authority of the United States be the constitutional resort for determining the line between the federal and state jurisdictions. Believing as I do that the general Convention regarded a provision within the Constitution for deciding in a peaceable and regular mode all cases arising in the course of its operation, as essential to an adequate system of government that it intended the authority vested in the judicial department as a final resort in relation to the States, for cases resulting to it in the exercise of its functions, (the concurrence of the Senate chosen by the state legislatures, in appointing the Judges, and the oaths and official tenures of these, with the surveillance of public opinion, being relied on as guaranteeing their impartiality); and that this intention is expressed by the articles declaring that the federal Constitution and laws shall be the supreme law of the land, and that the judicial power of the United States shall extend to all cases arising under them: Believing moreover that this was the prevailing view of the subject when the Constitution was adopted and put into execution; that it has so continued through the long period which has elapsed; and that even at this time an appeal to a national decision would prove that no general change has taken place: thus believing I have never yielded my original opinion indicated in *The Federalist* No. 39 to the ingenious reasonings of Colonel Taylor against this construction of the Constitution.

I am not unaware that the judiciary career has not corresponded with what was anticipated. At one period the Judges perverted the Bench of Justice into a rostrum for partisan harangues. And latterly the Court, by some of its decisions, still more by extra-judicial reasonings and dicta, has manifested a propensity to enlarge the general authority in derogation of the local, and to amplify its own jurisdiction, which has justly incurred the public censure. But the abuse of a trust does not disprove its existence. And if no remedy of the abuse be practicable under the forms of the Constitution, I should prefer a resort to the Nation for an amendment of the tribunal itself, to continual appeals from its controverted decisions to that ultimate arbiter.[71]

This argument, according to Roane and Taylor, was based primarily on policy and expediency, and in their opinion, so far as it was predicated on the language of the Constitution, was not supported by the facts. Like the arguments of the Federalists, it is founded on preconceived ideas and postulates which the facts do not substantially support. Madison's own views at the time of the making of the Constitution do not sustain such a broad power of review of state acts by the federal courts. The threat of nullification, which was now frequently advanced, apparently led Madison to retract somewhat from his earlier expressions of opinion against judicial supremacy in the field of constitutional construction.

Commenting on Jefferson's criticisms of the decisions of men like Justices Marshall, Story, and Washington, Kendrick C. Babcock contended that Jefferson did not understand that "the Constitution was being interpreted in these great decisions by men of the highest legal attainments and historical sense, men of the finest patriotism and devotion to the Constitution."[72] But Babcock misses the real point at issue. Both sides in the controversy had able, high-minded, and patriotic statesmen as leaders who were defending what they regarded as the sound interpretation of the Constitution. It was because the Supreme Court did not confine itself to the strict interpretation and application of the letter of the law, but went over into the realm of determining policy and expediency and of making the language of the Constitution sufficiently malleable to sanction a broad program of national powers, that these decisions called forth persistent and continuous criticisms from the Democrat-Republicans and the successor to this party, the Jacksonian Democrats.

Decisions of the Supreme Court from 1823 to 1828

The period from 1815 to 1825 was marked by repeated attempts of the states to check the centralizing tendencies of the federal government, particularly those tendencies which were reflected in the decisions of the Supreme Court. But on this issue Chief Justice Marshall was unyielding and unwilling to consider anything in the way of compromise. Whether or not his views accorded with public sentiment made no difference to him.

---

[71] *Writings* (Ford ed.), IX: 140–143.
[72] *The Rise of American Nationality, 1811–1819* (New York, 1906), 307.

On certain questions, however, Marshall readily concurred in the prevailing views of the people regardless of the apparent injustice or hardship which might result from the determination of the rights of individuals. When a cause came to the Supreme Court involving the validity of land grants made by Indian tribes, the Chief Justice assumed, with little in the way of argument, that titles to lands granted to individuals or companies by Indian tribes could not be recognized by the courts of the United States. The United States, he said, "have unequivocally acceded to that great and broad rule by which its civilized inhabitants now hold this country. They hold, and assert in themselves, the title by which it was acquired. They maintain, as all others have maintained, that discovery gave an exclusive right to extinguish the Indian title of occupancy, either by purchase or conquest; and gave also a right to such a degree of sovereignty as the circumstances of the people would allow them to exercise."[73] Contrary to apparent and indisputable facts, it was assumed that the Indians were uncivilized and hence had no recognized and approved forms of civil government which could grant and give sanction to valid legal titles to land. The decision merely gave federal judicial sanction to a practice which had been followed by the European powers in their discovery and settlement of the American continent and to the practically uniform procedure of the colonial and state governments in the United States. A contrary decision at this time would have proved so disastrous that it can scarcely be deemed possible that any court would have undertaken to rectify the injustices and the wrongs perpetrated in the seizure of the lands of the Indians.

Justice Story undertook to declare slavery to be contrary to the law of nations because it was in "violation of some of the first principles, which ought to govern nations" and was "repugnant to the great principles of Christian duty, the dictates of natural religion, the obligations of good faith and morality, and the eternal maxims of social justice." And in view of all the circumstances surrounding the traffic in slaves, Story thought that he was bound "to consider the trade an offense against the universal law of society."[74] This decision, Warren thinks, did credit to Story's moral fervor, though it was in advance of the morals of the times, and in conflict with established international law and the decisions of the English courts.[75] Chief Justice Marshall, however, admitting that trade in slaves was contrary to the law of nature, declined to follow in the footsteps of Story. Speaking for the Supreme Court in a decision refusing to condemn slavery, Marshall said: "Whatever might

---

[73] Johnson and Graham's Lessee v. McIntosh, 8 Wheaton 587 (1823).

[74] United States v. Le Jeune Eugenie, 2 Mason 449 ff. (1822).

[75] Warren, *op. cit.*, II: 45.

be the answer of a moralist to this question, a jurist must search for its legal solution, in those principles of action which are sanctioned by the usages, the national acts, and the general assent, of that portion of the world of which he considers himself a part, and to whose law the appeal is made. If we resort to this standard, as the test of international law the question . . . is decided in favor of the legality of the trade."[76] The resentments aroused during the discussion of the Missouri question indicated that public sentiment was not likely to support a far-reaching judicial pronouncement affecting the slavery interests. Though Marshall was willing, when occasion required, to build law upon "the eternal maxims of social justice," this was deemed to be an instance in which the solid basis of governmental sanction for the enforcement of such principles was necessary.

The rights and privileges of the states were also treated somewhat considerately in a case arising under the admiralty jurisdiction of the federal courts. A District Court was held to have no jurisdiction in a suit for wages earned on a voyage from a port within a state and back to the port of departure as a cause of admiralty and maritime jurisdiction. Examining the act of 1790 regulating merchant seamen, Justice Story said: "It merely recognizes the existing, and does not intend to confer any new, jurisdiction. Whether, under the power to regulate commerce between the States, Congress may not extend the remedy, by the summary process of admiralty, to the cases of voyages on the western waters, it is unnecessary for us to consider. If the public inconvenience, from the want of a process of an analogous nature, shall be extensively felt, the attention of the legislature will doubtless be drawn to the subject. But we have now only to declare, that the present suit is not maintainable as a cause of admiralty and maritime jurisdiction, upon acknowledged principles of law."[77]

It had been previously decided that the admiralty and maritime jurisdiction of the federal courts extended to similar cases on the rivers of Kentucky. The assertion of admiralty jurisdiction by the federal courts over inland waters was strongly opposed by the states bordering on the navigable rivers. Senator Johnson of Kentucky called this extension of federal authority "the most serious encroachment upon the constitutional jurisdiction of the state tribunals and the most dangerous inroad upon state sovereignty." A bill confining admiralty jurisdiction to places within the ebb and flow of the tide was favorably considered in Congress but failed of enactment.[78] The situation was temporarily relieved by

[76] The Antelope, 10 Wheaton 121 (1825).
[77] The Thomas Jefferson, 10 Wheaton 429 (1825).
[78] 17th Cong., 1st sess., Feb. 13, 1822. 17th Cong., 2d sess., Feb. 15, 1823.

the decision of the Supreme Court in *The Thomas Jefferson* that admiralty jurisdiction did not extend beyond the ebb and flow of the tide.[79] This change in attitude by the federal Justices probably resulted from the public agitation for the reform of the federal Judiciary. It was later deemed necessary for the Supreme Court to reverse itself on this point.[80]

Despite seeming interferences with the contract clause, the Supreme Court refused to stand in the way of the developing public sentiment to abolish imprisonment for debt. In *Madison v. Haile*,[81] wherein a claim was made that such an act violated the contract clause of the federal Constitution, the Court declared that "this is a measure which must be regulated by the views of policy and expediency entertained by the state legislatures," for, said Justice Thompson, "such laws act merely upon the remedy, and that in part only. They do not take away the entire remedy, but only so far as imprisonment forms a part of such remedy." *Sturges v. Crowninshield* was quoted to the effect that "without impairing the obligation of the contract, the remedy may certainly be modified as the wisdom of the nation shall direct. . . . Imprisonment is no part of the contract, and simply to release the prisoner, does not impair its obligation."[82] Imprisonment for debt was now generally considered repugnant to reason and justice, and the Supreme Court did not stand in the way of the abolition of the inhuman practice which had prevailed for centuries. One of the most important cases which came to the Supreme Court during this period, *Ogden v. Saunders,* related to the interpretation of the contract clause.

Ogden v. Saunders.—This case[83] was first argued in March, 1824, following the decision in *Gibbons v. Ogden,* but because of a division of opinion among the Justices, no decision was rendered during this or the following term of the Court. After the appointment of Justice Trimble the case was again argued in January, 1827. One month later the decision was rendered, the Justices being divided four to three on this issue of whether a New York insolvent law was valid so far as it was applicable to contracts made after the passage of the law. By the same vote, but with a different line-up of the Justices, it was held that the New York law could not discharge a contract with a citizen of another state.

Henry Wheaton, arguing against the validity of the state bankrupt

---

[79] 10 Wheaton 428 (1825). It is interesting to note that before this decision Justice Story had been extremely liberal in construing the extent of admiralty jurisdiction. See Warren, *op. cit.,* II: 95.

[80] See The Genessee Chief v. Fitzhugh, 12 Howard 443 (1851).

[81] 12 Wheaton 378 (1827).

[82] 4 Wheaton 200, 201 (1819).

[83] 12 Wheaton 213 (1827).

acts, contended that the prohibition on the states against the passage of laws impairing the obligation of contracts was intended to establish "a great conservative principle" under which contracts might be protected from unjust acts of legislation in any form.[84] The authority in the power granted to the federal government to enact a uniform bankruptcy law was declared to be vested exclusively in the federal government. To the claim that the prohibition on the states in the passage of bankrupt laws applied to acts operating on existing contracts only, Wheaton replied that "retrospective laws, applicable to civil cases, hardly required any positive and express prohibition. In every system of jurisprudence, such laws are considered as contrary to the first principles of natural justice. . . . The Constitution meant to preserve the inviolability of contracts, as secured by those eternal principles of equity and justice, which run throughout every civilized code, which form a part of the law of nature and nations, and by which human society, in all countries and all ages, has been regulated and upheld." The obligation of contract does not spring from municipal law alone. It is derived from a higher source—"from those great principles of universal law, which are binding on the societies of man as well as on individuals."[85]

For the state, counsel insisted that it was by this time the settled doctrine of the Supreme Court that the states could pass bankrupt laws provided these laws did not impair the obligation of existing contracts and that if Congress enacted a uniform law the state acts would be suspended only so far as they were in conflict with the federal statute. The obligation of contract, which by the Constitution the states could not impair, was defined as the local laws which were then in force and were intended to give effect to the contract. These laws could clearly be changed if made to apply only to subsequent contracts.

Webster, in support of the contentions of Wheaton, said: "The Constitution was intended to accomplish a great political object. Its design was not so much to prevent injustice or injury in one case, or in successive single cases, as it was to make general salutary provisions, which in their operation should give security to all contracts, stability to credit, uniformity among all the States, in those things which materially concerned the foreign commerce of the country, and their own credit, trade,

---

[84] *Ibid.*, p. 216.

[85] 12 Wheaton 221, 222. Counsel, in arguing the case of *Ogden v. Saunders*, explained that the obligation of contract which the Supreme Court enforced in *Green v. Biddle* (8 Wheaton 1) was one presented and required by the law of nature and of nations and not one specifically demanded by the language of the Constitution. See argument of Wheaton, 12 Wheaton 223 and confirmation of this view by Justice Washington, *ibid.*, p. 258.

and intercourse among themselves."[86] Agreeing also with Wheaton, Webster thought that the obligation of contract did not arise solely from the provisions of municipal law but that the duty to provide that the terms of agreements entered into are fulfilled springs from universal law. The authorities on natural law and the law of nations such as Vattel, Grotius, Burlamaqui, Pothier, and Rutherforth were cited in support of this view. "We differ from our learned adversaries on general principles," said Webster, "we differ as to the main scope and end of this constitutional provision. They think it remedial: we regard it as preventive. They think it adopted to secure redress for violated private rights: to us it seems intended to guard against great public mischiefs. . . . We think its main scope to be general and political."[87] Webster then took issue with the opinion of the Court as expressed in *Sturges v. Crowninshield*[88] to the effect that the authority to enact bankrupt laws was not granted exclusively to the federal government. He respectfully requested the Justices to reconsider this point, for "one great political object, intended by the Constitution, would be defeated, if this construction were allowed to prevail."[89]

The Justices delivered their opinions *seriatim*. To Justice Washington the most important issue to decide was "whether the obligation of a contract is impaired by a state bankrupt or insolvent law, which discharges the person and future acquisitions of the debtor from his liability under a contract entered into in that State after the passage of the act."[90] Interpreting the prohibition of the Constitution so as to enforce the notions of the universal law relating to the performance of contracts would, thought Washington, restrict the sphere of state legislation beyond that which the sovereign states of the union would have consented to, for, said he, "it will be found upon examination, that there are few laws which concern the general policy of a State, or the government of its citizens in their intercourse with each other, or with strangers, which may not in some way or other affect the contracts which they have entered into, or may thereafter form."[91] The term "obligation" then, maintained Washington, can refer only to the municipal law of the state, whether that be written or unwritten, which is the law of the contract made within the state. "To the decision in the case of *Sturges v. Crowninshield,* and to the reasoning of the learned Judge who delivered that opinion," Washington said, "I entirely submit; although I did not then, nor can I now, bring my mind to concur in that part of it, which admits the constitu-

---

[86] 12 Wheaton 237.
[87] *Ibid.*, p. 247.
[88] 4 Wheaton 122 (1819).

[89] 12 Wheaton 253.
[90] *Ibid.*, p. 254.
[91] *Ibid.*, pp. 258, 259.

tional power of the state legislatures to pass bankrupt laws, by which I understand, those laws which discharge the person and future acquisitions of a bankrupt from his debts. I have always thought that the power to pass such a law was exclusively vested by the Constitution in the legislature of the United States. But it becomes me to believe that this opinion was, and is, incorrect since it stands condemned by the decision of a majority of this Court, solemnly pronounced."[92] It was then concluded that a bankrupt law which operates prospectively, or so far as it does so operate, does not violate the Constitution of the United States. In Washington's opinion the power to pass bankrupt laws was exclusive in Congress, and, since affirmative federal action would prevent unreasonable interference with contracts as affected by such laws, the intention must have been to apply the constitutional prohibition only to retrospective laws.

After calling attention to errors or misinterpretations of the reporters in the cases of *McMillan v. McNeill*[93] and *Sturges v. Crowninshield*,[94] Justice Johnson explained that the Court in the latter case was "greatly divided in their views of the doctrine, and the judgment partakes as much of a compromise, as of a legal adjudication. The minority thought it better to yield something than risk the whole. And, although their course of reasoning led them to the general maintenance of the state power over the subject . . . yet, as denying the power to act upon anterior contracts, could do no harm, but, in fact, imposed a restriction conceived in the true spirit of the Constitution, they were satisfied to acquiesce in it, provided the decision were so guarded as to secure the power over posterior contracts, as well from the positive terms of the adjudication, as from the inferences deducible from the reasoning of the Court."[95] The limitations of the reasoning and judgment in the *Sturges Case* were then asserted to the effect that a state may pass a bankrupt law provided it does not impair the obligation of contracts, and provided there is no conflicting act of Congress, and that so far as such state act relates to contracts made before its passage, it is void. These propositions were thought to have disposed of the claim that Congress had exclusive authority to enact a bankrupt law. But since the question of the exclusiveness of the federal authority in this field was again raised by counsel and supported by Justice Washington, Johnson gave his reasons for rejecting this interpretation of the language of the Constitution. The grant of authority to Congress, he thought, was in such form that nothing short of a direct prohibition on the states against the exercise of such authority would

[92] *Ibid.*, pp. 263, 264.
[93] 4 Wheaton 209 (1819).
[94] *Ibid.*, p. 122.
[95] 12 Wheaton 272, 273.

have sanctioned exclusive federal power over bankruptcy. Appealing to history, Johnson made the following suggestion:

Let any one turn his eye back to the time when this grant was made, and say, if the situation of the people admitted of an abandonment of a power so familiar to the juris-prudence of every State; so universally sustained in its reasonable exercise, by the opinion and practice of mankind, and so vitally important to a people overwhelmed in debt, and urged to enterprise by the activity of mind that is generated by revolutions and free governments. I will with confidence affirm, that the Constitution had never been adopted, had it then been imagined that this question would ever have been made, or that the exercise of this power in the States should ever have depended upon the views of the tribunals to which that Constitution was about to give existence. With regard to the universal understanding of the American people on this subject, there cannot be two opinions. If ever contemporaneous exposition, and the clear un-derstanding of the contracting parties . . . could be resorted to, as a means of expound-ing an instrument, the continuing and unimpaired existence of this power in the States ought never to have been controverted.[96]

Johnson concluded that the exclusive power of Congress over the relief of insolvents was untenable and that the dangers apprehended from the contrary doctrine were unreal.

The obligation of contract, then, which the Constitution protects was given a very broad application. The right and power involved in such an obligation, said Johnson, "will be found to be measured neither by the moral law alone, nor universal law alone, nor by the laws of society alone, but by a combination of the three—an operation in which the moral law is explained and applied by the law of nature, and both modi-fied and adopted, to the exigencies of society by positive law."[97] Since the broad ground which he was predicating for the protection of contracts might be deemed applicable to contracts made prior to the contested law as well as those made posterior to it and because his views in this respect were inconsistent with the decision in the case of *Sturges v. Crownin-shield,* Johnson replied, "I think this no objection to its correctness. I entertained this opinion then, and have no reason to doubt it since."[98] "It appears to me," he continued,

that a great part of the difficulties of the cause, arise from not giving sufficient weight to the general intent of this clause in the Constitution, and subjecting it to a severe literal construction, which would be better adapted to special pleadings. By classing bills of attainder, *ex post facto* laws, and laws impairing the obligation of contracts together, the general intent becomes very apparent; it is a general provision against arbitrary and tyranical legislation over existing rights, whether of person or property.[99]

If the term obligation of contract is held to apply to the remedy alone, Johnson believed that these words would have an ambulatory and uncer-tain meaning.

---

[96] 12 Wheaton 275, 277.   [98] *Ibid.,* p. 284.
[97] *Ibid.,* p. 282.   [99] *Ibid.,* p. 286.

After mature consideration Justice Thompson concluded that the New York law was valid. The law in question had been enacted in 1801, but this act was essentially a revision and reënactment of a measure adopted in 1788. To declare a law void after such a lapse of time, Thompson thought, should only be done for reasons of urgent necessity, and should be founded upon reasons and principles scarcely admitting of doubt. Such reasons had not been presented by counsel and were not otherwise apparent. To Justice Thompson it is the law of contract which forms its obligation, and not some features of agreements which find their sanction only in natural or universal law. But principles of natural law were not entirely discarded, for it was maintained that retrospective laws taking away vested rights should not be enforced, because "such laws are repugnant to those fundamental principles, upon which every just system of laws is founded."[100] With respect to the insolvent law in question, however, it was contended that, since the letter of the Constitution did not imperiously demand a construction which denied to the states the power to pass such acts, policy and expediency required a contrary construction.[101]

Justice Trimble approved the reasoning of the Court in the *Sturges Case,* and therefore did not consider the control of bankruptcy as belonging exclusively to the federal government; nor did he regard the obligation of contracts to be derived from natural or universal law. Obligation in the constitutional sense can mean nothing other than that which is recognized by, and results from, the law of the state in which the contract is made.[102]

Chief Justice Marshall, speaking for the minority, noted that Justices Duval, Story, and himself did not concur in the judgment pronounced. They conceived the prohibition as inserted in the Constitution to be general in its scope. "Language is incapable of expressing in plainer terms," said Marshall, "that the mind of the Convention was directed to retroactive legislation, and whether the thing to be prohibited be the exercise of mere political power or legislative action on individuals, the prohibition is complete and total. There is no exception to it. Legislation of every description is comprehended within it."[103]

Marshall then turned to the nature of agreements and the obligation inhering in them in a state of nature. The obligation in such agreements is, he thinks, not conferred by positive law, but is intrinsic and is conferred by the act of the parties.[104] To support this reasoning Marshall

[100] *Ibid.,* p. 304.
[101] *Ibid.,* p. 310.
[102] *Ibid.,* p. 321.
[103] *Ibid.,* pp. 335, 336.
[104] *Ibid.,* p. 346.

appealed to the authority of writers on natural and national law "whose opinions have been viewed with profound respect."[105] From these premises it followed necessarily that the obligation of contract and the remedy provided for its enforcement are not identical, as the majority assert, but are distinguishable one from the other—the first is created by the act of the parties, the last is afforded by the government. It was concluded, therefore, that the words used in the Constitution relative to the protection of contracts "taken in their natural and obvious sense, admit of prospective, as well as retrospective operation."[106] Expressing grave fears at the results which were likely to follow if a great constitutional principle prohibiting all laws of an obnoxious character relating to contracts was to be applied only to the protection of preëxisting contracts, Marshall declared that the reasoning of the majority converted an inhibition to pass laws impairing the obligation of contracts into an inhibition to pass retrospective laws. Thus a vital provision of the Constitution—"one on which the good and wise reposed confidently for securing the prosperity and harmony of our citizens would lie prostrate, and be construed into an inanimate, unoperative, unmeaning clause."[107]

On the specific question raised in *Ogden v. Saunders* whether the New York insolvent law could discharge a contract made by a citizen of another state, Justice Johnson joined with the dissenters on the meaning of the contract clause and held that such a contract could not be discharged. Justices Washington, Thompson, and Trimble dissented from this decision. The grave uncertainties, which the meaning of the Constitution exhibited in the reasoning of the Justices and the obvious mixture of law and political expediency in the opinions rendered, fostered the growing criticisms directed against the federal Judiciary. Internal dissension was beginning to appear and to weaken the dominating position maintained by Chief Justice Marshall for nearly three decades.

The policy of enforcing judicially construed limitations on the states was again asserted in the announcement by the Chief Justice of the far-reaching "original package doctrine." In 1821 Maryland passed an act requiring all importers of foreign articles or commodities to take out a license. The fee for such a permit was fifty dollars with a fine and forfeiture of the tax for failure to obtain a license. Brown was indicted for failure to observe the provisions of this law and, failing to secure release from the indictment from the state courts, appealed by writ of error to the Supreme Court of the United States.

---

[105] Three Justices agreed with Marshall that there was a natural law which sanctioned the obligation of contracts, but to them the civil obligation was paramount.

[106] 12 Wheaton 354.

[107] *Ibid.*, p. 340.

Brown v. Maryland.—In this case the attorneys for Brown argued that the Maryland act violated the prohibition on the states to lay imposts or duties on imports as well as implied restrictions which necessarily result from the supreme and paramount authority of the union to regulate foreign and domestic commerce. Roger B. Taney and his associate counsel for the state replied that the state act was merely a tax on trade or business carried on within the state. The authority over commerce was declared to be concurrent, with full authority to act, so far as there was no conflicting act of Congress, belonging to the states. Congress not having regulated the sale of imported articles in the hands of the wholesale dealer, the state was free to regulate the business as it saw fit. To the contention that serious inconveniences would result from the exercise of conflicting authority if the state act were upheld, it was answered that in the adjustment of the relations between the nation and the states much dependence must be placed upon "the good sense and good feelings of the people," for "the Union cannot be preserved by the mere strength and power of the federal government. It is dissolved as soon as it shall forfeit the affection and confidence of the States."[108]

Chief Justice Marshall, rendering the opinion of the Court, stated the issue to be primarily whether the legislature of a state can constitutionally require the importer of foreign articles to take out a license from the state before he may sell an imported article. Turning to the ground of policy and expediency, which always loomed large when Marshall faced the issue of nationalism versus State rights, he maintained that the prohibition against the states on the control of imports and exports "would be as completely defeated by a power to tax the article in the hands of the importer the instant it was landed, as by a power to tax it while entering the port. There is no difference, in effect, between a power to prohibit the sale of an article, and the power to prohibit its introduction into the country."[109]

Recognizing that to a certain degree there must be concurrent authority by the federal and state governments over articles while in the process of importation into a state, Marshall formulated the well-known "original package doctrine." It is sufficient for the present to say, generally, Marshall observed,

that when the importer has so acted upon the thing imported, that it has become incorporated and mixed up with the mass of property in the country, it has, perhaps, lost its distinctive character as an import, and has become subject to the taxing power of the State; but while remaining the property of the importer, in his warehouse, in

---

[108] Brown v. Maryland, 12 Wheaton 433 (1827).
[109] *Ibid.*, p. 439.

the original form or package in which it was imported, a tax upon it is too plainly a duty on imports to escape the prohibition in the Constitution. . . .

The principle, then, for which the plaintiffs in error contend, that the importer acquires a right, not only to bring the articles into the country, but to mix them with the common mass of property, does not interfere with the necessary power of taxation which is acknowledged to reside in the States, to that dangerous extent which the counsel for the defendants in error seem to apprehend. It carries the prohibition in the Constitution no farther than to prevent the States from doing that which it was the great object of the Constitution to prevent.[110]

Maryland's act, then, was held to be repugnant to the clause of the Constitution which declares that "no state shall lay any impost or duties on imports or exports" and to the clause authorizing Congress to regulate commerce. Since importation was an ingredient of commerce, asserted Marshall, Congress has a right not only to authorize importation but to authorize the importer to sell. Any penalty, therefore, "inflicted on the importer for selling the article, in his character as importer, must be in opposition to the act of Congress which authorizes importation."[111]

Since the license imposed by Maryland was required for permission to sell goods in the internal trade of the state, Justice Thompson, dissenting, could see no reasonable ground for permitting such a tax on retail dealers and condemned it, at least so far as applicable to wholesale dealers who were engaged in the importation of goods from without the state. The power to regulate commerce was, in Thompson's opinion, clearly a concurrent power, for "it is to be borne in mind, that this was a power possessed by the States, respectively, before the adoption of the Constitution, and is not a power growing out of the establishment of the general government. It is to be viewed, therefore, as the surrender of a power antecedently possessed by the States, and the extent of the surrender must receive a fair and reasonable interpretation with reference to the object for which the surrender was made."[112] Chief Justice Marshall admitted in *Gibbons v. Ogden* that the states could regulate internal but not external commerce.[113] To Justice Thompson the only practicable line to draw between internal and external commerce was to recognize that federal power ceased when the article was imported and offered for sale in the state. The distinction which applied the prohibition on the state's power to tax, so far as the first sale by the wholesale dealer was concerned, was regarded by him as based on specious reasoning and as in no sense warranted by the express language of the Constitution. Speaking of Marshall's references to policy and expediency as justification for the condemnation of the state act, Thompson re-

---

[110] 12 Wheaton 441–444.
[111] *Ibid.*, p. 448.
[112] *Ibid.*, p. 452.
[113] 9 Wheaton 194, 208 (1824).

marked that "arguments drawn against the existence of a power from its supposed abuse are illogical, and generally lead to unsound conclusions."[114] Thompson's views against placing judicially construed limitations on the states were soon to be given greater weight by the Supreme Court, and the practice of the Chief Justice in this respect was to be largely repudiated by the members of the Court who were influenced by Democratic principles and doctrines.

In one more instance, however, the doctrine of implied powers was relied upon to construe as belonging to the federal government the authority to extend the territorial limits of the United States. Though the Constitution provided for the government of territory under the jurisdiction of the United States, no express authority was granted to the federal government to acquire territory. This defect or omission was slurred over by Chief Justice Marshall by regarding such a power as necessarily incidental to powers granted. "The Constitution confers absolutely on the government of the Union," said he, "the powers of making war and of making treaties; consequently, that government possesses the power of acquiring territory, either by conquest or treaty."[115] Since the authority of a territorial court of Florida was involved in this case, it was deemed necessary to define the status of such courts. They were declared to be not constitutional courts but legislative courts, created by virtue of the general right of sovereignty which exists in the government and sanctioned by that clause which enables Congress to make all needful rules and regulations respecting the territory belonging to the United States. Distinguishing these courts from those established under Article three of the Constitution, they were in essence declared to be "legislative courts" set up in the territories in accordance with the broad powers which Congress, both as a general and a local government, exercises over such territories. It was again held that the federal government, for certain purposes at least, possessed the rights and privileges of a sovereign government. No more irritating language could have been used to arouse the opponents of the authority exercised by the federal courts. This decision was subjected to criticism thirty years later in the debates on the power of Congress over slavery in territories.[116] The party realignments which took place during the decade from 1820 to 1830 and which resulted in the inauguration of Andrew Jackson to the presidency in March, 1829, were destined to have a marked effect upon the development of the Supreme Court and upon its principles of constitutional interpretation.

---

[114] 12 Wheaton 457.
[115] American Insurance Co. v. Canter, 1 Peters 511, 541 (1828).
[116] See Beveridge, *op. cit.,* IV: 142–144, and Warren, *op. cit.,* II: 160.

Part Five

THE DECLINE OF THE AUTHORITY
AND PRESTIGE OF THE
SUPREME COURT

CHAPTER XV

Constitutional Construction and the Issue of Nullification

THE FIRST PARTY DIVISIONS which prevailed during the periods of the Revolution and constitution-making followed the age-old conflict between the conservative groups and those inclined to accept and follow liberal and democratic doctrines in political outlook and attitudes. This type of political alignment frequently involved a contest between those who lived along the seaboard, in the lowlands, and in the commercial centers, and those who pushed westward into the first American frontier. Parties were thus based to a considerable degree on the differences in political points of view, as well as on geographic or sectional lines. In time, however, party alignments came to be more closely associated with sectional interests and antagonisms. Evidences of hostility between New England and the South, particularly as typified in the policies and leadership of Virginia, appeared in the federal Convention and grew in intensity as controversies arose over the interpretation and application of the provisions of the Constitution.[1] Sectional

---

[1] John Taylor, who at one time favored North-South separation, in his definition of parties, observed that on every question, domestic and foreign, the two parties were far apart. In his term in the Senate he described a conference with Rufus King and Oliver Ellsworth in which they suggested that steps be taken to bring about a peaceable dissolution of the union. In their opinion the conflict between the interests of the southern states and those of the north and east was of such a nature that adjustment of differences seemed impossible. Taylor thought it was still possible to preserve the union. See account of Taylor's memorandum on this conference, Henry H. Simms, *Life of John Taylor* (Richmond, 1932), pp. 61, 62. Jefferson wrote to Taylor on June 1, 1798, as follows: "It is true that we are completely under the saddle of Massachusetts and Connecticut, and they ride us very hard, cruelly insulting our feelings, as well as exhausting our strength and subsistence." But he concluded that "in every free and deliberative society, there must, from the nature of man be opposite parties, and violent dissensions and discords.... But if on a temporary superiority of the one party the other is to resort to a scission of the Union, no federal government can ever exist. If to rid ourselves of the present rule of Massachusetts and Connecticut, we break the Union, will the evil stop there? Suppose the New England States alone cut off, ... we shall see a Pennsylvania and Virginia party arise in the residuary confederacy.... If we reduce our Union to Virginia and North Carolina ... they will end by breaking into simple units.... If the game runs against us at home, we must have patience until luck turns, and then we shall have an opportunity of winning back the *principles* we have lost. For this is a game where principles are the stake." *The Writings of Thomas Jefferson*, ed. by Paul Leicester Ford (New York, 1892), VII: 263–266.

differences in point of view and interpretation were apparent in the resistance to the enforcement of the Alien and Sedition Acts, in the approval of and the resistance to the policies of the national administration in carrying out the embargo acts, and in the conduct of the War of 1812. Such differences characterized the opposition to and the support of the nationalistic program adopted following the war. The marked divisions between the New England Federalists and the Republicans of the South was shown in the reëlection of Madison. All of the states east of the Delaware except Vermont had voted for Clinton, and all of the states of the South and West except Delaware and Maryland had voted for Madison. The situation was now changed, for the Federalists charged that the freemen of the North were at the mercy of the slaves of the South. It was recognized that the political and geographical cleavages were nearly coincident. As early as 1820 it became apparent that slavery was an institution which was likely to foster these sectional differences to the point where peaceful methods of adjustment of divergent political issues might become impossible.[2]

The disappearance of the former party alignments following the War of 1812 tended to bring sectional viewpoints to the forefront. After 1815 the Federalist party split into three groups. Some condemned the Hartford Convention and joined the Republican party. A few, following the principles and policies of the Essex Junto, continued to oppose every act of the national administration. The majority of the party, however, joined Harrison Gray Otis in adopting a middle course based on the contentions that "the Republican party, having absorbed every Federalist principle of permanent value, did not intend to use its power to the detriment of New England's sectional interests, and that under these circumstances there could be no object in withholding Federalist support from Madison and Monroe."[3] The Federalist party was gradually reduced to a minority and protesting group in all of the states except Massachusetts where Federalist officials were elected until 1823. With the defeat of Harrison Gray Otis for governor in 1823, the Federalist party lost its last state and entered into a period of final dissolution. Massachusetts Federalism gradually blended with the conservative wing of the old Jeffersonian party.[4] In the other states the Federalist party had long since ceased to exist as an effective political organization.

In Monroe's Administration much of the bitterness of political feeling which had characterized the preceding decades disappeared. Historians

[2] Edward Channing, *A History of the United States* (New York, 1927), IV: 156, 157.

[3] Samuel Eliot Morison, *The Life and Letters of Harrison Gray Otis: Federalist* (Boston, 1913), II: 201, 202.

[4] *Ibid.*, p. 243.

sometimes object to the characterization of Monroe's Administration as "the Era of Good Feeling," because of the factional conflicts within the Republican ranks, but Morison observes that during Otis's sojourn in Washington from 1817 to 1822 "the distinction between Federalists and Republicans was as obsolete in Congress as it was in Washington society."[5] It is a mistake to assume, however, that the former issues between the Federalists and Anti-Federalists were no longer to dominate the debates and the political cleavages in Congress or in the states. The principles of the two parties were, indeed, "opposite and irreconcilable, the one believed in a government by the upper classes, the other in a government by the people."[6] The way was being prepared for the conflict between these two groups over the issue of nationalism versus State rights.

PARTY ALIGNMENTS FOLLOWING THE "ERA OF GOOD FEELING"

As the political battle lines were being drawn for this major issue, John Quincy Adams was elected President without having received a majority of the electoral vote. Hence, he took office in violation of an essential principle of democracy. This and other factors led to the gradual formation of a new Democratic party, the principles of which were in accord in part only with those of the party's founder, Jefferson. And the followers of Adams, Webster, and Clay combined to form a National Republican party which later took the name "Whig." The newly organized Democratic party, which still clung to the name "Republican" for the time being, espoused the cause of State rights and a strict construction of the federal charter. The Whigs, on the other hand, championed a loose or broad construction of the Constitution, directing their efforts primarily to the advocacy of Clay's "American system" with high protective tariffs and liberal federal aid to internal improvements.[7] Though party lines from 1820 to 1830 were loosely drawn and party doctrines were vaguely formulated, the contest over the Supreme Court and over divergent principles of constitutional construction was waged with intermittent fervor until new appointments to the Supreme Court by Andrew Jackson changed the political affiliations and attitudes of the Justices and thereby assured more favorable consideration to the interests of the states.

Following the arguments over the Missouri Compromise and over the nationalistic opinions of Chief Justice Marshall and Justice Story, it became fairly clear that most of the old and new Republicans, particularly those in the states of the South and West, looked upon the distribution of

---

[5] *Ibid.*, p. 213.

[6] *Op. cit.*, I: 62.

[7] Cf. William MacDonald, *Jacksonian Democracy*, American Nation Series (New York, 1906), pp. 34 ff.

powers under the Constitution as in effect establishing a league of states. The states were regarded as sovereign from the time of the Declaration of Independence and the adoption of the Constitution. It was assumed that the acceptance of the Constitution did not change this condition. But even if the language of the Constitution, with its supremacy clause and its broad grant of powers to the federal courts, appeared to place some marked limits upon state sovereignty, it was taken for granted that the adoption of the Ninth, Tenth, and the Eleventh Amendments rebuffing the Federalist's claim of national sovereignty as sanctioned by the Supreme Court,[8] the Virginia and Kentucky Resolutions with Madison's report, followed by the election to the presidency of Thomas Jefferson, the author of the most extreme of the resolutions, and the continuous and persistent denial of sovereignty in the federal government by almost every state in turn, had placed to the forefront the view that sovereignty resided ultimately and in a final sense in the states.

The Supreme Court had asserted its authority over the state courts in the interpretation of the federal Constitution and to make its view of federal supremacy prevail had neatly sidestepped the Eleventh Amendment. But the assertions of federal supremacy over the states occurred infrequently and they were strongly opposed. Furthermore, the grounds on which they were based were repeatedly declared in public pronunciamentos and frequent official statements to be indefensible upon a fair and reasonable interpretation of the language of the Constitution. It might be argued, as many historians have been inclined to do, that these pronunciamentos and statements were merely partisan diatribes presented for political purposes and that the nationalistic arguments of the Supreme Court and of leading Federalists were pure law undefiled by political implications. The facts of history have indeed been frequently distorted in this manner. No doubt the men who strove to defend the sovereignty of the states were doing so for political purposes, and their motives were often as unimpeachable as were those of the members of the Supreme Bench. Doubtless the statesmen who sat upon the Supreme Court for equally laudable political purposes aimed to advance the cause of nationalism. The vague and indefinite language of the written charter did not resolve the issue. Political arguments were necessary and they were indulged in freely both on and off the Bench.

To the Republicans the government established at Washington was a "general government" to which the states had accorded certain express powers which might be exercised for the general good so long as the states

---

[8] The Ninth and Tenth Amendments, according to Channing, "were actual changes in the nature of the fundamental law and were intended to place a limitation on the strong nationalistic tendency of the Constitution." Channing, *op. cit.*, IV: 158.

did not desire to take them away. It was taken for granted that the states became members of the union of their own free will and that if and when they saw fit to withdraw from the union they clearly had a right to do so.[9] Withdrawal from the union, though often discussed and generally regarded as within the realm of possibility both by the Federalists and the Republicans, was not to be decided lightly and without due consideration of the serious consequences involved. But few objections were raised to the frequently expressed sentiments of secession or nullification.

The Federalists, being estopped from the use of the word national and not daring to assert the claim of sovereignty for the central agency of the union, because of the resentment which the use of this term aroused in the minds of those who supported the independent authority, jurisdiction, and sovereignty of the states, concealed their purposes in the word "government." It was, they contended, a government, not a league which was established by the Constitution. And all of the connotations of nationalism were gathered in this general and inoffensive word.

Whereas the Republicans thought and spoke of the government at Washington as a "general government" carrying out powers expressly granted by a league of states, the Federalists and some of the conservative Republicans of the old school, gradually merging into a new political party and building upon the organic or nationalistic concepts expressed during the Revolutionary and post-Revolutionary periods, constructed a philosophy to support the current nationalistic designs. It was when the states had moved strongly in the direction of applying the doctrines of nullification that the Webster-Hayne debate and other public discussions renewed the argument of whether the Constitution had merely readjusted the relations between a league of states or whether the document formed a nation possessed of sovereign powers and privileges.

Despite the disappearance of the Federalist party from national politics and the decline of the influence of the party in all except a few states, the political ideas of the party continued to play a prominent role in national affairs for the next few decades. The essential doctrines of Federalism received the continued support of strong and effective minority groups. Writing to Gallatin in 1822, Jefferson commented on the fact that the old party alignments still continued and that the Federalists continued to support the generally discredited doctrine of centralization in government.[10] But, as Webster observed in 1824, party distinctions

[9] There were statements in the federal and state conventions that once a state had entered the union it could not withdraw, but little was heard of this notion afterward, and it was customary in most of the public discussions relative to the matter to assume that the states could if they saw fit withdraw from the union.

[10] *Writings* (Ford ed.), X: 235, 236.

were becoming confused. Some Republicans preferred the conservatism of Adams to the democracy of the Jeffersonians, whereas others joined the newly forming Democratic groups. For nearly a decade personalities rather than party principles came to be the central factors in the political activities of the time.[11] While Adams, Clay, Jackson, Calhoun, and Webster were engaged in the contests for political advantages and preferment, issues of constitutional construction were temporarily submerged under the machinations of personal and partisan politics. The significance of the work of the Supreme Court from 1825 to 1835, however, can be appreciated and understood only in connection with the controversies over constitutional construction which became the major issue before Congress and in public discussions throughout the nation. It was over the issues of national aid for internal improvements and of the enactment of protective tariff acts—issues which only indirectly involved the decisions of the Supreme Court—that the states attempted to give practical application to the Democratic-Republican doctrines formulated by Roane, Taylor, and Jefferson.

CONSTITUTIONAL OBJECTIONS TO NATIONAL AID FOR INTERNAL IMPROVEMENTS AND PROTECTIVE TARIFF ACTS

It was not a theory of government, thought Frederick J. Turner, but a political exigency which called forth the principle of state sovereignty.[12] With the industrial policy of the country under the control of the North and the West and the social system of the South endangered, an appeal was made to state sovereignty as a mode of recourse to meet what appeared to Turner to be a desperate condition. The growing popularity of Clay's "American system" which included generous aid by the federal government for internal improvements and the extension and increase of protective duties for manufacturers aroused the resentment of the whole planting sections. It was in South Carolina, however, where drastic action was taken, for, to the people of this state, "the triumph of loose construction principles and the possible election of a northern President seemed to presage not only the sacrifice of their economic interests, but even the freeing of their slaves." The Missouri controversy, the colonization society which began to agitate in favor of the emancipation of the negroes, and the dangers of insurrection among the negroes made South Carolina leaders feel that compromise was no longer possible.

The frequent and persistent assertions of the doctrine of state sovereignty by the separate states and by groups of states from 1789 to 1830

---

[11] E. Malcolm Carroll, *Origins of the Whig Party* (Durham, 1925), pp. 4, 5.

[12] Frederick J. Turner, *Rise of the New West*, American Nation Series (New York, 1916), pp. 304 ff.

in all sections of the union, however, gives evidence of other bases for the espousal of the doctrine than mere political expediency. There was a fundamental and vital difference of opinion with respect to the nature of the union established in 1789. The adoption of certain measures or modes of interpretation by those in charge of the public affairs of the nation brought this difference, which sometimes merely smouldered beneath the surface, to the forefront. Among the incidents which aroused emphatic responses were: the Alien and Sedition Laws, the Embargo Act and the War of 1812, the establishment of a national bank, and the extension of the powers of the federal government by the adoption of the principle of implied powers by both Congress and the Supreme Court. It was the acceptance of the nationalistic theory of the interpretation of federal powers with respect both to internal improvements and the tariff which called forth the most persistent and defiant reactions from the states. The proposition that surplus revenue should be raised by means of protective tariffs in order to pay for internal improvements mostly in the North and West seemed to southern statesmen to be outrageous. In the adoption of the Tariff Act of 1824, only one representative of the southern states, Johnson of Virginia, voted for the measure. In 1820 the house of representatives of South Carolina opposed the protective system on grounds of policy but apparently conceded its constitutionality.[13] A few years later the argument was shifted from a matter of policy to one of constitutionality.

By the close of Monroe's Administration, the forces of nationalism seemed to have triumphed in the field of internal improvements. And when measures were enacted by Congress, on the recommendation of President Adams, providing for internal improvements and for higher protective duties for American manufactures, state sovereignty sentiment, involving the conviction that the enforcement of these acts must be checked, grew rapidly in the South. Governor Wilson of South Carolina, in December, 1824, called attention to "the alarming extent to which the federal Judiciary and Congress have gone toward establishing a great and consolidated government, subversive of the rights of the States and contravening the letter and spirit of the Constitution of the Union." Wilson conceived it to be the duty of the states to act as public sentinels to give the alarm "in order that those who are friendly to the present Constitution may preserve it in its original purity."[14]

Both Jefferson and Hamilton appear to have regarded it necessary to

---

[13] See copy of a report adopted in Dec., 1820, Herman V. Ames, *State Documents on Federal Relations* (Philadelphia, 1906), pp. 134, 135.

[14] Ames, *op. cit.*, p. 137; see also *Annals of Congress*, 18 Cong., 1st sess. (1823–1824), pp. 2207, 2208.

secure an amendment to the Constitution to authorize the federal government to appropriate money and to engage in a program of internal improvements.[15] Jefferson, however, approved bills for the survey of the Cumberland Road and of the rivers and harbors along the coast. Although Albert Gallatin and Jefferson were the first to propose and to secure the enactment of internal improvement measures, it was John C. Calhoun who prepared a bill to set apart and pledge as a permanent fund for internal improvements the profits received from the national bank. When this bill was approved by Congress and submitted to President Madison, he vetoed it on the ground of "the insuperable difficulty of reconciling the bill with the Constitution." Though he admitted the desirability of federal aid for internal improvements to promote intercourse and to increase the share of every part of the country in the common stock of national prosperity, he suggested the adoption of an amendment to carry out such a plan.[16] President Monroe also agreed with this view and proposed an amendment to the Constitution to give Congress greater power in this respect. He vetoed every bill that came before him involving federal aid for improvements within the states.[17] Indicating the marked differences of opinion on the issue of the right of Congress to establish a system of internal improvements, the House of Representatives voted on a series of resolutions. It was first decided by a vote of 89 to 75 that Congress had power to appropriate money for the construction of roads and canals and for the improvement of watercourses. By a vote of 81 to 84 the House decided against the power to construct post roads and military roads; 71 to 95 against the construction of roads and canals necessary to commerce between the states; and 81 to 83 against the construction of canals for military purposes.[18] Writing to Martin Van Buren on September 20, 1826, Madison had the following to say on the validity of federal grants for internal improvements:

Give the power to the general government as possessing the means most adequate, and the objections are, 1. the danger of abuses in the application of the means to objects so distant from the eye of a government, itself so distant from the eye of the people, 2. the danger, from an increase of the patronage and pecuniary transactions of the general government, that the equilibrium between that and the state governments may not be preserved.

Leave the power exclusively with the States, and the objections are: 1. that being

---

[15] See Edward Channing, op. cit., V: 316–318.

[16] See Madison's last annual message to Congress, James D. Richardson, *A Compilation of the Messages and Papers of the Presidents* (Washington, 1911), I: 576, and his veto message on the bill to provide for internal improvements in the West, *ibid.*, p. 584.

[17] Kendrick Charles Babcock, *The Rise of American Nationality, 1811–1819* (New York, 1906), pp. 255, 256.

[18] Turner, op. cit., p. 229.

deprived by the Constitution, and even by their local relations (as was generally experienced before the present Constitution was established) of the most convenient source of revenue, the impost on commerce, improvements might not be made even in cases wholly within their own limits. 2. that in cases where roads, and canals ought to pass through contiguous States, the necessary cooperation might fail from a difficulty in adjusting conditions and details, from a want of interest in one of them, or possibly from some jealousy or rivalship in one towards the other. 3. that where roads and canals ought to pass through a number of States, particular views of a single State might prevent improvements deeply interesting to the whole Nation.

This embarrassing alternative has suggested the expedient which you seem to have contemplated, of dividing the power between the general and State governments, by allotting the appropriating branch to the former, and reserving the jurisdiction to the latter. The expedient has doubtless a captivating aspect. But to say nothing of the difficulty of defining such a division, and maintaining it in practice will the Nation be at the expense of constructing roads and canals, without such a jurisdiction over them as will ensure their constant subservience to national purposes? Will not the utility and popularity of these improvements lead to a constructive assumption of the jurisdiction by Congress, with the same sanction of their constituents, as we see given to the exercise of the appropriating power, already stretching itself beyond the appropriating limit.

It seems indeed to be understood, that the policy and advantage of roads and canals have taken such extensive and permanent hold of the public will, that the constructive authority of Congress to make them, will not be relinquished, either by that, or the constituent body. It becomes a serious question therefore, whether the better course be not to obviate the unconstitutional precedent, by an amendatory article expressly granting the power. Should it be found as is very possible, that no effective system can be agreed on by Congress, the amendment will be a recorded precedent against constructive enlargements of power; and in the contrary event, the exercise of the power will no longer be a precedent in favor of them.

In all these cases, it need not be remarked I am sure, that it is necessary to keep in mind, the distinction between a usurpation of power by Congress against the will, and an assumption of power with the approbation, of their constituents. When the former occurs, as in the enactment of the Alien and Sedition Laws, the appeal to their constituents sets everything to rights. In the latter case, the appeal can only be made to argument and conciliation, with an acquiescence, when not an extreme case, in an unsuccessful result.

If the sole object be to obtain the aid of the federal treasury for internal improvements by roads and canals, without interfering with the jurisdiction of the States, an amendment need only say, "Congress may make appropriations of moneys for roads and canals, to be applied to such purposes by the legislatures of the States within their respective limits, the jurisdiction of the States remaining unimpaired."

If it be thought best to make a constitutional grant of the entire power, either as proper in itself, or made so by the moral certainty, that it will be constructively assumed, with the sanction of the national will, and operate as an injurious precedent, the amendment cannot say less, than that "Congress may make roads and canals, with such jurisdiction as the cases may require."

But whilst the terms "common defence and general welfare," remain in the Constitution unguarded against the construction which has been contended for, a fund of power, inexhaustible and wholly subversive of the equilibrium between the general and the state governments is within the reach of the former. Why then, not precede all other amendments by one, expunging the phrase which is not required ... by this Constitution."[19]

The movement, which was sponsored by Madison and others who agreed with him, to secure the adoption of an amendment to the Constitution to authorize federal aid to improvements within the states was not seriously considered either in Congress or in the states. And it was not long before more vigorous opposition was engendered in the states to Congressional acts imposing protective tariff duties.

The argument over the constitutionality of the tariff involved the old contention between a strict and loose construction of the Constitution. Though the controversy had been waged with varying degrees of energy and bitterness from the time of the inauguration of the federal government, a radical change had occurred in the main issue between the two schools. In Washington's Administration the strict constructionists insisted that only expressly granted powers and those *indispensably* necessary to carry out a granted power were allotted to the federal or general government—as they preferred to call the political system established by the Constitution. The loose constructionists contended that in addition to the granted powers there were implied and resulting powers. Hamilton, as is well known, gave a very broad and extensive interpretation to the category of implied powers. By 1828, however, the advocates of loose construction had changed their ground. They had adopted the principle announced by Hamilton and approved by Marshall in *McCulloch v. Maryland*,[20] namely, that the federal government in carrying out the ends and purposes outlined in the Constitution might do whatever was not prohibited by the Constitution, provided the act was deemed necessary or desirable in the public interest or for the general welfare. It was thought by many that this change in method of interpretation was destroying the effect of the main principle adopted as a feature of the federal Constitution. Under such a scheme the idea of the reserved rights of the states could have little meaning.[21] It is only when this great underlying issue is appreciated that it is possible to understand the intensity with which men thought, felt, and argued on this and related constitutional questions.

The first real protective tariff, the act of 1816, resulted from the strong nationalist sentiment following the War of 1812 and the obvious necessity of rendering aid to American manufacturers to meet the ruinous competition of their English competitors. From 1816 to 1828 the senti-

---

[19] *The Writings of James Madison*, ed. by Gaillard Hunt (New York, 1908), IX: 252, 255.

[20] 4 Wheaton 316 (1819).   [21] MacDonald, *op. cit.*, pp. 76, 77.

ment in New England and the West moved in the direction of a continuance and an increase in protective duties, whereas the sentiment of the public men of the South changed, as indicated in the views of John Calhoun, from support of the protective system to an active opposition. Changes in economic conditions, particularly the decline in manufactures in the southern states, tended to foster the divergence in political opinions. When it became apparent, after the tariff acts of 1824 and 1828 were passed, that the majority of the representatives of the states of New England, of the West, and of the Southwest favored protection, the only recourse for southern leaders, who felt that the South had a real grievance so far as the revenue measures were concerned, was to attack the constitutionality of the tariff. The constitutional argument as set forth in resolutions and protests was, as MacDonald notes, "largely drawn from Jefferson's opinion in 1791, against the constitutionality of a national bank and the Kentucky and Virginia resolutions of 1798–1799, while that in favor of protection owed its substance to Hamilton's opinion in favor of the constitutionality of a bank, and the development of Hamilton's doctrine in the decisions of Chief Justice Marshall."[22] The year 1824 marked the beginning of active and aggressive opposition in certain southern states both to the policy and the constitutionality of the enactment of internal improvement and of protective tariff acts by the federal government.

Efforts to Check the Policy and Practice of Broad Construction of Grants of Power to Congress

Following the passage of the tariff act of 1824, the legislature of South Carolina approved the recommendations of a committee of the house of representatives condemning the acts of Congress relating to internal improvements and the tariff. Resolutions were adopted declaring in effect: that Congress does not possess the power, under the Constitution, to adopt a general system of internal improvements as a national measure; that a right to impose and collect taxes does not authorize Congress to lay a tax for any other purposes than such as are necessarily embraced in the specific grants of power and those necessarily implied therein; that Congress ought not to exercise a power granted for particular objects to effect other objects, the right to effect having never been conceded; that it is an unconstitutional exercise of power on the part of Congress to tax the citizens of one state to make roads and canals for the citizens of another state; that it is an unconstitutional exercise of power on the part of Congress to lay duties to protect domestic manufactures.[23]

---

[22] MacDonald, *op. cit.*, pp. 73, 74.
[23] *Acts of South Carolina*, 1825, pp. 88, 89, and Ames, *op. cit.*, pp. 139–140.

Virginia joined South Carolina in the movement to condemn the broad construction policy of Congress and of the Supreme Court. Both Jefferson and Madison from 1824 to 1826 expressed their disapproval of national legislation in aid of internal improvements. After President Adams had recommended to Congress a liberal policy of internal improvements, Jefferson wrote to Madison suggesting the desirability of the legislature of Virginia passing a new set of resolutions following the precedent of 1798 and declaring the obnoxious laws null and void. He enclosed a draft for such a set of resolutions.[24] In this draft Jefferson restated the original basis for the doctrine of state sovereignty on the dictum that "the States of North America which confederated to establish their independence of the government of Great Britain, of which Virginia was one, became on that acquisition, free and independent States, and as such authorized to constitute governments, each for itself, in such form as it thought best." Then commenting on the distribution of powers provided in the Constitution and to which the commonwealth of Virginia adhered and wished to sustain, Jefferson maintained that "the federal branch has assumed in some cases and claimed in others, a right of enlarging its own powers by constructions, inferences, and indefinite deductions, from those directly given, which this assembly does declare to be usurpations of the powers retained to the independent branches, mere interpolations into the compact, and direct infractions of it." It was then declared that the right to provide for internal improvements within the confines of the states was not granted to the federal government but belonged to the states alone. Jefferson again took occasion to condemn the doctrine that the power to levy taxes and impost duties gave Congress authority to do whatever might be regarded as conducive to the general welfare.

Although the states were prepared to raise objections to what they regarded as the usurpations of power by the federal government, Jefferson thought the advantages of the union were too great to make "every difference of construction a ground for an immediate rupture." Such a breach, he continued, was deemed to be one of the greatest calamities which could befall the states, "but not the greatest. There is yet one greater, submission to a government of unlimited powers. It is only when the hope of avoiding this shall become absolutely desperate that further forebearance could not be indulged."[25]

If the other states would not join in the protest of Virginia and were willing to acquiesce in the unwarranted assumptions of power by the

---

[24] *Writings* (Ford ed.), X: 348, and *Niles' Register*, XXXVII: 79, 80.
[25] *Writings* (Ford ed.), X: 349–352.

federal government, the only thing to do was to be patient and suffer "under the confidence that time, ere it be too late, will prove to them also the bitter consequences in which this usurpation will involve us all." Recoiling from the extreme device of direct nullification, Jefferson proposed that if the people wished to continue the policy of rendering aid to internal improvements within the states, an amendment should be adopted to carry out this purpose. In the meantime, to preserve peace and until the legislature otherwise decided, citizens were advised "to acquiesce under those acts of the federal branch of our government which we have declared to be usurpations, and against which, in point of right, we do protest as null and void, and never to be quoted as precedents of right."[26]

Madison disapproved of this plan because he doubted the advisability of Virginia taking the lead in opposing the obnoxious acts of Congress, owing to prejudices which had been aroused against her. He did not think that any advantage on the part of Virginia could be gained by such action as Jefferson proposed.[27] Jefferson thought it advisable, under the circumstances, to delay action in view of the protest of South Carolina and of the fact that a proposed amendment expressly granting the power to the federal government over internal improvements was before Congress. It seemed preferable to him that the proposal to disapprove such acts should be made by some other state than Virginia.[28] This conclusion

---

[26] *Writings* (Ford ed.), X: 352. See also letter to Edward Livingston, *ibid.*, pp. 300, 301.

[27] *Writings* (Hunt ed.), IX: 236–240.

[28] *Writings* (Ford ed.), X: 359. With respect to the issue of the validity of a general policy of federal aid to internal improvements, Jefferson wrote to William B. Giles as follows: "I see, as you do, and with the deepest affliction, the rapid strides with which the federal branch of our government is advancing towards the usurpation of all the rights reserved to the States, and the consolidation in itself of all powers, foreign and domestic; and that, too, by constructions which, if legitimate, leave no limits to their power. Take together the decisions of the federal court, the doctrines of the President, and the misconstructions of the constitutional compact acted on by the legislature of the federal branch, and it is but too evident, that the three ruling branches of that department are in combination to strip their colleagues, the State authorities, of the powers reserved by them, and to exercise themselves all functions foreign and domestic. Under the power to regulate commerce, they assume indefinitely that also over agriculture and manufactures, and call it regulation to take the earnings of one of these branches of industry, and that too the most depressed, and put them into the pockets of the other, the most flourishing of all. Under the authority to establish post roads, they claim that of cutting down mountains for the construction of roads, of digging canals, and aided by a little sophistry on the words 'general welfare,' a right to do, not only the acts to effect that, which are specifically enumerated and permitted, but whatsoever they shall think, or pretend will be for the general welfare. And what is our resource for the preservation of the Constitution? Reason and argument? You might as well reason and argue with the marble columns encircling them. The representatives chosen by ourselves? They are joined in the combination, some from incorrect views of government, some from corrupt ones, sufficient voting together to out-number the

was arrived at somewhat regretfully, for, said he, the majority of the people are against us on this question.

The legislature of Virginia in March, 1826, again expressed its approval of the doctrines of 1798 and its condemnation of the obnoxious policies of the federal government. In the course of the resolutions approved by the legislature, it was asserted that the legislature "views the powers of the federal government, as resulting from the compact to which the States are parties; as limited by the plain sense and intention of the instrument constituting that compact, as no farther valid than they are authorized by the grants enumerated in that compact; and that, in case of a deliberate, palpable and dangerous exercise of other powers, not granted by the said compact, the States, who are parties thereto, have the right, and are in duty bound, to interpose, for arresting the progress of the evil, and for maintaining, within their respective limits, the authorities, rights and liberties appertaining to them."[29] On March 6, 1827, the legislature of Virginia approved a set of resolutions condemning the tariff policy of the United States.[30] Following the adoption of resolutions favorable to the protective tariff policy at the Harrisburg convention, the legislature of South Carolina resolved that the Constitution of the United States is a compact between the people of the different states

---

sound parts; and with majorities only on one, two, or three, bold enough to go forward in defiance. Are we then *to stand to our arms,* with the hot-headed Georgian? No. That must be the last resource, not to be thought of until much longer and greater sufferings. If every infraction of a compact of so many parties is to be resisted at once, as a dissolution of it, none can ever be formed which would last one year. We must have patience and longer endurance then with our brethren while under delusion; give them time for reflection and experience of consequences; keep ourselves in a situation to profit by the chapter of accidents; and separate from our companions only when the sole alternatives left,, are the dissolution of our Union with them, or submission to a government without limitation of powers. Between these two evils, when we must make a choice, there can be no hesitation. But in the meanwhile, the States should be watchful to note every material usurpation on their rights; to denounce them as they occur in the most peremptory terms; to protest against them as wrongs to which our present submission shall be considered, not as acknowledgments or precedents of right, but as a temporary yielding to the lesser evil, until their accumulation shall overweigh that of separation. I would go still further, and give to the federal member, by a regular amendment of the Constitution, a right to make roads and canals of intercommunication between the States, providing sufficiently against corrupt practices in Congress, (log-rolling, &c.) by declaring that the federal proportion of each State of the moneys so employed, shall be in works within the State, or elsewhere with its consent, and with a due *salvo* of jurisdiction. This is the course which I think safest and best as yet." *Writings* (Ford ed.), X: 354–356.

[29] *Acts of Virginia, 1825–26,* p. 114, and Ames, *op. cit.,* pp. 141, 142; see also *Niles' Register,* XXX: 38.

[30] Ames, *op. cit.,* pp. 142–144. For Madison's reply to inquiry of Joseph C. Cabell concerning the resolution presented to the Virginia legislature proposing to condemn the validity of a federal tariff act, see appendix, pp. 573 ff.

with each other, as separate, independent sovereignties; and that for any violation of the letter or spirit of that compact by the Congress of the United States, it is not only the right of the people but of the legislatures, who represent them to every extent not limited, to remonstrate against violations of the fundamental compact. It was then declared that tariff laws, the object of which is not the raising of revenues, or the regulation of foreign commerce, but the promotion of domestic manufactures, are violations of the Constitution in its spirit and ought to be repealed. The legislature also disapproved of the policy of Congress of giving aid to internal improvements, declaring that the authority of Congress extended no further than to pass "the necessary and proper laws" to carry into execution their enumerated powers.

The legislature of Georgia joined with those of Virginia and South Carolina in condemning both the policies of giving aid to internal improvements and of a protective tariff. A number of the legislatures of the northern states passed counterresolutions supporting the authority of Congress in dealing with these matters under the Constitution. The passage of the "tariff of abominations" greatly increased the agitation against such legislation in the South. During the summer and fall of 1828, strong expressions of disapproval and even threats of resistance were common in the legislative halls, in popular meetings, and in the press.[31]

STEPS LEADING TOWARD NULLIFICATION

South Carolina again took the lead in opposing what were deemed to be unconstitutional measures. Following the recommendation of Governor Taylor that the tariff act of 1828 be declared void and that steps be taken to enforce the action of the state, the legislature adopted a report, the original of which had been drafted by John C. Calhoun. The argument in this report has come to be known as the "South Carolina Exposition." It was in this exposition that Calhoun first presented his views on the doctrine of nullification. This doctrine was based on the following propositions: that the people of each State were sovereign at the time of the ratification of the Constitution; that in the process of ratification each state acted as a separate and sovereign unit; that the Constitution was a compact between sovereign states; and, that each of the parties to the compact had a right to judge of the infractions of terms of the compact and to take such action as appeared necessary to maintain the rights of the people of the state. On this hypothesis the general gov-

[31] See *Niles' Register*, XXXIV: 288–290, 300, 301, 339, 340, 351–356; XXXV: 14, 15, 203–208; also John Bach McMaster, *A History of the People of the United States* (New York, 1900), V: 255–262.

ernment was merely the agent of separate and distinct sovereignties and the union was "a union of States as communities, and not a union of individuals." The people of a state could, therefore, declare an act of the general government void and hence not binding in the state and could take such action as was deemed necessary to protect the citizens of the state against the federal government.[32]

The most significant feature of the exposition, however, was its declaration regarding the means by which a state might protect itself against federal usurpations. Interposition was the remedy proposed and a state convention was the proper body to apply it. When convened, said Calhoun, "it will belong to the Convention itself to determine, authoritatively, whether the acts of which we complain be unconstitutional; and, if so, whether they constitute a violation so deliberate, palpable, and dangerous, as to justify the interposition of the State to protect its rights. If this question be decided in the affirmative, the Convention will then determine in what manner they ought to be declared null and void within the limits of the State; which solemn declaration, based on her rights as a member of the Union, would be obligatory, not only on her own citizens, but on the general government itself; and thus place the violated rights of the State under the shield of the Constitution."[33] Such an extreme remedy, Calhoun thought, should not be applied until ample time had been allowed for further consideration and reflection in the hope that "a returning sense of justice on the part of the majority" might lead to a repeal of the obnoxious acts.[34]

Georgia, Mississippi, and Virginia joined with South Carolina in protesting against the tariff act of 1828. Virginia reasserted the right of each state to construe the federal compact for itself, and declared that the tariff acts "are not authorized by the plain construction, true intent and meaning of the Constitution."[35] Though the citizens of South Carolina were nearly unanimous in their opposition to the tariff acts, they were not united in their support of the doctrine of nullification. It was not until after the passage of the tariff act of 1832 that public sentiment in the state veered strongly in the direction of the approval of nullification doctrines.

In Georgia, where from 1798 to 1823 there had been a reaction against the prevalent theories of state sovereignty, the attempt to secure aid from Congress for the African Colonization Society brought forth in

---

[32] See *The Works of John C. Calhoun*, ed. by R. K. Cralle (New York, 1864), VI: 1 ff.; Channing, *op. cit.*, V: 420, 421; and Turner, *op. cit.*, p. 329.

[33] *Works, op. cit.*, p. 45.

[34] *Ibid.*, p. 55.

[35] Ames, *op. cit.*, p. 157.

1827 an emphatic approval of state sovereignty. The legislature declared that the federal compact was an agreement "made between independent sovereignties for the general benefit and welfare of the whole, by which each, to effect that object, relinquished portions of its sovereign power, reserving to itself the residue, and by which all become mutual guarantees of each of the absolute and exclusive enjoyment of that residue. All the powers which could be exercised by each in a way sufficiently beneficial and without clashing or interfering with the exercise of the same powers by the others were intended to be retained and were retained by the States in their separate capacities. It irresistibly follows that Congress can not by implication, derive from that compact power to do any act which interfered with the just and full exercise by the States of powers which each can exercise itself in a way beneficial to itself. Such are the powers of each State to make roads and canals and regulate its slave population."[36] A year later, in a controversy over slavery between South Carolina and Ohio, Georgia resolved that the states had an unquestionable right, in case of a breach of the compact, to complain, to remonstrate, and even to refuse obedience to any act of the general government deemed manifestly violative of the Constitution.[37]

After 1824, when threats of nullification and secession were made with increasing frequency, it was maintained that nullification was "an entirely new doctrine, based upon conceptions of the nature of sovereignty and of the meaning of the word 'compact' which were strange to the men of 1798."[38] But it is apparent from a review of the evidence and the doctrines which were widely held and frequently expressed that ideas of nullification and secession were far from new. In the early years of American history men frequently spoke of the probability of disunion or secession. Many instances of the espousal of doctrines of nullification have been discussed in previous chapters. The Virginia and Kentucky Resolutions of 1798 and the Hartford Convention of 1814 were the most extreme manifestations of nullification doctrines. But scarcely a year went by without some expression of disunion sentiments by individuals, by groups, and by the states. Judge Tucker, in his edition of *Blackstone's Commentaries*, asserted as an inevitable deduction from his general scheme of political philosophy that the several states had an indefeasible right of seceding from any federation or union which they had entered or might enter.[39] In an attempt to nullify the disunion sentiment after

---

[36] Ulrich Bonnell Phillips, *Georgia and State Rights*, Annual Report of the Amer. Hist. Assn., 1901, II: 115.

[37] *Acts of Georgia*, Gen. Assem., 1828, p. 174, and Phillips, *op. cit.*, p. 116.

[38] Abbot Emerson Smith, *James Madison: Builder* (New York, 1937), p. 231.

[39] See appendix, pp. 573 ff., for Madison's reply to this contention.

1820, De Witt Clinton urged the building of the Erie Canal because, in his opinion, it would serve as a bond of union between the Atlantic and western states and hence might prevent the dismemberment of the American empire.[40]

Commenting on the attitude of the people of Georgia to the tariff, Phillips says: "As long as the South could make any effective opposition in Congress to the protective tariff the ballot box was trusted to secure the observance of the fundamental law. But as soon as the majority showed its determination to override the Southern opposition and disregard Southern interests, the cry of unconstitutionality was raised."[41] But there were many and convincing precedents for the recurrence to the ground of unconstitutionality when doubts were raised to the wisdom or expediency of the unexpressed or implied powers exercised by Congress and the Supreme Court.

Starting with the premise of the sovereignty of the states as it was customary for men to conceive it before 1787, it was contended that the states created the central government as their agent to perform certain specified functions. The general government, as the agent of the states and being subordinate to the sovereignties that created it, could not increase or expand its own authority and if any attempts were made to usurp powers, it was the duty of the states to resist such encroachments on their rightful domain. Nullification was thus regarded as a formula for the specific application of the doctrine of state sovereignty.

Attempts have been made to distinguish the procedures of Virginia and Kentucky in 1798 from that of South Carolina in 1832. Kentucky, in dealing with an instance of alleged usurpation of powers by the Federal government, adopted resolutions declaring the acts void. It then sent these resolutions to the other states and to the representatives from the state in Washington and requested the other states to join with Kentucky in securing the repeal of the obnoxious acts. The right of a single state or of several states acting together to nullify an act of Congress was, however, definitely asserted. When South Carolina passed her Nullification Ordinance, Madison denied that either Jefferson or himself meant by the proceedings in 1798 what Calhoun and others claimed for them. According to Madison, in 1798 the representatives in Washington had taken steps which most of the people disapproved. South Carolina, on the other hand, in 1832 objected to measures which were supported by a great number of the people and a majority of the states.

But the differences between the proceedings in 1798 and in 1832 may

---

[40] Turner, *op. cit.*, p. 32.
[41] *Georgia and State Rights*, p. 122.

well be exaggerated. There was more than a threat of nullification involved in the acts adopted by both Kentucky and Virginia. The language
of these resolutions, if it does not go to the full length of the way traveled
by South Carolina, did more than mark the road for the step of outright
nullification. Though there are substantial grounds for Madison's interpretation of the resolutions, this is not the interpretation which men
were generally inclined to place upon them. In numerous treatises, in
public addresses, and in formal documents these resolutions were interpreted as sanctioning a doctrine of state sovereignty which, when
a pertinent occasion arose, might normally and legally lead to nullification and, with serious enough provocation, to secession. Nationalist
sentiment was stronger in 1832, particularly in certain parts of the
country, than it was in 1798, and hence the Virginia and Kentucky Resolutions were frequently given a construction very different from that
which prevailed for nearly two decades. It is obvious that these resolutions, like the Declaration of Independence, the Articles of Confederation, and the federal Constitution may be interpreted either in the
direction of nationalism or of State rights. It is also clear that nationalism could be arrived at only by a process of strained or loose construction
of the language of these public documents and by eliding or suppressing
certain obvious historical incidents since 1776. To those who deemed it
wise and expedient that there should be an effective union of states on
the American continent, it was regarded as desirable and in fact necessary to make the essential constructions to attain this end. Following in
the footsteps of Alexander Hamilton and John Marshall, Daniel Webster was prepared to make the necessary constructions to have the federal
Constitution serve as a basis for a sovereign nation.

The Webster-Hayne Debate

It was the debate over the resolution of Senator Foot of Connecticut
instructing the Committee on Public Lands to inquire into the expediency of limiting for certain periods the sales of public lands which
brought to the forefront the smoldering sentiments regarding constitutional construction. The resolution was attacked by Senator Benton and
others as an indication of hostility to the West. Benton maintained that
the East, which held control in Congress, had no right to check immigration by withdrawing from sale the public lands. Senator Hayne of South
Carolina introduced into the discussion the consideration of the doctrine of State rights and the necessity of a strict construction of the Constitution. It has been customary, says David Franklin Houston, to state
that the great nullification debate of 1830 came on in the Senate by acci-

dent, but in his opinion deeper investigation may show that the issue was sought by Webster and that due preparation was made.[42] Whether the surmise of Houston is correct or not, it is evident that Webster knew what he meant to say and desired an opportunity to say it.[43] Advising Clay that it was desirable for him to come to the Senate, Webster wrote: "An array is preparing much more formidable than has ever yet assaulted what we think the leading and important public interests. Not only the tariff, but the Constitution itself, in its elemental and fundamental provisions, will be assailed with talent, vigor, and union. Everything is to be debated as if nothing had ever been settled."[44]

The occasion for which Webster had prepared arose when Senator Hayne, debating Foot's resolution regarding the sale of public lands, said that he objected to the policy which was being pursued in relation to the disposal of these lands. He saw a danger in the creation of a fund in the national treasury which might be used to corrupt American institutions. The establishment of such a fund would, he thought, be fatal to the sovereignty and independence of the states. He went on to say that he was one of those who believed that the very life of the system established under the Constitution was the independence of the states and that there was "no evil more to be deprecated than the consolidation of this government."[45]

Webster, in his reply to Hayne, defended the East and in particular Massachusetts against the charge of hostility to the West. From the time of the adoption of the Ordinance of 1787, he claimed "no portion of the country has acted either with more liberality or more intelligence, on the subject of the public lands in the new States than New England."[46] Consolidation was referred to as "that perpetual cry both of terror and delusion." And the consolidation of the framers of the Constitution and of General Washington was approved, for, said Webster: "I wish to see no new powers drawn to the general government; but I confess I rejoice in whatever tends to strengthen the bond that unites us, and encourages the hope that our Union may be perpetual." He expressed regret at some of the expressions used by the senator from South Carolina because, in his opinion, their obvious tendency was to weaken the bond of our connection. He also deplored the fact that "there are some per-

---

[42] *A Critical Study of Nullification in South Carolina* (New York, 1896), p. 86.

[43] Webster said he "was drawn into the debate with no previous deliberation, such as is suited to the discussion of so grave and important a subject." *The Works of Daniel Webster* (Boston, 1866), III: 341.

[44] Claude G. Bowers, *Party Battles of the Jackson Period* (Boston, 1922), p. 171.

[45] *Cong. Debates*, 21st Cong., 1st sess., Jan., 1830, VI, pt. 1, pp. 35, 38 ff.

[46] *Works*, III: 262.

sons in the part of the country from which the honorable member comes, who habitually speak of the Union in terms of indifference, or even of disparagement."[47]

Hayne replied to this speech by disclaiming unfriendliness to the people of New England. And he cited the "tariff of abominations" as an instance of consolidation leading to the destruction of the present balance of powers between the nation and the states. He felt it to be his duty to maintain a federal rather than a national union, that is, one in which federal powers were confined strictly within the limits of the written Constitution. To Webster's contention that the union would be "a mere rope of sand" if a state could intervene to prevent a deliberate violation of the Constitution, Hayne replied by quoting pertinent passages from the Virginia and Kentucky Resolutions and from the South Carolina Exposition. The South Carolina doctrine was declared to be the historical republican doctrine.

In Webster's second reply to Hayne, he stated the nationalist doctrine as against the State rights philosophy in bold and broad strokes and with the fervor and enthusiasm of an orator. The fundamental proposition of Hayne that "the States may lawfully decide for themselves, and each State for itself, whether, in a given case, the act of the general government transcends its power" was emphatically denied. To Webster there could be no middle ground between submission to laws enacted by the Legislative and Executive departments and declared valid by the courts, and rebellion or revolution. Hayne had contended that the states were sovereign under the Articles of Confederation, that as sovereign states they had adopted the Constitution, and, hence, that at no time had they relinquished their essential rights as sovereign states. Webster's answer to this argument was that even though the states were sovereign in 1787 and though the Constitution was ratified by the people acting through conventions called by such sovereign states, yet this act of adoption was really not the act of the several states, but of the whole people united into a political unity by a subjective feeling of nationality which is the ultimate foundation of every sovereign state. That is, the national state existed subjectively in the minds of the people and was made objective by the creation of the national government, and existing state organs and political machinery were used merely for convenience to carry out that purpose. This was, in effect, the "organic or nationalist" philosophy as described in a previous chapter.[48]

In one of his oratorical flourishes, Webster declared: "It is sir, the people's Constitution, the people's government, made for the people,

---

[47] *Works*, III: 257–258.   [48] Chap. iii.

made by the people, and answerable to the people. The people . . . have declared that this Constitution shall be the supreme law."[49] But this, admits Albert J. Beveridge, was the constitutional theory of the nationalists and as a matter of fact was not strictly true. It is apparent that most of the people did not favor the Constitution adopted by the Convention and ratified by the states, and that if the document had been submitted to a vote of the people, "it is highly probable that it would have been rejected."[50]

As to the authority to interpret the Constitution and hence to annul or declare federal laws void, Webster quoted the provisions of the Constitution declaring that the Constitution and the laws made in pursuance thereof shall be the supreme law of the land and that the judicial power of the United States shall extend to all cases in law and equity arising under the Constitution and laws of the United States. He further asserted that when the federal courts under these provisions had declared a law valid, the only legal recourse remaining was to change the law by a constitutional amendment. With these provisions, said he, "it is a Constitution; without them it is a Confederacy." But it is clear that these provisions of the Constitution must be understood and accepted with the customary hypotheses or assumptions of the Federalists to discover therein a final and conclusive authority to interpret federal laws, both with respect to the other departments of the federal government and to the states. Webster closed his argument by a strong appeal to expediency, painting in vivid colors the dangers of secession and disunion and voicing the well-known sentiment "Liberty and Union, now and for ever, one and inseparable."

Hayne, in his second reply to Webster, reiterated in clearer and more emphatic form the essential features of the doctrine of State rights. Before the adoption of the federal Constitution, the states had "all the rights and powers appertaining to independent nations"; after the adoption of the Constitution they remained "sovereign and independent as to all powers not expressly delegated to the federal government." The union was declared to be the result of a compact between sovereign states and, since there is no common superior, each party to the compact is the rightful judge of violations of its provisions. Under such circumstances the federal government did not have the authority to determine conclusively the extent of its own powers. Moreover, questions of sovereignty or the determination of the political relations of the nation and the states were not proper subjects for judicial investigation. The right of interposition by a state, when the terms of the compact had been vio-

---

[49] Works, III: 321.   [50] The Life of John Marshall (Boston, 1919), IV: 554 (note).

lated, is full and complete and it does not involve, as Webster contended, an act of war. It was asserted to be the duty of the federal government to recognize and accept the state decision, to the extent of appealing to the people for an amendment to the Constitution, and of refraining in the meantime from coercion.[51] Webster, in a brief reply, denied that the Constitution was formed as the result of a compact and again insisted that it was formed by the people of the United States.

It is not necessary to analyze and evaluate the relative merits of the arguments in this debate. The disputants were covering familiar ground, and they presented relatively little that was new[52] to the controversy which began with the adoption of the Declaration of Independence. The crux of the controversy centered around the Hamilton-Marshall device of expanding federal powers by means of an implied power doctrine. This doctrine, observes William MacDonald,

formulated in all essential particulars by Hamilton in his opinion on the constitutionality of a national bank,[53] elaborated by Webster in his great constitutional arguments before the Supreme Court, and stated with consummate clearness by Marshall in a long series of decisions, had given the federal authority a scope far beyond anything that could have been dreamed of by those who saw the national government inaugurated. "Implied powers" had chartered a national bank, enacted the alien and sedition laws, decreed an embargo, voted money for internal improvements, and established a protective tariff. If progress were to continue in this direction, the authority of the nation would soon be everywhere supreme, and the "sovereignty of the States" would become, ere long, only a memory and a name.[54]

Against this trend toward nationalism, Hayne defended the view that by the federal Constitution the sovereign states had created a federal government of delegated powers. And it was the duty of the states to see that the limits prescribed for the federal government should be strictly observed. The right of a state to protest and to refuse to obey a federal statute deemed unconstitutional seemed to follow as inevitable steps from the above premises.

To offset the growing sentiment toward nullification, Chief Justice Marshall and Daniel Webster defended the doctrine that the federal government, as framed and adopted in 1787 and 1788, was an act of the sovereign people. By this original act limits were placed not only on the

---

[51] See MacDonald, *Jacksonian Democracy*, chap. vi, for an excellent summary of the Hayne-Webster debate.

[52] According to Woodrow Wilson, Webster was supporting a new point of view, whereas Hayne was defending the old, and, in his opinion, "Webster's position was one toward which the greater part of the Nation was steadily advancing, while Hayne's position was one upon which the South was presently to stand quite alone in occupying." *Division and Reunion* (New York, 1910), p. 47.

[53] J. C. Hamilton, *Life of Alexander Hamilton* (Boston, 1879), IV: 104–138.

[54] *Jacksonian Democracy*, pp. 107, 108.

federal government but also on the states. Thus, what has been called "the most distinctive contribution to the theory of American constitutional law" was ably expounded by Webster in his debate with Hayne. But, according to MacDonald,

no theory could have had a slighter historical foundation. From the beginning of the ratification of the Constitution to the end, there never was a moment when "the people of the whole United States" acted in "their collective capacity," or in any other manner than as "the people of the several States." "The ratification of the conventions of nine States shall be sufficient for the establishment of this Constitution between the States so ratifying the same," is the declaration of the Constitution. If anything is clear beyond peradventure in the history of the United States, it is that the Constitution was established by the States, acting through conventions authorized by the legislatures thereof, and not by "the people of the United States" in any such sense as Webster gives to that phrase. In so far as the Constitution was ratified by popular conventions instead of by the state legislatures it is, in truth, "the people's Constitution," and not the creation of the state governments; but outside the geographical limits of the several States and the directions and conditions imposed by state constitutions and laws, the people of the United States have never yet had a voice in the establishment of their fundamental law. For the purpose of opposing Hayne's theory of the right of state interposition, Webster voiced a theory not only at variance with the facts, but so contrived also as to miss the only vulnerable point of his opponent's position. It was a glorious fiction, and it has entered into the warp and woof of our constitutional creed; but it was fiction, nevertheless.[55]

But even if Marshall and Webster had to build their theory of nationalism out of a slim foundation of fact and had to construe the language of the federal Constitution according to what they deemed to be its general spirit and purport, they were arguing for a point of view which an increasing number of people deemed more reasonable and practicable than the opposite one, which in their minds led only to nullification and secession. "In other words, Hayne argued for a theory which, however once widely held, had been outgrown, and which could not under any circumstances be made to work in practice. Webster argued for a theory which, though unhistorical in the form in which he presented it, nevertheless gave the federal government ground on which to stand. The one pleaded for the States, the other for the Nation. One looked to the past, the other to the present and future."[56] Thus, Webster had given new life and vitality to the cause of nationalism, though it was based rather upon extralegal grounds and grounds of expediency than upon a literal and logical interpretation of the Constitution. Webster charged

---

[55] MacDonald, *op. cit.*, pp. 109, 110.

[56] *Ibid.*, p. 111. "Webster's argument that the Constitution was a compact between the people of the United States, forming a single Nation, was not in harmony with the general opinion in 1787–1788 however congenial it may have been to the nationalistic spirit of his own section and generation." Robert Livingston Schuyler, *The Constitution of the United States* (New York, 1925), p. 166.

that Calhoun and Hayne could attain their objectives only by amendments to the Constitution or by rebellion, but was it not Hamilton,
Marshall, and Webster who were trying to secure by peaceful revolution
a change in the base of supreme authority from the states, where it essentially belonged for the greater part of the preceding decades, to the
nation, where the nationalists desired it should be?

Thomas H. Benton thought that Webster's view of the Court was leading to "a judicial tyranny and oppression," for, through the decisions
of the Court and the assumption of implied powers, the range of federal
authority was becoming unlimited. If the process of the expansion of
federal powers continued, he believed that the states would be reduced
to the condition of "provinces of the federal empire." When the Court
asserted its right to impose restraints upon the sovereignty of the states,
John Rowan maintained that it should be treated as "a usurper, and
driven back by the States within its appropriate judicial sphere," for he
viewed state sovereignty as the sheet anchor of the union and looked to
the states, not to the Supreme Court, for its strength and perpetuity. Levi
Woodbury of New Hampshire observed that since 1803 the Justices had
manifested a "sleepless opposition" in all cases of a political nature bearing on the strict construction of the Constitution approved by the people
in Revolution of 1801. Moreover, he condemned the strides being made
toward consolidation through construction of the Constitution, which
thus forged chains for the states never dreamed of at the time of the
formation of the general government. All of these men agreed with
Hayne that they were not attacking the Supreme Court, for which they
had high respect, but that they objected to the assumption of political
powers by the Court—powers not granted to the Judges and which they
could not safely exercise.[57] The primary issue of constitutional construc-

---

[57] In the opinion of Claude Moore Fuess, "it has been forcefully and correctly maintained that Webster's argument from history is untenable. He was certainly wrong in
his interpretation of the words 'We, the people,' and, although his view strengthened
our government politically, it had no foundation in fact. Separate States, like New
Hampshire and South Carolina, undoubtedly felt, when they voted to form the Union,
that they were entering an improved Confederacy, from which, if dissatisfied, they
could withdraw. The new government was primarily an agreement for mutual convenience and benefit, in which each State retained its autonomy. Utterances of public
men during the first quarter-century of the republic assumed that secession was within
the province of any state government. The facts indicate that the Constitution was
by many tacitly regarded as a compact between States; that the advisability of secession
was more than once considered, not only by Virginia and Kentucky, but by Connecticut
and Massachusetts; and that nothing but expediency prevented the breaking up of the
United States into smaller units.

"Gradually, however, a revised conception of the federal Union had become popular.
The admission of new States; the acquisition of Louisiana; the sense of harmony developed during the struggles with France and Great Britain; the growth of a healthy

tion was again brought forward both with respect to internal improvement legislation and a new tariff act.

As we have seen, the participation of the federal government in internal improvements began soon after the establishment of the federal government. A number of projects received government support until the movement was checked by Madison's veto of Calhoun's bonus bill. Monroe agreed with Madison on the invalidity of federal appropriations in aid of internal improvements. On the other hand, John Quincy Adams, approving the nationalistic views of Clay and Calhoun, encouraged the preparation of surveys and approved grants for the construction of roads and canals. Jackson, who had voted for several internal improvement projects while a member of Congress, indicated in his first annual message to Congress his disapproval of the policy of rendering aid for the improvement of projects within the states. He recommended the apportionment among the states, according to their representation in Congress, of the surplus revenue which was accumulating as the result of protective duties. Nothing must be done, said he, that would encroach upon "the legitimate sphere of state sovereignty," for the success of the union has been due primarily to "the watchful and auxiliary operation of the state authorities." The Constitution, he thought, was to be interpreted and applied as intended by its framers.[58] Carrying out his expressed intention in this respect, he vetoed a number of measures, including a bill authorizing a subscription of stock by the United States in the Maysville Road Company.[59] But the real test over constitutional construction versus the assertion of the doctrine of State rights came over the tariff issue.

SOUTH CAROLINA ADOPTS THE POLICY OF NULLIFICATION

South Carolina's opposition to the tariff began at an early date. When the first impost law was before Congress and it was proposed to include certain prohibitory duties, Pierce Butler of South Carolina threatened "a dissolution of the Union, with regard to his State, as sure as God was in the firmament."[60] "The dissatisfaction of South Carolina over the

national self-consciousness—all these had contributed to weld the sections together. But more important than any of these had been the influence of Chief Justice John Marshall, aided by Joseph Story and Daniel Webster, in emphasizing the authority of the Constitution and the Supreme Court." *Daniel Webster* (Boston, 1930), I: 380, 381.

[58] Richardson, *op. cit.*, II: 1015.

[59] *Ibid.*, pp. 1046–1056. See also Jackson's veto on a bill to subscribe to a turnpike road company, Richardson, *op. cit.*, II: 1047, and John Spencer Bassett, *The Life of Andrew Jackson* (New York, 1925), II: 475–496. This message put an end for a generation to the building up of a land transportation system at federal expense.

[60] William Maclay, *Sketches of Debate in the First Senate,* ed. by G. W. Harris (Harrisburg, 1880), p. 77.

action of Calhoun and others in voting for the tariff bill of 1816," notes David Franklin Houston, "was the beginning of the end. It marks the time when South Carolina began to feel that the interests of the South were not identical with those of the North; that the general government was falling into the hands of Northerners, for whose unselfishness there was no guaranty; that in short, the powers of the government were likely to be stretched more and more along lines not laid down in the Constitution."[61] Before 1823 the opposition to protective duties was based largely on the matter of the inexpediency and injustice in the levying of such duties, but after this date the opposition was based mainly on the ground of unconstitutionality. It was not until the enactment of the tariff act of 1824 that South Carolina leaders denied the right of the extension of federal powers through the implied power doctrine.

When Justice Johnson, in a federal District Court decision, held void an act of the state of South Carolina prohibiting the landing of free negroes in the state, the governor sent a message to the legislature in which he expressed "a firm determination to resist, at the threshold, every invasion of our domestic tranquillity and to preserve our sovereignty and independence as a state is earnestly recommended; and if an appeal to the first principles of the right of self-government be disregarded and reason be successfully combated by sophistry and error, there would be more glory in forming a rampart with our bodies on the confines of our territory than to be victims of a successful rebellion or the slaves of a great consolidated government."[62] Justice Johnson's opinion was disregarded by the officials of South Carolina for several decades. Public men in South Carolina were perhaps taking too literally the reasoning of Senator Gouverneur Morris in the Judiciary Debate of 1802, for in 1828–1829 her representatives were arguing in Congress that South Carolina could never consent to the dangerous principle that the majority shall rule. "If a majority is to rule," they contended, "away with your Constitution at once. All governments have fundamental principles; and so far as those of this government are correct, South Carolina agrees with them; but she protests against the principle that a majority shall rule."[63]

Houston refers to the confused conceptions of the nature and location of sovereignty which are to be found in the arguments and public documents which appeared in South Carolina. Thus, the instance is cited

[61] *A Critical Study of Nullification in South Carolina*, p. 5.

[62] See Elkison v. Deliesseline, 8 Fed. Cases 493 (1823); Charles Warren, *The Supreme Court in United States History* (Boston, 1922), II: 87; and *Niles' Register*, XXV: 13–16, XXVII: 242, 243.

[63] *Cong. Debates*, 20th Cong., 2d sess., Feb. 10, 1829, p. 54.

of the argument of Senator Hayne and others that the general government was one of the sovereign parties to the compact and that the issues at stake were between the sovereign federal government, on the one hand, and the sovereign states, on the other. In the opinion of the South Carolina legislature in 1827, the state should be urged to approach the national government as a sovereign and equal.[64] It is apparent that such confused conceptions were not confined to South Carolina.

Though George McDuffie exaggerated the influence of the tariff on prices and economic conditions, it is evident that the state had a real grievance. It could receive little if any benefit from a high tariff, as the tariff laws were becoming increasingly sectional measures in support of sectional interests. South Carolina had grounds for opposing the tariff separate from the institution of slavery, but it was slavery that helped to crystallize sentiment in the state and to furnish the basis for extreme measures to support the institution. The series of articles by Robert J. Turnbull entitled "The Crisis" or "Essays on the Usurpations of the Federal Government" written under the pseudonym of Brutus prepared the people to think in terms of drastic action. It is noteworthy that Turnbull directed some of his diatribes against the tendency toward consolidation which he thought had made progress rapidly since 1821. Seeing primarily nothing but hostility to the South in these consolidating measures, Turnbull advocated secession as the only effective remedy. The people became so aroused in 1828 that a resolution was approved by the legislature which insisted that no discussion or vote on slavery take place in the halls of Congress without being looked upon as a grave insult to the state.

Whether true or not, George McDuffie was able to prove to the satisfaction of most of the people of South Carolina that a protective tariff was a system of taxation which perverted the powers granted by the states to the national government—to the oppression of one part of the union for the benefit of another. To McDuffie there was an irreconcilable opposition between the manufacturing interests of the North and the agricultural interests of the South. The fact that a majority of the people through their representatives in Congress wanted protection did not convince McDuffie. The Constitution, he maintained, did not intend that the majority should rule unchecked. It was intended that minority rights must be protected. In this argument he was on the firm ground on which John Marshall had stood in a number of important controversies. The various ramifications of the meaning of due process of law had not yet been discovered, or he might have argued along lines of some

---

[64] Houston, *op. cit.*, p. 31.

of the classic statements of Justice Chase and Chief Justice Marshall that taking money from southern planters to give aid to northern manufacturers was clearly taking the money of A and giving it to B and was therefore a denial of due process of law.

Houston thinks that McDuffie was "unconscious that he was assuming a great deal in stating that our political system was a confederation of sovereigns; nor did he appear to himself to be absurd in claiming for the minority a right which could not safely be entrusted to the majority."[65] But was there not good ground historically for McDuffie's assumptions? And why should he appear either to himself or to others "absurd," when he was merely announcing and approving the doctrine which the Federalists wrote into the Constitution, so far as they could reasonably do so, and by which they defended the finality of judicial review of legislation by the courts after they were in the minority party? Why does the presumably sound and reputable doctrine of Gouverneur Morris in the debate of 1802 that the Constitution was designed to establish minority rule appear absurd at this time?

When Clay proposed to use the protective tariff as a device to consolidate the groups opposing Andrew Jackson and to foster his presidential ambitions, it was suggested that such a plan might be interpreted as "setting the South at defiance." Clay replied that "to preserve, maintain and strengthen the American system, he would defy the South, the President and the Devil."[66] To carry out partisan designs and to gain adherents from special interests that might profit from such legislation, a new act with high protective duties was drafted. The passage of the Tariff Act of 1832 was the signal for action by the proponents of State rights in South Carolina. After the passage of this act, which included a reduction of duties on a number of articles, but did not involve any important modification of the protective system, the South Carolina members in Congress issued a formal communication to the people of the state expressing the conviction that protection "must now be regarded as the settled policy of the country," and that "all hope of relief from Congress is irrevocably gone." It further expressed the opinion that it was for the people to decide "whether the rights and liberties which you have received as a precious inheritance from an illustrious ancestry shall be tamely urrendered without a struggle, or transmitted undiminished to your posterity."[67] By a two-thirds affirmative vote of the legislature, a convention was called to consider the conditions of affairs from the standpoint of the state.

---

[65] *A Study of Nullification in South Carolina*, p. 42.
[66] Bowers, *op. cit.*, p. 186.
[67] MacDonald, *op. cit.*, pp. 154, 155, and *Niles' Register*, XLII: 412–414.

On November 24, 1832, the convention met and adopted an ordinance of nullification in which the following sentiments were expressed: that the acts of Congress imposing duties and imposts on foreign commodities enacted in 1832 are unauthorized by the Constitution of the United States and violate the true meaning and intent thereof, and are null and void, and hence not binding upon this state; and all promises and obligations entered into with the purpose of securing the duties imposed by said acts, and all judicial proceedings to carry the same into effect, shall be deemed null and void. Appeal was prohibited to the Supreme Court of the United States in cases involving the interpretation of the ordinance or the validity of the state acts passed to enforce it. All officers except the members of the legislature were required to take an oath to obey and enforce the ordinance and the acts passed to carry it into effect. Finally, the ordinance made it clear that the state would not submit to force, and that if the general government undertook to resort to means of coercion, the people of the state would consider themselves absolved from all political connection with the people of the other states, and would organize a separate government.[68] The legislature was requested to pass the necessary enabling legislation to carry out the general purposes of the nullification ordinance. These acts were speedily passed by the legislature.[69] The unionists of the state, as well as those in other states, regarded these proceedings as revolutionary and treasonable. But, as in many similar controversies of this kind, much depended upon the assumptions or underlying principles with which one approached the issue.

In the campaign of 1832 the friends of Jackson repudiated the Calhoun heresy of nullification and featured the coalition of the nullifiers with the Whig groups opposing the President. They claimed that Calhoun, with the connivance of Clay, was laying the basis for a clash between South Carolina and the general government, in the hope that he might secure the sympathy and support of the entire South. When South Carolina's electoral vote, under Calhoun's direction, was given to Governor Floyd of Virginia, Bowers notes that Jackson, realizing the significance of the act, "girded his loins for a life-and-death struggle with Calhoun and Nullification."[70] For partisan reasons, as well as from motives of intense loyalty to the union for which he was now the chief executive officer and spokesman, Jackson made it clear that he meant what he said in the toast at the Jefferson birthday dinner: "Our Federal Union. It

---

[68] Houston, *op. cit.*, pp. 110, 111.

[69] For the text of the nullification ordinance, see William MacDonald, *Select Documents Illustrative of the History of the United States* (New York, 1907), p. 268.

[70] *Party Battles of the Jackson Period*, p. 251.

must and shall be preserved." While Governor Hayne was putting the state into a condition to take military measures if necessary, President Jackson was quietly and effectively preparing the federal forces to take such action to preserve the union as the situation demanded. He issued a proclamation declaring "disunion by armed force is *treason.* . . . On your unhappy State will inevitably fall all the evils of the conflict you force upon the government of your country. It cannot accede to the mad project of disunion, of which you would be the first victims. Its First Magistrate can not, if he would, avoid the performance of his duty."

"The Constitution of the United States, then," the President maintained, "forms a *government,* not a league; and whether it be formed by compact between the States or in any other manner, its character is the same. . . . Because the Union was formed by a compact, it is said the parties to that compact may, when they feel themselves aggrieved, depart from it; but it is precisely because it is a compact that they cannot. A compact is an agreement or binding obligation. It may by its terms have a sanction or penalty for its breach, or it may not."

Following this line of reasoning, Jackson declared, "I consider, then, the power to annul a law of the United States, assumed by one State, incompatible with the existence of the Union, contradicted expressly by the letter of the Constitution, unauthorized by its spirit, inconsistent with every principle on which it was founded, and destructive of the great object for which it was formed."[71] The President requested the passage of an act giving him powers adequate to meet the crisis and recommended a modification of the tariff system.

The President's proclamation was answered by a similar pronouncement by Governor Hayne. And the South Carolina legislature replied to the proclamation by adopting a series of resolutions among which it was declared that "the power vested by the Constitution and laws in the President of the United States, to issue his proclamation, does not authorize him in that mode, to interfere whenever he may think fit, in the affairs of the respective States, or that he should use it as a means of promulgating executive expositions of the Constitution, with the sanction of force thus superseding the action of other departments of the general government." The right of secession was supported in the resolution when it said "that each State of the Union has the right whenever it may deem such a course necessary for the preservation of its liberties or vital interests, to secede peaceably from the Union, and that there is no constitutional power in the general government, much less in the executive department, of that government, to retain by force such State

---

[71] Richardson, *op. cit.,* II: 643 ff.

in the Union.'"[72] It was also proposed that a convention of the states be called as early as practicable to consider the questions of disputed power that had arisen between the states of the confederacy and the general government.[73]

In January, 1833, an armed conflict appeared imminent with South Carolina calling for volunteers and taking the necessary steps to uphold her authority and with the President appealing to Congress for the grant of authority to enforce the tariff laws in South Carolina. While Congress was considering the enactment of a Force Bill and a modification of the existing tariff system, the political leaders of the state arranged for a suspension of the nullification ordinance and issued a call for a second state convention. When this convention met Congress had passed the Force Bill and a Compromise Tariff Act, providing for a reduction of duties for a period of ten years. The convention repealed the ordinance nullifying the tariff but approved another ordinance declaring the Force Bill null and void.[74]

To the proposal of South Carolina to call a convention of the states, the Delaware legislature replied "that the Constitution of the United States of America, which is a form of government established by the people of the United States of America, has expressly provided a tribunal in the Supreme Court of the United States, for the settlement of controversies between the United States and the respective States, and of all controversies arising under that instrument itself."[75] Almost all of the states agreed with the sentiment expressed by the legislature of Alabama that nullification as a constitutional remedy is unsound in theory and dangerous in practice and that "it is unconstitutional and essentially revolutionary, leading in its consequences to anarchy and civil discord, and finally to the dissolution of the Union."[76] Virginia requested South Carolina to repeal its nullification ordinance and to depend upon Congress for a speedy reduction of the objectionable duties and imposts. The doctrines of the resolutions and report of 1798 and 1799 were reiterated, but it was declared that the doctrines of these resolutions did not sanction the proceedings of South Carolina.

The crisis was temporarily averted by Clay's Compromise Tariff Act, which, as is usual in a compromise, pleased nobody. By this bill the tariff

---

[72] *Acts of South Carolina*, 1832, pp. 29, 30, 38; and Ames, *op. cit.*, pp. 174–176.

[73] Ames, *op. cit.*, p. 176.

[74] *Ibid.*, pp. 188, 189.

[75] *Ibid.*, p. 177. New Jersey, Maryland, and Kentucky joined with Delaware in supporting the Supreme Court as the proper and only tribunal for the final settlement of controversies relating to the relations of the federal government and the states.

[76] *Ibid.*, p. 181.

rates in excess of 20 per cent, as fixed by the act of 1832, were to be gradually reduced until by 1842 they would stand at the uniform rate of 20 per cent. Calhoun agreed to the compromise, though for him the reductions were in most instances too slow and hence the termination of unreasonably high rates too long deferred. To the representatives of South Carolina, despite objectionable features of the act, there was a choice only between acceptance or secession. Since secession now meant civil war, and the people of the state had thought largely in terms of peaceful secession, the compromise was accepted as in the nature of a peace offering. Clay was willing to compromise, for his constituents no longer supported him in his stand for high protective duties. Jackson favored similar action, for, as Houston observes, "Jackson and Webster were then in combination and all the advantage would have accrued to Webster if the controversy had ended without a compromise."[77] Hence the President signed the Tariff Act on the same day that he signed the Force Bill to compel South Carolina to submit to the enforcement of federal laws.[78] At this stage the state convention was again called into session and upon the advice of Calhoun and the moderate wing of the party the Nullification Ordinance was rescinded.

To the members of the convention, the attitude of the state had been the main factor in securing a reform of the tariff and hence a glorious victory had been won. It was contended that the state had now obtained the objects contended for over a period of more than a decade. Regarding the Force Bill as a dangerous precedent for the future, the convention proceeded to nullify it so far as its enforcement within the state of South Carolina might be concerned. As to the results of the controversy, Houston believes that it "was decidedly a victory for the general government, at least as far as principles are concerned."[79] There were those who thought that in the final settlement of the controversy there was little cause for pride and congratulations on the part of the leaders of the majority party in the state, but the people of South Carolina continued to boast of the glorious stand which the state had taken in the cause of liberty in 1832.

With the enactment by Congress of Clay's Compromise Tariff Bill of 1833 and with the suspension of South Carolina's Nullification Ordinance, civil war for the time being was averted. The real pass at arms had

---

[77] *A Study of Nullification in South Carolina*, p. 127.

[78] Representative McDuffie of South Carolina attempted to change the title of the Force Bill to "An Act to subvert the Sovereignty of the States of the Union, to Establish a Consolidated Union without Limitation of Powers, and to make the Civil subordinate to the Military Power." *Cong. Debates,* 22d Cong., 2d sess., p. 1903.

[79] Houston, *op. cit.,* pp. 134, 135.

merely been delayed. Marshall was aware of the storm he had helped to create, though he could only characterize opposition to his doctrines of nationalism as "madness." Viewing the aftermath of the nullification controversy which appeared as more of a victory for South Carolina than the nation, Marshall wrote with prophetic insight: "Have you ever seen anything to equal the exhibition in Charleston and the far South generally? Those people pursue a southern league steadily or they are insane. They have caught at Clay's bill, if their conduct is at all intelligible, not as a real accommodation, a real adjustment, a real relief from actual supposed oppression, but as an apology for avoiding the crisis and deferring the decisive moment till the other States of the South will unite with them."[80]

Some incidental effects of the controversy were the strengthening of the conviction that the interests of the North and the South were diametrically opposed, and, at least so far as South Carolina was concerned, the marked lessening of respect for the general government, and a disposition to look forward to secession as an ultimate necessity. Throughout the debates over the policies of the federal government regarding internal improvements and the tariff, the doctrine of secession was strongly and frequently affirmed. Recognizing the futility of resistance by a single state, the plan of a southern union was proposed. It was in this atmosphere, when the people of the state were aroused and irritated, that the abolition movement came as a measure to keep alive and foster the disunion sentiments which had gained a strong foothold in South Carolina from 1830 to 1832.

---

[80] Letter of Marshall to Story, April 24, 1833. Massachusetts Hist. Soc., *Proceedings*, (2d ser.), XIV: 356, 357. "The political world, at least our part of it, is surely moved *topsy turvy*. What is to become of us and of our Constitution? Can the wise men of the East answer the question? Those of the South perceive no difficulty. Allow a full range to state rights and state sovereignty, and, in their opinion, all will go well." Letter of Marshall to Story, Nov. 16, 1833, *ibid.*, p. 358, and John Edward Oster, *The Political and Economic Doctrines of John Marshall* (New York, 1914), p. 152.

APPENDIX

As THE ARGUMENTS *were taking shape in the beginning of the Administration of Andrew Jackson as President, it is well to recur again to the views of James Madison. There were no indications that Madison had changed his views on the undesirability of granting to the courts a final and conclusive authority to interpret the terms and phrases of the federal Constitution, so far as the powers of Congress and the Executive were concerned, or of placing similar authority in the hands of the state courts, so far as their interpretation of the powers and authority of the coördinate branches of these governments were concerned. It is apparent, however, that he had shifted his position somewhat from the views which might fairly and reasonably be deduced from the Virginia Resolutions and from his report on these resolutions to the legislature of Virginia, so far as the finality of interpretation by the Supreme Court was concerned when questions of federal and state authority were involved. At this time Madison, in a series of communications, wrote as follows:*

The extreme to which the Resolution goes in declaring the protecting duty as it is called unconstitutional is deeply to be regretted. It is a ground which cannot be maintained, on which the State will probably stand alone, and which by lessening the confidence of other States in the wisdom of its councils, must impede the progress of its sounder doctrines. In compliance with your request I offer a few hasty remarks on topics and sources of information which occur to me.

1. The meaning of the power to regulate commerce is to be sought in the general use of the phrase, in other words, in the objects generally understood to be embraced by the power, when it was inserted in the Constitution.

2. The power has been applied in the form of a tariff, to the encouraging of particular domestic occupations by every existing commercial nation.

3. It has been so used and applied particularly and systematically by Great Britain whose commercial vocabulary is the parent of ours.

4. The inefficacy of the power in relation to manufactures as well as to other objects, when exercised by the States separately, was among the arguments and inducements for revising the old Confederation, and transferring the power from the States to the government of the United States. Nor can it be supposed that the States actually engaged in certain branches of manufactures, and foreseeing an increase of them, would have surrendered the whole power (over) commerce to the general government unless expected to be more effectual for that as well as other purposes in that depositary, than in their own hands. Nor can it be supposed that *any of the States,* meant to *annihilate* such a power, and thereby disarm the Nation from protecting occupations and establishments, important to its defence and independence, against the subversive policy of foreign rivals or enemies. To say that the States may respectively encourage their own manufactures, and may therefore have looked to that resource when the Constitution was formed, is by no means satisfactory. They could not protect them by an impost, if the power of collecting one had been reserved, a *partial* one having been found impracticable; so, also as to a prohibitory regulation. Nor can they do it by an excise

on foreign articles, for the same reason, the trade being necessarily open with other States which might concur in the plan. They could only do it by a *bounty,* and that bounty procured *by a direct tax,* a tax unpopular for any purpose, and obviously inadmissible for that. Such a state of things could never have been in contemplation when the Constitution was formed.

5. The printed journal of the Convention of 1787 will *probably* show positively or negatively that the commercial power given to Congress embraced the object in question.

6. The proceedings of the state conventions may also deserve attention.

7. The proceedings and debates of the first Congress under the present Constitution, will show that the power was generally, *perhaps* universally, regarded as indisputable.

8. Throughout the succeeding Congresses, till a very late date, the power over commerce has been exercised or admitted, so as to bear on internal objects of utility or policy, without a reference to revenue. The University of Virginia very lately had the benefit of it in a case where revenue was relinquished; a case not questioned, if liable to be so. The Virginia Resolutions, as they have been called, which were proposed in Congress in 1793–94, and approved throughout the State, may perhaps furnish examples.

Every President from General Washington to John Quincy Adams inclusive has recognized the power of a tariff in favor of manufactures, without indicating a doubt, or that a doubt existed anywhere.

10. Virginia appears to be the only State that now denies, or ever did deny the power; nor are there perhaps more than a very few individuals, if a single one, in the State who will not admit the power in favor of internal fabrics or productions necessary for public defence on the water or the land. To bring the protecting duty in those cases, within the war power would require a greater latitude of construction, than to refer them to the power of regulating trade.

11. A construction of the Constitution practised upon or acknowledged for a period, of nearly forty years, has received a national sanction not to be reversed, but by an evidence at least equivalent to the national will. If every new Congress were to disregard a meaning of the instrument uniformly sustained by their predecessors, for such a period there would be less stability in that fundamental law, than is required for the public good, in the ordinary expositions of law. And the case of the Chancellor's foot, as a substitute for an established measure, would illustrate the greater as well as the lesser evil of uncertainty and mutability.

12. In expounding the Constitution, it is as essential as it is obvious, that the distinction should be kept in view, between the usurpation, and the abuse of the power. That a tariff for the encouragement of manufactures may be abused by its excess, by its partiality, or by a noxious selection of its objects, is certain. But so may the exercise of every constitutional power; more especially that of imposing indirect taxes, though limited to the object of revenue. And the abuse cannot be regarded as a breach of the fundamental compact, till it reaches a degree of oppression, so iniquitious and intolerable as to justify civil war, or disunion pregnant with wars, than to be foreign ones. This distinction may be a key to the language of Mr. Jefferson, in the letter you alluded to. It is known that he felt and expressed strongly, his disapprobation of the existing tariff and its threatened increase.

13. If mere *inequality,* in imposing taxes, or in other legislative acts, be synonymous with *unconstitutionality,* is there a State in the Union whose constitution would be safe? Complaints of such abuses are heard in every legislature, at every session; and where is there more of them than in Virginia, or of pretext for them than is furnished

by the diversity of her local and other circumstances; to say nothing of her constitution itself, which happens to divide so unequally the very power of making laws?[81]

And may it not be fairly left to the unbiased judgment of all men of experience and of intelligence, to decide which is most to be relied on for a sound and safe test of the meaning of a Constitution, a uniform interpretation by all the successive authorities under it, commencing with its birth, and continued for a long period, through the varied state of political contests, or the opinion of every new legislature heated as it may be by the strife of parties, or warped as often happens by the eager pursuit of some favourite object; or carried away possibly by the powerful eloquence, or captivating address of a few popular statesmen, themselves influenced, perhaps, by the same misleading causes. If the latter test is to prevail, every new legislative opinion might make a new Constitution; as the foot of every new Chancellor would make a new standard of measure.[82]

On the subject of an Arbiter or Umpire, it might not be amiss, perhaps, to note at some place, that there can be none, external to the United States, more than to individual States; nor within either, for those extreme cases, or questions of passive obedience and non-resistance, which justify and require a resort to the original rights of the parties to the compact. But that in all cases, not of that extreme character, there is an Arbiter or Umpire, as within the governments of the States, so within that of the United States in the authority constitutionally provided for deciding, controversies concerning boundaries of right and power. . . .

On comparing the doctrine of Virginia in 98–99, with that of the present day in South Carolina will it not be found that Virginia asserted that the States, as parties to the constitutional compact, had a right and were bound, in extreme cases only, and after a failure of all efforts for redress under the forms of the Constitution, to interpose in their sovereign capacity, for the purpose of arresting the evil of usurpation, and preserving the Constitution and Union: Whereas the doctrine of the present day in South Carolina asserts that in a case of not greater magnitude than the degree of inequality in the operation of a tariff in favor of manufactures, she may of herself finally decide, by virtue of her sovereignty, that the Constitution has been violated; and that if not yielded to by the federal government, though supported by all the other States, she may rightfully resist it and withdraw herself from the Union.[83]

But the Union of the States is, according to the Virginia doctrine in 98–99, a *Constitutional Union;* and the right to judge *in the last resort,* concerning usurpations of power, affecting the validity of the Union, referred by that doctrine to the parties to the compact. On recurring to original principles, and to extreme cases, a single State might indeed be so oppressed as to be justified in shaking off the yoke; so might a single county of a State be, under an extremity of oppression. But until such justifications can be pleaded, the compact is obligatory in both cases. . . . A political system that does not provide for a peaceable and effectual decision of all controversies arising among the parties is not a government, but a mere treaty between independent nations, without any resort for terminating disputes but negotiation, and that failing, the sword. That the system of a United States, is what it professes to be, a real government and not a nominal one only, is proved by the fact that it has all the practical attributes

---

[81] *Writings* (Hunt ed.), IX: 284–287. Letter to Joseph C. Cabell in answer to inquiry concerning the resolution presented to the Virginia legislature proposing to condemn the validity of a federal tariff act.

[82] *Writings* (Hunt ed.), IX: 334. Letter to Joseph C. Cabell, Sept. 18, 1828.

[83] *Writings* (Hunt ed.), IX: 342–344. Letter to Joseph C. Cabell, Aug. 16, 1829.

and organs of a real though limited government; a Legislative, Executive, and Judicial Department, with the physical means of executing the particular authorities assigned to it, on the individual citizens, in like manner as is done by other governments. Those who would substitute negotiation for governmental authority, and rely on the former as an adequate resource, forget the essential difference between disputes to be settled by two branches of the same government as between the House of Lords and Commons in England, or the Senate and House of Representatives here; and disputes between different governments. In the former case as neither party can act without the other, necessity produces an adjustment. In the other case, each party having in a Legislative, Executive, and Judicial Department of its own, the complete means of giving an independent effect to its will, no such necessity exists; and physical collisions are the natural result of conflicting pretensions.[84]

Is there then no remedy for usurpations in which the Supreme Court of the United States concur? Yes: constitutional remedies such as have been found effectual; particularly in the case of Alien and Sedition laws, and such as will in all cases be effectual, whilst the responsibility of the general government to its constituents continues:— Remonstrances and instructions, recurring elections and impeachments; amendment of Constitution as provided by itself and exemplified in the Eleventh Article limiting the suability of the States.

These are recourses of the States against the general government: resulting from the relations of the States to that government: whilst no corresponding control exists in the relations of the general to the individual governments all of whose functionaries are independent of the United States in their appointment and responsibility.

Finally should all the constitutional remedies fail, and the usurpations of the general government become so intolerable as absolutely to forbid a longer passive obedience and non-resistance, a resort to the original rights of the parties becomes justifiable; and redress may be sought by shaking off the yoke, as of right, might be done by part of an individual State in a like case; or even by a single citizen, could he effect it, if deprived of rights absolutely essential to his safety and happiness. In the defect of their ability to resist, the individual citizens may seek relief in expatriation or voluntary exile a resort not within the reach of large portions of the community.

In all the views that may be taken of questions between the state governments and the general government the awful consequences of a final rupture and dissolution of the Union should never for a moment be lost sight of. Such a prospect must be deprecated, must be shuddered at by every friend to his country, to liberty, to the happiness of man. For, in the event of a dissolution of the Union, an impossibility of ever renewing it is brought home to every mind by the difficulties encountered in establishing it. The propensity of all communities to divide when not pressed into a unity by external danger, is a truth well understood. *There is no instance of a people inhabiting even a small island, if remote from foreign danger, and sometimes in spite of that pressure, who are not divided into alien, rival, and hostile tribes.* The happy Union of these States is a wonder; the Constitution a miracle; their example the hope of liberty throughout the world. Woe to the ambition that would meditate the destruction of either![85]

It has been too much the case in expounding the Constitution of the United States that its meaning has been sought not in its peculiar and unprecedented modifications

---

[84] *Writings* (Hunt ed.), IX: 347–349. Letter to Joseph C. Cabell, Sept. 7, 1829.
[85] From an outline on a form of government in the United States, Sept., 1829. *Writings* (Hunt ed.), IX: 353–357.

of power; but by viewing it, some through the medium of a simple government others through that of a mere league of governments. It is neither the one nor the other; but essentially different from both. It must consequently be its own interpreter. No other government can furnish a key to its true character. Other governments present an individual and indivisible sovereignty. The Constitution of the United States divides the sovereignty; the portions surrendered by the States, composing the federal sovereignty over specified subjects; the portions retained forming the sovereignty of each over the residuary subjects within its sphere. If sovereignty cannot be thus divided, the political system of the United States is a chimera, mocking the vain pretensions of human wisdom. If it can be so divided, the system ought to have a fair opportunity of fulfilling the wishes and expectations which cling to the experiment.

Nothing can be more clear than that the Constitution of the United States has created a government, in as strict a sense of the term, as the governments of the States created by their respective constitutions. The federal government has like the state governments, its Legislative, its Executive and its Judiciary Departments. It has, like them, acknowledged cases in which the powers of these departments are to operate. And the operation is to be directly on persons and things in the one government as in the others. If in some cases, the jurisdiction is concurrent as it is in others exclusive, this is one of the features constituting the peculiarity of the system.

In forming this compound scheme of government it was impossible to lose sight of the question, what was to be done in the event of controversies which could not fail to occur, concerning the partition line, between the powers belonging to the federal and to the state governments. That some provisions ought to be made, was as obvious and as essential, as the task itself was difficult and delicate.

That the final decision of such controversies, if left to each of the 13 now 24 members of the Union, must produce a different Constitution and different laws in the States was certain; and that such differences must be destructive of the common government and of the Union itself, was equally certain. The decision of questions between the common agents of the whole and of the parts, could only proceed from the whole, that is from a collective not a separate authority of the parts.

The question then presenting itself could only relate to the least objectionable mode of providing for such occurrences, under the collective authority.

The provision immediately and ordinarily relied on, is manifestly the Supreme Court of the United States clothed as it is, with a jurisdiction "in controversies to which the United States shall be a party"; the Court itself being so constituted as to render it independent and impartial in its decisions; whilst other and ulterior resorts would remain in the elective process, in the hands of the people themselves the joint constituents of the parties; and in the provision made by the Constitution for amending itself. All other resorts are extra and ultra constitutional, corresponding to the Ultima Ratio of nations renouncing the ordinary relations of peace.

If the Supreme Court of the United States be found or deemed not sufficiently independent and impartial for the trust committed to it, a better tribunal is a desideratum: But whatever this may be, it must necessarily derive its authority from the whole not from the parts, from the States in some collective not individual capacity. And as some such tribunal is a vital element, a *sine qua non*, in an efficient and permanent government the tribunal existing must be acquiesced in, until a better or more satisfactory one can be substituted.[86]

---

[86] *Writings* (Hunt ed.), IX: 354, 355. Letter to N. P. Trist, Feb. 15, 1830. See *ibid.*, p. 355, for Madison's views on the compact theory.

CHAPTER XVI

The Trend of Supreme Court Decisions from 1828 to 1835

THE ADMINISTRATION of Andrew Jackson, notes William MacDonald, "marks, with greater distinctness than does the administration of any other President, the beginning of a new period in the political history of the United States. . . . There was to be still the same Constitution, but a new theory of it; the same administrative organization, but a new and un-heard-of spirit animating it; the same confidence in national honor and resource, but a more striking assertion of them; the same vigorous social life, but with strange and startling manifestations."[1] The doctrine of the "will of the people" was revived, and urged with a vigor which caused most people to believe it something new. The election of 1828 marked the breaking down of the Democratic-Republican system of more than a quarter of a century and the coming into power of the democracy of the next thirty years.[2] Through an analysis of some of the important decisions of the Supreme Court may be traced the mingling of the old doctrines of the Federalist and Republican periods with those of the new democratic society.

CHANGES IN THE DECISIONS OF CHIEF JUSTICE MARSHALL

Before the 1826 Congressional debate the Supreme Court had reached the peak of its authority and prestige under the regime of Chief Justice Marshall. The decline in the position and power of the Court was gradual for a few years, when even the Chief Justice gave indications of a recognition in his decisions of the changes in public opinion. It was ap-

---

[1] William MacDonald, *Jacksonian Democracy: 1829–1837*, American Nation Series (New York, 1906), pp. 3, 4, 32.

[2] See Edward Channing, *A History of the United States* (New York, 1927), V: 379 ff. "The ideal of the west," maintains Frederick Jackson Turner, "was its emphasis upon the worth and possibilities of the common man, its belief in the right of every man to rise to the full measure of his own nature, under conditions of social mobility. . . . It was certain that this society, where equality and individualism flourished, where assertive democracy was supreme, where impatience with the old order of things was a ruling passion, would demand control of the government, would resent the rule of the trained statesmen and official classes, and would fight nominations by congressional caucus and the continuance of presidential dynasties." *The Rise of the New West, 1819–1829* (New York, 1906), pp. 68, 69, 107.

parent before the election of Andrew Jackson to the presidency that the Court was giving some consideration to what Mr. Dooley called "election returns." But the decline in the Court's authority and effectiveness, which began in the middle of the decade from 1820 to 1830, grew more marked after the election of President Jackson, and the last five years of Marshall's Chief Justiceship was marked by such serious conflicts with the Executive and with the states that both Marshall and Story believed that the Supreme Court would be shorn by judicial construction, Congressional legislation, and Executive domination of the essential powers which were necessary to its functioning as an effective federal tribunal. The story of these uncertain and hesitant years form a marked contrast with that of the decade from 1815 to 1825 when, with something in the nature of a pontifical air, the Court was expounding and applying the principles of Hamiltonian nationalism. But it is interesting to review the steps by which the Court met the oncoming tide of sectionalism, of the militant assertion of State rights, and of the assertive attitude and principles of frontier democracy typified by Andrew Jackson and gradually adjusted itself to markedly new trends and tendencies.

In a suit brought by the president, directors, and company of the Bank of the United States upon a bond given to the bank to secure the faithful performance of the official duties of one of its cashiers, Marshall held on circuit that evidence of the execution and of its approval by the board of directors was inadmissible, as there was no written record of such approval. The Supreme Court reversed this decision in a lengthy opinion by Justice Story.[3] Story held that the same rule which applied to private persons was applicable under similar circumstances to a corporation. Daniel Webster, who argued the case for the bank, reported to Jeremiah Mason that "our friend Judge Story laid out his whole strength and made a great opinion."[4] Chief Justice Marshall, dissenting, admitted that his decision in the Circuit Court "gave general surprise to the profession, and was generally condemned," and in a letter to Story he recognized that the practice of banks had not conformed to his construction of the law. Nevertheless, he argued ably and effectively that a corporation, unless so exempted in its charter, could be bound only by acts under seal or for which there was evidence in a written record. Beveridge cites the *Dandridge Case* as another instance of Marshall's conservatism coupled with his dogged persistence. When all of the other Justices joined in reversing a wrong decision Marshall had

---

[3] United States Bank v. Dandridge, 12 Wheaton 64 (1827).

[4] See Letter, Apr. 10, 1827. Writing to the president of the bank, Feb. 24, 1827, Webster noted that the bank had not lost any case in the Supreme Court. *The Private Correspondence of Daniel Webster*, ed. by Fletcher Webster (Boston, 1857), I: 417.

rendered on circuit, "the unanimity of his brethren, the clear and convincing opinion of Story, the disapproval of his own views by the bench, bar, and business men of the whole country"[5] were not sufficient to make him yield.

The reaction against the strongly nationalistic bias of the Supreme Court in earlier decades was evident in *Willson v. Blackbird Creek Marsh Company* which again raised the question whether the power of Congress over commerce was exclusive or merely concurrent. Delaware authorized a company to build a dam across a navigable stream. The owners of a sloop licensed under the navigation laws of the United States broke the dam, and, through an action for trespass, the issue was brought to the Supreme Court. For the owners of the sloop it was argued that the rights of navigation are public rights and that they necessarily belong to the United States, subject only to such regulations as Congress may prescribe. Attorney General Wirt replied for the company that "it cannot be urged that the power to regulate commerce can interfere with the rights of the States over the property within their boundaries. While the waters of the United States belong to the whole people of the Nation, this creek continued subject to the power of the State in whose territory it rises."[6]

Chief Justice Marshall, rendering the opinion of the Court, disposed of the question raised by counsel relative to the jurisdiction of the Court. Though the pleadings in the state court did not raise the contention that the state act was repugnant to the Constitution and laws of the United States, Marshall thought that question must have been discussed and decided. To warrant the acceptance of jurisdiction by the federal court, said he: "It is sufficient to bring the case within the provisions of the 25th section of the judicial act, if the record shows that the Constitution or a law or a treaty of the United States must have been misconstrued, or the decision could not be made. Or, as in this case, that the constitutionality of a state law was questioned, and the decision has been in favour of the party claiming under such law."[7]

As to the authority of the state, Marshall observed that the act of the assembly, by which the plaintiffs were authorized to construct their dam, shows that this is one of those many creeks passing through a deep level marsh up which the tide flows for some distance. The value of the property on the banks of the creek was enhanced by excluding the water from the marsh, and the health of the inhabitants probably was improved. So far as such acts do not come into collision with the powers of the general government, they are regarded as undoubtedly within the powers

[5] Albert J. Beveridge, *The Life of John Marshall* (New York, 1919), pp. 482, 483.
[6] 2 Peters 245, 249 (1829).
[7] *Ibid.*, p. 251.

reserved to the states. It was clear that the act of the state authorizing the placing of a barrier in a navigable creek abridged rights of those who had been accustomed to ply their boats in it. "But this abridgement, unless it comes in conflict with the Constitution or a law of the United States," thought Marshall, "is an affair between the government of Delaware and its citizens, of which this Court can take no cognizance." Since there was no act of Congress applicable for the protection of the navigable waters of the state, Marshall did not regard the state act repugnant to "the power to regulate commerce in its dormant state."[8] It was difficult to reconcile the language of this decision with pertinent expressions in *Gibbons v. Ogden*,[9] but apparently Marshall adopted for the present case the concurrent power doctrine so strongly urged by counsel in the *Gibbons Case*. To reconcile the sentiments expressed regarding the "dormant state" of Congressional power over interstate commerce with some of the language in the *Gibbons Case* was a difficult task indeed, and the decision increased the uncertainty regarding the meaning of the commerce provision of the Constitution.

A similar attitude of caution was manifested in decisions which involved the giving of protection to vested rights contrary to state enactments affecting such rights. The principle of affording protection to vested rights by indirect construction of constitutional phrases against hostile state legislation was making headway slowly, as may be seen by the decision of the Court in *Satterlee v. Matthewson*.[10] In determining a controversy over land titles between Connecticut and Pennsylvania claimants, a Pennsylvania act defining the rights of landlord and tenant between such claimants was held not to impair the obligation of contracts. There is nothing in the Constitution of the United States, said Justice Washington, which forbids the legislature of a state to exercise judicial functions; nor does the Constitution prevent the divesting of rights which were vested by law.[11] A dictum to the contrary by Chief Justice Marshall in *Fletcher v. Peck*[12] was declared to have no binding effect, and the expressions of opinion favorable to the protection of vested rights in *Vanhorne's Lessee v. Dorrance*[13] and *Society for the Propagation of the Gospel v. Wheeler*[14] were explained as predicated upon the application of state constitutional provisions. The criticisms of the Court in Congress may have influenced the judgment and majority

[8] 2 Peters 250, 251.
[9] 9 Wheaton 1 (1824).
[10] 2 Peters 380 (1829).
[11] 2 Peters 412, 413.
[12] 6 Cranch 87 (1810).
[13] 2 Dallas 304 (1795).
[14] 8 Wheaton 464 (1823).

opinion in this case. For it was held that statutes may be made retroactive even to the extent of divesting acquired rights, even though such legislation might be deemed an unjust exercise of legislative power.

Justice Johnson concurred in the judgment, but disagreed with the grounds for the decision stated by the Court. To give efficacy to a void contract, he maintained, not only violates a contract, but also does that which is infinitely worse, for "it is advancing to the very extreme of that class of arbitrary and despotic acts, which bear upon individual rights and liabilities, and against the whole of which the Constitution most clearly intended to interpose a protection commensurate to the evil." The real difficulty in the case arose, in his opinion, out of "that unhappy idea, that the phrase 'ex post facto' in the Constitution of the United States, was confined to criminal cases exclusively; a decision which leaves a large class of arbitrary legislative acts without the prohibitions of the Constitution."[15] Johnson, appointed to the Court as a Jeffersonian Republican, had now repudiated the principles of Jeffersonian democracy to such an extent that he would have had the Court, by the simple process of interpretation, create a broad doctrine for the protection of civil rights against legislative attacks. It remained for future Justices to accomplish this result by the interpretation of the phrase "due process of law."

A retrospective law of Rhode Island was also held valid in *Wilkinson v. Leland.*[16] Justice Story admitted the "danger, inconvenience and mischief" of such legislation, but declared that the Court must decide "not upon principle of public policy, but of power." But, like Justice Chase in *Calder v. Bull,*[17] Story could not let the opportunity go by to affirm the doctrine favorable to the protection of vested rights which gave encouragement and support to his brethren in subsequent cases. Referring to the authority belonging to the government of Rhode Island under the charter granted by Charles II, Story said:

In a government professing to regard the great rights of personal liberty and of property, and which is required to legislate in subordination to the general laws of England, it would not lightly be presumed, that the great principles of Magna Charta were to be disregarded, or that the estates of its subjects were liable to be taken away without trial, without notice, and without offence. Even if such authority could be deemed to have been confided by the charter to the general assembly of Rhode Island, as an exercise of transcendental sovereignty before the Revolution, it can scarcely be imagined, that that great event could have left the people of that State subjected to its uncontrolled and arbitrary exercise. That government can scarcely be deemed to be free, where the rights of property are left solely dependent upon the will of a legislative

---

[15] 2 Peters 414–416.
[16] 2 Peters 627 (1829).
[17] Calder v. Bull, 3 Dallas 386 (1798).

body, without any restraint. The fundamental maxims of a free government seem to require that the rights of personal liberty and private property should be held sacred. At least, no court of justice in this country would be warranted in assuming that the power to violate and disregard them—a power so repugnant to the common principles of justice and civil liberty—lurked under any general grant of legislative authority, or ought to be implied from any general expressions of the will of the people. The people ought not to be presumed to part with rights so vital to their security and well-being, without very strong and direct expressions of such an intention. In *Terret v. Taylor*,[18] it was held by this Court that a grant or title to lands once made by the legislature to any person or corporation is irrevocable, and cannot be reassumed by any subsequent legislative act; and that a different doctrine is utterly inconsistent with the great and fundamental principle of a republican government, and with the right of the citizens to the free enjoyment of their property lawfully acquired. We know of no case, in which a legislative act to transfer the property of A to B, without his consent, has ever been held a constitutional exercise of legislative power in any State in the Union. On the contrary, it has been constantly resisted as inconsistent with just principles, by every judicial tribunal in which it has been attempted to be enforced. We are not prepared, therefore, to admit that the people of Rhode Island have ever delegated to their legislature the power to divest the vested rights of property, and transfer them without the assent of the parties."[19]

Justice Story was now giving judicial sanction in the form of dicta to the doctrines announced by Justice Chase in *Calder v. Bull*,[20] by Chancellor Kent in *Dash v. Van Kleeck*[21] and subsequent cases, and by Daniel Webster in his arguments before the Supreme Court. The ground was being prepared for the judicial construction of implied limitations on legislative powers favorable to the protection of vested or acquired rights of persons and of corporations. Another of the principles for which the Federalists contended from the time of the adoption of the Constitution was gradually being approved as a dictum of sound constitutional interpretation.

The judicial gloss which was being constructed as necessary to preserve federal supremacy and to protect vested rights led to another decision which stretched the process of judicial construction to its utmost limits. In *Weston v. The City Council of Charleston*[22] the Supreme Court was called upon to decide whether a city ordinance levying a tax on the stocks and bonds of the United States was valid. Answering a strongly nationalistic argument by Robert Hayne, attorneys for the city expressed apprehension at the difficulties which might be experienced if the Supreme Court reversed the decision of the state courts and attempted to

[18] 9 Cranch 43 (1815). Justice Story rendered the opinion of the Court in this case.
[19] 2 Peters 657, 658.
[20] Cf. above, p. 154.
[21] 7 Johnson 477 (1811). See also John Theodore Horton, *James Kent: A Study in Conservatism* (New York, 1939), pp. 161 ff.
[22] 2 Peters 449 (1829).

enforce its mandate. It was suggested that only an affirmative act of Congress could make interference by the federal courts effective. It was admitted that, in the field of taxation where the state and federal governments exercise concurrent powers, if the exercise of authority by the state interferes with a power of the federal government, the former must give way. But there was no federal act with which the ordinance conflicted. Forecasting difficulties which might arise if the implied prohibition contended for were adopted, it was pointed out that "the general government, by carrying their power to extremes in the creation of extensive loans, might furnish facilities of exempt investment, that would entirely absorb from the reach of state taxation all the funds of its citizens, and thus destroy one of its highest prerogatives and very existence."[23]

Chief Justice Marshall, rendering the decision, held that the Supreme Court had jurisdiction under the twenty-fifth section of the Judiciary Act, since powers granted under the Constitution were drawn in question and that a writ of prohibition was not only an appropriate remedy, but also that the hearing on the application for this writ in the state court constituted a suit which might be taken to the Supreme Court for review on a writ of error. Stating the main question whether stock issued for loans made to the government of the United States was liable to be taxed by states and local public agencies, Marshall declared the tax void. Relying again on matters of policy and expediency, the Chief Justice asked whether anything could be more dangerous or more injurious than the admission of a principle which authorizes every state and every corporation in the union which possesses the right of taxation to burden the exercise of the power of Congress to borrow money. Such a possibility during a state of war, when the honor, safety, and the independence of the nation were at stake, was deemed inconceivable. The contention on which the Court based its opinions in *McCulloch v. Maryland*,[24] that the power to tax involved the power to destroy, was strongly supported as a warrant for the denial of the authority now asserted as belonging to all state agencies.

Admitting that taxation is one of the most essential powers of the state governments and that the necessity of limiting its exercise is one of the delicate and difficult duties which devolve upon the Supreme Court, Marshall maintained that in the performance of this duty "we have considered it as a necessary consequence from the supremacy of the government of the whole, that its action in the exercise of its legitimate powers should be free and unembarrassed by any conflicting powers in the pos-

[23] 2 Peters 461.
[24] 4 Wheaton 316 (1819).

session of its parts; that the powers of a State cannot rightfully be so exercised as to impede and obstruct the free course of those measures which the government of the States united may rightfully adopt."[25] In accordance, then, with the reasoning in the case of *McCulloch v. Maryland*, it was held that a contract made by the government in the exercise of its power to borrow money on the credit of the United States is independent of the will of any state in which the individual who lends may reside. The restraint which was being applied to the state and its subordinate units was considered to be imposed by the Constitution, for, said Marshall: "The American people have conferred the power of borrowing money on their government, and by making that government supreme, have shielded its actions, in the exercise of this power, from the action of the local governments. The grant of the power is incompatible with a restraining or controlling power, and the declaration of supremacy is a declaration that no such restraining or controlling power shall be exercised."[26]

Justice Johnson, apparently moved by the insistence on the part of the Republicans that all of the Judges should state their views on constitutional issues, made it clear in his dissent that he wished his views on constitutional questions to appear "where they cannot be misunderstood or misrepresented." In the first place, Johnson objected to the Court taking jurisdiction of the case because in a situation where a writ of prohibition had been refused, as in this case, it was not final and conclusive. But because the majority of the Court had decided to take jurisdiction and to dispose of the issue as they conceived it, Johnson expressed his opinion on the main issue. Though agreeing with the majority of the Court that a tax which impeded the operation of the government of the United States in borrowing money could not be tolerated, Johnson regarded the tax in question as an income tax not applying unfairly or discriminatorily to government loans. In view of this fact, he asked "why should not the stock of the United States, when it becomes mixed up with the capital of its citizens, become subject to taxation in common with other capital? Or why should one who enjoys all the advantages of a society purchased at a heavy expense, and lives in affluence upon income derived exclusively from interest on governmental stock, be exempted from taxation?"[27] Thus, Johnson pointed out the fundamental defect in Marshall's reasoning on the doctrine of implied prohibitions.

It was this defect which caused the public authorities in two other federal systems of government, namely, Canada and Australia, to discard the Marshall doctrine and to render government salaries, stocks and

[25] 2 Peters 466.   [26] 2 Peters 468.   [27] 2 Peters 473.

bonds, et cetera, subject to nondiscriminatory taxation. President Franklin D. Roosevelt recently called attention to the unsatisfactory and impossible situation which developed in the United States in the continued application of the rule of implied prohibitions, and the Supreme Court, after indicating a tendency to reverse its earlier decisions and to adopt the more reasonable procedure suggested by Justice Johnson, has finally, one hundred and ten years after Marshall's doctrine was announced, brushed aside the judicial gloss which has no basis in the express language of the Constitution.[28] A large part of the inequities and unfair discriminations brought about by these early decisions of the Supreme Court in rendering it possible for governments to issue tax-exempt securities remain to be dealt with by subsequent legislation and by some necessary financial adjustments. The incidental effects of a few judicial decisions may have a far-reaching influence on the development of the political and financial policies of the government.

Justice Thompson, also dissenting, did not regard the Court as having jurisdiction of the case. Referring to the fact that the Supreme Court had no power to enforce its judgment or to give the party any relief against the imposition of the tax, Thompson thought the judgment of the Court was "no more than an opinion expressed upon an abstract question." The tax being small, one-fourth of one per cent, and applied generally to investments of every description including money to loan, but with the exception of stocks of states and cities and that of banks, Thompson, not finding any express prohibition in the federal Constitution against such action by an agency of the state, thought the ordinance should be upheld. *The Federalist* was cited as confirming this view, for, in discussing the independent and uncontrollable authority of the states to raise their own revenues, it was affirmed "that (with the sole exception of duties on imports and exports) they would, under the plan of the Convention, retain that authority, in the most absolute and unqualified sense; and that an attempt on the part of the national government to abridge them in the exercise of it, would be a violent assumption of power, unwarranted by any article or clause of the Constitution."[29] Thompson believed that great injustice was done to others "by exempting men who are living upon the interest of their money, invested in stock of the United States, from the payment of taxes; thereby establishing a privileged class of public creditors, who, though living under the protection of the government, are exempted from bearing any of its burdens,"[30]—a remarkably

[28] Graves v. New York, 306 U. S. 466 (1939).
[29] 2 Peters 477, and *The Federalist* (Ford ed.), pp. 197, 198.
[30] 2 Peters 478.

pertinent and accurate forecast. The Chief Justice no longer maintained the former dominating influence over his brethren, and both Justices Johnson and Thompson contended that the reasoning of the case of *McCulloch v. Maryland*[31] should be limited to direct taxation in the nature of an interference or impediment upon the operation of the agencies or instrumentalities of the federal government. To the nationalists the decision was another link in the chain by which the courts were rendering support to the federal government against what they regarded as threatening encroachments by the states. On the other hand, it increased the opposition to the Court, because the decision was looked upon as political in its background and implications.

Before the disagreements and dissensions among the members of the Supreme Bench became so serious as to be of considerable concern to Chief Justice Marshall, he again appeared to take delight in upholding a state act. In 1791 Rhode Island granted a charter of incorporation to a bank in Providence. About thirty years later the legislature imposed a tax on every bank in the state except the Bank of the United States. The Providence bank refused to pay the tax on the ground that it was repugnant to the Constitution in that it was a law impairing the obligation of the contract as contained in the charter. The Supreme Court, however, held that the law did not impair the obligation of the contract created by the charter granted to the bank.[32]

Marshall, though noting that it had been settled, did not undertake to retrace the steps by which this construction had been arrived at, which was that a contract entered into between a state and an individual is as fully protected by this section of the Constitution as a contract between two individuals and that a charter incorporating a bank was a contract. But the question whether the contract had been impaired in this case, he thought, must be answered by an examination of the charter itself. Turning to the legislative act, he found that it contained no stipulation promising exemption from taxation. The state, therefore, had made no express contract which had been impaired by the act of which the plaintiffs complained. To the arguments of the plaintiffs that the power to tax involved the power to destroy, Marshall replied

that the taxing power is of vital importance; that it is essential to the existence of government; are truths which it cannot be necessary to reaffirm. They are acknowledged and asserted by all. It would seem that the relinquishment of such a power is never to be assumed. We will not say that a state may not relinquish it; that a consideration sufficiently valuable to induce a partial release of it may not exist; but as the whole community has a right to insist that its abandonment ought not to be presumed, in a case in which the deliberate purpose of the state to abandon it does not appear . . . the

---

[31] 4 Wheaton 316 (1819).   [32] Providence Bank v. Billings, 4 Peters 514 (1830).

Constitution of the United States was not intended to furnish the corrective for every abuse of power which may be committed by the state governments. The interest, wisdom, and justice of the representative body, and its relations with its constituents, furnish the only security, where there is no express contract against unjust and excessive taxation, as well as against unwise legislation generally.[33]

This was a different attitude from that manifested by the Chief Justice in other cases[34] dealing with state acts, and it appeased some of those who were disposed to criticize the Court for its previous decisions unfavorable to the exercise of state powers.

On the death of Justice Trimble in September, 1828, it was thought by the Democrats that Andrew Jackson, the newly elected President, should nominate the new Justice. But Adams hastened to fill the position by offering the place in turn to Charles Hammond and Henry Clay. When these men declined, the nomination of John J. Crittenden of Kentucky was the next choice, but the Democratic majority of the Senate decided to defer action until the inauguration of the new President. Jackson nominated John McLean of Ohio, who was Postmaster General during the Administrations of Monroe and Adams. It was asserted that McLean differed with Jackson's policy regarding removals from office and that Jackson wished to remove him from the political arena as a possible political rival.[35]

When Jackson nominated Henry Baldwin of Pennsylvania for the place made vacant by the death of Justice Washington, Webster wrote: "This is another escape. We had given up all hope of anything but Chief Justice Gibson's nomination."[36] And John Quincy Adams said, "Judge Baldwin paid me a short visit. This is another politician of equivocal morality, but I hope will make a more impartial Judge. I told him I had been gratified by his appointment—which was true; because I had dreaded the appointment of Gibson as precisely the most unfit man for the office in the Union."[37] The opposition to Gibson was due to his opin-

---

[33] 4 Peters 560, 563 (1830).

[34] See *Fletcher v. Peck* and *Dartmouth College v. Woodward*, above, pp. 309 and 379.

[35] See *Life and Letters of Joseph Story*, ed. by William W. Story (Boston, 1851), I: 564. Writing of the appointment of McLean, Story observed: "It is a good and satisfactory appointment, but was, in fact, produced by other causes than his fitness, or our advantage. The truth is, that a few days since, he told the new President, that he would not form a part of the new Cabinet, or remain in office, if he was compelled to make removals upon political grounds. The President assented to this course, but the governing ultras were dissatisfied, and after much debate and discussion, Mr. McLean remaining firm to his purpose, they were obliged to remove him from the Cabinet, and to make the matter fair, to appoint him (not much to his will) a Judge." *Ibid.*

[36] See Letter, Jan. 6, 1830.

[37] *Memoirs of John Quincy Adams*, ed. by Charles Francis Adams (Philadelphia, 1876), VIII: 174.

ion in *Eakin v. Raub* and in other cases in which he opposed the authority which the courts were claiming in declaring legislative acts void.[38]

With the inauguration of Andrew Jackson to the presidency and with the appointment of two Justices to the Supreme Court, it was apparent that the period of Federalist domination of the Court would not continue much longer. The case of *Craig v. Missouri*[39] marked the beginning of differences of opinion, division, and dissent, which were gradually to change the point of view and trend of decisions favoring Federalist principles and nationalist doctrines which Marshall, Story, and Washington had rendered for a period of approximately thirty years, toward a point of view which veered in the direction of the democratic ideas and principles prevalent throughout the nation.

The Case of Craig v. Missouri and Attacks on the Jurisdiction of the Supreme Court

This case arose over the interpretation of an act of the state of Missouri establishing loan offices with authority to give promissory notes secured by personal property or securities which could be used to purchase loan certificates issued by the state. State resources were pledged for the redemption of these certificates which were negotiable. They were intended to serve as a local medium of exchange. The case involving the validity of this law, which had been upheld by the state courts, was held over for argument in the 1826 term of the Supreme Court, when the Justices decided against a motion to dismiss the cause on the ground of want of jurisdiction. It was argued in the 1828 term of the Court but held over again for reargument and decision until 1830.

The attorney for the plaintiffs argued that the state act violated the provision of the Constitution prohibiting the states from issuing bills of credit, that the issue of constitutionality had been definitely raised in the trial of the case in the state court, and that, therefore, it was an appropriate cause to be brought to the Supreme Court for determination in accordance with the grant of jurisdiction under the twenty-fifth section of the Judiciary Act of 1789. Where the rights of the individual protected by the Constitution were invaded by a sovereign state, it was declared to be the duty of the Supreme Court to intervene. Senator Benton, appearing rather as a "corps of observation" to watch what was going on, since he did not consider it necessary for the state to have an advocate to defend its rights, protested that "the State of Missouri has been 'summoned' by a writ from this Court under a 'penalty' to be and appear before this

---

[38] 12 Serg. and Rawle 330 (1825), and Wike v. Lightner, 1 Rawle 289 (1829).
[39] 4 Peters 419 (1830).

Court. In the language of the writ she is 'commanded' and 'enjoined' to appear. Language of this kind does not seem proper when addressed to a sovereign State, nor are the terms fitting, even if the only purpose of the process was to obtain the appearance of the State."[40] This language, he maintained, imputes a fault to the state, whereas no act has been done which was not within the full and ample powers possessed as a free, sovereign, and independent state. For the Supreme Court to thus humiliate a state, Benton declared, was "not calculated to promote harmony, and to secure a continuance of the Union. If, in questions of this kind, or if in any cases, the character of a sovereign State shall be made the subject of such imputation, this peaceful tribunal would not be enabled to procure the submission of the States to its jurisdiction; and contests about civil rights would be settled amid the din of arms, rather than in this hall of national justice."[41] The bills issued under the Missouri law, Benton asserted, could be refused by the citizens and were not legal tender in the ordinary significance of that term.

Chief Justice Marshall, speaking for the Court, dealt first with the question of jurisdiction. Since the validity of the state act in accordance with the federal Constitution was not expressly raised and discussed by the state court, the query arose whether the Supreme Court could assume the fact that it was made or determined in the tribunal of the state. The record showing distinctly that the cause arose primarily over the validity of the issuance of these certificates, Marshall held that "if in such a case, the mere omission of the court of Missouri, to say, in terms, that the act of the legislature was constitutional, withdraws that point from the cause, or must close the judicial eyes of the appellate tribunal upon it; nothing can be more obvious, than that the provision of the Constitution and of an act of Congress may be always evaded; and may be often, as we think they would be in this case, unintentionally defeated."[42]

The state court having upheld the validity of the contract and inferentially having supported the validity of the state law, the case was regarded as coming within the jurisdiction of the Court as defined by the twenty-fifth section of the Judiciary Act. Answering the question, then, whether the Missouri act violated the federal Constitution, Marshall first defined the term "emit bills of credit." This phrase, he thought, conveyed the idea of issuing a paper medium intended to circulate through the community for the ordinary purposes of society. In view of the conditions which led to the insertion of this prohibition in the Constitution, Mar-

[40] Craig v. Missouri, 4 Peters 419 (1830).
[41] 4 Peters 420.
[42] 4 Peters 429.

shall believed that if the words were not empty sounds they must comprehend the emission of any paper medium by a state government for the
purposes of common circulation.[43] Because of the fact that the certificates
were not called bills of credit was held to have no significance; nor was
any importance attributed to the fact that they were not made legal
tender in the full sense of this term; the state act was therefore held void
by a majority of the Court. We have been reminded, said Marshall, in
closing his opinion,

of the dignity of a sovereign State; of the humiliation of her submitting herself to this
tribunal; of the dangers which may result from inflicting a wound on that dignity. . . .
To these admonitions, we can only answer, that if the exercise of that jurisdiction
which has been imposed upon us by the Constitution and laws of the United States,
shall be calculated to bring on these dangers which have been indicated, or if it shall
be indispensable to the preservation of the Union, and consequently of the independence and liberty of these States, these are considerations which address themselves
to those departments which may with perfect propriety be influenced by them. This
department can listen only to the mandate of the law, and can tread only that path
which is marked out by duty.[44]

Justice Johnson, dissenting, thought it clear beyond doubt that the
framers of the Constitution intended to prevent the issuance of paper
money and that these certificates were not in the exact sense a circulating
medium. Though the state act came near to a violation of the Constitution, it was a doubtful case and, since the state had acted in good faith,
the act should be upheld. To Justice Thompson it was obvious that the
term "bills of credit" had no precise or technical meaning. Adverting to
the intention of the framers of the Constitution, he did not think it was
their intention to prohibit the issuance of loan certificates of this type.
Moreover, he believed that the judgment of the majority of the Court
would lead to serious embarrassment for state legislation, since the issuance of all bank notes by the states would fall within the category of bills
of credit and hence come within the prohibition.

On the question of jurisdiction Justice McLean had strong doubts
because the record did not present the issue of the validity of the state
act, but he yielded to the force of prior adjudications of the Court. Since
the state did not enforce the circulation of the certificates and the object
was a benign one, namely, to relieve the citizens from an extraordinary
pressure produced by the failure of local banks and the utter worthless-

---

[43] 4 Peters 432.

[44] 4 Peters 437, 438. "In this noble passage," thinks Beveridge, "Marshall is not only
rebuking Benton; he is also speaking to the advocates of nullification, then becoming
clamorous and threatening; he is pointing out to Andrew Jackson the path of duty."
He further observed that never did Marshall's genius shine more resplendently than
in his opinion in this case. *The Life of John Marshall,* IV: 510, 513.

ness of the available currency, McLean was disposed to uphold the act. Conceding that the power of review of federal and state acts to determine whether they were in accordance with the Constitution belonged to the Supreme Court, McLean expressed an attitude different from some of his Federalist brethren on the Bench when he said, "the act of Missouri having received the sanction of the legislative, executive, and judicial departments of the government, cannot be set aside and disregarded under a doubtful construction of the Constitution. Doubts should lead to an acquiescence in the act. The power which declares it null and void, should be exercised only where the right to do so is perfectly clear."[45] Believing the issue doubtful, McLean was inclined to affirm the judgment of the state court.

Considering the difficulties which had arisen and were likely to arise in determining the division of powers between the states and the federal government, McLean concluded:

The experience of many years may be necessary to establish, by practical illustrations, the exact boundaries of these powers, if, indeed, they can ever be clearly and satisfactorily defined. Like the colors of the rainbow, they seem to intermix, so as to render a separation extremely difficult, if not impracticable. By the exercise of a spirit of mutual forbearance, the line may be ascertained with sufficient precision for all practical purposes. In a State, where doubts exist as to the investiture of a power, it should not be exercised, but referred to the people; in the general government, should similar doubts arise, the powers should be referred to the States and the people.[46]

If such a practice had been followed in the interpretation of constitutional provisions, great changes would have resulted in the status and significance of written constitutions in the United States.

The decision in the *Craig Case* was rendered while the debate on the Foot Resolution was in progress in Congress and aroused great excitement in Missouri, Kentucky, and other states which were suffering from financial distress and which it was generally thought could be relieved only by some form of state guarantee for the issuance of currency. It was, however, the accumulation of grievances which brought a renewal of the attacks on the Supreme Court.

In the first session of Congress after the Craig decision was rendered, a bill was presented to repeal the twenty-fifth section of the Judiciary Act of 1789. If this section is repealed, wrote Justice Story, the Constitution is practically gone, for "our wisest friends look with great gloom to the future."[47] Marshall also expressed alarm when he said that "the

---

[45] 4 Peters 458, 459.
[46] *Ibid.*, pp. 464, 465.
[47] *Life and Letters*, II: 49.

crisis of our Constitution is upon us. A strong dispensation to prostrate the Judiciary is upon us."[48]

A majority report of the Judiciary Committee of the House was presented on January 24, 1831, favoring the repeal of the twenty-fifth section of the Judiciary Act under which the Supreme Court had annulled some of the most important laws of the states. The sponsors of the bill regarded the powers of the Court as so "vast and alarming that the constantly increasing evil of interference of federal with state authorities must be checked." Representative Davis, presenting this report, announced that the investigations of the Judiciary Committee had resulted in the conviction that this section of the Judiciary Act is unconstitutional and ought to be repealed. Analyzing the language of the Constitution relating to the organization of the federal courts and of their jurisdiction, it was maintained that the makers of the Constitution did not intend to provide for appeals from the state courts to the Supreme Court. And the contention of Chief Justice Marshall and Justice Story in *Martin v. Hunter's Lessee*,[49] *McCulloch v. Maryland*,[50] and *Cohens v. Virginia*[51] that there must be an appeal to the federal courts when the controversy involved an interpretation of a law, a treaty, or a provision of the Constitution of the United States was emphatically denied. It was pointed out that such a construction of the Constitution would confer on the federal courts vast political powers not only to control inferior courts but also to dominate the coördinate branches of the government. The federal courts under these admitted principles, the committee declared with a prophetic outlook, "will have the power to prohibit state legislation by writs of injunction; to sequestrate state treasuries, and to imprison state functionaries, whether governors, judges, or state legislatures, in a body. Indeed, the power will not stop here; the same reasoning will sustain a power in the federal court, to attach and imprison the President and both Houses of Congress."[52] To the contention that the

---

[48] In a letter to Story, Marshall wrote, "I find our brother McLean could not acquiesce in the decision of the Court in the Missouri Case. I am sorry for this, and am sorry too to observe his sentiments on the 25th section of the judicial act. I have read in the last volume of Mr. Peters the three dissenting opinions delivered in that case, and think it requires no prophet to predict that the 25th section is to be repealed, or to use a more fashionable phrase to be nullified by the Supreme Court of the United States. I hope the case in which this is to be accomplished will not occur during my time, but accomplished it will be at no very distant period." Massachusetts Hist. Soc. *Proceedings*, 2d ser., XIV: 342, 343, and John Edward Oster, *The Political and Economic Doctrines of John Marshall* (New York, 1914), pp. 130, 131.

[49] 1 Wheaton 394 (1816).

[50] 4 Wheaton 316 (1819).

[51] 6 Wheaton 264 (1821).

[52] *Cong. Debates*, VII, 21st Cong., 2d sess. (1830–1831), appendix, pp. lxxx–lxxxi.

federal government would be crippled by the repeal of the twenty-fifth section of the Judiciary Act, it was replied that it is the imperative duty of Congress to repeal without delay any of its acts in contravention of the Constitution, be the consequences what they may, for "necessity and expedience are the pleas of the tyrant; amendment, the dictate of the Constitution. By pursuing the former course, we trample upon the Constitution; by following the latter, we go back to the people, the original source of all power."[53]

James Buchanan presented a report for three minority members of the committee in which it was contended that the repeal of section twenty-five would seriously endanger the existence of the union. The framers of the Constitution, it was maintained, intended "to create a government which should have the power of construing and executing its own laws, without obstruction from state authority." Repudiating the state sovereignty philosophy of the majority report, the minority asserted that "we have in this country an authority much higher than that of sovereign States. It is the authority of the people of each State. In their state conventions they ratified the Constitution of the United States; and so far as that Constitution has deprived the States of any of the attributes of sovereignty, they are bound by it, because such was the will of the people."[54]

The debate aroused deep feeling and resentment. To the friends of the Supreme Court, the proposal to repeal section twenty-five was equivalent to a movement to repeal the union of the states; to the opponents of judicial review of state acts, it was a necessary step to protect the states against "the assaults of this gigantic tribunal." The strong feeling of opposition against the decisions of the Supreme Court which pervaded the legislative halls was expressed by Representative Gordon of Virginia, who exclaimed: "I declare to God . . . that I believe nothing would tend so much to compose the present agitation of the country . . . as the repeal of that portion of the Judiciary Act."[55] John Quincy Adams rejoiced in the defeat of the bill and spoke of a visit with Justice Thompson who expressed alarm for the fate of the Judiciary, since the administration was resolved to transform the government of the union "into the national imbecility of the old Confederation."[56] Though the bill was defeated by a vote of 138 to 51, the almost solid vote of the representatives from the southern states against the nationalistic views of the Court indicated a very unsatisfactory and dangerous situation relative to the relations be-

[53] *Cong. Debates*, VII, appendix, p. lxxxi.
[54] *Cong. Debates*, VII, appendix, p. lxxxv.
[55] *Cong. Debates*, VII, 21st Cong., 2d sess., pp. 620, 621.
[56] *Memoirs*, VIII: 302–304.

tween the nation and the states. It was in the contests with the state of Georgia, however, that the authority of the Supreme Court received its most drastic rebuffs.

CONFLICTS WITH THE STATE OF GEORGIA

When Georgia decided to take over the lands of the Creek and Cherokee Indians situated within the borders of the state, despite treaties negotiated by the United States guaranteeing to the Indians full control and possession over these lands, the Supreme Court became involved in a political controversy which seriously affected the prestige of the Court.[57] The issue, which was the last of the great controversies over federal versus state powers during Marshall's Chief Justiceship, arose through an attempt of the authorities of the state to secure control over the land of the Creeks.[58] The governor and legislature of Georgia openly defied President Adams and resisted the assertion of his authority under treaties with the Indians. Congress was not inclined to stand by the President, and Georgia proceeded against the Indians according to her own discretion.[59] After the contest had continued for more than two years, during which time a voluminous correspondence had merely tended to reveal the weakness of federal power and to arouse the wrath of the state authorities,[60] the suggestion was made that the whole case be turned over to the Supreme Court of the United States. The governor advised the state representatives in Congress that he could not acknowledge a power in the federal government to bring before its judicial tribunals for trial and judgment the governor, judges, or representatives of the state. He was not wanting, the governor claimed, in confidence in the Supreme Court of the United States in all cases falling within its acknowledged jurisdiction. But according to his conception the Supreme Court was not made the arbiter in controversies involving rights of sovereignty between the states and the United States. The states could not therefore consent "to refer to the Supreme Court, as of right and obligation, questions of sovereignty between them and the United States, because that Court, being of exclusive appointment by the government of the United States,

---

[57] In the account of the two controversies with the state of Georgia, some extracts have been used from my study on *The Conflict over Judicial Powers in the United States to 1870*, published in the Studies in History, Economics and Public Law of Columbia University (New York, 1909), XXXV: 122–131.

[58] For an account of the origin of the contests over the Indian lands in Georgia, see Ulrich B. Phillips, "Georgia and State Rights," Amer. Hist. Assn., *Reports*, 1902, II: 39 ff.

[59] *House Executive Documents*, 19th Cong. 2d sess., iv, p. 59; Reports of House Committee, iii, p. 98.

[60] Extracts from this correspondence are given in Herman V. Ames, *State Documents on Federal Relations* (Philadelphia, 1906), pp. 115 ff.

will make the United States the judge of their own cause; this reason is equally applicable to a state tribunal."[61] The failure of Congress to support the President in his attempt to enforce the treaties and uphold national authority finally led to the acknowledgment of the contention of the state and brought an end to the Creek controversy.

Cherokee controversy.—While the controversy over the lands of the Creeks was under way, Georgia took steps to secure the lands of the Cherokee Indians. This Indian tribe, with the tacit support of the United States government, drew up a constitution and proceeded to set up an independent government. The procedure was in line with the past policy of the national government toward the Indians: to treat them as independent communities within the states, to be dealt with by the national government and then only by treaty. Encouraged by President Jackson's announcement of his Indian policy,[62] Georgia passed an act incorporating the land of the Cherokee nation into the territory of the state, and annulled all laws as well as the constitution of the newly formed nation.[63]

When the state authorities had shown every indication of incorporating the Indian lands regardless of federal treaties, Mr. Wirt of Maryland, who had been secured as counsel for the Indians, wrote to Governor Gilmer. He reminded the governor of the difference of opinion regarding the rights of Georgia to deal with the Indians, and suggested that "fortunately there exists a tribunal before which this difference of opinion may be quietly and peaceably settled," namely, the Supreme Court of the United States.[64] The governor in reply charged Mr. Wirt with having encouraged the spirit of resistance against the state and with having fostered the idea that the state had usurped authority. Through such men as Mr. Wirt, the governor maintained, the Cherokees were persuaded that the right of self-government could be secured for them by the power of the Supreme Court in defiance of the legislation of the general and state governments.[65] "Your suggestion," the governor continued, is "an evidence of the state of that contest in which the advocates of power, are exerting themselves to increase the authority of the departments of the general government, whilst the friends of liberty and the rights of the people are in opposition, endeavoring to sustain the sovereignty of the State."[66]

---

[61] *Niles' Register*, XXXII: 20.

[62] James D. Richardson, *A Compilation of the Messages and Papers of the Presidents* (Washington, 1911), II: 457.

[63] *Niles' Register*, XXVIII: 328, 329.

[64] *Ibid.*, XXXIX: 69.

[65] *Ibid.*, p. 70.

[66] *Ibid.*, p. 71.

The opportunity to bring the question at issue before the Supreme Court of the United States was soon presented, when, in the execution of the statutes over the Cherokee territory, an Indian by the name of George Tassels was tried, convicted, and sentenced to death. On an appeal to the Supreme Court a writ of error was granted, the purpose of which was to bring the case before the federal courts for reconsideration.

The governor, having received the order from the Court, submitted a message to the legislature in which he referred to a communication "purporting to be signed by the Chief Justice of the United States, and to be a citation of the State of Georgia to appear before the Supreme Court, . . . to answer to that tribunal for having caused a person who had committed murder within the limits of the State, to be tried and convicted therefor," and he declared that "so far as concerns the executive department, orders received from the Supreme Court for the purpose of staying, or in any manner interfering with the decisions of the courts of the State, in the exercise of their constitutional jurisdiction will be disregarded, and any attempt to enforce such orders will be resisted with whatever force the laws have placed at my command."[67] The legislature immediately resolved "that they view with feelings of the deepest regret, the interference by the Chief Justice of the Supreme Court of the United States, in the administration of the criminal laws of the State, and that such an interference is a flagrant violation of her rights." The governor and every other officer of the state were requested to disregard any and every mandate that might be served upon them "purporting to proceed from the Chief Justice or any Associate Justice of the Supreme Court of the United States, for the purpose of arresting the execution of any criminal laws of the State."[68] The order of the Supreme Court was ignored and Tassels was executed according to the verdict of the state tribunal.[69] Following the execution of Tassels, the Supreme Court being impotent to assert its authority, John Quincy Adams wrote: "The Constitution, the laws and treaties of the United States are prostrate in the State of Georgia. Is there any remedy for this state of things? None. Because the Executive of the United States is in league with the State of Georgia. . . . This example . . . will be imitated by other States, and with regard to other national interests—perhaps the tariff. . . . The Union is in the most imminent danger of dissolution."[70]

A later case was dismissed by the Supreme Court for want of juris-

---

[67] *Niles' Register*, XXXIX: 338.
[68] *Niles' Register*, XXXIX: 338; Ames, *op. cit.*, pp. 125–127.
[69] *Niles' Register*, XXXIX: 353.
[70] *Memoirs*, VIII: 262, 263.

diction but with some caustic remarks from the Court.[71] In delivering the opinion, Chief Justice Marshall reviewed briefly the history of the proceedings and held that the numerous treaties made with the Indians by the United States recognized them "as a people capable of maintaining the relations of peace and war, of being responsible in their political character for any violation of their engagements, or for any aggression committed on the citizens of the United States by any individual of their community. Laws have been enacted in the spirit of these treaties. The acts of our government plainly recognize the Cherokee nation as a state, and the courts are bound by these acts."[72] The Cherokee Indians had, he noted, established a constitution and form of government, the leading features of which were borrowed from that of the United States. Nevertheless, Georgia had assumed authority contrary to these laws and treaties of the United States, and a writ of error allowed by the Chief Justice of the Supreme Court to the final sentence of the court of Georgia had been ignored. If courts were permitted to indulge their sympathies, Marshall thought, a case better calculated to expiate them could scarcely be imagined. The request of the Indians was denied, however, because the Court did not regard the case as coming within its jurisdiction. Though the Indian tribes were considered to be separate political communities under the guardianship of the United States, they could not, as foreign states, maintain an action in the courts of the United States. Furthermore, continued Marshall, "the bill requires us to control the legislature of Georgia, and to restrain the exertion of its physical course. The propriety of such an imposition by the Court may well be questioned. It savors too much of the exercise of political power to be within the province of the judicial department. . . . If it be true that wrongs have been inflicted and that still greater ones are to be apprehended, this is not the tribunal which can redress the past or prevent the future."[73]

The agitation to require the giving of opinions *seriatim* was apparently having effect, for Justice Johnson, in presenting his views favoring the dismissal of the suit, stated that in pursuance of his practice in giving an opinion on all constitutional questions, there was, in his opinion, no doubt that the case was "one of a political character altogether, and wholly unfit for the cognizance of a judicial tribunal."[74] There was, in effect, in Georgia an appeal, not to laws, but to force between two political entities claiming sovereign powers. Justice Baldwin concurred in the dismissal of the suit on the ground that the Indians could not appear as

[71] Cherokee v. The State of Georgia, 5 Peters 15 (1831).
[72] 5 Peters 15.
[73] 5 Peters 19, 20.
[74] 5 Peters 28.

plaintiffs before the Supreme Court. Following an extensive survey of the negotiations with the Indians, he concluded that from colonial times the colonies and states had exercised the rights of sovereignty over the territory occupied by the Indians. The Supreme Court was, therefore, not regarded as having authority or jurisdiction to reverse a principle on which all governments had acted for fifty-five years.

Though he disclaimed any authority for the Supreme Court to exercise jurisdiction upon any matter properly falling within the realm of political power, Justice Thompson, speaking for himself and Justice Story, dissented. Accepting the definition of a sovereign state by Vattel, he said: "It is not perceived how it is possible to escape the conclusion, that they [the Indians] form a sovereign state. They have always been dealt with as such by the government of the United States; both before and since the adoption of the present Constitution."[75] Differing with Justice Baldwin in his interpretation of the facts, Thompson contended that from the year 1775 the uniform practice of all branches of the government of the union was to treat the Indian tribes "not only as sovereign and independent, but as foreign nations or tribes, not within the jurisdiction nor under the government of the States within which they were located."[76] The matter of the violation by Georgia of the laws of the United States and of the treaties made with the Cherokee nation was declared to be "a pure question of law," and, hence, it was deemed appropriate for the Supreme Court to grant an injunction to prevent the further execution of such laws. It was not long before the Supreme Court was again called upon to intervene in the controversy between Georgia and the Indians.

Worcester v. Georgia.—A new law of the state imposing more stringent regulations for the Cherokee territory was defied by several missionaries who were working among the Indians, with the result that they were tried, convicted, and sentenced to imprisonment.[77] On application to the Supreme Court, another writ was issued demanding that the authorities of the state appear before the Court. Governor Lumpkin, instead of obeying the writ, referred the whole matter to the legislature in a message which is typical of the attitude assumed when the courts of the nation asserted jurisdiction over matters with which the state governments were inclined to deal and to admit of no interference. "My respect for the Supreme Court of the United States," said the governor,

---

[75] 5 Peters 53, 54.

[76] 5 Peters 59. In the *Cherokee Case*, Justice Story wrote: "The subject touches the moral sense of all New England. It comes home to the religious feelings of the people; it moves their sensibilities, and strikes to the very bottom of their sense of justice. Depend on it, there is a depth of degradation in our national conduct, which will irresistably lead to better things." *Life and Letters*, II: 46.

[77] *Niles' Register*, XL: 244–248.

"as a fundamental department of the federal government, induces me to indulge the earnest hope, that no mandate will ever proceed from that Court, attempting or intending to control one of the sovereign States of this Union, in the free exercise of its constitutional, criminal or civil jurisdiction."[78] The object of the proceeding was considered to be nothing less than an attempt to call into question and to overthrow the essential jurisdiction of the state.

The Supreme Court not only assumed jurisdiction but decided the case against the state in no uncertain language.[79] To the argument of lack of jurisdiction in the case, Chief Justice Marshall replied that the indictment and plea drew in question the validity of the treaties made by the United States with the Cherokee Indians and that, therefore, the act of Congress constituting this Court has given it the power and imposed on it the duty of exercising jurisdiction in the case. Recognizing the rights acquired by war or by conquest which are conceded by the world and cannot be controverted, the Chief Justice maintained that European nations, in taking possession of the American continent, did not regard the Indian title to lands as extinguished by discovery, exploration, and settlement.[80] The English policy which had been continued by the United States aimed to acquire territory by conciliation, by treaty, and by compromise. Following this practice, several treaties between the United States and the Cherokee nation were adopted. The last of these treaties, explicitly recognizing the national character of the Cherokees and their right of self-government, guaranteeing their lands, and pleading the faith of the United States for their protection, was declared to be still in force. It was held, then, that "the treaties and laws of the United States contemplate the Indian territory as completely separated from that of the States; and provide that all intercourse with them shall be carried on exclusively by the government of the Union."[81] As a consequence of this reasoning, the laws of Georgia could have no force or effect within the territory of the Cherokee nation, and the citizens of Georgia could not enter this territory except with the assent of the Cherokees themselves. Hence the act of Georgia in dispute was declared to be null and void.

---

[78] *Niles' Register*, XL: 313; Ames, *op. cit.*, pp. 129, 130.

[79] Worcester v. The State of Georgia, 6 Peters 515 (1832).

[80] But see Marshall's opinion in Johnson and Graham's Lessee v. McIntosh, 8 Wheaton 543 (1823).

[81] Worcester v. The State of Georgia, 6 Peters 557. Beveridge calls Marshall's opinion "one of the noblest he ever wrote." The opinion "closes with a passage of eloquence almost equal to, and of higher moral grandeur than the finest passages in McCulloch v. Maryland and in Cohens v. Virginia." *The Life of John Marshall*, IV: 549, 550.

Justice McLean, concurring in the opinion of the Court, announced some nationalistic principles in opposition to the antifederal doctrines which were being strongly urged at this time. Supporting the jurisdiction of the Court under the twenty-fifth section of the Judiciary Act, McLean conceived that the use of the name of the state in the proceedings was a mere form. And on the question whether the Constitution was the result of an act of the people or of the states, it was his judgment that "there was an expression of popular suffrage and state sanction, most happily united, in the adoption of the Constitution of the Union."[82] Some of the doctrines of nationalism espoused by McLean were as follows: "It is in vain, and worse than vain, that the national legislature enact laws, if those laws are to remain on the statute book as monuments of the imbecility of the national power. . . . It has been asserted that the federal government is foreign to the state governments; and that it must consequently be hostile to them. Such an opinion could not have resulted from a thorough investigation of the great principles which lie at the foundation of our system. . . . No one can deny that the Constitution of the United States is the supreme law of the land; and consequently, no act of any state legislature, or of Congress, which is repugnant to it, can be of any validity." Referring to the objections raised to the authority claimed by the courts, federal and state, to declare legislative acts void, McLean observed, "such an argument must end in the destruction of all constitutions, and the will of the legislature, like the acts of the Parliament of Great Britain, must be the supreme and only law of the land. . . . The powers of this Court are expressly, not constructively, given by the Constitution; and within this delegation of power, this Court is the Supreme Court of the people of the United States, and they are bound to discharge their duties, under the same responsibilities as the supreme court of a State; and are equally, within their powers, the Supreme Court of the people of each State."[83] Agreeing with the Chief Justice, McLean believed that the control over Indian affairs had been confided exclusively to the federal government. In this case there did not appear to be any doubt in the mind of Justice McLean.

On the justice or policy of the laws enacted by the state, McLean did not regard himself as at liberty to speak, but he observed: "They have, no doubt, been enacted under a conviction of right, by a sovereign and independent State, and their policy may have been recommended by a sense of wrong under the compact. Thirty years have elapsed since the federal government engaged to extinguish the Indian title, within the limits of Georgia. That she has strong ground of complaint arising from

[82] 6 Peters 569.   [83] Ibid., pp. 569–572.

this delay, must be admitted; but such considerations are not involved in the present case; they belong to another branch of the government."[84]

Justice McLean referred in the above comments to the fact that Georgia, in ceding to the United States the territory constituting the states of Alabama and Mississippi, stipulated that the United States should extinguish for the use of Georgia the Indian title to lands within the remaining limits of the state. The United States not only failed to perform its agreement but adopted a policy which aimed to develop the Cherokees into a civilized community. An Indian tribe permanently established within its borders, claiming independent powers and authority, and exemption from the jurisdiction of the state, led to drastic action by the state. Georgia asserted its authority over the Cherokees and declared that the federal government could not bind a state by a treaty made with Indians. The discovery of gold on the land claimed by the Indians complicated the situation. It was expected that the state would defy the decision and judgment of the Court.[85] "John Marshall has made his decision:—now let him enforce it," was said to be the reply of Andrew Jackson;[86] both the governor and the legislature met the decision "with a spirit of determined resistance." Additional acts were passed to hasten the distribution of the Cherokee lands.

The mandate which was issued in accordance with this decision was disregarded. Governor Lumpkin reported to the legislature that the decision of the Court was an attempt to "prostrate the sovereignty of this State in the exercise of its constitutional criminal jurisdiction" and that he would oppose the usurpation with determined resistance. He congratulated the people of Georgia for sustaining the sovereignty of their state.[87] There were opinions in the press of the state strongly favoring the use of force, and frequent references were made to the dangers of judicial despotism.[88] The case was supposed to demonstrate the absurdity of the doctrine that the federal courts were granted a supreme and absolute control over the states. A writ of error issued by the Supreme Court in the case of James Graves was also ignored by the state. The governor submitted the writ to the legislature and the proceedings in the state court were carried out without hindrance.

---

[84] *Ibid.*, p. 595. Justice Baldwin dissented on the grounds stated in the *Cherokee Case*.

[85] See the prediction of Story, *Life and Letters*, II: 83.

[86] See Horace Greely, *The American Conflict* (Hartford, 1866), I: 106, and Phillips, *Georgia and State Rights*, p. 80. "It is not sure that the words were actually uttered," says John Spencer Bassett, "but it is certain, from Jackson's views and temperament, that they might have been spoken." *Life of Andrew Jackson* (New York, 1910), II: 690, 691.

[87] Phillips, *op. cit.*, p. 82.

[88] *Niles' Register*, XLII: 78.

In the controversy with the Creeks, the state authorities succeeded in gaining control of the lands because Congress failed to uphold President Adams in his attempt to enforce the treaties with the Indians. The Supreme Court was humiliated in the Cherokee difficulty because President Jackson supported the policy of the state government. In his first annual message, on December 8, 1829, the President informed the country that

if the general government is not permitted to tolerate the erection of a confederate state within the territory of one of the members of this Union against her consent, much less could it allow a foreign and independent government to establish itself there.

Actuated by this view of the subject, I informed the Indians inhabiting parts of Georgia and Alabama that their attempt to establish an independent government would not be countenanced by the Executive of the United States, and advised them to emigrate beyond the Mississippi or submit to the laws of those States.[89]

As a result of the lack of unity of action among the departments of the federal government, Georgia felt at liberty to resist judicial mandates and enforce her own laws regardless of orders from the federal courts. The missionaries were finally pardoned by the governor, and the question at issue was then settled by an act of Congress providing for the removal of all Indian tribes to the territory beyond the Mississippi River.[90] A few references to the controversy are to be found in the campaign literature of the time, when the failure of the President to secure the enforcement of federal judicial decrees was used as political capital against Jackson and his party.[91] Marshall wrote to Story on the proceedings following the decision of the Court in *Worcester v. Georgia,* as follows:

I yield slowly and reluctantly to the conviction that our Constitution cannot last. I had supposed that north of the Potomac a firm and solid government competent to the security of rational liberty might be preserved. Even that now seems doubtful. The case of the South seems to me to be desperate. Our opinions are incompatible with the united government even among ourselves. The union has been prolonged thus far by miracles. I fear they cannot continue.[92]

The successful resistance of Georgia in this dispute was a decided victory for the Jacksonian Democrats, and the bank controversy, where the authority of the Court was successfully challenged from another

---

[89] Richardson, *op. cit.,* II: 457, 458.

[90] *Statutes at Large,* IV: 411, 412.

[91] *The Works of Daniel Webster,* ed. by Edward Everett (Boston, 1866), I: 269; *Niles' Register,* XLIII: 140.

[92] Massachusetts Hist. Soc. *Proceedings,* 2d ser., XIV: 352. "For the time being," says Beveridge, "Marshall was defeated; nationalism was prostrate; localism erect, strong, aggressive. Soon, however, Marshall and nationalism were to be sustained, for the moment, by the man most dreaded by the Chief Justice, most trusted by Marshall's foes. Andrew Jackson was to astound the country by the greatest and most illogical act of his strange career—the issuance of his immortal Proclamation against nullification." *The Life of John Marshall,* IV: 552.

quarter, may be looked upon as the beginning of a new era in the history of the Court—an era when many questions heretofore determined by the Court were voluntarily turned over to the political departments of the government; when the doctrine of implied powers, under which the authority of the federal government had been greatly enlarged, received a more restricted application; when the states were given a greater freedom from interference by the federal Judiciary. It was the period which led to a reversal of the nationalistic policies of Hamilton and Marshall and a return to the principles of Jefferson and Jackson. The Federalist party lost control of its only stronghold; the Democratic party, for the first time, held full sway in all departments of the government. Four of the fundamental policies of the government pointed toward a strict construction of the Constitution. These were: the treatment of the Indians, the refusal of the United States government to take part in internal improvements, the reduction of the tariff, and the attack upon the national bank.

OPPOSITION TO A NATIONAL BANK

The issue of the national bank raised a constitutional question of prime importance. The Supreme Court, in the case of *McCulloch v. Maryland*[93] and later in *Osborn v. The Bank of the United States*,[94] had emphatically upheld the authority of the federal government in the establishment of a national bank. The chief argument against the bank was on the ground of its unconstitutionality. This argument had been exhaustively treated by the Court and strongly denied. The bank had continued to do business under a charter granted by Congress and was upheld in all its features by the Supreme Court of the United States. But the managers of the bank wielded great political power and made many enemies. Under the leadership of President Jackson a movement was begun to destroy the bank.

Jackson and some of his party associates detested the bank. Its power, prestige, and it was charged, some of its money had been used to perpetuate the Administration of John Quincy Adams. The corporation was attacked on all sides but in no way so emphatically as on the issue of its unconstitutionality. In his first annual message to Congress on December 8, 1829, President Jackson noted that "both the constitutionality and the expediency of the law creating this bank are well questioned by a large portion of our fellow-citizens, and it must be admitted by all that it has failed in the great end of establishing a uniform and sound currency," and recommended that Congress should enact a

---

[93] 4 Wheaton 316 (1819).   [94] 9 Wheaton 738 (1824).

measure for the establishment of a bank "which would avoid all constitutional difficulties and at the same time secure all the advantages to the
government and the country that were expected to result from the present bank."[95] These views were reiterated in subsequent messages and
a vigorous campaign on behalf of the renewal of the charter was conducted by the friends of the bank under the leadership of its president,
Nicholas Biddle. Jackson did not appear to be influenced by this campaign and regardless of the threat that the recharter of the bank would
be made an issue in the forthcoming election for the presidency, Jackson opposed the plan to renew the charter. To Clay and the National
Republicans, the bank controversy was regarded as a favorable issue
to oppose the Jacksonian Democrats at the polls, and with the aid of
the forces friendly to the bank a bill was hurriedly pushed through
Congress.[96]

In the forceful veto with which Jackson returned the bill to Congress,
we have the President's opinion on judicial powers.[97] "It is maintained
by the advocates of the bank," said Jackson,

that its constitutionality in all its features, ought to be considered as settled by precedent, and by the decisions of the Supreme Court. To this conclusion I cannot assent. . . .
If the opinion of the Supreme Court covered the whole ground of this act, it ought not
to control the coordinate authorities of this government. The Congress, the Executive
and the Court must each for itself be guided by its own opinion of the Constitution.
Each public officer who takes an oath to support the Constitution, swears that he will
support it as he understands it, and not as it is understood by others. It is as much
the duty of the House of Representatives, of the Senate, and of the President, to decide
upon the constitutionality of any bill or resolution which may be presented to them
for passage or approval, as it is of the Supreme Judges when it may be brought before
them for judicial decision. The opinion of the Judges has no more authority over
Congress than the opinion of Congress has over the Judges; and on that point the
President is independent of both. The authority of the Supreme Court must not, therefore, be permitted to control the Congress or the Executive, when acting in their legislative capacities, but to have only such influence as the force of their reasoning may
deserve.[98]

Jackson gave a very different turn to one of Marshall's fundamental
maxims of interpretation. "Where the law is not prohibited and is
really calculated to effect any of the objects intrusted to the government," said Marshall, "to undertake here to inquire into the degree
of its necessity would be to pass the line which circumscribes the judicial

---

[95] Richardson, op. cit., II: 462.

[96] John Spencer Bassett, The Life of Andrew Jackson (New York, 1925), chaps. xxvii,
xxviii.

[97] Senate Journal, 22d Cong., 1st sess., p. 1296.

[98] Senate Journal, 22d Cong., 1st sess., appendix, p. 76, and Richardson, op. cit., II:
1144, 1145.

department and to tread on legislative ground." To Jackson this language meant that "it is the exclusive province of Congress and the President to decide whether the particular features of this act are *necessary* and *proper* in order to enable the bank to perform conveniently and efficiently the public duties assigned to it as a fiscal agent, and therefore constitutional, or *unnecessary* and *improper,* and therefore unconstitutional." In short, the President insisted that the Legislative and Executive departments had authority to determine the constitutionality as well as the expediency of a national bank.[99] Jackson's veto message was regarded as a political manifesto and was criticized as a demagogic appeal to the voters, but the President was aware that the presentation of a memorial for a recharter four years before the expiration of the existing charter was made by Clay and his friends to aid the cause of the National Republicans in the forthcoming campaign.

Andrew Jackson, as the champion of the people, dared to attack the constitutional opinions of John Marshall who was looked upon as the protagonist of vested interests. To Justice Story, Marshall expressed his disgust and disappointment. "We are up to the chin in politics. Virginia was always insane enough to be opposed to the bank of the United States, and therefore hurras for the veto."[100] Marshall hoped that some of the other states might come to the defense of the bank.

DECISIONS OF THE COURT FROM 1831 TO 1835

During the last years of the Chief Justiceship of Marshall, the Supreme Court ceased temporarily to be a center of political attack, but marked differences of opinion arose among the members of the Court on constitutional questions. The time of the Court in these years was taken up mostly with commercial and land questions. In *Fisher v. Cockerell*[101] the Justices refused to take jurisdiction of an action to review state decisions of ejectment arising out of disputes concerning land titles alleged to be

[99] Richardson, *op. cit.,* p. 1146. Charles Warren quotes an extract from a letter of Chief Justice Taney to Van Buren denying that Jackson ever doubted his duty to carry into execution an act of Congress regularly passed, regardless of his own opinion of its constitutionality. It was Taney's contention that Jackson in his bank veto merely insisted on his right in performing his legislative duties to exercise his own independent judgment on the constitutionality of a measure. Apparently the Chief Justice, after the lapse of nearly thirty years and when the Supreme Court's authority was again being defied, was inclined to interpret Jackson's words as well as his actions in relation to the Court in the Indian and bank cases in such a way as to minimize his resistance to and defiance of its authority, as the final and authoritative expounder of the Constitution. See Warren, *op. cit.,* II: 221 ff., and *Maryland Historical Mag.* (March, 1915), X: 23.

[100] Letter to Story, Aug. 2, 1832. Massachusetts Hist. Soc., *Proceedings,* 2d ser., XIV: 349, 350, and Oster, *op. cit.,* p. 140.

[101] 5 Peters 247 (1831).

protected by the compact between Virginia and Kentucky. Holding that there was no substantial basis for intervention in the controversy by the federal courts, Chief Justice Marshall again reiterated the view that the Supreme Court in its decisions was guided only by the necessities and compulsions of the law. Said he: "In the argument, we have been admonished of the jealousy with which the States of the Union view the revising power intrusted by the Constitution and laws of the United States to this tribunal. To observations of this character, the answer uniformly given has been, that the course of the judicial department is marked out by law. We must tread the direct and narrow path prescribed for us. As this Court has never grasped at ungranted jurisdiction, so will it never, we trust, shrink from the exercise of that which is conferred upon it."[102]

Charles Warren calls the opinion rendered by the Court in the *Barron Case* at the opening of the 1833 term "the last of the series of vital decisions on constitutional law which had made the Chief Justiceship of John Marshall so memorable an era in American history." "It was a striking fact," Warren remarks, "that this last of Marshall's opinions on this branch of law should have been delivered in limitation of the operation of the Constitution, whose undue extension he had been so long charged with seeking."[103]

The case of *Barron v. Baltimore* arose over an action against the city of Baltimore to recover damages for injuries to wharf property of the plaintiff resulting from the acts of the city. Conceding that damage had been done to the plaintiff's property, the city denied any liability on the ground that the damage was occasioned by the construction and repair of the streets under authority granted by the state legislature. The plaintiff appealed to the Supreme Court of the United States on the ground that the city's acts contravened the provision of the Fifth Amendment to the Constitution which declares that "private property shall not be taken for public use without just compensation."

Raising the query whether the Supreme Court could take jurisdiction of the case under the twenty-fifth section of the Judiciary Act, Chief Justice Marshall said:

The Constitution was ordained and established by the people of the United States for themselves, for their own government, and not for the government of the individual States. Each State established a constitution for itself, and, in that constitution, provided such limitations and restrictions on the powers of its particular government as

---

[102] 5 Peters 258. Justice Baldwin, dissenting, thought that Marshall had declined to take jurisdiction in a case wherein a cause plainly presented on the record an issue which was properly before the Supreme Court for determination.

[103] *The Supreme Court in United States History* (Boston, 1922), II: 240, 241.

its judgment dictated. The people of the United States framed such a government for the United States as they supposed best adapted to their situation and best calculated to promote their interests. The powers they conferred on this government were to be exercised by itself; and the limitations on power, if expressed in general terms, are naturally, and, we think, necessarily applicable to the government created by the instrument. They are limitations of power granted in the instrument itself; not of distinct governments, framed by different persons and for different purposes.

If these propositions be correct, the Fifth Amendment must be understood as restraining the power of the general government, not as applicable to the States. In their several constitutions they have imposed such restrictions on their respective governments as their own wisdom suggested; such as they deemed most proper for themselves. It is a subject on which they judge exclusively, and with which others interfere no farther than they are supposed to have a common interest.[104]

Turning to history with a different outlook and approach from that which had been manifested in numerous judicial pronouncements, the Chief Justice concluded his last important opinion affecting the constitutional law of the country with these observations:

It is universally understood, it is a part of history of the day, that the great revolution which established the Constitution of the United States, was not effected without immense opposition. Serious fears were extensively entertained that those powers which the patriot statesmen, who then watched over the interests of our country, deemed essential to union, and to the attainment of those invaluable objects for which union was sought, might be exercised in a manner dangerous to liberty. In almost every convention by which the Constitution was adopted, amendments to guard against the abuse of power were recommended. These amendments demanded security against the apprehended encroachments of the general government—not against those of the local governments.

In compliance with the sentiment thus generally expressed, to quiet fears thus extensively entertained, amendments were proposed by the required majority in Congress, and adopted by the States. These amendments contain no expression indicating an intention to apply them to the state governments. This court cannot so apply them.[105]

Thus the amendments to the federal Constitution constituting a bill of rights were held to establish limitations on the authority of the federal government and not on the states. It required another amendment to the Constitution, namely, the Fourteenth Amendment, and a broad stretch of constructive interpretation to apply at least a part of the protection designed by these amendments against governmental interference with private rights to state action.[106]

The January, 1834, term of the Supreme Court marked the end of Marshall's control of the Court. Justice Washington's poor health had caused the removal from the Court of a strong supporter of the views

[104] Barron v. Mayor and City Council of Baltimore, 7 Peters 247, 248 (1833).
[105] 7 Peters 250.
[106] See Gitlow v. New York, 268 U. S. 652 (1924), and Charles Warren, "The New Liberty under the Fourteenth Amendment," 39 *Harv. Law Rev.* (Feb., 1926), 431.

of the Chief Justice. Johnson was ill, and Duval was aged and infirm. These two Justices, who were members of the Republican party, usually approved the nationalist decisions of Marshall. Justice Story was the only member of the Court who could be relied upon to maintain the principles of the Chief Justice. Three new Justices, Thompson, McLean, and Baldwin, soon made it clear that they were unwilling to follow Marshall in his constitutional interpretation.

Recognizing the change in the trend of decisions on constitutional questions, Marshall was compelled regretfully to announce the inability

TABLE I

THE DECISIONS OF THE SUPREME COURT

Years	National	State rights	Protection of vested rights	Protection denied vested rights
1801–1805	2	1	2	0
1806–1810	6	0	1	0
1811–1815	3	1	3	0
1816–1820	8	5	2	1
1821–1825	9	1	3	0
1826–1830	5	9	0	6
1831–1835	1	8	0	4
Total	34	25	11	11

of the Court to decide several important cases. Though it is difficult to classify Supreme Court decisions into clear and well-defined categories, particularly with relation to the tendencies to support either the doctrine of nationalism or the doctrine of State rights, it is apparent that in the decade from 1816 to 1826 there was a marked trend to uphold the powers of the federal government and to restrict the powers of the states. And though the trend is not so well marked, it is also apparent that from 1826 to 1835 the Supreme Court was more inclined to support the contentions of the states as against the federal government and less disposed to interfere with state acts so far as they affected vested rights. These trends are reflected in tables I and II.

When a law of Kentucky authorizing the issuance of bills which were made receivable for taxes and were to be accepted in satisfaction of judgments against debtors was attacked as an attempt to emit bills of credit, and when a New York law attempting to prevent the entrance to the city of undesirable aliens by requiring the masters of ships to furnish to the mayor a report on all passengers was resisted, the Chief Justice delivered the following opinion:

The practice of this Court is, not (except in cases of absolute necessity) to deliver any judgment in cases where constitutional questions are involved, unless four Judges concur in their opinion, thus making the decision a majority of the whole Court. In the present cases four Judges do not concur in opinion as to the constitutional questions which have been argued. The Court therefore directs these cases to be reargued at the next term, under the expectation that a larger number of the Judges may be present.[107]

These cases were again continued when the Court was unable to reach an agreement during the 1835 term. By this time the vacancy caused by the death of Justice Johnson had been filled by the appointment of James M. Wayne of Georgia; but Justice Duval had resigned, leaving one vacancy on the Court. Against the decided opposition of Justice Story and himself, Marshall was unwilling to announce a decision in

TABLE II

THE DECISIONS OF CHIEF JUSTICE MARSHALL

Years	National	State rights	Protection of vested rights	Protection denied vested rights
1801–1805	2	1	2	0
1806–1810	6	0	1	0
1811–1815	1	0	1	0
1816–1820	6	2	2	1
1821–1825	6	0	1	0
1826–1830	4	2	1*	1
1831–1835	1	4	0	1
Total	26	9	8	3

*This was a dissenting opinion in Ogden v. Saunders, 12 Wheaton 213 (1827)— the only dissent Marshall wrote in a constitutional case during his career on the Supreme Bench. For the preparation of these tables, I am indebted to Vincent M. Barnett, Jr., "An Appraisal of the Decisions of Chief Justice Marshall Relative to Constitutional Law." (Thesis submitted for degree of Master of Arts, Los Angeles, University of California, June, 1936).

which only three Justices concurred. When the cases were finally decided, after Marshall's death, Justice Story, dissenting, expressed the views in which he and the Chief Justice concurred.[108]

Similar differences of opinion and uncertainty developed in the case of the *Charles River Bridge v. Warren Bridge*. This case was first argued in March, 1831. It was continued after the close of the 1832 term because of the facts that "one Judge before whom the case was argued at the last term being absent and the Judges differing." The division of the Court was reported to be as follows: Marshall, Story, and Thompson supported the Charles River Bridge, McLean thought jurisdiction doubtful, Baldwin supported the Warren Bridge, and Johnson and Duval were absent. In the final decision, after Marshall's death, seven Justices decided against the proprietors of the Charles River Bridge in an opinion delivered by Chief Justice Taney; Justices Story and Thompson dissented.[109]

[107] Briscoe v. Bank of Kentucky, and New York v. Miln, 8 Peters 121 (1834) and 9 Peters 85 (1835).
[108] 11 Peters 328 (1837).
[109] 11 Peters 420 (1837).

It was during the last few years of Marshall's Chief Justiceship that the Supreme Court confirmed the rule previously laid down that claims to land titles, even though founded on rather flimsy pretexts, must, whenever possible, be preserved and protected by the Courts. Justice Baldwin, speaking for the Court in *United States v. Arredondo*[110] pertaining to Spanish land grants made in Florida, held that a grant made by a public official purporting to be in accordance with the laws of the sovereign power for which he was acting was deemed to be a valid act, and the burden rested upon the government to prove lack of authority. Warren calls Baldwin's opinion superb because it favored the claimants rather than the government, though he admits that "it is undeniable that the Court's decision resulted in the unjust enrichment of many speculators whose claims possessed no legal foundation."[111] Similar principles were announced and followed in other cases at this time and in the later determination of the validity of land grants in California and New Mexico, despite the fact that wholesale frauds, forgeries, and collusions were thereby given legal sanction.[112] The last case in which Marshall spoke for the Court was a Florida land claim case involving title to more than a million acres of land derived from grants made by the Indians and ratified by the local authorities of Spain. He disposed of a motion to continue the cause for another term, and Justice Baldwin rendered the opinion of the Court confirming the title for the claimants.[113]

In a suit by Wheaton, the former reporter of the Supreme Court, against Peters, the present reporter, Wheaton, having failed to comply with all of the technical requirements of the copyright laws of the United States, attempted to maintain his copyright at common law. Rejecting his claim, Justice McLean said: "It is clear there can be no common law of the United Statees. The federal government is composed of twenty-four sovereign independent States, each of which may have its local usages, customs, and common law. There is no principle which pervades the Union and has the authority of law that is not embodied in the Constitution or laws of the Union. The common law could be made a part of our federal system only by legislative adoption."[114]

It was apparent in this, and in other opinions of the recently appointed Justices, that the country was entering upon a new era of constitutional

---

[110] 6 Peters 691 (1832).

[111] *History of the Supreme Court*, II: 244.

[112] Referring to Marshall's opinions during this term, Beveridge thinks "the last words Marshall ever uttered as Chief Justice sparkle with vitality and high ideals." *The Life of Marshall*, IV: 585. See United States v. Clarke, 8 Peters 436 (1834).

[113] Mitchel v. United States, 9 Peters 711 (1835).

[114] Wheaton v. Peters, 8 Peters 591 (1834).

interpretation. From the time of the establishment of the Supreme Court in 1789, the Justices had conceived it to be their duty to foster and to engraft upon the American constitutional system some of the essential principles and policies of Hamiltonian Federalism. The Jeffersonian revolution retarded but did not seriously interfere with the warping of the Constitution into the Federalist mold. Thus the Supreme Court was thrust into the political arena and because of this fact was subjected to political influences and controls. The Federalists used the Court as an agency to stem the tide of Jeffersonian Democracy and to a considerable extent succeeded in checking democratic tendencies. It was not until the accession into power of the Jacksonian Democrats that the opportunity came to bring all three departments of government under the control of the Democratic party. By 1835, however, a constitutional structure had been formed which, though it might be changed in some important phases, was destined not to be destroyed or seriously undermined. Another great Chief Justice was called upon to carry out the program of development and conservation of constitutional theories and principles.

CHAPTER XVII

Political Phases and Implications of the Marshall Era of Constitutional Interpretation

Dean roscoe pound pointed out some years ago that the customary nineteenth-century modes of legal interpretation largely ignored the element of creative activity of lawyers, judges, text writers, or legislators. They considered legal phenomena as if men had no part in securing the results or determining the trends of juristic endeavors. After noting that the omission of men in juristic reckoning bore fruit in the jurisprudence of conceptions with some unfortunate effects on both private and public law, Dean Pound raised some queries: "May we interpret law and legal history in terms of the element which the last century ignored? Is it possible to make a great-lawyer interpretation of legal custom? May we tell the story around the personality of judges and law-givers and jurists? If we may do so is the interpretation valid?"[1] The answer to these queries is given in the affirmative, and it is admitted that great minds and masterful personalities aid in the explanation of many phases of legal history. Among the illustrations cited is the fact that "in American law, Marshall has been pronounced rightly the creator of the Constitution in the sense that his statesmanlike legal exposition of it in the formative period made it an effective instrument that stood the test of civil war."[2]

The account of certain phases of the work of the Supreme Court in the preceding pages—and it is necessary again to call attention to the fact that only selected parts of the Court's work have been subjected to consideration and analysis—has shown in clear perspective that the individual members of the Court, and the Court as an institution, played an important role in the scenes and acts of the political drama enacted from 1789 to 1835. As the date 1835 marks a distinct change not only in the personnel of the Court but also in the trend of judicial decisions, it may be well to undertake a brief review of the relations of the Court

[1] *Interpretations of Legal History* (New York, 1923), p. 124.
[2] *Ibid.*, p. 139.

and of its individual members to the development of certain distinctively American political and economic doctrines.

Although primary consideration will be given in this résumé to the career and the decisions of Chief Justice Marshall, with only incidental references to the other Chief Justices and the Associate Justices, it is obvious that the Supreme Court as an institution, the mere outlines of which were incorporated in the Constitution, accounts in part for some of the unique contributions to the philosophy and the doctrines which are characteristic of the American political and legal system. It may be said that men were largely responsible for the peculiar evolution of the institution, but they in turn were influenced and their views were molded by the institution.[3]

Before the appointment of Chief Justice Marshall to the Supreme Bench, the Court, under the leadership of Chief Justices Jay and Ellsworth, had paved the way for some of the most distinctive contributions of federal jurisprudence. As was noted in previous chapters, it was clearly indicated that when appropriate occasions arose, the federal Courts would hold void acts of Congress if deemed in conflict with any of the provisions of the federal Constitution, and in *Ware v. Hylton*[4] a state act was declared void on this ground. It was then decided that the Court would hear and decide only actual controversies and hence would not render advisory opinions. The Court assumed that it was its duty to aid in the establishment and maintenance of federal supremacy and in checking the powers of the states—in short, to sustain national as against state sovereignty. In certain cases in the Supreme Court and in the inferior federal courts, the doctrine was asserted that these courts were not confined to the express language of the Constitution concerning their jurisdiction or the mode of interpreting the fundamental law. Federal Justices regarded it as well within their province to engage actively in the political controversies of the day and to use the courts as agencies to accomplish political or partisan ends. The judicial department had been given the special mold and features which were designed for the Judiciary by the Federalist party, dominant during the period of the framing and adoption of the Constitution and during the Administrations of George Washington and John Adams.[5] Thus, a good foundation was laid for the career of Chief Justice Marshall.

---

[3] "Why is it," inquired Attorney General (now Justice) Robert H. Jackson, "that the Court influences appointees more consistently than appointees influence the Court?" *The Struggle for Judicial Supremacy: A Study of a Crisis in American Power Politics* (New York, 1941), p. vii.

[4] 3 Dallas 198 (1796).

[5] See above, chaps. iv, v.

MARSHALL'S FEDERALISM IN CONSTITUTIONAL CONSTRUCTION

It was owing to the peculiar nature of the Court over which Chief Justice Marshall presided and because he presided during the formative period of American history, when it was possible to exercise the molding influence of a statesman, that the Chief Justice has been given so high a rank among the men of his time.[6] But how did it come about that a member of a judicial tribunal, in discharging the functions of a Judge, could show the highest skill in statesmanship? A variety of answers has been given to this query. In the opinion of Judge McClain, a partial answer may be found in a Constitution stated in broad and general phrases which was to be adapted by interpretation to meet new and changing conditions. And in the process of interpretation and adaptation which was confided to the Supreme Court, McClain admits that Judges as human beings "are capable, even though honest and sincere in their convictions, of entertaining the prejudices and passions of other human beings."[7] He concluded, however, that it was not as a Federalist or a partisan that Chief Justice Marshall dominated the Court and determined the trend of its decisions on constitutional questions. Because his judgments were the judgments of a Court, his reasoning was legal reasoning and his conclusions were legal conclusions. This has become the accepted verdict of history. But Marshall's contemporaries did not usually so regard his work as a member of the Supreme Court. It becomes necessary, therefore, to consider the political views and partisan prejudices of the Chief Justice.

Despite the well-known fact that John Marshall was a Federalist before his accession to the Supreme Bench and that he continued to support and announce in his decisions some of the most important doctrines of that party, it is frequently contended by historians and jurists that as a Judge he was in no sense a partisan. He belonged, it is maintained, to no particular school of construction and had no theories of government which he desired to maintain. Naturally possessed of a judicial temperament, it is believed that he could not be a partisan.[8] The view

---

[6] See Emlin McClain, "Chief Justice Marshall as a Constructive Statesman," *Iowa Journal of History and Politics* (Oct., 1903), pp. 427–466.

[7] *Ibid.*, p. 437.

[8] Marshall's opinions, according to William Draper Lewis, "show that he adhered closely to the words of the Constitution; indeed, no one who has attempted to expound our fundamental law has confined himself more strictly to the examination of the text. In the proper, though not in the historical sense, Marshall was the strictest of strict constructionists; and as a necessary result, his opinions are practically devoid of theories of government, sovereignty, and the rights of man." "John Marshall," in *Great American Lawyers* (Philadelphia, 1907), II: 378. For a different judgment rendered by Lewis about thirty years later, see below, p. 623.

which has been generally approved by members of the Bench and Bar was expressed by E. J. Phelps in his address before the American Bar Association in 1879, as follows: "Federalist as he was, and whatever may be said of his party or their views, we can find no more trace in any line of those great judgments that would indicate the political sentiments or bias of the Chief Justice than if we were to study his opinions upon charter-parties or policies of insurance."[9]

On the other hand, many public men, including prominent members of the legal profession, have frankly conceded that Marshall was a partisan and that his political views influenced his judicial decisions. "By reason of the appointment of Marshall in the last months of the Adams administration," said Jeremiah Smith, "the Federalist theories of the Constitution prevailed in that tribunal for more than a generation, and indeed long after the Federalist party had ceased to exist as a political organization."[10] According to James C. MacRae, the opinions of Marshall by which he worked into the warp and woof of the Constitution his theories of nationalism were to be expected from him, for "he was a Federalist upon principle from the beginning."[11] No one was in a better position to evaluate his partisanship or his consistent adherence to Federalist principles than Justice Story, who said of Marshall that

there was throughout his political life a steadfastness and consistency of principle as striking as they were elevating. During more than half a century of public service he maintained with inflexible integrity the same political principles which he begun. He was content to live *by, with,* and *for* his principles.... He was, in the original, genuine sense of the word, a Federalist—a Federalist of the good old school, of which Washington was the acknowledged head, and in which he lived and died. In the maintenance of the principles of that school he was ready at all times to stand forth a determined advocate and supporter. On this subject he scorned all disguise; he affected no change of opinion; he sought no shelter from reproach. He boldly, frankly and honestly avowed himself through evil report and good report, the disciple, the friend, and the admirer of Washington and his political principles.[12]

Marshall was in fact "a party man of hard fibre."[13] And why should he not have been a party man, for, regardless of the development of a tradition to the contrary, it has frequently been observed that Judges, when appointed to the Bench, carry with them their political principles and political biases. Since constitutional questions usually have political

---

[9] *John Marshall: Life, Character and Judicial Services,* compiled and edited with an introduction by John F. Dillon (Chicago, 1903), III: 394.

[10] *Ibid.,* I: 139.

[11] *Ibid.,* II: 75.

[12] *Ibid.,* II: 367; and Story, *Miscellaneous Writings of Joseph Story,* ed. by William W. Story (Boston, 1852), p. 683.

[13] From address of Henry Cabot Lodge, Dillon, *op. cit.,* II: 314.

bearings and implications, Judges, in disposing of them, are inclined to that construction of the Constitution which conforms to their political views.[14]

At the time of his appointment to the Supreme Court, John Marshall was looked upon as one of the most popular Federalists in the United States. And after the decision in the case of *Marbury v. Madison*,[15] Jefferson and the members of his political party believed that the Judiciary was being used by Marshall to uphold the principles of the Federalist party contrary to the definitely expressed will of the nation. There were unwarranted indications of partisanship during the Burr trial, and the Chief Justice joined the New England Federalists in their defiance of President Madison and of the national Administration during the War of 1812, and he assisted the extreme wing of the party in their efforts to end the war by overthrowing the Administration.[16] It was, however, in his decisions after 1815 that Marshall's political theories and principles were embodied in his constitutional opinions. The political principles on which the views of the Chief Justice were assertive and unyielding were the authority of final and conclusive interpretation of the Constitution by the Supreme Court, the supremacy of the federal government over the states, not only in the exercise of granted powers, but also in the development of such resultant or implied powers as Congress and the Courts might approve, and the protection by the courts of acquired or vested rights against legislative attacks. Martin Van Buren observed that: "Under a disposition the most genial, and a childlike simplicity and frankness of manner he cherished during his whole life ... Federal principles and Federal prejudices of the most ultra character."[17]

The partisan character of much of John Marshall's work, though seldom commented upon by historians or legal scholars, was clearly recognized by Vernon Louis Parrington.[18] Parrington regards it as an ironical

---

[14] From address of J. M. Bartholomew, *ibid.*, III: 139.

[15] 1 Cranch 137 (1803).

[16] See Albert J. Beveridge, *The Life of John Marshall* (Boston, 1919), IV: 40 ff.

[17] *Inquiry into the Origin and Course of Political Parties in the United States* (New York, 1867), p. 282. See also Professor Phillips' comment that: "In 1803 John Marshall began his series of vigorous nationalistic decisions which averaged more than one per year for the next thirty years, accompanying the decisions of his Court in most of these cases with fulminations from his own pen to preach the doctrines of broad construction." Ulrich B. Phillips, "Economic and Political Essays in the Ante-Bellum South," in *The South in the Building of the Nation* (Richmond, 1909), VII: 192.

[18] Describing Marshall as "the last of the Virginia Federalists," Parrington observes that "unlike John Taylor of Caroline, whose fame lies buried with his cause, the reputation of John Marshall has taken on immense proportions with the later triumph of his principles. There is abundant reason for the veneration in which he has come to be held by present-day disciples of Hamilton. More than any other man he saved the

fact that Marshall should have come out of Virginia, for he belonged rather to Boston than to Richmond. He was profoundly influenced by Alexander Hamilton and Robert Morris and found the Federalists of Boston and New England more congenial in temper and outlook than his associates in Virginia and in the South.[19]

Indicative of his judicial statesmanship, Albert J. Beveridge, the fore-

---

future for Federalism. During the critical years of the Jeffersonian and Jacksonian assaults upon the outworks of nationalism, he held the inner keep of the law, and prepared for the larger victories that came long after he was in his grave. His strategic judicial decisions served as a causeway over which passed the eighteenth-century doctrine of the sovereignty of the law, to unite with the new philosophy of capitalistic exploitation. The turbid waters of frontier leveling and states-rights democracy washed fiercely about him, but he went on quietly with his self-appointed work. He was one man who would not bow his neck to the majority yoke, would not worship the democratic Baal. He profoundly distrusted the principle of confederation. Convinced that the "continental belt" must be buckled tightly, he gave unstinted service to the cause of consolidation. The imperative need of a sovereign political state to curb the disintegrating forces of America was axiomatic in his thinking. Looking upon all democratic aspirations as calculated to destroy federal sovereignty, and convinced that the principle of equalitarianism was a bow strung to wield against society, he stoutly upheld the principle of minority rule as the only practical agency of stable and orderly government. Holding such views it was a matter of high and patriotic duty with Marshall to use his official position to prevent the majority will from endangering interests which were far more sacred in his eyes than any natural rights propagated in the hothouse of French philosophy. He was the last of the old school of Federalists and the first of the new. . . .

"The narrowness of his outlook intensified the rigidity with which he held to his fixed opinions; and his extraordinary courage coupled with a dominant personality clothed his strategic position as Chief Justice with fateful influence on the later institutional development of America.

"Although Marshall's fame is the fame of a lawyer, he was in reality a politician whom fate in the person of John Adams placed on the Supreme Court bench at a critical moment, where his political opinions translated themselves into the organic law of the land, and shaped the Constitution to special and particular ends. Masterful, tenacious, manipulating his fellow Judges like putty, he was a judicial sovereign who for thirty-five years molded the plastic Constitution to such form as pleased him, and when he died the work was so thoroughly done that later generations have not been able to undo it. His political opinions, therefore, became a matter of very great importance to the historian, for they help to explain the peculiar direction taken by our constitutional development." *The Romantic Revolution in America, 1800–1860* (New York, 1927), pp. 20–22.

[19] Justice Story, in his eulogy on Marshall, refers to a meeting which took place in Philadelphia in 1796 while the case of *Ware v. Hylton* was being argued before the Supreme Court between Marshall and the leading members of the Federalist party who were then in Congress. Among this group were Messrs. Cabot, Ames, Dexter, and Sedgwick of Massachusetts, Wadsworth of Connecticut, and King of New York. I was delighted with these gentlemen, he was reported to have said, and the high opinion he formed of them, Story notes, was cherished by him throughout his life. Dillon, *op. cit.*, III: 354. See also letter of Timothy Pickering to George Cabot at the time President Adams was considering John Marshall for the position of Associate Justice, Henry Cabot Lodge, *Life and Letters of George Cabot* (Boston, 1878), pp. 181–183.

most authority on Marshall's work, maintains that the purpose of his life was to strengthen and enlarge the powers of the national government, or, to use another phrase, he was the "constructing architect of American nationalism." He was passionately devoted to what he regarded as the fundamental principles of government and to the constitutional theories the application of which, in his opinion, were indispensable to the sound development of the American nation. Hence, Beveridge commends his "statesmanlike foresight" which has few parallels in judicial history. In fact, his opinions are called nothing less than "state papers of the first rank."[20] The use of the Supreme Court as a platform to announce political doctrines is conceded by Beveridge and regarded by him and by many other historians as signally brave and noble conduct. Considering the circumstances under which the decision in *United States v. Judge Peters*[21] was rendered, Beveridge thinks Marshall's opinion was not confined to the case before him; it was meant for the whole country and especially for those localities where national laws were being denounced and violated."[22]

To Marshall, the politician and statesman, it is generally conceded, was due more than to any other person the establishment of the principle of nationality in the American system of government.[23] By the sheer force of intellect, claims Hampton L. Carson, Marshall underpinned and then uplifted the Judiciary to a plane of independence beyond the reach of the executive and legislative branches, "there to remain as the controlling power under the Constitution."[24] So great was his work in this respect that an eminent lawyer has asserted that "we are indebted to Chief Justice Marshall for the American Constitution. . . . He was not the commentator upon American constitutional law; he was not the expounder of it; he was the author, the creator of it."[25] Thus, he was at once a statesman and a judge—a dual role in which he performed to the end of his career. Continuing the work of Washington and Hamilton, Chief

---

[20] *The Life of John Marshall,* III, preface, and pp. 15, 75, 109, 132, 178, 179; IV: 117, 169.

[21] 5 Cranch 135 (1809).

[22] Beveridge, *op. cit.,* IV: 20.

[23] This principle, as defined and defended by Marshall, maintains John F. Dillon, "has profoundly affected our national life. It has determined our destiny. It has made us a Nation in fact as well as in name, a power and not a mere painted semblance. It held the Nation intact against the heresies of nullification and secession. It received its complete, final and now unquestioned triumph with the overthrow of the Confederacy, whose forces, as has been said, surrendered not more truly to Grant in the field than to Marshall's great judgments expounding the Constitution." Dillon, *op. cit.,* I, introduction, p. xiii.

[24] Address before the Cleveland Bar Association, Feb. 4, 1901, Dillon, *op. cit.,* II: 252.

[25] E. J. Phelps, address before the Amer. Bar Assn., *Reports,* 1879, p. 176.

Justice Marshall transformed a document essentially confederate in nature into a charter for a national union.[26]

Adept in using the camouflage of legal logic to conceal his partisan or political designs, Marshall aimed to give the impression that he was a "just judge," uninfluenced by the partisan and political influences of his time. When the pressure against the assertion of the doctrines of nationalism in judicial decisions grew menacing, he called to his aid the chief assumption of the mechanical school of jurists, whose work has been described in a previous chapter,[27] and announced to the country that "this department can listen only to the mandates of the law."[28] And after indulgence in some amazing stretches of interpretation to formulate and express the legal philosophy and principles of the Federalist party as a part of the constitutional law of the United States, he tried to counteract the persistent criticisms and objections by saying: "This Court has never grasped at ungranted jurisdiction."[29]

Marshall, then, did not cease writing diplomatic and political state papers when he became Chief Justice. The Supreme Court became an appropriate forum for this purpose. As time went on, the papers became increasingly political and displayed a minimum of diplomacy, which customarily entails compromise, adjustment, and due consideration for all the factors and conditions involved. The Chief Justice became more and more a partisan—a protagonist of nationalistic doctrines—and he strayed from the path of strict duty as a Judge to announce these doctrines with, at times, an utter disregard of the consequences. Historians with a federalist or nationalist bias have lauded in glowing terms the political efforts of the Chief Justice and have condemned in disparaging phrases and epithets the efforts of those who disagreed with him.[30]

[26] "Chief Justice Marshall transformed the words of the Constitution into authority and made them spell national power. He found the organic law full of silences which he made articulate. He gave the Constitution resiliency and made it, what it claimed to be, the supreme law of the land." Forrest Revere Black, "Constitutions and Democracy," *The Annals* of the American Academy of Political and Social Science, Vol. 169 (Sept., 1933), p. 73.

[27] Cf. above, chap. i.

[28] Craig v. Missouri, 4 Peters 410 (1830).

[29] Fisher v. Cockerell, 5 Peters 259 (1830).

[30] According to Henry Cabot Lodge the Federalist party was "the party of order, of good government, and of conservatism. Against them was ranged a majority of their fellow citizens. But this majority was wild, anarchical, disunited." *Life and Letters of George Cabot,* p. 415. See, in this connection, reference to Beveridge's "notoriously partisan but masterly biography of Marshall," in Henry Steele Commager's review of *John Marshall in Diplomacy and Law* by Lord Craigmyle. Commager notes that the thesis of Craigmyle's work is "the not unfamiliar one of the triumph of order and justice over the forces of anarchy and chaos through the instrumentality of Marshall's decisions on the great questions of the relation of the States to the central government

Speaking of Marshall's greatest decisions, William Draper Lewis says "the approval accorded these decisions by later generations has caused them to be regarded as the inevitable result of any fair reading of the Constitution. The fact has become obscured that the views of Marshall which time has proven best for the national progress were neither the views of the majority of the Nation during the period of their adoption by the Court, nor the only rational views which could be entertained."[31] Much of American legal and political history ignores the fact that because of the great divergency of political concepts of the two contending parties, each of which was supported by men of imposing ability and acumen, the nation stood at the parting of the ways. One was determined by every device and stratagem to form the people of the United States into a single sovereign nation. By the process of interpretation the language of the Constitution was to be construed to support the nationalistic designs. The other party insisted that the general government was merely the accredited agent of independent sovereignties which had delegated to such agent certain strictly defined powers which the states could abrogate or withdraw whenever they saw fit. Members of the latter party strenuously dissented from the strengthening and consolidating ideas of the Federalists and the inevitable weakening and final destruction of the sovereignties of the separate states.[32] Of even greater significance than the espousal of the cause of nationalism was Marshall's persistent and uncompromising hostility to democratic ideals and principles.

MARSHALL'S OPPOSITION TO DEMOCRATIC IDEALS AND PRINCIPLES

Contrary to the prevailing view regarding Marshall's judicial temperament and his detachment from political influences in rendering his constitutional decisions, Beveridge asserts that everyone knew that he was the most determined nationalist in the country and that he was the most unyielding enemy of Jefferson and the Republican party.[33] His antidemocratic notions were equally well known. Fundamentally, Marshall seems never to have changed his view, as expressed in 1787: "I fear, and there is no opinion more degrading to the dignity of man, that these have truth on their side who say that man is incapable of governing himself."[34]

---

and the sanctity of contract and of property. Every Federalist historian has rendered the same verdict." *The Saturday Review of Literature*, May 13, 1933.

[31] *Interpreting the Constitution* (Charlottesville, 1937), p. 49.

[32] See orations of Wayne MacVeagh, Dillon, *op. cit.*, I: 27, and of James C. MacRae, *ibid.*, II: 72.

[33] *The Life of John Marshall*, III: 161.

[34] *Ibid.*, I: 302.

By the time he was appointed Chief Justice, Beveridge notes, he had become "obsessed with an almost religious devotion to the rights of property, to steady government by 'the rich, the wise and good,' to 'respectable society.' " The stoutest champions of Marshall's views on the stability of institutions were the Federalist leaders. These men became his intimate comrades and associates.[35]

The views which Marshall held on the relations of government to business were expressed early in his judicial career, as follows: "I consider the interference of the legislature in the management of our private affairs, whether those are committed to a company or remain under individual direction, as equally dangerous and unwise. I have always thought so and I still think so. I may be compelled to subject my property to these interferences, and when compelled I shall submit; but I will not voluntarily expose myself to the exercise of a power which I think so improperly usurped."[36]

But Marshall's lack of appreciation and understanding of democratic ideals and impulses were especially manifested in his opinions concerning and his relations with Jefferson. Early in the public life of the two men, Marshall expressed the view that the Democrats were divided into "speculative theorists" and "absolute terrorists," and with the latter he was disposed to class Jefferson. Though, as Chief Justice, Marshall did not in the beginning of their association join in the personal attacks on Jefferson, he never gave any expression of praise or appreciation for his work. On his attitude in this respect Beveridge comments as follows: "Holding to the old-time Federalist opinion that Jefferson's principles were antagonistic to orderly government; convinced that, if they prevailed, they would be destructive of the Nation; believing the man himself to be a demagogue and an unscrupulous if astute and able politician—Marshall, nevertheless, said nothing about Jefferson to anybody except to Story, Lee, and Pickering; and, even to these close friends, he gave only an occasional condemnation of Jefferson's policies."[37] But as time went on and as criticisms of his decisions grew more frequent and insistent, Marshall was inclined to charge Jefferson with the responsibility for the foremost ills of the nation. In 1832 he wrote: "We are now gathering the bitter fruits of the tree even before that time planted by Mr. Jefferson, and so industriously and perseveringly cultivated by Virginia."[38]

---

[35] *The Life of John Marshall*, IV: 4.

[36] Letter to Greenhow, Oct. 17, 1809, see Beveridge, *op. cit.*, IV: 479–480.

[37] *Ibid.*, pp. 579, 580.

[38] Letter to Story, Massachusetts Hist. Soc. *Proceedings*, 2d ser. (Boston, 1901), XIV: 354. The State rights philosophy and the philosophy of consolidation, as Parrington

America had made a choice between the Federalist and Democratic-Republican theories of government. It had repudiated the rule of the "rich, the wise and the good," as the Federalists liked to refer to themselves. But to this mandate of the people, Marshall declined to yield. The political nature of Marshall's decisions was generally recognized at the time, and this accounts for the continuous and acrimonious opposition of the Republicans and the extravagant praise of the Federalists when these decisions were rendered. For thirty-five years John Marshall labored unceasingly to counteract the political and constitutional principles of Thomas Jefferson.[39]

The most striking characteristic of Marshall's legal and political thinking was his persistent and unyielding conservatism. Beveridge, his leading biographer, maintains that, like Jefferson, he began his political career as a liberal with democratic inclinations and that it was his experience during the Revolutionary War and during the critical period that made him a confirmed conservative. Whether or not this observation is correct, by the time of Marshall's appointment as Chief Justice, he had accepted and was prepared to defend most of the principles of the Tory or conservative party which were in large part espoused by the Federalists.[40] In his first important decision interpreting the Constitution, that of *Marbury v. Madison*,[41] which was for most purposes a moot case, he brushed aside judicial proprieties and proceeded to announce as constitutional law some of the foremost Hamiltonian doctrines concerning the nature of a written constitution and the place of the Judiciary in its interpretation and application. At the earliest opportunity he denounced the Jeffersonian doctrine of a strict interpretation of the Constitution. With Justice Story, the Chief Justice joined in the assertion of the view that property rights must be protected by the courts, whether statutory provisions or the Constitution guaranteed such protection.

---

observes, "were at swords' points; the agrarian and capitalistic economies were engaged in a mortal duel; that it should have been a Virginian who saved the day for the Hamiltonians, erecting the old Federalism into the law of the land, and conducting by his decisions straight to an augmented, consolidated state, under the shadow of whose power the development of corporate finance might go forward without agrarian let or hindrance, was a bitter brew for the Jeffersonian planters to drink." *The Romantic Revolution in America, 1800 to 1860*, p. 26.

[39] "For thirty-five years," says Edward Channing, "Marshall remained at the head of the national Judiciary, and for thirty-five years he remained a Federalist. Moreover, as one of the old Federalist Justices after another died and his place was filled by a Republican appointed by one of the Virginia Republican Presidents, he fell immediately under the overwhelming influence of the Chief Justice. . . . In death, indeed, the Federalist party triumphed." *A History of the United States* (New York, 1927), V: 309, 310.

[40] For an account of these doctrines, see above, chap. ii.

[41] 1 Cranch 137 (1803).

European doctrines of natural law were relied upon to sanction judicial preservation and protection of the sacred rights of property and of contract.

The unyielding conservatism of the Chief Justice was shown in *Sturges v. Crowninshield,*[42] when he held invalid a law which relieved creditors from contracts made before the passage of the law and used language in the opinion which was regarded as applying to contracts made after the enactment of an insolvency statute. Because of the great public discontent caused by the *Sturges Case,* the Supreme Court limited the application of the contract clause to contracts made before the passage of the law in the case of *Ogden v. Saunders.*[43] It was in this case that Marshall delivered his only important dissenting opinion. He predicted that a provision of the Constitution "on which the good and the wise reposed confidently for securing the prosperity and harmony of our citizens, would lie prostrate, and be construed into an inanimate, inoperative, unmeaning clause."[44] In his opinion the prohibition in the contract clause was complete and total, and all contracts, past or future, were subject to its inhibitions. "No group of his cases," observes Benjamin Fletcher Wright,

so well illustrates his conservatism as does that concerned with the contract clause. By employing a far broader conception of contract than had been prevalent in 1787, and by combining this conception with the principles of eighteenth-century natural law, he was able to make of the contract clause a mighty instrument for the protection of the rights of private property. His personal dominance of the Court, at least until 1827, made it possible for him to give to that clause a breadth of meaning which not only exceeds that intended by the Framers, but also goes beyond the views expressed by Wilson, Paine, the members of Congress who took part in the Yazoo lands debate, and even Paterson and Hamilton. His four great contract opinions[45] written between 1810 and 1819 are among the most important opinions, economic as well as legal, which have ever come from the Supreme Court. Had he been able to carry the Court with him in *Ogden v. Saunders*[46] the scope of the clause would have been complete. For lack of one more vote he fell short of his goal, but his accomplishment was a remarkable one.[47]

Chancellor Kent and Justice Story agreed with Marshall in his conservative and antidemocratic doctrines and in the condemnation of the views of Jefferson. In a eulogy on the life and character of Marshall

[42] 3 Wheaton 122 (1819).

[43] 12 Wheaton 254 and 358 (1827).

[44] Note the use of the phrase which is frequently found in the writings of the foremost Federalists.

[45] Fletcher v. Peck, 6 Cranch 87 (1810), New Jersey v. Wilson, 7 Cranch 164 (1812), Sturges v. Crowninshield, 4 Wheaton 122 (1819), Dartmouth College v. Woodward, 4 Wheaton 518 (1819).

[46] 12 Wheaton 213 (1827).

[47] *The Contract Clause of the Constitution* (Cambridge, 1938), pp. 28, 29.

written by Kent, he referred to the adoption of "the great political principles, which constituted the guide of all his future life—to which he clung with a steadfast and unshrinking devotion, and which he supported with a zeal and ability rarely equalled, and perhaps never surpassed."[48] Moreover, Jefferson, who declined to approve these "political principles" or the methods by which they were being fostered by the process of interpretation, was criticized by Kent.[49] To Kent, "Democracy was unpardonable not only because it was evil in itself but because it was the root of all other evils."[50] American Jacobinism, Kent said, was as menacing to freedom as to property. Like Marshall, he regarded charters as contracts, the obligation of which the federal Constitution prohibited the states from impairing. "I cannot," said Kent, "conceive of anything more grand and imposing in the whole administration of human justice than the spectacle of the Supreme Court sitting in solemn judgment upon the conflicting claims of the national and state sovereignties and tranquilling all jealous and angry passions, and binding together this Confederacy of States in peace and harmony, by the ability, the moderation and the equity of its decisions."[51] Kent agreed with Marshall and Story in finding barriers to be applied by the courts to check unwise legislation which interfered with acquired or vested rights in doctrines of higher or natural law.

Marshall played the role of the "supreme conservative" in the Virginia constitutional convention of 1829. He opposed, among other things, a new constitution for the state, the extension of the suffrage, and any

---

[48] *New York Review* (1838), III: 334.

[49] "Nothing in our judgment," said Kent, "is more deserving of public reprehension than the constant attempts of Mr. Jefferson, almost to the very hour of his death, to heap public odium upon some of the great men of the country, who had been his rivals for public favor, or his opponents in his political measure. . . . His comments upon the constitutional opinions of the Chief Justice, have little of the urbanity of a gentleman, and less of the acuteness or skill of a jurist. He accuses him of sophistry, without any offer of proofs; of false reasoning, without being able to point out his errors; and of insidious cunning, without a shadow of evidence to sustain the charge." *Ibid.,* pp. 342, 344. Expressing his sentiments on Jacksonian democracy, Kent said: "I look upon Jackson as a detestable, ignorant, reckless, vain and malignant tyrant, and I think the country begins to open their eyes in astonishment and see things in the true light. This American elective monarchy frightens me. The experiment, with its foundation laid on universal suffrage and an unfettered and licentious press, is of too violent a nature for our excitable people. We have not in our large cities, if we have in our country, moral firmness enough to bear it." To this letter Story replied, "Your views of politics and men run exactly in the same mold as mine." *Life and Letters of Joseph Story,* ed. by William W. Story (Boston, 1851), II: 182; see also 5 *Amer. Law Rev.* (1871), 368.

[50] John Theodore Horton, *James Kent: A Study in Conservatism* (New York, 1939), pp. 126, 237, 289.

[51] *Commentaries,* pt. ii, lect. xix: 444.

legislative interference with business. The convention, influenced to a considerable degree by Marshall, voted to sustain the Federalist doctrine repudiated by the Repeal Act of 1802, namely, that judges should continue to hold their positions despite the abolition of their offices. He was not only unsympathetic to the rule of the people, but he also believed the more they directly controlled public affairs, the worse the business of government would be conducted. In fact, Beveridge concludes that "on every issue over which the factions of this convention fought, Marshall was reactionary and employed all his skill to defeat, whenever possible, the plans and purposes of the radicals."[52] As Marshall grew older, he became more conservative and less inclined to approve changes in political affairs. "Should Jackson be elected," he wrote in 1828, "I shall look upon the government as virtually dissolved."[53] "Nearly a century has passed since these happenings," concludes Beveridge,

and Marshall's attitude now appears to have been that of cold reaction; but he was as honest as he was outspoken in his resistance to democratic reforms. He wanted good government, safe government. He was not in the least concerned in the rule of the people as such. Indeed, he believed that the more they directly controlled public affairs the worse the business of government would be conducted.

He feared that sheer majorities would be unjust, intolerant, tyrannical, and he was certain that they would be untrustworthy and freakishly changeable.[54]

It was Marshall's conservative and antidemocratic views which are particularly in evidence in the decisions asserting the superiority and supremacy of the Judiciary in interpreting the Constitution, in expanding the meaning of the contract clause so as to lay the foundation for a broad rule for the protection of vested rights from legislative interferences, and in checking some of the incipient efforts of the states to control property and civil rights both by taxation and by regulation.

Toward the end of Marshall's service on the federal Bench, the former party divisions between the conservative and aristocratic groups, on the one hand, and the Democratic-Republican groups, on the other, were developing new forms of organization and were influenced and inspired by somewhat different ideals and principles from those which were prevalent at the time of the establishment of the American system of government. When party spirit appeared to be at a low ebb during the "era of good feeling" of the Monroe Administration, the Republican party was breaking up into conservative and democratic factions. The conservatives, who supported the National Republican Party and later formed the Whigs, were chiefly concerned with the strengthening of the bonds of the union against the growing tendencies toward particularism and

---

[52] *The Life of John Marshall*, IV: 488.   [53] *Ibid.*, p. 463.   [54] *Ibid.*, p. 507.

the assertion of State rights; they supported the movement to develop and protect manufacturing and industrial interests; and they gave enthusiastic support to the Supreme Court as the "sheet anchor," not only to foster and preserve doctrines of nationalism, but also to protect property from the dangers of legislative tinkering.[55] The new Democratic party set as its goal the removal of the restrictions on suffrage, as well as the property qualifications for office; they desired to have as large a share of the government as possible in the hands of the people, and hence preferred elective to appointive officials and short terms of service with the principle of rotation in office; their thinking was characterized by the spirit of individual initiative and assertiveness and therefore they were frequently skeptical regarding the efforts to secure government aid for industry, commerce, and transportation, though the needs of a frontier civilization often prompted them to favor federal aid for internal improvements and protection to manufacturers.

To many of the Democrats, the American system of government was an experiment in democracy—an experiment in which the people would ultimately decide what they deemed to be best in public policy. And it was rather to be expected that they would look with disfavor upon the practice of the federal courts declaring void state and federal legislation. The major assumption of the conservatives in most of the discussions regarding the legislative functions of the federal Judiciary were that the people could not be trusted in the exercise of the ultimate powers of government and hence that the courts must act as a check to preserve the people against themselves. The Democrats, on the other hand, took it for granted that all governmental powers could be safely entrusted to the people without specially appointed guardians. Marshall used all of his intellectual powers and his indomitable will against the rising tide of democracy and the determination to place all the powers of the government under more direct popular control.[56] His method and technique in

---

[55] Arthur B. Darling observes that "the National Republicans, their successors the Whigs, and those descendants of the Whigs, the native Americans, all displayed themselves as conservatives and, at times, reactionaries. They all stood for the established order and invariably were to be found on the opposing side of any issue which seemed to involve a change." "Jacksonian Democracy in Massachusetts," 29 *Amer. Hist. Rev.* (Jan., 1924), 286.

[56] "The popularity of John Marshall, therefore, and the prestige acquired by the Supreme Court during his regime," says Carl Brent Swisher, "resulted largely from the fact that he wrote into constitutional law the beliefs and prejudices of a class, the class, incidentally, from whose records and in terms of whose judgments most of the history of the period has been written. Outside that class he and his Court were anything but popular, as is shown by the wrathful outpourings of Thomas Jefferson, Judge Spencer Roane and others during his early years as Chief Justice, and by the criticisms of the partisans of Old Hickory during the Jackson period." *Roger B. Taney* (New York, 1935), p. 350.

deciding cases, however, tended to conceal the political nature of his decisions and the consequent effects upon the principles and processes of government.

MARSHALL'S METHOD AND TECHNIQUE IN DECIDING CASES

One of the most striking phases of Marshall's long judicial career was his domineering attitude and his dictatorial control of the Court. The practice of delivering *seriatim* opinions had become well established, and because no Justice had assumed the role of oracle to speak for the Court, the Chief Justice began to deliver all of the opinions. During the first five years Marshall delivered the opinion of the Court in every case except in those in which he was disqualified because of personal interest. In the next seven years he rendered the opinion in one hundred and thirty cases, whereas the Associate Justices prepared only thirty opinions.[57] Practically no decisions were announced by the other Justices in cases involving constitutional questions unless, owing to personal interest, the Chief Justice was disqualified.[58] An indication of Marshall's method of disposing of cases was shown in *Rose v. Himely*[59] in which he delivered the leading opinion and ordered the judgment of the Circuit

[57] Speaking of the dominance of Marshall in the affairs of the Court for the first decade after his appointment, Hampton L. Carson observes that "owing to the age and infirmities of Chase and Cushing and the frequent absences of Todd, two Judges sometimes practically became a majority of six and three a majority of seven, *The History of the Supreme Court of the United States* (Philadelphia, 1904), I: 229; see also John M. Shirley, *The Dartmouth College Causes and the Supreme Court of the United States* (St. Louis, 1879), p. 311.

[58] Justice Johnson occasionally dissented from the views of the Chief Justice, but on the issue of nationalism versus State rights, he became in some respects a more confirmed nationalist than Marshall. In seventeen years on the Court, Justice Livingston wrote the opinion in only seventeen cases and none of these involved a constitutional question. During nearly twenty years of service, Justice Todd wrote approximately a dozen opinions, none of which were of any special import. Justice Thompson differed from the views of the Chief Justice in three cases: *Brown v. Maryland, Ogden v. Saunders,* and *Craig v. Missouri.* Accepting the most important Marshall doctrines, Justice Baldwin differed with the Chief Justice merely concerning the appropriate methods of constitutional construction. Justice Duval, the lone dissenter in the *Dartmouth College Case,* gradually came to accept the nationalistic views of the Chief Justice. Though a Republican, he was so violently opposed to Jackson that he refused to resign, even after he was incapacitated from any effective judicial service, because he feared the President would appoint a politician such as John McLean in his place. Justice Washington and Chief Justice Marshall were frequently referred to as a single Judge, because their views on major issues seldom differed. The opinions of Justice Story, which usually coincided with the Chief Justice, have been considered in the preceding analysis of cases. The only Justice during the Marshall period to challenge seriously some of the constitutional doctrines of the Chief Justice was McLean, who was appointed by Andrew Jackson. See Hampton L. Carson, *The History of the Supreme Court of the United States* (Philadelphia, 1904), I: 230; and Carl Brent Swisher, *Roger B. Taney* (New York, 1935), p. 311.

[59] 4 Cranch 241 (1808).

Court to be reversed when only a single Judge agreed with him.[60] Whether intended as a facetious comment or not, the reporter of the Court observed, in connection with one of the cases, that after argument the Chief Justice rendered the opinion with "all the other Justices being present." Having assumed the role of the only competent spokesman for the Court, one is not surprised at the view expressed by Justice Story with respect to Marshall that "no one ever possessed a more entire sense of his extraordinary talents and acquirements than he."[61]

It is true that no weak Judge could have faced unmoved the active hostilities which he had to encounter during what John F. Dillon calls his "long judicial reign." He knew the direction in which he was going and nothing could deter him from his course. In fact, it has been said of him that "he kept on in the orbit of his duty, like the planets in their courses, silent and irresistible."[62] As Chief Justice he not only brought around to his way of thinking a majority of the Justices who were appointed as Republicans to counteract his Federalist views, but he also consistently rendered decisions which, in certain respects at least, were contrary to the preponderant public opinion of the nation.

Lawyers belonging to the school of realistic jurisprudence, whose views respecting constitutional interpretation were briefly considered in a previous chapter,[63] may well regard John Marshall as an exponent of one of the primary doctrines of the school. Realistic jurists not only give a foremost place in the process of judicial decision to the personal feelings, attitudes, and opinions of judges, but they also accord great weight to the intuitive method or the so-called "hunch" in resolving legal controversies.[64] It is well known that Chief Justice Marshall in his constitutional decisions seldom cited precedents; in fact, it has been frequently intimated that he had only a meager knowledge of legal precedents.[65] Whether or not this intimation is correct, and there are those who think

[60] See explanation given in Hudson v. Guestier, 6 Cranch 281 (1810). For an admission that a similar mistake had been made in *Bollmun's Case*, see United States v. Burr, 25 Fed. Cases 161 (1807). For an indication of the marked change in the handling of cases after Marshall's accession to the Bench, see *The American Doctrine of Judicial Supremacy* (2d ed., Berkeley, 1932), pp. 352 ff.

[61] Dillon, *op. cit.*, III: 363.

[62] *Ibid.*, I: xiii, xiv.

[63] See chap. i.

[64] Cf. Joseph C. Hutcheson, "The Judgment Intuitive: The Function of the Hunch in Judicial Decisions," 14 *Cornell Law Quar.* (Apr., 1929), 274.

[65] Justice Story in his eulogy on the Chief Justice remarked that "it is due to truth as well as to his memory to declare that his juridical learning was not equal to that of the great masters in the profession, living or dead, at home or abroad. He yielded at once to their superiority of knowledge, as well in the modern as in the ancient law." From discourse by Joseph Story, Dillon, *op. cit.*, III: 376, 377. See also James Bradley Thayer, *John Marshall* (Boston, 1901), p. 56.

that Marshall's knowledge of the law has been underestimated, it is true that the opinions of the Chief Justice which have profoundly influenced American public law were, as Justice Story characterized them to a considerable extent, "the fruits of his own unassisted meditations."[66] In the words of Horace Binney, "he looked through the Constitution with the glance of intuition."[67] Justice Gray thought that Marshall had an intuitive perception of the real issue of every case, however complicated, and of the way in which it should be decided—an illustration of the method of the hunch at its best. By the intuitive method the Chief Justice was able to discover the "hidden treasures of the Constitution" or, as commentators are wont to observe, to read between the lines. Because the framers of the Constitution did not express in that instrument in plain terms all they would have expressed had not the people of the time opposed so strenuously the centralization or consolidation of powers in the central government, much room was left for a nationalist, such as Marshall, to read between the lines. It was through the intuitive process or the reading between the lines that some of the most important doctrines of American public law were evolved by means of legal interpretation with comparatively little or no basis in the express language of the written document.

Many lawyers and judges who have discussed the work of Chief Justice Marshall comment on his "marvelous," "remorseless," and "commanding" logic. It would be easier, so they say, to challenge a proposition of Euclid than to attack the irrefutable logic of one of his masterly opinions. Occasionally it is admitted that if the premises or assumptions are accepted the logic is irrefutable. But when one approaches the problem resolved by one of these opinions from a different set of premises the question immediately arises whether the so-called "remorseless logic" involved much more than the reading into the vague and indefinite language of the Constitution of the political and economic views which Marshall regarded desirable from the standpoint of expediency and the public welfare.

Nothing in the work of Chief Justice Marshall has received such frequent and enthusiastic commendations as his opinion in the case of *Marbury v. Madison.*[68] The commemorative addresses dealing with Marshall's judicial career give special attention to this case and laud Marshall's reasoning as the greatest landmark in the field of constitutional jurisprudence. A few extracts are: "The premises seem so undeniable, the reasoning so logical, the conclusion so irresistible, that men are wont to

---

[66] Dillon, *op. cit.*, III: 379.

[67] *Ibid.*, p. 317.

[68] 1 Cranch 137 (1803).

wonder that there ever had been any question at all";[69] "an adamantine piece of reasoning, an invincible fortress of nationality, like the pyramid of Cheops, unshaken by the barking of jackals at its base."[70] But the praise accorded to the Chief Justice is not always so unstinted, for James Bradley Thayer, referring to Marshall's opinion in this case, said: "It may reasonably be wondered that he should have been willing to give the opinion in such a case; and especially that he should have handled the case as he did. But he was curiously regardless of conventions."[71] With much doubt and uncertainty having been expressed regarding the authority of the Judiciary to review acts of Congress and with full recognition of the prevailing views repeated over and over again during the debates on the Judiciary Repeal Act of 1802 that the Congress had at least an equal right with the Judiciary to put a construction on the Constitution and that neither ought to be required to surrender its judgment to the other, Marshall undertook to establish the supremacy of the Supreme Court in the field of federal constitutional construction. It has been shown elsewhere[72] that none of the reasoning in this case will stand the tests of fact or of logic except the Federalist assumption that Judges are better qualified to interpret constitutional provisions than any other persons, official or unofficial, particularly so far as the support of the tenets of nationalism and the preservation of the rights of property and contract are concerned. Justices Bland and Gibson pointed out the weaknesses in this so-called "adamantine piece of reasoning" in illustrations, analyses, and logic which leave little to be said for Marshall's reasoning, except that he was, in his calm and unperturbable assumptions, laying the basis for an ideal system to assure the supremacy of the Judiciary in the American system of government, thereby placing, in accordance with the well-known conservative doctrines of the day, effective if not almost insuperable barriers in the way of the extension and development of the popular control of government in the United States.

Historians have as a rule joined with the lawyers in approving the decision as well as the reasoning of Chief Justice Marshall in *Marbury v.*

---

[69] From address of Rawle, Dillon, *op. cit.*, III: 422.

[70] From address of Hampton L. Carson, Dillon, *op. cit.*, II: 254.

[71] *John Marshall* (Boston, 1901), p. 77. Regarding this decision, Thayer also observed: "So far as any necessary conclusion is concerned, it might fairly have been said, with us, as it is said in Europe, that the real question in all these cases is not whether the act is constitutional, but whether its constitutionality can properly be brought in question before a given tribunal. Could Marshall have had to deal with this great question, in answer to Chief Justice Gibson's powerful opinion in *Eakin v. Raub,* in 1825, instead of deciding it without being helped or hindered by any adverse argument at all, as he did, we should have had a far higher exhibition of his powers than the case now affords." *Ibid.*, p. 101.

[72] See chap. vii.

Madison. According to Samuel Eliot Morison and Henry Steele Commager, "the power of judicial review, already familiar to the framers of the Constitution, was conferred on the federal Judiciary in the Constitution, with full intention that it should be exercised;

> Of that there is no manner of doubt—
> No probable, possible shadow of doubt—
> No possible doubt whatever!"[73]

It is admitted, however, by these authors that although the authority of the Judiciary to review acts of Congress is explicit in the Constitution, it is not "very explicit." Any defects in this respect, it is claimed, were soon obviated by Alexander Hamilton's discussion in the seventy-eighth number of *The Federalist* and in the setting up of the machinery to test the constitutionality of acts by the Judiciary Act of 1789. But it seems strange that neither Hamilton in *The Federalist* nor Gouverneur Morris, speaking for the Federalists before the Senate in 1802, could find any explicit grant of such authority in the Constitution. Hamilton gathered the American doctrine of judicial review from the general spirit and tenor of a written constitution with specific limitations on legislative powers,[74] and Gouverneur Morris based the doctrine on an authority superior to the Constitution—derived "from the constitution of man, from the nature of things, from the necessary progress of human affairs."[75]

Most of the authorities on American legal history have not found a grant of authority or any explicit language to support the right of the federal courts to declare acts of Congress invalid. This authority, they contend, must be gathered by the process of interpretation from language which was probably intended to give support to the courts in the exercise of the power of judicial review.[76] From this standpoint the most

---

[73] *The Growth of the American Republic* (2d ed., New York, 1937), I: 180.

[74] *The Federalist* (Ford ed.), p. 522.

[75] *Annals of Congress*, 7th Cong., 1st sess., p. 180.

[76] "As to any method of protecting the federal system within its own household, that is to say, as against Congress, it was proposed in the convention, for one thing, that each House of Congress might call upon the Judges for opinions; and, again, it was urged, and that repeatedly and with great persistence, that the Judges should be joined with the Executive in passing on the approval or disapproval of legislative acts,—in what we call the veto power. It was explicitly said, in objecting to this, that the Judges would have the right to disregard unconstitutional laws anyway,—an opinion put forward by some of the weightiest members. Yet some denied it. And we observe that the power was not expressly given. When we find such a power expressly denied, and yet not expressly given; and when we observe, for example, that leading public men, e.g., so conspicuous a member of the convention as Charles Pinckney of South Carolina, and afterwards a Senator from that State, wholly denied the power ten years later; it being also true that he and others of his way of thinking urged the express restraints on state legislation,—we may justly reach the conclusion that this question, while not overlooked, was intentionally left untouched. Like the question of the bank

important powers exercised by the federal Judiciary and the most significant and far-reaching feature of the American federal system of government, the doctrine of judicial review of legislation, is sanctioned only by the implications which follow from the language of the Constitution.

Though the provisions of the Constitution, viewed from a conservative and nationalistic standpoint, may be regarded as authorizing the courts to declare acts of Congress invalid, it requires an extraordinary stretch of interpretation to extract from these provisions the power claimed by the Judiciary to place a final and authoritative interpretation upon the words and meaning of the Constitution which all other public officials as well as all private citizens are required to accept and obey. The distinction between the preliminary type of judicial review in which the Judges as well as all other public officers might take steps to prevent the carrying out of an act deemed to be unconstitutional and the claim of the high prerogative of placing a final and conclusive interpretation on the provisions of the Constitution is frequently ignored by historians as well as by jurists, and the greatest issue of the first half century of American history is inadequately considered and, at times, misunderstood. It was the assumption throughout his reasoning in *Marbury v. Madison* and subsequent cases, not only that it was the duty of the Judges to declare an act of Congress deemed unauthorized by the Constitution invalid, but also that such a declaration was a final and conclusive interpretation of the Constitution subject to change only by an amendment to the Constitution that gives to Marshall's opinions their great significance for the future growth of American public law. These decisions were designed to change the ordinary process of judicial review of legislation to a form of judicial supremacy with Judges wielding broad powers in the determination of political and economic policies.

Marshall's method of reasoning in constitutional decisions was shown at its best or its worst in the *Cohens Case*,[77] depending upon the point of view from which one approaches the decision. The constitutional issue could readily have been avoided, but the opportunity to restate the principles and the philosophy of nationalism seemed too appropriate and vital to let pass. Assuming jurisdiction, Article III, section 2 of the Constitution defining the jurisdiction of the federal courts was considered separate from and independent of the necessary modifications

---

and various others, presumably it was so left in order not to stir up enemies to the new instrument; left to be settled by the silent determinations of time, or by later discussion." From James Bradley Thayer, *John Marshall,* pp. 65, 66. Attorney General Jackson thinks that "any explicit grant of this power was omitted and that it was left to lurk in an inference." *The Struggle for Judicial Supremacy,* p. 4.

[77] Cohens v. Virginia, 6 Wheaton 264 (1821). See above, chap. xii.

and implications resulting from the adoption of the Tenth and Eleventh Amendments. To withdraw cases from the broad grant of jurisdiction given to the federal courts in this section, Marshall contended that there must be an express prohibition or exception—a reversal of the fundamental hypothesis which pervades the entire Constitution. Following this chain of reasoning, he arrived at the conclusion that the Supreme Court was authorized to decide all cases of every description arising under the Constitution and laws of the United States. The proposition was not denied that states are suable only when they have given their consent to be sued. But to meet this proposition, Marshall adopted one of the main assumptions of the "organic school" of thought, namely, that consent to be sued was granted when the states, by adopting the Constitution, surrendered a part of their sovereignty. Thus, it was taken for granted that in the framing and adoption of the Constitution, a nation was called into being. The real purpose in forming a nation with supreme powers was gathered from the Preamble to the Constitution and was, in Marshall's opinion, merely amplified by subsequent provisions of the document.[78]

And, then, the Chief Justice turned to the line of reasoning in which he was particularly proficient—the argument for a broad review of the judgments of state courts from the standpoint of policy or expediency. Attention was called to the "mischievous consequences of the construction contended for on the part of Virginia." From such a contention it followed that each member of the union would possess a veto on the will of the whole nation, and state tribunals would not be impartial in the determination of such questions. For a government to endure "for ages to come," Marshall thought, it must contain authority to execute its own laws. Courts are the only appropriate agencies to assure such execution, and with this background it was declared that a defendant who removes a judgment rendered against him by a state court into the Supreme Court, for the purpose of reëxamining the question whether that judgment violates the Constitution or laws of the United States, does not commence or prosecute a suit against a state. In the consideration of such a question, the federal courts may not be considered as foreign tribunals in relation to the state courts. And, above all, the necessity of uniformity of decision and of "correctness in expounding the Constitution and the laws of the United States" rendered a single tribunal the only appropriate method of deciding such cases. How could a "more perfect Union" be established if federal tribunals were not accorded such powers?

---

[78] Evidence was available with which Marshall should have been familiar that no such intention was involved in the adoption of the Preamble.

In conclusion, it was asserted that the argument for the state was founded, not on the words of the Constitution, but on its spirit, and resulted from a particular view of the nature of the union and of the great principles on which the fabric stands.[79] But did not Marshall's arguments also result from the same sources? For Felix Frankfurter has well said: "By shifting terms in the formula of federalism, the counterpart of Marshall's doctrine could be invoked to limit the affirmative exercise of Congressional power; though we are a Nation we are also a federation of States, as declared by the Tenth Amendment, and Congressional authority may therefore be subjected to such limitations as the Court deems necessary for the protection of the independent existence of the States."[80] In like manner judicial powers might have been curtailed rather than extended so as to limit the authority of state tribunals.

The main emphasis throughout this study has been given to the decisions of the Supreme Court on constitutional issues, but other phases of the work of the Court which have influenced political doctrines or political practices have not been neglected. Among the most important groups of cases of this kind are those which relate to questions in the field of international law. Some of the outstanding decisions in this category have been considered in their appropriate time and setting. Because, from 1801 to 1835, more cases were decided within the scope of international law than within the field of constitutional law and because some of these had marked political implications, a few comments and observations concerning these decisions will not be inappropriate.

Marshall recognized a principle in dealing with questions in the field of international law which might have been appropriately applied by the Court in some important constitutional law cases, namely, that "such questions are generally rather political than legal in character. They belong more properly to those who can declare what the law shall be; who can place the Nation in such a position with respect to foreign powers as to their own judgment shall appear wise; to whom are entrusted all its foreign relations; than to that tribunal, whose power, as well as duty, is confined to the application of the rule which the legislature may prescribe for it."[81]

Questions relating to the acquisition of territory, to a change of sov-

---

[79] This opinion of the Chief Justice, which was bitterly assailed by many of the leading Republicans at the time it was rendered, was lauded in 1901 by Hampton L. Carson, who said: "What intellectual strength, what far-seeing statesmanship, what superb moral courage are here displayed! Every mind assented to his logic, every heart was filled by his intrepidity, and every eye was transfixed by the white light of judicial rectitude which shone in every sentence." Dillon, op. cit., II: 259, 260.

[80] The Commerce Clause under Marshall, Taney and Waite (Chapel Hill, 1937), p. 19.

[81] United States v. Palmer, 3 Wheaton 634 (1818).

ereignty, to the making and enforcement of treaties, and to the declaration and termination of war were regarded as rather in the political than in the legal realm and, hence, courts should defer their settlement to the political departments of the government. With this principle in mind, it was held that the rules which have been adopted by the political departments of the government must whenever possible be adhered to by the Judiciary; and as a corollary it was maintained that the rules of conduct which have been generally consented to by the civilized nations of the world must be deemed a part of international law. The Hamiltonian doctrine that the law of nations is a part of the common law and by adoption a part of the law of the United States was accepted by Marshall soon after his appointment to the Supreme Bench.[82] Congress, he asserted, would not be presumed to violate the principles of international law and "till such an act be passed the Court is bound by the law of nations, which is part of the law of the land."[83] And following his inclination to accept and apply principles of natural law, he declared that "the law of nations is a law founded on the great and immutable principles of equity and natural justice."[84]

In cases relating both to constitutional law and international law, Marshall followed a practice which Beveridge notes distinguished him sharply from other jurists,[85] namely, of discussing principles which were not directly or necessarily involved in the controversy before the Court. It is in the discussion of these principles that the major biases of the Chief Justice become apparent, that is, the bias in favor of the protection of private property and that in favor of the extension of neutral rights and privileges. On the basis of a thorough analysis of the opinions and judgments of Marshall relating to international law, Benjamin Munn Ziegler concludes that "one cannot make any study of Marshall without coming quickly to the conclusion that above all he had such a high regard for the sanctity of private property that it acted almost as an obsession upon him—an obsession that at times led him into dubious paths of reasoning."[86] It is generally agreed, however, that Marshall's treatment of controversies in the field of international law displayed "the same traits of mind, the same breadth and originality of thought, the same power in discovering and the same certainty in applying funda-

---

[82] See Murray v. The Charming Betsy, 2 Cranch 118 (1804), and The Nereide, 9 Cranch 423 (1815); *The Works of Alexander Hamilton* (Lodge ed.), VII: 436; also, Benjamin Munn Ziegler, *The International Law of John Marshall* (Chapel Hill, 1939), pp. 5 ff.

[83] The Nereide, 9 Cranch 423.

[84] The Venus, 8 Cranch 297 (1814).

[85] *The Life of John Marshall*, IV: 121, 122.

[86] *The International Law of John Marshall*, pp. 47 ff., and chap. xiii.

mental principles" as in the field of constitutional law.[87] It was in the latter field that the Chief Justice made of the Supreme Court one of the primary agencies for the formulation and announcement of governmental policies. By this means some of the foremost principles of Hamiltonian Federalism were incorporated into the constitutional structure.

THE SUPREME COURT'S ADOPTION OF PARTS OF THE PROGRAM OF HAMILTONIAN FEDERALISM

Among the foremost issues of the formative period of the American government, as discussed in previous chapters,[88] was the question whether the real source or sanction of public authority was to be found in the majority of the people or in a minority comprised of the rich, intelligent, and well-born. The early debates over the organization and jurisdiction of the federal courts brought this issue, together with the contest over Federalism and State rights, to the forefront.[89] It was in the debate over the Judiciary Repeal Act of 1802 that the question regarding the source of public authority was most clearly defined and discussed. This debate has been called "the battleground for two philosophies of government." The Federalists, led by Senator Morris of New York, argued against the repeal of the Judiciary Act because in their opinion the courts were to be preserved and strengthened "to save the people from their most dangerous enemy, to save them from themselves."[90] Morris admitted that defending the Supreme Court as something in the nature of a check department was not a popular doctrine, but he trusted that the Court would not only keep the people in a safe course but that it would also save the Constitution from the democratic or popular waves which might have a tendency to overturn it. In order that the federal courts might serve as an effective check department, the Federalists insisted that the judges should be the chief guardians and the protectors of the Constitution, and should be authorized to declare acts of Congress unconstitutional, thus placing a final and authoritative interpretation upon the language of this document.

Senator Breckenridge, who was the administration leader and who favored the passage of the Repeal Act, surmising that the primary objective of the Federalists was to secure an extension of federal powers by means of judicial construction of the Constitution, said that he wished

---

[87] John Bassett Moore, "John Marshall," 16 *Pol. Sci. Quar.* (Sept., 1901), 405.

[88] See especially chaps. iii, xi, xii.

[89] See Charles Warren, "New Light on the History of the Federal Judiciary Act of 1789," 37 *Harv. Law Rev.* (Nov., 1923), 49, and Charles Raymond Kummer, "Congress and the Supreme Court, 1789–1860" (unpublished dissertation, Los Angeles, University of California, 1939), chaps. ii, iii.

[90] *Annals*, 7th Cong., 1st sess., p. 41.

the federal government to possess and exercise all its rightful powers and he wished the states also to be left in the exercise of theirs. He further maintained that he did not desire an extension of federal legislation and adjudication so that one mighty and consolidated sovereignty might be collected from the ruins of all of the state sovereignties. The Republican contention that the Judges should be independent did not mean that they should be independent of the nation itself, nor in the opinion of the Republicans was the Judiciary designed to control the other departments of government. Senator Breckenridge could not find any warrant in the Constitution for the Federalist claim of authority in the courts to declare void acts of Congress. Such a transcendent power could be derived from the Constitution by construction only, but if Judges may be permitted to enlarge their own powers by such astute constructions, the Constitution could be warped to accomplish whatever ends they thought desirable.[91]

The Federalist argument, the Republicans contended, was equivalent to the proposition that the people are incapable of governing themselves and that hence their rights and liberties can be preserved by the Judiciary alone. The Republicans, however, asserted that the Constitution was fundamentally based upon the will of the people and the primary principle for carrying out this will was the provision making all public agents responsible, mediately or immediately, to the people. According to one theory, the people were, as Hamilton characterized them, a great beast which needed to be tamed and controlled, whereas, according to the other theory, the people were to be the ultimate source and sanction of all public powers, or, to repeat Jefferson's dictum: "Every government degenerates when trusted to the rulers of the people alone. The people themselves are its only safe depositors."[92] The underlying issue has been rightly described as a phase of "power politics" with the ultimate location of public power at stake.[93]

The Federalists desired as large a share as possible of the control of public affairs to be placed in those agencies not directly subject to popular interference or domination. To carry out this program, the clause was inserted in the Constitution that no state shall impair the obligation of contract. Believing that acquired or vested rights of property should be preserved whether or not given constitutional protection, Chief Justice Marshall decided in *Fletcher v. Peck*[94] that a grant of land made

---

[91] *Annals*, 7th Cong., 1st sess., pp. 178–180.

[92] *The Writings of Thomas Jefferson*, Mem. ed. (Washington, 1905), II: 207.

[93] See Charles Kummer, "Congress and the Supreme Court, 1789–1860" (unpublished dissertation, Los Angeles, University of California, 1939), and Robert H. Jackson, *The Struggle for Judicial Supremacy*, chap. 1.

[94] 6 Cranch 87 (1810).

by a state was a contract and hence not subject to annulment by a subsequent state act. In the *Dartmouth College Case*,[95] the protection of the contract clause was given a broader interpretation, and the rights of property and contract, so far as comprehended within the grants of charters to corporations, were given further protection against legislative attack. By this time, the main features of Hamiltonian Federalism had been accepted by the Supreme Court and by its decisions made a part of American constitutional law. Among these features, which were pointed out in a previous chapter,[96] were the following: (1) a strong federal government whose powers were to be expanded by an implied power doctrine permitting those things to be done by the federal government which were deemed of national importance; (2) a Judiciary independent of the other departments and in many respects independent of the nation itself; (3) a doctrine of judicial review of legislation whereby the judicial department, independent of any effective popular control through its function as guardian and protector of the fundamental law, could hold in check all departments of the government; (4) a theory requiring the preservation of vested rights by the courts whether or not constitutions expressly provided for such protection, and hence the development of the principle of political and economic *laissez faire* under judicial guardianship. The cornerstone of the whole structure was the Supreme Court of the United States, which was armed with the authority to declare legislative and administrative acts invalid and with the authority to interpret the Constitution finally and conclusively subject only to the process of amendment which was purposely made extremely cumbersome and difficult.[97]

To those who saw with apprehensions the marked trends toward the development of local and sectional views frequently associated with the doctrine of State rights, there was a grave emergency which required bold and unequivocal action. The tide of localism, it was determined, must be checked, and the people must, as the historians sometimes express it, be "kidded" into the acceptance of a vigorous and assertive nationalism. For this reason Marshall "seized every opportunity to educate the country to a spacious view of the Constitution, to accustom the public mind to broad national powers, and to restrict the old assertiveness of the States. He imparted such a momentum to these views that it carried the Court in his general direction beyond his own time."[98]

---

[95] 4 Wheaton 518 (1819).

[96] Chap. iv, p. 118.

[97] See my article on "Histories of the Supreme Court of the United States Written from the Federalist Point of View," 4 *Southwestern Pol. and Soc. Sci. Quar.* (June, 1923), 1.

[98] Felix Frankfurter, ed., *Mr. Justice Holmes* (New York, 1931), p. 44.

The result of the adoption of so large a part of the Federalist program as features of American constitution, notes Arthur Twining Hadley, accounts for the fact that the whole political and social system of the United States is based on the preservation of property rights far more completely than such rights have been protected in any European country.[90] Clauses in the Constitution, said Hadley, "which were at first intended to prevent sectional strife, and to protect the people of one locality against arbitrary legislation in another, became a means of strengthening vested rights as a whole against the possibility of legislative or executive interference. . . . They indirectly became a powerful means of establishing the American courts in the position which they now enjoy as arbiters between the legislature and the property owners." The essential ideas and much of the preliminary groundwork for the doctrines of political and economic *laissez faire* which characterized political thinking and many judicial decisions during the nineteenth century are to be found in the decisions of the Supreme Court from 1810 to 1835. Constitutional doctrines were thus formulated and announced which, though remaining dormant for many years, could readily be called forth again when a due process clause was added to the Fourteenth Amendment and when the extension of the regulatory powers of the states afforded an opportunity for the exercise of enlarged supervisory powers by the Supreme Court over acts affecting property rights.

The antidemocratic or antirepublican doctrines which the Supreme Court gradually adopted and fostered in its opinions gave a political cast to the work of the Court which was frequently commented upon in the public press and in the halls of Congress. In the debate on the Force Bill giving President Jackson authority, if necessary, to coerce South Carolina, Senator Bibb characterized the most important phases of the Court's work as follows:

If the Judges of the Supreme Court are to have the final and exclusive authority to settle political questions, touching encroachments upon the reserved powers of the States, and all other political questions arising under the Constitution, then, superadded to those qualifications which have heretofore been thought essential for a judge, the primary considerations in selecting him ought to be, in what political school has he been brought up? What are his political opinions on certain great contested political questions? To what political party does he belong? I respect a court of justice, but I abhor a party court. Let us, not by construction, transform a court of justice into a political council of state. Let us not transform the emblem of justice into the emblem of power. Let us not defile the sanctuary of justice with the passions of political parties contending for political powers.

If the Supreme Court is once acknowledged to be the ultimate tribunal for settling the boundaries of political power between the federal government and the state gov-

---

[90] *Undercurrents in American Politics* (New Haven, 1915), pp. 33, 42.

ernments, so as to bind the parties to the compact, then it will inevitably follow that the Court will be the subject of political party strife. Reform in the court, by infusing a new spirit by other or additional Judges, will become the subject of political party strife as much as reform in the executive administration. The majority of Congress and the Executive might at any time add to the Bench of the Supreme Court a sufficient number of Judges to carry an important question of political power.[100]

It was the attempted settlement of the conflicts of power between the nation and the states which made the Supreme Court the center of public discussion and controversy for almost two decades.

THE SUPREME COURT AND THE ISSUE OF NATIONALISM VERSUS STATE RIGHTS

In evaluating the work of the Supreme Court from 1789 to 1835, so far as its relations to government and politics are concerned, it is necessary to review some of the ground previously covered, particularly certain phases of the problems and issues involved in the adjustment of federal and state relations. During the period of the Revolution and of the government under the Articles of Confederation, the preponderance of evidence indicates that the colonies as they were transformed into states regarded themselves as independent political units. It is true that from the beginning of the Revolution there was a central agency to which were delegated some of the most important functions of common defense and protection. The Continental Congresses, acting as this central agency, not only performed functions that were delegated to them, but also assumed the position of a *de facto* government to conduct the war for the states and to deal with foreign powers in bringing the war to a successful conclusion. But at this time no one would have doubted the right of any one of the states to withdraw from the central agency and to discontinue its participation in the war or to engage in a separate war in accordance with its own discretion. Some of the states conducted their own military and naval campaigns and engaged in such foreign relations as appeared to them desirable. The *de facto* condition of independence and of state sovereignty was explicitly sanctioned and confirmed in the Articles of Confederation adopted in 1781.[101]

There were, of course, some colonial and state leaders who as nationalists or imperialists placed the common interests uppermost. They thought in terms of the formation of a permanent national government for the states, and they deprecated the extreme tendencies toward separateness and independence among the states. Such national or "organic"

---

[100] *Cong. Debates,* IX, pt. 1, p. 293.
[101] Cf. above, chap. iii.

conceptions,[102] as they are sometimes called, were undoubtedly concerned with the future and with the hope that these ideas might be put into enduring institutional form. But from 1776 to 1789 the nationalists represented a small minority group. The conduct of the war, the negotiation of peace, and the consequent national and international problems tended to foster the doctrines and theories of nationalism. Moreover, economic and social problems following the war and the depression which ensued exaggerated the weaknesses of the state governments, which were largely under the control of the radical and democratic groups, and brought to the forefront the failures of the central agency as an effective government for the union of states. These conditions prepared the way for the calling of the Constitutional Convention at Philadelphia and for the strengthening of the bonds of the union. But at this time the states, as states, were dominant.

The conservative reaction against the democratic theories and philosophy which prevailed during the period from 1776 to 1787 gave the conservatives an opportunity to embody in the draft of the Constitution some of the "organic" or nationalist doctrines. But the majority of the people in most of the states belonged to the Democratic or radical parties, and it was necessary to win over some members of those parties in order to secure the adoption of a new form of government. For this reason, some of the provisions designed to secure a stronger and more effective union were drafted in such a way as not to offend the liberal and democratic leaders of the states. These provisions were so worded as to be susceptible of interpretation either favorable to the union or to the states. If the testimony of Gouverneur Morris may be accepted as true, the provisions relating to judicial powers were among those left purposely vague.[103]

Some of the delegates to the Convention desired to subordinate the states to the authorities of the union and thus to establish a real federal state in place of a confederate form of government. Supporters of the Constitution, as well as a few of its opponents, said that the states would no longer be sovereign if the Constitution were adopted and put into operation. But it does not seem likely that the Constitution would have been adopted if such views had been freely expressed and had been fully understood. The entire process of adoption of the Constitution was carried out with the general understanding that states could adopt or reject the instrument, that they could adopt it provisionally, and that once a resolution of adoption was passed, important changes in the federal rela-

---

[102] Cf. above, chap. iii.
[103] Jared Sparks, *Life of Gouverneur Morris* (Boston, 1832), III: 323.

tionship could be made to meet persistent objections. The procedure was frankly regarded as experimental, and there was little in the public discussions of the time to indicate that such a revolutionary change was taking place as that from a confederacy to a federation with coercive powers over the states and from which a state that joined could not withdraw.

But the Federalists who desired to see a strong and permanent union established were largely responsible for the adoption of the Constitution, and it was mainly the members of this party who were placed in office in order to set the machinery of the federal government in motion.[104] It was not long before the members of this party attempted to assert authority which involved a definite and emphatic subordination of the states to what was declared to be a "sovereign union." The radical and the democratic groups which in many of the states strongly opposed the adoption of the Constitution, partly on the ground that state sovereignty was in danger, now joined the new Democratic-Republican party and opposed the interpretation of the Constitution in such a way as to form an effective federal union. This party secured the adoption of the Eleventh Amendment to counteract the assertive nationalist views of the Supreme Court in the *Chisholm Case,*[105] was responsible for the adoption and circulation of the Virginia and Kentucky Resolutions in which the doctrine of state sovereignty was first formally declared, and secured the election of Thomas Jefferson to the presidency on a platform distinctly antinationalistic. Whatever gains had been made toward the establishment of a real federal state in the adoption of the Constitution and during the Federalist Administrations of Washington and Adams, it was now evident that the trend was more nearly in the direction of the conditions prevailing under the Articles of Confederation than in accord with the policies of Washington, Hamilton, and Adams.

It was not only the Democratic-Republican party which espoused doctrines favorable to the support of state powers in preference to the development of a virile and assertive nationalism, but when Jefferson was in the presidential office, the Federalists also talked freely of secession from the union. They attempted to found a northern, in opposition to a southern, confederacy, and finally advocated nullification doctrines in opposition to Jefferson's embargo policies and Madison's conduct of the War

---

[104] In the opinion of Charles A. Beard the Constitutional Convention did not dissolve until the economic measures which were necessary to make the Constitution a living instrument were fully realized. *Economic Origins of Jeffersonian Democracy* (New York, 1915), pp. 105, 106.

[105] 2 Dallas 419 (1793).

of 1812. The antinationalist activities of New England culminated in the Hartford Convention which presented its program for a reconstruction of the Constitution at the inopportune time when the War of 1812 was coming to a close and the nationalistic views engendered by the conflict were in the ascendancy. Nationalist doctrines prevailed a few years after the close of the war when the national bank was rechartered and when the policies of protection to manufactures and of federal aid for internal improvements were favored by members of the Democratic-Republican party who later, as advocates of State rights and a strict construction of the Constitution, opposed both of these policies of the party.

In the last few years of the decade 1810–1820, the leaders of the Democratic-Republican party, including Jefferson, Madison, and Monroe, turned toward a strict construction of the Constitution. The Supreme Court, however, began in 1816 its great series of nationalistic pronouncements with Justice Story's opinions in *Martin v. Hunter's Lessee*[106] and Chief Justice Marshall's opinions in *McCulloch v. Maryland*[107] and *Cohens v. Virginia*.[108] In opposition to the views expressed in these opinions, the doctrines of State rights and of a strict construction of the Constitution were ably expounded by Spencer Roane and John Taylor with the support and approval of Jefferson. The period of the Revolution, of the Confederation, of the formation of the Constitution, and of the Virginia and Kentucky Resolutions were reviewed to demonstrate that public men generally thought in terms of a confederation, with the states being sovereigns instead of being absorbed into the union of states, except for the time when the Federalists unsuccessfully tried to put into effect their extreme centralizing principles. Nationalistic principles were so definitely repudiated by the people that men might rightfully feel and think that the attempt to foist these principles upon the nation by means of legislative action or judicial construction was quite indefensible. From this feeling was fostered the spirit of opposition to the Supreme Court and resentment at its repeated interferences with the powers of the states which threatened a thorough reorganization of the Court and culminated in an effort to repeal the twenty-fifth section of the Judiciary Act of 1789.

Though the Court was not directly involved in the controversy over nullification in South Carolina, the proceedings taken to sustain the authority of the federal government, in part at least, were in accord with the doctrines formulated by the Justices in their opinions. Following the President's proclamation and message relating to nullification, Justice Story wrote: "The Chief Justice and myself have become his

---

[106] 1 Wheaton 394 (1816).   [107] 4 Wheaton 316 (1819).   [108] 6 Wheaton 264 (1821).

[Jackson's] warmest supporters, and shall continue so just as long as he maintains the principles contained in them."[109] With Andrew Jackson, John Marshall, and Daniel Webster joining in support of the supremacy of the federal government, the Supreme Court, which had been under attack since the rendering of its decisions in *Fletcher v. Peck*[110] and *Martin v. Hunter's Lessee*,[111] found its position and constitutional doctrines somewhat strengthened. But it was the doctrines of nationalism as opposed to State rights, repeatedly asserted by the Court in its opinions, which more than any of its other pronouncements made the Court the center of political attacks.

With nullification of federal laws by the states threatening, with disagreements among the Justices on constitutional issues, and with Jacksonian democratic ideas beginning to prevail in state and federal judicial construction, Marshall surveyed the situation with a melancholy outlook. "Things to the South wear a very serious aspect," he wrote to Justice Story in 1832,

if we can trust appearances the leaders are determined to risk all the consequences of dismemberment. I cannot entirely dismiss the hope that they may be deserted by their followers—at least to such an extent as to produce a pause at the Rubicon. They undoubtedly believe that Virginia will support them. I think they are mistaken both with respect to Virginia and North Carolina. I do not think either State will embrace this mad and wicked measure.[112]

Because the people of his own state as well as those throughout the South generally repudiated his political and constitutional doctrines, Marshall regarded them as insane.[113] In this section he thought political prejudice was too strong to yield to any degree of merit, and he did not see any hope for the adoption of sound principles in any other part of the nation.[114] Though Jackson and many of his party approved Marshall's doctrine, so far as the issue of nullification was concerned, it was evident that they disapproved of other phases of Hamiltonian Federalism which the Chief Justice had also consistently interpreted as a part of the federal fundamental law.

Writing of the period of American history from 1816 to 1860, John W.

---

[109] *Life and Letters*, II: 119.

[110] 6 Cranch 87 (1810).

[111] 1 Wheaton 394 (1816).

[112] Letter to Story, Oct. 6, 1834, Massachusetts Hist. Soc. *Proceedings*, 2d ser., XIV: 350–352, and John Edward Oster, *The Political and Economic Doctrines of John Marshall* (New York, 1914), pp. 141, 143.

[113] In Dec., 1834, he wrote: "We are insane on the subject of the Bank. Its friends, who are not numerous, dare not, a few excepted, to avow themselves. You will perceive by the message of our governor that he is a complete nullifier in the Georgia sense of the term." Massachusetts Hist. Soc. *Proceedings*, 2d ser., XIV: 359.

[114] See Story, *Life and Letters*, II: 172, 173.

Burgess maintained that there is not one scintilla of justification for secession and rebellion, and that

the South must acknowledge its error as well as its defeat in regard to these things, and that, too, not with lip service, but from the brain and the heart and the manly will, before any real concord in thought and feeling, any real national brotherhood, can be established. This is not too much to demand, simply because it is right, and nothing can be settled, as Mr. Lincoln said, until it is settled right. Any interpretation of this period of American history which does not demonstrate to the South its error will be worthless, simply because it will not be true; and unless we are men enough to hear and accept and stand upon the truth, it is useless to endeavor to find a bond of real union between us. In a word, the conviction of the South of its error in secession and rebellion is absolutely indispensable to the establishment of national cordiality; and the history of this period which fails to do this will fail in accomplishing one of the highest works of history, the reconciliation of men to the plans of Providence for their perfection.[115]

With this purpose in mind, many American histories have been written. And others, aiming to confirm the view expressed on a monument erected in honor of Confederate soldiers who died for the cause of the Confederacy, have defended the cause of the South. The epitaph reads: "Erected in honor of the brave soldiers who died to preserve and protect rights guaranteed by the Constitution." The preceding pages have not been written to defend or to oppose the doctrines of nullification or secession. An attempt has been made rather to reëvaluate the evidence relating to federal relationships during the first decades of the American republic concerning which able, conscientious, and high-minded statesmen differed. This evidence shows that there were at least defensible grounds for the contentions of each of the major parties to the greatest political and constitutional dispute of the nineteenth century, and each party using the Constitution as a background could claim that they were contending for rights guaranteed by that instrument.

The last years of Marshall's Chief Justiceship were embittered by the attacks on the Court, by the appointment of new Justices who disagreed with his constitutional doctrines, and by the threats of nullification which gave support to the view that a confederacy and not a federation had been formed in 1789. But when the future looked so dark to Marshall that he forecast the destruction of the union, forces and influences were at work which did not appear promising to those who undertook to put into effect doctrines of nullification and secession. Though the historical background before 1830 gave stronger confirmation to the doctrine of State rights than to that of nationalism or consolidation (as it was often called), the creative work of the Federalist party in the forma-

---

[115] *The Middle Period: 1817–1858* (New York, 1901), preface, p. xi.

tive years of the federal government, the nationalist movement which accompanied and followed the War of 1812, and the extension of the terms and phrases of the Constitution by Chief Justice Marshall and by Justice Story were beginning to bear fruit. Sentiment in New England and in the West began to support nationalist principles and a liberal construction of the Constitution, at the same time that southern statesmen espoused more vigorously than ever doctrines of State rights and a strict construction of the Constitution. Public opinion throughout most of the country supported Webster rather than Hayne in the debate over the Foot Resolution. Much to the surprise of Marshall, Andrew Jackson, supporting the Federalist doctrine that a federation had been formed in 1789, refused to permit a state to defy federal authorities in the enforcement of the laws. Conciliatory measures, both on the part of the federal government and of the state of South Carolina, averted, for the time being, civil war. But the issue whether the government of the United States was a federation or a confederation remained undetermined, and with the issue of slavery, to which it became irrevocably attached, it furnished a fruitful ground for controversy until both sides saw no other alternative than an appeal to arms. This appeal, however, was deferred long enough to give an opportunity for the new political order which Marshall envisaged to gain a firmer foothold upon the sentiments and imagination of the people—a new order which was to be modified but not radically transformed by the impact of democratic doctrines and the revival of the spirit of localism.

The Spokesman for a New Political Order

The presentation of Chief Justice Marshall's contributions to American constitutional law in the preceding pages gives an inadequate evaluation of his work. It is in fact necessary to view this work, not only in relation to the preceding decades, but also in relation to future developments, the course of which were either determined or strongly influenced by Marshall's decisions. Only in this manner can the nature and significance of the new political order which Marshall was constructing be understood. According to one of the estimates of the work of the Supreme Court from 1801 to 1835, there were 1215 reported cases and 1106 opinions filed, 519 of which were delivered by Chief Justice Marshall. In this same period, 62 decisions were rendered in the field of constitutional law, and in 36 of these Marshall spoke for the Court.[116] The Chief Justice dissented in

[116] Henry Hitchcock, "Constitutional Development in the United States as Influenced by Chief Justice Marshall," in *Constitutional History of the United States as Seen in the Development of American Law* (New York, 1889), pp. 36 ff.

eight cases. Only a few important decisions affecting the public law of the country were delivered by Marshall's Associates.[117] In one of these, *Martin v. Hunter's Lessee*,[118] Marshall was personally interested because of the purchase with his brother of a tract of land originally belonging to the Fairfax heirs; in another, *Ogden v. Saunders*,[119] the Chief Justice joined with the dissenters. The few decisions rendered by Marshall involving constitutional questions profoundly affected political and economic trends in the United States.

The significance of *Marbury v. Madison*[120] in the establishment of judicial review of acts of the state and federal legislatures is generally known and appreciated. This decision was soon followed by a broad and elastic interpretation of the grant of jurisdiction of the federal courts with respect to the review of inferior tribunals. And in these early years of Marshall's Chief Justiceship, Justice Story's opinion in *Swift v. Tyson*[121] was foreshadowed in the comment that there was a general commercial law to be applied by the federal courts. The organic or nationalist philosophy concerning the founding of the American government was accepted and incorporated as one of the constitutional dogmas, despite countervailing facts and prevalent opinions to the contrary. But acceding to the persistent criticisms and demands of the Democratic-Republicans, Marshall joined his Associates in the declaration that the federal courts had no common law jurisdiction. The scope of the contract clause was extended to include a grant made by a state legislature, and hence such a grant was not subject to revocation so as to divest vested rights, nor was a state permitted to revoke a grant of immunity from taxation.

Marshall approved Story's strongly nationalistic reasoning in *Martin v. Hunter's Lessee*[122] and soon thereafter supported the cause of nationalism in one of his greatest opinions, that rendered in *McCulloch v. Maryland*.[123] In this case Congressional authority to establish a national bank was approved, and the Hamiltonian doctrine of implied powers was declared to be a necessary phase of constitutional construction.

---

[117] Twenty-six decisions involving constitutional questions were rendered by the Associate Justices. Another estimate of the constitutional opinions rendered from 1801–1835 is 64. In these cases, 40 opinions were rendered by Marshall, 10 by Story, and 14 by all the other Justices. Vincent M. Barnett, Jr., "An Appraisal of the Decisions of Chief Justice Marshall Relative to Constitutional Law" (Thesis submitted for degree of Master of Arts, Los Angeles, University of California, June, 1936).

[118] 1 Wheaton 304 (1816).

[119] 12 Wheaton 213 (1827).

[120] 1 Cranch 137 (1803).

[121] 16 Peters 1 (1842).

[122] 1 Wheaton 304 (1816).

[123] 4 Wheaton 316 (1819).

About the same time a state grant of a charter to a college was held to be irrevocable except with the approval of the trustees of the institution and the donors of funds for its support, and, as a consequence, private educational institutions as well as other corporate agencies were placed in a semi-independent status in the American economy. These outstanding decisions in their political and social effects were soon followed by two others which greatly limited the effect of the Eleventh Amendment, so far as the prohibition of suits against the states was concerned, and made the states subject to the surveillance of the federal courts with respect to the rights claimed under the federal Constitution, laws, and treaties. With a denial of the Jeffersonian principle of a strict construction of the Constitution, the term interstate commerce was defined so as to include traffic and commercial intercourse within the confines of the states, and, by the famous "original package doctrine," the transportation of goods into a state could not be restricted or interfered with by state action until the goods were offered for sale or had mingled with the general property within the state.

The Chief Justice, dissenting in *Ogden v. Saunders*,[124] defended a doctrine favoring the protection of vested rights which, though not accepted by his Associates, was later to be included in the broad scope given by interpretation to the phrase due process of law as included in the Fifth and Fourteenth Amendments. Concerning this and related decisions of Marshall, Harold J. Laski observes that:

In no other country has economic development been so largely shaped by judicial decision. Anyone who examines the first fifty years of the court's history will find the clue to its attitude in that line of decisions of which *Fletcher v. Peck*[125] and the *Dartmouth College Case*[126] are the most notable, where the purpose of the Judges was to protect the vested interests of property from invasion by state legislatures which were being driven by the economic difficulties of their constituents to inflation, the reduction of debts, and the cancellation of property rights. This epoch of judicial nationalism, so remarkably inaugurated by Marshall, was obviously an expression of Federalist effort to secure the conditions under which commerce could flourish without interference from those who had suffered through the poverty resulting from the Revolutionary War. This explains the court's view both of the Commerce Clause, as in *Gibbons v. Ogden*,[127] and the "obligation of contract" clause in the Constitution.

These first fifty years summarize a period in the history of the United States in which the pattern of a modern industrial society is only beginning to emerge. The work necessary for that stage was well accomplished by Marshall and his immediate successors. From 1830 until the Civil War the court hardly needed to do more than apply the canons of constitutionalism it had already laid down.[128]

---

[124] 12 Wheaton 213 (1827).
[125] 6 Cranch 37 (1810).
[126] 4 Wheaton 518 (1819).
[127] 9 Wheaton 1 (1824).
[128] *The State in Theory and Practice* (New York, 1935), pp. 156–159.

The doctrine that one of the necessary agencies or instrumentalities of a federal system of government may not be interfered with, either by taxation or regulation, by one of the other agencies of such a system was given a wide scope, so as to lay a basis for a vast system of tax-exempt securities. And the states were denied the authority to provide for the issuance of any form of paper currency which might be expected to circulate as a legal tender within the state. During the last few years of Marshall's service on the Bench, the strongly nationalist viewpoint in *Gibbons v. Ogden* was modified by the adoption of Chancellor Kent's principle of concurrent power over commerce both by the states and the nation, when Congress had not assumed authority over a special phase of the subject. But despite this modification of earlier views, ground was broken for an effective control over state action affecting commerce by refusing to permit the states to interfere with the free flow of commerce within their borders. The limitations of the contract clause were relaxed somewhat by the requirement that to be valid an exemption from taxation by a corporation against state action must be expressly provided in its charter. There was a tendency to decline jurisdiction in certain cases affecting the validity of titles to lands as defined by state law, and the amendments to the Constitution providing for the protection of personal and individual rights were held applicable only to the federal government. These modifications of earlier views did not materially affect the substantial and far-reaching features of the constitutional structure which Marshall outlined and envisaged.

The Chief Justice, through his decisions and through his views elsewhere expressed, had gone a long way toward the establishment of the supremacy of the Judiciary over the other departments of the government in the interpretation of the federal Constitution, laws, and treaties: he had taken long steps toward the establishment of the supremacy of the federal government over the states, not only where express grants of power were concerned, but also where the federal authority could be based upon mere implication; he supported the authority of the federal government in its right to lay a general and indefinite embargo on foreign imports, to control the state militia, and to promote internal improvements; he developed the doctrine of implied powers, thus giving broad scope to the necessary and proper clause and the general welfare clauses of the Constitution; he greatly restricted the states' control over contracts and over corporations; and he upheld the paramount obligation of treaties and aided in the extension of the admiralty and maritime jurisdiction of the federal courts.

It is generally recognized that the federal Constitution was framed to overcome defects in the Articles of Confederation, but, Max Farrand notes, "it does not seem to be recognized that experience had shown certain specific defects to exist, that the Convention was called for the purpose of correcting those specific defects, and that the Constitution embodied in itself little more than the remedies for those defects."[129] But building on the mere framework for the establishment of a government for a nation, Chief Justice Marshall had filled in the gaps and had found federal powers, not only in the vague phrases of the document, but also in the unexpressed intentions or silences of the Constitution. "His work of building up and working out the Constitution was accomplished," maintains Lord Bryce, "not so much by the decisions he gave, as by the judgments in which he expounded the principles of these decisions, judgments which for their philosophical breadth, the luminous exactness of their reasoning, and the fine political sense which pervades them, have never been surpassed and rarely equaled by the most famous jurists of modern Europe or of ancient Rome."[130]

Using the general phrases of the Constitution as a lever, Marshall lifted the American system of government out of the morass, as he saw it, of the dominance and control over public affairs by separate and independent state sovereignties. He thought the American republic was "not destined to perish, if it shall perish, by the overwhelming power of the national government; but by the resisting and counteracting power of the state sovereignties. . . . In our government the centrifugal force was far greater than the centripetal."[131] But the centripetal forces were destined to overwhelm the centrifugal. Marshall's decisions and the Civil War were the main factors in accomplishing a shift in sovereignty from the states to the nation. This shift was in the nature of a revolution just as the framing of the Constitution and its adoption by nine States instead of the required unanimous action was a revolution. It was a revolution sanctioned not only by military force but also by the predominant public sentiment of the nation. Marshall, in outlining the directions of the new political order, thus prepared the way for the future course of development of the American Republic, with the control of government and public affairs primarily in the hands of judges rather than in executives or legislators.

In explanation and extenuation of the support of these doctrines by a Judge of the Supreme Court, it may be noted again that it was customary in the early years of our history for the Judges, while serving on the

---

[129] "The Federal Constitution and the Defects of the Confederation," 2 *Amer. Pol. Sci. Rev.* (Nov., 1908), 532.

[130] *The American Commonwealth* (New York, 1912) I: 386.

[131] *Miscellaneous Writings of Joseph Story*, p. 684.

Bench, to take a much more active interest in politics than current ideas and practices would approve today. But more significant is the fact that the federal Constitution necessarily dealt with issues of great political and economic significance. The Court might have adopted the common practice and procedure followed in most other countries where written constitutions have formed the basis for official action of regarding these political and economic questions as not appropriate for judicial consideration and determination. The prevailing ideas, however, gave encouragement and sanction for Judges to deal with questions primarily political in nature. Certain provisions of the federal Constitution furnished at least an implied sanction for the assertion of such authority, and, finally, Federalist political principles made it imperative that the written Constitution be interpreted and applied by the Judiciary rather than by the departments subject to more direct popular influences and controls. It is readily understood, then, why Chief Justice Marshall for more than thirty years bore a large share of the brunt of the attacks on localism, particularism, and State rights. He has been rightfully lauded as a statesman and a constructive jurist for his share in carving a real federation—a nation—out of the discordant and disparate elements which were dominant during the greater part of the time he served on the federal Bench.

The process of changing and molding the meaning of the fundamental law to accomplish this end, important as it was in the building of the nation, ran counter to the prevailing political feelings and sentiment of the time and caused much feeling of resentment, bitterness, and opposition to the federal government. Westel W. Willoughby has pointed out that "the circumstances that the Constitution was so indefinitely worded that it could be interpreted as creating a national state, without doing too much violence to the meaning of terms, enabled the people, through Congress and the Supreme Court, to satisfy their desire for political unity without resort to open revolutionary means. Still it must be conceded by those who take this view, that however peaceably and gradually the transformation to a federal state was effected, the change was revolutionary in character. It does not help them to point to the manner in which its steps were clothed in apparent legal form."[132]

Those viewing American history from the nationalist standpoint have applauded Marshall for his constructive statesmanship and have condemned Roane, Taylor, Jefferson, and Calhoun for supporting a type of local, selfish, and sectional politics which led in the direction of secession and civil war. From a different perspective, the work of Marshall may

---

[132] *The American Constitutional System* (New York, 1904), pp. 32, 33.

well be regarded as preparing the way for civil strife. The process of construing the states out of their rights and privileges, laudable as it may seem today, aroused antagonisms which needed only an appropriate incentive to lead men to the point where rational adjustment and compromise were regarded as impossible. Was not the stage set for the conflict of 1860 during the decades from 1815 to 1835 while the Supreme Court was engaged in the process of the development of new concepts of nationalism differing markedly from the disparate, local, and independent political ideas which characterized the periods of the Revolution, of the critical period, and of the postwar administrations of the Democratic-Republican party?[133]

Marshall is frequently credited with having saved the Constitution and the union established by it. "We feel almost sure," said John F. Dillon, "that a narrow, rigid, iron-clad, jealous construction of the Constitution would have changed our whole history and perhaps have led to the shipwreck of the Union."[134] Or, as it is frequently put, the union could not have withstood the strain of the Civil War had it not been for Marshall's work in support of nationalism. But it is significant that the enduring character of the Constitution as a charter for the establishment of a truly federal or national government was settled only through the arbitrament of war—a war the responsibility for which is usually placed upon Jefferson, Roane, Taylor, and Calhoun. It is merely a matter of conjecture, however, that the union might not have survived if the Jeffersonian doctrines of constitutional interpretation had prevailed.

If more complete ideas of popular control had prevailed, the process of centralization would no doubt have moved more slowly with perhaps some temporary setbacks. It is doubtful whether broad construction of the Constitution, the purpose of which was to extend the power of the federal government, would have become such a grave political issue as it was from 1815 to 1835 when the Court was to a large extent the center of attack. It was in this period, when the Court in its political inclinations had marked Federalist tendencies and the other departments of government were under Democratic control, that resistance to federal encroachments developed a spirit of bitterness which often brought threats of rebellion. The states feared federal encroachments on commerce and transportation, on slavery, and on internal improvements, and the sentiment was frequently expressed that it was better to endure

---

[133] "So it came to pass that John Marshall and the Supreme Court became a center about which swirled the forces of a fast-gathering storm that raged with increasing fury until its thunders were the war of cannon, its lightning the flashes of battle." From Beveridge, *op. cit.*, IV: 370.

[134] Dillon, *op. cit.*, I: 384; see also address of E. J. Phelps, Dillon, *op. cit.*, III: 389.

rebellion than to become "slaves of a great consolidated government." The Federalists, under the leadership of Hamilton, Marshall, and Webster, wished to convert by means of interpretation what was thought by the majority of the people to be a confederate form of government with the center of gravity in the states to a federal government with undoubted national supremacy and an unlimited opportunity for development of federal powers. And they tried to make it appear that an attack on the centralizing tendencies of Congress and the Supreme Court was an attack upon the union. When a court participates in the settlement of such a grave political issue, it must of necessity be subject to acrimonious public attacks. The fact that this department was beyond the ordinary reach of popular control made the resentment of opponents of its decisions having political implications all the greater. It was generally believed that the Court was quietly and unostentatiously absorbing the rights of the states, and destroying those of the people, without a full realization of the revolutionary character of its decisions.

If Democratic policies and principles had prevailed, the spirit of bitterness which developed from the covert undermining of state powers would have had less occasion for vigorous development. With a more natural and direct outlet for political feelings and prejudices and with greater freedom for the expression of particularist tendencies, may it not have been that the issues of expansion and of slavery could have been settled without such long and bitter controversies?

Moreover, if the Federalist doctrines of judicial protection to vested rights and of implied limitations on legislatures in favor of private rights of person and of property had been rejected, the economic and industrial development of the country through private capital would no doubt have been less rapid. Public interests would have prevailed where private interests gained ascendancy under the Federalist regime. Private property and corporate interests would not have become so impregnably intrenched as to be in many respects beyond public control,[135] and the doctrines of political and economic *laissez faire* which prevailed during the latter part of the nineteenth century would not so readily have found judicial support. Of greatest import, however, was the extraordinary and, at times, unwarranted mingling of constitutional law and politics.

The issue whether the federal Constitution, as put into effect in 1789,

---

[135] See my article on "Histories of the Supreme Court of the United States Written from the Federalist Point of View," 4 *Southwestern Pol. and Soc. Sci. Quar.* (June, 1923), 1, from which a few extracts have been used in the preceding paragraphs; also, "Judicial Review of Legislation in the United States and the Doctrines of Vested Rights and of Implied Limitations on Legislatures," 2 *Texas Law Rev.* (Apr., June, 1924), and 3 *Texas Law Rev.* (Dec., 1924), and *The Revival of Natural Law Concepts* (Cambridge, 1930), especially pts. ii, iii.

was a supreme law to be interpreted authoritatively and finally by the Courts, or a political document whose interpretation and application belonged equally to the three great departments established by the Constitution, remained undetermined, as Marshall surveyed the situation from 1830 to 1835.[136] During the first few decades of American history, the Constitution was regarded as more in the nature of a political document than a supreme law in the legal sense. Constitutional law and politics were freely mingled. For more than thirty years Chief Justice Marshall had used every available opportunity to uphold the supremacy of the terms and provisions of the Constitution, the supremacy of the federal over the state agencies, and the supremacy of the Judges over all other public officials as interpreters of the Constitution. The theory that the Judges were the mechanical mouthpieces of the law was used as a cloak to conceal the regular and persistent announcement of political opinions in the field of constitutional law. These opinions were prepared and presented on the hypothesis that they were necessary to save the union. In fact, beginning with the defeat of John Adams by Thomas Jefferson for the presidency, the advocates of Federalism began to propagandize the people by saying that the fate of the union depended upon the acceptance of the main principles of this party.

It is, of course, difficult to refute the contention that Federalism saved the union and that the views in opposition, had they been adopted, would have destroyed the union. Jefferson and many of his followers, after believing in a somewhat mild form of judicial review of legislation and in certain other checks on popular rule, came to the conclusion, as a result of political experience, that on vital issues it was better that the will of the people, or more literally the will of the electorate, ought to prevail, rather than to set up an oligarchy of judges or other officials who were presumed to know what the people wanted. Just as Hamilton, Marshall, and Webster thought it better from the standpoint of political expediency to keep certain matters, especially those relating to property and contracts, out of the hands of the electorate, so the Democrats on the same grounds tended to favor ultimate popular control even over private rights. In most respects the Hamilton-Marshall theories have been adopted in American constitutional law and the Jeffersonian popular control theory has been discarded, at least so far as fundamental personal and private rights are concerned. It is true, indeed, that "federalism and conservatism rallied under the captaincy of Chief Justice Marshall, and from behind the Supreme Court barricade developed a subtle offensive of ideas—the supremacy of the nation and the sanctity

[136] See above, chap. i.

of property—that in due time would leave little of Jeffersonian democracy but a memory and a tradition."[137]

Marshall did not live to see the triumph of the conservative, nationalist, and anti-Jeffersonian doctrines which he had struggled to make a part of constitutional law. But certain fundamentals of American politics and public law were not merely well formulated and effectively expressed—they were also gaining in public favor. Among these were the following principles or doctrines: that in accordance with the terms and provisions of the written fundamental law, the government was divided into three separate and coördinate departments, with the Judiciary set apart from the regular machinery of government to serve, not only as an umpire for the adjustment of the relations between the nation and the states, but also to perform the duty of seeing that the other departments keep within their prescribed limits; that the Constitution, though written, could grow by interpretation as well as by amendment and that there were distinct advantages in the slow and case-by-case growth by interpretation; that corporate bodies created by the states to engage in multitudinous functions could operate without too drastic or serious interference with their activities after the charters were granted; that the protection of acquired or vested rights both as a constitutional requirement and as a feature of natural law was one of the plain and unmistakable duties of the Judiciary; and that the process of constitutional interpretation necessarily required that the Judges participate in the settlement of political and economic policies. In short, the essential features and principles of what has appropriately been termed the American doctrine of judicial supremacy[138] were so well formulated that future Justices could add little that was new.

It is not within the scope of this study to undertake to give an estimate of the significance of Chief Justice Marshall's work in the light of the political and constitutional developments of the past century. Whether, as Justice Holmes phrased it, "after Hamilton and the Constitution itself, Marshall's work proved more than a strong intellect, a good style, personal ascendancy in his Court, courage, justice and the convictions of his party"[139] may well be a matter of doubt. Viewed from the vantage ground of American law and politics of 1835, however, the Chief Justice had made an enviable record—a record which was regarded as laudable and impressive even by those who disagreed with his political doctrines. President Jackson voiced what appeared to be the prevailing opinion

---

[137] Morison and Commager, *op. cit.*, I: 293.
[138] See my work under this title, 2d ed., pp. 27, 28.
[139] *Collected Legal Papers* (New York, 1920), p. 269.

among the Democrats, when he wrote that "having set a high value upon the learning, talents and patriotism of Judge Marshall, and upon the good he has done his country in one of its most exalted and responsible offices, I have been gratified at seeing that sentiments equally favorable have been cherished generally by his fellow citizens, and that there has been no disposition, even with those who dissent from some of his expositions of our constitutional law (of whom it is perhaps proper that I should say I am one), to withhold from his memory the highest tribute of respect."[140] Even John C. Calhoun, whose views on federal relations Marshall abhorred and did all in his power to counteract, commended the Chief Justice as "that pure and upright magistrate who has so long, and with such distinguished honor to himself and the Union presided over its deliberations, with all the weight that belongs to an intellect of the first order, united with the most spotless integrity."[141]

It is fortunate, indeed, that the American government as it grew and prospered contained some of the essential ideas and doctrines not only of Hamilton and Marshall but also of Jefferson and Jackson. Andrew C. McLaughlin, commending the principles of Jeffersonian freedom— "principles which blossomed in America, and made America to be, not Europe but itself," observed that "there were many things to be done in America besides making a national Constitution and holding the Union together, wonderfully appealing as these deeds are to us. America had in addition to find expression for her real self, live out the fundamental purposes of democratic life, make actual, if she could, the philosophy of belief in men, and their capacity for self-control, widen and strengthen popular participation in government, make government the actual representative of an uncowed people, believing in themselves."[142] There was in Marshall nothing of what Beveridge calls "the humanitarian fervor"

---

[140] *Jackson Papers*, MSS, Letter of Sept. 18, 1835. On the other hand, William Leggett, editor of the *New York Evening Post*, expressed the view with which many Democrats concurred. Giving due recognition for his ability, attainments, and exemplary character, Leggett observed that "his political doctrines unfortunately were of the ultra-federal or aristocratic kind" and that, agreeing with Hamilton, he "distrusted the virtue and intelligence of the people, and was in favor of a strong and vigorous general government at the expense of the rights of the States and of the people. His judicial decisions of all questions involving political principles have been uniformly on the side of implied powers and a free construction of the Constitution." Leggett felt that it was gratifying that "the enormous powers of the supreme tribunal of the country will no longer be exercised by one whose cardinal maxim in politics inculcated distrust of popular intelligence and virtue, and whose constant object in the decision of all constitutional questions was to strengthen government at the expense of the people's rights." *New York Evening Post*, July 8, 10, 13, 28, 1835.

[141] *The Works of John C. Calhoun*, ed. by R. K. Cralle (New York, 1864), VI: 166.

[142] From review of Albert J. Beveridge's, *The Life of John Marshall* in 7 *Amer. Bar Assn. Jour.* (May, 1921), 231–233.

or, as expressed more emphatically in a recent work, "there was not a spark of liberalism in John Marshall."[143] Discounting the encomiums and laudatory comments frequently inspired by partisan feelings in addresses commemorating the career of Marshall, and recognizing the limitations concerning his outlook and interests with respect to democratic doctrines and humanitarian affairs, the record, as it stood in 1835, warranted the judgment made many years later by Justice Holmes "that if American law were to be represented by a single figure, sceptic and worshipper alike would agree without dispute that the figure could be one alone, and that one, John Marshall."[144] It would have been difficult at this time, however, to foresee the great powers and authority in the American federal system which the Supreme Court was destined to exercise and to exercise not only with marked success but also with profound effects upon government and politics both in the states and in the nation.

As Chief Justice Marshall was finishing his notable judicial career, Alexis de Tocqueville surveyed the American political scene and put his impressions into enduring form in his *Democracy in America*. He was struck by the growth of democracy in the United States where the people were supposed to reign without impediment. But to him more significant was the fact that effective barriers were placed in the way of the rule of the majority. Viewing American society in the third decade of the nineteenth century, de Tocqueville observed that the lawyers formed the most powerful counterforce to the democratic element, for, armed with the power of declaring laws to be unconstitutional, the American judge frequently interfered in political affairs. And, as he saw it, "scarcely any political question arises in the United States which is not resolved, sooner or later, into a judicial question." The power to declare an act of the legislature void, because being in conflict with the Constitution, is, in his opinion, the only power

which is peculiar to the American magistrate, but it gives rise to immense political influence. . . . The political power which the Americans have intrusted to their courts of justice is therefore immense. I am inclined to believe this practice of the American courts to be at once most favorable to liberty and to public order. . . . Within these limits, the power vested in the American courts of justice, of pronouncing a statute to be unconstitutional, forms one of the most powerful barriers which has ever been devised against the tyranny of political assemblies. . . .

The peace, prosperity, and the very existence of the Union are vested in the hands of the seven federal Judges. Without them, the Constitution would be a dead letter: the Executive appeals to them for assistance against the encroachments of the legislative power; the Legislature demands their protection against the assaults of the Execu-

[143] James Truslow Adams, *The Living Jefferson* (New York, 1936), p. 299. See this work for a favorable estimate of Jefferson's contribution to American life and thought.
[144] *Collected Legal Papers*, p. 270.

tive; they defend the Union from the disobedience of the States, the States from the exaggerated claims of the Union, the public interest against private interests, and the conservative spirit of stability against the fickleness of the democracy.[145]

Though the peculiar characteristics of the American system of government were taking shape slowly, it was apparent by this time that judicial tribunals were to become "forces of reserve in the army of civilization" and that the American people were to be essentially a "judge-ruled people."[146] Whereas lawyers in other countries had relatively little concern with the legal phases of the constitutional principles of government or with the basis on which the public administration operated, in the United States, lawyers and judges were charged with the "safekeeping of the Constitution." Owing to the relative infrequency of amendments to the fundamental law and to the steady and persistent process of judicial construction, it was becoming clear that in the field of constitutional law it was lawyer's law and not the people's law that was to prevail. And the method of the settlement of vital governmental policies through the medium of lawsuits between private individuals was well on its way to firm establishment as a fundamental feature of federal public law.

By placing the "safekeeping of the Constitution" in the hands of the Judiciary, some of the highest duties of statesmanship and some of the most delicate and difficult political problems were transferred for final determination from the halls of legislation to the Supreme Court.[147] The reason that the Supreme Court has gained so great a preëminence is due not a little to the fact that it is a political as well as a judicial body. In the performance of this dual function, it is, indeed, "safe to say that no man has left a greater impress, not only on the jurisprudence of the country, but upon the very framework of our institutions, than John Marshall. While he did not make the Constitution of the United States, he shaped it by his powerful and lucid opinions and by his influence with the great Court over which he presided."[148]

At the same time that Supreme Court decisions were being defied and the Court was being subjected to violent attacks in Congress and other public forums because of its nationalistic and antidemocratic bias, a spirit of veneration or worship was developing which, despite the setbacks of the Jackson era, the upheaval resulting from the Dred Scott decision, and the rebuffs encountered during the Civil War period,

---

[145] Alexis de Tocqueville, *Democracy in America*, trans. by Henry Reeve and edited with notes by Frances Bowen (Boston, 1882), I: 128–130, 191.

[146] See orations of Wayne MacVeagh and Charles J. Bonaparte, Dillon, *op. cit.*, I: 38 and II: 29.

[147] See address of A. B. Cummings, Dillon, *op. cit.*, II: 450 ff.

[148] From address of William B. Hornblower, Dillon, *op. cit.*, I: 340.

was to be revived with extraordinary vigor during the latter decades of the nineteenth century. The beginnings of such veneration or worship are difficult to trace. There was indeed little of veneration during the early decades following the establishment of the Court. For the better part of two decades after John Marshall's appointment as Chief Justice, the position and authority of the Supreme Court was too uncertain and precarious to find any marked evidences of veneration. There are occasional indications during the period from 1810 to 1820 of the emerging notion of the sanctity of the Constitution and of its primary oracle—the Supreme Court. Regardless of notable encounters in which his state, by 1825, had twice been the loser, Senator Barbour of Virginia thought well enough of the Court to describe it as "the sheet anchor which secured the safety of the vessel."[149] And Senator Van Buren of New York commented on the development of a sentiment of idolatry for the Supreme Court "which claims for its members an almost entire exemption from the fallibilities of human nature."[150] Slowly and with occasional setbacks people were becoming impressed, not only with the importance of the federal Judiciary, but also with the sanctity of the Supreme Court. In 1834 Edward Everett, commenting on Justice Story's career on the Bench, observed that he "rose immediately above the sphere of party; and with the ermine of office, put on the sacred robe of the Constitution and the law."[151]

As an institution which had very unpromising beginnings, the Supreme Court was gradually capturing the respect, loyalty, and admiration of the people, and, with the appointment to the Bench of a majority of Justices in sympathy with the principles and policies of Jacksonian democracy, criticisms of the Court quickly subsided. Moreover, the advocates of the extension of judicial powers supported it, not only as a conservative safeguard, but also as a means of protecting popular rights. The Constitution, which was essentially an instrument prepared to carry out the program and policies of one of the two leading parties in the country, had come to be looked upon much more than formerly as the people's law. The impression was gaining ground that the Supreme Court was a protecting agency that would stand between the people and their governments and in its interpretation and application of the Constitution would carry out the people's will.

---

[149] *Cong. Debates*, I, p. 586. See Frank I. Schechter, "The Early History of the Tradition of the Constitution," 9 *Amer. Pol. Sci. Rev.* (Nov., 1915), 707. This article exaggerates the sentiment for and the worship of the Constitution in the early decades.

[150] *Cong. Debates*, II, pt. i, pp. 420, 421. For similar views expressed by Senator Rowan of Kentucky, see *ibid.*, p. 442.

[151] *North American Review*, XXXVIII: 83 (1834).

Table of Cases

Index

Active, capture of, 270 ff.

Adams, James Truslow, quoted on: Hamliton, 191, 195; Jefferson, 219; Marshall, 409 n. 109

Adams, John: appointed partisan judges, 41–42, 117; favored dominance of rich, 62; lauded First Continental Congress, 99; device of, of checks and balances, 118; judiciary reorganization act in Administration of, 149, 177; recommended revision of judicial system, 149, 178, 180 and n. 87; few Supreme Court cases during Administration of, 153, 182; appointed Marshall Chief Justice, 179–180; nominated judges, 181

Adams, John Quincy: quoted on Chase impeachment, 261–262; criticized Marshall in Burr trial, 287; cited on common law jurisdiction, 307; declined Supreme Court appointment, 332; quoted on piracy, 350; prophesied Civil War, 372, 598; elected President, 541; for liberal policy on internal improvements, 550; cited on repeal of section 25 of the Judiciary Act, 595

Adams, Samuel, 18, 56, 58, 103

Addison, Judge, 176, 260–261

Admiralty jurisdiction, 182, 525–526

Agriculture: foundation of American republic, 218; depredations on, by tariff, 449

Albany Plan, 101

Alien and Sedition Laws: prosecutions for libel preceded, 159–160; unfair enforcement of, 161, 260; constitutionality of, assumed, 161, 172, 359; sovereignty of states under, 165; claim that common law might apply to, 174; expired, 182, 224; Republicans denounced, 185; coöperation between Kentucky and Virginia on, 296; agitation against, 338; sectional differences in enforcement of, 540; response of states to, 545

Ames, Fisher: quoted on government protection of property, 61–62; in debate of 1802, 235–236

Amos, Sir Maurice Sheldon, quoted on history of law, 29

Articles of Confederation: radical doctrines in, 58; terms of, 59–60; criticized by commercial interests, 63; recognized state sovereignty, 90–97, *passim*, 140, 440, 454, 559, 643; submitted to states, 91; influence of, on development of central government, 94 ff., 137; defects of, 95; contribution of, 96; as law, 97; reservation of state independence in, 140–141; two interpretations of, 557; Constitution to overcome defects in, 653

Bank, national: established, 116; Maclay opposed, 117; Hamilton favored, 194–195, 351; Jefferson opposed, 196, 203–204, 351; constitutionality of, questioned, 203–206, 212, 217 and n. 65, 351–352, 444, 605; issue of validity of state tax on, 278–279, 352 ff.; attacked by Taylor, 338, 444, 446; second charter granted to, 339; charter expired, 351; inauspicious beginning of second, 352; mismanagement of second, 353; attempt to confine, to District of Columbia, 367; opposition to, in Jackson Administration, 606–607. *See also* McCulloch v. Maryland

Bankruptcy law: distinction between insolvency laws and, 368–369; question of state, 369, 526–527, 531. *See also* Sturges v. Crowninshield, Ogden v. Saunders

Barbour, James: quoted on Sedition Act, 42, 364; cited on ordinances of District of Columbia, 431

Beard, Charles A.: quoted on Constitution, 73–74, and early political parties, 116; cited on party machine, 187

Beveridge, Albert J., quoted on: Federalist campaign, 70; judges, 177; Republicans, 179; Marbury Case, 247, 249, 257; cited on court divided politically, 280–281; in praise of Marshall, 282, 284, 306, 357, 409, 488, 490, 621, 638; on Dartmouth College Case decision, 396, 398 and n. 71, 410–411 and n. 111; on Cohens v. Virginia, 427, 436; on constitutional theory of nationalists, 500, 560; on Marshall's persistence, 580–581, 623–624

DATE DUE